The Rise of
NEW YORK
PORT

From a painting by J. G. Chapman   *Engraved by J. W. Bennett*

NEW YORK FROM THE BAY, 1835

The lower tip of Manhattan is at the left, with the Brooklyn shore at the right and Castle William on Governors Island at the extreme right. The ship in the foreground was the Havre packet *Charles Carroll*, which incidentally carried Charles X of France to exile in England after the 1830 revolution, and later served as a whaler until wrecked off the African coast in 1862

The Rise of
NEW YORK
PORT
[*1815-1860*]

by Robert Greenhalgh Albion

with the collaboration of

JENNIE BARNES POPE

DAVID & CHARLES : NEWTON ABBOT

Published in Great Britain 1970 by
David & Charles (Publishers) Limited
South Devon House   Newton Abbot   Devon

ISBN 0 7153 5196 6

Printed in the United States of America

PREFACE

THIS BOOK originally appeared in 1939, that year of the beginning of World War II, yet the fundamental aspects of this study seem to have retained their original validity during the past three decades. New York's long and continuing status as a great metropolis has overshadowed its equal rise as a great seaport. As we wrote in 1939, "the world's greatest seaport has been too busy with its present and its future to be bothered with its past. Many sleepy little New England ports, with rotting wharves and vanished commerce, have received fuller treatment. Those now-deserted waterfronts suggest the days of 'wooden ships and iron men,' but at New York one must carry on research within earshot of the humming traffic of a crowded midtown corner, or of penetrating harbor whistles at the busiest of Custom Houses."

Now, in 1970, there has been a rise of serious interest in the port's past. More and more one finds an awareness of this wonderful heritage along the waterfront that has been left to rot too long. Evidence of this has been the "South Street Seaport" project on the East River. Coming from the vision and enthusiasm of a few young men, its sudden and far-reaching growth has brought support from leaders in shipping and civic affairs. Within a few years, its membership has risen into thousands. Many tireless volunteers have been a factor in implementing the ambitious program. Difficulties and obstacles have been surmounted with striking success. Not only has there been public indoctrination in New York's maritime background, but a basic section of the old waterfront has been acquired for restoration. In addition, a collection of early vessels is increasing, to be dominated by the masts and spars of the old square-rigger *Wavertree*.

The South Street restoration centers particularly on the period covered by this volume, between the War of 1812 and the Civil War, when New York really shot to the front. We had originally planned

v

to cover the port's entire history since the early Dutch days, but once this mid-period was completed, the pre-1815 and post-1860 seemed anticlimactic.

The research for this study ranged far and wide, from dusty records in the basement of the New York Custom House to manuscript collections, statistical records, and a wide variety of books and periodicals. The most valuable and time-consuming element, however, consisted of fighting through 45 years of daily "marine news" at the rate of a month an hour, in the newspaper files at the New York Public Library. These not only yielded a wealth of factual information, but also reflected the atmosphere of the developing situation. This was at its best in the "golden age" around 1850, in the columns of James Gordon Bennett's *New York Herald*.

As we forged ahead in our research, our findings were to undermine the popular tradition that the opening of DeWitt Clinton's Erie Canal in 1825 had been the reason for New York's primacy among American cities. It became clear to us that long before the triumphal procession of canal boats from Lake Erie in 1825, several other factors had given New York such a lead over its rivals that they were never able to catch up. A particular lucky break came from the British. With the coming of peace in 1815, they decided to concentrate their dumping of industrial products at New York. To a Yorkshireman, Jeremiah Thompson, New York owes much. It was through his initiative that the city prospered so much from two other British projects—the inception of the transatlantic packet service, and the "Cotton Triangle" to provide return cargoes for the packets. Thus it was the British—not the building of the Erie Canal—who gave impetus to New York in these three ways. A fourth major boost came from the Auction Law, passed by the New York State legislature. It is evident that even before 1825, the city was well on the way to become, as the phrase went, "the great commercial emporium of America," while Boston, Philadelphia and Baltimore were in for a frustrating stern chase.

This interpretation was subjected to scrutiny in 1966 at a symposium on "The Growth of the Seaport Cities, 1790–1825" attended by more than a hundred economists and historians. The meeting was held at Greenville, Delaware, under the sponsorship of the Eleutherian Mills-Hagley Foundation. It was stated prominently at the outset that: "Since the appearance of Robert G. Albion's *The Rise of New York Port* in 1939, there has been very little work of a comparative nature on the growth of the seaport cities. More recently, doubts have been expressed regarding the formative role of maritime commerce in the rapid growth of the nation's economy, a factor emphasized by Albion to explain the rapid rise of New York to commercial and financial supremacy. What then made the cities grow?" After lengthy and wide-ranging discussion on matters of population, urban expansion, manu-factures, and economic thought in connection with Boston, New York, Philadelphia, and Baltimore, the chairman, Dr. Carter Goodrich, in summing up such consensus as could be reached, confirmed our 1939 view of "the rise of New York to a position unmistakably ahead of the others, even before the opening of the Erie Canal." He also declared that "the impression left by the discussion is that the four cities were commercial at their core; throughout the period the central determining activity was the commercial one."

As we had realized from the beginning, the story of a general sea-port like New York cannot be limited to mere local history. The economic activity of the whole world passed in review along the wharves and in the countinghouses of South Street. One must, there-fore, consider the textile factories of Manchester, the hongs of Canton, the flour mills of Rochester, and the cotton-laden levees of New Orleans, as well as much else. To place such varied elements in their proper setting; to show the workings of the waterfront and business district; and to explain New York's successful competition with the other American seaports are the main objectives of this book.

Plenty of books tell *how* the old ships sailed; too few tell *why* they sailed. A port history, therefore, has to be made up of more than sailors' yarns and speed records, however thrilling they may be. Save for the opening background chapters, our treatment is topical rather than chronological.

To avoid littering the text with too much detail, a large amount of pertinent statistical data has been crowded into as compact a space as possible. The publishers, more generous than many others in this respect, allowed 34 pages of this, in addition to 46 pages of bibliog-raphy. The achievements of other major American ports, in addition to New York, in various branches of maritime activity, are shown year by year for the whole period, reduced to their simplest terms in thousands or millions.

Because of the many-sided nature of the subject and the wide dispersion of the source material, a large number of institutions and individuals have assisted in various stages of the work. The heaviest demands, in point of time, were made upon the staffs of the Princeton University Library, the Newspaper and Manuscript Divisions of the New York Public Library, and the Marine and Records Divisions of the New York Customs House. The same courteous cooperation, in quality if not in quantity, has been experienced in the authors' relations with the National Archives, the Library of Congress, Harvard College Library, Baker Memorial Library of the Harvard Business School, Yale University Library, Columbia University Library, Rutgers University Library, the library of the Stevens Institute of Technology, the Chamber of Commerce of the State of New York, Public Record Office (London), Free Public Library of Liverpool, New-York Historical Society, Marine Museum of the City of New York, New York Society Library, India House, Historical Society of Pennsylvania, Essex Institute, Maine Historical Society, Portland Public Library, New Jersey State Library, United States Court of the Southern District of New York, Surrogate Courts of New York and Kings Counties, the Atlantic Mutual Insurance Company, the United States Lighthouse Bureau, and the United States Consulate at Liverpool. Grants from the Princeton University Research Fund, the Social Research Council, and the American Council of Learned Societies were of great assistance in gathering some of the material which lay at a distance from Princeton.

The Princeton University Press granted permission to utilize some of the material in our *Square-Riggers on Schedule: The New York Sailing Packets to England, France and the Cotton Ports* (1938) which was a by-product of our general New York research. For facilitating the use of family manuscripts, we are indebted to Mr. William Gilman Low of Bristol, R. I.; Mr. Alexander O. Vietor and Mr. Blair S. Williams of New York City; Mr. George Griswold and Mr. Carleton O. Pate of Greenwich, Conn.; Mr. Thomas Gamble of Savannah, Ga.; Mr. Elwin M. Eldredge of Kingston, N. Y.; Mr. Vernon Tate of Alexandria, Va.; Miss Jennie A. Evans of Burlington, N. J.; the estate of Laurence John Brengle; the Pennsylvania Museum of Art; the Frick Reference Library, and the Prints Division of the New York Public Library. The Chamber of Commerce of the State of New York graciously loaned several cuts from its *Catalogue of Portraits* for reproduction in this study. The Yale University Library granted permission for the quotations from its Bostwick manuscripts.

Space prevents mentioning by name the still larger number of individuals who helped in many other ways. Some have answered questions upon subjects in which they are experts, sometimes furnishing material from their own works in progress or reading portions of the book in manuscript or proof.

Except for this Foreword, the original text is preserved. Those who seek an up-to-date bibliography may consult the authors' *Naval and Maritime History: An Annotated Bibliography* and its supplements.

R. G. A. and J. B. P. A.

South Portland, Maine

CONTENTS

ILLUSTRATIONS

CHAPTER I

TWO CENTURIES AND A DECADE

THE names of Liverpool and Hamburg suggest the sea and little else. At New York, as at London, the seaport tends to be overshadowed by the manifold aspects of the metropolis. Yet Broadway, Wall Street, and Fifth Avenue would not be what they are today had it not been for the activity on the waterfront a century or so ago. Only recently has New York become the world's leading port. Although from the outset it was one of the chief American ports, it secured national primacy only after two centuries. A third century was necessary before it also won the world title by passing London, Liverpool, and Hamburg in the volume and value of its commerce. In 1614, New York's first chartered commerce began. Exactly two hundred years later, in 1814, the port was ready to enter upon a new era, as the War of 1812 was brought to a close. Just a century after that, in 1914, the World War began to cripple the trade of New York's transatlantic rivals, with which it had been running neck and neck. From that time on, it has been the world's busiest seaport; a title more secure than its claims to be the world's largest city.

In all those three centuries, the most significant period of the port's development lay between the years 1815 and 1860. To narrow things down still more radically, it may be said that the first decade of peace, from 1815 to 1825, determined that New York would outstrip the other seaports of America. One may even fix upon the year 1817 as the *annus mirabilis* when the all-important innovations were decided upon. Twenty years earlier, to be sure, New York had pushed ahead of its rivals in volume of trade; but in 1815 Boston and Philadelphia were still close enough astern to render the primacy very uncertain. Ten years later, they had dropped almost hopelessly far behind. During the intervening period, New York had struck while the iron was hot and by means of packets, steamboats, canals, and other well-timed devices had caused the main channels of commerce to flow in its direction. The long period of peace after 1815 gave this leadership an uninterrupted chance to develop and New York became, as the phrase went, "the great commercial emporium of America." That decade was to prove of more value to New York than the whole two centuries which had gone before.

It is somewhat surprising, in view of its manifold natural advantages, that New York took as long a time as this to gain such leadership. Not only did it have the best geographical setting of any American port, but it also possessed a unique commercial heritage. It was founded for purely trading purposes by the Dutch, who held it during that portion of the seventeenth century when their remarkable maritime activity was at its height. From the viewpoint of old Amsterdam, the busiest port in the world at that day, the commerce of this New Amsterdam must have seemed negligible. With their East Indies trade sometimes yielding profits of a million guilders and their commerce with the Baltic and the Mediterranean still heavier, Dutchmen must have thought little of the occasional cargoes of beaver skins from the Hudson. This fur trade was the *raison d'être* of New Amsterdam—yet at its peak it seems to have consisted of only 85,000 skins a year. It is not surprising that the Dutch West India Company sneered at "the trifling trade with the Indians or the tardy cultivation of uninhabited regions," when the capture of a Spanish plate fleet once brought them 15,000,000 guilders' profit at a single stroke.

On a summer day in 1664, four English frigates swooped down to change New Amsterdam into New York. The port thus passed into England's hands just as she was successfully challenging Holland's supremacy on the seas and was welding her overseas possessions into a coordinated commercial system. New York soon found a profitable, if unimpressive, niche in the mercantilist plan for a self-sufficient empire. It was not one of those ideal colonies, from the mother country's point of view, like the West Indian islands with their sugar, Virginia with its tobacco, or South Carolina with its rice and indigo. It was not, on the other hand, considered as "prejudicial" as the New England colonies, whose ships and fish competed with home activities.

Not long after that capture, the flour barrel began to replace the beaver skin as the port's most valuable offering to the world of commerce; and would remain so for more than a century. A significant step was taken in 1678 when the colony passed an act requiring that the sifting or "bolting" of flour for export be concentrated at the port in order to facilitate inspection and to safeguard its uniform quality, which was important for the port's reputation. This shift from the fur economy to the stimulus of agriculture paved the way for a more normal expansion of both the port and the hinterland. The growing of wheat and milling of flour meant not only a more widespread market but also a more stable population. The act, although not long in force, greatly stimulated the port. In 1678, there were said to have been only three ships, eight sloops, and seven boats at New York, whereas sixteen years later the number had risen to sixty ships, sixty-two sloops, and forty boats.

The flour barrel led to the triangular trade. The triangle was as popular in early American commerce as it became in modern fiction. Where two regions, such as England and Virginia, had a mutual desire for each other's wares, a direct shuttle trade was possible and satisfactory, but for the northern colonies, the triangular system was a necessity. England did not want enough of the products of New England, New York, and Pennsylvania to pay for what they wanted of her in return. The solution lay in the West Indies and southern Europe, which would buy enough New England fish and lumber and New York flour to enable the colonists to pay for their English wares. The New Yorkers consequently peddled their flour down among the sugar islands, to the southern European nations, and along the Atlantic seaboard, while they sent only a fraction of it directly to England.

In this early English period, New York did not confine its activity to flour exports. Scarcely was that business getting under way when more exciting diversions arose. In 1689, England and France entered upon the first act of their "Second Hundred Years' War," that intermittent duel for empire, which did not reach its final phase until the peace settlement of 1815. For years, it would give New Yorkers and other colonies recurrent opportunities to sally out, under letters of marque, and prey upon enemy commerce—an exciting and sometimes lucrative occupation. Privateering was common for most Atlantic ports, but New York in particular became more closely involved than any other colonial port in the next stage—outright piracy.

In a bizarre interlude around 1700, Captain Kidd and various other pirates made New York a rendezvous, where they might dispose of loot wrested from distant Indiamen. They swaggered about the streets, abetted by many leading merchants who were glad to buy their booty at bargain prices, while officials winked at their shady activities. Captain Kidd himself, strange to say, held the King's commission to suppress piracy. Yet, when he picked up at New York a crew of 150 "men of desperate fortunes," the governor had serious misgivings, which proved well-founded. In 1698, when a ship arrived from the pirate base at Madagascar, to cite an instance of this merchant co-operation with piracy, her cargo was put ashore "by hasty and secret efforts in the night." When officers were sent to seize it, "the whole body of merchants interposed" with violence. One New York merchant, hearing that another such cargo was on the way to him from Madagascar, sent his son in a vessel to take off the East India loot at sea and carry it to some other port. Things went to such a length that eventually the governor urged the Admiralty to send over a swift vessel "which would discourage and destroye these vermine who have hitherto made New York their nest of safety."

During most of its first seventy-five years under English rule, New York was overshadowed commercially by Boston. While the New Yorkers were playing with the pirates, the Bostonians were busily cementing more prosaic and permanent contacts. The New Yorkers awoke to this situation before the eighteenth century had progressed far. They realized that a considerable share of their goods from England was reaching them by way of Boston instead of direct and that their financial transactions were likewise routed by way of Massachusetts. This was perhaps the only time in its history that New York found itself on the passive end of such a relationship—it would later force many another port into such a position. Boston, moreover, at this time was aided by a hinterland with a larger population than New York's sphere of commercial influence, which was limited to the sparsely settled province of New York with adjacent parts of New Jersey and Connecticut.

To combat this competition, New York at last laid a heavy duty on goods which came from England by way of Boston and gradually caught up with its New England rival, which was having to share its business with Salem, Newport, Portsmouth, Falmouth (Portland), and other neighbors. By 1742, New York had built up its trade with England so that it exceeded that of all New England. For a few years, the port enjoyed a foretaste of the leadership which would belong to it in the next century.

Then opposition suddenly arose to the southward. Philadelphia was founded more than half a century after New York and Boston, but in 1749 its trade made a threefold jump. For most of the next fifty years, it enjoyed a slight lead over the other rivals.

The customs figures for the period down to 1769 are satisfactory only for the direct trade to and from England and give only occasional glimpses of the general distribution of colonial exports. A three-year average for 1715–1718, for instance, shows that New York was sending annually 112 vessels to the West Indies, 71 along the coast, 21 to Great Britain, and 11 to other parts of Europe, but the vessels averaged only 35 tons each. Boston, in those same years, was sending nearly twice as many vessels and they averaged 50 tons each. The increased vigilance and activity of the customs officials during the years immediately preceding the Revolution left more ample records which give a fuller picture of the situation.

In 1770, for example, New York stood fourth among the American ports in the total tonnage arriving and clearing. The figures for the arrivals, which were about equal to the clearances, show Philadelphia leading with 47,000 tons, Boston next with 38,000, and Charleston third with 27,000, closely followed by New York in fourth place with 25,000. The heaviest item in that New York total was the West Indian trade, at 8695 tons. Great Britain and Ireland accounted for 5722 tons, southern Europe for 3124, and Africa for 230. These old reports have a unique value, for they are practically the only ones before the twentieth century to give figures for the coastwise trade. The New York total in that field was 7768 tons, far behind Philadelphia and Boston, but slightly ahead of Charleston. Of that figure, trade with nearby Rhode Island and Connecticut accounted for some 3000 tons. The trade with the southern ports, which would later reach an important figure, did not yet amount to much.

The value of a colony in those days was determined largely by its record in the customs ledgers of the mother country. So all-important was this aspect that the British came very close to taking the rich little sugar island of Guadeloupe instead of Canada, in 1763. From that point of view, New York was not outstanding, for as a consumer of British goods it took only 3 per cent of the mother country's exports. In fact the port was relatively less valuable to England when it was a colonial possession that it became seventy or eighty years later as a foreign port in trade with England.

By 1770, of course, New York's days in the British Empire were numbered. In one way, that imperial connection had been rather more in evidence at New York than in most of the other ports. Its central location made it the western terminus of the government packets, established in 1755 to bring the American mails from Falmouth, England, by way of Halifax or Bermuda; and it was also the center of such general administrative authority as existed on this side of the Atlantic. During the Seven Years' War, the port did a rushing business with the movement of supplies and troops, but that successful conflict was no sooner over than trouble began with the new British fiscal methods. England was determined, as every one knows, to make the colonies pay their share of the cost of defense and other expenses. The merchants of New York joined with those of Boston and Philadelphia in the non-importation agreements, with which they opposed the Stamp Act as well as many of the subsequent measures. On the whole, however, the New York group was more moderate than that in either of the other two cities.

During the Revolution, New York played an unusual role as a Tory port. It was occupied by the British in the summer of 1776 after the battle of Long Island and remained in their possession for seven years. Not until late in 1783 did they finally evacuate the city. During the occupation, it was the center of British authority in America and there was much official business as well as lively Tory privateering. For much of this time, the British zone was limited to a radius of only twenty or thirty miles around the city and for a while this cut off the port from trade with the countryside. Consequently, instead of its usual shipping of flour to others, New York had to receive its foodstuffs from overseas. On the other hand, the last months of the British occupation in 1783 were the busiest that the port had ever seen. The evacuation of the army and that of nearly 30,000 loyalists as well taxed the shipping facilities to the limit.

Then, with the peace, the port encountered several extremely lean years. Its mercantile personnel had been more violently disrupted than in the case of Boston and Philadelphia, where the British occupation had been very much briefer. Certain of the New York merchants had been able to keep on doing business under the various successive changes, but many of the Tory merchants, who had flourished during the war, sailed away to Nova Scotia or London. The patriots who returned from seven years of exile found a radically reduced population in the city, as well as the ruins of a great fire which had swept away a thousand buildings. They also awoke to the disheartening realization that their pre-war debts to English merchants were now by the treaty terms collectible at accumulated interest; with the energetic, determined Alexander Hamilton among the most active of the debt collectors. To be sure, New York was better off than Boston at this time as far as outside trade conditions were concerned. British regulations in 1783 disrupted the old triangular trade with the West Indies. This exclusion of American vessels from trade with the British West Indies bore more heavily upon the New England shipping centers than upon New York or Philadelphia. The new laws discriminated against New England's lumber and fish, while still permitting in British bottoms the shipments of flour from the middle states. Altogether the combination of circumstances left Philadelphia in the most favored position, and for thirteen years after the peace, it maintained first place in American commerce.

New York made various attempts to adjust itself to the new situation. It was the scene of the heaviest dumping of British manufactures in the first three years of peace, but the Hessian fly ruined the grain with which it hoped to pay for its purchases. The French effort to capture American trade, by means of vessels sailing regularly to New York, soon ended in failure. The pioneer voyage of the *Empress of China* from New York to Canton in 1784 was the most conspicuous attempt to find a new avenue of trade. Interstate rivalry and the jumbled condition of the state currencies, however, seriously hampered the merchants—a depressed and at times desperate tone runs through their letter-books of those years. Their realization of the need for a united American front in the outside commercial world made the ratification of the federal Constitution particularly acceptable to New York City, which, for a brief period, was the national capital.

One ray of hope buoyed some of the merchants during the gloom of the 1780s. Late in 1787, one of these New Yorkers wrote to his Jamaica correspondent, "Should a war (O, horrid war!) take place between Great Britain and France, will not your ports be open to us, and our commerce with you as neutrals be an object of consideration?" In a few years the hoped-for war had come, when England entered the French Revolutionary struggle early in 1793. The British West Indian regulations became a dead letter; France needed neutral bottoms for the commerce of its sugar islands; and in many directions American tonnage and American grain were at last in active demand.

This European war brought a boom period to all the American ports, and especially to New York. Its exports, which amounted to $2,500,-000 in 1792, rose to $5,400,000 in 1794, $13,300,000 in 1797, and reached a peak of $26,300,000 in 1807. Its registered tonnage doubled in five years and trebled in fifteen. The year 1797 had a particular significance in the history of the port, for in that year, when it lost the state capital to Albany, it passed Philadelphia and thus jumped into national first place both in imports and in exports. It has kept that position ever since with but two brief exceptions. This lead, however, was to remain insecure until after 1815.

The swelling customs figures tell only part of the story. As American shipping penetrated into the ports of the belligerents, it ran afoul of their stringent and rapidly changing commercial regulations. France was the first offender, chiefly with high-handed seizures in the West Indies, but Britain was soon doing worse as its frigates snapped up New York merchantmen all the way from Sandy Hook to Java Head. Nevertheless, New York's commerce continued to grow even after the stringent terms of Napoleon's Berlin and Milan decrees and the British orders in council were proclaimed, and this increase continued to the very end of 1807. In fact, the volume of trade in that year was scarcely approached again for almost a quarter century. The passage of Jefferson's Embargo Act, barring American vessels from foreign trade, shut down with deadening effect after 1807. A British traveller, who had marvelled at the busy East River wharves in the summer of 1807, returned the following year to count 500 idle vessels in port. A fair recovery was under way after the repeal of the act, when the War of 1812 interrupted everything.

Although popular accounts of "Old Ironsides" and her consorts give the impression of striking American naval success, the experience of New York during that sorry conflict reveals quite another story. At first, when vessels were able to come and go fairly freely, many New York privateers slipped to sea and there a few met with unusual luck. By the summer of 1813, however, the British clapped down a blockading squadron off Sandy Hook and by the end of the year were patrolling the Sound as well. New York began to feel the influence of sea power, thus exercised by the Royal Navy. Foreign commerce was almost at a standstill and the southern coastwise movements likewise had almost ceased. A few little vessels slipped in from the Sound but not many were able to get through the blockade. The prices of textiles, salt, and other imports more than doubled in value, while flour and other domestic goods were a drug on the market. By 1814, the city was certain that the British were going to attack and worked feverishly to throw up defenses. The tireless British patrol of the sea lanes outside did not slacken, although there was no attack on the port. All trade languished while the merchants and many other New Yorkers as well grew heartily tired of "Mr. Madison's War."

On the day before Christmas in 1814, British and American negotiators drew up at Ghent the peace terms which would go into effect as soon as they were ratified in both capitals. Communications were so slow that the belligerents did not hear of the peace in America for several weeks and continued their fighting. During that interval, Andrew Jackson won his victory at New Orleans, and at New York two episodes occurred in the blockade. The *President,* New York's favorite frigate, a sister ship of the *Constitution,* and the product of an East River shipyard, tried to escape to sea but pounded her bottom on Sandy Hook bar; in her crippled condition she was overtaken by the British and captured. The inhabitants of Southampton on Long Island watched with mixed emotions when one of the blockading vessels pounded to pieces on their shore and most of the crew perished.

Then came February 11, 1815, one of the most significant dates in the whole history of the port and the beginning of the period of this study. It was a bitterly cold night and there were only three men at the *Gazette* office in Hanover Square instead of the usual group who gathered nightly to discuss the affairs of the town and of the world. As those three were about to leave for home, a pilot breathlessly staggered into the room with the news of the peace. The British sloop-of-war *Favourite* was lying below with an American legation secretary and a British King's messenger aboard, the bearers of the official tidings of the seven-weeks-old treaty at Ghent.

The news spread like wildfire throughout the city. In spite of the freezing night and snow in the streets, every one turned out to celebrate. No one bothered about the peace terms; it was enough that the war was over. All through the night, with torchlight parades and with shouts of "a peace!" the city rejoiced over the end of "Mr. Madison's War." Had those New Yorkers been able to look into the future, their joy would have been increased manifold, for their port was on the eve of its spectacular rise.

That news of peace marked a turning point in the rivalry of American ports. Although New York had stood first in exports and imports since 1797, its lead had not been decisive. Its New England rivals, moreover, were deliberately treated leniently by the British blockade because they were known to be bitter and rebellious toward their government for declaring war and might even secede. Boston had consequently once more forged ahead.

For more than fifty years, most of such progress made by the rival ports had been impermanent, because commerce had been carried on under abnormal conditions in the rapid succession of wars and in the periods of tension or dislocated trade. Now, however, conditions were different, for, though the men of that day could not perceive it, the nation was settling down to almost a half century of peace, broken only by the distant Mexican War. Anything accomplished from 1815 onwards would have far more lasting effect than any earlier efforts. Thus it was that New York was able to compensate by singularly well-timed initiative during this coming decade for those two centuries, in which it had failed to capitalize adequately its magnificent natural advantages.

At the risk of a certain amount of repetition, it might be well to glance briefly at that noteworthy decade of port history before turning to the various particular aspects of it. Those years gave the chance of a fresh start to the various ports in their rivalry for trade—therein lay their chief significance. New York alone struck while the iron was hot, to make the streams of commerce flow to its wharves. It drew to itself the three major trade routes—from Europe, from the southern ports, and from the West. Without producing many of the important articles of commerce itself, New York made itself into an entrepôt where goods of every sort from every place were exchanged and the New Yorkers grew rich from the profits, commissions, freights, and other excuses for levying toll upon that volume of business. It was in like manner that Amsterdam and London in turn had become the foremost seaports of the world, while the accumulated profits from such business had made them the world centers of finance. New York was on the threshold of a similar career when the peace news arrived on that February night; had the crowds realized what was in store, they might have cheered even more lustily.

It took a while for the seaboard to shift from war to a peace basis. Although the peace terms were ratified at Washington on February 17, officially ending the war, a time allowance was given to let the news spread to the ships at sea. The treaty contained a sliding scale of dates until which captures of enemy craft would still be "good prizes," ranging from twelve days for the coasting trade and thirty for the Atlantic shuttle to three or four months for the distant seas. This interval was employed to good advantage by the shipwrights and riggers in fitting out the merchantmen which had been lying idle up the Hudson during the blockade, removing the tar barrels ("Mr. Madison's night caps"), inverted over the mastheads, and the salt shovelled in to preserve their timbers.

New York had a constant series of interesting episodes during those first months of peace. February saw fireworks at Governors Island and a great dinner and celebration to show the city's joy over the end of the war. Robert Fulton died, just before the completion of his final brain-child, the first steam warship, which came on the scene just too late to be used against the King's ships at Sandy Hook. During March, privateers kept slipping in to port from their final cruises; and there was a hint of new trouble when a New York-bound Spanish ship was plundered by pirates. In April, the *Cyane*, late a sloop of the Royal Navy, arrived at New York as a prize to "Old Ironsides," which had captured her off Madeira late in February. Ships from Bermuda and Halifax brought in American seamen who had been confined there, while over in England several New York sailors were killed in a prison riot at Dartmoor. The governor of New York meanwhile proclaimed a day "devoted to public prayer, thanksgiving and praise" for peace, but scarcely was it over when news came of Napoleon's escape from Elba for the "Hundred Days." Early in May, a French frigate hurried in from the West Indies, and her commander, after some deliberation, hauled down the Bourbon lilies and hoisted the tricolor. British warships from Halifax returned to their familiar patrol off Sandy Hook and snapped up two French merchantmen from Guadeloupe. In that same month, the navy sold off 44 little gunboats and Decatur sailed from New York with a squadron for the Mediterranean to punish the Barbary pirates. By the beginning of August, the news of Waterloo arrived by way of Boston; and real peace at last settled down upon New York, which proceeded to organize a Peace Society.

In the meantime, commerce was getting underway with a rush. As soon as the "safe" period approached, vessels began to clear for foreign ports. Apparently, the first was the *Diamond*, which left for Havana the 1st of March. Five days later, the *Othello* opened the transatlantic business by clearing for Ireland. A week after that,

Astor's *Seneca* cleared for Canton, then the *Emily* and the *Kensington* sailed for India.

More significant than these clearances were the arrivals. The British seem to have settled upon New York as the best port for the bulk of their "dumping" of manufactures. It seemed better for their purposes than Boston, where the British had played upon the anti-war feeling by tolerating a reasonable amount of leakage and which consequently had not been deprived of European goods to the extent of New York. New York's central location made it preferable to the ports to the southward, which had also been rigidly blockaded and where imported goods were likewise scarce and prices high. Anticipating the peace news, the British had sent a considerable number of well-laden merchantmen to Halifax, Bermuda, and other nearby vantage points from which they might hasten to New York with the lifting of the blockade and take full advantage of the situation. Several such cargoes had reached New York before the first American ship arrived direct from Liverpool in mid-May. She was the *Massachusetts,* with a cargo valued at a million dollars, the vanguard of a flotilla of British and American merchantmen which poured woollen and cotton cloth, hardware, cutlery, and other articles into the empty market in such profusion that it was soon glutted. The subsequent sale of the surplus goods in auction rooms at sacrifice prices drew customers from far and wide to the city.

That British decision to "dump" at New York rather than at some other city was the first step in the port's remarkable rise at this time. New York itself, of course, could claim no credit for this step, which was all-important in setting one of the main currents of world commerce flowing in its direction.

The magnitude of the movement may be judged from the customs figures. The full statistics for imports by states are not available for the years before 1821, but a fair idea of the relative volume of imports may be gained from the amount of duties collected in each state. The ports of New York and Philadelphia accounted for almost the whole total for their respective states, while the Massachusetts figures had to be divided among Salem, Portland, and several other active ports in addition to Boston. In 1811, the last year of fairly normal trading before the war, the rivals were still running pretty much neck-and-neck, with $2,700,000 for Massachusetts, $2,400,000 for New York, and $2,300,000 for Pennsylvania. Four years later, the British dumping had given New York an impressive lead. For the year ending September 30, 1815, representing only about the first six months of active trading after the peace, Massachusetts stood at $5,900,000 and Pennsylvania $7,100,000, while New York had a larger total than both of those combined, at $14,600,000.

Although it was simply New York's good luck that the British gave it that initial advantage, its own initiative deserves full credit for keeping that stream of manufactures coming in its direction two years later, when it seemed probable that the British would turn their shipments from New York's overstocked market to some of the other ports. New York took two steps which helped to maintain its lead in the import business in 1817. The first of these was the enactment of favorable auction legislation which became law at Albany on the same day, as we shall see, as the Erie Canal bill. Abraham Thompson, a New York auctioneer, claimed credit for the measure, which was designed to secure final sales of all goods put up for auction. By discouraging the withdrawal of goods in case the bidding ran low, it was expected that more buyers would be attracted by the prospect of bargains. More important in keeping the foreign wares coming to New York was the announcement on October 24th of that same year of the first regular ocean liners, sailing on schedule to Liverpool. This pioneer packet line, which came to be known as the Black Ball, went into operation in the first week of 1818. The new regularity of service, as anticipated, attracted shippers almost at once and helped to clinch New York's leadership as the chief receiving port for the offerings of European markets.

In view of the attitude of many historians in oversimplifying the explanation of New York's rise by attributing everything to the Erie Canal, it cannot be emphasized too strongly that New York's distinction as an importing port has always been greater than in exporting, which was the main advantage of "Clinton's Ditch." Even before this canal was opened in the fall of 1825, the packets and other devices had strengthened New York's hold on the Atlantic shuttle. Its import duties for the year ending a few weeks before the canal opening totalled $15,700,000, as compared with $5,700,000 for Massachusetts (now separate from Maine), and $5,200,000 for Pennsylvania. Baltimore, handicapped by its geographical position, lagged far behind in imports, for the Maryland duties came to only $1,300,000.

The route which led down the bay, past Sandy Hook, and then turned sharply eastward, across the Atlantic to Europe, was only one of the four directions in which a vessel might leave New York. On the other three routes as well, New York made innovations. One of these also led down the bay, but upon reaching Sandy Hook, bore southward along the New Jersey coast toward the cotton ports. Another, starting with the East River and the tortuous channel of Hell Gate, led to the quiet waters of Long Island Sound and toward New England. The fourth route was up the Hudson, from which a vessel might connect with New York's unique water-level way to the West.

On the southern coastal route, New York developed what was perhaps the cleverest step of all, by diverting the commerce between Europe and the cotton ports some two hundred miles out of its normal course, in order to collect toll upon it and at the same time to provide eastbound cargoes for Liverpool. Cotton became New York's most important article of export and the South received most of its foreign imports by way of New York. The South passively allowed New York to gain this strangle hold on its trade and to strengthen the arrangement with the packet lines to the cotton ports. In several ways this fitted admirably into New York's concentration of commerce, giving it an excellent market for the distribution of its imports and at the same time providing return cargoes for the eastbound transatlantic shipping. Without those the Atlantic shuttle could not have operated successfully, while British markets were closed to flour and grain, the principal northern offerings.

From the commercial standpoint, the route through Hell Gate to the Sound was the least important of all, for the New Englanders to the eastward were too energetic traders themselves to be as easy subjects of exploitation as the southerners. The Sound, however, was admirably adapted for an extension of New York's energetic use of the steamboat. The successful introduction of steam navigation slightly antedates our period, for it was 1807 when Fulton's *Clermont* began its runs on the Hudson. Steamboat traffic on that river had steadily developed, but the British blockading squadron had prevented such service on the Sound until the first weeks of peace in 1815, when the *Fulton* began her runs to New Haven. Before long, this was extended to Providence and intermediate points, greatly facilitating traffic to the eastward and helping to bring southern and western New England within New York's sphere of commercial influence. Steamboat service was also rapidly developed during the decade on the route across the

FULTON'S *CLERMONT* ON THE HUDSON RIVER

This is said to be the only contemporary picture of the celebrated pioneer steamer. It was presumably drawn around 1810, and shows her as enlarged in 1808

LAUNCHING OF THE STEAM FRIGATE *FULTON THE FIRST*

This first steam warship, originally named the *Demologos*, was launched at New York on October 29, 1814 but was not ready for sea until late in February, 1815, after the death of Fulton and the arrival of the peace news. She was finally destroyed by an explosion at Brooklyn Navy Yard in 1829

Bay to the Raritan, making much simpler the trip to Philadelphia and points beyond. In the use of the steamboat, New York rapidly gained and kept a lead over all the other coastal ports—one more significant factor in drawing business to its waterfront.

Finally, there was the Hudson route which was made to lead to the West. The great ridge of the Appalachians stood between the western farmers and the eastern seaboard. A fortune awaited the port which could first provide them with a cheap and easy means of marketing their flour and other products. The first successful solution of the problem came in 1817, as the most conspicuous act of that vital year of port development. DeWitt Clinton pushed through the state legislature an act which provided for the digging of the Erie Canal. He lifted the first spadeful of earth at Rome on the Fourth of July of that year, just six months before the first Black Ball packet sailed; but the canal took eight years to dig.

The great decade may be said to have reached its close on November 4, 1825, with the arrival at New York City of a procession of canal boats, which had come the entire way from Buffalo by water. That triumphal opening of the Erie Canal was the event which captured the public imagination more than the Black Ball packets, the "cotton triangle," or the extension of the steamboat service. Yet without those other examples of New York initiative in that decade, "Clinton's Ditch" alone could not have made New York what men were already calling it—"the great commercial emporium of America." Only then did the other ports awaken to all that New York had been quietly accomplishing and by that time it was too late for them to catch up. The first appendix shows concisely the effects of the resultant rivalry in a dozen branches of maritime activity; Boston and New Orleans shared the second places, but New York stood first in every case. Those ten years had done more for the port of New York than the whole two centuries which had gone before.

CHAPTER II

PREDESTINATION

NATURE can do a good deal, but not everything, to determine the success of a seaport. Human initiative also counts for something; otherwise American maritime history would have less to say of Salem with its mediocre physical setting and more to say of Norfolk with its rich endowment of natural advantages. Geographical considerations were all-important in the story of New York port. Other places have surpassed it in particular respects, but at no other spot on the North Atlantic coast was there such a splendid harbor so favorably situated for the combination of transatlantic, coastal, and inland trade. Yet even New York trailed behind less favored rivals for many years until local initiative finally took full advantage of nature's bounty.

As approached from the sea, the beautiful harbor of New York lies at the apex of a large sandy angle, interminable stretches of beach upon which the surf pounds incessantly. One arm of this is the outer shore of Long Island, stretching eastward 104 miles from Coney Island to Montauk Point. The other arm is the New Jersey coast, extending 110 miles from Sandy Hook to Cape May. Along the former ran the main sea lane to Europe; the latter was skirted by shipping for the southern and the Caribbean ports. In normal weather, vessels were usually in sight of those endless beaches. In bad weather, those sandy arms formed menacing lee shores for New York shipping. All the way to Montauk and Cape May, there was not a single harbor of refuge for anything larger than schooners. Year after year, vessels by the dozen would pile up on the sands of that desolate angle, uninhabited at that time save for a few scattered fishing villages. Society had not yet discovered Southampton and the Jersey coast was still innocent of boardwalks. Yet strangely enough, a wreck quickly drew a crowd of Long Islanders, who generally succored the victims, or of wild Jerseymen, who too often looted them. That absence of good harbors, however, helped to prevent the development of rival ports to share New York's commercial influence over the region; while Long Island shut off New Haven and the other Sound cities from direct contact with the open sea. As for the Jersey ports within the limits of the sheltered Bay at New York, Perth Amboy and Newark have from time to time entertained hopes of maritime greatness. Newark's efforts belong more to present; but Perth Amboy, at the mouth of the Raritan River, some three miles nearer the open sea than New York, offered inducements to shipping in our period, with loopholes for evasion of New York's customs, quarantine, and immigration regulations. But the Raritan was not the Hudson and the great stream of shipping left it at one side.

At some prehistoric period, before the sea receded, the area within that angle was probably dry land, for hydrographers have recently discovered the ancient bed of the Hudson, running far out to sea, and roughly bisecting the present sandy angle. For some eighty-five miles, it leaves a track of mud only a few fathoms deeper than the surrounding sandy angle; then it deepens for forty-five miles into a gorge deeper and wider than the Grand Canyon, where the river had once apparently cut its way through to the sea. Even in the mid-nineteenth century, before this was known, a mariner, seeking his bearings in thick weather, knew from the *American Coast Pilot* that in coming from the eastward his soundings would reveal more than twenty miles of gray sand with sixteen fathoms of water "which depth will carry till you get into what is called the Mudhole, where are from twenty to thirty-six fathoms water, marl or green ooze, and sometimes pebbles."

In clear weather, however, the incoming mariner, whether approaching from Europe or the southward, realized he was nearing his objective when, miles offshore, he spied the Highlands of Navesink. This steep bluff, colloquially known as Neversink and now called Atlantic Highlands, rises sharply from the shore to some 282 feet, an unusual feature in the flat seacoast of the region. At its foot, the Jersey coast terminates in a sandspit some five miles long, aptly known as Sandy Hook because its shape resembles a fishhook curving inward from the sea. Sandy Hook, lying about seventeen miles from the tip of Manhattan, has always been regarded as the conventional outer limit of the port of New York. To the uninitiated, six miles of good, clear water seem to lie between Sandy Hook and Coney Island at the end of Long Island. Actually, however, a broad sandbar, perilously close to the sur-

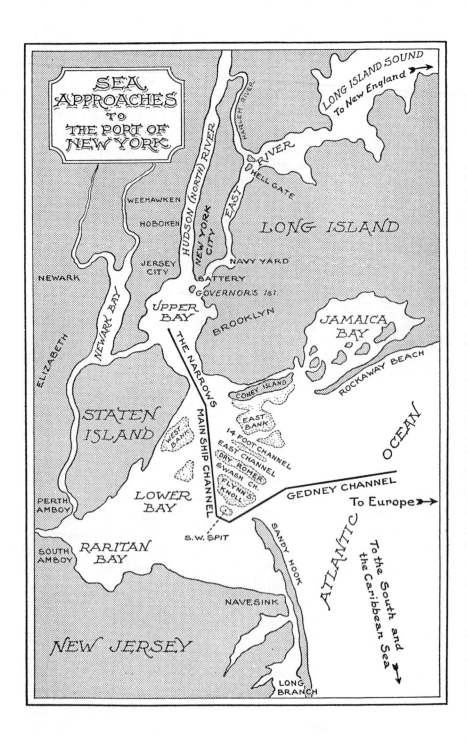

face at some points, joins the two shores, and has made it necessary for vessels to be guided into the bay by pilots.

The waters of the port of New York within this entrance fall into five main divisions—the Lower Bay, the Narrows, the Upper Bay, the East River, and the Hudson (or North) River. The Lower Bay, being exposed to the sea by that six-mile gap at Sandy Hook, did not offer adequate security to shipping. Upon clearing Sandy Hook, a vessel might be headed westward into Raritan Bay to Perth Amboy or, as was far more likely to happen, be steered northward through the Lower Bay to the Narrows between Staten Island and the present Brooklyn end of Long Island.

The Narrows, two miles long, and at one place only three quarters of a mile wide, form a bottle-neck through which has passed more than a third of all the nation's foreign commerce. The Narrows became the obvious place for quarantine inspection and harbor defenses and also served a far more valuable end in giving New York a virtually land-locked harbor, almost completely protected from ocean gales.

The incoming vessel emerged from the Narrows into the Upper Bay or harbor proper, which is some four miles wide. In the pre-dredging era, shallow flats extended for a considerable distance from either shore, but there was always adequate room in the center for a deep channel and for the anchorage of a large number of ships. Manhattan Island splits the upper end of the harbor into two parts—the East and Hudson Rivers. The dividing point is the Battery at the southern tip of Manhattan, off which lies Governors Island.

Until fairly recent times, the more sheltered East River was the scene of the principal business at the port. This stream is about sixteen miles long and at present, after extensive fillings on each side, varies from 600 to 4000 feet in width. It is a tidal strait rather than a river proper. It makes Long Island an island by joining the Upper Bay with Long Island Sound. Incidentally, Manhattan Island itself owes its insular status to the Harlem River, a similar but even narrower, double-ended tidal strait, with its beginning and end in salt water. In the first mile or so of the East River towards the Bay were to be found most of the important wharves of the port during the period before the Civil War; beyond them, near the great bulge of Manhattan at Corlear's Hook, were the shipyards. Roughly midway between Bay and Sound, the East River formed at our period one of the most-cursed stretches of water on the Atlantic coast. The English had to alter its

old Dutch name only slightly into the appropriate Hell Gate. The
tides rushed through it at five or six miles an hour; each of its rocks
acquired a sinister familiarity to the skippers of the eastern coasters,
who named them Flood Rock, Mill Rock, the Gridiron, the Pot, Bald-
Headed Billy, and the like. Nevertheless, plenty of mariners were glad
to use Hell Gate because that short bad passage led to a hundred safe
miles in the sheltered waters of Long Island Sound.

The Hudson, on the other side of Manhattan Island, was often
called the North River, a relic of the Dutch days when the Delaware at
the other end of New Netherland was the South River. About a mile
wide at New York, the Hudson was broader and less turbulent than
the East River, but shipping at its wharves was less protected from
the elements because of its broad sweep and the danger of floating ice.
As an element of the New York waterfront, its utility was limited
at first to the traffic with the upper Hudson region. The foretaste of its
future came in 1847 when the Cunard wharves were built across the
river at Jersey City. Some ludicrous accidents to the first French steamships in the narrow, crowded East River emphasized the fact that the
Hudson, with its ample room for turning, was the better berthing place
for ocean steamships. From that time on, the North River piers have
accommodated most of the largest liners afloat. The Hudson is a tidal
estuary to the head of navigation, some 150 miles inland from New York
at Troy. Unlike the East River, it is a real freshwater stream in its
upper reaches. While the rise and fall of the tide are noticeable as high
as Albany and Troy, salt water generally penetrates only as far as
Poughkeepsie, seventy-odd miles upstream.

The Hudson and Long Island Sound have been vital factors in New
York's geographical importance. The Hudson gave easy access to the
rich hinterland of its own valley, and was the first stage in the "water-
level" route to the West, which was to give New York a marked advantage over the other ports. The stream afforded a good depth of water
until one reached a sandbar known as the "overslaugh" a few miles
below Albany. Little sailing sloops took full advantage of the river
from its earliest days and later it furnished a practically ideal setting
for the first permanently successful application of steam.

Long Island Sound was even more unusual as a body of water.
Lying between Long Island and the Connecticut coast, it is about a
hundred miles long and averages from ten to twenty miles wide, with
ample depth of water and plenty of convenient harbors. Its most

valuable feature is the shelter which it offers from the sea, for the outer shore of Long Island catches the full brunt of the ocean waves. While the Sound can at times grow very rough with waves of its own production, vessels are safer than they would be on the outside. The trade of Bridgeport, Norwalk, New Haven, and the other Sound ports naturally gravitated to New York; and the Sound afforded a valuable "back door," utilized by most of the vessels trading to other parts of New England and points eastward. It gave, besides, an alternative approach to New York when weather conditions made it difficult to enter past Sandy Hook. Adverse winds might keep all arrivals away for days at a time at other ports, but at New York because of the alternative entrance to the harbor, it was a rare day when the marine intelligence did not herald the arrival of several vessels. In time of war, the Sound gave an added chance to escape from blockaders. Finally, this body of water offered another excellent setting for the use of steam.

The two entrances from the sea brought in two distinct tidal movements. Arriving at different times, they helped to keep the East River turbulent. The normal rise of tide in New York harbor is about four and a half feet. Twice a month, however, the so-called "spring" tides rise about a foot higher than normal, while at the first and third quarters of the moon each month, the "neap" tides run about a foot less than usual. The naval Hydrographic Office has minutely calculated the ebb and flow of the tides and from their detailed tables, one may plot the progress of each tide as it comes in through Sandy Hook and up the Sound. On a particular day, for instance, when the tide was high at Sandy Hook at noon, high tide reached the Narrows at 12.11 and the Battery at 12.36. Leaving for a moment that portion of the main tide from Sandy Hook which passed into East River, we may follow the rest of the tide up the Hudson, where high tide reached Tarrytown at 2.26, West Point at 3.25, Poughkeepsie at 5.21, Hudson at 7.41, Albany at 10.22, and Troy, the head of navigation, at 11.52, which was just before the next high tide was coming over the Sandy Hook bar. The rise of tide varies at different parts of the Hudson, ranging from two and a half feet at West Point to four feet at the town of Hudson. Those are modern figures, affected by the deepening and straightening of the channel; in 1831, the tide rose only a foot at the Troy dam; in 1931, it rose three feet.

In the meantime, the second tidal "wave" was coming up the Sound, much later than the one from Sandy Hook, because it had much farther to travel from the open sea. On our typical day, when one high tide reached Sandy Hook at noon, another reached Montauk Point, at the tip of Long Island, at 12.25, but in its slow progress up the Sound it did not reach New Haven until 3.04, Throgg's Neck at the Sound end of East River until 3.24, and Flushing, just east of Hell Gate, until 4.04. Meanwhile, of course, part of the Sandy Hook tide passed the Battery into East River at 12.36. To complicate matters, at the Bay end of East River the tide rose about four and a half feet; at the Sound end it rose seven feet. The two currents had to find a common level in that narrow stream, where, in the words of the Army Engineers, "the water level approximates a plane surface, sloping between the heights of tide at the extremities." The result was that Hell Gate, on our particular day, had its high tide at 2.24, two hours later than the Bay end of the river and one hour earlier than the Sound end.

The coming and going of such a tremendous volume of water into and out of the harbor with its narrow entrances naturally produces strong currents which were a matter of much greater concern in the days of sail than at present. Such currents are generally stronger on the ebb than on an incoming tide. For an hour or so at the turn of the tide, their effect is not marked; at their maximum strength with a normal ebb tide, they run nearly three miles an hour at Sandy Hook and in parts of the Upper Bay, reaching a maximum velocity of more than five miles in the East River where Blackwell's (Welfare) Island divides the river into two streams. At Hell Gate, the velocity is about five miles both on ebb and flood tides. Twice a month, however, on the "spring" tides, the velocity is about one-fourth stronger, giving more than six miles an hour at Hell Gate and Blackwell's Island. Even with a favorable wind, a sailing vessel could scarcely make headway against such a current and with the wind ahead tacking would be out of the question and the vessel would have to wait for the tide to turn. That was one feature which gave the steamboats such an advantage over sail on the Sound.

So much for the description of the port—although one might like to quote the impressions made upon travellers even in the pre-skyline era by the beauty of the approach through the Narrows into the Upper Bay. Instead, we shall turn to a brief comparison of the port with some of its potential rivals in respect to certain features which contribute to a seaport's success or failure. Nine other ports seem worthy of inclusion in the list of those which had good reason to hope that they might either overtake New York as the chief commercial outlet of North America or at least secure a generous share of the seaborne trade: Montreal, Portland, Boston, Philadelphia, Norfolk, Charleston, Savannah, and New Orleans. Several names, such as Salem, Newport, and Mobile, are deliberately omitted since they were never serious competitors in general trade, while San Francisco and the other Pacific ports were in a separate category. The considerations about Montreal apply in general to Quebec, which first monopolized the seagoing trade from the St. Lawrence. Even though situated outside the United States, these Canadian ports had good cause to hope for a liberal share of our western trade.

In the days before acts of Congress might cause thirty feet of water to flow where only ten had flowed before, the natural depth of water at the entrance of a port was an all-important consideration for its success. Bars from river silt or from the shifting of shore sands had an exasperating habit of forming before some of the most likely locations. Both the normal depth of channel at low tide and the average rise of tide affected a port. Some ports had plenty of water even at low tide to accommodate the largest ships; some were accessible only at high tide; while the least favored were unable to admit a ship, bark, or brig at any stage of the tide.

The draft or depth of keel on various types of vessels at different periods was an essential point since the problem was the amount of water under a keel at high or at low tide. The Navy was most vitally concerned for, in the period before the Civil War, its vessels had deeper draft than most merchantmen. For instance, it reported in 1836, that with full equipment ships of the line drew from 25 to 26 feet and frigates from 21 to 22½ feet. The steam vessels, built shortly after that by the Navy, had somewhat lighter draft. The draft of merchantmen was not given in the regular customs measurements and is somewhat elusive. It affected chiefly the pilots, whose rates were based on so much per foot of draft, and might vary from trip to trip according to the weight of the cargo. Until after the Civil War, however, 23 feet seems to have been a general maximum both for sail and steam. The celebrated frigate, *Constitution,* built in 1797, drew more water than the maximum merchant shipping of a half century later. If "Old Ironsides" could visit a port, the largest packet or steamship need run no risk there.

Channel depths fluctuated from time to time, making it rather difficult to state categorically the "controlling depth" or shallowest part of
the main channel in the pre-dredging period. Portland and Boston had
no bars and were safe for the largest ships at all stages of the tide. They
did not need their nine-foot rise of tide which would have been a
boon to some of their southern rivals. Quebec and Norfolk likewise had
no cause to worry about depth of water, but not so Montreal with less
than eleven feet at low tide. Vessels in all sizes could ascend the
Delaware until just below Philadelphia, where a bar cut the depth to
some 18 feet even at high water. Baltimore, too, had a controlling
depth of 18 feet—"three fathoms of water, soft bottom, being the
most you will have in this channel, common tides." Charleston had
some 12 feet at low water and 17 feet at high, while south of that the
situation grew worse. Savannah at one time had a channel seven feet
deep at low water and about double that at high tide. Large vessels
could ascend Mobile Bay until about six miles from the port, where a
bar reduced the depth to some 11 feet at high tide, which in the
Gulf meant generally only a one foot rise. At New Orleans, the situation was reversed. Ample water was available at the city and down
the Mississippi to within a mile of the Gulf; but there, at the entrance
to all five passes, the river silt piled up bars of soft mud, so that
there was at the deepest only 13 feet at times at low tide and 14 at
high. Had it not been for New Orleans' unsurpassed connections with
the interior, the port would have suffered keenly as ships grew larger.

Many other ports had such shallow entrances that they never had a
real chance to develop. For instance, in 1833 a dismasted brig, naturally
lighter with her masts gone, was said to have been "the first square-
rigger that ever entered" Little Egg Harbor on the Jersey coast near
the present Atlantic City. Inadequate draft prevented the North Carolina ports from developing much of a direct foreign trade because
the Cape Fear River kept vessels of more than 300 tons away from
Wilmington, while Ocracoke Bar, the entrance to most other ports of
the state, was often hazardous even for schooners.

It was one thing to have adequate depth of water under one's keel
and quite another to find easily the channel where that water lay. Every
port had its records of mishaps to vessels which failed to strike the
channel. Some were better situated than others, but even at the best,
pilots were a virtual necessity for all vessels except the smaller coasters.
It was appropriate that pilot charges were estimated at so much for

each foot of draft, for naturally, the deeper a vessel lay, the more chance she ran of grounding. In this matter of easy access, few ports could rival Portland with its straight, deep channel, and with only three and a half miles from open sea to docks. Boston had similar deep water, but the channel wound among many rocky islands, dangerous in darkness, storm, or fog. The long winding channels leading to Philadelphia, Baltimore, Savannah, and New Orleans offered numerous chances for grounding.

With the conditions at the other ports in mind, one may appreciate the advantages and the limitations of the Sandy Hook bar, which controlled the depth of water and the ease of access for New York. As far as depth of water was concerned, New York was well fixed. The old Main Ship Channel over the bar had a natural minimum depth of 21 feet at low water, with four to five feet more at high tide. In 1837 Lieutenant R. T. Gedney, U. S. N., improved this channel as a result of Coast Survey soundings by discovering an outer extension in the alternative channel, which still bears his name. This gave a minimum depth of 23 feet at low tide and also, by bearing southeast upon leaving the bar, saved three or four miles and gave shipping a wider range of winds. As a result, virtually all the pre-Civil War shipping might enter and leave New York at all stages of the tide.

To find the channels was another matter and the Sandy Hook bar was a bad one in this respect. In the six miles of bar, which stretched from Sandy Hook to Coney Island, there were only the few hundred yards of the Main-Gedney Ship Channel available for larger vessels and that ran close to Sandy Hook. Smaller craft might use one of the three lesser channels, the Swash, "Fourteen Feet" or East (today deepened into the 40-foot Ambrose Channel), but close to each lay dangerous sandbanks. One of the latter was only two feet under water at low tide and sometimes exposed at spring tides—hence its name of Dry Romer. Vessels which gave Sandy Hook too wide a berth were liable to run on the Southwest Spit, while the so-called East Bank and West Bank were also lying in wait for the unwary. The bar was composed of hard sand, a continuation of the shifting sandy beaches of the Long Island-New Jersey angle; not a deposit of river silt, for the Hudson leaves that well upstream. For a while, it looked as if Sandy Hook might move outward some time to close the Main Channel. A Coast Survey chart showed a marked outward movement around

1800—an outcome devoutly desired, it was said, by Philadelphians. It did not; but the sand was there, to be plowed by many an unwilling keel.

Only twice until the close of the nineteenth century did the depth of water at Sandy Hook bar have any important influence. Both instances occurred during the rare emergencies when war came to New York harbor; and both gave the responsible officers the excuse of the bar to account for their failures. In the summer of 1778, a French fleet crossing the Atlantic to co-operate with the Americans headed for New York, where Lord Howe with a weak squadron of smaller vessels awaited it just inside Sandy Hook. The French admiral, aware that in wartime the channel buoys were removed and that his first-rate flagship, the *Ville de Paris,* one of the largest vessels afloat, would have scant margin for clearance anyway, gave the bar as his reason for withdrawing to Newport, thus saving Howe from an action under desperate handicaps. In the other episode, early in 1815, the frigate *President,* as we have seen, fell into British hands after being crippled by pounding on the bar. Her commander also used the bar as an excuse and prejudice remained in naval minds. In 1817, a commission of naval and army officers, inspecting potential navy yard sites at eastern ports, rated Boston as perfect in all respects, but pointed out that capital ships could not enter New York at low tide. One influential old commodore seems to have continued this grudge against New York as a naval base for many years afterwards.

The Sandy Hook channel was put to a severe test in the last months of our period with the first arrival of the *Great Eastern* on June 28, 1860. That giant ship, some 22,500 tons by the old reckoning and 18,900 gross tons by the new measurement, was far ahead of her time in size; fully loaded, she drew 30 feet. There was talk at first of sending her to Portland, but finally, it was decided to try the Sandy Hook approach to New York. After an 11-day run, she reached the lightship early in the morning, drawing nearly 27 feet aft. She had to wait nearly seven hours for high tide; the time was spent in adjusting the cargo to place her upon an even keel. *The Herald* next day told of the crossing:

It is now about two o'clock—the tide is at its height and the moment has arrived when the fact is to be demonstrated whether or not the *Great Eastern* can cross the bar. Much has been said pro and con on the subject, and it is quite natural that the liveliest interest should prevail. The offi-

cers are all at their stations. . . . Capt. Vinehall and Mr. Murphy, the
New York pilot, with his associate, Mr. Van Duzer, are on the wheel
house, cool, calm, and collected; the engineer is at his station, looking
down into the huge vault where revolves the massive machinery. . . .

The order is finally given by Mr. Murphy, under whose command the
ship has now passed, to "Go ahead." The engineer waves his hand, the
officer below repeats the order to those still further below, and in a minute the great wheels commence their revolutions. . . . Gradually the point
of danger is neared. The perilous bar is at hand. Speed is accordingly
slacked, and Mr. Murphy from his position silently gives his orders. . . .

Once, it is said, the noble vessel barely touched the bottom, but this is
uncertain. . . . Among those cognizant of the fact, it was generally agreed
that the discolored water which marked the spot was only the stirring up
of the great deep by her screw.

The bar was safely crossed and the great ship proceeded triumphantly
past the booming guns of Fort Lafayette in the Narrows to her North
River pier where cheering thousands greeted her arrival.

The Hell Gate entrance to the port was still worse; the water was
deep enough but it swirled so violently around the reefs that the channel was a dangerous one for large vessels. It was considered a superb
feat of seamanship during the Revolution when the British frigate
Roebuck was taken through East River into the Sound; and during
the War of 1812, smart handling was required to steer the still
larger American frigate *President* through the same passage. During
the Revolution, however, another British frigate, the *Hussar,* struck
a rock near Hell Gate and went to the bottom too quickly to save the
gold, estimated at several million dollars, which she was carrying as
pay for the redcoats. Ever since, that huge treasure has presumably
lain buried in East River mud but the swift current has so far frus-
trated repeated efforts at salvage.

Human ingenuity applied itself to modifying these natural disadvantages along the coast. The first step, before serious efforts were
made to secure deeper water, was to build vessels with shallower draft.
As we shall see, New York shipwrights were very successful with
large "flat-floored" ships for the Mississippi entrance, while in the
lesser craft, sloops and schooners were made with centerboards instead of fixed keels for use in still shallower waters. But the deepening
of harbors and rivers became the usual method to deal with the problem. For many years, such a project was part of the internal improvement plan of the Whig party, but congressional "river and harbor"
appropriations were not common before the Civil War.

The first effort to improve upon nature at New York was a municipal appropriation of $13,861 in 1851 to remove some of the Hell Gate rocks and a reef at the harbor entrance to East River. Two years later, Congress appropriated $20,000 for similar work. The main entrance at Sandy Hook, however, was regarded as adequate until 1884 and not until the turn of the century were heavy appropriations needed for the accommodation of the largest liners. About that time, the East Channel through the bar, with its 16 feet minimum natural depth, was converted into the Ambrose Channel with 40 feet at low tide and also the North River docks, in extensive operations, were made accessible to the liners. Long before that, the army engineers had built huge jetties to sluice deep channels through the bars at Charleston and New Orleans, while many lesser ports and would-be ports had dipped into the "pork barrel." It is an evidence of the natural advantages at New York that up to 1911, only $21,000,000 of a national total of $800,000,000 in river and harbor appropriations had been spent in improving the port which handled so much of the nation's foreign commerce.

Like depth of water, shelter from the sea was an all-important prerequisite in a good harbor. It is obviously essential that shipping in port have protection from the violence of ocean waves in storms either by nature or by artificial breakwaters or moles. The river and bay ports, lying far inland from the sea, had naturally little to worry them in this respect, and luckily even the major American harbors opening directly upon the ocean were relatively well protected against the intrusion of stormy seas. To appreciate this good fortune, one has only to read of the extensive and expensive efforts required to secure shelter at numerous foreign ports, such as Port Said and Madras, or even at Plymouth and Cherbourg, where breakwaters were needed to guard the harbor openings. Well-sheltered harbors were needed not only for the protection of the shipping anchored in the stream or lying at the wharves but also, if possible, as refuges for vessels caught in storms at sea. Such havens of distress were fairly common along the New England coast, but between New York and Charleston, Norfolk was the only place of refuge for large vessels until the government built a huge breakwater just inside Cape Henlopen at the mouth of the Delaware.

Of the ten major ports under consideration, five lay far up rivers or bays and the other five enjoyed the rare combination of shelter and deep water, close to the open sea. New York possessed a landlocked harbor, which offered more perfect natural shelter than that of any other major American port as close to the sea. A century ago, a prominent engineer remarked that even if the sandy mass of Long Island might have no other use, it justified itself as a natural breakwater for New York. Staten Island served a similar purpose. Even if a southeast gale should drive high waves through the Narrows, they would come at such an angle that their force would be spent on the New Jersey flats. Shipping in the Lower Bay or at the Narrows might catch the force of a gale, but the waters around Manhattan were spared the surges of stormy seas.

Even at that, the almost annual gales at times made things uncomfortable in the Upper Bay. The harbor might grow very rough, but this was simply the effect of the winds; and the same results were evident on inland lakes. Year after year, particularly at the period of the September "line" storms, a fairly consistent list of casualties would appear in the daily press as soon as the wind subsided. Generally the story was pretty much the same—a few little sloops, loaded with stone or timber, sinking at the wharves; a brig or two, insecurely fastened, breaking loose; the harbor ferries and the Sound steamers suspending service; a few small craft capsizing in the Upper Bay; perhaps a vessel or two dragging anchor at the Narrows and running aground. A December gale in 1833, however, was an exception and inflicted "a vast amount of damage," according to the *Evening Post*. Blowing directly down the Sound and East River, it accumulated the water at high tide in the bay and drove it up into the streets of the lower city, flooding cellars and kitchens, putting out fires. On the day of the gale, the *Evening Post* stated, "The water is so high that small boats from the vessels in the harbor pass over the wharves. A sailboat has passed up Maiden Lane from South to Front Street."

Rarely, however, did one read of the larger ships inside New York harbor sustaining any damage beyond loss of spars. For instance, in September, 1815, a series of gales "covered the Atlantic seaboard with the wrecks of vessels, floating spars, casks, boxes & c." The worst of the gales, blowing from the northeast, swept the New York waterfront for thirty hours. The next issue of *The Shipping and Commercial List* reported, "Last Saturday a severe gale of wind done (*sic*) considerable damage to the wharves and shipping in the city; no vessels lost. To the eastward, the violence of the gale exceeded all recollections, doing incalculable damage on the land and water." The reports from

New England confirmed that last remark. At Boston, where the harbor lay somewhat exposed to northeasters, numerous vessels at the wharves were "stove in and sunk," several wharves were badly smashed, while "of all the vessels at anchor in the stream at the commencement of the gale, only two vessels (schooners) held on and rode it out." From Stonington, Connecticut, came word that "A new ship belonging to N. York is in the street, by Mr. Franklin's with the bowsprit over the house. The sloop *Volunteer* went over the wharf, and now lies in Mr. Cheesbrough's meadow." Providence, likewise, had "a sloop standing upright in Pleasant street before the door of Col. Webb, and a ship in the garden of General Lippett." Altogether, shipping might count upon New York as a pretty safe harbor of refuge in storms. Most of the damage was caused by the winds, and relatively little by the waves, except at the Narrows, where the damage inflicted served to emphasize the greater security inside.

Ice was an occasional nuisance at New York; but only on very rare occasions did the harbor freeze over so as to prevent the going and coming of shipping past Sandy Hook. There was no repetition of the great freeze in the winter of 1779–80, while the British were occupying the port during the Revolution. For several weeks the Narrows and Upper Bay were frozen so solid that on one day the commissary was able to send eighty wagons loaded with provisions across the harbor to Staten Island. On occasions during our period temporary cold snaps tied up shipping for a few days. In February, 1818, for example, no vessels arrived or cleared for six days. Another short stoppage occurred in January, 1821, when one day the thermometer dropped to 7° below zero. Rarely if ever, however, was New York cut off from the open sea for a whole week—the strong tidal currents through the Narrows generally prevented that.

On the other hand, the floating ice from the Hudson many times caused trouble in the harbor. This was particularly true at the beginning of our period before iron anchor cables and steam towing came into vogue. Vessels at the Narrows were frequently driven ashore after the ice cakes cut their hempen cables; and on one occasion a schooner arriving from Curaçao sank near the Narrows after an ice floe crushed her planking. The East River and the Hudson were occasionally so jammed with ice that for a few hours men could walk from Manhattan to the Brooklyn or the Jersey shore. Packets sometimes missed their sailing dates in January or February when ice cakes kept them hemmed in at their piers. Vessels tied up at the outer end of wharves were particularly vulnerable. On a December day in 1831, after a huge ice floe had drifted from the Hudson into East River so that hundreds crossed "free of toll," *The Post* remarked:

It often happens that a temporary bridge of this kind is formed, and is the cause of great damage, carrying before it all vessels at anchor. In one instance we recollect a brig, loading at the end of one of the docks, was cut in two, from stem to stern . . . she sunk so quickly that the stevadores in the hold had great difficulty in escaping with their lives.

While the harbor itself remained relatively ice-free, New York was annually affected when the freezing of the Hudson cut it off from Albany and the interior. Various tables are available showing the date of the closing and opening of navigation on the river—a hundred days was the general average for ice, extending from late November to early March. Sometimes unlucky sloops were held imprisoned in the ice for months; and one of the crack river steamers, wintering at Albany, was carried down river to destruction when the ice went out. The shallow Erie Canal was frozen solid for an even longer period each year—an average of more than four months. The New York end of Long Island Sound was also frequently liable to long obstruction by ice. In the early days of steamboats, service was generally suspended both on Sound and river from mid-November to mid-March.

To appreciate New York's relative advantages in the matter of freezing, we might turn to a few of the rival ports for comparison. Naturally, most of those to the northeast suffered more severely. Montreal and Quebec were generally cut off from the open sea about five months each year, a situation which would give Portland some seventy years of prosperity as the winter port of Montreal. Even Portland, however, sometimes had its harbor frozen solid as far out as House Island in the ship channel. Boston, too, suffered far more often than New York from freezing. Wide publicity attended the action of the Boston merchants who subscribed several thousand dollars to saw a seven-mile channel through the harbor ice so that one of the first Cunarders might sail on time. Portsmouth alone of the eastern ports was apt to remain ice-free, thanks to the swift rush of the currents which accompanied its abnormally heavy rise of tide. In compensation, however, that same current was pretty much of a nuisance to shipping during the rest of the year.

Even to the southward, several ports suffered more than New York, particularly Philadelphia and Baltimore with their quieter river water. The Delaware River was liable to be frozen solid for several weeks in the colder winters; at times even Delaware Bay froze too. One need only examine the marine intelligence in the Philadelphia newspapers to note the scarcity of arrivals in January and February, or to read of icebound flotillas tied up just below the great bend in the river. A year-by-year summary outlined this situation from 1681, when three vessels with settlers from England remained icebound all winter at Chester, to 1828, when it was remarked, as unusual, "during the winter, the navigation has been uninterrupted." In 1817, the river was closed for 50 days and in 1822 for 52 days. Consequently the lists of marine arrivals at New York contained scores of such notes as "Ship *Nautilus*, 65 days from Liverpool, belonging to Philadelphia, put in here on account of the ice." Doubtless many shipowners diverted their trade elsewhere and, even though shipping movements were lightest in winter even at ice-free ports, it is probably safe to say that Philadelphia ranked next to Montreal and Quebec as a victim of ice.

Baltimore suffered somewhat less, as Chesapeake Bay generally remained free from all but floating ice, although the Patapsco River, leading to the port, often froze over. In February, 1831, for instance, Baltimore reported nearly a hundred vessels of all classes in the river and bay waiting for the ice to break up, while many people were amusing themselves on the ice, patronizing "travelling shops with refreshments and strong drinks" and admiring "a sailboat on runners" which "beat up very handsomely to windward." A year later, Baltimore shipowners "contracted for the opening of a channel to the termination of the ice." Other ports in the Chesapeake region were sometimes affected by ice, as Richmond for instance. Norfolk, however, seems to come off well in this as in most other natural respects although the floating ice in the bay was sometimes troublesome. In 1840, according to a report from Norfolk, "all the vessels in Hampton Roads are cut through with ice. Two ships and four brigs have come up for repairs." Naturally only an unusually cold winter brought ice farther southward as, for instance, in the record-breaking great freeze early in 1827 when "all our great rivers with the exception of the Mississippi are either frozen over or obstructed by ice."

The steamboat, as it gradually came into use, helped to keep channels open where sailing vessels could not have moved. Several early Hudson and Sound steamers did valiant work in opening channels, sometimes straining their engines to the breaking-point in the process.

Apparently the first instance of towing at New York occurred in February, 1818, during a period of floating ice. By 1835, enterprising Baltimore had its steamboat, *Relief,* especially designed as an ice-breaker, with a bow bearing "a close resemblance to the bowl of a tablespoon." She proved so useful that in 1839 a more powerful ice-breaker was built by popular subscription. By that time, the Philadelphia authorities had appropriated $70,000 for a "City Ice Boat."

Compared with ice, fog was a less important natural handicap. It was most prevalent at New York from December to March. The northern seaboard from the St. Lawrence to New York felt its effects most severely; further south, with the Gulf Stream running closer to the shore, it was less troublesome. Modern fog statistics of the Lighthouse Service, based on the average hours per year for a quarter century or so in which fog signals were operated at various stations, show that New York's Ambrose Lightship had the heaviest score at any port south of Maine with 876 hours, as compared with 832 for Boston Lightship, 602 for the mouth of the Delaware, 331 for the approach to Chesapeake Bay, 192 for Charleston, 173 for Savannah, and 528 for the lower Mississippi.

At almost every seaport the fog was heavier just outside rather than inside the harbor. At Robbins Reef, in the Upper Bay at New York, the total was only 438 hours and at Hell Gate, 192. "True ocean fogs," report the Army Engineers, "seldom reach the inner part of New York Harbor," although troublesome light fogs more frequently settle over the water during the morning hours. They demonstrate statistically that for only about 52 hours during the average year is the visibility in the inner bay less than a quarter of a mile, more than half of which comes between December and February. Off the Hook, of course, conditions are worse and in the old days often led to grounding on the bar. Fog generally implied an absence of wind so that collisions were rare, but not unknown, with sailing vessels in and around the harbor. Shipping might often be held up by fog for hours or even days and the harbor would resound with the clanging of ships' bells; quieter to be sure than the modern raucous chorus of deep-throated whistles which at present penetrate lower New York on a foggy day. At its worst, however, fog was only a temporary nuisance and would seldom, if ever, divert shipping from one port to another.

Another natural harbor consideration is the capacity for expansion in waterfront and other port facilities. In this respect, the exceptionally compact configuration of New York harbor gave it a marked advantage over its American rivals. Both sides of Manhattan Island, the Brooklyn and Jersey shores, as well as Staten Island, were always available and recent dredging has opened channels from the Upper Bay to yet further potential waterfront. Compared with this accessible and compact area, river ports such as Montreal, Philadelphia, Savannah, or New Orleans are at a disadvantage, for their waterfronts may be expanded only by spreading out for long distances up and down the stream or by elaborate docking systems "dug out of the mud," as in the cases of London, Liverpool, Hamburg, and some other foreign ports. The remarkable concentration of commerce at New York, however, has saved its rivals from too severe problems of expansion. The modern port of New York has a tremendous waterfront, estimated by the most extreme standards at some 771 miles of potential wharfage. In addition, New York has exceptionally ample space for anchorage. Port experts, however, claim that all this available room for expansion has caused the port to spread out in an inefficient manner. Even before the Civil War, New York shippers were wrestling with this problem of port expansion.

Turning from the harbor to more general geographical considerations, nearness of the open sea was a factor of importance, more vital in the days of sail than in modern times with steam or other artificial power. Since sailing vessels in an extra fifty or hundred miles of river channel were more apt to be delayed by vagaries of the wind than in an equivalent extra distance between ports on the open sea, the ports lying up rivers were thereby handicapped. Ice and fog, as well as wind conditions, were liable to cause more complications in reaching such ports. The danger of collision was an added liability in the narrow approaches. From this situation arose increased charges for pilotage or towage, and even at times for marine insurance.

Six of the ports considered lie fairly close to the sea. Although the distances from "bar to berth" are susceptible to juggling, there seems to be a general concurrence in the mileage from the principal docks to the open sea. Portland has the least distance with 3½ miles, followed by Charleston, Boston, New York (with 17 miles), Savannah, and Norfolk (with 30 miles). There is, naturally, a considerable jump to Philadelphia and New Orleans, each just over 100 miles; Baltimore,

152 miles; and Montreal, 500 miles from the Gulf of St. Lawrence and about 1000 from the Straits of Belle Isle.

To offset that long approach with its liabilities of ice and fog, Montreal is the closest of the ten ports to northern Europe. Portland is the nearest United States port to Europe, followed by Boston, New York, Philadelphia, Norfolk, Baltimore, Savannah, and finally New Orleans, with its handicap of the long trip around the Florida peninsula. Thanks to the studies of Lieutenant Matthew F. Maury and others in connection with ocean currents, combined with years of experience, the modern Hydrographic Office figures, given in the appendix, for these distances, probably represent shorter sea lanes than those in use a century ago; but the relative position of the ports remains much the same.[1] The distances between these ports and Gibraltar are in identical order except that Montreal is in third place.

In the routes to the Caribbean, New Orleans and Savannah are about tied as the closest ports to Havana, while the eight other ports are, as one would expect, in almost exactly reverse order from their proximity to Liverpool. The sea lanes to South America, on the other hand, present a surprise. Among the seaboard ports, there is a difference of only 123 miles to South America. One would scarcely believe that Portland is 414 miles nearer Rio de Janeiro than is New Orleans, or only 19 miles farther than Savannah! Since vessels from all these ports had identical routes after passing the great bulge of Brazil, the figures for Rio represent the same relative situation as for Buenos Aires, the west coast of South America, and the clipper route to California. All the ports had a fair start with few favors in that competition, and since the Havana distances are pretty much in reverse order of the European, the eight ports from Portland to Savannah were fairly evenly matched in their locations for foreign trade.

For general coastwise trade, a central position is the most desirable, facilitating as it does the interchange of products up and down the coast. A port which lies too far "off side" is thus seriously handicapped. A glance at the map would give the impression that Philadelphia and Baltimore occupy the positions closest to the center of the coastline in general; that, however, is offset by their distance from the sea, a handicap more serious than mileage alone would indicate. The relative advantages of the ten port locations for coastwise trade may be determined roughly by averaging the distance from each port to the other nine.

[1]See Appendix, xxiv.

In this respect, New York is a close second, being 20 miles more than Norfolk. After these two, come in order Philadelphia, Baltimore, Boston, Charleston, Portland, and Savannah. New Orleans has a coasting average almost double that of any of those eight ports and Montreal has an even worse position. In colonial days, New York was regarded as the most central of the ports, but the opening of New Orleans threw that advantage to Norfolk. New York naturally had another asset in Long Island, whose shelter was of more help than the 15 miles which it saved in comparison with the outside route.

Curiosity has prompted a carrying of this arithmetical geography to an arbitrary conclusion by combining the distances in the three most significant fields of trade: the Liverpool and Havana mileage added to the coastal average. Charleston, with 4997 miles, has a slight lead over Norfolk, with 5007, and New York, with 5039. Then comes Savannah, followed by Philadelphia and Boston nearly tied, Portland, and Baltimore. New Orleans and Montreal have their usual excessive totals. The significance of these differences may be partly appreciated by remembering that a hundred miles a day at sea was a good average run for a sailing vessel; in the port approaches, the rate would be normally slower. This game, of course, might be carried to greater lengths; most of the rivals are so close that by taking other standards than the Liverpool and Havana routes, the order might be altered in minor details.[1]

Yet the fundamental relationship would be much the same. No port along the seaboard from Portland to Savannah suffered under a serious handicap or enjoyed an undue advantage in the length of its major sea lanes. New York was among the most favored but it did not, as is sometimes claimed, have a commanding position in this respect.

One must look to the land, as well as to the sea, to appreciate fully the location of a seaport. New Orleans and Montreal, in spite of the length of their sea lanes, became major ports because they were situated on rivers which penetrated far inland and gave them, and them alone, natural water communication with the rich interior of the continent. Of the other eight, Baltimore and Philadelphia were closest to the West—Baltimore being more than a hundred miles nearer Chicago than was New York. In estimating inland routes, however, altitudes must be considered. Therein lay New York's geographical advantage—the principal explanation of the rise of the port, according to popular ac-

[1] See Appendix, xxiv.

count, which exaggerates the situation. Unlike the other ports with the Appalachians rising between them and the West, New York was able to take the mountains in flank, use canals, and thus have a water-level approach to the West through the Hudson and Mohawk valleys. As we shall see later, New York utilized this Hudson-Mohawk route at just the right moment, before the railroads came on the scene to make the mountain barrier less of an obstruction for the other ports. This proved of tremendous value to the port, but it may be possible to demonstrate that New York's rise as a seaport was caused more by its capitalization of its sea routes than by the building of the Erie Canal.

All told, nature had distributed her advantages among the ports with a fairly even hand. The northern ports had ice and fog; the southern had sandbars. All had fairly adequate shelter. The two ports most handicapped in the matter of sea lanes had the best natural connections with the West. Yet the fact remains that New York, while superlative in few of these considerations, was not seriously handicapped in any of them. Norfolk alone seemed to offer a similar happy sum of such advantages—but perhaps the more bracing climate of Sandy Hook was a further natural asset in New York's favor!

CHAPTER III

THE FIRST LINERS

O F THE innovations which made the first decade of peace memorable in the history of New York port, the invention of the
ocean liner was about the first to produce immediate results.
At that critical period of port rivalry, these sailing packets did much
to cause the channels of trade with Europe to flow toward New York
rather than to Boston or Philadelphia.

The inauguration of the celebrated Black Ball Line in the first week
of 1818 marked the successful beginning of the practice of running
several vessels under common private management between two or
more ports on regular schedule. The first liners were square-rigged
sailing packets but the line principle was extended to the steamships,
which gradually supplanted them. Whether under sail or steam, most
of the crack liners of the world have made New York their western
terminus ever since that initial venture.

Most of the merchantmen in that day were tramps or "transients,"
to use the more respectable term then current. They knocked around
from port to port, wherever cargoes might be had—cotton ports, Caribbean islands, northern Europe, the Mediterranean, or "down east."
They offered the sailor the best chance to see the world, for he might
visit a half-dozen lands and cross many strange seas before returning
home.[1] The stories of thousands of such rambling voyages lie hidden
in the old log books. During boom periods, a transient with a shrewd
captain and well-selected agents might earn a substantial profit but in
times of depression she was at a disadvantage in competing for cargoes with the vessels which were operated on a more regular basis.

The next stage was the "regular trader," which was fairly common
in the first quarter of the last century. She differed from the tramp in
that she confined herself to a single sea lane between two or three

[1]See Appendix, xxiii.

ports. The regular traders, which were generally ships ranging from 300 to 400 tons, were usually owned by merchants trading with those particular ports. Frequently two or more firms owned such a ship jointly and sometimes two or three regular traders might be under the same ownership. The owners used them to carry their own cargoes but tried to fill up the holds by carrying freight for others. Passengers and mail increased the earnings of such trips. A regular trader in the transatlantic service ordinarily made two voyages or round trips during the year, a "spring sailing" and a "fall sailing." In the boisterous winter months when both the seas and the cargoes were at their worst, regular traders normally lay comfortably in port.·

While their fixed routes gave these ships more regularity than the transients, they still lacked two of the essential attributes of liners— co-ordinated sailings of several ships and punctuality of departure. Each regular trader was usually operated without regard to the sailings of the others. A half dozen might clear for Liverpool in a single week and after that there might be no sailings for five or six weeks. Then, too, it was an all-too-common practice to postpone their advertised departure from day to day and even from week to week in order to secure as much freight as possible. This was an annoyance to the merchants, who had freight aboard or mail deposited in the letter bag; perhaps even more, it was particularly irritating for the passengers who had to cool their heels while awaiting the filling of the hold or the coming of a favorable wind.

A few vessels, to be sure, ran to and from New York on fairly regular schedules. The British government mail brigs, as they had done since colonial times, sailed on a fixed day each month for Falmouth but their roundabout voyages by way of Halifax or Bermuda helped to make their passages much slower than those of the regular traders; and they carried no freight. By 1817, steamboat lines on the Hudson and the Sound made daily departures at a specified hour and for steamboats, of course, it was also possible to predict the hour of arrival, which could never be done for sailing vessels. Finally, some of the little coasting sloops and schooners were being advertised as "lines," with sailings in succession at fairly regular intervals.

The establishing of ocean packet service was to consist of taking regular traders as instruments and operating them on a fixed schedule after the manner of these other services. This transition from regular trader to packet is best shown in the experience of the old *Pacific,* a ship of 384 tons and one of the fastest regular traders between New York and Liverpool. She was built in 1807 for Isaac Wright, a Quaker merchant from Long Island, who was active among New York's importers of British textiles. He soon associated with him in the ownership not only his son and partner, William Wright, but also Francis Thompson, a Quaker who had come to New York to market the woollens manufactured by his father and brothers in the West Riding of Yorkshire. By 1816, the joint owners of the *Pacific* also included another Quaker, Jeremiah Thompson, nephew of Francis. Jeremiah was both an importer of woollens and one of the most extensive exporters of southern raw cotton to Liverpool. The fifth owner was Benjamin Marshall, another native of Yorkshire, active in importing Lancashire cotton goods and likewise an exporter of raw cotton, for which purpose he frequently spent several months annually in Georgia. Not only was religion a common bond among four of the owners, but marriage also cemented the relationship. Francis Thompson married the daughter of Isaac Wright while Marshall married the daughter of the *Pacific's* captain. In 1816, the Wrights, Thompsons, and Marshall became joint owners of two new regular traders, the *Amity* and the *Courier,* almost identical in size with the *Pacific,* and early in the following year, they built a fourth and slightly larger one, the *James Monroe* of 424 tons.

Four little ships in a row appeared in the New York newspapers in late October, 1817. For years, marine advertisements had been designated by the cut of a single ship; but this grouping of four ships at the head of a notice was significant. The public was informed that beginning with the first week of January in 1818, the *Amity, Courier, Pacific,* and *James Monroe* would sail in regular succession, on a specified day, each month throughout the year from New York and from Liverpool. "The ships," according to this advertisement, "have all been built in New York, of the best materials, and are coppered and copper fastened. They are known to be remarkably fast sailers, and their accommodations for passengers are uncommonly extensive and commodious." "The commanders of them," the notice continued, "are all men of great experience and activity; and they will do all in their power to render these packets eligible conveyances for passengers. It is also thought that the regularity of their times of sailing, and the excellent condition in which they deliver their cargoes, will make them very desirable opportunities for the conveyance of goods." The new service

was to start with the sailing of the *Courier* on January 1 from Liverpool and with the *James Monroe* on January 5 from New York. Such
was the announcement of the celebrated "Black Ball Line."

This radical alteration of the habits of ships was attended with certain risks as well as with prospects of increased gain. There were arguments pro and con in this combining of four regular traders into
a compact packet line. The ships were pledged to sail at their scheduled
date "full or not full," as the Liverpool advertisement of the line declared. That involved the risk of running the ships at only a fraction
of their potential freight-earning capacity. The announced schedule of
sailings meant that each ship would make three round trips a year instead of the two to which the regular traders had been accustomed.
The third voyage had to fall in the winter months when the North
Atlantic was at its worst. Gales would impose a cruel strain on hulls,
masts, and men, while less was to be expected in the way of cargoes at
that season. The winter westbound passage of the packets was to be
one of the most gruelling tasks assigned to ships in that day. On the
other hand, the third trip meant that 50 per cent more service would
be derived from the capital invested in the ships and probably the
extra earnings of the ships, even in the meager winter months, would
more than compensate for the wear and tear of the winter crossings.
The principle of punctuality, it was hoped, would be appreciated by
travellers and merchants who would henceforth give packets, rather
than regular traders, the most lucrative and desirable branches of the
shipping business. This included "fine freight," which represented
large value in small bulk and paid high rates; specie or coined money,
which was constantly crossing and recrossing the Atlantic to rectify international balances; mails, where regularity and speed were all-important; and cabin passengers. There was less competition for the carrying of cheap and heavy freight or of steerage; these the new line operators were willing to leave to the regular traders. As far as initial
financial outlay was concerned, no new capital was needed since the
ships were already at hand and their total value anyway was probably
less than $140,000. This was not excessive, considering the fact that
Jeremiah Thompson, who is credited with the inspiration of the line
organization, was one of the wealthiest merchants in the country and
his four colleagues were all well-to-do. Finally, unlike investments in
turnpikes, canals, or railroads, the capital was not irrevocably bound
up with the success or failure of a particular route, for ships, like

motor trucks later, might be shifted to another run or used as transients if the line did not measure up to anticipations.

Mere advertised promises of regularity and punctuality were not enough to impress mercantile communities. They were too familiar with the time-honored custom of definitely announcing sailing dates and then postponing them, possibly several times. A curious and probably skeptical crowd, therefore, gathered during the forenoon of January 5, 1818, to see whether the *James Monroe* really would sail as advertised. It was snowing hard, which in itself would have been regarded as a valid excuse for delay by any regular trader. Nevertheless, the owners were determined that the public must be impressed by the punctuality of this initial departure from New York, else this most distinctive feature of the new service might be wasted. With seven passengers in the cabin, a cargo of small value, consisting mostly of apples below decks, and the letter bag brought down from the coffee house at the last minute, the *James Monroe* lay ready at her wharf. Captain James Watkinson carefully watched the time and as St. Paul's clock struck ten, the little ship was backed out of her berth and stood down the harbor into the snowstorm at exactly the hour appointed. That punctuality helped to convert her from just another regular trader into proud distinction as one of the first of the ocean liners. In appearance she was much like a dozen or more New York regular traders, except that as her fore-topsail was unfurled a large black ball, the symbol of the new service and later the popular name for the line, came into view. By four in the afternoon, she had passed Sandy Hook and had headed eastward for Liverpool.

By the margin of a single day, the *James Monroe* missed the honor of being the first packet to sail. The *Courier* had been advertised to inaugurate the westbound service from Liverpool on New Year's Day, but the English agents of the line seem to have taken the principle of punctuality less seriously than did the New York owners. Not until January 4, six months to a day after DeWitt Clinton had lifted the first spadeful of earth for the Erie Canal, did Captain William Bowne finally leave Liverpool to wrestle with the winter westerlies. The *Courier* carried seven men in her cabin, in addition to a Mrs. Irving, the first woman packet passenger. Below decks was a cargo of British textiles and manufactures, far more valuable than that which was coming eastward aboard the *James Monroe*. The prevailing west winds stretched the *Courier's* trip to 49 days, twice as long as it took the

James Monroe, with those same winds astern, to cross from New York to Liverpool.

Once started on its scheduled runs, the Black Ball continued for sixty years, which subdivide into three periods of almost exactly twenty years each. During the first twenty years from 1818 to 1838, the functional importance of the packets was at its height. Fulfilling the anticipations of the promoters, the liners conveyed most of the cabin passengers, specie, mail, "fine freight," and news between Europe and America. Most significant of all, from the owners' point of view at least, were those cargoes of "fine freight." Although most of the commercial houses on South Street in New York had their own vessels, the dry-goods merchants, auctioneers, and manufacturers' agents on Pearl Street did not ordinarily own shipping and were intensely interested in obtaining their goods from abroad as quickly and easily as possible. This service of the packets to shippers was the chief explanation of the permanent success of the line principle.

During the second twenty-year period, from 1838 to 1858, this functional importance of the packets was reduced by steam competition, particularly after regular line service to New York was established by Cunard in 1848. The steamships took over mail and the other communication services almost at once but only gradually did they lure away the cabin passengers and fine freight from the packets. The latter for a while fell back on the steerage business, which was at its height. In the third period, after 1858, the packets lost even the immigrants to the steamships. Nothing remained to them except the carrying of iron, coal, and other heavy freight. They had become packets in name only, robbed of the business which had once made their arrivals a matter of widespread interest. The last Black Ball sailing came in 1878; one London line extended the packet era three years beyond that.

Turning from the functions of the packets to the ships themselves, we find the development somewhat different. The early packets, being regular traders brought together from various sources, lacked uniformity. There was a rapid turnover during the 'twenties but by the mid-'thirties, a distinctive type of tough, fast ship of moderate size had been developed. Whereas the coming of the steamships in 1838 marked the beginning of the decline in packet functions, it also saw the first 1000-ton packet. The ships continued to grow in size into the middle 'fifties, and these later ships, though speed no longer mattered with the decline in their functions, were generally faster too. By the late 'fifties, the sailing liners shared the general depression, which settled down upon American sailing vessels; few new packets were built and the old square-rigged liners were kept at work on the shuttle until they wore out.

Returning to the early Black Ballers, we find them maintaining their schedule of monthly sailings with rigid promptness. Not long after the line had started, business in general slumped badly in 1819 and for three years the Black Ball freight earnings fell off seriously. Time and again the packets had to fill up their holds on the westbound crossings with salt or coal instead of the fine textiles for which $10 a ton might be charged. Fortunately the owners had deep pockets and could afford to continue with the experiment, while awaiting better times. At any rate, the regular traders were suffering more, for the packets had already taken away their best business. Those first four years, during which the Black Ball alone was trying out the packet idea, demonstrated clearly to New York the advantages of the liner over the regular trader or the transient.

In 1822, with business at last emerging from the depression, a remarkable expansion occurred in packet service. Several other lines, closely imitating the Black Ball model, sprang into existence. A "Second Line" to Liverpool, later known as the Red Star from the symbol on its fore-topsail, was announced on January 3. Its first ship, the *Meteor,* sailed from New York on the 31st of that month, after being delayed six days by ice in the harbor. Its operators were Byrnes, Trimble & Co., a firm of flour merchants who traded heavily with the Chesapeake region. The Black Ball countered in March by doubling its fleet to eight ships and its sailings to twice a month. That increased service was reckoned as the "third line" to Liverpool although never so designated. The line as a whole was now called the "Old Line" until the name Black Ball was later substituted. Late in July of that same year, Fish & Grinnell, who had come from New Bedford, announced a "Fourth Line" to Liverpool, later known as the Blue Swallowtail because of the flag borne by the ships. Its service began with the sailing of the *Robert Fulton* from New York on September 8.

In less than ten months, therefore, the Liverpool packet service had undergone a fourfold expansion. For the next fourteen years, four liners a month sailed for Liverpool on fixed days—a Black Baller on the 1st, a Red Star on the 8th, another Black Baller on the 16th, and a

SOUTH STREET FROM MAIDEN LANE, 1828

This is the best of the contemporary waterfront scenes. Many of the packets docked in this section, with the countinghouses of the operators across the street. The ship in the left foreground was the Swallowtail packet *Leeds*, wrecked later that year in the Thames

Swallowtail on the 24th. They sailed in the same order from Liverpool but on different days of the month.

Liverpool, as the outlet of the world's most extensive manufacturing district, had naturally received first attention in the development of the New York packets, but during the boom of the 'twenties lines were quickly started to other ports also.

An abortive attempt was made in 1818 to run a line to the French port whose name was rapidly reduced, in New York parlance, from Havre-de Grâce to Le Havre, and then simply Havre. In 1822, with the Liverpool boom in full swing, Francis Depau, a native Frenchman and son-in-law of Admiral DeGrasse, inaugurated the so-called "Old Line" to Havre, sharing its ownership with a Connecticut Yankee and an Irish sea captain. The following year, a Second Line to Havre was organized, with the backing of the powerful old house of Leroy, Bayard & Co., and operated, as Havre packets would be for some forty years, by John J. Boyd, a product of their countinghouse. Also in that same summer of 1822, John Griswold, a shipping broker from Lyme, Connecticut, tried to organize a line to London but was unable to establish it firmly until 1824, when he secured the co-operation of Fish & Grinnell. Actually the London service from that time on might be termed two lines in one—Griswold's "Black X" and Fish & Grinnell's (later Grinnell, Minturn & Co.'s) "Red Swallowtail." These were separately owned and operated but during most of the time were run in close correlation as a single London line. The Liverpool lines enjoyed an almost constant superiority over the other ocean packets in the size of their ships and in the speed of their passages, while the second Havre line lagged farthest behind.

Two other lines later joined the competition on the Liverpool run. On the eve of the 1837 panic, the "Dramatic Line" was organized by Edward K. Collins, the most conspicuous of the individual operators, already successful with Vera Cruz and New Orleans packets. His *Shakespeare, Garrick, Siddons,* and *Sheridan* were the largest packets afloat when built; his *Roscius,* added in 1838, was the first to reach 1000 tons. He secured some of the ablest captains and provided excellent service. In 1843, Woodhull & Minturn started a "New Line" which six years later was absorbed in the Blue Swallowtail. Altogether, the total number of packets on the three major transatlantic runs rose from 4 in 1818 to 28 by 1825, 36 by 1830, 48 by 1840, and a maximum of 52 by 1845. This last figure meant an average of three regular transatlantic sailings from New York and an equal number to New York each week.

The packet boom of the early 'twenties had not stopped with those three major runs. A rather short-lived line to Greenock, the port of Glasgow, was started and later shifted to Belfast in Ireland. A large number of lines, composed of everything from sloops to ships, radiated from New York to numerous ports up and down the coast. Some of the lines to the cotton ports of Charleston, Savannah, Mobile, and New Orleans consisted of full-rigged ships. Those coastal packets, which performed a vital role in focusing trade at New York and in gathering and distributing the cargoes of the ocean packets, will be considered later.

Some of New York's rivals sought to take advantage of the new packet idea. Thomas P. Cope, a Philadelphia Quaker, began a long-lived line to Liverpool from that city in 1821. It met with steady but moderate success. During most of the period, Philadelphia's packet service was limited to this single four-ship line, with monthly sailings, long after New York's packets were numbered by the dozens. In spite of three attempts, Boston failed to achieve even that modest degree of permanence in ocean-packet service, largely because of the difficulty in securing adequate eastbound cargoes. Boston even complained that the New York lines, in order to lure business in their direction, offered its importers a 20 per cent reduction from the normal freight rates. Later, three old New York packets were purchased to form a Baltimore-Liverpool line, but it never amounted to much. Spasmodic attempts to inaugurate ocean packet service from Charleston and other cotton ports met with even less success. Foreign packet competition was negligible. Except for a short-lived line of British brigs between Hull in England and New York, and the Hamburg-American Line before it turned to steam, almost every ocean packet flew the Stars and Stripes, and most of them had "of New York" painted on their sterns as their hailing port.

The early packets were little ships. The smallest of all, the Havre liner *Henry*, measured only 257 tons; 93 feet in length and 25 feet in beam. That tubby proportion characterized most of the earlier sailing liners. The ratio of length to beam gradually increased until, at the end, it occasionally exceeded 5 to 1. Most of the regular traders assembled to form the first lines, ranged from 300 to 400 tons. The combined tonnage of the first four Black Ballers was less than that of the frigate *Constitution* or that other most celebrated of American sailing ships, the clipper *Flying Cloud*. The reason for the small packets was not the inability of the local yards to build larger vessels, for New York had produced a sister ship of the *Constitution* and was turning out merchantmen of 900 tons. On the contrary, the packet owners themselves showed great moderation in adapting the size of their ships to the business of the moment, and later, when larger packets seemed likely to pay, they ordered them built. Gradually, over a period of more than thirty years, the tonnage of the packets steadily crept upwards, passing the 600-ton mark in 1826, 700 tons in 1834, and 1000 tons in 1838. It reached its maximum in 1854 with the 1771-ton *Amazon*, 215 feet long and 42 feet in beam, only 11 tons smaller than the *Flying Cloud*, which was 13 feet longer and 16 inches narrower.

The packets gradually changed somewhat in outward appearance as they grew in size. Of course, all of them, from the little *Henry* to the huge *Amazon*, shared the beauty inherent in the full-rigged ship, with yards and canvas on foremast, mainmast, and mizzenmast at right angles. The packets might often be distinguished from ordinary merchantmen by the naval smartness of their appearance. Decks, hulls, and rigging reflected this; and in dock, the yards were kept rigidly squared instead of hanging askew as was apt to be the case on ordinary craft. The arrangement of the topsides, or upper deck, however, underwent a progressive change. The earliest ships were flush-decked, with the upper line of their hull running in an unbroken gentle curve from stem to stern. The upper deck was relatively clear of encumbrances, save for the "barnyard," which every packet carried to provide for the table of the cabin passengers—with a cowpen and with pigs, sheep, and poultry crowded into the jolly boat lashed over the main hatch. The principal profits of a packet came from the " 'tween decks" below. Aft lay the captain's cabin and the passengers' quarters; midships and forward was considerable space for fine freight or, if occasion required, for steerage; still further forward was the forecastle for the crew's living quarters. Beneath that was the lower hold, generally used for the bulkier and less valuable freight. Gradually the passengers' quarters were brought out of the 'tween decks to better ventilated space on deck. At first, this simply took the form of a "roundhouse," which might be used as a lounge. Later, the "poopdecked" packets had their whole cabin passenger quarters in an additional deck aloft, sometimes running forward from the stern almost a third of the length of the ship. These innovations helped to make conditions more comfortable for the passengers, but many of the old sailors complained that they could not work the ship properly with this littering of the deck. The earlier ships were "bright-sided," with a broad band in natural finish or light colors around the hull; later this gave way to a conventional black, with a white band broken by imitation black gun ports. The inner finish of the topsides is said to have been light green at the start, gradually changing to white. On the more subtle question of hull design, more will be said later in connection with shipbuilding in general.

Finally, whatever their tonnage, deck arrangements, or design, the packets were among the toughest ships that sailed the seas. The smashing and wracking which every packet had to withstand in her westbound winter passage made this a necessity. For that reason, the builders sent south at considerable extra expense for locust, cedar, and above all live oak in order to make the hull as sturdy and durable as possible. Ordinary ships might be built more cheaply to the eastward with the white oak, which grew there, but the packet owners demanded the best, and were ready to pay for it.

Considerable homogeneity was given to the packets by the fact that most of them were built along a half-mile stretch of the East River, and the three most important shipyards there accounted for some two-thirds of them. A few were built in other East River yards and a few in Connecticut and New Bedford; by the late 'forties, the packet owners often sent further eastward to Boston, Newburyport, Portsmouth, and even to Maine, but in their origin as in their active service, the sailing liners were intimately linked with the East River.

The toughness of their construction is apparent in the long service of many of those old ships. For the first twenty years, at least, their actual line service was relatively brief, and they were soon replaced by larger ships with innovations to attract the passenger business. Seven years was a normal maximum for that earlier period and many were discarded after even briefer service. It was only in the later days, after the cabin passengers were patronizing the steamships, that the really long service records were achieved. Up to 1848, the longest steady line service was 19 years for the Havre packet *Sully*. That was barely half the total for the longest service record, that of the *Liverpool,* which was built in the spring of 1843 and battled the seas steadily on the Liverpool or London routes until the very last months of the packets in the autumn of 1880, a total of more than thirty-seven years. By a strange coincidence, the shortest packet record was that of an earlier *Liverpool,* which struck an iceberg on her maiden trip and went to the bottom forty days after she was launched.

Dismissal from line service did not, however, necessarily mean the end of a packet's usefulness. Nearly forty of the earlier packets were absorbed in the whaling fleet. The pioneer Black Baller, *Pacific,* built in 1807, chased whales around the seven seas until she finally fell apart in Panama Bay at the ripe age of seventy-five years. Many others remained in steady employment far beyond the allotted span of twenty years, which has been regarded the normal life of a ship both in those early days of wood and sail and the later days of steel and steam.

That gruelling grind of the packet service, wherein the liners made their regular sailings in times of harsh weather when other ships were lying snugly in port, required tough men as well as tough ships. It was a matter of survival of the fittest. Captains who could not make satisfactory speed records were in danger of being thrown quickly into the discard, while seamen who could not keep their footing aloft in a January gale soon received a two-line obituary in the marine news.

Until the clippers and steamships presented rival opportunities in the later days of the period, the packet captains were the cream of the American merchant marine. The position called for first-rate seamanship in order to maintain as much regularity as possible on that stormy route; it required sufficient force of character to keep the crews well in hand; and it also called for social attributes, since the captain had to play host for weeks on end to the cabin passengers. For those who stood the test, the rewards were generous. The captain's salary was only nominal but he could count on "primage" or 5 per cent of his ship's freight earnings, together with a larger portion of the income from passengers, and all the receipts from mails. Possibly $5000 a year was a fair average, and that income meant much more then than it does now. Many captains were part owners of their commands; a few owned the whole packet outright. They had the opportunity to associate with the nobility, diplomats, admirals, generals, literary lights, and merchant princes who crossed in their ships. Travellers often arranged their trips in order to sail with a favorite captain and sometimes the passengers would present the captain with silver plate or other valuable presents. Joseph Bonaparte, one-time king of Spain, used to engage the whole cabin on Captain Elisha E. Morgan's packet, when he crossed the Atlantic with his entourage to or from his New Jersey home, while Queen Victoria was received by Captain Morgan at London aboard the packet which was named for her. Along with profits and social contacts went the gratification of professional pride in receiving the command of a crack new liner—and during the 'twenties and 'thirties, that represented the pinnacle of American seagoing ambitions.

There were three principal approaches to that pinnacle. The first packet commands naturally went to captains who had already built up reputations as commanders of regular traders, Indiamen, or transients, with perhaps a little privateering on the side. By the 'thirties, however, when the service had become well established, men trained in packets were more likely to become their captains. A considerable number were promoted to ocean runs after good records in command of New Orleans or other coastal packets, but by far the largest number of later appointments went to mates on ocean packets. Mates' berths were not sought because of the pay, which was little more than that of ordinary seamen. The immediate recompense was psychological rather than material, for a packet mate had an unusual amount of immediate authority over the crew, since the presence of the passengers ordinarily forced the captain to remain aloof from the sort of roughness often needed in keeping a crew in order. A man might, moreover, pass up the command of an ordinary merchantman to become mate of a packet because that was the chief stepping-stone to the captaincy of a crack liner. The turnover in captains was even more rapid than in ships in the packet service. Many lasted only a year or two; and few made the rare record of twenty years of continuous packet command. Except in the London service, where most of the long records were achieved, the rapid turnover meant constant openings for able and ambitious mates.

If packet quarterdecks were the most sought after of all, the same could not be said for packet forecastles. Popular tradition has left the impression that all packets were "blood ships" with brutal "bucko mates," who gave clumsy or recalcitrant foremast hands a steady diet of "belaying pin soup." That picture doubtless fits many of the Liverpool packets during the period of decline in the late 'forties and in the 'fifties, but the testimony of a passenger on an early Black Ball trip paints an idyllic picture of studious youths reading in the forecastle library, when off duty. As time went on, the rapid expansion of the merchant marine opened up more attractive opportunities for this type of seagoing young men, who were usually New Englanders, and the supply of foremast hands definitely deteriorated. The packet forecastles came to be filled either with greenhorns, incompetent for the work aloft, or with tough "packet rats," living in a constant state of hostility with the "'old man" and the mates. The famous shanty "Blow the Man Down!" describes the supposed conditions aboard a Black Baller in those later days.

Until steam competition gradually cut into their monopoly, the three particularly important functions of the packets were as principal links between America and Europe. They generally bore the latest news from the other side of the Atlantic; they carried most of the trans-Atlantic travellers; and they took in their holds the most valuable cargoes in American commerce of that day. The arrival of the latest packet from overseas was, therefore, a matter of vital interest to the business world and often to the public at large.

In these days of instantaneous communications around the world, it is hard to realize how stale was Europe's news of America and how even more stale, because of the prevailing westerly winds on the North Atlantic, was America's news of Europe. The direction of those winds was unfortunate, for Americans were more curious about what was happening in Europe than Europe was about events on this side of the ocean. American business, too, was on the whole more sensitive to overseas conditions than was the European.

In view of the general American thirst for overseas information, the packets did what they could to bring it as speedily as possible. But in spite of punctual sailings and hard driving, the date of their arrival depended upon the winds out on the North Atlantic. Whereas the eastbound passages from New York usually took only three weeks or so with following winds, the trips to New York generally required at least five weeks, and during the winter months, sometimes eight. That was the best the packets could do; but it was decidedly faster than the transmission of news across the Atlantic in the pre-packet days. One has only to examine the newspaper files of that earlier period to appreciate the steady performance of the packets. The passages of the 97 vessels, arriving at New York from Liverpool in 1816, for instance, averaged seven weeks (49.4 days). The record for the British government mail brigs from Falmouth was almost identical, for their speed was offset by the roundabout route via Halifax or Bermuda.

An analysis of 4160 westbound crossings on the Liverpool, the London, and the Havre runs during the first forty years of packet service shows an average of 36.2 days. The Liverpool packets were fastest, at 35.3 days; the London record was almost as good, at 36.1 days from Portsmouth; while the Havre liners lagged, as usual, at 37.7. There was a gradual improvement during the period. During the first five years the Liverpool average was just 39 days; in the five years 1848–52, it was at its best at 33.3. The bulk of the trips lasted from thirty to forty days—passengers could bet, as they often did, with about equal prospects of success on any particular figure within that range. Occasional trips, however, fell far outside that range. The two fastest passages were the 16-day crossings of the Black Ballers *Yorkshire* and *Harvest Queen*. These were made possible because the winds blew from the eastward for a change. The slow trips generally came in the winter months when gales or ice could sometimes, but only rarely, stretch out a trip to ten or twelve weeks. The slowest passage of them all was the 89-day passage of the *Patrick Henry* late in the period. A freak passage, which illustrates well the uncertainty of dependence upon the winds, was the 69-day crossing of the Black Baller *South America* under Captain Robert H. Waterman in the winter of 1833–34. She had one of the fastest general averages of all the packets; while Waterman later set up a series of all-time speed records as a clipper commander, yet there were only a dozen or so slower packet trips in the whole forty years!

The information sought from overseas consisted both of regular news and of particular commercial information. American newspaper editors complained that second-rate gossip from abroad was read more eagerly than important items about domestic affairs. The American public, for instance, followed with intense curiosity the lively details of Queen Caroline's divorce proceedings in 1820 and sometimes a quarter or third of the whole space in a daily issue would be given over to the latest account. It was, however, a case of "to be continued in our next" with no sure knowledge of when that next would come—depending as it did upon how hard the winds happened to be blowing in mid-Atlantic. Possibly such suspense added zest to the news, when it eventually arrived.

The New York newspapers took very seriously their unique position as purveyors of foreign news to the American public and went to great pains to secure it at the earliest possible moment. Frequently a packet might be becalmed or fogbound for several days off Sandy Hook or Long Island. Then the newspapers sent little sloops or schooners out to meet them. Often the news boats reached the incoming ships long ahead of the pilots and then raced for port so that an extra might be quickly published. Some of the papers co-operated to support a single news boat and thus reduce the expense, but generally one enterprising competitor would have a boat of its own and the resultant keen rivalry brought the overseas tidings even faster to the waiting public.

To many Americans, the news from abroad often meant something far more vital than the gratification of idle curiosity. A temporary suspension of the British corn laws, which would mean the chance to export flour or grain to England, or a rise of twopence a pound in the price of cotton at Liverpool might mean fortunes to those who learned of it before the general public. This advance knowledge would, of course, make it possible to buy flour or cotton at normal prices before the news produced a boom. That was one of the advantages of packet ownership. The incoming liner bearing news of financial moment often sent a mate ashore on Long Island with instructions to carry such information to the owners privately. The packet, meanwhile, would dawdle along toward Sandy Hook to give ample time for profits to be made by the advance information. Even when the news was published, New York had a decided advantage over Philadelphia and its other rivals. It was charged on more than one occasion that the regular mail carriers were bribed or otherwise delayed while private couriers dashed southward in order to "clean up" at Philadelphia or Baltimore. During the cotton boom of 1825 and the panic of 1837, such advance news brought by the packets was of special economic significance.

The other two distinctive functions of the early packets—the carrying of passengers and fine freight—need only brief mention here, for they will be discussed elsewhere. It is enough to say that the regularity of the line sailings and the relative speed of the packet passages quickly lured travellers away from the British mail brigs and the regular traders. In 1826, for instance, 454 cabin passengers arrived at New York from Liverpool by packet and only 131 by other vessels. The steerage passengers were in reverse proportion, for the packets, which were not eager for that trade, brought only 295, while the other vessels carried 2032. Most of those important in government, business, letters, and society were to be found travelling by packet. The cost of an eastbound cabin passage during most of the early period was "40 guineas, wines included"; for the slower westbound crossings, when the passengers would have to be furnished meals for a longer period, the charge was a guinea higher. Only the Havre packets carried any considerable number of immigrants during the early years; not until the steamships had cut into the cabin trade and the fine freight, did the Liverpool packets devote their " 'tween decks" to this less attractive form of business.

As for the "fine freight," the same advantages of fixed sailings and quick crossings transferred much of the business from the regular traders to the packets. Instead of the old irritating uncertainty about the relative chances of early sailings of various vessels, the shippers found it much more satisfactory to send their freight to the packet agents. They found that by patronizing the packets their freight was forwarded quickly and that the period during which their goods lay unproductive in port or on the ocean was materially reduced. Even for shipments from Liverpool, say to Boston, Philadelphia, or Charleston, it was at any rate easier and generally quicker to send them to New York by packet and have them distributed by the coastal steam or sailing lines from that port. Once these advantages were realized and habits formed, not only was the success of the packets assured, but New York was in a position to take its profits on business which, before the packets, would not have come within a hundred miles of Sandy Hook. Even the opening of the Erie Canal did not blind certain contemporaries, such as Hezekiah Niles, the Baltimore editor, and Lieutenant Maury, the oceanographer, to the significance of this fact.

In that, more than in anything else, the ocean packets contributed to the rise of New York port. The tremendous volume of trade on the Atlantic shuttle assured constant cargoes, some of which represented high value in small bulk. In the course of her three annual voyages, a packet would probably carry more valuable freight than an East Indiaman in her single annual voyage and the duties collected on these packet cargoes at the New York Custom House paid a considerable part of the running expenses of the United States government. Ultimately, of course, the very considerations of speed and regularity which had shifted this business from regular traders to packets moved it on again from packets to the ocean steamships.

CHAPTER IV

DRY GOODS, HARDWARE, AND WET GOODS

IN THEIR dresses and "unmentionables," the women of 1855 probably carried around more yards of cloth than any others before or since. From the rather scanty directory gowns at the beginning of the century, a gradual increase reached its culmination in the huge bell skirts, supported by half a dozen petticoats. A prominent authority on the history of costume, when consulted on this matter, estimated that the average dress of 1855 required some thirty yards of material, while the petticoats and other garments underneath brought the total close to a hundred yards. This was about eight times the amount needed for all purposes in 1800, and it was sufficient to clothe fourteen women in the nineteen twenties when the cycle of styles had once more swung around to scantiness.[1]

The relationship of feminine fashions to commercial history may seem obscure until one recalls that the prosperity of New York, New Orleans, Liverpool, and certain other ports rested primarily upon trade in the raw materials or finished products of such textiles and that the more the women wore, the more business there was for all concerned. Those bell skirts, with their voluminous underpinnings, might be termed a style that launched a thousand ships, but we shall not go so far as to claim that the decline of the American merchant marine was caused by the substitution of the wire hoop for four or five of the petticoats around 1856.

A correspondent in a Liverpool newspaper complained of this trend toward fullness as early as 1829, when its effects began to be noticeable:

Among the novelties of the times, the fashions of ladies' dresses are peculiarly remarkable, when contrasted with those in vogue twenty years ago. At that time five and a half or six yards of cloth were considered sufficient

[1] See Appendix, xxv.

for the making of a lady's gown of fashionable cut, so closely was that garment fitted to the shape. . . .

If the ladies of 1800 were guilty of scanty garments, those of 1829 are delinquents in the opposite extreme, by enlarging and modelling their lovely forms to the beau ideal of female beauty, by means of bustles, cushions, plaiting, stuffing, puffing, and other elegant et ceteras of the toilet. . . .

We should not feel inclined to reprehend this profuse expenditure of clothing material, were it observed without rendering its objects somewhat ridiculous, for it must tend greatly to increase the consumption of goods, and thus benefit the manufacturing interests of the country. . . .

Supposing a man should marry a woman thus built and inflated to the roundness and symmetry of beauty on the supposition that such shape was her own : how would he look when he found that all he admired was the effect of mere padding and stuffing? that she was inflated into symmetry . . .? Might he not demand an annulling of the marriage contract? might he not plead that he had been cheated and deceived? Might he not say, "I married, as I thought, a fine, robust, well formed woman : I find her divested of her borrowed plumes and stuffing, an ordinary feeble-bodied object, as shapeless as a post !"

It seems singularly inappropriate that such a plaint should have come from Liverpool of all places, for its whole prominence and prosperity rested on the volume of textiles which it handled. New York, which was also vitally concerned in the business, was more ready to sacrifice æsthetic to practical considerations. The *Evening Post,* commenting upon the Liverpool article, remarked, "We sincerely hope that the present amplitude of female drapery will not cease to be the mode. . . . It contributes to the warmth if not the adornment of the person."

The changes in men's styles were less violent during those years. Throughout the period, the well-dressed man required only about twelve or thirteen yards of material, but the proportion of woollen goods increased as long trousers gradually replaced the former silken knee breeches.

These textiles composed the most valuable part of the freight carried westward by the packets and other vessels on the Atlantic shuttle from England and the Continent to New York. Numerous other articles of various sorts were brought across the North Atlantic in the teeth of the westerly gales in return for the cotton, flour, tobacco, naval stores, and other American products shipped eastward. Iron in its various forms from penknives to railroad rails figured prominently and so, too, did the various kinds of alcoholic stimulants from wines to gin. All of these were dwarfed into insignificance, however, in comparison with the textiles, which, as Britain's chief article of export and the United States' chief article of importation, towered above all else in the world of commerce in that day. For New York in particular, textiles were of outstanding importance since in such imports its leadership was more pronounced than in any other branch of the nation's commerce.

As the result of being the pioneer in the Industrial Revolution, England easily led in the field of manufactured products by 1815. For a half century English industry had been shifting from the old handicraft stage of the spinning wheel and hand loom to the use of power machinery concentrated in factories. The inventions of Hargreaves, Arkwright, Crompton, and Cartwright had enabled the English to make cloth far more cheaply and in much larger quantities than had been possible under the old methods. The textile business was not new to England, since for centuries the nation's commercial prosperity had rested upon some form of it. Back in the Middle Ages, England had limited itself to the production of raw wool, which outsiders had carried away to spin and weave, a passive economy similar to that of the American South with its cotton in our period. By an energetic economic policy, England finally achieved a more active rôle and by the days of Elizabeth, Merchant Adventurers were offering finished woollen cloth in every foreign market where they were able to wedge their way. This business continued to expand for two centuries more, with the growing market for England's woollen goods resting more upon commercial aggressiveness than upon advantages in production, since other nations could, if they would, use the same sort of spinning wheels and hand looms. By the late eighteenth century, England added to this long-established and successful system of world marketing the new and vital advantage of cheap, large-scale production of the Industrial Revolution. This enabled the English to undersell their rivals in most kinds of woollen and cotton goods—and to make their country the "workshop of the world" for nearly three-quarters of the nineteenth century.

The customs statistics show that throughout our period most of the American textile imports came from British ports, principally from Liverpool. In 1825, for instance, of a total $39,800,000 in value, $24,-300,000 came from the United Kingdom, $6,700,000 from France, $3,300,000 from China, $1,900,000 from Hamburg and Bremen, and $600,000 from India. The commanding position of the British was particularly marked in woollen and cotton goods, with 94 per cent and

88 per cent respectively. They also sent 54 per cent of the linen and other manufactures of flax, chiefly produced in Ireland, but in silks, which were almost as valuable as the woollens or cotton goods, they sent only 2 per cent. In 1860, those proportions were much the same, with some $85,000,000 out of a total of $120,000,000 for all textiles coming from British ports. The only important difference at the later date was the marked increase in silk shipments from England, amounting to slightly more than half the total. These figures do not necessarily imply that all the goods shipped from a particular country were manufactured there, but at least they indicate why the Liverpool-New York shuttle was so important.

Of the textiles shipped from non-British ports, those from France, particularly from Havre, stood second. It was the outlet for the manufactures of Switzerland, and of part of Germany and Italy, as well as for the French industrial centers. Silk, manufactured at Lyons and other French centers, bulked largest in this category. In 1825, 55 per cent of the silk imports came from France, while the shipments of the other textiles were negligible. In 1860, the French silk shipments had dropped to 40 per cent. Ribbons, laces, and "luxury" articles of various sorts were more common than ordinary cloth in these arrivals from Havre.

Linen, which was gradually losing its earlier importance in competition with cheaper cotton goods, came not only from Ireland but also from Germany. In 1825, it stood first among the textile imports from Hamburg and Bremen. By 1860, those "Hanse towns" were also sending a considerable quantity of hosiery and other knit goods, both cotton and woollen.

While most of the textile imports arrived by way of the Atlantic shuttle, a modest and decreasing amount came from more distant regions. In 1825, the silk imports from China amounted to $3,000,-000, or 30 per cent of the total; by 1860, this had dropped to $900,000, or about 3 per cent. China and India also sent a modest quantity of nankeens and other cheap cotton goods at the outset; but these were among the first victims of the protective tariff, and were generally reshipped to Latin America, with the duties refunded.

The magnitude of the textile trade warrants a still further parading of statistics, for it overshadowed all else in the world of commerce. Throughout our period, textiles amounted to nearly 60 per cent of England's domestic exports and about one third of the imports of the

United States. As far as England was concerned, the upstart cotton industry rapidly overtook the long-established manufacture of woollens, the cotton exports being about double those of all other textiles combined. In American imports, however, woollens maintained a slight lead over cotton goods throughout most of the period in value though not in volume. One yard of woollen goods, of course, was worth as much as several yards of cotton cloth. In 1821, for instance, the per capita imports, for every man, woman, and child in the United States, amounted to 69 cents in woollens and 61 cents in cotton goods. By 1860, increasing prosperity and voluminous styles had apparently offset the inroads of domestic manufactures, and those figures had nearly doubled, standing at $1.36 for woollens and at $1.00 for cotton goods. At the latter date, the end of our period, the nation's textile imports amounted to $37,900,000 for woollens, $32,900,000 for silk goods, $32,500,000 for cotton goods, $10,700,000 for linen and other manufactures of flax; exclusive of $4,000,000 for lace, $2,100,000 for ready-made clothing and a few other minor items. The relative importance of this trade is evident if we realize that the woollen, silk, and cotton manufactures were each more valuable than the highest non-textile imports, which were sugar at $31,000,000, coffee at $21,800,000 and iron and steel close behind at $21,500,000. The cargoes of tea from China, so suggestive of wealth, totalled only $8,900,000.

These textile imports were the outstanding feature of New York's whole business as a seaport in this period and the port had almost a monopoly of them. Adequate figures are lacking for commodity imports by ports in the early years, but by 1860, New York had become the distributing center for the United States to such an extent that out of the national total of some $120,000,000 worth of textile imports, about $101,000,000 arrived by way of Sandy Hook. The other ports lagged hopelessly behind, with Boston not quite $8,000,000; New Orleans, $4,600,000; Philadelphia, $3,700,000; San Francisco, not quite $1,000,000; and Baltimore, less than $700,000. New York port thus played a distinctive role in clothing the American people. This was doubtless its most profitable single activity.[1]

At this distance, and with the old customs manifests burned, we are often able only to guess the amount of textiles carried by particular ships or handled by particular merchants. The incoming textile cargoes were designated merely by the vague phrase "merchandize." The bales,

[1]See Appendix, x.

cases, and square hair-covered trunks, moreover, were an elusive basis for estimating values, compared with the fairly uniform staple articles such as barrels of flour or bales of raw cotton. Besides, a bewildering variety of cloths were made from each of the major textiles. The merchants of that day knew their names and respective attributes, but today even many of the old names are obsolete. Broadcloths, satinets, kerseys, blankets, and flannels covered only a part of the woollen cloth, while cotton goods included much else besides muslins, calicoes, sheetings, and shirtings. It took a practiced eye to know, for example, whether a consignment of blue broadcloth was dyed with indigo, which would hold fast, or had gained its color more cheaply with logwood, which might run or change color. Altogether it was a complicated trade.

New York's rapid commercial rise, as we saw, was stimulated when the British selected it as the center of their "dumping" operations early in 1815. A huge surplus of textiles and other manufactures had been piling up in England during the years when war had interrupted trade with America and the Continent; and manufacturers were naturally ready to sell them for whatever they might bring. At New York, on the other hand, textiles had become increasingly scarce as the War of 1812 dragged on, while the few lots which found their way to the port by devious means commanded high prices. Scoville, the chronicler of the old New York merchants, tells the story of one young New Yorker, who had recently entered the textile business without much capital. Early in February, 1815, he attended an auction of these scarce imported cloths and bid to the limit of his resources for one lot which went, however, at an abnormally high price to his former employer. News of the peace treaty arrived that night and the bottom dropped out of the textile market. The young merchant realized his good fortune, for a week later he found that he was able to buy similar goods at only a fraction of that earlier price. Many others were not as fortunate and were caught with considerable stocks of woollens and cottons, which they had to sell at tremendous losses. One young Connecticut Yankee, Stephen B. Munn, extricated himself from the situation by exchanging his cloth for the land warrants, which had been given the soldiers. Then he laid the basis of a big fortune by swapping those frontier lands in turn for New York real estate.

It took presence of mind and luck of that sort during the early period of peace to keep on one's feet in the Pearl Street textile business. Even before the *Massachusetts* arrived in May direct from Liverpool with her million-dollar cargo, various other vessels, which had been awaiting the peace at Halifax or Bermuda, had poured a generous stock of British manufactures into the empty market. This new rush of imports, instead of being handled by importing merchants who had bought outright from British manufacturers or exporting merchants in the usual way, was put up for sale by the manufacturer's agents at auctions, which will be discussed further in a later chapter. The importing merchant, unable to compete with the violent price fluctuations of the auction rooms, dropped out of the picture for the time being. New York jobbers and country merchants from far and wide flocked to the Pearl Street auctions, lured by the ever-present chance for bargains. This established a custom which would last for years, for even when more normal importing returned after a quarter century or so, the southern and western merchants kept on coming to Pearl Street to make their purchases. Thus lured to New York for textiles, they would also buy other articles of every sort, and so strengthened the port's commanding position as the great entrepôt of American trade.[1]

This flood of British textiles became the storm center of violent tariff disputes. The Pearl Street auction rooms and the "damned Yorkshiremen," as Hezekiah Niles called the manufacturers' agents in his protectionist weekly, were distasteful not only to the old importers, whose business was thus undermined, but also to the cotton-mill operators who had built up that "infant industry" during the period of interrupted trade between the Embargo Act and the coming of peace. The little cotton mills in New England could not count on adequate returns for their wares with the British manufactures selling in vast quantities at sacrifice prices; and many of them folded up quickly.

This clamor from the domestic manufacturers and importers led to a moderate protective tariff in 1816, with changes at frequent intervals thereafter. Woollen and cotton goods, because of their volume in trade, naturally were particularly subject to attack in the perennial disputes but here there is no occasion to follow the historians of the tariff through the maze of changes. The New Yorkers divided on the merits of protection and free trade. The principal local excitement occurred in connection with the passage of the irrational "Tariff of Abominations" in 1828. It was passed in the middle of May and its increased rates were to go into effect, as far as textiles were concerned, on the

[1]See Appendix, xvii.

first of July. This was a time of cruel anxiety for those who had ordered from abroad, for the passage of the bill came too late to countermand orders in those days of slow communications. Excitement increased as the July deadline approached, for numerous cargoes were on the high seas and it was difficult to predict within ten days how long a westbound passage might take. The Swallowtail packet *Silas Richards* slipped in under the deadline on June 29 with a valuable cargo. Two days later, the *Evening Post* gave an appreciative account of the last minute rush:

Today that unblessed act, the *tariff,* commences to operate, and we are pleased to learn that all the gentlemen connected with the revenue department manifest a very proper solicitude for the shipping and commercial interest. Yesterday we understand that Capt. Benjamin Wood, the boarding officer at Quarantine Ground, continued to board the inward bound vessels and endorse their manifests till 12 o'clock at night, thereby saving to the merchants large sums of money which would have been payable under the new tariff, if the same service had been deferred until this morning. Such generous and praiseworthy conduct deserves the commendation and thanks of all classes of our citizens, except the woollen manufacturers.

Some vessels, however, came too late to take advantage even of that act of grace. The ship *Franklin,* for instance, left Liverpool on May 18, six days ahead of the lucky *Silas Richards,* but she did not reach New York until July 6. It was estimated that the additional duties on the green baizes, fine flannels, carpeting and low-priced cloths in her cargo amounted to $70,000. "The greater portion," remarked the *Post,* "will probably be entered in bond, and reexported in British bottoms to another market." Such instances help one to appreciate the changes later wrought by steam and the cable on the Atlantic shuttle.

At times, however, tariff legislation met more favor with the merchants of the port. Their agitation helped to secure the Warehousing Act of 1842, which facilitated the storage of imported goods in bonded warehouses, with payment of duties only when they were withdrawn for internal consumption. This simplified the shipment of British manufactures to Canada by way of New York. The achievement of moderate tariff reciprocity with Canada and other parts of British North America in 1854 further stimulated the trade to the northward.

The tariff affected the New York textile market in another way, by stimulating the competition between domestic and imported goods. A significant feature between 1816 and 1832 was the establishing of a minimum *ad valorem* rate on cotton and woollen goods. This meant, for instance, that a duty of 25 per cent was charged on all cotton goods, but the minimum basis for reckoning was 25 cents a yard, which meant a duty of 6¼ cents. As the price of the cheaper and coarser grades gradually dropped to less than nine cents a yard, this afforded very powerful protection to that type of domestic cotton goods. Similar protection was granted to woollen manufactures, but was partly offset by a duty on raw wool. The American factories had not yet developed adequate technique to produce satisfactory substitutes for the finer grades of imported textiles but they steadily increased their production of the cheaper sorts. Factories by the score were constantly springing up, particularly in New England. In the cotton industry, the total number of spindles in the country was reckoned at 8000 in 1807, 87,000 in 1810, 130,000 in 1815, 800,000 in 1825, 2,300,000 in 1840 and 5,200,-000 in 1860. That final total was about equal to the number in France, more than double the number in Germany, but still very far behind the British total of 30,000,000. By 1860, the output of the domestic cotton factories was valued at $115,000,000, more than three times as much as the imported cotton goods, while the American woollen output was reckoned at about $69,000,000, as compared with imports of nearly $38,000,000.

For a while, it looked as though Boston, as the center of the New England factory district, would profit at New York's expense as the increasing domestic production relieved the dependence upon foreign textiles. For several years, Boston held great annual auctions of domestic cloths which attracted buyers from many parts of the country. New York's well-established position as a general entrepôt stood it in good stead here as in many other ways, and gradually drew the business from Boston to Pearl Street. The merchants from the South and West found it more convenient to buy all their stocks in New York rather than to go up to Boston for "domestics" after ordering their imported goods on Pearl Street. As a result, by the 'forties, the products of the New England mills were being brought to New York either by Sound steamers or by the little packet schooners around Cape Cod. New Yorkers were thus handling and taking profits on most of the nation's textile supply, whether spun and woven at Manchester, Leeds, Lowell, or Fall River.

Closely related to the importation of textiles was the trade in ready-made clothing. Some of this was imported but still more was made up

at New York of imported and domestic fabrics in about equal proportion. The pioneer in this business is said to have been James Chesterman, a journeyman tailor who migrated to New York about 1800 from
Bolton, one of the most active manufacturing centers in Lancashire.
During the 'twenties, Chesterman and two associates "commenced importing ready-made clothing from Europe, in which business they realized a handsome fortune," Chesterman being rated as a millionaire by
the mid-'fifties. Although most people in the East had their clothing
made by tailors, dressmakers, or at home, there seems to have been a
good business in making up garments, more durable than fashionable,
for laborers and for the South and West. One enterprising New Yorker
went into this business heavily, later establishing branches at New
Orleans and other centers. Not all the ready-made clothing was of ordinary sort, however, and as early as 1831 there was advertised at auction
a stock of 5000 garments, "part of a stock of a fashionable clothing
store," and including "superfine blue, black, brown and green cloth
dress, frock and short coats and pantaloons; cloth, camblet and tartan
plaid cloaks; cloth, violet, marseilles, valence and silk vests; seasonable
pantaloons and round jackets; cotton shirts, linen collars & c." The
word cloth, it will be noticed, was used in a narrow sense, denoting
a particular type of woollen goods. According to census figures which
cannot be taken too literally, New York led all other states in the
manufacture of clothing, turning out products worth $16,000,000 a
year in 1850 and nearly $25,000,000 in 1860, more than a third of the
national total in each case. A large part of this state total came from
New York City and its vicinity. In addition, the imports of ready-made
clothing and wearing apparel amounted to some $820,000 in 1850 and
$2,000,000 in 1860, New York's share at the latter date being $1,500,-
000. England furnished about half of the total and France about a
third, most of the remainder coming from Hamburg and China.

The world of fashion was not interested in ordinary ready-made
clothing, but it furnished a constant market for certain articles in the
latest styles, imported from Havre. This "luxury" trade included not
only silks, ribbons, laces, and fancy vest materials, but hats and bon-
nets as well. As early as 1817, one Mme. Devaux was advertising that
on the following Saturday she would "open one case of spring hats,
just received from Paris, of the newest fashion; and also one case of
ladies' black crape dresses," while she had "just received the latest
number of *The Journal of Fashions,* containing a description of the

NEW YORK FROM BROOKLYN HEIGHTS IN 1837

The East River is in the foreground; beyond it in turn are New York City, the Hudson River and the New Jersey shore

latest that have been adopted in that metropolis." In 1835, Aaron Burr appeared as one of the counsel for Eugene Martineau, a dealer in these luxury imports, who was suing one John Odronaux, a sugar refiner, for the balance of a $1236.34 bill. This had been run up in four months by his estranged wife in purchases for herself, three daughters, and the fair of the Catholic Asylum. The items, only part of which are listed below, with the original spelling, give an idea of the sort of articles which helped to make the Havre trade important:

A black uncut velvet hat trimmed with gauze and black artificial feathers, gauze ribbons, blond lace inside	16.00
3 Donna Maria gauze scarfs with tassels at 2.00	6.00
A real bird of paradise (entire)	40.00
A circular box for the above bird	2.00
A rich pearl buckle	4.50
A Paris made pink satin tippet wadded all through and trimmed with swan fur	20.00
An embroidered pink crape dress	26.00
A bug colored real thibet shawl	10.00
16¼ yards pink poule de soie at 1.25	20.30
A pair of chaly fancy shoes	2.50
A pair of long white silk lace gloves	4.00
A blue satin French hat trimmed with two blue feathers, wreath inside	16.00
A blond thulle inside handkerchief trimmed with rush and blond lace	4.50
8 rich striped and figured Hernani shawls at 4.00	32.00
A blond lace hdkf. a la Paysanne, trimmed with gauze ribbon and rush	10.00
2 doz. watered and embroidered with gold and silver bead bags	96.00
8 boxes French sugar plums and fruits from the Fidel. Berger, at 22s	12.00
1 small poule de soie Dress with embroidered sleeves	5.00
A fancy smelling cushion for Hdkfs.	7.00
6 embroidered silk stockings at 3.00	18.00
A long pink figured sattin Pellarine trimmed with swan	20.00
6 bottles cologne water	3.00
A bunch of fine rice papered flowers	3.00

Some of the material imported from Havre was intended for reexport to the southward. An advertisement of DeRham, Iselin and Moore, an outstanding house in this field, headed by Henry C. DeRham, Swiss consul, included, along with ribbons, Florences, Gros de Naples, Satin Russe, Plush, sewing silk and Leghorn Hats, "embroidered Swiss muslin robes, adapted to the Mexican market," listons (whatever they might be) in assorted high colors "put up with great attention for the southern markets," and French printed muslins, "suitable for exportation." A Havre packet was named for DeRham in recognition of the large amount of business which was brought to the line.

The packet service with its regularity was of particular importance in this luxury trade with its emphasis on the latest Paris modes. By 1825, a Boston critic of New York's increasing business pointed out that the regular traders, bringing cargoes twice a year to Boston, could not compete with the Havre-New York packets. The frequent sailings of the latter enabled merchants to keep their stock constantly up to the minute without having to load up with articles which might go out of style before they were sold.

Iron in its manifold forms stood next to dry goods in importance in the cargoes which came westward on the Atlantic shuttle. As in the case of textiles, the technological advances of the Industrial Revolution had given a tremendous stimulus to a long-established British industry. In both cases, the United States depended almost entirely upon England and other overseas nations before American industry reached a position to meet local demands. The relief from such foreign dependence came more slowly in iron than in dry goods and as late as 1850, three-fifths of the nation's iron needs were still being supplied from abroad.

As far as value went, the different imports of iron amounted to only a sixth of the textile total and consequently they were of less concern to the importing merchants. With the shipowners, it was a different story because the weight and bulk of the iron cargoes created a much greater demand for tonnage than the textiles, which represented large value in small bulk.

England figures about as impressively in this trade as in dry goods, but, because of the difficulty of handling the material, there was less tendency to concentrate the business at particular ports. Because of its bulk, "heavy iron," such as rails, was usually shipped from the port closest to where it was produced to the port nearest to the place of ultimate consumption. Liverpool and New York figured more heavily than their rivals, but they did not enjoy the remarkable concentration of business which they commanded in the textile trade. In 1860, for instance, when New York received more than 80 per cent of the nation's textile imports, it handled only 57 per cent of the arriving iron.

The iron trade fell into three major parts. First, and at the beginning by far the most important, came the finished cutlery and hardware manufactured at Birmingham, Sheffield, and other centers of the industry. These knives, pots, pans, and much else were usually shipped from Liverpool. Throughout the period heavy importations of iron and steel were made in semifinished form, such as bars, sheets, rods, and the like. The third major group consisted of the heavier manufactures, particularly railroad rails, increasing in importance as time went on and generally shipped from Bristol or some other outlet of the South Wales industry. While steel in its finer forms was represented, of course, in Sheffield cutlery from the beginning, the great age of steel did not come until after Bessemer's experiments at the very end of our period.

Sheffield and Birmingham became in the iron and steel business what Manchester and Leeds were in textiles. For centuries, Sheffield blades had been celebrated and its only rival in steel production in the early nineteenth century was Essen in Germany. Sheffield furnished a considerable part of the knives, scissors, edged tools, and similar steel products used in the United States a century ago. The city was so closely connected with the New York trade, that when the Red Star Line named one of its packets the *Sheffield,* the merchants there engaged in the American export business presented her with a flag.

The same line had already named another ship the *Birmingham,* for that more versatile city on the edge of the "Black Country" was turning out a remarkably variegated array of articles, chiefly but by no means wholly made from iron. In the summer of 1815, a New York importer advertised the contents of forty-two casks of assorted Birmingham wares, imported in one of the ships which swarmed from Liverpool in the "dumping" rush which followed the news of peace. The scores of items, thrown together with the illogical lack of sequence and relationship common to the commercial notices of that day serve to indicate the wide scope of the factories of "Brummagem" as the city was popularly called. There were compasses, thimbles, pincers, hammers, gimlets, tap borers, trunk handles, nails, commode knobs, binding wire, knitting pins, brushes, curtain rings, cloak and curtain pins, bells, fencing foils, skates, tongs, shovels, pokers, clock balls, pinions, forged work, castings, eyes, cranks, knobs, locks, fishhooks, watches, spoons, shuttles, snuffers, corkscrews, bodkins, mainsprings, screws, keys, coal "scoupes," hods and buckets, hinges, dustpans, sifters, gridirons, coffee mills, stair rods, staples, tea urns, block-tin teakettles, tea and coffee pots, inkstands, caddies, graters, carpenters' rules, squirrel chains, dog calls, powder flasks, Norfolk and thumb latches, spittoons, tenterhooks, hobnails, beefsteak tongs, dog collars and chains, gigging irons and surveyors' chains, as well as such non-metallic products as glass gauges, brushes (hearth, bottle, clothes, hair, nail, tooth, etc.), children's rattles, game boards, pencils, backgammon boards, chessmen, green wax, "segar boxes," corals, shot belts, gun charges, gunflints, gun picks, bellows, saddlery, fishing tackle, and morocco cases of needles. Another cargo, which arrived that autumn, included such additional items, probably from Sheffield as well as Birmingham, as knives, forks, pens, "chissels," plane irons, Britannia metal teapots, gilt and plated coat and vest buttons, fowling pieces and pistols, spectacles, frying pans, anvils, and files. The following year a merchant advertised, among his imports from Birmingham, a most amazing item, indicating that the British had not taken the late war too seriously—"victory furnitures" celebrating the recent American victories on land and sea! Apparently the ingenuity of the Birmingham manufacturers of that day knew no limit. As for the reputation of these products, old Rufus King, the former minister to the Court of St. James's, once compared a certain New Jersey senator to "Brummagem ware"—shiny, brittle, and made for the American market.

In the importation of partly finished iron from abroad for the purpose of working it into its final form on this side, the bar, pig, and sheet iron, together with steel, amounted to between one-third and one-half of the total value of iron imports. About a half of the national imports came to New York, where the firms of Blackwell, McFarlane & Co., Boorman, Johnson & Co., and Phelps & Peck made a specialty of it. This was the branch of the iron trade where England's monopoly was less secure, because considerable amounts came from Sweden and other parts of the Baltic. At the very beginning of our period, in July, 1815, for instance, Blackwell & McFarlane were advertising "300 tons Swedes, Russia and English Iron—flat, square and round, of all sizes . . . landing from different vessels." Phelps & Peck, whose business was so extensive that Anson G. Phelps became the leading metal importer of the country, did not limit themselves to iron; but also brought in large quantities of brass, lead, tin, and copper, with copper sheathing for vessels a particular specialty.

Gradually, "heavy" iron manufacture began to grow up in the South Wales region, with shipments from the old port of Bristol and from Newport, as well as from the new port of Cardiff, opened after a huge capital outlay by the Earl of Bute. In 1824, New York received from Bristol the iron pipes for its new gas system.

Within a few years, a far more extensive business began when the new American railroads sent abroad for rails, or "railroad iron" as the phrase went. Some of this consisted simply of flat iron strips fastened to the top of wooden rails. Robert L. Stevens of Hoboken, however, was not satisfied with this crude device. The same versatile genius which led him to invent many of the significant steamboat devices made him consider a solid iron rail. When the Stevens family undertook the building of the Camden & Amboy Railroad to link New York and Philadelphia, Robert went to England to secure rails. Crossing on the Black Baller *Hibernia,* he one day picked up a block of wood and began some thoughtful whittling. When he was through, he had produced a section of the "T" rail, very much as we know it today. An iron manufacturer in South Wales, after some arduous experiments, managed to turn out a satisfactory product. The first cargoes were shipped to Philadelphia, as that end of the line was to be completed first. Ships carried some 600 tons at a time—one of them, a former Black Baller, bound from Bristol to Philadelphia, struck a shoal near Cape Henlopen where the heavy cargo pounded her bottom out. New York, in the meantime, soon began to receive rails for the new series of railroads running parallel to the Erie Canal.

From that time on, the rapid increase of the American railroad net meant that ships by the score loaded up with two or three miles of rails when no better cargo offered. New York was more passive than its rivals in railroad construction until the late 'forties. Consequently there were some years when Boston, Philadelphia, and Baltimore ran well ahead. It was not bad when a ship merely filled out part of her cargo with rails, but when they were the chief item, there was apt to be trouble. In 1841, for instance, the ship *Echo,* bound from Liverpool to New York, encountered a heavy gale at sea. Losing two of her masts, she rolled heavily in the trough of the sea. "She was laden principally with railroad iron, eighty tons of which were between decks, which during the storm got loose, and at every roll was thrown against the side of the ship with tremendous violence." Numerous other accidents occurred, either in foundering at sea because of increased stiffness or from the added risk in running aground. The marine insurance rates jumped sharply when a ship's cargo of iron amounted to more than half of her registered tonnage.

During the late 'forties, occasional efforts were made to produce rails on this side of the Atlantic, notably by Abram Hewitt at Trenton, but it was difficult to compete in price with the British manufacturers, some of whom were accepting railroad bonds in payment. By the mid-'fifties, American industry began to take over part of the steadily increasing demand, but as late as 1860, the imports of railroad iron into the United States amounted to 122,000 tons, valued at $3,700,000. New York by that time stood first among the ports, with just about a third of the total, followed by New Orleans with a fifth.

The changes in women's styles which swelled the consumption of dry goods were mild when compared with the innovations which stimulated the use of "heavy" iron. The spread of railroads, with their demand for rails and bridges, was the chief factor in this, but by the mid-'fifties the use of iron beams in buildings pointed the way to still further demand. By that time, however, Pittsburgh was developing to a point where it could more and more relieve the dependence upon British sources; and not long after our period ends, the domestic iron and steel industry would make an even more spectacular rise than that made in the textile industry.

After dry goods and iron, the importation of wines and spirits was the most interesting aspect of the cargoes from Europe. In this branch of trade, as in textiles, New York played a prominent role. In several ways the trade in alcoholic beverages differed from that in dry goods and hardware. England's participation was slight compared with that of France, Holland, Spain, Portugal, and the wine islands. Linked with that was the fact that the Industrial Revolution did not affect this trade to any extent. Also, instead of showing a relative increase during the period, it showed a falling off in per capita consumption. This arose not so much from the temperance propaganda of the 'fifties as from the increasing use of domestic whiskey. The stills of the West were more immediately effective in relieving dependence upon Europe than were the spindles of Lowell and Fall River or the furnaces and foundries of Pittsburgh.

The range of New York tastes in drinking at the outset can be judged from the advertisement of James Farquhar & Son, liquor importers, in October, 1815. Their offerings consisted of

London Particular Madeiras, 5 to 20 years old; Lisbon Port, Sherry, Teneriffe, Marseilles and Sweet Sicily Wines, in whole, halves, and quarter pipes, demijohns and bottles; Claret, sparkling Champagne, very old Hoc, Barsac and Grave Wines; Bitters; old Batavia Arrack; Old Cognac Brandy; Real Irish Whiskey; Jamaica and Antigua Rum; Holland Gin; and London Bottled Brown Stout.

Tastes of various sorts could be gratified at no great expense. A British visitor to New York in 1818 wrote:

The markets of New York are well supplied with provisions of all kinds, which are in price less than in the metropolis of England . . . and with the exception of malt liquor, the votaries at the shrine of Bacchus may enjoy, for a fourth part of the sum, the glorious and exhilirating blessings of the Jolly God.

He added, however, that "The continual use of ardent spirits from the cradle, on the part of the males, ruins the constitution, for at thirty, nature becomes torpid." The advertisement of one New Yorker who sold "Groceries—cheap for cash," two years later, gives an idea how cheaply one might ruin one's constitution. Wine prices ranged from seven shillings a gallon for claret to twenty shillings for Madeira. Cognac and Jamaica rum both sold at nine shillings a gallon; Holland gin at eight shillings sixpence; Pierpont's gin, apparently domestic, at five shillings; and common rum, probably from New England, at four shillings sixpence. Those figures were in New York currency with the shilling at twelve and a half cents. Philip Hone's diary, however, tells of choice wines which commanded $11 a bottle.

Scoville, the chronicler of the old New York merchants, describes the business of one debonair Irishman who ranked high as a wine dealer:

Dominick Lynch kept a very large wine store in William Street, three doors from Wall, and opposite the Merchants' Exchange. In 1829 he was burned out, and a splendid stock of wines was consumed. I was at that fire, and never did the firemen of New York suck such delicious wines as then.

The fire did not burn up Dominick Lynch. He was more energetic after than before the fire. He commenced in 1830 his importations of the great Lynch's "Chateau Margeaux." A man was nobody in those days if he had not subscribed for a box of that almost inaccessible wine to anybody but Lynch. The subscription lists for three hundred cases contained all the principal people of New York. The cases were about three feet long and four feet round, and contained four dozen quart bottles. A smaller size contained four dozen pints. The price, I believe, was about $75 a case.

In 1833, *The Journal of Commerce* published some pioneer temperance propaganda which included the "curious and not unuseful calculation" concerning the importation of ardent spirits (not including wines, of course) into the United States:

Enough has been brought into the country since the beginning of 1790 to fill a canal from New York to Trenton four feet deep, twenty feet wide and sixty miles long, with a surplus of twenty-five million gallons of rum to provide against leakage and the draughts of the boatmen.

By the year of this propaganda, the trade was beginning to fall off and the per capita consumption to decrease.

By the end of the period, when we may distinguish the imports for the particular ports in the customs records, New York's leadership was clear. In 1860, it imported about $3,400,000 out of the national total of $5,100,000 for distilled spirits; $2,900,000 of the total $4,700,000 for wines; and nearly $300,000 of the almost $800,000 total for ale, beer, and other malt drinks. Altogether the port had about two-thirds of the whole business.[1]

France was the source of about two-thirds of the alcoholic imports. Its brandy alone amounted to $3,700,000 in 1860 followed by its champagne at $1,300,000, while other wines made the rest of the $6,300,000 total. At the outset, much of this came from Bordeaux, which had shipped out wines for centuries. The establishing of the Havre packet service, however, caused much of the wine and brandy to travel up the coast to the Seine port for shipment to America. Nearly every Havre packet reached New York with scores of cases and hundreds of hampers of French drinks of one sort or another. A lesser amount came to New York from Marseilles.

The names of port and sherry, derived from the ports of Oporto in Portugal and Jerez in Spain, indicate the prominence of those two countries in the wine business, while the islands which they owned out in the Atlantic contributed still further to the total. Madeira was a particular favorite at New York from early in the eighteenth century. A considerable amount of this wine did not come directly from Portuguese or Spanish ports but came by way of London or Hamburg.

"Holland gin" was the source of much business with Amsterdam and

[1]See Appendix, x.

stood high among the imported drinks in value, amounting to nearly $900,000 in 1860. Scoville relates that Frederick Gebhard was the first to make a specialty of the gin trade at New York. His imports of Swan gin were tremendous and the mainstay of his "packets" plying between the two ports. Effective rivalry came by the late 'thirties from Udolpho and Joel Wolfe, who established a distillery in Amsterdam and shipped large quantities of Schiedam Schnapps to New York where they bottled it. Scoville also tells the story of another enterprising New Yorker who had gin distilled at Baltimore and then, because of the preference for imported liquors, had it shipped to New York by way of Amsterdam. Occasionally, shipments of juniper berries were advertised at New York for the domestic manufacture of gin.

The importation of malt liquors lagged far behind brandy, gin, and wine in both volume and value, although nearly every London packet brought a moderate amount of ale, porter, or stout. This was because it was easier to produce adequate beer in this country and the domestic beer business gained a tremendous impetus with the coming of the Germans in the 'forties.

The domestic production of whiskey in the inland states also cut radically into the demand for imports in that line. By 1830, the amount of domestic spirits carried through the Erie Canal toward New York exceeded the total national imports of ardent spirits, which had fallen off radically. Large amounts of whiskey also found their way down the Mississippi to New Orleans, and some of that was carried northward to New York. Rum was always a strong rival of brandy; and the West Indian supply was supplemented by the distilleries at Medford, Portland, and elsewhere along the coast.

On the other hand, the efforts of Nicholas Longworth of Cincinnati and others to create a demand for their domestic wines was not particularly successful in reducing the imports of wine from France. The consumption of imported beverages, like the use of French luxury goods, tended to center in the larger cities along the coast. Consequently the imports did not keep pace with the growth of population to the westward because domestic whiskey or beer answered cheaply the desires of that region.

The trade in "dry goods, hardware, and wet goods" by no means accounts for all the business on the Atlantic shuttle, but there is no space here to do more than mention some of the remaining commodities. Crates of earthenware from British potteries were a bulky form of freight which shipping from Liverpool carried, if fine textiles, with their higher rate of freight, were not available. The better grades of "chinaware" usually came from Canton at the outset, but as time went on, the products of Wedgwood and others in England, together with the French wares from Limoges, added to the business of the shuttle.

British coal was constantly coming into New York throughout the period. At the beginning, it was superior to the Virginia coal which then formed the only local offering, and there still remained certain uses for bituminous from Liverpool, Newcastle, and other British ports after Pennsylvania anthracite became popular for fuel in the 'twenties. The steamboats on local runs, as we shall see, ordinarily used wood and were not at first successful in their experiments with anthracite. The British transatlantic steamships to New York were usually supplied with Liverpool coal, brought over in sailing vessels. Even the proud packets were occasionally reduced to cargoes of coal, along with Liverpool salt, in depression periods when fine freight was lacking. From Havre, "burr" stones, to be used in grist mills, were regularly carried in lieu of ballast.

The Baltic and Mediterranean furnished a constant but modest stream of cargoes to New York. Aside from Swedish iron, a fairly regular trade existed in iron, hemp, and tallow from St. Petersburg, while an occasional cargo of those same commodities came from icebound Archangel on the White Sea. The Mediterranean ports offered a richer variety with raisins, figs, oranges, lemons, and almonds from Malaga; rags, marble, olive oil, and silks from Leghorn, Naples, Palermo, or Trieste; wool, opium, and tobacco from Smyrna; and a wide variety of wares from Marseilles.

In both the Baltic and the Mediterranean New York ran into stiff competition from Boston, which held the upper hand in some branches of that trade. It cannot be too strongly emphasized that New York's real distinction in its transatlantic contacts lay in its much larger trade with the western Atlantic ports of Europe and there it was without effective rivalry.[1]

Many strange miscellaneous items and episodes were to be found in this European trade. Some of the pioneer locomotives for American railroads reached New York from Liverpool. Race horses and other animals for breeding were frequently to be found in the cargoes. Several residents of New York, including the radical William Cobbett during

[1] See Appendix, vi.

his temporary sojourn, imported seeds and plants, sometimes trying to introduce new varieties. Grant Thorburn, for instance, author of some interesting reminiscences, was advertising in 1820 the merits of Cape Broccoli, with its "taste almost equal to a cauliflower." Many watched for the arrival of the London packets because they carried the latest books and magazines. In 1815, when New York had been cut off for nearly three years, one circulating library advertised that it would pay the full original price for any books which travellers might have brought with them.

Probably the greatest value in smallest bulk of any of the shipments coming to New York across the shuttle were the consignments to Tiffany & Young who, from starting a little store on Broadway in 1837, began to send one partner abroad each year to pick up jewelry and novelties and gradually went into the trade in precious stones. This reached a climax when the widespread revolutions of 1848 led many of the old continental aristocracy to sell their diamonds. Tiffany and his partners decided to put all their available capital into taking advantage of this opportunity at a time when prices were cut in half and the stones which they purchased that year and brought back to New York did much to establish their primacy in that business.

New York's participation in the business of the Atlantic shuttle, altogether, was the most impressive part of world commerce by the close of our period. In 1860, 904 vessels, totalling some 975,000 tons, arrived at New York from the ports of western Europe, about two-thirds of them from England. Not only was New York's total far and away greater than that of any other American port, but the steamships coming to New York on that run, like the packets which preceded them, were the finest ships in the world's merchant marines. The value of the articles brought to New York, as we have seen, made a similar impressive total. Finally the distribution of a considerable part of those imported wares throughout the nation was doing more than anything else to clinch New York's position as the greatest seaport in America and one of the greatest in the world.

CHAPTER V

HINTERLAND AND CANAL

Back in the inland counties, where men never smelled salt water and probably would not recognize a brig if they saw one, the country storekeepers carried on an activity almost as essential to the success of the port of New York as were the movements of its shipping.

A farmer in our period would drive up to the store with sixty bushels of wheat, for instance, in his wagon. After a dicker with the storekeeper, he would sell the grain and then make purchases from the variegated stock of the general store. When he started back home, he might be carrying in place of his wheat, a few yards of calico, some bushels of salt, a scythe, a kettle, a bag of coffee, and a gallon or so of rum, or some similiar assortment. No cash had changed hands; the storekeeper had simply set down the grain in his ledger on the credit side of the farmer's account and the various articles taken away on the debit side, which was generally the heavier of the two.

Such an episode represented the Alpha and the Omega of the port's commerce. The farmer was the original producer of many of the articles which the port offered as exports in the world of commerce, while he was also the ultimate consumer of the goods collected by the port's merchants from beyond the seas. The shipowners and merchants had already taken their import profits on the calico and hardware brought from Liverpool, the salt from Turks Island or Cape Verde, the coffee from Rio or Samarang, and the rum distilled from Caribbean molasses. They could anticipate further profits from selling the wheat, once it was ground into flour, either to Boston or to some port beyond the seas.

The country storekeeper, consequently, served an invaluable function in collecting goods for export and distributing the imports. No port could grow great simply by catering to the needs of its own inhabitants. Its success would depend to no small extent upon the number of such little storekeepers who might be persuaded to trade through its merchants rather than through those of some rival port. It naturally had first call upon those who lived close at hand in its immediate back country or hinterland, to use the German equivalent less grating to inland ears.

New York's original hinterland consisted of the valley of the Hudson and other upstate regions, together with adjacent parts of Long Island, New Jersey, and Connecticut. In the Hudson valley, there was no serious threat of outside competition, but some of the trade of the southwest portion of the State was drained down the Susquehanna toward Philadelphia or Baltimore, while the counties of the "north country" had an easy natural outlet through Montreal and Quebec. Until after 1800, the population of New York State had lagged behind that of Pennsylvania, where a more liberal land policy had attracted settlers to Philadelphia's hinterland. By 1810, New York State ranked second to Virginia in population, with 959,000 inhabitants to Pennsylvania's 810,000.

When pushing its commercial activities sideways into New Jersey and Connecticut, New York naturally encountered competition. The two college towns of Princeton and New Haven were disputed outposts of New York's sphere of influence. New Jersey, then as since, was a "cask tapped at both ends." East Jersey traded through the Raritan and New Brunswick with New York; and west Jersey through the Delaware River towns with Philadelphia. The Connecticut towns and western New England in general represented a three-cornered dispute between New York, which had the advantage of proximity and the convenient Sound approach; Boston, which had a considerable trade with the region in spite of its remoteness; and, finally, the local maritime enterprise of New Haven and New London along the coast and in the Caribbean. Altogether, if one combines the population of New York State with half of New Jersey's and a third of Connecticut's, the population of New York's hinterland numbered about 1,170,000 in 1810 and 1,600,000 in 1820, roughly one-sixth of the national total in each case.

That had previously been about New York's share of the nation's commerce, but by 1820 it already handled more than a third of the total imports and would steadily increase its proportion of the country's commerce. That was largely brought about by two clever strokes which greatly increased the number of country storekeepers whose wares came and went through New York. The "cotton triangle," as we shall see, added a considerable part of the South to New York's sphere of influence, while the Erie Canal gave the West as well.

Before turning to that celebrated ditch which has been credited with so great an influence on New York's rise, it might be well to consider what the port's immediate hinterland had to offer as potential exports. Obviously, the back country would be of no use to the port as a consumer of imports unless it could offer something of commercial value wherewith to pay for them. The more remote and primitive farmers might live in a state of fairly complete self-sufficiency, raising their own food, making their own homespun and crude utensils, while meeting their other needs locally. If they expected to have articles from beyond the seas—and most of them sooner or later had such expectations—they had to produce some sort of "cash crops" which could be carried away for trading purposes. This was an easy matter for the southerners, who could raise cotton, rice, tobacco, or sugar which Europe desired in large quantities, but the northern states had much the same climate as Europe and consequently their ingenuity was put to the test in developing hinterland products which would be negotiable in the world of commerce.

The New York hinterland managed to produce a few such commodities—ashes, flaxseed, salted meats, and, above all, flour. Lumber was never an important output of the old New York hinterland—New England to the eastward was exploiting that trade. The trees which had to be cleared away before crops might be raised, however, could at least be burned and their ashes sold. A French traveller, visiting the back country in the last years of the eighteenth century, described the process. The ashes from the burned trees were shovelled into large tubs with double bottoms. Water was poured over them and the resultant lye trickled through the holes into the lower part, whence it was drawn off through a spigot. Until it was strong enough for an egg to "swim" in it, it was poured through the ashes again. Then the lye was boiled in large pots until a black or gray salt known as "pot ashes" or potash was left. It might either be marketed in this form, or roasted in a kiln whence it would come out as "pearl ashes." These ashes, barrelled and sent to the coast, were familiar items in the old export records, for they might be used abroad in the making of soap (from pearl ashes) and glass (from pot ashes), as well as in bleaching and in various other ways.

Hogs and cattle, often elderly oxen which had outlived their usefulness at the plow, were slaughtered, cut up, and barrelled in brine. Such meat as was not needed for home consumption might be sent to the seaports where it met with a demand, not only for export to the Caribbean and coastwise, but also as the companion of hardtack in the monotonous diet of the mariner. The United States naval specifications in 1829 called for beef "packed from well fatted cattle, weighing not less than 480 pounds in quarter or 800 pounds on the hoof," with all "legs, leg-rounds, clods, cheeks, skins and necks" wholly excluded and the rest cut into pieces as near ten pounds each as possible, so that twenty pieces would make a barrel of 200 pounds net weight. The pork specifications were similar, except that eight-pound pieces with not more than three shoulders were designated. Beef and pork were both to be packed in salt from Turks Island in the Bahamas, the Isle of May in the Cape Verdes, or St. Ubes in Portugal "and no other," while five ounces of pure saltpetre were to be put in each barrel. Bacon and hams were likewise in demand at the port. The beef and pork generally began to arrive at New York in October or November.

A considerable part of the linen produced in Ireland during the early part of our period came from flax grown there from seeds which came from America. The Irish flax growers generally harvested the plants before they were mature enough to bear seeds and consequently had to look elsewhere for flaxseed, or linseed as it was sometimes called. The United States furnished a considerable part of this, New York in particular. From the colonial period until the late 'twenties, many vessels carried flaxseed from New York to Belfast or some other Irish port and then proceeded to Liverpool for a return cargo. The first transatlantic clearance at New York after the coming of peace in 1815 was for just such a trip. New York handled most of the flaxseed exports while they lasted; by 1860, they had dwindled to almost nothing.

Flour, of course, overshadowed all those and other lesser offerings of the New York hinterland. When a new seal had been drawn up for New York back in 1686, the flour barrel had been included with the beaverskin as the basis of the port's prosperity and it had continued to be the principal local offering. In those early days of the English occupation, we remember, there had been an effort to concentrate bolting at New York itself on the excuse that it would be a better guarantee of quality in the export world but by 1700 that monopoly was broken and little mills up and down the Hudson valley were producing flour for the market. Kingston, or Esopus as it was then called, was a particularly rich wheat region, while the Albany section also grew and milled wheat, as did the adjacent Mohawk valley as time went on.

England, on the occasions when it wanted breadstuffs from America, preferred to import wheat and do the milling itself, but for most of the other markets, New York offered the finished product of flour, packed in barrels weighing 196 pounds net. About five and a half bushels of wheat were needed to make a barrel of flour and the New York farmers might receive anywhere from 15 to 25 bushels from an acre. A barrel of flour was worth anywhere from $5 to $10 at New York, according to the supply and demand at the moment. Six dollars was perhaps a fair average for the period.

Most of the little New York mills were of the type known as "country mills"; that is, they charged for grinding wheat into flour and "bolting" it through a sieve of fine cloth, but their connection ended with that service. Occasionally one found a "merchant mill," managed upon a larger scale, by a proprietor who bought the grain himself and marketed the finished product. Philadelphia had several such, in addition to the Brandywine mills at Wilmington; Baltimore had the Ellicott mills; and Richmond, the Gallego and other "city mills," whose products were known in the flour trade by the mill's name. Most of the New York flour was anonymous though Ely and other names at Rochester became celebrated.

The equipment of the little mills was fairly simple. Except on Long Island, where a few windmills were relics of the Dutch period, a stream was generally dammed up to furnish power. The wheat was fed through a hopper into a hole in the upper of the two millstones, each of which was about four feet in diameter and a foot thick. The better mills had "burr stones," quarried near Chateau Thierry on the Marne and brought from Havre or Rouen. Caught between the two millstones, the grains of wheat were ground into flour which gradually worked its way out to the edge through grooves, hot from the friction. After cooling, the flour was "bolted" through a screen of silk, linen, or woollen cloth and was finally ready for packing.

The merchant millers made their own marketing arrangements at the port. The flour ground in the "country mills" frequently belonged to the storekeepers, who had taken the grain in exchange for purchases from their stock. They would often send it by wagon or sleigh to Albany, Troy, Schenectady or some other collection point. During the height of the season dozens of loads would be brought in on a single day and ambitious flour dealers would go out to meet the incoming teamsters to drive their bargains before their rivals had an opportunity to bid. Farmers from the Berkshires in western Massachusetts often sent their grain over to the nearest river town on the Hudson. During the winter months huge stocks accumulated at Albany and the other towns; as soon as the ice began to go out of the river, sloops by the score would carry it down the Hudson to New York. A similar process was going on in New Jersey, which in the late eighteenth century was the leading wheat producing state in the union. The sloops from New Brunswick and Raritan Landing brought the flour up through the Narrows and added it to the stock accumulating from the upper Hudson. Some New York commission merchants specialized in handling this material and a few had huge warehouses where, in times of low prices, the flour might be stored in anticipation of better times, though there was always the danger that it might turn sour.

Before any flour was sold at New York, the barrel had to be branded by the state flour inspector, who indicated its grade—middling, fine, or superfine. This inspection was a perennial source of discussion for a century and a half after the beginning of New York's flour industry in the 1670's. It had been one of the chief arguments for concentrating the bolting of flour at Manhattan, where the merchants argued strongly that the reputation of New York flour in foreign ports depended upon the rigidity and honesty of the inspection. A final strenuous agitation broke out in the early 'twenties after the publication of a letter from abroad saying that New York flour sold at a considerably lower price than the flour from Baltimore or Philadelphia because of lack of confidence in its quality.

This led to a searching examination of the situation, continuing for weeks in the columns of the press. The chief source of trouble seemed to be that the office of flour inspector yielded such a rich total of fees that it was one of the choicest plums in state patronage. Political jockeying at Albany meant a frequent change of inspectors and too often they were apparently ready, because of carelessness, political expediency or even, it was hinted, bribery, to pass flour which did not deserve to pass. A particular practice which was hurting the reputation of New York flour was the effort to salvage the loss on old, sour flour by regrinding it and mixing it in with fresh flour which would eventually be contaminated. Each barrel, before it came up for state inspection, usually already had the private brand of the upstate miller or dealer. The brand of Ely, the prominent Rochester merchant miller, was said to have meant more in the world of commerce than that of the state inspector.

The widespread demand for an improved reputation of New York flour finally led in 1821 to the appointment of a competent and fearless inspector, John Brown. On entering into office, he found on hand 60,000 barrels of flour already passed by his predecessor as superfine. The merchants refused to purchase it for export until it received Brown's brand as well—he passed only 1000 barrels as superfine and reduced the remainder to lower gradings. So successful was Brown's "inflexible perseverance" in raising the standard that a legislative committee could report early in 1825 that New York flour had "resumed its former good character." Instead of selling for a dollar or two a barrel less than the flour of Pennsylvania, Maryland, and Virginia, it was actually being carried to the rival flour ports and commanding a premium there. The year after Brown entered office, 10,000 barrels of New York superfine were sent to Philadelphia where they sold at 75 cents a barrel higher than the best Pennsylvania brands, while New York western flour was "sold at a high advance for family use" at the active flour ports of Petersburg and Richmond. This improved standing came at a decidedly propitious time, for the opening of the Erie Canal was about to put New York in first place as the center of the flour trade.

While white flour was the chief item in the breadstuffs trade, the hinterland also sent down unground wheat as well as other grains, ground or unground, in considerable quantities. Indian corn, together with ground corn meal, ranked next to flour, while rye, oats, buckwheat, and barley came in smaller quantities. New York did a fairly good business in the making of "ship bread" or hardtack, one of the major items of sailors' diet, baked to the consistency of modern dog biscuit so that it would not spoil too quickly on long voyages. A German named Lydig had come from Hamburg and prospered in this business, gradually branching into extensive flour milling in the Hudson valley.

During the first years of peace, New York lagged behind Philadelphia and Baltimore as a flour market. Both of those rivals had richer and more extensive hinterlands, Baltimore in particular having made a remarkably rapid rise since the late colonial period. In 1817, however, New York took a step which was to give it a long lead over both those rivals by increasing its hinterland to much greater proportions.

The story of the Erie Canal has been told so often that it does not seem necessary to follow it here in any detail, but the high points must be mentioned because it was one of the vital factors in New York's commercial ascendancy.

Even before the Revolution, settlers from the seaboard colonies were beginning to pass beyond the Alleghenies to take advantage of the opportunities offered by the apparently limitless tracts of rich land in the West. By the end of the Revolution, they were so numerous that Washington and others began to consider the problem of communications between the coast and the new settlements.

The most pressing economic problem of the frontiersmen was the marketing of their products. Even in the absence of good roads, it was practicable to carry imported goods, representing high value in small bulk, over the mountains on packhorses, but there could be no trade in such wares unless the western farmers could pay for them with some sort of "cash crop." Wheat, ashes, and other agricultural products could not pay their way—it cost $100 or so to transport a ton of goods from the Great Lakes to New York and about $70 from Pittsburgh to Philadelphia. That was more than those bulky articles were worth when they finally arrived at market. The only feasible way to reach the sea was to send the stuff in rafts or boats down the Mississippi to New Orleans, but even after that port passed into American hands in 1803, it was not perfect as an outlet. Most of the products came down with the spring freshets and, arriving more or less all together, found the market so glutted that the wares had to be sold at sacrifice prices. Until a more satisfactory outlet developed, the frontiersmen were forced to live on a primitive subsistence basis, denying themselves the outside products which they had no means of purchasing. There was no point in raising wheat which could not be sold and the best they could do was convert their corn into pork or whiskey which could be transported more easily. At the same time, both they and the easterners knew that the rich virgin soil beyond the Alleghenies could produce excellent wheat if it might only be brought through to the coast at a rate which would not be prohibitive.

Washington had been familiar with the West in his younger days and no sooner was the Revolution over than he began to consider the development of communication over the mountains. A remark of his in 1784 showed his keen foresight:

The western settlers . . . stand as it were upon a pivot. The touch of a feather would turn them any way . . . smooth the road, and make easy the way for them, and then see what an influx of articles will be poured upon us; how amazingly our exports will be increased by them, and how amply we shall be compensated for any trouble and expense we may encounter to effect it.

His own preference, quite naturally, was for the route up the Potomac and across the mountains to the Ohio. It was, to be sure, the shortest route as far as mileage was concerned, but the mountains rose a full half mile in height across its path. The quest for a western route, as every one knows, helped to pave the way for our federal constitution, for delegates were brought together at Annapolis in 1786 to discuss the problem and that led to the constitutional convention at Philadelphia a year later. Even before the eighteenth century was out, there were various pioneer attempts to solve the problem by means of canals or turnpikes and Philadelphia had sunk a considerable amount of money in abortive efforts. Baltimore was the first of the ports to receive any sort of adequate communication, for its connections made it the eastern terminus of traffic over the Cumberland Road started by the federal government in 1811 and opened for traffic in 1818, between the headwaters of the Potomac and the Ohio at Wheeling.

Geographical considerations gave New York a tremendous advantage over its rivals for easy communication with the West. The "water-level route" from Albany westward to Lake Erie was the one point where the Appalachians could be taken in flank. As early as 1724, the surveyor general of the province had pointed out the possibilities of this route and the matter was already being discussed by the eve of the Revolution. In the last years of the century, a corporation actually constructed some locks to make the navigation of the Mohawk River easier and numerous proposals were being made for improving the waterways to provide communication with Lake Erie or Lake Ontario.

The more ambitious proposal to construct an artificial canal all the way from the Hudson to Lake Erie, rather than simply to improve natural waterways, might be dated from 1810 when the State legislature appointed a commission to investigate the possibilities. The ultimate success of this plan may be attributed largely to the vision and tireless energy of one of the commissioners who made the arduous trip over the proposed route that year. This was De Witt Clinton, of prominent old New York stock, son of a general, nephew of a governor and at the time mayor of New York City, a man of wide cultural and scientific interests. Two years later he would give James Madison a close run in the presidential election and he was involved in many ups and downs in state politics. Through all that, however, he maintained his eager interest in the canal project. Temporarily postponed by the War of 1812, the issue was brought to the fore again in 1816 by Clinton. He persistently pointed out how New York would benefit from the opening of communication not only with its own western counties but also, by way of Lake Erie, with Ohio and the regions further west. The project gained such widespread support that even the seasoned politicians, who disliked Clinton thoroughly, felt it wise to back the idea.

Early in 1817, the legislature received the canal bill drawn up largely by Clinton, who had mastered both the technical and financial aspects of the problem. The State of New York was to pay for the canal, build it, and operate it. The bill passed both houses and became law on April 15. On the Fourth of July, three days after he first became governor, Clinton lifted the first spadeful of earth at Rome (Fort Stanwix), on the upper Mohawk River.

It was a stupendous undertaking for that day, considering that America had few trained engineers and that the steam shovel had not yet been invented. Even on the simpler, straightaway stretches of the middle section, there were forests to be cleared away and miasmic swamps which threatened fever to the workers. Though the route was relatively level, 83 regular locks, each 90 feet long, had to be constructed of masonry. Such things offered problems enough to inexperienced contractors, but the canal also involved several more arduous engineering feats, such as the 750-foot aqueduct to carry the canal over the Genesee River at Rochester; the great embankment, nearly a mile long, to carry it across the Irondequoit Valley; and as a final difficulty, the piercing of the ridge at Lockport. There, just east of the Buffalo terminus, a double series of five locks had to be constructed to raise the level of the canal nearly sixty feet within two miles. The total length of the canal from Buffalo to Albany was 363 miles.

The middle section, because it was the simplest to build and politically the most expedient, was tackled first. Three thousand men, 500 horses, and 200 yoke of oxen were kept steadily at work; and by the spring of 1820, traffic was opened on the 96-mile stretch from Utica westward. The eastern section came next and on October 8, 1823, the

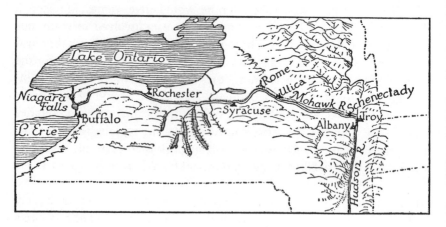

ERIE CANAL

canal was open for 280 miles for through traffic from Rochester to Albany and on to New York. On November 16, the schooner *Mary & Hannah* reached New York from Hector Falls at the head of Seneca Lake with a cargo of wheat and butter. "We hope our citizens will pay some attention to this arrival," said one newspaper, "it being the first vessel that has reached this city through the Great Western Canal."

With the Erie or "Great Western" Canal thus partly open, we might note the opening of its junior partner, the Champlain or "Great Northern Canal." Authorized on the same day in 1817 as part of the State program, it was designed to connect Lake Champlain with the Hudson and thus provide an outlet for the northern regions which were being lured toward Montreal. It was 64 miles long, following natural waterways part of the distance. Since it entailed much less work, it was naturally finished first. About ten weeks before that first boat arrived from the Erie Canal, the "sloop-rigged boat *Gleaner,* Capt. Mills," came from St. Albans, Vermont, with a thousand bushels of wheat and thirty-five barrels of pot ashes, "the first that has come through the whole distance of the Northern Canal." Since this was New York's first tangible evidence of canal activity, the *Gleaner* got a rousing welcome. A pleasure craft, decked out with flags, rode up the Hudson to greet her, she received a salute from the Veteran Corps of Artillery and the "cheers of the multitude assembled on the Battery."

That, however, was mild compared with the celebration of the final opening of the Erie Canal in October, 1825. With the ridge at Lockport finally pierced, water from Lake Erie was let into the western end of the canal and a procession began its ten-day triumphal progress over the route of more than 500 miles from Buffalo to New York. Cannon, placed at intervals, served in lieu of a telegraph to spread the news. The first boat entered the canal from Lake Erie at 10 A.M. on October 26, and New York, more than 500 miles away, learned of it a hundred minutes later. De Witt Clinton, once again governor, was the hero of the group on the canal boat *Seneca Chief,* receiving tremendous ovations as she passed eastward through Rochester, Syracuse, Rome, Utica, Schenectady, and on to Albany. There the steamer *Chancellor Livingston* took her in tow for the final stages of her trip down the Hudson to New York City. The eventual arrival made November 4, 1825, one of the red-letter days in the history of the port, ranking with January 5, 1818, when the first Black Baller sailed for Liverpool, and April 23, 1838, when the arrival of the *Sirius* and *Great Western* marked the beginning of transatlantic steam navigation. Twenty-two steamboats, gaily decked with bunting, participated in the welcome—a flotilla which scarcely another port in the world at that day could muster. The city fathers, on the steamer *Washington,* rode out to meet the procession from upriver. They hailed the *Seneca Chief,* "Whence come you and where are you bound?" "From Lake Erie—bound for Sandy Hook!" came the reply. Off Sandy Hook, Clinton poured into the sea a keg of water from Lake Erie, symbolizing the completion of the great task which he, more than any other man, had pushed through to success in fifteen years of tireless promotion. That night New York celebrated with fireworks and three nights later with a great canal ball. All these things impressed the Erie Canal upon men's minds as the chief cause for New York's rise—overshadowing the equally significant development of the "cotton triangle" which had already tremendously extended New York's sphere of commercial influence without the attendant blare of trumpets.

The canal was a success from the very start—and it should be remembered that for two years before its final grand opening it had been bringing to New York the products of the rich middle section as far west as Rochester. In 1825, for instance, the canal statistics show that during the open season an average of 42 boats a day had passed through Utica, carrying nearly a thousand passengers a day. The eastbound cargoes from the hinterland totalled 185,000 tons, including 221,000 barrels of flour, 562,000 bushels of wheat, 435,000 gallons of "domestic spirits," mostly whiskey, and 32,000,000 board feet of lumber. It is significant that the westbound cargoes, consisting chiefly of imported goods and domestic manufactures, weighed only 33,000 tons, little more than a sixth as much as the bulky freight travelling in the opposite direction, though probably equal in value. The heavy movement of westbound passengers, swarming to new lands on the frontier, helped to equalize the business.

A new sort of craft was developed to handle the canal business. Typical, perhaps, was the canal boat *Congress* enrolled at New York in 1831 with Benjamin Taber of Ithaca as builder, master, and owner. Nearly 77 feet long, she had a beam of 14 feet, 3 inches, which left 9 inches of clearance in the locks, and a depth of 4 feet, 10 inches, measuring altogether 49 tons, and probably costing between $1000 and $1500. Such a boat was generally hauled by two horses who trod the towpath. Many did not unload their cargoes at Albany but entered the Hudson and were towed, dozens of them at a time, by steamers, down to New York. Many of the boats, like the above, were "transients," but the line principle was quickly extended to canal service. Comfortable passenger packets, with ample sleeping accommodations, could travel at a hundred miles a day, while some of the freight boats were organized into lines operated by "forwarding companies."

A new type of floating population developed in the "canallers" who lived aboard the boats throughout the season from the breaking up of the ice in the spring until the canal finally froze over in November. Families, not always bound together by matrimony, made their homes on these freighters, as admirably depicted by the historical novelist who has re-created so ably the conditions attendant upon the building and workings of the canal. In 1830, a convention of delegates from the towns along the canal gathered at Syracuse. Alarmed by the "gambling, drinking, blasphemy, licentiousness of every kind" and "the actual pillage of property transported on the canal," they sought, without much effect, to "promote the moral and religious improvement" of the canallers.

The canal naturally wrought tremendous change in the hinterland

THE ERIE CANAL

The celebration in New York Harbor November 4, 1825 on the completion of the canal. The revenue cutter *Alert* accompanied by river craft is firing a salute. (The middle panel joins the top on the left.) Below is an upstate scene on the Canal from a watercolor by J. W. Hill

of New York port. The Hudson River counties had opposed the canal for obvious reasons. Scoville, in referring to David Lydig, whose father had manufactured sea biscuit, states that as the canal approached completion

> Mr. Lydig foresaw with the foreshadowing sagacity of the penetrating merchant, that flour would be ultimately manufactured in the great grain growing valleys of the West, at a cost in production that would annihilate all competition on the part of the manufacturers in the southern part of the state, and to the astonishment of all those engaged in the business, he sold out his extensive mills at Buttermilk Falls, at what appeared to be a foolish sacrifice, commenced to curtail, and finally wound up his business. By this timely movement he saved a fortune, the greater part of which would have been swept away in the revolution which followed very speedily upon the opening of the Erie Canal.

The western counties of New York, along the route of the canal, quickly replaced the Hudson Valley as the center of the flour industry. The virgin lands of the Genesee Valley could produce far richer wheat crops than the long-used fields closer to New York. The Mohawk Valley, which had long thrived on wheat and flour production, turned to dairying and began to offer tons of cheese instead. The city which most immediately profited by the change was Rochester. With only 15 inhabitants in 1812 and 331 in 1816, it was the natural center for the Genesee region. It had had a moderate start already, for the Ely mills were established in 1814, but the opening of the middle section of the canal meant an immediate boom. On October 29, 1822, the first canal-boat load of Rochester flour left for Little Falls and the following spring the local paper remarked, "10,450 barrels of Rochester flour were shipped on the canal from this village during the last ten days. So much for 'Clinton's big ditch.'" By 1840, Rochester with 20,000 inhabitants was the leading flour-milling center of the country, with its closest rival Oswego, located just north of the canal on Lake Ontario where it had access to the Canadian grain supply. It, like numerous other points, was provided with a "feeder" canal which connected it with the Erie. Another short branch, to the State salt works at Salina, helped to relieve the previous dependence upon salt imports from Turks Island, Portugal, and the Cape Verdes.

Along with Rochester, Buffalo also underwent an immediate expansion, not so much as a manufacturing center as from its strategic relation to the Lake trade. Westward on Lake Erie lay Cleveland, the

natural northern outlet for the Ohio region. A brisk Lake trade between Buffalo and Cleveland rapidly sprang up, partly with steamers
and partly with schooners. Within a few weeks after the opening of
the canal at Buffalo in October, 1825, fifteen vessels sailed with cargoes
for Ohio, chiefly with material which had come from New York.
The following year, Ohio products began to arrive at tidewater. The
first cargo of Ohio pork, 182 barrels, reached Albany by the canal
on May 17 and within a week a vessel arrived there, the first to
come direct from Ohio. She was the canal boat *Eclipse,* which had
been loaded at Monroe in Ashtabula County with whiskey, pork,
and pot ashes, towed down the lake by steamer to Buffalo, and then
dragged through the canal by horses which had come overland. Three
months later, the 50-ton sloop *St. Clair* arrived at New York with
a cargo of furs and ashes from Mackinaw in Michigan, "an inland
voyage of more than 1000 miles."

Just before the Erie Canal had opened, New York participated in
a new venture which would further extend its sphere of influence
in Ohio. On the Fourth of July in 1825, Clinton was present at the
formal start of the Ohio Canal which that state was undertaking
to connect Cleveland on Lake Erie with Portsmouth on the Ohio
River. Realizing that this would help to divert Ohio's commerce from
the natural route southward to New Orleans, New York bankers had
arranged a large loan, after first stipulating guarantees of the state's
financial soundness. Part of the new canal was opened in 1830 and
the whole in 1835, while another state canal later opened up the
western portion of the state with an outlet on Lake Erie at Toledo.
By 1840, produce was beginning to arrive at Buffalo from Chicago.
At the outset, those regions were inclined to send wheat to Rochester
or other New York centers for milling, but by the close of our period,
crop pests were crippling the western New York supply and the
center of flour milling was extended westward. No matter where
the flour might be milled in the old northwest, however, the canal
continued to bring the supplies to New York.

Financially, the Erie Canal's success was clear, for tolls soon
totalled more than $1,000,000 a year. The state was before long
reimbursed for the initial cost, some $7,000,000, and for the subsequent
charges for maintenance and enlargement, which were needed because of increasing volume of traffic. The impressive figures of that
rapidly growing volume of business are reproduced in the appendix

and it will be enough here to mention that the 218,000 tons carried in 1825 had swelled to 1,417,046 in 1840, 3,076,617 in 1850, and 4,116,082 in 1856. The value of the freight was $73,000,000 in 1840, $144,000,000 in 1850, and $204,000,000 in 1856.[1]

As for the effect upon the commerce of the port of New York, it would seem that while the canal had a very definitely stimulating influence, the western trade did not for some time rise to equality with the southern trade developed by the cotton triangle. The chief importance was not in the flour and other articles brought eastward, for New York's exports were always relatively less important than its imports. The main significance was the rapid growth of the number of little country stores which came under New York's influence in the hinterland as distributing points for the imports which the port brought from Europe, China, and Latin America. As far as the physical transportation of the goods went, they represented sufficient value in small bulk to have paid their way under the older and more costly system of transportation. The chief influence of the Erie Canal upon the growth of the port of New York apparently lay in the opportunity which it gave to the westerners to send to the seaboard the "cash crops" wherewith to pay for the imports they desired. Eventually, even though they might ship their produce to tidewater at other eastern cities or at New Orleans, they were apt to buy their imports and domestic manufactures through New York.

Unfortunately, there is no adequate yardstick for measuring the regional distribution of New York's offerings to the interior, for the same reason that it is difficult to draw definite conclusions about the packet cargoes from Liverpool to New York or from New York to New Orleans. Unlike flour barrels and cotton bales, which make computations and comparisons easy, dry goods, hardware, and similar wares were too diversified. In view of the fact that New York was before long handling two-thirds of the nation's imports, it would be interesting if we might trace the distribution of a Liverpool packet's cargo, to see how much was consumed at New York itself, how much was spread among the adjacent coastal ports, and how much found its way into the little country stores of the South and of the West. Until 1840, probably, westbound shipments by the Erie Canal were overshadowed by the cargoes which went southward along the coast. The latter, as we shall see, included merchandise not only for

[1]See Appendix, xviii.

southern consumption but also for many of the western storekeepers as well.

We may, however, draw more definite conclusions about the trade in flour. The influence of the Erie Canal in making New York the principal flour market is clear. We have, for example, the statistics of flour inspection at the chief ports during the 'twenties. In 1820, Baltimore led with 577,000 barrels, followed by Philadelphia with 400,000, and then New York with 267,000. By 1823, when part of the canal was already open, New York had passed Philadelphia but Baltimore was still in the lead. In 1827, however, the western flour put New York in first place, with a score of 625,000, followed by Baltimore at 572,000, and Philadelphia at 351,000. New York's lead increased steadily after this.

The foreign flour market was subject to violent fluctuations. With the coming of peace in 1815, the flour trade declined from the relative importance which it had enjoyed during the long period of the Anglo-French wars when America played an active part in feeding overseas regions. In 1807, for instance, the national exports (adequate figures by separate ports are not available until 1856) totalled nearly 1,200,000 barrels and in 1812 more than 1,300,000, but in 1816 this had dropped to 620,000 and remained at that level for a decade or more. One important reason for the decline was the success of the British landowners, who dominated Parliament, in passing the Corn Laws which protected their income by curbing foreign competition. At the outset, they prohibited the importation of breadstuffs until wheat should reach a certain high price. In such cases, the government might temporarily suspend the prohibition on imports, whereupon there would be a sudden boom in prices in the American ports and big profits might be made by those who first received the news. New York with its packet service was in a fortunate situation for that. The effect of the Corn Laws is shown by the fact that flour exports to England amounted to nearly 480,000 barrels in 1801 and only 5500 in 1816, rising and falling spasmodically thereafter in too uncertain a manner to form a sure and steady market. In 1816, nearly half the total exports went to the Caribbean, where Cuba was a market of constantly increasing importance. Spain and Portugal took about a quarter of the total, while part of the remainder went to British North America. During the coming decades Latin America would offer a further outlet for flour.

In the meantime, there was a steady and very important market closer at hand, but it did not show in the customs records. Eastern New England never raised enough wheat for its own needs—rocks were the principal crop of the farms in that region. Even before the Revolution, New York, Philadelphia, and Chesapeake Bay had furnished considerable flour to Boston and ports eastward and this trade increased, particularly as an industrial population developed in the New England towns. As we shall notice, in connection with the coastal trade, Boston ranked as one of the best customers for Erie Canal flour and a constant procession of schooners carried it eastward around Cape Cod. A considerable number of them snubbed New York completely and sailed directly up the Hudson to Albany, carrying New England manufactures or Boston imports in exchange.

Any increased demand for flour meant more business for New York, because it was handling most of this trade. In 1846 occurred a tremendous stimulus to the flour industry with the repeal of the Corn Laws, hastened by the Irish potato famine. American flour and grain were at once in great demand. The repeal represented the victory of the manufacturers over the landlords in England and from that time on, the British looked more and more beyond the seas for their food. At New York, the flour exports jumped from 469,000 barrels in 1845 to 1,193,000 in 1846, and wheat exports from 304,000 to 1,472,000 bushels, in addition to other grain shipments, while cotton exports fell from 262,000 to 187,000 bales. Exact statistics of value are lacking for the New York exports that year, but it seems certain that for once the northern breadstuffs were worth more than the southern cotton.

There had been a period, ten years earlier, when that situation had been reversed. The crops went bad in 1836 and 1837 on this side of the Atlantic. The price of flour and bread soared and New York had a severe bread riot in the early months of 1837, just as the panic was coming on. The story went around that two of the leading domestic commission merchants in New York, Eli Hart & Co. and S. B. Herrick & Son, were hoarding large amounts of flour for a further rise. Their warehouses were attacked by an angry mob and considerable flour carried off. That summer many strange sights were seen in the port which normally exported flour in such quantities. Grain-laden craft of every description came in from Danzig, Stettin, Odessa, and numerous lesser European ports, some of which had never enjoyed direct connection with New York before that time. The harbor presented a strange motley of flags, hulls, and rigs, while the marine news heralded passages of 130 or 140 days in length, establishing new duration records for the Atlantic crossing.

The Hart and Herrick concerns, whose warehouses were attacked by the mob, were leaders among the domestic produce merchants who handled flour and grain from the interior, generally on a commission basis. They helped to draw the business to New York by advancing a considerable part of the purchase price several months in advance. A southern writer commented on this practice in 1854 as follows:

> Last autumn, the rich regions of Ohio, Indiana and Illinois were flooded with banknotes of the eastern states, advanced by the New York houses on produce to be shipped by them by way of the canals in the spring. These moneyed facilities enable the packer, miller and speculator to hold on to their produce until the opening of navigation in the spring and they are no longer obliged, as formerly, to hurry off their shipments during the winter by way of New Orleans in order to realize funds by drafts on their shipments. The banking facilities of the East are doing as much to draw trade from us as the canals and railways which eastern capital is constructing.

By paying for the flour before it was milled, just as it paid for the southern cotton before it was planted, New York derived a triple benefit from its position as the nation's chief financial center. By placing the farmers and planters in a chronic state of debt, it drew a steady stream of interest in return for the advances; it had first call on the products of the interior for export from its own port; and above all, the money which it advanced generally inclined the country storekeepers to replenish their stocks with imports and domestic manufactures which came through New York rather than through some rival port. Even though much of the flour, beef, and pork might go down the Mississippi to New Orleans instead of eastward through the Erie Canal, the chances were great that the proceeds would be spent for New York goods anyway.

This meant that, except for the immediate spheres of influence of Boston, Philadelphia, and Baltimore, most of the country had become New York's hinterland at least two decades before the Civil War. The Erie Canal had played its part in adding the West, and the financial bonds which resulted were so strong that the subsequent efforts of the rival ports to tap that region with railroads did not shake the predominance of New York.

CHAPTER VI

THE COTTON TRIANGLE

SOUTHWARD from Sandy Hook past storm-swept Hatteras to the cotton ports ran a sea lane second in importance only to the Atlantic shuttle, as far as New York was concerned. Coastwise trade has been consistently slighted in writing of the sea, but unlike the little schooners which came to New York with lumber from Maine or grain from the Chesapeake, these vessels along the Gulf Stream were no ordinary coasters. In their size; in the risks they encountered on that stormy, hazardous course; and particularly in the cargoes they bore; they could hold their own with much of the shipping which left Sandy Hook to cross the Atlantic. The ingenious trade in which they were employed, moreover, was one of New York port's most profitable and original achievements.

By creating a three-cornered trade in the "cotton triangle," New York dragged the commerce between the southern ports and Europe out of its normal course some two hundred miles to collect a heavy toll upon it. This trade might perfectly well have taken the form of direct shuttles between Charleston, Savannah, Mobile, or New Orleans on the one hand and Liverpool or Havre on the other, leaving New York far to one side had not it interfered in this way. To clinch this abnormal arrangement, moreover, New York developed the coastal packet lines without which it would have been extremely difficult to make the east-bound trips of the ocean packets profitable.

At the three corners of the "cotton triangle" were the cotton port (Charleston, Savannah, Mobile, or New Orleans), the European port (generally Liverpool or Havre), and New York. On this triangular course there were two distinct major movements.

Many vessels, usually the majority, actually sailed around the three sides. They carried cotton directly from the southern port to Europe; returned to New York with general freight or immigrants; and finally

95

returned southward on the coastwise run with freight or in ballast. In that trade New York, as we shall see, had an interest even in the eastbound cotton cargoes which went direct.

The port was much more vitally concerned, however, with the alternative course which utilized only two sides of the triangle, eliminating the normal direct run between, say, New Orleans and Liverpool. A considerable part of the southern cotton and other products was carried to Europe by way of Sandy Hook and the wharves of the East River, even though that involved some two hundred extra miles of carrying and the extra charges for unloading and reloading. This gave the packets on the Atlantic shuttle their eastbound cargoes. In return, an even larger proportion of the European goods reached the South by travelling the two sides of the triangle via Sandy Hook instead of going direct from a European port to a cotton port.

This trade around the two sides naturally affected New York more directly than the sailing around the three sides of the triangle, but New York business circles profited by both. They actually took over a large share of the South's commercial activity. The combined income from interest, commissions, freight, insurance, and other profits was so great that, when the southerners finally awoke to what was happening, they claimed that the New Yorkers with a few other northerners were getting forty cents of every dollar paid for southern cotton.

This interference with the commerce of the cotton ports may well be called impudent because unlike the development of the Atlantic shuttle or the digging of the Erie Canal, there was no logical need for it. In the case of the ocean packets or of the Erie Canal, inlets for European wares and outlets for western products were so essential that the business would have been divided among the big northern ports anyway, whether or not New York had shown its timely enterprise in attracting the major share of it. The South, on the other hand, needed no such service nor any such northern interference in their commerce at all. New York, however, had very good reasons for interfering. Without the cotton and other southern products, it would have been hard pressed to provide return cargoes for the vessels which brought imports from overseas. The uncommercial attitude of the southerners, who found it more congenial to have the Negroes raise cotton than to engage in countinghouse routine and risks, gave New York port its opportunity. Yankee representatives of New York concerns, backed with adequate capital to make loans, swarmed into the

SANDY HOOK FROM NAVESINK HIGHLANDS

The east tower of the twin lights and the news semaphore are at the left

southern ports and, provided they survived the yellow fever, found it a simple matter to absorb the lion's share of the business.

The varied groups profiting by the cotton trade were summed up by Israel D. Andrews in his well-known report to Congress in 1852:

Cotton employs upwards of 120,000 tons of steam tonnage, and at least 7,000 persons engaged in steam navigation in its transportation to southern shipping ports. In some sections it pays freight to railroads for such transportation. Its first tribute to the underwriter is for insurance against casualties in its transportation from the interior.

Cotton affords employment and profit to the southern commission merchant or factor, and to the many and various laborers engaged in carting, storing it, &c., in the southern port; and a second tribute is paid to the underwriter for insurance against fire whilst in store. The "compressing" and relading it for shipment coastwise to eastern Atlantic cities, or to foreign ports, and insurance against the danger of the seas, give additional employment and cause additional charges.

The transportation of that portion of the crop sent along the gulf coast to the principal gulf ports, or coastwise to eastern cities, employs upwards of 1,100,000 tons of *American* shipping in the gulf and Atlantic coasting trade, and upwards of 55,000 American seamen engaged in such trade. As no foreign vessel can participate in the trade, the freights are highly profitable. They ordinarily average from the gulf ports to New York not less than five-eighths of a cent per pound freight.

In the eastern Atlantic cities, the wharfinger, those who unlade the vessel, the drayman, the storekeeper, the commission merchant, the cotton-broker, the weigher, the packers who compress the bales by steam power or otherwise, the laborers, and those who charge for "mendage," "cordage," &c., &c., the fire insurer, and the shipper, the stevedore, and numerous other persons in those ports, find profitable avocations arising from cotton, whether destined for a home or for a foreign market. . . .

More than 800,000 tons of the navigation of the United States engaged in the foreign trade are employed in carrying American cotton to Europe and elsewhere, and upwards of 40,000 American seamen are given employment in such vessels. It is estimated that the foreign tonnage and seamen employed in carrying American cotton to Europe and elsewhere to foreign countries amount to about one-sixth of that of the United States so employed.

Since this is a history of the port, it will not be necessary to go into all the financial ramifications of New York's contacts with the cotton ports. This will be merely the story of the major coastwise trade, from Charleston southward. The bringing of naval stores from North Carolina and of tobacco and flour from the Chesapeake will be dealt with later in connection with the lesser coastal trade.

By the time our period opens, the cotton bale had become the most important single unit in American commerce. Wrapped in burlap and tightly bound, it contained 400 pounds of cotton more or less, tightly pressed into a round or square shape so that it would take up as little room as possible in a vessel's hold. Its value, of course, fluctuated from month to month and gradually declined as the supply increased. By and large, $50 was a fair average value for "uplands," grown in the hinterland of Carolina and Georgia. "Louisiana" cotton from the Gulf region might command a few dollars more, while the occasional bales of choice "sea island," grown off the Georgia coast, might be worth twice as much as ordinary uplands. A trunk of broadcloths from Liverpool or a matting-covered chest of tea from Canton would generally be worth more than a single bale, but the southern cotton output grew at such a tremendous rate during our period that it overshadowed all other individual items of import or export.

That importance, however, was only of recent date. The cotton bale was conspicuously absent in the commerce of the colonial period. The mills of Lancashire in the late eighteenth century were being supplied with cotton from the Mediterranean, the West Indies and, to a lesser degree, from India and Brazil. The very few bales which arrived at England from American colonial ports before the Revolution had probably been brought originally from the West Indies.

No sooner was the Revolution over, however, when Carolina began to grow cotton of its own. There is an unconfirmed legend to the effect that when an American ship brought eight bags of Carolina-grown cotton to England in 1784, the customs officials at first declared it an illegal importation because they had never heard of cotton being grown in the United States. A survey of the Liverpool shipping lists gives no record of those eight bags, but it yields the significant revelation that almost from the very start the southern cotton was carried to Liverpool by way of New York. The story of the cotton triangle goes back to a beginning just thirty years before the arrival of the peace news in 1815. The first arrival of American cotton recorded at Liverpool was a "bag" direct from Charleston in January, 1785. The following month, a second bag of cotton reached there—this time by way of New York, in the ship *Tonquin*. That was apparently the beginning of the roundabout trade which was to reach such tremendous proportions later.

Until after Eli Whitney invented the cotton gin about 1792, the "bags" of southern cotton were not numerous and they commanded a high price. At first the shipments consisted of only a few scattered bags, but by 1789, one ship from New York had brought more than 330 bales in a single trip. By the end of 1789, New York had sent some 572 bales to Liverpool, while Philadelphia's total was some 521. Both of those ports had a larger total than the 133 from Charleston whence most of the cotton had come originally. The first direct shipment of two bags from Savannah did not reach Liverpool until 1790.

The invention of the cotton gin made it possible to produce marketable cotton far more cheaply than before, and led to a remarkable expansion of planting which was to give southern economic life its distinctive aspect. By 1806, the United States had passed the West Indies as a source of cotton and by 1810 its 240,000 bales amounted to more than half of the British cotton imports. From that time on southern cotton dominated the Liverpool market and was the most valuable single item in British imports.

Looking at it from the standpoint of American exports, cotton enjoyed an even higher relative importance. In 1821, the national total of exports, excluding specie, was $54,000,000. In that amount, cotton was an easy first at $20,000,000; next in order, but trailing far behind, came tobacco at $5,000,000 and flour at $4,000,000. Thirty years later cotton was relatively still more a leader, for out of the export total, excluding specie, of $188,000,000, cotton accounted for $112,-000,000 or nearly 60 per cent, with flour at $10,000,000, and tobacco at $9,000,000.

It was small wonder that New York, seeing how completely its local offerings of flour, meat, ashes, and the like were overshadowed by the cotton trade, was eager to participate in this grand prize of American commerce. The creation of the cotton triangle, however, was a very gradual and very quiet affair, unaccompanied by the fanfares which called public attention to the beginnings of the Erie Canal or even to the Black Ball Line. For them, we may ascribe very definite dates and bestow credit upon particular men. New York, however, was not anxious to advertise its activity to the southward, lest the cotton ports become alarmed and safeguard their direct trade. Consequently, it is only by delving in the analyses of individual cargoes that one may trace New York's development of the practice which started with the shipping of that bag of cotton in the *Tonquin* in 1785.

Gradually, during the early years of the century, the "cotton triangle" began to assume a definite form. To Jeremiah Thompson, the

Yorkshire woollen importer, New York is indebted not only for the inspiration which led to the Black Ball Line but also for the decided stimulus which he gave to the shipping of British goods southward and the bringing back of cotton wherewith to pay for his textiles at Liverpool. His Yorkshire colleague, Benjamin Marshall, was also active in this business, frequently spending his winters in Georgia purchasing cotton from the planters, a pioneer among the hundreds who would later go south from New York on similar missions. Possibly there were others who were even more active in those formative years in routing southern commerce by way of Sandy Hook. There is an opportunity for some patient scholar to analyze the coastwise cotton consignments in the New York shipping news and reveal the parts played by those who developed the trade. That lies before the period of this study and it will be enough here to note what progress had been made on the eve of the War of 1812.

The first issue of *The Liverpool Mercury* appeared just a year before that conflict started; and a tabulation of its lists of incoming cargoes for those intervening twelve months reveals that New York had already made good progress. It shipped some 15,000 bales, in forty different cargoes, almost a quarter of the whole amount arriving at Liverpool from the United States. Nearly every ship from New York brought at least a few bales; and in two or three cases more than 700 came by a single ship. The cotton from New York was more than the combined shipments from Philadelphia, with nearly 3000; Boston with 2200; and Baltimore with nearly 1000.

With that good start before the war, New York was in a position to make rapid advances in perfecting the cotton triangle as soon as peace came. By the early 'twenties, the old secrecy was removed and various commercial periodicals gave detailed analyses of the cotton movements. In 1822, for instance, cotton was far and away the most valuable of New York's domestic exports, while certain other commodities from the southward demonstrated the success with which the triangular arrangement was operating. The total value of the port's domestic exports was $9,228,000. Some 40 per cent of this was represented by cotton at $3,925,000. Flour, the principal northern offering, was a poor second at $794,000, closely followed by tobacco, brought chiefly from the nearer South, at $754,000. Then came a sharp drop to pot and pearl ashes, a northern product, at $464,000; followed by undressed skins and furs, brought in part from the South, at $291,000; and northern flaxseed at $277,000. Then, just ahead of northern salt beef and pork, came two southern items, naval stores at $232,000 and rice at $213,000. Altogether the purely southern products of cotton, tobacco, naval stores and rice accounted for 55 per cent of the total, to which should be added part of the skins together with part of the barrel staves and other lumber. Without this southern connection, New York would certainly have been hard pressed for eastbound cargoes on the Atlantic shuttle.

Approaching the situation from another angle, New Orleans in that year shipped out 156,000 bales of cotton, of which 64,000 went direct to Great Britain, 33,000 direct to France, and 51,000 coastwise, including 28,000 to New York, 10,000 to Philadelphia, and 7000 to Boston. Three years later, during the great speculative boom in cotton, the New Orleans total was 204,000 bales, of which 101,000 went direct to Great Britain, 32,000 to France, and 69,000 coastwise. By that time, New York had increased its proportion with 51,000 bales, compared with only 7000 to Boston, and 3000 to Philadelphia.

So common had been this preponderance of southern exports from New York that when, in 1843, the new packet *Queen of the West* sailed on her maiden trip, Philip Hone wrote in his diary:

Saturday, Sept. 16—A state of things exists in the commerce of this country unprecedented and worthy to be noted down among the memorabilia of the day. This ship has taken out to England a cargo consisting of articles all (with the exception of the naval stores) of Northern production, and the *Ashburton,* which sailed a day or two since, has not a Southern article on board. Not a single bale of cotton in both cargoes. The *Stephen Whitney* has only 119 bales of cotton. . . . The large shipments of provisions may be accounted for by Sir Robert Peel's new tariff. Cotton is higher in the United States than in England, and rising.

By that time, the coastwise shipments of cotton to New York were being frequently overshadowed by the cargoes to Boston, destined for domestic industry. In the 1836–37 season, for instance, New Orleans sent 39,000 bales to Boston, 23,000 to New York, and 6000 to Philadelphia. This was the general proportion for many years to come, though there were still seasons such as 1843–44 when New York led with 82,000, followed by Boston at 72,000, and Philadelphia with 6000.

This surfeit of statistics has been given to demonstrate the extent to which New York's participation in the physical movement of cotton and other southern products had developed at the beginning of our period. Since coastwise figures were not gathered and published by the government, these are not as readily obtainable elsewhere as are statistics for foreign trade. The other part of New York's share in the cotton triangle—the carrying of imported goods and northern manufactures southward—may be postponed for the moment.

By 1822, then, when the Erie Canal was only partly finished, the cotton triangle was a well-established and strongly functioning business. Even after that much-touted ditch had been opened, it would seem reasonable to argue that the cotton and other southern products brought north by coasters far exceeded in value the flour and other western offerings carried by the canal boats. The South, moreover, probably ranked before the West as a distributing point for the imports and domestic manufactures which New York had to offer. At any rate, advertisements in the New York newspapers were addressed to "Southern and Western Merchants," and it was only toward the end of the period, after the West was filling up rapidly, that its merchants were placed first.

Of the four major cotton ports, involved in the triangle, the business at first centered in the two old and well-established seaboard cities of Charleston and Savannah. Gradually they were overtaken in volume of business by the old French ports on the Gulf, New Orleans and Mobile. In some ways, the conditions at the seaboard ports were different from those on the Gulf, as far as New York was concerned.

The early leader was Charleston, oldest, and perhaps proudest, of the four cotton ports. Situated on a narrow peninsula between two rivers, it was the only one of the ports opening directly on the sea, and had the only first-rate harbor for miles in either direction along the barren sandy Carolina coast. Founded around 1670, it had soon developed a shuttle trade with England, whither it sent large quantities of rice and indigo. By the eve of the Revolution, it stood third among the American ports, with a greater volume of trade than New York. Its imports in 1772 were actually heavier than they were to be during the period between 1837 and the Civil War. With exports it was a different story, for the opening of the cotton era found it the chief outlet for the upland cotton grown in the back country. With its old, proud, and wealthy society and long-established mercantile houses, Charleston was to be the most difficult of the four ports for Yankee traders to penetrate. Nevertheless, enough of them were there in 1819 to form a New England Society, and many a name in the commercial columns of the *Mercury* betrayed the merchants who flocked south from Connecticut by way of New York. Even after the Gulf ports finally overshadowed Charleston in the customs figures, it was ready, as the most intensely southern of the ports, to take the lead on several occasions against what it considered northern aggression.

About a hundred miles farther south lay Savannah, some twenty-four miles inland from the sea on the Savannah River, which penetrated far into the interior. Founded in 1733, it never managed to catch up with Charleston in trade. On the eve of the Revolution, its commerce was only a fifth or a sixth of the Charleston total. Savannah likewise became an outlet for upland cotton and at the beginning of our period it was showing marked initiative in steam navigation, not only on inland waters but also in sponsoring the pioneer transatlantic steamship which bore the city's name. Its mercantile community was not as large, nor as wealthy, nor as exclusive as Charleston's and consequently offered better openings to the ubiquitous Yankees. They also swarmed into Augusta, up the river in the cotton country, the chief gathering point for Savannah's cotton cargoes.

Unique in many ways was Mobile, which lay some thirty miles from the Gulf at the head of the beautiful Mobile Bay, near the mouths of two rivers which ran far into the Alabama hinterland. It was the second oldest of the cotton ports, for in 1702 the French explorer Iberville had planted a near-by settlement which seven years later was moved to the present site. For more than a century, however, under the three flags of France, England, and Spain, it had been a slumbering little hamlet with virtually no trade at all. The customs figures during the period of British occupation just before the Revolution showed the arrivals of only a vessel or two each year. Andrew Jackson occupied it during the War of 1812 and under its fourth flag, Mobile began to awaken. By the time Alabama was organized in 1818, planters from the seaboard states were flocking to the rich virgin soil of the hinterland while New Yorkers and other northerners began to swarm to Mobile and its upstart rival Blakely near by. Corner lots in both towns were being advertised in the New York newspapers and, since the old inhabitants of the former had developed virtually nothing in the way of business, the New Yorkers had a clearer field for action than in any of the other ports; and New York's ascendancy was probably highest there. More than any of the other cotton ports, Mobile depended upon New York for its imports, developing almost no direct trade with Europe during the years in which it gradually surpassed Savannah and then Charleston in the volume of its exports. In 1851, for instance, its exports amounted to $18,000,000 and its imports to only $413,000, a ratio which was probably never equalled elsewhere.

Finally, destined to outrank all the other cotton ports and for a while to overshadow even New York in exports, came New Orleans. A hundred miles up the Mississippi from the mudbars at its mouth, it was the natural outlet for the inland produce of the thousands of miles of that great river and its tributaries. With this fortunate location for commercial growth, it was able to tap a good part of the interior of the continent. Like Mobile, it was of French origin, having been established by Bienville in 1718, and like Mobile, it also passed later into Spanish hands. From the beginning, it was more important than its Alabama rival, gathering together a colorful, variegated, and rather turbulent population. Its commercial potentialities were not realized under the French or Spanish régimes, but by 1803, when the Louisiana Purchase brought it into the United States, the opening of the West meant an almost immediate stimulus of business. It also offered rich opportunities for newcomers from the North. Vincent Nolte, the international financial adventurer, described its population at the time of his first visit there in 1806.

In the city itself the French number at least three-fifths of the inhabitants; one other fifth was of Spanish race, and another Americans, among whom were some Germans. The city numbered about 16,000 souls, of whom one-third were people of color or slaves. The mercantile class was made up of four or five French establishments, springing from the neighborhood of the Garonne, and founded during the continuance of the French rule; three Scotch counting-houses, one German concern, and eight or ten commission-houses, lately opened by young American merchants from New York, Philadelphia, and Baltimore.

As the trade of the port expanded, the last group grew rapidly. In certain summers, the newspapers carried long casualty lists of the northerners dying of yellow fever, most of the victims being in their twenties or thirties.

The river brought an ever-increasing amount of cotton and western produce to New Orleans, at first in flatboats which were broken up at the port for lumber. The first river steamer reached there in 1811; and by 1840 there were scores of them at the levees, unloading cargoes which would be hoisted into seagoing vessels for New York or overseas. In 1834, the rapidly growing city ran ahead even of New York as the first port of the nation in the value of its exports. It continued in that position for nearly a decade, winning a place among the foremost seaports of the world.[1]

Lapsing into figures once more, it is possible to indicate briefly the relative growth of the cotton ports in trade and population. In exports, by millions of dollars, the standing in 1815 was Charleston 6, New Orleans 5, and Savannah 4, Mobile not yet having come on the scene. In 1822, New Orleans overtook Charleston for first place. By 1836, Mobile had won third place from Savannah and four years later passed Charleston as well, the score in 1840 standing: New Orleans 34, Mobile 12, Charleston 10, and Savannah 6. They remained in that order for the rest of our period, but the Gulf ports drew steadily ahead of the old seaboard centers. By 1860, the score was: New Orleans 108, Mobile 38, Charleston 21, and Savannah 18. A moderate amount of cotton was shipped from the Florida Gulf ports of Pensacola and Apalachicola as well as from Galveston in Texas, but none of these could compare with the four big cotton ports.

Whereas New Orleans grew to be a good-sized city, Charleston remained moderate in population, while Mobile and Savannah were small, in view of the size of their trade. New Orleans had about 5000 inhabitants in 1785, 17,000 in 1810, and 168,000, almost the size of Boston, in 1860. Charleston's growth was more moderate. In 1790, it had 16,000 inhabitants, just below Boston and just above Baltimore. In 1860, this had grown to only 40,000. Mobile, which numbered less than 800 in 1785, had only 1500 in 1820 and 29,000 in 1860, while Savannah, the smallest of the four, had about 5000 in 1810 and only 22,000 in 1860.[2] The census figures in 1850 throw light on the origins of the population of the various cities. In the four cotton ports, there were 5637 natives of New York and 3822 who were born in New England, where Massachusetts stood first, followed by Maine and Connecticut. This New York-New England element was proportionally strongest at Mobile, with 1324, approximately 10 per cent of the white population. It was lowest at Charleston, with less than 3 per cent. In the business districts of those ports, however, those New York-New Englanders were prominent out of all proportion to their numbers.

As for the shipping between New York and these ports, maritime history has been constantly neglectful of coastwise navigation. One

[1]See Appendix, i, ii.   [2]See Appendix, xxix.

reason for this is that, while statistics are available in generous quantity for foreign commerce, the customs authorities were not required to keep such records for the even larger volume of traffic which passed between the ports of our own coasts. The story of the coastwise trade consequently involved deeper searching. A second and equally cogent explanation is the false impression that coastal navigation is apt to seem a simple matter of skirting along the shore—mere child's play compared with venturing into deep water. Actually, a vessel out at sea, with plenty of room to maneuver, is much safer than one in frequent danger of contact with the shore, the source of most accidents. It may be a surprise to know that, in the eyes of the marine-insurance experts, whose business it was to estimate the probabilities of accident, the trip from New York to New Orleans was regarded as more risky than to Liverpool, London, or Havre and almost as dangerous as the route halfway round the world to China. In 1825, for instance, the rate of insurance from New York to New Orleans was 1¼ to 1½ per cent, while to the British Isles and France it was 1 to 1¼ per cent and to Canton in China only 1¾ per cent. The shorter routes to Charleston and Savannah, of course, were considered safer with a rate of ½ per cent.[1] A third reason for slighting the coasting trade may be in part a borrowing of the attitude of the English, whose coastal voyages were much shorter affairs. A vessel from London might arrive in a dozen different foreign countries in shorter trips than that from New York to New Orleans, while it might reach several within the limits of the much briefer run from New York to Charleston. Altogether, the coastwise voyages to the cotton ports were tasks requiring first-rate vessels and first-rate men.

For all four ports, the early stages of the passage from New York were the same. Passing Sandy Hook, a vessel skirted the Jersey coast until halfway down, about at Barnegat, where it stood out to sea to clear Cape Hatteras, the stormy outer tip of the huge sandy barrier which runs along the Carolina coast. That "graveyard of the Atlantic," with its dangerous offshore shoals, caught victims year after year, both because of its constant storms and because of the fogs which involved the danger of a premature landfall. The southward passage was particularly dangerous, since shipping had to stand well in toward the shore to avoid the current of the Gulf Stream, running in the opposite direction.

[1]See Appendix, xix.

Beyond Hatteras, there was a parting of the ways between the vessels bound for the seaboard ports and those headed for the Gulf. The former skirted the two other Carolina capes, Lookout and Fear, and by that time were not far from their destinations. To Charleston, the closest of the four ports to New York, the distance was only 627 miles. The Savannah run averaged 700 miles, roughly one day's farther sailing.

Meanwhile, the shipping bound for the Gulf was encountering the meanest part of its passage. It was necessary to pass through the long barrier of islands, keys, and reefs which separate the Gulf from the Atlantic. The shortest route lay through the Providence Channel, cutting through the Bahamas northeast of Nassau at a place appropriately termed "Hole-in-the-Wall." Then, after dodging numerous reefs and keys on either hand, one reached the Florida coast which offered similar perils. Complicating all this was the presence of the Gulf Stream, which was at its narrowest and swiftest off the Florida coast. Between August and November, moreover, shipping faced the ever-present risk of violent hurricanes. "Wrecking" became a thriving industry at Key West. Once past the Dry Tortugas off the tip of Florida, the trip across the Gulf was generally fair sailing. The vessels for Mobile bore northward but, after making the bay, were usually forced to anchor some miles below the port and have their cargoes carried the rest of the way in lighters. The distance from New York to Mobile was 1658 miles, whereas it was 1711 to New Orleans, which offered the added annoyance of traversing the shallow muddy bars at one of the various entrances to the river. Then one had still a hundred miles of river to travel, which was ordinarily slow work unless the cargo was of sufficient importance to warrant the hiring of a steamboat for towing.

For the larger ships, these trips averaged a hundred miles a day. That, at least, was the result of tabulating more than three thousand northward packet passages from the cotton ports to New York. From Charleston, the average was 6.5 days; from Savannah, 7.3; from Mobile, 17.7; and from New Orleans, 18.0. These fluctuated from month to month, usually being at their best in the spring and worst in autumn and winter. Those records were made by full-rigged ships, operating on fairly regular schedule. Part of the trade with Charleston and Savannah was carried on in brigs and even schooners, and for them the average passage would be apt to be somewhat longer.[1]

[1] See Appendix, vi, xxiv.

During the early 'twenties, the success of the Black Ball service to Liverpool led to the organization of similar packet lines for the cotton ports. For many years before that, the term "packet" had been used for many vessels, more properly regular traders, which linked New York and Charleston or Savannah without regular scheduled service. Since the packet lines to the cotton ports have been analyzed by the author in a separate work, only a few of their more significant features will be mentioned.

As in the case of the ocean sailing packets, the original operators of these lines were generally merchants actively engaged in business with those ports. They were bringing cotton northward and shipping general cargoes southward on their own account anyway, and believed that regular service would bring them added profit by carrying similar wares for others. Their agents in the cotton ports were frequently partners or close associates in business, and were generally part owners in the ships. In two conspicuous cases, packet captains became operators of coastal lines, but, along with that, both developed a general commission business specializing in the southern trade.

The first really regular line was established in the spring of 1822 to Charleston with four, and soon five, ships of moderate size. The most conspicuous of the merchants who joined forces to organize this service was Anson G. Phelps, who, we recall, was one of the nation's outstanding importers of metals. To provide return payments, he engaged heavily in cotton exports by way of New York. This Charleston "Ship Line" continued until 1855, being operated for a considerable period by George Sutton, one of Phelps's original captains. The New York-Charleston packet service also included a short-lived "brig-line" and a more permanent line, which started with schooners and gradually progressed through brigs to ships.

Savannah packet service began in 1824 with two rival ship lines. The close relation of the coastal and ocean packet trade, involving the cotton triangle, was indicated by the fact that one line was started by John Griswold, operator of London packets, and the other and more lasting service, by William Whitlock, Jr., prominent in the service to Havre. Many changes of ownership and management occurred in the Savannah service, until, around 1840, most of the ships were transferred to the New Orleans run. A more modest service continued to Savannah mostly with brigs.

The Mobile packets, operated by Elisha D. Hurlbut, began in 1826 but were so irregular in their performance that they scarcely deserve the name of packets at all, particularly after 1840. Instead of keeping to the New York-Mobile shuttle, they were more inclined to sail around the triangle, like many of the transient tramps. They would carry cotton from Mobile to Liverpool or Havre; bring back immigrants and general freight to New York; and there load other general cargoes for the return trip to Mobile.

The New Orleans packets, like the New Orleans trade in general, soon overshadowed all the others. This service had been started in a modest way with three brigs in 1821 by John W. Russell, originally from New Bedford, who advertised a "line of packets" but did not observe a regular schedule. Silas Holmes, a Stonington mariner who had commanded one of Russell's brigs, began a rival line of his own in 1824. This second line, under Holmes and his successor, William Nelson, established a distinguished record for duration and performance. It continued to run regularly until the Civil War interrupted the business. During all that time only one of its vessels was totally wrecked, whereas one of the later rival lines lost six ships in a decade. In 1831, keen competition came with the appearance of the "Louisiana and New York Line," which suddenly sprang into being with five new and almost identical ships, particularly designed with "flat-floored" construction in order to carry heavy cargoes over the shallow Mississippi bars. This line quickly passed under the management of Edward K. Collins, who was later to win a high reputation with sailing packets and steamships on the Liverpool run. By this time, the New Orleans packets compared favorably with those on the Atlantic shuttle. The 741-ton *Shakespeare*, built for Collins in 1835, was larger than any ocean packet at the time, while several of the able captains assembled by Collins for this New Orleans run later won outstanding reputations in the Liverpool service. The New Orleans packet service continued to grow, especially after 1840, when most of the Savannah ships were transferred to that longer and more profitable run to the Mississippi. There would be no point, however, in following here the various shifts in lines and operators.

Altogether, New York's coastal packet fleet was an invaluable adjunct to its ocean packets and the fact that they were "mere coasters" should not obscure the fact that in size, performance, and earnings the ships plying to the cotton ports were among the finest afloat.

While cotton was by far the most important item carried by these vessels on their northbound trips, it was by no means their only source of freight to New York. A detailed analysis of the individual coastal packet cargoes arriving at New York in 1835, as a typical middle year of the period, has been reproduced as an appendix in the author's packet study. It indicates not only the range of products from each of the ports but also the marked seasonal fluctuations.

The cotton season extended from early autumn until late spring. During the summer, news would often arrive that the "first bale" had reached tidewater, usually at Savannah, where one particular planter made it a point to win this distinction, if possible. Other bales would trickle in during September, but not until October was the season really under way; and the statistics for a cotton crop were ordinarily given for the year beginning in October. By midwinter, the movement was in full swing until it began to taper off after April. During the summer, cotton shipments were almost at a standstill. In 1835, for instance, the receipts of cotton at New York by coastal packets from New Orleans dropped from 2577 bales in April to 119 in September. The changes at Charleston and Savannah, while less violent, followed the same trend, while from Mobile packet movements simply ceased during the summer months.

One reason for the irregularity of the Mobile packets was the fact that that port specialized so intensively in cotton that it had few alternative offerings for the dull season except skins and hides, which came in varying quantities from all the southern ports. It happened that whereas the summer months were the dullest season on the coastal run, they were the busiest on the Atlantic shuttle. Consequently, more money was to be made in having the coastal packets carry cotton directly to Europe and on the return trip participate in the regular Atlantic shuttle business to New York.

New Orleans, on the contrary, had numerous alternative cargoes with which the packets might be filled during the off-season. More regular service, therefore, could be maintained throughout the year on a fairly profitable basis. The naming of the New Orleans packet *Galena* was a recognition of the importance, during the slack season in cotton, of the shipments of lead mined at that town in Illinois. From February through April, for instance, the New Orleans packets brought 7185 bales of cotton and only 300 pigs of lead; from July through September, the cotton fell to 2330 bales while the lead rose to 33,188 pigs (about 1100 tons). A moderate amount of flour was brought north during the summer months. Tobacco, chiefly from Kentucky, and sugar from Louisiana's rapidly developing industry were brought in considerable quantities. The tobacco shipments were spread fairly evenly throughout the year but the sugar season coincided almost exactly with that of cotton. Nearly $2,000,000 in specie, chiefly from the Mexican silver mines, was carried to New York, most of it arriving in November and December. Numerous other articles in wide variety but smaller quantities were to be found in the packet cargoes from New Orleans —hams, bacon, pork, lard, flaxseed, pig iron, molasses, buffalo robes, and much else in addition to the ever-present hides, skins, and furs. This wide diversity and good seasonal spread were the chief reasons why the New Orleans packet fleet rivalled in size and in profits the sailing liners to London and Havre.

Charleston and Savannah were in an intermediate position between New Orleans and Mobile in this respect. They had an important alternative in rice, but unfortunately, from the line operators' standpoint, the rice and cotton seasons were almost identical. From January to March, for instance, Charleston sent by packet 2899 bales of cotton and 7810 casks, or their equivalent, of rice. From June to September, the total shipments were only 1554 bales of cotton and 106 casks of rice. Outside of hides and skins, no other commodity was sent in any considerable amount, though both ports from time to time shipped small quantities of Spanish moss, wool, peanuts, and lumber. Savannah occasionally sent reeds and Charleston shipped a little cotton seed. Naval stores, which today constitute the principal offering of Savannah, were entirely absent from all the cotton port cargoes except for a single small shipment of turpentine from Charleston. The large quantities of tar, rosin, and turpentine which the ocean packets carried to Europe had been brought, as we shall see, in smaller craft from the North Carolina ports where the sandbars kept larger vessels from entering in safety. The result of this poor seasonal spread was that during the summer the Charleston packets sailed only twice a month instead of weekly, while the Savannah packets were quite irregular. Rather than sail only partly full, the packets were ready to carry cheap and bulky freight at low rates. Large quantities of firewood were brought northward during the dull seasons, particularly from Savannah, while baled hay and granite paving blocks were frequently carried southward from New York.

The major portion of the cotton brought northward to New York was simply shifted from one wharf to another on South Street and carried to Liverpool or Havre in the ocean packets. In 1835, for example, the packets carried northward 47,952 bales of cotton, worth more than $3,000,000. From New Orleans, Charleston, and Savannah came the equivalent of enough for the Liverpool packet cargoes that year, while Mobile sent nearly enough for the Havre packets. Naturally, they were not all those same identical bales, since some of the cotton brought to New York was taken by Sound steamers to Providence for the southern New England mills.

While New York was most vitally interested in the cotton and other products brought directly to the East River in the packets and other vessels, it also had a definite concern in the much larger amount of cotton shipped directly overseas from the southern ports. A considerable part of that business was in the hands of New York firms or their representatives.

The first stage in that process lay in the relationship between the planter and the "factor" resident in some such inland town as Augusta. These factors were in many cases New Englanders, who had established New York connections before moving southward. The key to their success lay in their ability to advance long credit. The average planter was inclined to be at least one year in debt, receiving from the factor, at a substantial rate of interest, a considerable part of the value of his next year's crop. This chronic state of debt arose in part from the desire to buy more land and more slaves. New York's constantly increasing importance as a financial center placed it in a better position than any other city to take advantage of this situation, for the banks, if not the New York merchants themselves, could carry the cotton crop during those months of waiting and prosper from the accumulation of interest.

The methods under which business was carried on by one of those inland factors are revealed in rich detail by the letter books, journals, ledgers, memorandum books, and other commercial records of William Bostwick, preserved at Yale. Bostwick, apparently from Connecticut, operated as a cotton factor and merchant at Augusta, Georgia, from the mid-'twenties to the mid-'forties, sometimes in partnership, at other times alone. The ledgers reveal accounts with scores of scattered planters as well as with occasional storekeepers further inland. From them he received cotton; to them he advanced credit and sold various wares, chiefly from New York. The informal store memorandum books supplement the ledgers, indicating the details of this business:

John Thornton will send in Sdy next 8 bales of cotton—sell them at not less than 13, and apply the money to pay his note for $325. If it will not command 13c keep it for his further instructions. . . .

Benj. Bugg's waggon will be in tomorrow with six bales cotton, to be stored with Baird & Rowland, and keep warehouse net. Send by the waggon 6 bush. salt, 1 qtr. rice, 3 small packages (paper bundles). . . .

In store for Jones & Hester which send by first waggon from Elbert County with a bill 100″ lead, 2 bundles shot and bags, 1 coil rope, 5 casks nails (nails to be sent when they arrive from New York). . . .

In store for P. F. Maragne bot. this day—send bill—to go by Edwards' boat or any other boat if this does not arrive soon. 50″ coffee, (?) bus. salt, 1 jug wine, 1 bundle of 14 blankets, 1 bag rice 20″, 1 box cheese from Morse. When Baird & Rowland sell Mr. M's cotton call on them for money enough to pay Cross & Turpin's bill & also the amt. he owes on my books. C. & T. must be paid *soon* tho' the cotton be not sold.

The Georgia hinterland did not monopolize Bostwick's attention. He was in very frequent communication with New York, particularly with Thaddeus Phelps, a commission merchant who dealt in cotton and much else, a relationship which Bostwick summarized in 1841:

In my case, every bale of cotton that I have shipped to your market in the last *ten years* has been consigned to you. Every order I have had executed has been by you. Every draft I have drawn, in short every transaction in your city during that period upon which I have paid a commission has been with yourself.

The occasion for those remarks was discontent with Phelps's increase of the interest rate on his account, for he was in a fairly constant state of debt to New York just as the planters were to him. He drew notes steadily against Phelps for purchases, chiefly from New York, and informed him every month of those about to mature. A typical routine letter ran:

Above I hand you check for $500, which please place to my credit. You will please pay my 4 notes as they come to maturity in March as at foot. You may send me by Savannah 1000 lbs. bar lead in boxes or casks—the bars must be small, say about ¾ of a pound each—1 pound will not do— James McCullugh, Tucker & Carter and James Kelso are the men I buy it of. The last I bot was at 6 months. Our cotton market continues to advance.

At times, he ordered directly from New York wholesale grocers or textile jobbers, rather than through Phelps, generally stipulating that the goods be sent by the schooner line of packets to Savannah. A little set of pocket memorandum books contain the scrawled notes made during his annual summer visits to New York, when in accordance with the regular custom, he purchased a considerable part of his stock from the jobbers, importers, or auctioneers.

From the factors in the inland towns, the cotton generally passed to other New York-New Englanders in the cotton ports. Samuel St. John, for instance, the leading cotton dealer in Mobile, came originally from New Haven and was closely linked with Elisha Hurlbut and other New York merchants. These men at the ports might ship the cotton to New York, which was becoming the chief American center for speculation, or to New England, for domestic industrial use; or, a still more likely possibility, directly overseas to Liverpool, Havre, or some other port. Even in the latter case, New York again profited, for the major part of the cotton was carried either in New York transient "cotton drogh-ers" or in New England vessels, for whose service some New York shipbroker was apt to have received a commission. The chances were also good that the marine insurance premiums on such cargoes would go in large part to one of the New York companies. In interest, com-missions, freight, insurance, and from other similar sources, New York took its toll even on the cotton which never came past Sandy Hook.

The man who perhaps did more than any other to inaugurate this system was, as we saw, Jeremiah Thompson. By the early 'twenties, he rated as the foremost cotton trader in the world. His Liverpool dealings were with the house of Cropper, Benson & Co., also Quakers, whom he selected as agents for the Black Ball packets. He consigned tremendous quantities to them, shipping some cotton by way of New York in the Black Ballers, and the rest directly in his own ships from the cotton ports. In the mid-'twenties, when he was at the height of his success as a cotton trader, he was likewise one of the heaviest shipowners in the United States.

The very nature of the cotton trade made it an object of speculation. Thompson and his associates in Liverpool were in the thick of the boom in 1825, the biggest orgy in cotton speculation. At the end of 1824, it was announced that the stock of cotton on hand in Liverpool was about one-third less than usual and consequently prices rose rapidly. Cropper, Benson & Co. and a few other Liverpool traders decided to gather all possible American cotton into their hands, and by achieving a corner in the material, force prices still higher. When the news reached New York by packet a few weeks later, a similar boom resulted. Thompson despatched a fast pilot boat to New Orleans with word to his agents, including Nolte, to buy up as much as possible. One of the coastal packets beat the pilot boat, however, and Russell's correspondents, receiving the news nearly two days ahead, were able to make heavy advance profits by buying in the still-normal market. From that time on, the boom ran its course of rise and collapse at Liverpool, then at New York, and finally at the cotton ports, with an interval of several weeks between those cities, depending upon the speed with which the packets could carry the news. In 1824, Charleston and New Orleans each had export totals of about $8,000,000; in 1825, these jumped to $11,000,-000 and $12,000,000 respectively. The infant trade of Mobile increased by only $130,000 while Savannah actually fell off. The most violent jump in exports occurred at New York, indicating that a considerable amount of the cotton was brought up the coast to that more sensitive market, closer in touch with the latest news from abroad. From $22,000,000 in 1824, New York's total suddenly rose to $35,-000,000. Cotton exports, rather than the opening of the Erie Canal, apparently accounted for that.

By the middle of April, the market began to crack in Liverpool. One Scottish firm threw a small amount on the market at a reduced price, while an unexpectedly large arrival of Brazilian cotton further threw off the calculations of the speculators. The Manchester manufacturers, in the meantime, had curbed their purchases and were running on a hand-to-mouth basis. Prices suddenly tumbled at Liverpool but continued at an abnormally high level in New York, where the speculators were ordering even more from the southward. With the arrival of the Black Baller *Florida* in May, prices likewise dropped at New York but New Orleans still remained in ignorance of the change and Nolte was far up the river buying cotton at top prices. By midsummer, the cotton market was prostrate at all three ports and the boom left a trail of failures in its wake. Jeremiah Thompson weathered the storm and emerged apparently richer than ever, only to meet his doom three years later when Cropper, Benson & Co. passed a virtual financial death sentence upon him, since, in view of a declining market, they refused to honor his drafts for heavy consignments of cotton. Afterwards, from time to time, other speculative attempts were made to corner the market, particularly the ambitious but unsuccessful scheme of Nicholas Biddle in the next decade, but none reached the magnitude of the 1825 boom.

By the mid-'fifties a change took place in the cotton movements. Its principal feature was a sharp diminution of the amount of cotton sent northward to New York for transshipment to Europe. A considerable part of that amount had always been for speculative purposes and the speculators gradually found that it was enough to send the bills of lading and samples to New York. In this way, the speculative trade might be handled without having the bales themselves incur the added charges of freight and handling involved in going abroad by way of Sandy Hook. The first annual report of the Chamber of Commerce of the State of New York called attention to this trend in 1859:

> In discussing the cotton trade of New York, it must not be forgotten that the import of cotton from the Southern States has been materially diminished by the mode of selling cotton at this port by sample, while on its way from Southern ports to Europe—especially to Liverpool—or, as the phrase is, "in transit."
>
> This mode of conducting the more speculative portion of the cotton trade only began to be commonly resorted to four or five years ago, and has been constantly on the increase since. There has always been a class of adventurers who wished to have the option of terminating their operations by a sale in New York. A few years ago, this class—a very important one in moving the cotton crop—ordered the cotton to be shipped to New York; but this necessarily involved double freights, insurances, and expenses on the cotton with only the small advantage of selling for home consumption. Now, however, the plan is to ship the cotton direct to Liverpool, from the Southern port, and to send the samples and bills of lading to New York, where it can be sold, if the adventurer is unwilling to take the risk of the Liverpool market.

The report cited the statistics of shipments from New Orleans and Mobile for several "cotton seasons." For the latest one, ending in mid-May, 1859, the total was only 28,800 bales to New York as compared with 310,400 to other coastwise ports (chiefly in New England) and 1,866,000 direct to foreign ports. Those figures stood in sharp contrast to the annual average for 1850–53, when 94,000 bales were sent to New York, 176,000 to the other coastwise ports, and 982,000 to foreign ports. It was pointed out, on the other hand, that the "transit" transactions with samples at New York had probably risen to 200,000 bales a year by 1859, but that was cold comfort to the shipowners who lost the freights from the former profitable, if irrational, extra trip up the coast to New York. By that time, the British demand for American grain had increased and New York was not as dependent upon cotton for its eastbound cargoes. Even in 1860, however, cotton remained an easy first in New York's exports.[1]

[1]See Appendix, ix.

Drawn by F. E. Palmer

Lithographed by Currier & Ives

STATEN ISLAND AND THE NARROWS FROM FORT HAMILTON

Fort Lafayette (Fort Diamond), shown in the foreground surrounded by water, was used for the detention of prisoners during the Civil War

The freight movements in the opposite direction along the cotton triangle are more elusive. Cotton bales were convenient units for comparison but the variegated cargoes of manufactures and other wares were not adequately described to make possible a similar survey of just what happened. As in the westbound ocean traffic, the blanket phrase "merchandise" covered a large variety of articles. The extent of this trade may be deduced in part by comparing the figures for exports and imports for the southern states as given in the appendix. In 1822, for example, the combined exports of South Carolina, Georgia, Alabama, and Louisiana amounted to almost $21,000,000 and their imports to only $7,000,000.

The South received, therefore, only a relatively small amount of imports direct from Europe, compared with the exports which it sent thither. This does not mean necessarily that it consumed a total of European goods equivalent in value to its heavy cotton exports. In the absence of statistics for the coastal trade, we may do no more than guess. One student of the subject has declared that the South, with its simple rural economy, probably did not consume much more in the way of imported articles than it received directly from overseas. That is probably too extreme a statement, for it is certain that a considerable amount arrived at the southern ports by way of New York. As time went on, it seems likely that the cargoes carried southward from New York to the cotton ports contained an increasing amount of northern domestic manufactures, which gradually took the place of previous similar wares from Europe. Southern industry was in its infancy, so that northern manufactures made up for much of the region's needs. Altogether, the South was essentially a one-crop region, specializing as it did in cotton. It received a large amount of foodstuffs from the West, while the bulk of the remaining portion of its outside needs came by way of New York port.

Whereas the northbound packet cargoes, as we saw, were pretty much limited to a few staple articles, the table of packet freight rates in 1836 lists literally scores of articles regularly sent southward. European textiles formed a part of these, but manufactures of iron and leather also bulked large. The packet *Newark* was named in recognition of the large amount of business which the line received from the factories of the New Jersey metropolis, where leather in particular was a flourishing industry. Furniture was also a common article in southern shipments, Duncan Phyfe and the father of "Boss" Tweed being among those most prominently engaged in the business. Carriages of various sorts were also so commonly carried that freight rates were regularly quoted—$25 for a coach and $20 for a barouche. The Charleston packets even carried south the English and New York made locomotives for South Carolina's first railroad. Altogether, the cargoes shipped to the cotton ports resembled those which New York was sending to Cuba and to other parts of Latin America.

One of the important seasonal activities in New York's business district was the coming of the southern merchants early in the summer to lay in their stocks for the coming year. Arriving by packet in June or July, sometimes accompanied by their families who summered at some near-by resort, the southerners would spend several weeks among the New York jobbers selecting what they wanted from the stocks of imported and domestic goods. The day of the jobber's "drummer" who went out to solicit business among the customers had scarcely arrived —the customer still came to the jobber. Some southern writers later represented this practice as a burden to the merchants, but it seems likely that to many it was a welcome opportunity to get away from home at a time when business and weather were bad, and a good excuse not only for a trip but also for a sojourn in a city whose hotels and theatres were even then making life attractive for transient visitors. The trip north was not really a necessity—the factors who bought the cotton could also bring down anything needed and there were plenty of New Yorkers in southern cities who carried a considerable stock. It was significant that in later days, when the travelling salesmen removed the excuse for such trips, business men developed conventions of one sort or another to gratify their wanderlust. At any rate, as autumn approached, the southern merchant started back, frequently in the same packet which bore his purchases. At times, these southbound cargoes were more valuable than those arriving from Europe. When the Savannah packet *Louisa Matilda* was wrecked near Hatteras in 1827, for instance, it was pointed out that her cargo was worth between $350,000 and $400,000 and that the loss of those goods would represent a serious inconvenience to the Georgia merchants.

As time went on, a new inland triangle developed, complementary to the cotton triangle. The two had a common base in the sea route between New York and New Orleans but the opposite angle of the new figure was Cincinnati or some other western city, instead of Liverpool or Havre. The interest in this new geometrical figure lay in the rivalry

between its sides—whether the western storekeepers would replenish
their stocks from New York by way of packets and river steamers
through New Orleans or by way of the Erie Canal and its northern
connections. There was also the question of which route to use in sending their flour, pork, and other products to the sea. Since the South
and the West both lay in New York's sphere of commercial domination,
the metropolis stood to gain, whichever route was used.

In the beginning, the coastal route to New Orleans had the advantage but as time went on the Erie Canal gradually cut into its business
in handling freight to and from interior ports. In 1833, the canal commissioners, contemplating a reduction of rates in order to stimulate
business, sent questionnaires to many inland merchants asking for
opinions on the relative merits of the two routes. A firm in Nashville
replied that it secured merchandise from New York by both routes.
The sea route was cheaper but the canal route was quicker. To bring
a ton of merchandise from New York by packet to New Orleans and
thence by river steamer up the Mississippi, Ohio, and Cumberland cost
about $20 less than the alternative route by way of the Erie Canal,
lake transportation, Ohio Canal, and steamer down the Ohio and up
the Cumberland; but the latter was ten to twelve days quicker. With
the frequent reduction of canal rates, the northern route gradually
drew more and more of the shipments to the interior; but New Orleans still attracted the bulk of the heavy outward traffic in flour and
the like. In 1852, Cincinnati tobacco dealers reported that it was both
cheaper and quicker to use the northern route. The freight on a 1200-
lb. hogshead to New York cost some $15 by way of New Orleans and
ship; $8.50 by way of the Erie Railroad and $7.50 by way of the Erie
Canal. By rail the trip took 6 to 8 days; by canal about 18 days; and by
New Orleans a month or two more. The freight arrived by rail or canal
in better condition than if it had "sweated" in the hold of a packet.
The previous year, however, just as railroads were about to complicate
the situation, statistics showed that at Albany and New Orleans combined, the total value of the goods going inland was $173,000,000, ex-
actly equal to the amount coming out. At Albany, the goods going
west, chiefly from New York but partly from Boston, were worth
$135,000,000, while the freight from the interior came to only $65,-
000,000. At New Orleans, the situation was exactly the reverse. The
"up trade" amounted to only $38,000,000, while the heavy "down
trade" totalled $108,000,000.

Whether it travelled by New Orleans or by Albany, however, much of the westbound "merchandise" destined for the shelves of country stores had originally come from New York, which took its profits in either case. Even the foodstuffs sent from the West to feed the South helped New York indirectly, for they enabled the inland farmers to purchase imports and domestic manufactures from New York. With the hinterland grown to national dimensions, South Street, Pearl Street, and Wall Street would profit, whichever route the freight might follow to and from the back country.

By the mid-'thirties, the South began to awaken to just what New York was doing. Boston had fully appreciated and analyzed the situation back in 1825, but the first serious rumblings from the South came in 1836 when Charleston sought unsuccessfully to establish a packet line to Liverpool. "Direct trade" was the objective, eliminating New York's profitable participation.

The southerners tried to take advantage of the temporary setback to New York after the panic of 1837. Six commercial conventions were held within eighteen months. These culminated in a convention at Charleston in 1839, which drew up a lengthy report attacking New York's position in the southern trade. It was bad enough, the report said, to have a national tariff which discriminated against the South. In addition, "the direct trade, which was her own by every law of commerce and nature, and which should have grown and increased every year, grew less and less until it almost disappeared, being by this unpropitious policy transferred to the northern ports and people. . . . The importing merchants of the South became an almost extinct race, and her direct trade, once so great, flourishing and rich, dwindled down to insignificance." The report included a detailed analysis which attempted to prove that the southern shopkeepers could procure their imports more cheaply direct through Charleston than by way of New York. In the flood of rhetoric appeared the remark, "The South thus stands in the attitude of feeding from her own bosom a vast population of merchants, shipowners, capitalists, and others, who without the claims of her progeny, drink up the life-blood of her trade." The movement, once begun, continued spasmodically down to the Civil War with conventions held in various cities from time to time. Lieutenant Matthew F. Maury, the oceanographer, and J. D. B. DeBow in his *Review* persistently kept the propaganda alive, but nothing much came of it.

Though the European manufacturers and merchants showed an inclination to go halfway in developing a direct trade and a few short-lived attempts were made to establish packet or steamship lines, the southern shopkeepers kept on making their annual pilgrimages to New York to replenish their stocks. When the Civil War broke out, the cotton triangle was still one of the major features in American commerce. The news of Fort Sumter, however, placed in a difficult position those New York merchants who had been happily exploiting southern commercial passivity.

CHAPTER VII

QUODDY TO CAPE FEAR

THE COASTING trade of the United States is great and New York ingrosses a very large proportion of it," reported the British consul at Philadelphia in 1817. New York continued to "ingross" it throughout our period with the same thoroughness which it was showing with the virtually equal volume of foreign commerce. With its admirable central position and the added advantage of the Sound, New York was better situated for coastwise shipping than was any other port, except perhaps somnolent Norfolk.

Cape Fear, close to the boundary between the two Carolinas, divided New York's coasting trade into two distinct parts. These differed sharply both in vessels and in cargoes. Proud square-riggers were generally employed for the trade to the southward where, as we saw, cotton gave a homogeneity to the cargoes of those aristocrats of the coasters. Our concern here is with the hundreds of lesser coasters, chiefly schooners, operating as transients, regular traders, or packets, all the way from Wilmington inside Cape Fear, the furthermost port of North Carolina, to Passamaquoddy Bay at the northeastern tip of Maine and of the nation.

These lesser coasters kept New York in constant contact with scores of major and minor ports, which helped to absorb part of New York's imports and in return sent the products of their particular regions past Hell Gate or Sandy Hook. Probably their heterogeneous cargoes did not differ materially from the freight later carried by land eastward and southward from New York; but a brig has more appeal than a dozen box cars while motor trucks cannot compete with schooners in matter of interest.

Even more than the cotton ships, these lesser coasters are a neglected virgin subject. The absence of tangible statistics has been one reason why maritime historians have shied away from the subject, for even such compact units of measurement as cotton bales are lacking in the diversified work of the smaller craft. Estimates of the value of their cargoes can be only guess work. Many of the schooner-loads of coal were worth only $1000 or so, and flour cargoes about $5000 or $6000, but it is recorded that the mixed cargo of one packet sloop, bringing tea, spices, and other exotic imports from Boston to New York, was insured for $200,000!

As far as their movements are concerned, it is possible to dig statistics of sorts out of the marine news in the absence of ready-made accounts. The appendix contains the results of such a study for 1835, our typical middle year of the period.[1] Omitting local traffic with ports in the same and immediately adjoining states, a tabulation of some 8000 coastwise arrivals at New York, Boston, and Philadelphia gives a rough idea of the volume of trade from each port with various parts of the coast. By separating the arrivals into ships, brigs, schooners, and sloops, the approximate tonnage on each route may be estimated. Steamboats are not included, as they were chiefly engaged in the passenger business at that time.

New York's total coastwise trade was almost equal to that of its two chief rivals combined. The tonnage ratio was roughly New York 3, Boston 2, and Philadelphia 1; but Boston almost equalled New York in lesser coasting. New York's lesser coasters totalled a much greater aggregate tonnage than the larger vessels from the cotton ports. Of the former, there were 2869 arrivals at some 302,000 tons; of the latter, 718 arrivals at about 172,000 tons. The combined tonnage of these 3587 coastwise arrivals (almost ten a day) about equalled that of the almost 2000 vessels arriving at New York from foreign ports. If one includes the local traffic with Long Island, Connecticut, and New Jersey, the coastwise total becomes still greater, while the regular steamer service to Charleston, Providence, and nearer points would give it a still further boost. Boston and New Orleans stand out as the two chief ports with which New York traded coastwise. The 494 vessels from Boston were almost equivalent in tonnage to the 203 arrivals from New Orleans and the same was true of the even larger volume of shipping going in the opposite direction toward those two ports which, between them, absorbed nearly a quarter of New York's coastwise movements. In total tonnage arriving at New York, Liverpool was an easy first, followed in turn by New Orleans, Boston, Philadelphia, Havre, Charleston, Savannah, London, and Mobile.

[1]See Appendix, v.

The little schooner of a hundred tons or so became the favorite instrument on these lesser coastal trips. Of the 2869 arrivals, 2521 were schooners; 6 were ships; 2 were barks; 193 were brigs, mostly from Baltimore or the extreme runs from Quoddy and Wilmington; and 147 were little sloops, principally from Philadelphia, Providence, or New Bedford. This record stands in marked contrast to the cotton-port trade, where 82 per cent of the vessels were square-rigged ships, barks, or brigs.

The schooner was admirably adapted to the trips of moderate length, up to about 500 miles. Sloops, with their single mast, had been commonly employed at the outset, but the schooner was becoming increasingly popular by the 'twenties. The relative advantages of the various types and rigs will be considered later in connection with shipbuilding. Many of the old coasting schooners were remarkably tough and long-lived. Three little lumber schooners which appeared in Penobscot Bay in 1938 were found to be more than eighty years old, one having been built on the Hudson in 1853, the second on Mount Desert in 1855, and the youngest of the trio at Westerly, R. I., in 1857.

Some of them came to grief, for even the shorter coastal trips were not child's play. If, unlike the ships for New Orleans and Mobile, the lesser coasters were spared the treacherous reefs and keys of the Bahamas and Florida, their courses nevertheless kept them continuously closer to the coast; and that was where accidents generally occurred. It required a fair degree of seamanship to guide the little vessels to the eastward beyond the Sound, through the baffling waters of Pollock Rip and around the storm-swept sands of Cape Cod. To the southward, the coasters for North Carolina had to round Hatteras and negotiate the treacherous swell over the shallow bar leading to the quiet waters inside that cape. Even the trade with the Delaware and with Chesapeake Bay had its occasional perils. There were times after heavy northeast gales when a dozen or more little coasters, unable to claw off the inhospitable Jersey coast, were reported ashore between Cape May and Sandy Hook. There are scores of lively tales in this connection but they must wait until a separate volume on the subject affords more room.

The movements of the little local craft, which connected New York with near-by points of New Jersey, Long Island, and the Sound, perhaps did not deserve the name of coastal traffic. Yet even before the Revolution, garden produce and firewood for the city's consumption had meant brisk business for the farmers of eastern New Jersey and western Long Island. Both regions were blessed with good soil; and the farmers found that often the richest returns per acre were to be obtained by growing crops for the tables of Manhattan. These farmers were among the first to develop intensive agriculture in this country and to make energetic efforts to fertilize the soil. According to a writer about 1800, they gathered manure from miles around and in addition "they have swept the Sound, and covered their fields with the immense shoals of white fish." Occasionally they raised a surplus of onions and beets for export to the West Indies.

New York's need of fuel gave constant employment to one sort of coasters or another. Before coal came into general use, the city depended upon the sloop loads of split and seasoned oak, chestnut and hickory, which were sold to city "cartmen" who peddled the wood around the city. The difficulty in such a supply lay in the fact that when a bitter cold spell struck New York in midwinter, the wood sloops generally lay icebound in their little creeks and inlets. The steamboats developed a demand for pine wood as fuel and this gave business to sloops which ventured down the Jersey coast as far as Egg Harbor.

The Connecticut towns along the Sound found a good source of income from early days onward in the cattle and dairy products which they gathered from the back country. Sometimes New London and New Haven shipped live cattle and horses, together with butter and cheese, direct to the West Indies, often bringing the return cargoes of sugar and molasses to New York. Yet they also did a good business in supplying the city's own demands for these products.

The little vessels which came and went on this business were small and operated with a minimum of formality and of personnel. Frequently the farmer and his son would load the produce into a homemade sloop and run it across the short distance to the East River slip or pier which was the center of that particular business. For the shallow streams which ran back into the New Jersey farmlands, centerboard sloops and little two-masted "pettiaugers," of which more later, were developed. For bringing wood from Brookhaven on outer Long Island, or dairy products from the Sound ports, sloops of a more conventional design were employed. In the days before steamers took over their business, most of the Connecticut towns, and those of Rhode Island as well, had a sloop or two which operated as a "packet," with weekly sailings to and from New York, carrying passengers and freight, while the captain would execute, while in town, the commissions of various residents who might want to purchase anything from ladies' hats to schooners.

Leaving this local traffic, which seldom felt the force of the open sea, we come to the well-distributed coasting proper. Here were several distinct spheres. In 1835, 494 vessels came from Boston, 410 from Maine, 422 from Philadelphia, 823 from Chesapeake Bay, and 467 from North Carolina, while the rest of them arrived from scattered points along the coast.

On the important New York-Boston shuttle, vessels encountered some tricky sailing and special pilots advertised their services for the uninitiated. After leaving the shelter of the Sound and passing Block Island, vessels bound to the eastward had to negotiate Vineyard Sound and then the "rips," where the tides swirled among the treacherous shoals north of Martha's Vineyard and Nantucket. In bad weather coasters by the score took refuge in Holmes's Hole, now Vineyard Haven. Once through Pollock Rip and its difficult neighbors, there was still Cape Cod to round, for the canal through its neck was not dug till early in this century. Skippers skirted the south side of the Cape, often praying that gales and fogs would not add them to its toll of victims. Once clear of the tip, it was fair sailing across Massachusetts Bay until one reached the island-studded approach to Boston.

Numerous busy and successful packet lines—with sloops at first and then schooners—maintained constant service on this run. They were often owned and generally manned by Cape Codders, whose families watched their comings and goings and signalled them in passing. The pioneer in this service was old Captain Benjamin Hallett, who began to run his sloop as a regular trader from Boston to New York and on up the river, shortly after the Revolution. He continued on into our period, finding time between trips to organize the first "seamen's bethels," where mariners could get religion, first at New York and then at Boston. In the place of the lone sloop, the Despatch Line, the Tremont Line and other rivals soon began to offer regular service, each with a weekly sailing on a specified day. Three days was good time for the run; fog or bad weather sometimes stretched it to a week or more.

Boston, of all the cities in the United States, was least likely to come under New York's domination because it was exceedingly enterprising itself. Other ports, such as New Orleans, might handle at times a heavier export trade than New York itself, but they usually joined with the rest of the country in purchasing their imported goods through New York. Boston was the only port to compete strongly in New York's specialty of importing. In some regions, such as the Baltic, the Levant, and India, it traded more heavily than New York throughout our period.

The coastal trade between the two, therefore, consisted in part of a mutual exchange of surplus imports. The packets from Boston to New York were often loaded with Russian duck for sailcloth, figs from Smyrna, pepper from Sumatra, or cotton goods from India. Numerous cargoes of the same sort likewise came from Salem. In return the packet schooners might carry to Boston some of the surplus New York imports from Havre, and, until Cunard sent his steamships to Boston, from Liverpool and London as well. Both ports traded a great deal with China, Latin America, and the Caribbean; and until the Bostonians finally began to send their ships directly into New York on the return trips from abroad, one city might order tea, coffee, or sugar sent along the coast if prices at the other happened to be lower at the moment. Such exchanges of import surpluses meant that at times, as we saw in the case of the $200,000 cargo in the sloop *Macdonough,* a coastal vessel might well carry much of value.

Boston, as the center of the rapidly growing New England textile and shoe industries, furnished constant cargoes of "domestics" and footwear for New York. Gradually the latter port supplanted Boston as a distributing point for those goods. The letter book of Eveleth & Wood, shoe and leather brokers in Boston, shows that they gave the coastal packets considerable business in both directions. In 1833, for example, they wrote to one of the big New York leather dealers: "We wish you to forward the several lots of leather purchased at your sale on Oct. 31st and left in your store. Ship 247 sides by first vessel, 297 by next vessel and 300 by next after." Mingled with such instructions were letters to dealers in New York and Newark, enclosing bills of lading for boots and shoes shipped from Boston. The firm of Spofford & Tileston had its origin when the two young New England partners went to New York to act as commission agents for Haverhill shoes and other manufactured wares. That led to their serving as operators of one of the Boston-New York packet lines as the first step in their conspicuous career as packet and steamship operators.

Textiles apparently travelled in both directions on the shuttle. The papers of Thomas K. Jones & Co., Boston auctioneers and commission merchants, contain numerous letters from Francis and Jeremiah Thompson concerning consignments of textiles brought from Liverpool to New York in their Black Ballers in 1818 and 1819 and shipped on to Boston to "try the market." On the other hand, the manuscript diary of Frederick S. Wolcott, a New York dry goods merchant, contains a mournful entry late in 1849. He recorded that for twenty years he had served as New York agent for the "domestic" cotton output of two of the largest New England mills; during that time his sales had amounted to some $10,000,000; but he had just learned that the Bostonians were sending down two of their own number in order to keep in their hands the lucrative commissions arising from the business.

The Herrick family became Boston packet operators because of their interest in a commodity which travelled in the opposite direction and overshadowed in volume most of the other branches of the lesser coastal trade. This was flour, which together with cornmeal and other breadstuffs was absorbed by Boston in large quantities. New England, as we saw, depended upon the coastwise trade for its bread from early times and, at least until the repeal of the Corn Laws, Boston was one of the best customers for New York flour.

At the same time, Boston's need for flour led to one of the few cases of snubbing New York by direct trade with Albany in sloops or schooners, which sailed past Manhattan's wharves without stopping to land or take on cargo. As early as 1788, Captain Hallett had begun his coastal packet career by running a sloop between Boston and Albany; and others followed in his wake. Albany welcomed this trade for it had hopes of becoming an important port in its own right at the expense of New York, just as Baltimore was doing to Norfolk and Montreal to Quebec. One New Yorker had tried to do a similar thing by sending his ships directly up the Mississippi to Natchez without stopping at New Orleans. The purpose in both cases was to save the cost of transshipment at New York or New Orleans and in the former case the vessels were able to bring domestic manufactures in exchange. Neither Albany nor Natchez, however, seriously cut into the business of its great rival closer to the sea. In 1827, Albany claimed that 123 vessels were steadily engaged in its direct trade with eastern New England, each making several trips a year. In 1835, Boston received not only 667 cargoes from New York itself, but also 137 from Albany, 39 from Kingston, and 14 more from other Hudson River towns: a total of 857 by way of the East River! Four years later, the statistics of flour receipts at Boston indicate that out of the total of 451,000 barrels, New York led with 153,000, followed in order by Baltimore with 61,000, Richmond with 55,000, New Orleans with 47,000, and Albany with 39,000. Soon after that, Boston pushed through its Western Railway to Albany and the sea route diminished in importance. In 1859, when Boston received more than a million barrels, only 64,000 came from New York and 810 by sea from Albany.

In the earlier days, however, the coastal flour trade between New York and Boston called for far more cargo space than the packet schooners could provide. That links up the Boston trade with our next consideration, the coastal traffic with Maine. An analysis of the number of coastwise arrivals and clearances at New York, Boston, and Portland for the year 1816 reveals some interesting discrepancies. The clearances from New York for Boston were much more numerous than the arrivals from there; in the trade between New York and Maine, exactly the reverse was true. At Boston that year 264 vessels arrived from New York but only 150 cleared for there. On the other hand, only 285 arrived at Boston from Maine but 419 cleared for Maine at Boston. Combining the total clearances and arrivals of New York and Maine vessels at Boston, one finds that the totals from the two regions almost exactly balance. The New York figures in the appendix confirm the conclusion that many of the vessels which carried lumber, granite, lime, and fish from Maine to New York took flour back to Boston and then proceeded eastward with imports and other goods purchased at Boston for Maine use.[1] Maine was still under Boston's, rather than New York's commercial influence and the commodities carried to the latter simply paid for the goods bought from Boston merchants.

In 1825, it looked as though New York might capture that Maine market. In April of that year, Portland started a line of packet schooners to New York with sailings every Saturday from each port. "Our merchants," wrote the Portland *Eastern Argus,* "who have for some years past transacted business largely with New York, will now find an opportunity of receiving their goods with nearly as much celerity and with as little delay as from Boston." In that same month, the *Argus* gave a stronger indication of the port rivalry:

We learn from a paper printed at Gardiner on the Kennebec that an
[1]See Appendix, vi.

agent from New York is now in that vicinity for the purpose of opening an intercourse between the merchants of New York and those on the Kennebec. It is said that a considerable trade from the Kennebec is already carried on at the New York market, owing, in no small degree, to the hostile array of the Boston banks and their onset upon the Kennebeckers.

We should be happy to shake the hands of more of our Kennebec friends in this town, and we doubt not, that in a considerable portion of their trade we can give them as good satisfaction as they can obtain in Boston or New York.

In other words, Portland had ambitions of establishing itself as a distributing center for the State of Maine, collecting its profits on goods passing between New York and the eastward.

At that same time, a remark emanated from Boston revealing a curious defensive attitude toward New York's commercial advances, which were becoming more evident as the opening of the Erie Canal approached. A meeting was held at Boston to promote the digging of a Cape Cod canal, which would shorten the New York-Boston run by some sixty miles and eliminate the dangerous rounding of the Cape. A lengthy Boston analysis of the general rivalry between the cities voiced opposition to this project, in order to protect Boston's trade with Maine:

The risk in doubling Cape Cod and the Shoals, and the length of the passage thereby created in our intercourse with the south and west, give to New York an advantage over us; but then by means of this barrier between us and the southward, we ought to be benefitted by retaining to ourselves all the eastern trade. Boston is in consequence their natural mart. *We want, therefore, no Buzzard's Bay Canal,* for eastern vessels to slip through to the great Commercial Emporium.

Boston had already established regular steam service to Portland and the eastward and this continued on a permanent basis, with new or second-hand boats from New York, whereas the New York-Portland line of packet schooners did not survive and it was only at the end of our period that through steamer service between the two ports was inaugurated.

Though Boston might retain its hold on the Maine market, coasters constantly carried Maine products to New York. This trade consisted principally of building materials—lumber, lime, granite, and occasionally bricks. Even in ordinary years, the constant growth of the city meant a steady demand for such articles. The year 1825, however, saw a remarkable building boom there. Hundreds of new structures were put up in record time, with a resultant stimulus of the purchases from Maine. Another boom came in 1836, following the fire of the preceding December, which wiped out more than seven hundred buildings in the business district.

Lumber was the most conspicuous of these items in the coastal cargoes from Maine. The "Pine Tree State" was slashing recklessly into its huge stand of virgin forest. Sawmills along its various rivers were cutting the soft white pine logs into boards, which were marketed far and wide, with a considerable amount carried to New York. In 1816, for instance, the 138-ton schooner *Lucretia* arrived from Bangor with "60 M ft. dimension timber, 25 M ft. merchantable pine boards, 1500 ft. 1½ in, merchantable plank, 1500 ft. clear boards, 7000 ft. finished oars, 6000 hogshead staves, and 10 M pine shingles" in addition to ten tons of plaster of paris. She was typical of hundreds of similar schooners with similar cargoes—about 100,000 board feet of lumber, part of it stowed below and more piled high on deck, so that her scuppers were probably not far above water. A few of that sort may still be seen taking refuge at Portland when storms are brewing. At the outset, these cargoes came from many different little ports along the coast. As late as 1835, there were 46 arrivals from Machias and only 20 from Bangor, but the latter port, twenty-odd miles up the Penobscot, rose rapidly in the trade until, by the middle of the century, it was the busiest lumber port in the world. The New York shipyards also looked to the Maine coast for masts and spars.

Another Maine offering which filled many a schooner for New York was lime, to be used in mortar for the brick buildings which were common at New York. General Henry Knox, Washington's chief of artillery in the Revolution, was a pioneer in developing the lime quarries near his home at Thomaston. Dug from the many quarries and then burned in kilns, lime made a dangerous sort of cargo, for it was liable to burst into flames upon contact with water. Time and again the marine news told of lime-laden schooners which burned after running on the rocks or even after having their cargoes drenched by heavy seas. Shortly after 1850, the lime-producing section of Thomaston was set off as Rockland, the name more intimately associated with the trade in its later days.

A third bulky Maine offering for the New York builders was granite, which began to rival the output of the famous quarries at Quincy near Boston. The Kennebec River offered this in considerable quantities and several little islands "down east" were almost cut to pieces to meet the heavy demands. Occasionally a cargo of bricks came down from Maine, but New York received most of that supply from points closer at hand.

Other sorts of articles occasionally arrived from Maine, particularly from Portland, which was a major port with its own foreign trade. At times it ranked third, after New York and Boston, in the importation of West Indian molasses, received in exchange for the local production of staves and shooks for sugar and molasses hogsheads. Some of this molasses was shipped to New York, and some of it also went thither after being distilled into rum. Fish and salted beef were also frequently found in its offerings.

At the extreme eastern corner of the State and nation was Passamaquoddy Bay, often contracted then and later into Quoddy. Eastport and Lubec, its chief ports, enjoyed a unique role as the "jumping-off place" for the trade with the Maritime Provinces of British North America (the term "Canada" was not extended to those Bluenose regions until 1867). The nature of the Bay's active business may be judged by a quotation from *The Eastport Northern Light* in 1831:

> More than *thirty* British vessels, with full cargoes of plaster, grindstones &c which they exchange with our merchants for flour and other articles of American produce, were entered at the custom houses at Eastport and Lubec on Monday last—the largest number of entries ever made in one day in the District.

Several other foreign and coastwise arrivals were also recorded on that same day. In the earlier years of the period, this trade fluctuated violently as the British opened and closed the colonial ports to American commerce, in alternating moods of reprisal and reciprocity. Quoddy's business was at its best when American vessels were excluded from the colonial ports. Rather than let the British vessels profit by the whole freight receipts from New York and other points to the southward, the American coasters carried their flour and other offerings as far as they could, which meant Quoddy, before turning the business over to the Bluenoses.

While Quoddy represents the technical outer limit of the coasting trade in that direction, it would seem appropriate here to cross the border into British North America to mention the trade carried on directly between New York and the Maritime Provinces. Strictly speaking, it was foreign trade, but essentially it was simply an extension of the coasting trade. A considerable part of this direct business, which did not go by way of Quoddy, was carried on in British bottoms.

The geological formation of Nova Scotia yielded three products which found a market at New York. Mines near Pictou on the Gulf of St. Lawrence, Sydney on Cape Breton Island, and Cumberland at the head of the Bay of Fundy produced soft bituminous coal of fair quality which competed with British bituminous, particularly for use in blacksmiths' forges in the days before the domestic soft coal supply was developed. The same region also produced large quantities of plaster of paris or gypsum, which was used extensively as fertilizer, although later the Erie Canal opened up an ample domestic supply. Also, just as most of the best millstones came from a quarry near the Marne in France, so most of the grindstones were from the Maritimes.

In addition, large quantities of "soused mackerel" were brought to New York. On one occasion, a consignment, arriving from Halifax, was found to have a few mackerel at the head of each barrel "and the rest is stones and seaweed." That may have helped to redress the grievances of the British who often found cotton bales packed with stones or well soaked with water to give added weight. A collection of miscellaneous customs manuscripts hints at another irregularity from that port. In 1835, the collector of customs at New York received an anonymous "tip" from Halifax:

> The brig *Halifax* of this port has, I am credibly informed, many barrels of fish under the plaister which the same vessel is chiefly freighted with, and the fish and other articles are placed there with a view of evading the duty. She is to sail for New York this day—if you cause a close search you will certainly find this information correct.
>
> **M----**

Newfoundland at times came into this trade. Sealskins were brought from there and flour sent in return. With Canada proper, sea trade was very infrequent, for the distance to Quebec and Montreal was vastly shorter by land; and a heavy trade was conducted across the northern boundary or by the Great Lakes. When the ship *Washington* arrived at New York, late in 1828, by way of Pictou, where she had picked up a cargo of coal, the marine news stated "the W. is the first American ship that has been to Quebec."

In 1860, the arrivals from British North America amounted to 276,000 tons at Boston, 79,000 tons at New York, and since American

vessels might now trade direct, only 68,000 tons at Quoddy. This represented 2089, 478, and 410 vessels respectively. Boston, because of its
proximity, naturally was more heavily engaged than New York in this
seaborne trade to the northward.

Turning to the southward, Philadelphia was the first important objective of the coasters from New York. At the outset, this resembled
the trade with Boston, for the interchange of import surpluses provided
considerable business. As a consequence, the sloops and schooners
carried heterogeneous assortments back and forth. When the schooner
William Tell capsized off Barnegat, for instance, mariners were asked
to keep a lookout in the hope of recovering boxes containing valuable
"anatomical preparations in wax, obtained in Europe and intended for
the lectures in the Jefferson Medical College in Philadelphia." Local
products were also exchanged—fresh peaches sometimes arriving from
Philadelphia.

This was one of the first routes to have fairly regular packet service.
In 1816 appeared the notice of the Union Line, which would operate
six schooners in succession between the two ports, although not on
regular schedule. The device of combining the cuts of several little vessels in a row, adopted by the Black Ball line in its early notices, seems
to have been first employed in the advertisements of this line late in
the spring of 1816. It was estimated in 1823 that 60,000 tons of freight
were annually carried coastwise between the two ports.

By the mid-'thirties, these coastal schooners had lost all except the
bulkiest freight. Instead, lines of barges on the newly opened Delaware & Raritan Canal were getting the trade. This canal crossed the
"waist" of New Jersey between New Brunswick and Bordentown,
roughly parallel to the Camden & Amboy Railroad which was procuring
most of the passenger traffic. The configuration of the coast was such
that canals could radically reduce the distance from New York not only
to Philadelphia but also to Baltimore and the ports of North Carolina.
By 1835, a small vessel could travel all the way from Connecticut to
Wilmington, N. C., by inland waterways without once being exposed
to the open sea—through the Sound, the East River, New York Bay,
the Delaware & Raritan Canal, the Delaware River, the Delaware &
Chesapeake Canal, Chesapeake Bay, the Dismal Swamp Canal, and the
North Carolina sounds. This inland route lured much of the Philadelphia business from the coasters and a certain amount of the Baltimore freight as well, but from the rest of Chesapeake Bay and from

the North Carolina ports, it was generally quicker and cheaper to travel by open sea.

Several years before that inner route was opened, Philadelphia had entered upon the one branch of maritime activity in which it surpassed New York and in which it also enjoyed national primacy. This was the coastwise distribution of coal from the anthracite mines of its immediate hinterland in the Schuylkill, Lehigh, and Lackawanna regions.

Until the 'twenties, the use of coal in this country was pretty much limited to industrial purposes. Blacksmiths, brewers, and others required a moderate amount and usually preferred some sort of soft coal. Part of this was brought from Nova Scotia mines; part from Liverpool, Newcastle, and other British ports; and part from the domestic mines near Richmond, where a rather mediocre variety was obtained.

Until overshadowed as a coal port by Philadelphia, Richmond had an excellent coasting trade in the first decade of peace through this Virgina coal from the Heath and Randolph mines, together with flour. In fact, in 1816, more vessels arrived at New York from Richmond than from any other port in the world. A remark of a coasting skipper shows this Richmond prominence in the coal trade. Reaching Philadelphia with a cargo of Richmond coal in the mid-'twenties and engaged to carry Lehigh anthracite back to Richmond, he said while signing the bills of lading, "Well, this comes devilish near carrying coal to Newcastle." He did not realize that Philadelphia, instead of Richmond, was by then rapidly becoming the Newcastle of America.

Few major commercial changes have come as quickly as the use of anthracite. As late as 1820, only 365 tons reached tidewater. It was not until 1823, when the total approached 7000 tons, that Philadelphia, New York, and other eastern cities became "coal conscious." Thereafter, the jump was amazingly rapid: 34,000 in 1825, 174,000 in 1830, 868,000 in 1840, 3,555,000 in 1850, and 7,288,000 in 1855!

Heavy and bulky in comparison with its value, coal was naturally carried whenever possible by water, rather than overland. Throughout the rest of the century, it would give the coasters more business than any other commodity. At first, there was not shipping enough to keep up with the demand—Philadelphia was constantly sending word along the coast that schooners could find good employment as colliers. Eventually, it developed a huge fleet of them. The tonnage tables in the appendix show that whereas seagoing Boston had far more shipping registered for foreign trade than enrolled for coasting purposes, and

New York, with its more central position, had about an equal amount in each, Philadelphia showed a heavier proportion of enrolled tonnage for the coal business.[1] In 1834, 1614 coal-laden vessels, including 72 brigs, 1122 schooners, and 420 sloops, cleared from Philadelphia.

Naturally, many of these colliers were soon beating their way down the Delaware, around Cape May, and up the Jersey coast to Sandy Hook. Several cargoes of "Lehi" coal, brought to Philadelphia from Mauch Chunk, found their way in 1823 to New York, where a campaign of education was inducing many to install grates to heat their homes or countinghouses with coal instead of wood. The following year, the rival Schuylkill mines at Mount Carbon began to send their coal by canal and river to Philadelphia. On November 23 there arrived at New York the "Schr. *Superior,* Tunnell, 5d from Philadelphia, with coals &c for the Schuylkill Coal Co. The first load of coal from that place." Thereafter, the colliers came in increasing numbers. A tabulation from the newspaper marine news, probably incomplete, shows that in 1826 there arrived at New York seventy-two colliers from Philadelphia, forty-six from Richmond, and two from Rhode Island, which made a brief attempt to mine and peddle its "obstinately uncombustible" coal. In 1835, of the 519 vessels which went from New York to Philadelphia, only 422 returned, many of which were doubtless coal-laden.

A typical trip on a Philadelphia-New York collier is graphically described in the first of the yarns in Captain Samuel Samuels' robust autobiography, as part of his initiation into a sea career, which covered the seven seas and culminated with the command of the fastest clipper on the Atlantic. Running away from home at eleven, he shipped, after one or two minor trips, as cook and cabin boy on the schooner *Hampton Westcott.* He was made helmsman, being too light to help in hoisting the sails. It took two days to work down the river and the second night they anchored in the lee of Delaware Breakwater for shelter from a dirty southeaster. "At daylight the wind hauled to the south-west, and having gotten under way and cleared the capes, with the wind dead aft, we shaped our courses up the beach, wing and wing, for New York," with the water swashing over the decks. Both the captain's wife and his sister, the wife of the mate, made their home aboard and attended to the cooking. They won the boy's gratitude, sympathizing with him in his first pangs of seasickness and interposing when the captain threat-

[1]See Appendix, i, xi.

ened to beat him. When Horace, his bunk-mate, tried a practical joke, Deborah, the mate's wife, "was quite beside herself at the treatment I had received. She was a muscular woman, and seizing a belaying pin, she used it with the skill of a Liverpool packet-mate on the funny man." The wind lasted just long enough to allow the schooner to work around Sandy Hook, where she anchored in the Horseshoe inside the tip, with an anchor watch set for the night as a precaution against harbor pirates. The next morning, she worked her way up through the Narrows to the coal yard at the foot of Rector Street in the North River. It took three days to unload the cargo and prepare for the return, the whole group remaining aboard during the stay in port. When sailing time came, however, young Samuels jumped ship and soon found himself aboard an even more informal schooner bound up the Sound for Newport.

New York enterprise soon developed a few short cuts which brought the coal by canal across New Jersey without going to Philadelphia or using the coasters at all. The Delaware & Hudson Co., beginning to exploit the Lackawanna mines, built a short railroad from them to the Delaware at Honesdale, Pennsylvania (named for Philip Hone, New York's diarist-mayor), together with a 106-mile canal across to the Hudson near Kingston, New York. The first sloop laden with the coal brought by this route reached New York on December 11, 1828. Even at that, the city's coal supply ran short that winter and in February not a ton was to be had. In the mid-'thirties two other canals across New Jersey also short-circuited the coasters. The Delaware & Raritan, which we have already seen as part of the inner water route to the south, brought a considerable amount of coal to New Brunswick, while the Morris Canal carried coal from the mouth of the Lehigh River across New Jersey to Newark, whence 24,000 tons were shipped in 1834 by sloop or schooner. In spite of those rival waterways, a very large quantity of coal was still brought up the coast in schooners from Philadelphia throughout our period.

Chesapeake Bay, with its numerous tributary rivers, conducted an even heavier coasting trade with New York than did Philadelphia. It was a long and roundabout route, for the schooners, employed in this trade, had to skirt the Eastern Shore, which cuts off the Bay from the sea, before they reached the entrance to the Bay between Capes Henry and Charles. By sea, the distance to Norfolk, just inside the capes, was almost identical with the route around Cape Cod to Boston, but to reach Baltimore, near the head of the Bay, the coasters had to double back to the northward and travel a total equivalent of 476 land miles. The overland route was considerably less than half that distance. Baltimore and Norfolk were by no means the only Chesapeake objectives of the coasters. Some ascended the Potomac to the national capital or the near-by towns of Alexandria and Georgetown. There was a great deal of trade with three river "ports," which would figure prominently in Civil War annals: Fredericksburg on the Rappahannock, Petersburg on the Appomattox, and, more important in the trade than either, Richmond on the James. The coasters also found their way into many lesser places: Snow Hill on the Eastern Shore, which offered shingles; Little York, near Yorktown, celebrated for its oysters; Suffolk, Folly Landing, and many other outlets for Chesapeake products.

Flour and tobacco were the chief objectives of this Chesapeake trade. The region was a rich center for both products. Especially before the Erie Canal gave New York its extended supply from the West, large quantities of flour were carried northward from Baltimore and Richmond with their big merchant milling establishments, as well as from Fredericksburg, Petersburg, and Alexandria. Many concerns with one or two partners in New York and one or two in the Chesapeake region engaged prominently in this flour trade. The silent partner of Byrnes, Trimble & Co., who started the Red Star line of Liverpool packets, for example, was Silas Wood who handled the Fredericksburg end of the business.

Whereas, from New York's standpoint, this Chesapeake supply was only one source of flour and a decreasingly vital one, the Chesapeake tobacco filled at first a very conspicuous niche in the port's general scheme of affairs. Like cotton and naval stores, it helped provide east-bound cargoes to European ports which did not have an adequate call for other northern products. An ever-increasing amount of Kentucky tobacco came down the Mississippi to New Orleans and was brought to New York from there, but in the beginning the Chesapeake was the main source. Baltimore, Richmond, and Petersburg shipped a considerable part of the Chesapeake output direct to Bremen or other Continental ports, but their geographical setting prevented such easy communications as were enjoyed by New York. In consequence, a large quantity was brought by the coasters to New York to be transshipped by packets to Havre for the French government monopoly.

Much of this business fell into the hands of Lewis Rogers, a native

Virginian. According to Scoville, he organized the companies of Rogers, Harrison & Gray at Richmond, James Gray & Co. at New Orleans, Rogers & Co. at New York, and Lewis Rogers & Co. at Havre. In addition, he had the powerful financial backing of a great banking house at Paris and had influence enough to secure a huge contract with the French government monopoly. It is said the business sometimes amounted to a million dollars a month. Some of the Chesapeake tobacco was also carried by the New York packets to London, where Rogers was associated with another Virginian, W. S. Warwick, whose house of Warwick & Claggett was the largest in the London tobacco trade. In 1822, New York's tobacco exports amounted to $754,000, which was almost equal to its flour shipments abroad. In 1860, New Orleans had become the leading tobacco exporting port, with New York trailing just behind Baltimore and Richmond.

The foreign exports, however, were only one consideration in bringing tobacco hogsheads up from the Chesapeake. A heavy domestic business, as well, increased in importance as New York became the general distributing center for the nation. Before the tobacco finally reached the little country stores in the hinterland, New York had generally added to its value by manufacture. Cigarettes had not yet come into use and cigars came chiefly from Havana, but there was a good business in preparing snuff, smoking tobacco and, above all, plugs for chewing. Most European travellers were amazed and disgusted by the readiness of the average American male to fresco every object in sight with tobacco juice. The house of Lorillard had begun its distinguished career in tobacco manufacture at New York as early as 1760 and a century later, in 1855, New York and Brooklyn had forty-five establishments, producing finished products worth $795,000 from tobacco which cost $476,000.

The Chesapeake had other offerings, which did not bulk as large as those two staples. Shingles, staves, and other forms of lumber came frequently—in a single day four cargoes of shingles arrived from Norfolk and four more from Snow Hill. The East River shipbuilders sent to the Chesapeake for tough locust to be used for treenails. Watermelons and peaches were often brought in season, and during the brief early period when a pioneer coastal steamer plied between Norfolk and New York, green peas were brought long before they were available from local gardens. Norfolk was something of an entrepôt for the region and its shipments were generally more variegated than those from further up the Bay. In a single cargo in 1819 the schooner *Tell Tale,* which plied for years as a regular trader to New York, brought wheat, apple brandy, peach brandy, coffee, hams, molasses, corn meal, lard, and second-hand sheathing copper. Norfolk, however, might have done infinitely more as a Chesapeake entrepôt—alone of the bay ports it had an admirable location for the coastwise trade, fully equal to New York's, but most of the coasters snubbed it and sailed past on their way to the remoter river ports up the Bay.

The return cargoes from New York are less easily identified. Since there was relatively little shuttle trade between the Chesapeake and Europe, the imported products, brought to New York in the packets, found a constant market there. It is probable that the storekeepers throughout that region carried on their shelves a considerable stock of goods which had come from abroad by way of Sandy Hook.

Quite early in the period, many of the schooners trading with the Chesapeake were organized into packet lines, sailing at first in regular succession and later on specified days of the week, much as in the case of the Boston service. In 1836, five lines went to Baltimore, two to Petersburg, and one each to Norfolk and Richmond; while Doane, Sturges & Co., who were leaders among the coastal packet operators, announced that their packets to Alexandria, Georgetown, and Washington "sail every day," which was something of an exaggeration.

Finally, there was New York's trade with the North Carolina ports. These were cut off from the open sea by the long, narrow outer barrier of sand, which comes to a point at stormy Cape Hatteras. Inside that barrier lay a series of broad sounds—Albemarle, Pimlico, and the rest. Beyond these, up the sluggish rivers, which penetrate far inland, were the various little ports of Elizabeth City, Edenton, Newbern, Washington, Plymouth, Swansborough, and, most important of all, Wilmington. The chief navigating difficulty lay in the fact that, except for Wilmington which had its own entrance at the mouth of the Cape Fear River, the only opening from the sea was Ocracoke Inlet below Hatteras. Not only was the depth of water over its bar so shallow that larger square-riggers were virtually barred from the trade, but in order to reach the more northern ports, it was necessary to go way down below Hatteras and then double back for a considerable distance. The North Carolinians urged the opening of the old Roanoke inlet, much further north, arguing that it would greatly reduce the distance to and from New York, but nothing came of the project. Norfolk made one of its rare exhibitions of energy in the period by cutting the Dismal Swamp Canal to give North Carolina a short and sheltered outlet to Chesapeake Bay but it did not succeed in luring much of the trade. In consequence, the constant procession of schooners and sloops, with occasional brigs, had to make the stormy passage around Hatteras and negotiate shallow bars and channels where the course was apt to change after every gale. Blunt, whose *American Coast Pilot* gave minute directions for most of the rest of the coast, remarked in this connection:

We decline giving directions for sailing into many ports in North Carolina, as all the harbors are barred, and always subject to alteration by every gale, particularly in the equinoctial storms; but the bars create only a part of the danger in sailing into those ports; it is the vast bed of shoals that lie within the bars, with their innumerable small channels which give to tide so many different directions that even the pilots who live on the spot find it difficult to carry a vessel in without some accident.

In spite of all that, the trips were made, dozens of times each month, for beyond those bars and shallows lay most of the nation's supply of naval stores in that day. Scorned by its proud neighbors to the immediate north and south, North Carolina was dubbed the "Tar Heel State," for its chief business in early days consisted of extracting tar, resin, and turpentine from the pines which abounded in the coastal regions. These products were in steady demand, both from domestic shipbuilders and for export. These gave New York a third southern product, besides cotton and tobacco, for its eastbound cargoes. Many a packet stowed away a few score or hundred barrels of naval stores to round out her cargo for England or France. The North Carolina ports also exploited the red oaks of the region and sent northward annually a million or more hogshead staves, along with shingles and some forms of lumber. In return, these ports served as distributing points for New York's imports.

Whereas schooners carried on most of the traffic over Ocracoke bar, brigs were often employed on the Wilmington route. The *General Manning* ran for years as a regular trader between there and New York, for instance. In later days, it was reported that ten splendid "tar packets," well equipped with passenger accommodations, were constantly employed on that route.

From Quoddy, then, all the way down to Cape Fear, New York drove a thriving business with these forgotten lesser coasters. If the wind blew from the east, the marine news next day would report schooners bearing lumber from Maine or the more costly offerings of Boston or Salem. Let it blow from the south, and a different squadron made port, laden with coal, flour, tobacco, or tar. Back they would all go, a few days later, helping to extend New York's sphere of commercial influence by carrying the variegated offerings of the metropolis to replenish the stocks of storekeepers not reached by the port's other agencies of distribution. They were simple little vessels, compared with Liverpool packets or Canton traders, but they played their part in the rise of New York. The 'longshore business called for real men, too, as evidenced by the timbers of wrecked schooners on sandy shores from Cape Cod down to Hatteras.

CHAPTER VIII

STEAM ON RIVER, SOUND, AND BAY

ROBERT FULTON died within two weeks of the arrival of the news of peace at New York in 1815. Less than eight years before, on August 17, 1807, he had started the *Clermont* from New York on her epoch-making run up the Hudson. In that brief period, the steamboat had fully demonstrated its value as a mechanical and financial success. New York, moreover, had already attained the position which it would keep for many years to come as the most active of ports in the construction and use of the new device. Steam did not contribute as much to the port's rise as did the packets, the cotton triangle, or the Erie Canal, but it gave New York a unique distinction and it played its part in directing the lines of travel and trade toward Manhattan.

Fulton, of course, had not invented the steamboat. There is no need to revive the old disputes of those who support various pioneers for that honor. Perhaps the most deserving of them was "Poor John Fitch," who had built a workable steamboat at Philadelphia twenty years before the *Clermont's* famous trip and who had furnished fairly regular service on the Delaware for two or three years between Philadelphia and the upriver towns. Fulton had been able to profit by two decades of trial and had, moreover, the intelligent co-operation, ample financial support, and highly useful political influence of Robert R. Livingston. A member of one of New York's rich old landed families, Livingston had been chancellor of the state, minister to France, and a purchaser of Louisiana. Whereas, Fitch, broken-hearted at the lack of support for his project, had drifted out to Kentucky and committed suicide, Fulton had enjoyed profit, honor, and the gratification of achievement in his last years, and was no sooner dead than New York began to bestow his name upon everything from a street and a market to vessels of various sorts.

Those first few years of steamboating before 1815 might properly be annexed to our period because during that time New York had made substantial progress in developing the new device. No other American port, to be sure, had quite such a natural combination of sheltered waterways, both splendidly adapted to the use of the new steamboats, and leading toward important objectives. By 1815 and Fulton's death several New York steamers were in operation, not only on the Hudson, but also on the harbor and the Bay, while a boat was ready for service on the Sound just as soon as the British blockading squadron should leave.

The significant work of these early steamboats lay in facilitating travel rather than in the movement of freight. Passengers were consequently their main interest. Until that time, the traveller to Boston, Albany, or Philadelphia had his choice of stagecoaches, which were fairly regular but decidedly uncomfortable, or of sailing sloops, which offered more chance to stretch one's legs but which were most uncertain in time of arrival. The steamboat combined the merits of these two competitors, except in the winter months when frozen waterways threw all business to the stagecoach. Steam also eliminated the two chief disadvantages of coach and sloop, for the steamer was able to perform with the regularity of the former and at the same time provide considerably more comfort than even the sloop. Leaving the hauling of freight to wagons or sailing vessels, the early steamers quickly found a good source of profit in the passenger business.

The Hudson, as the first step in New York's pathway to the West, was admirable in this respect. With the tide rising and falling even at Albany and Troy some 150 miles inland, it did not have such strong downward currents as the Mississippi or Ohio, which could not be used by sailing vessels and called for a special type of steamer. Those inland river boats are entirely outside our scope of interest beyond the fact that a New Yorker, Nicholas J. Roosevelt, built the first one at Pittsburgh in 1811.

The *Clermont* took over part of the Hudson travel, much of which had been carried on in scores of sloops, which might take anywhere from three to nine days for the trip from New York to Albany. The sloop captains more than once tried to ram the *Clermont* and disable her paddle wheels, realizing full well what she meant to their business. With fares of about five cents a mile, the *Clermont* did so well that she soon had as companions on the route, the *Car of Neptune* and the

Paragon. These Hudson steamers made three sailings a week and a smaller boat in addition plied between New York and Poughkeepsie. The Fulton-Livingston combination was able to enjoy this lucrative business without fear of competition for it was safely entrenched behind a monopoly granted by the New York State legislature.

Within two years of the *Clermont's* first trip, steamboats also appeared on the New York-Philadelphia run, where geography gave them an unusual advantage. The land route between those two cities was nearly a hundred miles, whereas by sea the course down the Jersey coast, around Cape May, and up the Delaware River was almost three times as far (271 land miles or 235 nautical miles). That circuitous and often stormy sea route was all right for slow freight in sloops or schooners but few passengers had the time for such a trip. Steamboats, however, could radically reduce the cramping stage ride across New Jersey. From New York, they could cross the Bay and ascend the Raritan River to New Brunswick. From Philadelphia, they could go up the Delaware to Trenton. That left only some twenty-five miles or so of coaching across the narrow "waist" of New Jersey. This was so much more comfortable than the old, long, all-the-way-by-stage run that the steamboat owners were quick to seize upon it.

From the very outset, the Raritan route became the battleground over the Fulton-Livingston monopoly. Among the men who most deserve to share honors with Fulton as the promoter of steam navigation at New York was John Stevens, who lived just across the Hudson at Hoboken. An inventor of versatile genius, he had operated a little boat with twin screws on the Hudson in 1804 and by 1808 had built a full-sized steamer, the *Phœnix,* machinery and all—more American than the *Clermont* with her English engines. Stevens had hoped to run her on the Hudson, where he was confident that she could beat the five miles an hour of Fulton's boat. Attempts at compromise failed and Fulton and Livingston cited their monopoly rights to keep him from the river. Stevens consequently started the *Phœnix* on the New Brunswick run only to find a rival in 1809 in the *Raritan,* owned by the Chancellor's brother. Once more the monopoly was invoked, so that Stevens decided to send his boat around to the Delaware for the other part of the run. In July, 1809, the *Phœnix* ventured out past Sandy Hook along the long, surf-beaten Jersey coast, the first time that a steamer had appeared on the open sea. Despite widespread misgivings, she arrived safely and immediately began service between Philadelphia and Trenton. A line of stages through Princeton linked the two steamboat services and travellers were quick to take advantage of the more comfortable trip.

The peculiar conformation of Long Island Sound gave the steamboats a similar opportunity to improve travel conditions between New York and Boston. By land, the distance between the two cities was more than two hundred miles. By sea, the route around Cape Cod was well over three hundred miles in the century before the canal was cut through its base. Most of the travel was by stagecoach but it was a tedious trip. At the beginning of 1815, for instance, the advertisements stated that a traveller who left New York by coach at 6 A.M. on Monday morning would spend that night at New Haven and the second night at Ashland, Mass., arriving at Boston in time for dinner Wednesday evening. By water, it was possible to tap the route to Boston at numerous points—one could even go by water all the way from New York to Providence, which left less than fifty miles to cover by land with a total saving in distance of a full hundred miles over the sea route around Cape Cod. Some travellers, who were not in too much of a hurry, had avoided part of the stage trip before 1815 by taking packet sloops from Providence, New London, Norwich, or some other port, but of course, as usual, their time of arrival was a gamble.

Here was evidently another golden opportunity for the steamboat and, as early as 1813, a company paid Fulton and Livingston for permission to operate on the Sound; and built the steamer *Fulton* for that purpose. That year, however, the British sent a blockading squadron into the Sound and the route could not be used until the war ended. In March, 1815, less than a month after Fulton's death, Captain Elihu Bunker began regular service to New Haven in the *Fulton*. The travellers could at least eliminate the first day of the tedious stage trip. The Sound steamers carried more freight than those on the Hudson or the Bay and helped New York to challenge successfully Boston's commercial relations with western New England.

Another important "first time" in steam occurred at New York during these opening years. The insular position of Manhattan made ferry service vital, both to cross the mile-wide Hudson to New Jersey and the narrower East River to Brooklyn. The shorter the distance to be covered, the more significant was the value of steam in relieving shipping of dependence upon winds and currents, because a delay under such conditions was relatively more disrupting to service. The Hudson crossing was an especially difficult one upon which to maintain frequent ferry service, for the trips might vary from fifteen minutes to three hours or more. The first steam ferryboat in the world was the *Juliana,* which John Stevens, of whom we have already heard, placed upon the New York-Hoboken run in 1811, after securing temporary permission from Fulton and Livingston. By 1815 the Fulton steamers *York* and *Jersey* were crossing the Hudson to Jersey City, while the *Nassau* was doing similar work on the East River.

Towing, the other important harbor service, was a trifle slower in coming. At times, weather conditions might delay a sailing vessel several days in coming up from the Hook or in putting out to sea. This was particularly true in late winter when the harbor and Bay were filled with floating ice. The first instance of using steamboats to remedy this situation has hitherto escaped attention, but a day-by-day perusal of the newspaper files would seem to establish the date as January 26, 1818, when the harbor was particularly choked with ice. On that day, the Bay steamer *Nautilus,* owned by Vice President Daniel D. Tompkins, "towed the ship *Corsair* from one mile below the Narrows to the quarantine dock in three-quarters of an hour." For some time to come, towing would be a part-time job for steamers employed around the harbor or Bay; and disgusted commuters from Brooklyn would have to secure a law forbidding ferryboats from leaving their regular beats to pick up extra dollars in that way. It was to be several years before the *Hercules* was built to specialize in that business.

With the various branches of New York's steam activity thus set in operation, we might notice a few aspects in which the service created new maritime occupations. The men most apt to be mentioned in connection with a steamboat were her operator, her captain, and her builder. None of these three functions was essentially different in steamboating from the conventional situation in sailing vessels. Operation was naturally much the same; command was an easier job than in sailing vessels where tacking was necessary; while the building of a steamer's hull did not differ especially from fashioning a ship or a brig. The two distinctive new occupations, for which there were no precedents in sailing vessels, were the building of machinery and operating it aboard ship.

The early marine engineers, whose job it was to keep the new machinery going, are pretty much forgotten men. History has not recorded the name of the first of all, the Scot who nursed the *Clermont's* engines on the first trip up the Hudson. Legend does tell us, however, that upon arrival at Albany he celebrated his relief from the unusual strain by drinking himself into such a condition that for the return trip Fulton fired him and gave the job to the assistant engineer, Charles Dyke. The latter thereafter served not only on the Hudson, but on harbor ferries, Bay steamers, and on western waters, and incidentally participated in the defense of New Orleans in 1815. Aside from him, the names of the engineers generally appeared in print only after an explosion—either in the list of those badly scalded or in testifying that they had plenty of water in the boiler and were not racing. In those primitive days they had to be resourceful, without the benefit of experience to sustain them. In 1818, for instance, the hand beam of the *Paragon's* engine broke when she was near Hudson and it was necessary for her to wait until the broken beam could be sent overland to Canaan, Connecticut, for repairs. Two years later, the *Olive Branch* broke the iron strap of her air-pump off Perth Amboy. It was reported that it could have been quickly repaired "if the Captain had not been obliged to travel 3 or 4 miles in quest of a blacksmith."

It took a while to find the proper title for these engineers. In 1820, it was remarked concerning one steamer "on a thorough consultation with the artists and machinerist it is found unnecessary to make these alterations in the boiler." The firemen and "wood passers" were humbler engine-room additions to marine personnel. The word "stoker" crept in only slowly.

The men who made the engines were a somewhat more conspicuous group. Until after the Civil War, when the center of steam construction moved south from New York to the Delaware, the hull and machinery of a steamer were constructed by entirely separate establishments. The hull would be fashioned in one of the regular East River yards, some of which tended to specialize in steamboat work while others carried it on as part of their general shipbuilding. The engines and boilers were built in establishments known as "iron works," most of which were in the vicinity of the East River yards.

New York enjoyed unusual pre-eminence in this field. No other American port could rival the assemblage of talent concentrated in its "iron works." Nowhere else in the world, in fact, was there such a group except on the banks of the Clyde around Glasgow. During that important transitional period, from sail to steam and from wood to iron, in shipbuilding, New York and Glasgow led the way. No small part of that leadership came from the clever pioneer work of those who experimented with new devices for propelling steamships. Orders came to New York for steamers to serve at other American ports and in foreign waters, while for repairs steamers were sent hundreds of miles to the skilled technicians in the New York yards.

Outstanding in this group was James P. Allaire, whose Huguenot ancestors had settled at New Rochelle a century before. At a time when skilled mechanics were rare in this country, he showed ingenuity in assembling the machinery brought from England. Around 1815, he established a brass foundry in New York. Soon after Fulton's death, Allaire took over "the extensive steam engine factory erected by Messrs. Livingston and Fulton at Jersey City, together with a dry dock, models, tools, utensils and mill machinery, forming together one of the most complete establishments of the kind in the United States." He soon moved most of the equipment over to New York, where he established his extensive ironworks near Corlear's Hook in the vicinity of the East River yards. A newspaper article, describing a new Sound steamer and its thirteen-ton copper boilers in 1829, remarked, "Mr. Allaire, who is constructing the engines and boilers, politely showed us the whole of his extensive works. He has two hundred hands in his employ, all hale, muscular and contented looking men." The reporter was impressed by a sign which read, "Any person that brings, or drinks, spirituous liquors on my premises will be discharged, without any pay for the week." Allaire told him that he had put the sign up nine years before and had discharged only two men. He was receiving most of the important orders for machinery by that time and had developed the compound engine which used more than one cylinder. On the side, Allaire had his "Howell Works" in New Jersey to smelt bog iron with charcoal and produce ironware of various sorts in addition to meeting the needs of his engine and boiler works at New York. The growth of anthracite smelting in Pennsylvania finally checked this, and his other chief outside venture, the establishing of steamer service to Charleston in the 'thirties, came to grief with the loss of two of his vessels.

He was by no means alone in the business. Gradually he was overtaken by the "Novelty Works," which derived its name from having constructed the boilers and engines for the pioneer coal-burning river steamer *Novelty* in 1836. During the period of its great success in the early 'fifties, the business was operated by Stillman, Allen & Co. The junior partner was Horatio Allen, who had built the first regular

American locomotive for Charleston's railroad and had gone south to manage that road for several years.

Ranking third in general volume of business was the plant started by Theophilus Secor. Around 1850, it was purchased by Charles Morgan, the Gulf steamboat magnate, who named it the Morgan Iron Works and entrusted the management to his heavy-jowled Connecticut son-in-law, George W. Quintard, one of the few New Englanders in this particular branch of business.

A distinctive role was played by Cornelius Delamater, from up the Hudson, in partnership with Peter Hogg for a while and then alone. When John Ericsson, the great Swedish engineer, came to New York in 1839 to promote the steam propeller, he threw most of his work to Delamater, who became a close friend. The engines for the *Monitor* were built in the Delamater Iron Works. Had the other engine builders been as ready to turn from paddle wheels to propellers, New York might have retained longer its commanding position in the field of steam.

Among others conspicuous in this work were Pease, Murphy & Co., and, toward the end, John Roach, an Irishman who after the Civil War followed the shift of steam construction to the Delaware. The versatile Robert L. Stevens had an ironworks at Hoboken where he produced part of the machinery for the family steamers. He is credited with having introduced more new and fundamental features into the river steamers than any other man of the day.

Many of the important marine-engine builders of the country received their initial training in these New York ironworks. The men who played leading rôles in steam engineering in the Navy were in many cases graduates of these plants—Charles B. Stuart, Charles H. Haswell, and Benjamin F. Isherwood in particular.

With the exception of the Delamater plant, which was over on the west side, most of these ironworks were in the shipyard region on the East River. The Novelty Works in 1850 stretched for a thousand feet along the river from Twelfth to Fourteenth Street and had two slips capable of accommodating eight or ten of the largest steamers. The plant in that year had some 1170 employees, divided into 18 departments. The three largest groups were the 359 machinists, 248 iron founders, and 242 boilermakers. The plant even manufactured its own clocks and thermometers. The workers received an average of $1.50 for a day extending from 7 A.M. to 6 P.M. This was the largest of the iron works

—in 1847, when the Novelty had 1000 employees, there were some 800 apiece in the rival plants of Allaire, Secor, and Pease, Murphy & Co.

The anti-monopoly agitation on the Bay run was the outstanding feature of the new steamboat business during the first decade of peace and culminated in the famous Supreme Court decision in *Gibbons vs. Ogden* in 1824. Chancellor Livingston's brother, we recall, had been operating his *Raritan* to New Brunswick by 1809, safeguarded from competition by the monopoly. Then Aaron Ogden came on the scene, closely followed by Thomas Gibbons. Ogden, a Princeton graduate, had had a brilliant record in the Revolution, particularly in the assault on the lines at Yorktown, and later had served as governor of New Jersey. Gibbons, an irascible Georgian from Savannah, had had a somewhat shady record as a Tory in the Revolution and had managed a political campaign for Anthony Wayne in such a manner that a congressional committee denounced "this person, Gibbons, whose soul is faction and whose life has been a scene of political corruption." He had fought a duel and had served as mayor of Savannah. Like many other southerners, he established a summer home in New Jersey, selecting Elizabeth for the purpose. One has only to look at the pictures of those two tough, fighting faces to understand why the names of Gibbons and Ogden became linked in a lawsuit.

At first their relations had been amicable. Ogden, deciding to break into the Bay steamboat game, attempted to fight the monopoly rights of Fulton and Livingston, covering the New York end of the Bay run. Unsuccessful, Ogden soon purchased from the Chancellor's brother a license to run to New York from Elizabethtown Point, near the northwest corner of Staten Island. From there, Gibbons began to operate a connecting steamer to New Brunswick and thus passenger service was provided on the first leg of the Philadelphia route. No license was necessary for this latter service, of course, since the route did not enter New York waters.

Soon friction developed between the two men, not from steamboats in the beginning but from a private matter. It seems that as a friend of the family, Ogden tried to smooth out a quarrel between Gibbons and his son-in-law, whom Gibbons accused of seducing his daughter before marrying her. Gibbons turned on Ogden, and posted a threatening note on his house. Thereupon Ogden won a trespass decision against Gibbons. The quarrel shifting to steamboats, Gibbons suddenly began in 1818 to operate his *Bellona* between Elizabethtown Point and New

York in competition with Ogden's *Atlanta*. Ogden, since he had, we know, bought a license from the monopolists, received the support of the New York courts in opposing this Gibbons intrusion. It is scarcely necessary here to follow that long court battle. All that time Gibbons's *Bellona* managed to keep up service of sorts in spite of zealous New York officials who tried to serve injunctions against her. Her captain was none other than young Cornelius Vanderbilt from Staten Island, who was thus graduating from little sailing vessels to this first connection with steamboats, with which he was to be conspicuous for many years. With impudence and resourcefulness, he managed to land his passengers at one place or another along the New York waterfront, despite all the efforts of sheriff and process-servers.

Gibbons, thoroughly aroused, appealed the adverse decisions of the New York courts to the United States Supreme Court, which eventually heard the case in 1824. Gibbons claimed that his federal coasting enrolment was enough permission for the run. Sparing no expense, he retained Daniel Webster and Attorney General William Wirt; and in order that the case might be continued in the event of his death before the settlement, he provided $40,000 for the purpose in his will. The case ended with one of Chief Justice Marshall's celebrated decisions, which invoked the power of Congress to regulate interstate commerce and declared illegal the monopoly, which had sheltered the Fulton-Livingston combination.

The decision became a landmark in steam navigation, which was thus thrown open to free competition after seventeen years of monopoly. Grateful New Yorkers named two steamers for Marshall almost at once and the effects of the decision were felt in the various spheres of steamboating.

The Bay run, after producing that significant result, gradually sank in importance in comparison with the Hudson and the Sound. Ogden and Gibbons soon disappeared from the scene. Vanderbilt secured control of the *Bellona,* while his wife supplemented the family income by running the Bellona Tavern at the New Brunswick terminus. Gradually the Stevens family became all-important on this route, whence the elder John had been ejected by the monopoly in 1809. Not only did they have steamers on both the Raritan and the Delaware but also operated stages on the intervening link until in the early 'thirties they completed their Camden & Amboy Railroad across the "waist" of New Jersey. For a while that meant more business than ever for the Bay steamboats,

ROBERT FULTON
1765–1815

*Engraved by G. Parker after the portrait
by Benjamin West*

CORNELIUS VANDERBILT
1794–1877

Courtesy of the Chamber of Commerce

THOMAS GIBBONS
1757–1826

*From T. Gamble,
"Savannah Duels and Duelists"*

GOV. AARON OGDEN
1756–1839

*From W. O. Ogden,
"The Ogden Family in America"*

STEAMBOAT MEN

but by 1839 there was through rail service from Jersey City, part of the present Pennsylvania route, and thereafter only the less desirable part of the business fell to the Bay steamers.

On the Hudson, the influence of *Gibbons vs. Ogden* was felt with surprising emphasis. The comfortable and profitable days when the North River Steamboat Company operated without fear of competition gave way to years of violent cutthroat rivalry. Strangely enough, a steamboat named the *Olive Branch* was the one which brought contention to the river. She was transferred from the New Brunswick route and advertised for Albany, a few weeks after the Marshall decision. The monopoly group, however, immediately secured an injunction against her on the ground that the Hudson trade was not interstate traffic, and therefore was not affected by the decision. Thereupon the *Olive Branch* was qualified for interstate traffic by having her start at Jersey City before picking up passengers at New York. Not long afterwards, she crashed into the *Chancellor Livingston* of the monopoly line above Poughkeepsie, as the two boats were racing, close together, to round a point. It was charged that after an interchange of retorts between the pilots, the captain of the *Olive Branch* ordered his pilot, "Damn her, put your helm aport and we're plump into the ladies' cabin." Nevertheless, the ensuing crash damaged the *Olive Branch* more than it did the *Chancellor!*

Early in 1825, however, the New York Court of Errors put an end to the monopoly for state waters also; and the river was henceforth open to further rivalry. The opening of the Erie Canal later that year meant an increased volume of business for the Hudson, naturally, and several rival lines appeared. In 1826, the North River Steamboat Company, which had carried on the Fulton-Livingston monopoly, went out of business. Its most conspicuous successor was the Hudson River Association, in which the Stevens family was prominent with several fast steamers embodying Fulton's ingenious innovations. It is said that the Association paid a dividend of 70 per cent from its profits in its first year.

That naturally stimulated further competition, which was intense during the late 'twenties. Passengers approaching the steamboat wharves, apprehensive perhaps of boiler explosions which had been rather frequent, were told by persistent and noisy runners that the boilers of the opposition boat were all ready to burst, while the runners' boat had no boilers at all. Rate wars were carried to extremes. It was no longer possible to exact a $7 fare to Albany as Fulton had charged at the outset. Five dollars was the best to be expected and at times during the rate wars, the fares dropped to a dollar or even to fifty cents. On one occasion, passengers were carried free, though the line hoped to make something once the traveller was aboard, by stiff charges for stateroom and meals.

Only well-established lines were able to survive such competition. Any firm operating on a shoe-string soon had to withdraw, while those which had enough backing to maintain persistent opposition were likely to be bought out at a good price or taken into the more firmly established line. This latter type of "blackmail" was well illustrated by two masters of the art: Cornelius Vanderbilt and Daniel Drew. With passenger steamers offering one of the best chances to grow rich in that day, these two practised on the Hudson and on the Sound the tactics which they would later use in railroad manipulation.

Vanderbilt, who had shifted operations from the Bay to the river, organized a line to Peekskill. Drew, a product of upstate New York and one-time cattle drover, whose religious pose in no way cramped his sharp practices, persuaded the farmers of Putnam County that Vanderbilt's line was overcharging and thus raised capital to build an opposition boat. So successful was this, that Vanderbilt had to reduce his Peekskill fare to the bone. In 1832, however, Drew sold out to Vanderbilt without telling the other stockholders, who were furious.

Then Vanderbilt practised the first of the "blackmailing" which he was to repeat on the Sound and the ocean. Putting two good boats on the Albany run, he cut into the Association's profits so that after two years they bought him out on the condition that he would stay off that route for ten years. Thereupon Drew tried the same thing, and after a year was made a director by the Association, which gave his boats a share of the profits. That was not enough for Daniel. Disguising his own connection with the matter, he placed another steamer in opposition, with the captain's brother as dummy owner. Drew then persuaded his fellow directors of the Association to buy off this competitor. They decided upon a price and sent Drew to negotiate with the "owner." The story goes that he simply walked around the block, and returned with word that the owner insisted upon $8000 more, and after some discussion that price was met.

Meanwhile similar developments were taking place upon the Sound. Whereas the Hudson service had been a through New York-to-Albany affair from the first trip of the *Clermont,* the Sound steamers had crept eastward only gradually. At the beginning in 1815, the *Fulton* had gone only to New Haven, but when the *Connecticut* was added to the service a year later, New London at the end of the Sound became the terminus.

A further extension resulted from the fight against the Fulton-Livingston monopoly, which affected the Sound also. In 1822, Connecticut passed a law forbidding steamboats from New York to enter her ports as long as that monopoly remained in force. Various ingenious ways were improvised to meet this situation; but the chief consequence was the substitution of Providence as the terminus for the principal steamers. Long Island did not shelter this extension of the route and the sea was often very rough off "P'int Judy," as Point Judith was called. Many had misgivings about this longer route, when the veteran Elihu Bunker took the *Connecticut* on the first trip around the stormy point to Newport and Providence. The latter wharves were loaded with an enthusiastic crowd when he arrived there safely on June 6, 1822.

For the next fifteen years, this 210-mile route to Providence remained the most important of the Sound lines for through travel because it left less than fifty miles of stage-coaching to Boston. Hartford and several other Connecticut ports acquired steamboats to New York during that time, but not until 1837 did Providence, which by then had a railroad to Boston, lose its primacy in the through traffic.

The new rival was Stonington, that prolific breeder of bold mariners on the eastern edge of Connecticut close to the Rhode Island line. New York business men built a railroad from Providence to Stonington, where it connected with their Sound steamers from New York. By reducing the water trip, this meant a quicker through connection. The Stonington Line attracted the best and fastest boats; and for many years it carried the "Great Eastern Mail" to and from New England.

By the late 'forties, however, further railroad construction gave it serious rivalry. The Norwich & Worcester road ran to a terminus at Allyn's Point on the Thames between Norwich and New London, where it connected with Sound steamers for New York. This route meant 104 miles by rail instead of the Stonington's 90, with a slightly shorter boat trip. In 1847, the Fall River Line began its celebrated 90-year career, running past Newport to the Massachusetts cotton manufacturing town which had just completed rail connections with Boston. This involved a train trip only half as long as the rival routes, with a correspondingly longer boat trip.

The traveller from New York to Boston had still other options. For a brief period, the Long Island Railroad enabled one to go all the way by rail except for a short crossing of the Sound to Connecticut. Then a railroad was pushed through from Boston to New Haven. One could leave New York at 6 A.M. by steamer for New Haven and then proceed by a daylight rail trip to Boston. In 1849, the New York & New Haven road was completed and at last New York and Boston had a through rail connection. There were no sleepers, Pullmans, or even comfortable coaches at that time, however, and the majority of travellers, for many years to come, preferred the night boats on the Sound.

Whereas New York's steamers on the short Bay run were all day boats, and the Hudson steamers offered both day and night service, the Sound liners were usually night boats. They generally left New York about five in the afternoon and the passengers were delivered in Boston by train the next morning. Around 1850, the Stonington, Norwich, and Fall River lines were all charging five dollars for the trip to Boston and six dollars a ton for freight. The Stonington and Norwich lines stressed their sheltered route, which avoided the rough water off Point Judith. The Fall River countered with the fact that its passengers might "sleep till half past three or four o'clock in the morning," instead of being routed out to shift to the cars at an ungodly hour shortly after midnight, as was necessary at Norwich or Stonington. All three joined in praising the superiority of a comfortable night on the water to the hot and dusty through trip by rail.

The Sound lines also had their rate wars and sharp maneuvers. In 1833, Vanderbilt was carrying passengers for a dollar to Hartford, where the rate had been five. The Providence and Stonington lines remained in fairly compact control, like the Association on the river.

Whereas Drew was simply a shrewd manipulator with no apparent interest in improvement of service, Vanderbilt was eager to lure business by offering the best service possible. His son might later say, "The public be damned," but the "Commodore" owed no small part of his early fortune to his success in catering to the travelling public. His only rival in that respect was Isaac Newton, for years president of the People's Line which succeeded the old Hudson River Association. Those two men were largely responsible for the "floating palaces" which began to appear on river and Sound by the 'forties. Realizing how every little addition in comfort or luxury might lure extra passengers, the owners made lavish outlays and developed an ornate style of finish.

The forty years which separated the *Clermont* from these "floating palaces" had brought tremendous changes in the appearance of the steamers. Fulton's pioneer and the other early steamboats were all of the same general paddle-wheel sort and were so much alike that boats were frequently transferred between river, Bay, and Sound. The *Clermont* resembled a canal boat in its lines and had little above decks except a single tall stack. The later steamers, almost invariably painted white, had high superstructures with ample open-deck space where travellers might enjoy the view. The longitudinal "hog frames," invented by Robert L. Stevens to enable the slender hulls to support the weight of the engines, somewhat marred the external appearance, which was further rendered unusual by the Hudson River practice of placing engines and boilers on deck at either side, rather than in the hold. It was in the interior finishings that the new changes were most apparent. Newton is credited with the inspiration of the grand saloon, two decks high, surrounded by galleries onto which the individual staterooms opened. Ornate joiner work, generally finished in white and gold, was combined with rich upholstery to give an air of luxury.

The developments in size and speed were no less remarkable. The *Clermont,* when remodelled after her early trips, was 133 feet long, 18 feet wide, and 8 feet deep—in all these steamers the proportion of length to beam was much greater than in the seagoing sailing vessels which averaged about four to one and even in the clippers seldom reached six to one. It was exactly eleven to one in the *New World,* the largest river steamer built before the Civil War. With a beam of 35 feet and a depth of 10, she was 371 feet long—the newspapers by that time were referring to "our mile-long steamers." The Sound steamers, exposed to rougher water at the eastern end of their route, did not reach quite such an extreme. The largest before the Civil War was the *Plymouth Rock,* built for the Stonington Line in 1854, 330 feet long, with a beam of 40 feet and a depth of 12 feet 8 inches. On occasions, such boats sometimes carried a thousand passengers in a single trip.[1]

The development in speed was likewise remarkable during those years. Wind and tide could make some difference. It took twelve hours for a tide to run from Sandy Hook to Albany and a steamer might

[1]See Appendix, xvi.

thus have it with her or against her all the way. On the Sound, the tide counted most in East River, where, we recall, it sometimes reached a velocity of six miles in Hell Gate—too much for some of the early steamers which could make only five. The *Clermont's* running time from New York to Albany on her first trip was thirty-four hours, an average of slightly less than five miles an hour. In 1828, the *North America* of the Stevens Line set up a new record with ten hours and ten minutes. The fastest of all the runs, and one that seems to have escaped previous attention, was a down-river trip of seven hours and twenty-one minutes by the *South America* on April 19, 1843, an average of twenty-one miles an hour. On the Sound, the *Connecticut's* running time was twenty-nine hours on the first trip to Providence in 1822. When the *Lexington* made it in twelve hours on her maiden trip in 1835, one New York paper expressed the belief that she was the fastest boat in the world.

Racing was common on all the routes. Aside from the fact that the fastest boat was inclined to get the most business, it was a sport generally enjoyed, except by the more cautious passengers, who feared the danger of overstrained boilers. The most famous of the river races was a prearranged affair from New York to Sing Sing and back on June 1, 1847, for a $1000 stake. The contestants were the Sound steamer *Cornelius Vanderbilt,* owned by the Commodore, and the *Oregon,* owned by George Law, a burly, bewhiskered, self-made Irishman, who would later figure prominently in subsidy lines to Panama. Huge crowds turned out for the race and hundreds of side bets were made. On the up-river stretch the two boats ran neck and neck; but the *Oregon* was slightly ahead at the turn, when her rival bumped her and damaged her wheelhouse. On the return, the *Oregon's* coal gave out. Thereupon cabin furniture was tossed into the furnaces, followed by all other woodwork that could be ripped down. That did the trick, for the *Oregon* reached the Battery nearly a quarter mile in the lead. She had run the seventy-mile course in three hours and a quarter. It was the Commodore's first defeat and one of the very few he encountered in his long career but he had only himself to blame. Steering his own boat, he had lost headway by failing to slow down properly at the turn at Sing Sing.

Gradually the steamboat operators came to realize that, apart from other considerations, racing was a costly game because of the added fuel consumption. Down to the mid-'thirties, dry pine wood was the

Lithograph after F. E. Palmer

HUDSON RIVER STEAMERS IN THE 'FIFTIES

The 1332-ton *Isaac Newton*, built in 1846, and the 1235-ton *Francis Skiddy*, built in 1852, were examples of the "floating palaces" of the later period. They are shown racing through the Highlands

From the Eldredge Collection

THE BURNING OF THE *LEXINGTON*

The New York-Stonington steamer is shown burning in Long Island Sound on January 13, 1840, with the loss of more than 100 lives. The loaded lifeboat at the stern was an incorrect detail, as all the boats were swamped in the wash

ordinary steamboat fuel and the boats at night presented a striking sight with flames sometimes leaping from the tops of their tall stacks. On short runs, there was no particular trouble, but for the longer trips the necessary fuel was so bulky that it cluttered up much of the deck space. The *Clermont* used a dozen cords or so on her trips to Albany and by 1831, the larger steamers consumed about sixty-four cords on the Providence run. They could not carry all that at once, so a wood sloop used to be picked up off Fisher's Island near the far end of the Sound and her cargo transferred without losing headway.

Ten years later the same trip could be performed with a dozen tons of coal, which occupied far less room. Steamboat men had appreciated the advantages of coal long before, but the right kind was not available. Whereas the British steamers had plenty of soft coal from the outset, the American mines were not yet producing good bituminous and the hard anthracite offered serious problems in combustion. Numerous early experiments were made, in which Philadelphia claimed priority, but the successful use of anthracite in the steamers was dated by the New Yorkers from June 23, 1836, when the *Novelty* made a trial run on the Hudson. Among her ingenious devices invented by Doctor Eliphalet Nott, president of Union College, were twelve boilers fed by anthracite, with blowers to stimulate combustion.

Philip Hone entered in his diary for that day:

A party of gentlemen, consisting of the managers of the Delaware & Hudson . . . and others, went on board the *Novelty* this morning at six o'clock, at the foot of Chambers Street in New York, and came to Albany in twelve hours.

This was the first voyage ever made from New York to Albany by a steamboat propelled by anthracite coal. Dr. Nott has been engaged for several years in contriving to accomplish this important object, and has now succeeded completely. The great desideratum was to contrive the means of igniting the coal, and producing a flame sufficient to create the steam. This has been effected by condensing hot air, which by injection into the bottom of the furnaces accomplishes this object, and forces the flame into a chamber in which are a great number of iron tubes of the size of gun-barrels, placed vertically. There are four of these furnaces. The quantity of coal consumed on this trip was about twenty tons (something less), which at $5 per ton amounts to $100. The same voyage would have consumed forty cords of pine wood, the present price of which is $6, making a difference of more than one half. . . . Dr. Nott has succeeded completely in this invention, which establishes certainly that coal will succeed wood in all our steamboats, and the Delaware & Hudson Company will hereafter be able to sell all the coal they can bring down the canal at an advanced price.

From that time on, coal gradually supplanted the bulky pine sticks.

Four years later, however, the new blowing device led to one of New York's worst steamboat disasters. Vanderbilt's fast *Lexington,* which he had recently sold to the Stonington Line, had been newly equipped for burning coal. She left New York for Stonington on the afternoon of January 13, 1840. About seven that evening, when she was off Bridgeport, the stack, red hot from the pressure of forced draft under the coal, set fire to some of the cotton bales which had been piled dangerously close to it. The officers and crew seem to have lost their heads, the flames gained rapid headway and the boats, being launched before the engines were stopped, were swamped in the wash. A young New Orleans packet captain lowered himself onto a cotton bale and after a freezing night, was eventually picked up by a sloop the next forenoon. He was the only one of the 78 passengers to survive, while the pilot and one fireman alone escaped of the 34 officers and crew.

The only Sound disaster approaching that in magnitude was the loss of the *Atlantic,* a crack steamer on the Norwich run in November, 1846. She was not stout enough to stand a veritable hurricane which caught her as she left the Thames River with the passengers, who had arrived by train from Boston just before midnight. One of her steam pipes burst as she strained in the heavy seas, and she drifted helplessly, in the freezing cold, toward Fisher's Island. One anchor cable after another gave way and forty-eight hours later she struck stern first on a ledge and went to pieces in five minutes. As in the case of the *Lexington,* passenger travel was light in the winter and only about eighty persons all told were aboard her, about half of whom were lost.

Daniel Webster seems to have led a charmed life. He and some friends are said to have arrived at Allyn's Point on the boat train from Boston but decided not to sail on account of the threatening weather. A year earlier he had a similar close shave in one of the worst wrecks on the Hudson. He was aboard one of three steamers which were coming down the river together, apparently racing, on the night of April 7, 1845. In a narrow passage near Hudson, one of the other boats, the *Swallow,* drew ahead in order to secure the lead. Suddenly she ran full speed into a rocky little island, broke in two, and caught fire. She had more than three hundred passengers aboard and the

number of lives lost was never definitely determined, probably amounting to at least fifty. An even worse river disaster was the loss of the
Henry Clay on July 28, 1852. Racing down river against a rival steamer,
she was discovered to be afire near Sing Sing. Apparently her wood-
work had ignited from the excessive heat of the boilers or stacks. The
captain ran her bow ashore, but most of the passengers were trapped
by the flames in the stern, which was in deep water. The sixty-odd victims included several prominent New York residents, including a sister
of Nathaniel Hawthorne.

Various other steamers were lost through collision, running aground,
or fire, but the most common cause of accident, and the one which
caused the most frequent anxiety, was the exploding of boilers. Most
of the New York boats had low-pressure boilers and the explosions
were not as frequent or as deadly as the appalling disasters to the high-
pressure steamers on the inland rivers. Racing doubtless strained many
boilers severely and it took a while to learn that lack of water was apt
to mean an explosion. New York had an epidemic of six fatal explosions in 1824 and 1825 on river, Sound, and Bay, the worst occurring
in the harbor when the boiler of the Bay steamer *Ætna* gave way, killing thirteen and painfully scalding several more. This led to the novel
device of the "safety barges" on the Hudson. Two of these, the *Lady
Clinton* and the *Lady Rensselaer,* were built at New York in 1825, to
be towed by steamers on the night run. They were equipped with commodious sleeping quarters for those who wanted to travel without
danger of being blown up, but the service was so slow that it did not
last long.

In an attempt to curb steamboat accidents, Federal legislation in
1838 established inspectors of hulls and boilers at the chief ports. The
testimony of the veteran New York inspectors, a Sound captain and
a boiler maker, at the *Lexington* inquest of 1840, however, revealed
how casual and superficial those inspections were. Old Captain Bunker
argued that more care was unnecessary, since they knew the waterfront
reputation of every boat anyway. "I think that there could not be found
in the United States two other inspectors possessing the information
that we happen to possess." On August 30, 1852, just a month after
the *Henry Clay* disaster, Congress passed more stringent inspection
legislation, which included the licensing of pilots and engineers. During
the next year, the inspectors at New York passed upon 135 steamers
totalling 52,000 tons and licensed 161 pilots and 365 engineers, more

than Boston, Philadelphia, and Baltimore combined. It is not to be supposed, of course, that accidents were the order of the day—many steamers ran for years, carrying hundreds of thousands of passengers without a single mishap.

The steamboat had one marked effect upon the habits of New Yorkers. By 1827, according to *The Evening Post,* "the summer emigrations from this city are every year becoming more numerous." Short excursions and longer vacations became both more feasible and pleasanter, when a tedious trip by stage or sloop was no longer entailed. In mid-June, 1845, another editor made much the same comments on the annual emigration, with some off for Saratoga, "the summer headquarters of flirting, politics, and liver complaint," while "at the great wooden eating-houses of Long-Island's sea-girt shore, strangers are daily taken in" and "honest, sensible people are seeking out quiet and sequestered retreats," so that "the city will soon be abandoned to the dog-killers, cabmen, and police justices at the Tombs." Those who could not leave their business might at least commute from Hoboken with its cool and shady groves and its vistas of the Bay. Steamer excursions of every sort were advertised—trips to Coney Island or Long Branch for sea bathing, which was still a novelty; trips to the "sea bass fishing banks"; special trips for Yale commencements or Long Island camp meetings; Fourth of July excursions on river, Sound, or Bay, with bands, dancing, and turtle soup.

The steamboats also stimulated travel in general, as another New York editor noted in 1827:

It is a common observation that the amount of travel from one important commercial place to another in our country has lately increased in an astonishing degree. The mere growth of our population is not sufficient to account for this effect, for the increase of population has been infinitely short of the increase of travel. It must be owing, therefore, to the reduction of fare and the greater speed of the passage.

The increase of travel on the North River is a striking exemplification of the truth of this remark. The bringing of such a number of steamboats on that river seems to have multiplied rather than diminished the number of passengers in each. Every new boat is immediately filled, and yet the decks of the old ones seem only to swarm with additional numbers.

Since New York had more steamboats than any other port, it profited most by the new means of transportation. From the standpoint of its commercial growth, this was most helpful from its influence in determining the inland storekeepers, who were going to the coast to re-

From a painting by Stanley M. Arthurs

THE SAFETY BARGE

These passenger barges were built in 1825 in response to the fear of boiler explosions

plenish stocks, to utilize the speed and comfort of New York's boats.

While passengers were the main business of the New York steamers, they served other functions as well. Express service, which later grew to such tremendous proportions, started in 1839 when William F. Harnden, a conductor on one of the new Boston railroads, saw an opportunity to render an important service at good profit. A considerable amount of specie, banknotes, and other articles of great value in small bulk was constantly passing to and fro between New York and Boston banks and business houses. The steamboat companies did not accept responsibility for these and it was expensive to send a private messenger every time. He consequently started a "carpet bag messenger service," using the Stonington steamers and proceeding by rail to Boston. Within a year, business had increased so that a trunk was substituted for the carpet bag. His brother Adolphus was among the victims of the *Lexington*—his "express car," designed to float, contained an iron chest with some $10,000 in gold and $20,000 in bank notes. Others soon developed a similar service on other lines—in 1843 a young German stole the Pomeroy express chest, containing a half million in drafts and money, from the deck of the river steamer *Utica*. It was all recovered except a thousand dollars which went for honeymoon expenses. Henry C. Plant, later celebrated for his Florida developments, started as a deckhand on a New Haven steamer and soon became the New York head of Adams Express.

Another enterprising group likewise took advantage of the opportunities offered by the steamboats. A volume exposing the *Secrets of the Great City* in the late 'sixties contained the remark that "The various night lines of steamers running from New York City are literally overrun with abandoned women, seeking companions. The Albany and Boston lines are made intensely disagreeable by such persons."

As for bulky freight, the Sound steamers often carried a considerable amount, but, on the Hudson, steamboats were used for towing specially constructed lighters or dozens of canal barges. This became the usual fate for old steamers discarded from line service and some of them lasted on for many years as towboats. The most amazing endurance record was built up by the old *Norwich,* which was built in 1836 and was still towing barges on the Hudson well into the twentieth century. The sloops hung on stubbornly in the freighting business throughout our period, but they had constantly increasing competition from "the long lines of canal boats lashed together four and five abreast and strung out for nearly half a mile, being towed down the river, so slowly that the movement is hardly discernible."

More than two million passengers were carried on New York's three main steamboat routes during the year ending in July, 1851. The Hudson River boats came first with nearly a million, 995,000 to be exact. The New York-Philadelphia route, which apparently included the Delaware as well as the Bay steamers, came next at 840,000, while the Sound lines were third at 302,000.

In the very weeks when that period ended, however, the opening of the Hudson River Railroad to Albany marked the completion of the third of the all-rail routes which would, as time went on, lure both passengers and freight from the steamers on river, Sound, and Bay. All three runs were to feel the new competition with constantly increasing force and the Bay steamers would finally succumb completely as part of the Philadelphia route.

Yet even today there are still "floating palaces" on the Hudson and the Sound, not essentially different from their ancestors of the 'fifties, and they still attract some of us who, if time permits, will take advantage of the opportunity for a quiet and refreshing night on the water in preference to the later and speedier rival modes of transportation.

CHAPTER IX

THE CARIBBEAN AND LATIN AMERICA

THOUGH peace had come to much of the world in 1815, there was one region within New York's commercial sphere where ships still went armed during most of the next decade. From Mexico down to Chile, Spanish America had commenced its wars of liberation in 1810 and by 1825 Spain's former mainland colonies were independent. Brazil, too, had thrown off the yoke of Portugal. The spasmodic fighting on land and sea during those wars meant high adventure for some New Yorkers and rich commercial opportunity for many more.

From the days when the Elizabethan sea dog John Hawkins had peddled slaves along the Spanish Main at the cannon's mouth, the economic possibilities of Latin America had appealed strongly to the imagination and to the cupidity of outsiders. New York had a double inheritance of this covetous attitude. The Dutch and the English had made the most energetic efforts to drive entering wedges into the rigid monopolies, by which Spain and Portugal guarded the commerce of their American colonies for their sole profit. Not only were the silver and gold of those regions a powerful lure to those interlopers, but such born traders hated to see a potential market being allowed to go to waste, as they felt this one was, through the trade restrictions imposed by the mother countries.

New York had been initiated into this game in its infancy. The island of Curaçao, off the Venezuelan coast, was acquired by the Dutch West India Company in 1634 and made a first-rate smuggling base for operations in Latin America, as was evident from the size of its trade, which was all out of proportion to its own rather barren resources. The route between there and the Hudson became a familiar one.

After New York became English, the records give scant account of its exploits in that field, for such trading was apt to run foul of English as well as Spanish restrictions. Possibly some New York vessels may have been among the English craft which took undue advantage of the trade concessions granted by the Spanish to England in 1713. The British holdings on the Honduras coast served, like Curaçao, as bases for illegal operations. During the brief period in which England held Havana, after seizing it in 1762 in the Seven Years' War, Cuban trade flourished as never before. The lesson was not lost on the Spanish king, and beginning in 1766, many of the most rigid of the old commercial regulations were relaxed. Imports and exports rose, but still foreign shipping was for the most part excluded and customs duties remained high.

The first real chance for North American shipping in Latin America arose when England and France renewed their long struggle in 1793. Spain, involved as an ally on one side or the other during most of the contest, found it expedient to open some of her colonial ports to foreigners, because of the disruption of normal shipping. Vessels from New York, Baltimore, and other United States ports were quick to take advantage of the long-awaited opportunity. Between 1795 and 1799, exports from the United States to Spanish America jumped from $1,300,000 to nearly $9,000,000, with the imports even higher. In 1807, before the Embargo Act, the exports passed $12,000,000, more than three-fourths of which was the re-exportation of European goods. The British interpretation of international law, however, did not countenance many aspects of this trade, with the result that many Yankee vessels were snapped up by British frigates or by privateers. During these first years of Spanish-American trade, the wanderings of a few New York vessels, such as the *Cotton Planter* and the *Ambition,* may be traced from the elaborate briefs that were prepared for the appeal of their seizures before the British High Court of Admiralty. We find these vessels having to wander far and wide with their cargoes to make their rich profits in those years of European war. Such voyages, ranging to and from New York and including European ports, the African slave coast, and diverse other ports of call besides the West Indies and South America, may be fairly typical; but the captures were not. Enough vessels escaped the clutches of the British to make profitable business for Yankee merchants and shipowners as well as for the Spanish colonists, who welcomed the new trade.

The outbreak of the Spanish-American revolutions in 1810 does not seem to have made any immediate, perceptible difference in the exports from the United States; import figures are not available. In 1809, 1810, and 1811, the totals are about the same, roughly three millions in domestic products and three millions in re-exports. In 1808, however, the ports of Brazil were thrown open to the shipping of all friendly nations and the old rigid colonial regulations were completely discarded. In 1807, the American exports to Brazil had been barely $5000; in 1809, they reached $883,000; and a year later rose to $1,-610,000. Then the War of 1812 cut sharply into both the Spanish-American and Brazilian trade until, with the peace, it was necessary to start pretty much from scratch.

Following 1815, however, trade conditions remained abnormal as the royalists and revolutionaries struggled in Latin America. Consequently, although England and the United States were at peace, their shipping encountered the familiar hazards of blockading squadrons and marauding privateers for several years as both nations tried to exploit those newly opened markets. Toward the end, their vessels were exposed to piratical attacks of a far more brutal sort.

New York had participated in one of the first preliminary acts of violence in the Latin-American struggles for independence. In the summer of 1806, the ship *Leander* was made ready in the East River for a filibustering expedition of the Venezuelan Miranda to the Spanish Main. With the assistance of Federal officers, who believed that the authorities at Washington favored the project, she was loaded with a considerable amount of military stores, while about a hundred volunteers joined the revolutionaries. The premature revolt ended in failure and some of the New York volunteers languished for months in Spanish dungeons.

By 1816, however, the revolutions were in full swing and offered ample opportunities to the American privateersmen, who were loath to return to normal trading after the excitement of the war years. The swift privateers besides lacked sufficient cargo space to make them profitable in peacetime commerce. The Spanish Americans, on their side, although not trained for the sea, saw full well the value of raids on Spanish shipping. The two major scenes of action were the West Coast of South America, where the maritime situation was fairly orderly, and the Caribbean, where matters soon degenerated into piracy. During the next decade, New Yorkers were to be found both chasing with the hounds and running with the hares.

Out on the remote West Coast, where harbors were few, the head of the revolutionary government, soon in control of Chile, realized the advantage that sea power would give him over the royalists in Peru. Admitting "there was not a sailor to be found among all the people of Chile," he sent two agents to the United States, well equipped with funds from the rich silver mines. They were soon in touch with a successful New York commander of a privateer in the War of 1812, Captain Charles W. Wooster, the Connecticut-born grandson of a Revolutionary general. Wooster, accepting a commission in the Chilean Navy in October, 1817, soon sailed from New York with a heavy load of munitions under a layer of more innocent cargo in the fast bark *Columbus,* which joined the Chileans under the name of *Araucana.* Wooster, in command of another warship, captured a Spanish frigate, but soon resigned and went whaling when a Britisher became commander of the sea forces. Four years later, Wooster succeeded to this command and retained it for fifteen years.

In the meantime, the State Department at Washington buzzed with complaints from the Spanish minister because Chilean agents had contracted for the building of two warships at New York. These vessels, built by two of the East River's best shipbuilders at good profit to themselves and the merchants who arranged the terms, eventually joined the Chilean navy. Several other warships were built on South American account either at New York or on contracts sublet by New Yorkers to yards at Philadelphia and Baltimore. When the Spaniards protested this as a violation of neutrality, Henry Clay pointed out that Spain had bought a ready-made fleet from Russia and that the New Yorkers had been building warships for Spain also. In fact, he added, "the very singular case has occurred of the same shipbuilder having sold two vessels, one to the King of Spain, and the other to one of the Southern Republics, which vessels afterwards met and encountered each other at sea."

While New York was furnishing men and ships to the Chilean blockaders, it was also helping evade that same blockade. In June, 1817, John Jacob Astor's famous ship *Beaver,* a veteran of ten years in the Canton trade, sailed from New York for Valparaiso. Her commander, Captain Richard J. Cleveland, had persuaded Astor of the rich possibilities for profit in the Chilean region and below decks she carried a cargo worth $140,000, including a moderate amount of munitions. She was cleared for "Canton and the North West Coast," to disguise her destination. A shortage of wood and water forced her to put in at Talcahano in southern Chile, where she fell into the hands of royalists. The cargo was condemned and about $100,000 worth removed. After much intricate wire-pulling, including diplomatic negotiations at Madrid, she was released and for the next two years operated profitably along the coast from Callao up as far as Quito under special royalist permits. She successfully evaded the ships of the blockading navy, some of which were, like herself, products of the East River. After three years' absence, Cleveland returned to New York with more than 40 tons of Ecuador cocoa, together with some specie. This was New York's first major voyage in the new trade area.

The release of the *Beaver* and several other captured American vessels was undoubtedly facilitated by the presence of the American warship *Ontario* off the West Coast to protect American shipping in 1818. Possibly Astor's vigorous representations at Washington had something to do with this showing of the flag in those parts. For some time British frigates had been quite regularly stationed at various ports down there and several official representatives of the United States had been asking for American warships on similar duty. In July, 1812, not having learned that our small navy was fully occupied elsewhere, the consul at Buenos Aires wrote that "the presence of a national ship would give security to American trade," and increase respect for "our citizens." Another consul naively called attention to "how much more weight the character of an agent arriving in a vessel of War would have . . . than if he arrived in a simple merchant vessel." The combined considerations of prestige and security brought eventual results. In 1817, the *John Adams* was sent on a "good will" mission to various ports under Oliver Hazard Perry, whose naval status freed Washington from the embarrassment of accrediting a diplomatic representative. The *Ontario* carried three commissioners to Buenos Aires on her way around the Horn in 1818. The Americans at Valparaiso persuaded her commander to remain there for a while. Their letter of appreciation of his presence resembles many other documents drawn up by American shipmasters and merchants at other Latin-American ports, begging in almost pathetic terms for naval commanders to tarry with them longer. From that time, a regular succession of warships came to the Pacific station as well as others to the Gulf of Mexico and the South Atlantic.

Such assignments were profitable to the commanders, who were able to pocket generous charges for conveying gold and silver on private account. The United States Navy, in order to avoid misunderstandings between royalists and revolutionaries, tried to curb the practice but without much effect. The captain of the *Ontario* was charged by the Chileans with covering "property of the enemies of Chile" when he carried from Peru $201,000 for Astor and other merchants in New York, Boston, and Rio. His successor on that station is said to have made $55,000.

The situation on the West Coast led to an occasion, perhaps the only one, where the Navy abused its presence in those waters. As a result of the effective Chilean blockade of the Peruvian coast in 1821, the price of flour rose abnormally in Peru. Stephen Whitney, a Connecticut-born New York merchant, who had made a fortune in smuggling out cotton during the War of 1812, and three other merchants loaded a merchantman with flour, pork, and white lead for Peru, adding a few naval supplies to give her the protected status of a naval store ship. This was done with the knowledge of a friend of Whitney, Commodore Stewart, commander of the frigate *Macedonian,* which was preparing to sail for the Pacific station. A luckless lieutenant on the *Macedonian* entered into a contract with the merchants, whereby he would accompany the "store ship" to ensure her official character in return for one-fifth of the net profits. With the flour costing $5 a barrel in New York and selling for $24 at Lima, the $24,785 cargo altogether sold for $110,-716; a net profit of $61,823. The lieutenant, upon his return to New York, was courtmartialled and cashiered. An equity action, moreover, in the New York courts cost him his share of the profits by annulling his contract on the ground that, if his actions were part of his normal duties, he was entitled to no compensation, and if they were not, the contract was illegal.

Whereas New York was represented year after year in the Chilean squadron patrolling the West Coast as well as among the blockade runners, its ships and men were more often found among the hunted in the Gulf of Mexico and the waters around Cuba. Here the situation was less clean-cut and finally degenerated into one of the most brutal episodes in maritime history. In these waters it was primarily privateering which soon sank into piracy. The East River shipyards, to be sure, received several lucrative contracts for warships from Colombia and other revolutionary governments, but the "regular" navies were less in evidence than on the West Coast.

Here the North American privateers, with their officers and crews, found a welcome after peace ended their adventurous raiding of British commerce. The various revolutionary governments, lacking adequate vessels and seamen of their own, gladly furnished letters of marque authorizing the seizure of Spanish shipping. Some of these fast little vessels obtained this status without even visiting the countries whose flags they flew. The United States consul at Buenos Aires even sent a batch of blank commissions to his associates in Baltimore, which was more heavily involved than any of the other ports. Its little clippers were noted for their speed and its customs officials seemed strangely apathetic. A letter from Baltimore in 1818 remarked, "Privateers continue coming and going to this port as to their home. Two arrived this week, one of which landed at midnight eight dray loads of gold and silver!"

New York's hands were not entirely clean. Some vessels did not even change their names with their colors. The *True-blooded Yankee,* Captain Jewett, was fitted out at New York and operated under Chilean colors without visiting Chile; she was seizing Spanish vessels near Haiti in 1817. That same year, Ruggles Hubbard, the high sheriff of New York County, sailed south in his brig *Morgiana* to join the nest of freebooters organized under a Scotch adventurer at Amelia Island, whence she soon was operating under Buenos Aires colors. The New York pilot boat *Penguin* had undergone three changes of names and of colors by 1818, becoming the *Pelican* of Jamaica, the *Aquila* of Havana, and finally taking the appropriate name of a more aggressive bird of prey, the *Condor* of Venezuela.

These vessels were licensed to capture Spanish vessels, but according to a New York editor in 1817: "They board and overhaul everything they meet, and the character of the vessel is generally determined by the number of Spanish dollars that may be found aboard. If she has none of these on board, why their *patriotism* will let her run." Some even left the Caribbean to haunt the wine islands and the very coast of Spain, as well as the high seas. The ship *Robert,* for example, owned at New York and bound thither from Liverpool, was overhauled in May, 1818, "by one of these patriot picaroon cruisers." After pouring "a whole broadside of great guns and small arms" into her, they not only robbed her steerage passengers and officers of clothing as well as money, but slashed the rigging and carried off most of the food.

That was mild, however, compared with the practices of the next decade. Congress in 1819 passed legislation designed to curb United States vessels from this privateering. The energetic collector of customs at New York did his best to detain suspicious vessels and the Spanish consuls sought to prosecute offenders under the new law. In 1819, the son of the Spanish consul at New York, a vice-consul himself, brought action against one Robert Goodwin, the black sheep of a good family, for "piracy" but, meeting Goodwin on a New York street, was stabbed to death by him with a sword cane. Gradually most of the vessels and men from the United States withdrew from the business, even at Baltimore. The later freebooters, a mongrel lot, of various nationalities and colors, did not bother with letters of marque or revolutionary colors but became out-and-out pirates. The more ambitious continued to cruise in the long, low black schooners, which were the nightmare of every honest merchant crew sailing southward, but many others operated on a smaller scale with large rowboats or cutters along the coasts of Cuba and Haiti, ready to pounce on any brig or schooner which was unlucky enough to be becalmed in their neighborhood.

Gruesome tales of their atrocities appeared with alarming frequency in the northern papers throughout the 'twenties. Numerous vessels disappeared completely, probably having been treated on the principle that "dead men tell no tales"; in other cases, a solitary survivor brought back a blood-curdling story. Case after case might be cited of pirate ruthlessness, but space prevents their retelling here.

A force of small, fast naval vessels was sent to the Caribbean as early as 1821 to protect commerce, but a mass meeting at New York in 1824 petitioned Congress for still further action. Advertisements in the New York newspapers stated that the New Orleans packets went fully armed as did those from Vera Cruz with their valuable specie cargoes. A pirate plot to seize the steamer *Robert Fulton* when carrying specie from New York to New Orleans is said to have been hatched but it leaked out and a naval vessel convoyed the steamer. Marine insurance rates reflected the constant jeopardy of shipping in those waters. By 1828, according to the Secretary of the Navy in his annual report, the West Indian piracy had been stamped out. Yet the next year the brig *Attentive,* bound from Cuba to New York with a cargo of molasses, sugar, and coffee, was boarded six hours out. According to the one survivor, the second mate who hid in the hold, the captain and then the crew were "one by one . . . butchered in detail."

The brig was scuttled but the mate managed to swim ashore, clinging to a plank.

Occasionally New York had the excitement of the hanging of a captured pirate. In 1824, a sailor walking up Broadway recognized a passing Spaniard as one of a pirate crew who had looted a schooner off the Cuban Coast. He reported it; and the fellow was speedily tried in Federal Court and hanged. A more notorious victim was Charles Gibbs of a respectable Rhode Island family, whose story was included in some of the old anthologies of pirate yarns. He and a confederate were sentenced to death by a Federal judge in 1831 and Gibbs made a lengthy confession of his horrible deeds, including the death at his hands of over a hundred officers, seamen, and passengers, including women. Eager spectators crowded Ellis Island, where a gallows was erected, and hundreds of boats dotted the bay to witness his hanging. That was New York's last direct contact with West Indian piracy.

For years thereafter, however, rumors of long, low piratical schooners haunted the seafarers from New York and other ports. As late as 1837 a pilot's false report that a Philadelphia-Liverpool packet had been seized off the Delaware Capes caused a temporary panic. Collins thereupon advertised that his packets were built almost as strongly as warships and would go armed. Even in 1845, when trouble was brewing with Mexico, the Havre packet *St. Nicholas* reported that she had had to crowd on all sail to escape two low fast brigs which had made suspicious advances.

Returning to normal commercial transactions, we find that the Latin-American trade would amount to more than one-fifth of the total imports and exports of the United States between 1825 and 1860. Yet, strange to say, the trade with the two still-Spanish islands of Cuba and Puerto Rico was to be heavier than the commerce with all the far-flung independent republics. In this trade, as in so many fields, New York was gradually to win the lion's share and to become the chief American market for sugar, coffee, hides, and silver, the leading products of those lands.

From one point of view, this new commerce was simply an extension of the old triangular trade with the British West Indies which had loomed large in New York's trade before the Revolution. It was nothing new to bring sugar and other Caribbean products to New York; the chief difference was in the sources of those wares. In the colonial period, Jamaica, Antigua, Barbados, and the other British islands had generally been the destination of the little New York craft which had headed southward with "corn and cattle" to exchange for sugar, molasses, and rum. Despite British commercial regulations to the contrary, they had sometimes visited the French or Dutch islands, where better bargains might be driven. Jamaica, however, loomed head and shoulders above all others in volume of trade. The Revolution had broken up much of that trade which had been of value both to the New Yorkers and to the sugar planters. For nearly a half century after that, British commercial policy was constantly throwing obstacles in the way of free intercourse between the islands and the United States and this proved a boomerang, as we shall see, for the Yankees found it simple to substitute Cuba for Jamaica in their economy.

Almost as soon as peace came in 1815, an excellent trade was therefore underway with Cuba and certain other parts of the Caribbean, whereas trade with the British colonies was barred or hampered by regulations for the next fifteen years. It also took some time to develop much with Brazil and the war-torn republics of the mainland. A tabulation of the marine news indicates that only nine vessels arrived at New York from the mainland in 1816: three from Rio de Janeiro, three from Buenos Aires, and one from Puerto Cabello on the Spanish Main. In 1820, 10 vessels arrived and in 1821, 16. Thereafter, the increase was rapid as the revolutions succeeded: 52 in 1822, 52 in 1823, 86 in 1824, 111 in 1825. The principal increase in those last two years came from the opening of the ports in Mexico and on the Spanish Main. Altogether during the six years, 1820–25, there were 119 arrivals from Colombia and other parts of the Spanish Main; 79 from Brazil; 65 from Mexico; 39 from Buenos Aires or Montevideo; 14 from Chile or Peru, including six whalers; and five from the Guianas. In addition the trade was heavy with Curaçao, just off the Venezuelan coast, and a busy distributing point for the mainland: 40 vessels arrived from there in 1822 and 1823 alone. By 1825, with the revolutionary wars over, Latin-American trade was ready to settle down to a fairly normal basis and New York moved in to grasp a generous part of the American share in that business.[1]

One great New York house stood head and shoulders above all others in the field by 1830. At first, Leroy, Bayard & Co. and the Griswolds took the lead but soon the primacy passed to G. G. & S. Howland, later Howland & Aspinwall, which developed an ascendancy ri-

[1] See Appendix, vi, viii.

valling that of W. R. Grace & Co. in later days. According to Scoville, who described their business in the 'thirties, they "worked along by degrees, until they got into a very heavy Mexican and West India business," as well as with Venezuela with which they "did the largest business." He adds that their Pacific trade was "an immense concern" with "cargoes valued as high as $250,000" each, and that they "sent out supercargoes with these ships . . . in most cases clerks in the employ of the house." Other houses developed considerable trade with particular regions, such as the DeForests with Buenos Aires, the Aymars with Jamaica and the Virgin Islands, and Peter Hargous with Vera Cruz, as well as Moses Taylor and many other participants in the Cuban trade. No one of them could compare with the Howlands, however, in the volume or wide sweep of their trade in those regions.

The exports which New York offered to Latin America were pretty much the same for most of the different regions, but the imports varied widely. The chief export items were flour, wherever it might be sold, and manufactures, re-exported from England, the Continent, and India, together with an increasing amount of "domestic" textiles.

The Bayard manuscripts contain a memorandum drawn up about 1820, outlining a cargo for the Peruvian market. It lists various sorts of medicine, silk goods, ribbons, shawls, silk hose, Valencia velvet, Windsor chairs, shaving soap, Spanish "segars," Kentucky and Havana tobacco, earthenware, chocolate cups, hams, salmon, butter, lard, candles, boots and shoes, tea, quicksilver, paper, iron, cider, pale ale, red vinegar, New England rum "to be high colored." This bewildering variety resembles Scoville's description of the Howland shipments to the West Coast a decade or so later with "cargoes composed of everything from a cambric needle to a hoop pole" and he gives as lengthy a list with crockery ware and costly shawls along with muskets, steel, and salt: "in fact a country store on a mammoth scale."

Scoville further stated that New York was the only place in the world where such a cargo might be collected, but that superlative is a bit strong in view of London's trade of that day. New York was, however, undoubtedly the chief American entrepôt, with, as the appendix shows, a larger re-export trade in goods imported from other foreign countries than any of its rivals.[1] Part of the cargoes brought from England and the Continent were loaded at New York into brigs and schooners bound for the Caribbean and points southward, just as an-

[1] See Appendix, i, vii, ix.

other part found its way from New York to the cotton ports. An interesting old series of customs ledgers shows that New York did not limit itself to goods imported past Sandy Hook. Wares originally imported at Boston, Philadelphia, and other ports were carried coastwise to New York and thence sent to the Latin regions, while the duties originally paid at the other port were refunded at New York in the form of "drawbacks."

As far as manufactures were concerned, New York was at an obvious disadvantage in comparison with Liverpool and London, for it was pretty much dependent upon England even for its own needs and naturally goods could be shipped more cheaply direct than by a roundabout route. Geography aided New York, to be sure, in the Cuban and other Caribbean markets, but Buenos Aires and Valparaiso were nearly as close to England as they were to New York. At the beginning of our period, moreover, the British were adapting their offerings to the particular demands of the inhabitants, in the same way in which the Germans would be successful a century later. The early British shipments, according to one of the American commissioners sent to Buenos Aires in 1818, had included such articles as skates and warming pans, "but their merchants are now better acquainted with the wants of the inhabitants; ponchos, rugs, saddles, bits, lassos, balls, and, in short, every article formerly supplied by their domestic manufactures are now brought from England." Considering the backward state of American industry, it is not surprising that the British cargoes overshadowed the American at least two to one in value, if not in bulk.

One hope for the American trade lay in the strong liking of the Latin Americans for Continental fabrics, such as German linens and ribbons, silks and gay-colored textiles and shawls from France. Even the British exporters testified at a Parliamentary hearing in 1820 that an assorted cargo of French, Dutch, German, and British manufactures would yield a profit where a purely British one would not. Frequent re-exporting of this sort occurred at New York, as indicated by numerous advertisements in the local newspapers. In 1815, for instance, James G. King, who had not yet advanced from commerce to finance, advertised 15 bales of Flemish linens "of a superior quality, suitable for the Spanish market." Importers from Havre described goods as "adapted to the Mexican market," "suitable for exportation," or "put up with great attention for the southern markets." The ledger for drawbacks for 1835 shows that New York was sending to Latin

America a considerable quantity of the cheap India cotton goods, imported at Boston from Calcutta.

In wares produced in the United States, the Americans were able to compete more successfully. First and foremost came flour, which New York could offer in abundance, and which found a fairly constant market along the Spanish Main, in some of the West Indian islands, and in Mexico. Elsewhere even flour ran into obstacles. Chile soon became self-sufficient and Buenos Aires slowly followed. Restrictive regulations, of course, hampered the old market in the British West Indies. Cuba at one time imposed a tariff of $10 a barrel, nearly double its original cost, in order to provide a market for inferior Spanish flour which paid only $2.50 a barrel in duties. Even in Brazil, which was ready to use large amounts, New York suffered severe competition from Baltimore's choice "Howard Street" flour, which was supposed to stay fresh longer in hot climates.

The same commissioner, who reported upon the British catering to Latin-American needs, pointed out that "furniture, cordage, canvas, naval stores, liquors, and strong black tobacco" would "find a ready sale and . . . bear the duty." All of those items figured in New York's exports year after year.

The furniture trade was a particularly thriving one for New York. Windsor chairs seem to have been in steady demand all over Latin America, but were only a part, naturally, of the output of the Duncan Phyfe, Tweed, and other west-side establishments for this trade.

The carriage makers also did a flourishing business and the bulkiness of their products meant more freight for shipping. James Brewster, a celebrated coachmaker with establishments on Broad Street in New York, and in New Haven, had agencies in various Cuban ports as well as in New Orleans and Charleston. He advertised in 1828 "probably the greatest variety of carriages ever offered for sale in this country, more than twenty different kinds and those calculated for Spanish and other markets." In 1844, C. & A. Beatty built "some splendid omnibuses for service from Havana to a few miles in the country." As Cuban transportation progressed, New York continued to provide the instruments. Richard H. Dana, travelling by train from Matanzas to a near-by plantation in 1859, remarked, "The car I entered had 'Davenport & Co., makers, Cambridgeport, Mass.,' . . . familiarly on its front, and the next had 'Eaton, Gilbert & Co., Troy, N. York.' "

The plantation which he visited had American-made machinery, operated by an American engineer. It was not unique in that respect, for the Novelty Works at New York, we recall, built a large amount of sugar-mill machinery. By that time, American industry had developed to an extent which relieved much of the old dependence upon England and had more to offer beyond furniture and carriages. Colgate and some of the other New York manufacturers of that order had shipped a moderate amount of their soaps for the minority who used such things, and in 1823 one Samuel G. Redmond had advertised "Crimson, blue and green umbrellas, very elegant, and well adapted to the Spanish and South American markets," but by the end of our period the range of offerings had increased tremendously. Locomotives, hardware, domestic cottons, and much else were by then being sent not only to Cuba but also to other Latin lands, while numerous steamboats, built, and engined in the East River, went south under their own power for use in those waters.

One final important article of export was livestock, especially horses and mules for the West Indian islands. These came chiefly from Connecticut and were sometimes shipped directly from New Haven or New London, along with cheese and other local products. In the early years of the period, however, when American vessels were barred from British West Indian ports, the livestock was carried by sloop to New York and there transshipped in British vessels. In January, 1816, for example, the British brig *Martha,* bound from New York to Demarara in British Guiana, with a deckload of horses and with lumber in her hold, went ashore on Sandy Hook and the animals were rescued with difficulty. Later that year, another British brig sailed "with a deckload of horses for Barbados."

In marked contrast to the heterogeneous assortments sent southward, the cargoes brought back to New York consisted chiefly of a few staples. Here again, the Latin-American trade resembled that of the cotton ports, with sugar, coffee, hides, and a few other articles substituted for the cotton.

Sugar and coffee were the two outstanding offerings of the region. In value, they ranked directly after textiles among all the articles imported into the United States. At the beginning of our period, Jamaica, Cuba, and Brazil all produced both sugar and coffee. As time went on, each experienced a marked change. Jamaica dropped quickly from its exalted position and by the end of the period was selling relatively little sugar, coffee, or anything else. Cuba gradually dropped coffee and became the foremost sugar producer of the world. Brazil did exactly the reverse, specializing in coffee until it gained a similar commanding position as a coffee producer.

The sugar cane had been brought from the Mediterranean to America by the first Spaniards; and the Caribbean soon supplanted the Levant as the sugar bowl of the world. This specialization in raising cane had made the West Indian islands the most sought after of old colonial possessions and the flags of half a dozen European nations flew over the various sugar islands.

On all of them, the process of producing sugar was much the same. Negro slaves from the Guinea Coast performed the manual labor, planting, tending, and harvesting the cane, which was generally grown on large plantations. When cut, the cane was run through rollers to extract the juice. A series of processes resulted in a syrup, in which crystallization began. This was placed in large hogsheads with holes in the bottom, through which the important by-product of molasses was allowed to drain off for three or four weeks. The residue in the hogshead was raw brown sugar, known in trade circles as "muscovado." These hogsheads, containing a half ton or so, became the ordinary commercial units. An alternative form of raw sugar was the "clayed" variety, poured into conical pots which, after the molasses had been drained off, were sealed with moist clay. The cones were then packed for shipment in large wooden boxes, which sometimes later saw service as coffins. Havana specialized in this latter clayed variety, which commanded a somewhat higher price than ordinary muscovado.

New York received most of its sugar raw, either as muscovado in hogsheads or clayed in boxes. Some of it was distributed to the retailers in that form, because at the outset the lumpy brown sugar was purchased in large quantity by those who could not afford the refined white sugar. The usual final marketable form, however, was the large cone or loaf which had had further impurities removed in refining. This at first cost much more than the raw sugar from which it was made. Consequently, instead of having it refined in the Caribbean, the New Yorkers, like the British, usually reserved that lucrative process for themselves. Like tanning and the furniture trade, it was an important branch of commerce which led to the growth of industries at New York.

The first sugar refinery in the American colonies is said to have been established at New York in 1730. By 1855 fourteen such plants were located there. They employed more than 1600 hands and produced finished products worth $12,100,000 from raw materials costing $4,500,-000. It is small wonder that comfortable fortunes were amassed by the three generations of Havemeyers, who figure prominently in the refining business, one of them serving three times as Mayor of New York. Gradually the development of the refining process narrowed the price gap between brown and white sugar. By the last years of our period, the Havemeyer plant was producing granulated and lump sugar in addition to the old cones.

The molasses drained from the brown sugar was gathered into hogsheads containing a hundred gallons or so. Most of it was shipped to New York and the other northern ports in that form. Part of it was retailed as molasses, which figured heavily in the diet of the northeastern states, while part of it was distilled into rum. Like sugar refining, this was a process in which New York industry could increase the value of imports before distributing them. In 1860, all the rum was distilled in three states. Massachusetts, where Medford rum was famous, led with 2,300,000 gallons; New York came second with 1,300,000; and Maine third with 450,000. Against that total of some 4,000,000 gallons distilled after importation, only a fifth as much was imported in the form of rum. Most of it came from the old British islands or from St. Croix and the other Danish Virgin Islands, and more than half was brought to New York or near-by New Haven.

For more than a century before our period began, New York, as we know, had been looking to Jamaica and the other British West Indies as the chief source of its sugar supply. On the eve of the Revolution the single island of Jamaica bulked almost as large in the British customs ledgers as did the whole Thirteen Colonies. The Revolution interrupted that trade; at its close there began the restrictive British measures which were partly to exclude the United States for almost half a century from trade with the sugar islands. These regulations were frequently relaxed during the Anglo-French wars and in the last years of Napoleon's sway these islands, temporarily free from competition with French and Spanish Caribbean planters, thrived as never before.

With the coming of peace in 1815, however, that prosperity suddenly gave way to a swift decline from which Jamaica and the others never recovered. The British restrictions returned in full force and for a considerable time during the next fifteen years, Yankee vessels were virtually barred from British Caribbean ports. Britain's remaining North American colonies were unable to fill adequately the role of the lost thirteen in supplying the plantations with food. Slaves actually starved by the hundreds for want of the flour and fish which New York and Boston might so easily have supplied. The British planters, too, went bankrupt by the scores or lost their mortgaged estates, for there were other complications. At the peace, British Guiana, Trinidad, and several other former enemy colonies were brought in to share the privileges of British imperial preference. With their virgin soil, they could raise sugar more cheaply than the old islands. The British abolition of the slave trade in 1807 meant the end of fresh cheap labor reinforcements from the Guinea Coast while Cuba and Brazil were still importing "black ivory." Later, the abolition of slavery throughout the British Empire by Parliamentary decree, effective on the first day of 1834, greatly accelerated the decline of the islands.

In the meantime, England and the United States did not cease their duel of commercial regulations, alternating restrictions and relaxation, until 1830. For a while around 1822, trading was brisk, but it rested on an uncertain basis and was liable to be shut off without warning. On one occasion a revenue cutter turned back a British ship from Jamaica at Sandy Hook, while a New York vessel was seized at Bermuda for violating the regulation against importation in American bottoms, simply because the captain had landed a bonnet purchased in New York at the request of a friend. By 1830, the islands were beginning to pick up what trade they could with New York and other ports when the blow fell—the end of slavery. For a while the Aymars and other New York merchants maintained a fair amount of trade with Jamaica and ran packets to Kingston, but this dwindled to a minor part of New York's Caribbean commerce. Anthony Trollope, visiting that region in 1859, left a striking picture of the dull, hopeless attitude of the old British islands, with their stagnating trade, in contrast with the increasing prosperity of Cuba; the only contented spot in the British possessions was Demarara in Guiana, "a despotism tempered by sugar." In 1772, 47 per cent of the arrivals at New York in foreign trade came from the British West Indies; by 1860, that proportion had dwindled to little more than 1 per cent.

The rise of Cuba was as sudden and spectacular as the decline of Jamaica. Lying athwart the main sea route between New York and the Gulf, it was easy of access and rich in possibilities. Proximity gave the New Yorkers and their neighbors an advantage over British competitors here and they made the most of it. Spain, having relaxed her former rigid colonial restrictions during the Anglo-French wars, never revived them again. If she had, Cuba and Puerto Rico might have broken loose along with Spain's mainland colonies. As it was, the "ever faithful isle" had its occasional mutterings of revolt, while England, France, and particularly the United States talked more than once of annexation. Spain retained Cuba and Puerto Rico by allowing fairly free trade, hampered, to be sure, by high duties and at times made uncomfortable by high-handed officials. In the eyes of the New York sugar merchants, this was a more dependable region than Jamaica, where an Order in Council might stop all trade without warning.

Sugar gained its real ascendancy in Cuba after 1844, when a terrific hurricane uprooted the coffee trees, which had heretofore yielded an important rival export commodity. In a single year, the island's coffee shipments dropped from 18,000,000 pounds to only 1,000,000 and thenceforth remained at that low level. Thereafter sugar became more and more the major item in the economy of Cuba. With tobacco and "segars," it was the mainstay of the island's trade and a powerful lure to the merchants of South Street.

Cuba, while still belonging to Spain, became more and more an economic dependency of the United States in general and of New York in particular. New York added it to its sphere of commercial influence by the same methods it used in the cotton kingdom. New Yorkers, backed by South Street and Wall Street, settled as commission merchants at Havana, Matanzas, and other ports. Some even bought plantations, but anyway they brought the Cuban planters into a state of chronic debt, resembling that of the cotton raisers in Georgia and Alabama. Pledging their coming crop to the commission merchants, the planters were advanced credit wherewith to buy slaves, land, New York-made steam-sugar machinery, and the wide variety of articles "selected for the Spanish market" and shipped south from East River. When some day the great cases of papers of Moses Taylor in the New York Public Library are opened for research, there will be a chance for an illuminating study in the early stages of economic imperialism. That former clerk of the Howlands established himself first as a commission merchant in Cuba; then returned to New York as a sugar importer and operator of Havana packets; and finally became president of the City Bank, an institution which later, as the National City, continued to retain a warm interest in the "Pearl of the Antilles." It was remarked in the mid-'fifties that Taylor paid heavier customs duties every year than any other American save A. T. Stewart, the great dry-goods merchant.

Such commercial relations help to explain the steady stream of brigs and schooners which came and went between Sandy Hook and the Cuban ports. The largest number headed for the Cuban capital, for Havana had one of the finest harbors in that part of the world. It pretty much monopolized the exports of clayed sugar and also shipped cigars by the million. The headquarters for muscovado was Matanzas, even more accessible to shipping from the north and a special center for New York commercial connections. Little coasters gathered a considerable part of the sugar at those central ports, but the vessels from New York and New England were apt to pick up their molasses cargoes at numerous lesser ports. Santiago, the principal port of the south coast, did not figure as heavily in the New York trade, chiefly because it involved a longer, roundabout trip. The Bacardi family, moreover, did not begin until 1862 the manufacture there of that rum which was to make their name world-famous.

Puerto Rico was simply Cuba on a smaller scale. Vessels by the score came from its various ports, San Juan, Guayama, and the rest, with muscovado and molasses. It was the one region in foreign trade during the period where New London and New Haven continued any amount of trade; even here the materials which they received in exchange for horses, cattle, and cheese were brought back to New York in many cases.

There were, of course, other sugar-producing regions in the Caribbean, but none could compare with those two Spanish islands. Of the 211,000 tons imported at New York in 1860, the smashing total of 171,000 came from Cuba; 22,000 from Puerto Rico; 5000 from Brazil; and 3000 from the East Indies. Jamaica's contribution had fallen to 5000, while the other British colonies in the region yielded only 3000 more. In addition, some 15,000 arrived coastwise from Louisiana and other domestic plantations. Just as Cuba stood head and shoulders above rival producers, so New York outclassed the rival ports in sugar imports. The closest runner-up to its 211,000 total was Boston's 44,000, while Philadelphia and Baltimore were tied for third place at 28,000. These quantity figures, and others of the same sort which follow, are based on the calendar year as given in the Chamber of Commerce reports. They consequently do not coincide with the value figures, based on the fiscal year, as tabulated from government reports in the appendix.[1]

It was much the same story with molasses. Of the 8,500,000 gallons imported that year, 6,000,000 came from Cuba and 2,000,000 from Puerto Rico, with the old British sugar islands of Barbados next at 428,000. An additional 2,000,000 arrived coastwise, about half from Louisiana. New York's share of the molasses imports was not as large as in sugar. Of the national total of 31,000,000 gallons, it stood first with 8,500,000; but Portland was a fairly close second at 5,700,-000, received in exchange for hogshead staves. Then came Boston's 5,300,000, some of which went into Medford rum; Philadelphia's 3,200,000; and New Orleans's 2,200,000. Even little Gloucester received 350,000 gallons in exchange for its codfish.

Coffee stood next to sugar in importance as an article of importation; and coffee, as time went on, meant Brazil. The three trade names of Mocha, Java, and Rio sum up briefly the story of the expansion of the coffee trade. Back in the Middle Ages, coffee started in Arabia and became a favorite drink among the Turks. The Dutch later carried it to their spice islands where it flourished in Java, Sumatra, and some of the others. In the early years of our period, New York imported a good deal of "Java," but gradually attention centered in the regions closer at hand. Coffee plants had been brought to the Caribbean around 1700, where they grew well on many of the islands. The rich French colony of Haiti produced a tremendous amount under its old regime; but when the Negro insurrection wiped out the old planter society, many of the émigrés went to Cuba, where coffee flourished until the hurricane of 1844. Jamaica likewise had been a leading center of coffee production until it underwent the same dismal decline as sugar after 1815.

It has been remarked that in the seventeenth century, coffee was regarded as a medicine; in the eighteenth, it was the drink of the fashionable and the intellectual; and in the nineteenth century, it "went democratic." Some nations became heavier coffee drinkers than others. England, steeped in love of tea, was cold to coffee; but France, Germany, northern Europe, and above all the United States developed a

[1]See Appendix, x.

NEW YORK FROM GOVERNORS ISLAND IN 1846

The Battery is shown in the center background, with the Hudson River on the left and the East River on the right

big demand for it. This taste was steadily increasing as our period gained headway.

As it did so, Brazil came on the scene as the world's leading producer. The initial successful experiments there dated from about 1770; and the first cargo of Brazilian coffee reached the United States in a ship arriving at Salem in 1809. The new "empire" of Brazil, under a scion of the old Portuguese royal house, had achieved its independence with less violence than did the Spanish-American lands, so that trade, stimulated by a liberal policy, was not seriously interrupted.

Southern Brazil was admirably suited for raising coffee. There was plenty of land in the requisite moderately high altitudes, with the best kind of soil for the purpose, while Brazil, like Cuba, was one of the few regions still importing slaves. The planters had some trouble and expense in carrying to the coast the bags, which contained 150 pounds or so of the "green" coffee beans, but once the bags arrived there, vessels of many nations were ready to carry them away.

The Brazilian coffee trade centered almost exclusively at Rio de Janeiro. New York vessels picked up hides and other commodities at the other Brazilian ports—Para at the mouth of the Amazon, Maranham (Maranhão), Pernambuco, and San Salvador (Bahia)—but Rio remained the world's coffee port until at the end of the century the hitherto neglected and unhealthy port of Santos sprang into prominence.

Rio's harbor, one of the most beautiful in the world, was both convenient and commodious; but the New Yorkers found Havana a much better place for trading. At Rio, they encountered a double rivalry which reduced to a negligible amount the demand for those New York offerings which the Cuban ports accepted in generous quantities. England furnished a lion's share of Brazil's imports, as we know, while the French sent several times as much as the United States, whose flour alone was taken in any amount. Even in flour, we recall, Baltimore was favored over New York in these hot climates. As a result Baltimore often throughout the period gave New York a close run in coffee importations and New York was faced with a decidedly unfavorable balance of trade with Rio. According to the report of the United States consul there in 1835, which shows in minute detail the cargoes of American vessels entering and leaving that port, many vessels bringing coffee to New York returned with flour from the Chesapeake rather than from the East River. Twenty vessels, which arrived

at Rio direct from New York, brought cargoes averaging only $17,-
500 in value, five having come in ballast. Those same vessels carried
back coffee cargoes worth $70,000; but the extreme case was the ship
Cowper, which arrived in ballast from New York and carried back a
$120,000 load of coffee. The coffee had to be paid for by juggling
trade balances with other parts of the world, or in specie. On more
than one occasion, it was charged that New Yorkers were trying to
rectify the situation by carrying kegs of counterfeit coin to Rio!

Trade conditions were rather better for New York in the ports
of the Spanish Main, which offered a somewhat better grade of coffee
than Rio, though far below it in quantity. The Venezuelan ports of
LaGuaira, Puerto Cabello, and Maracaibo had a steadily increasing
amount of good coffee, once the revolutionary wars were over. They
were ready, too, to take New York's flour and other commodities in
exchange. The Howlands enjoyed a strong position in the Venezuelan
trade through the favor of President Paez. The coffee of Costa Rica,
which later would command a high price, had scarcely begun to
reach the United States at the end of our period.

Slightly surpassing the combined output of the ports of the Spanish
Main in volume were the coffee exports of Negro Haiti. In the eighteenth century, it will be recalled, the flourishing sugar and coffee
trade of Haiti had made it the richest of the Antilles. After the Negro
revolt and the flight of those planters who had escaped massacre, the
island remained in black hands. For a while it was governed by the
bizarre self-styled emperors and gradually became a Negro republic.
The smaller former Spanish colony of Santo Domingo at the other end
of the island was united with Haiti for about twenty-five years of our
period and thereafter was an independent republic, much less important commercially than Haiti. The Negroes were averse to the strenuous work of sugar planting, which virtually disappeared. The tending
of the coffee trees was apparently more congenial labor. The old plantations were broken up into small holdings, which produced a considerable supply, excellent in flavor but graded and packed with such
lack of uniformity that it sold at the lowest price in the New York
market. With that coffee, together with a fair amount of mahogany
and dyewoods, the Haitians were able to pay for a moderate amount
of flour, textiles, and other imports. A few American and other foreign commission merchants established themselves in the ports and
brigs and schooners carried on a steady, if not impressive, business with

Port-au-Prince, Cap Haitien (the former Cap François), Jeremie, Jacmel, Gonaives, Aux Cayes (whence it is said the expression O.K. originated) and Santo Domingo.

Of the 72,000,000 pounds of coffee imported at New York in 1860, Rio had a long lead with 46,000,000. Then came Haiti with 10,000,-000 and Venezuela with 7,600,000, three-quarters of which came from Maracaibo. Jamaica sent 2,600,000, while the total from Costa Rica and New Grenada (Colombia) was only 500,000. Java and Sumatra, which had once furnished a relatively much heavier proportion, sent 1,500,000, which was topped by 1,700,000 from the new Ceylon supply. In 1860, Rio and Venezuelan coffee commanded an almost equal price at $13.69 and $13.83 a hundred pounds respectively, while Java fetched $16.15 and Haitian coffee trailed at $12.39. Two years earlier, however, "Maracaibo and Laguayra" were rated at $12.04 when Rio was only $10.96.

Whereas New York handled nearly two-thirds of the nation's sugar imports in 1860, it attracted less than half of the coffee. Of the national total of 1,259,000 bags, New York received 510,000. Second place went to New Orleans at 284,000, chiefly for the westerners who drank little except Rio. Baltimore's 243,000 was a drop from its earlier proportion which had once rivalled New York's. Philadelphia and Boston received 102,000 and 86,000 bags, respectively.

Unlike sugar and hides, coffee offered New York little extra profit from industrial processing. A moderate amount was roasted at the port before distribution but most of it was sold by the wholesale grocers to the retailers in the "green" state.

Hides, the raw material of boots, shoes, and saddlery, were the third major offering of the Latin lands. Though the national coffee imports were worth about double the hide imports, New York's share of the latter trade was so heavy that the port's hide receipts were worth almost as much as its coffee. New York State made extra profit by tanning the hides into leather, an industry in which it led the nation; and the finished product resulted in still further trade for the port.

The quest for hides took New York vessels far afield to dozens of scattered ports all along the coasts of Latin America. Whereas sugar production involved a large capital outlay in lands, slaves, and machinery, hides could be furnished by regions in a primitive stage of economic development. The wild cattle which roamed the pampas of the Argentine and many other regions were to be had pretty much for the catching. From them came not only the hides, but additional marketable products such as horns, tallow, and smoked beef. It was with such offerings that many ports were able to pay for what they wanted from foreign lands. During the initial boom of British enthusiasm for Latin-American trade, an English company collected a generous amount of capital for the project of sending milkmaids to the Argentine in order to produce cheese from the wild cows. The venture is said to have ended unfortunately for the milkmaids as well as for the investors. While that additional source of income from Latin America's bovine wealth never materialized, the other products were the basis of a prosperous trade. As early as 1817, Buenos Aires alone is said to have shipped out a million hides worth about three dollars apiece, while the other products from those same cattle were worth another three million.

Buenos Aires and Montevideo, facing each other across the broad estuary of the Rio Plata, were the chief centers of this trade. Their hinterland was splendid cattle country and the climate made it a "white man's country," too. Millions of cattle roamed the flat, treeless, prairielike pampas, "a boundless, silent sameness," and thousands of gauchos or cowboys rounded them up for market. Many foreign merchants resided in the two ports, with the Englishmen outnumbering the Americans, since England was almost as close as New York; and as we know, the British enjoyed here as at Rio the bulk of the importing business.

New York, however, had a heavy demand for those Plata hides. The South Street house of the DeForests made a specialty of the business. For a while they ran brigs as regular traders between New York and Buenos Aires. The conventional return cargo was several thousand dried or salted hides, weighing twenty-odd pounds apiece, sometimes accompanied by casks of horns. New York had little use for the tallow and even less for the dried jerked beef, but its transients often made extra profits by carrying it to Havana or other Caribbean ports where such food was eaten.

The Plata ports by no means monopolized the hide supply. Scores of New York schooners worked their way up the Orinoco into Venezuela to take on cargoes at Angostura. Others found hides waiting their coming at the lesser Brazilian ports all the way from Para down to Rio Grande. Dozens of other places in Latin America sent a few hundred or a few thousand each year. Readers of *Two Years Before the Mast* recall Dana's vivid picture of the primitive methods of sliding hides down the steep banks to the shore out in California in the 'thirties; but Dana was in a Boston brig and New York only occasionally sought hides on the far side of Cape Horn until after California came into the Union.

While coffee outranked hides two to one in value among the nation's imports, the two were almost equal at New York. More than two-thirds of the national hide importations arrived past Sandy Hook, while Boston received most of the remainder. Almost a million hides were imported at New York in 1860 and an additional three-quarters of a million came from domestic sources. Buenos Aires led with 263,-000 and Montevideo sent 82,000 more. Brazil furnished about 150,000, and the Orinoco nearly as many. About half of the domestic supply came from the former Spanish lands of Texas and California.

That trade helped to make New York the leader of the nation's leather industry. Boston might be the center of the boot and shoe industry, but more hides were tanned into leather with the help of hemlock and other bark in the "Swamp" at New York and elsewhere in the state, than any other part of the Union; and the value of the hides was nearly doubled in that process. Much of the finished leather was carried coastwise to Boston; some was used at Newark and again found its way southward from New York in the form of boots, shoes, saddlery, and the like. The port thus reaped several profits from the cargoes of hides it had fetched from those distant sources.

Three other products deserve mention. The habits of the male population of the city were affected most by the millions of "segars" brought annually from Havana—sometimes a million came by a single packet. Good ones cost only three cents apiece in New York and the young men carried a handful of them in special linings inside their hats. There were many newspaper references early in the period to their annoying habit of blowing smoke in the face of passing women; but foreign observers found that less disgusting than the target practice with quids of native Virginia or Kentucky tobacco. New York imported 243,000,000 cigars in 1860, more than half the national supply, and valued at only a cent apiece wholesale.

Part of the silver from the famous mines of Mexico found its way to New York as soon as the fighting quieted down around 1825. Until then, a moderate amount was shipped from Tampico or Alvarado, but after that Vera Cruz was the outlet. The Mexican market absorbed a large quantity of New York's conventional offerings, from flour to gay-colored textiles, carriages, and Windsor chairs. By that means, the port could acquire casks of coined "dollars Mex" for its needs in the trade with Canton and other ports, which had little use for its commodity offerings. Edward K. Collins, we recall, started his conspicuous career as a shipping operator with a line of fast, armed packets to Vera Cruz in 1827. Outward bound, they carried heterogeneous cargoes; on their return, the shipping news usually mentioned simply "specie and cochineal." Part of the Mexican output was carried to New Orleans, whence some of it found its way to New York by the coastal packets during their dull season. Relatively little silver came from Potosi or the other old mines of Peru.

The last major item worthy of notice came on the scene later than the others. Not until about 1845 did New York really become conscious of guano, but thereafter it came with a rush. Guano was the old Peruvian word for manure. It was the collected droppings of countless generations of sea birds and it made one of the most potent of natural fertilizers. Some of the first guano came from the island of Ichaboe, off the South African coast; the island being nearly half shovelled away in the course of six months. A far more permanent and prominent supply was located on the Chinchas Islands, off the southern coast of Peru. Quantities began to reach the United States, and farmers gradually became convinced of its value. Here, as at Rio, Baltimore gave New York a close run; and at times led the country in guano imports, for its adjacent agricultural regions used much of it. As time went on, clippers, which could not negotiate a return trip from San Francisco by way of Canton, reluctantly came home around the Horn, with their holds full of dirty cargoes picked up at the Chinchas.

The trade was not regarded as wholly respectable for a while. During the first burst of interest in the new fertilizer in the mid-'forties, the *Herald* printed the alleged plea of Mrs. Parvenue for her husband to withdraw from the guano trade; she had tried to impress people that he was an importer of teas and silks by the shipload, only to have little daughter come home from school taunted with her father being a manure dealer!

Almost simultaneously with the first guano cargoes, a rival fertilizer began to arrive from that same region. In September, 1845, the bark

Childe Harold brought "2294 bags nitrate of soda to E. Bartlett" in 97 days from Arica, lying near the border between Peru and Chile. The Chilean nitrate did not get off to as quick a start as the Peruvian guano, but it remained longer as a prominent article of commerce. Aside from that, arrivals from the West Coast were infrequent before '49, except for occasional whalers or copper cargoes from Chile and sometimes vessels from Mazatlan on the western coast of Mexico.

Many lesser commodities were, of course, brought to New York from the Latin and Caribbean regions. In the days before the Germans perfected their chemical dyes, logwood, fustic, Nicaragua wood, and other dyestuffs from various island and mainland Caribbean ports were in steady demand. Mahogany came from Cuba and Santo Domingo. The pioneer schooner loads of oranges from Florida were overshadowed by more numerous shipments from the islands, while a few, but only a few, bunches of bananas now and then came from Cuba. Just outside the Caribbean, Turks Island and Ragged Key in the Bahamas were among the most constant sources of imported salt. The turtles from the Bahamas, too, meant turtle soups for the gourmands. That by no means exhausts the list, though it has doubtless long since exhausted the reader.

The Caribbean and Latin commerce as a whole had a few distinctive characteristics. Probably in no other branch of New York's commerce might the phrase "venture" be as truly used as for the cargoes sent hopefully southward. The British and European markets were well organized and the packets brought fresh information; the tea trade at Canton was likewise well co-ordinated. Each little Caribbean port, however, had its own particular situation. There was no telling whether an arriving schooner would find an empty market, with flour selling at $15 or $20 a barrel, or whether it had been so glutted by the coming of other brigs and schooners that the cargo could scarcely be given away. The marine news consequently recorded scores of clearances for "West Indies," "Spanish Maine," or "South America," rather than for some particular island or port. With such roving commissions, the schooners or brigs were able to try out port after port until they found the one, if any, where the cargo might be disposed of to best advantage. The old logs at the Essex Institute contain detailed records of many such transient voyages. Sometimes it was necessary to go in ballast from port to port, hoping to find a chance to carry horses from some South American port out to the islands or to take jerked beef in the same direction. In no other field of New York trade were conditions as irregular.

To catch the full flavor of New York's commerce with the Latin lands, one can do no better than to dip into the *Voyages* of Captain George Coggesshall. Born in Milford, Connecticut, he went to sea as a boy; by the time he was twenty-five, in 1809, he was a captain. From then until after 1840, he made, generally from New York, a constant series of transient voyages, interrupted only by lively privateering in the War of 1812. Unlike the work of those other captains who plied regularly between New York and Liverpool or Canton, scarcely two of Coggesshall's "tramp" voyages were identical, as the summary in the appendix will indicate.[1] Though he occasionally crossed the Atlantic, most of his trading was concentrated in the Caribbean and Latin America, all the way from Havana and Matanzas around to Valparaiso and Callao. He recounts shipboard experiences, on everything from sloops up to full-rigged ships, but there are plenty of other marine narratives for that purpose. His unique contribution lies in the full account of the cargoes he carried, the profits which he made, the ports which he visited, and numerous similar details which are ordinarily difficult to find. His business experiences ranged from dealings with the big commission houses at Havana and Rio down to peddling cargoes retail in little ports of the Spanish Main. His compensation ranged from a meager salary in Howland employ up to generous profits when he sailed and traded "on his own." One seven-month voyage from New York to the Cape Verdes, Rio, New Orleans and back yielded a net profit of $10,000. Numerous travellers' tales describe the major ports of the region, but here one may also find the second- and third-rate ones as well, with the added value of excellent descriptions of the business methods employed at each. As if all that were not enough, he gives good thumbnail sketches of the passengers he carried, of the pirates he escaped, and of revolutionary executions which he witnessed. If one started quoting from him, there would be no stopping—the best we may do is to recommend him highly as first-rate collateral reading.

The trade also had its distinctive atmosphere; a combination of glamor and squalor. The journal of one young captain at Havana tells proudly of donning his best whites to go ashore; and the picture arises of moonlight, señoritas, guitars, and all that sort of thing. Then a

[1]See Appendix, xxiii.

vivid passage in Joel Poinsett's journal shows a miserable night in an inn at Tampico, listening to the last hours of a Yankee sea captain dying of yellow fever in the next room. The region offered abundant experiences of both kinds. It also held the threat, which the other trading zones did not, of hurricanes around the end of summer. Marine insurance rates were usually jumped one-fourth in those waters during those months, for there was real danger. The hurricane, which nearly wiped out the coffee plantations of Cuba, left a terrific toll in the shipping in Havana harbor and elsewhere in the island.

All those elements, then, were involved in that commerce: uncertainty, glamor, disease, and hurricane. But with all that, sugar, coffee, hides, silver, and the rest came in a steady stream northward past Sandy Hook throughout the period. And they played their part in making New York the chief American exchange of the world's commodities.

CHAPTER X

DISTANT SEAS

LOOK at the customs ledgers and you find the Atlantic shuttle overshadowing all other sea lanes from New York. Glamor, however, dwells more upon those routes plowed by fewer keels but leading to ports less prosaic than Liverpool or Havre. Tea and silks from Canton, coffee from Samarang, ivory from the Guinea Coast, or sealskins from bleak islands off Cape Horn might leave New York merchants less rich in pocket than Manchester calicoes or Sheffield penknives, but they made the old merchant marine far richer in legend. Massachusetts showed valiant initiative in those far-flung adventures and has laid claim to the "Salem East Indies," but vessels from New York blazed the trail to the Orient and sooner or later the ships and brigs returning from those distant wanderings set their course for Sandy Hook.

The old China trade, of course, held an easy first place among those centrifugal activities. Its cargoes of Bohea and Hyson tea were, ship for ship, as precious as any which entered the nation's ports, although in volume they did not approach the profits from the busy traffic of the Atlantic shuttle. Those cargoes from the Orient with their origin in the remote and aloof land of the mandarins appealed strongly to the imagination. They suggested wealth, for it took abundant capital to figure prominently in that distant trade. The little brigs from Rio and the Spanish Main, ministering to the American preference for coffee, piled up as impressive a total in the import registers, but they and those who sent them have failed to capture the popular fancy as did the ships and men bound for China. Writer after writer has told of this old China trade but some aspects of New York's participation deserve their place in any history of the port.

The story starts immediately after the Revolution. The old colonial system, under which New York and its rival ports had carried on a flourishing business, was knocked askew. After fighting for eight years to be free from the political implications of membership in the British Empire, the Americans were indignant at being deprived of the economic privileges which went with such membership. A substitute had to be found for the old swapping of flour for sugar in the British West Indies, from which Yankee vessels were now barred. Of the various innovations suggested, the most promising was that of sailing halfway around the world to Canton.

It was under such conditions that the *Empress of China* set sail from New York for the first American voyage to China on February 22, 1784, barely three months after the British had evacuated the port. While New York was the starting-point and terminus of that voyage, it cannot claim the complete credit. Robert Morris, the financier of the Revolution, was among the Philadelphians who owned the 360-ton ship, which had been built at Boston, whence came several of the personnel. Financial backing for the venture came from all three ports.

She traced the route which would become familiar to the scores of American vessels following in her tracks. Cutting down across the North Atlantic and South Atlantic, past St. Helena, which was then only a name, and the Cape of Good Hope, she crossed the Indian Ocean, past Mauritius and Ceylon. Then, by some minor miracle, considering the crude navigating devices of the day, she passed Java Head and the Straits of Sunda, the bottle-neck where Malay pirates for years to come would lurk to waylay any vessel unlucky enough to be becalmed. Thence her course led on through the China Sea, luckily avoiding numerous hidden reefs as yet uncharted, until she finally arrived at Canton, the one port in all China where trade was tolerated with the outsiders. The French, the Danes, and even the recently hostile British extended every courtesy at this first showing of the Stars and Stripes in Far Eastern waters. With her cargo finally swapped for tea and the other conventional offerings of Canton, the *Empress* retraced her course around Good Hope. Nearly fifteen months after she had set out, she slid in past Sandy Hook with a cargo which yielded a profit of $30,000, a return of 25 per cent upon the capital hazarded in the venture.

The second American voyage to Canton was also despatched from New York. In many ways it was an even more audacious episode, for it was undertaken in the tiny *Enterprise,* a sloop of only 84 tons! The gods were good, however, and she, too, was back in a year or so with a cargo which returned an even higher rate of profit.

All that had occurred thirty years before our period proper opens. During the intervening years several other ports had crowded into this trade opened by the vessels from New York. Boston, Salem, Providence, Philadelphia, and Baltimore all participated, while occasionally a lesser port might send a vessel or two.

The major problem in those early years was to find an outward cargo acceptable to the Chinese in return for the desired tea, silks, and chinaware. A few kegs of Spanish "pillar dollars" would answer the purpose best, but that tied up a considerable amount of capital, and public opinion resented such a drain at a time when specie was scarce. There was little that the self-sufficient Chinese wanted in the way of outside commodities, but Yankee ingenuity found a few ways to relieve, if not to obviate, the demand for silver. The *Empress of China* and the *Enterprise* had carried out a large quantity of a root which grew wild in the Hudson valley and elsewhere, resembling the ginseng to which the Chinese ascribed great powers in restoring vigor to old men. It sold well but soon the business was overdone. Furs met with more permanent success, for they were welcome in the unheated houses during the cold winters of northern China. By 1790, it was discovered that furs of the sea otter could be secured cheaply from the Indians of the Northwest Coast in exchange for trinkets. Boston, however, monopolized most of that early trade, as it did the carrying of sandalwood from Hawaii to Canton. Around 1815, experiments showed that cotton goods, either American or British, might find a market even in the country which exported cheap nankeens of that material. British commercial bankers, like the Barings, made it possible to pay at Canton with drafts which could be met by shipments of American cotton to Liverpool.

As time went on, China, which had once sent its cheap nankeens to New York, took more and more cotton cloth of domestic American manufacture in return. Philip Hone, referring to the maiden sailing of the exquisite new clipper *Rainbow* for Canton on February 1, 1845, remarked upon her cargo of American manufactures as a "strange revolution in trade."

> The same articles which we formerly imported from China, and for which nothing but dollars would pay, are now manufactured here at one third the cost, and sent out to pay for teas. The difficulty now is to find

sufficient returns for the American cargoes. We do not send them specie
—not a dollar."

The quest for furs, in the meantime, had given rise to some colorful episodes in connection with the China trade. One of New York's
outstanding figures in the early commerce with Canton was John Jacob
Astor, to whom it was simply part of his larger business in furs. He
had despatched his first ship in 1800, sending some of the pelts which
had been gathered by his far-flung system and brought overland to
New York. His tough and long-lived *Beaver,* built in 1805 and of
which we have already heard on the West Coast of South America,
paid for herself several times over by an impudent ruse. At the time
when the embargo was prohibiting all American ships from making
foreign voyages, New York was amazed to see the *Beaver* clear and
sail for Canton. Astor had received permission from President Jefferson, in the interest of "international comity," to carry home a distinguished "mandarin" stranded in this country. Amazement gave
way to indignation when it developed that the "mandarin" was a very
ordinary Chinaman dressed up for the purpose and envy was well
mixed with admiration when the *Beaver* returned with a profit of
$200,000 from a voyage in which all American competition had been
legally debarred.

At the same time, Astor decided to invade the Northwest fur field
where the Bostonians had been very prominent. He planned to build
on a more permanent basis than they had, by planting at the mouth
of the Columbia River a settlement which would serve as an outlet for
the furs of the interior and also, in Astor's dream, as the nucleus of
a great American colonization on the Pacific. This Astoria, of which
Washington Irving has written in such graphic detail, encountered
misfortunes which soon ended its existence. Natives massacred the
crew of the *Tonquin* which Astor had sent out with supplies from New
York and the War of 1812 gave the *coup de grâce* to what might
otherwise have been a great success. At the threatened approach of a
British frigate, Astor's representatives sold out to their Scottish rivals.
The liquidation of this episode lasted down into our period, for the
Beaver, which had carried men and supplies out to Astoria in 1811
and then picked up furs for China, had lain idle in Canton during the
war, and arrived back at New York in March, 1816, with a valuable
cargo of china, cassia, and silks in addition to teas "selected and des-

tined for the Holland market." Meanwhile hardy Connecticut mariners, often operating from New York, were killing seals for the Canton market down in the Cape Horn region.

With the return of peace, the trade settled down to a more purely business basis. Astor continued for a while in the activity, but for the time being he was overshadowed in the field by the meteoric rise and fall of Thomas H. Smith, a spectacular plunger who during the early 'twenties carried on most of New York's Canton trade. He was aided in this operation by the government policy of allowing eighteen months in which to pay the heavy duties, thus releasing capital for still more cargoes. Finding that the collector of customs at New York was rather rigid in the extension of credit, Smith built wharves and huge warehouses at Perth Amboy which was ever ready to lure business away from its big rival by relaxing the regulations, whether in customs, quarantine, or immigration. Smith's ships turned sharply to the westward upon reaching Sandy Hook, instead of continuing through the Narrows. In the marine news of arrivals, there occasionally appeared such items as "Sloop *Hobert,* Seguine, from Amboy, with teas to T. H. Smith & Son." Together with one Thompson at Philadelphia, Smith overdid the Canton business until the market became hopelessly glutted in 1826. The price of tea dropped so sharply that he went into bankruptcy, owing the government three millions in unpaid duties.

For a while, his failure gave a setback to the business. The house of N. L. & G. Griswold brought in numerous cargoes from Canton as part of their manifold activities, but as an individual specialist in the China trade, Smith's most conspicuous successor was his former subordinate and agent at Canton, Daniel Washington Cincinnatus Olyphant. He formed the firms of Talbot, Olyphant & Co. at New York and D. W. C. Olyphant & Co. at Canton.

· Out at Canton, such permanent American commercial houses were beginning to replace the old practice of sending a business man, called a "supercargo," in each ship to handle the business on arrival. As a result, there was a group of commercial exiles cooped up in the foreign settlement, rigidly restricted from contacts with the city at large, and forbidden to bring foreign women ashore. These were generally young bachelors, who normally planned to make their fortunes in a few years before returning home. There is no need here to go into the familar story of the general setup of business relations at Canton, with the foreigners permitted to deal only through a small group of officially appointed "hong" merchants, who were responsible for the conduct of the outsiders—a group of men most of whose names ended in "qua" and of whom old Houqua was the particular favorite of the Americans.

Foremost among the Americans at Canton was the house of Russell & Co., organized in 1823 by Samuel Russell of Boston. It was customary for a number of young men, especially from Boston and New York, to serve as partners in this house. In many cases, they were related to the importers at Boston or New York, who threw their business to the company. Partnership in this company was the basis of many seaboard fortunes. Prominent among the young New Yorkers who served in this capacity was John Clive Green, born near Trenton. He started at New York with the Griswolds, married George Griswold's daughter, and after serving as supercargo on several of their ships for ten years, became a Russell partner. He had risen to be the head of the house and president of the new American Chamber of Commerce at Canton, when the opium troubles broke out in 1839. He came home with a comfortable fortune, joined forces with another former Russell partner in taking over the Michigan Central Railroad, and eventually amassed several millions, part of which he used as the principal benefactor of Princeton in the nineteenth century. A later Russell partner was Warren Delano, Jr., from New Bedford, whose brother was a partner in Grinnell, Minturn & Co., of New York. By his day, the prohibition on foreign women was removed, and he was joined at Canton for a while by his daughter, Sarah, who would later marry a Roosevelt and be the mother of a President.

If Russell & Co. transacted the largest business, the house of Olyphant played the most unique role at Canton. Olyphant was an extremely religious man and threw his influence wherever possible in the support of missionary efforts, so that the firm's quarters became known as "Zion Corner." Several missionaries were carried out free of charge in Olyphant's ships, including one from New York who served as chaplain to the American community and the sailors at Canton. He also supported the publication of the *China Repository*, a collection of information about the country. Charles W. King, a silent partner of Olyphant, resided at Canton from 1826 to 1845, in charge of the business there, except for three years back at New York. With some missionaries, he participated in an unsuccessful effort to open relations with Japan in 1837. With the return of several ship-

wrecked Japanese sailors as an excuse, they sailed in the Olyphant ship
Morrison, named for a prominent missionary, but were fired upon at
two Japanese ports and returned without accomplishing their objective.

The house of Olyphant, alone among the foreigners at Canton, sacrificed an opportunity for much additional profit by abstaining from
the traffic in opium. A moderate amount of this had been picked up in
the Levant and carried to Canton by American ships earlier in the period; but the real opportunity came in 1834 with the abolition of the
East India Company's monopoly of the trade between China and India.
India was the principal source of the drug, which the Company had
been selling for some time. At last, here was something adequate as a
substitute for specie, even though its importation was contrary to Chinese law. Smuggling was easy and the East River shipyards in New
York turned out some of the fast little schooners used for bringing it
into China. This profitable situation lasted for five years, but, in 1839,
the Chinese Government sent to Canton a commissioner who meant
business. A huge amount of opium, practically all in British hands,
was confiscated. The British merchants withdrew in protest but the
Americans stayed on and for a while their ships made more money
than ever in carrying tea down to the British. The situation, as every
one knows, led to the "Opium War" in which British arms were successful in forcing a wide breach in the old regulations. Not only were
most of the old restrictions removed at Canton, but several "treaty
ports" were opened to foreign trade. Foremost among these was
Shanghai in northern China, which gradually overtook Canton in the
volume of foreign trade. The Americans soon took advantage of these
same terms, but Canton was an easy leader in the arrivals at New
York until well into the fifties.

Even before that, most of the China cargoes were making their way
to Sandy Hook. In 1815, several other ports equalled or exceeded
New York in the volume of this trade. The New York newspapers
carried advertisements stating that the cargo of a ship just arrived
from Canton would be auctioned at Providence, Boston, or Philadelphia. New York, however, developed so rapidly as an entrepôt where
goods of almost every sort could be sold to best advantage that vessels
which had sailed to Canton from Boston, Providence, or Philadelphia
generally put into New York to dispose of their cargoes. The major
profits still went to the owners in the outside cities but the customs

figures showed a constantly increasing proportion of the China trade arriving at New York until, by the end of our period in 1860, its tea imports amounted to $8,315,000 out of a national total of $8,915,000. The value of the tea imports had barely doubled in the course of forty years, while the total imports of all commodities had made a twenty-fold gain; so that the relative importance of the China trade was much less in the later days than it had been in the beginning, when it amounted to nearly one-third of the total.

During the 'thirties, there was no particular concentration of the China trade in the hands of a single house at New York. Olyphant did a respectable business as a specialist, but so, too, did the great general houses of Howland & Aspinwall as well as the Griswolds, whose succession of ships named *Panama,* according to Scoville, made "Panama teas" a byword among the grocers. One bizarre and short-lived innovation in the field was the reproduction of French goods at Canton by two New York brothers named Carnes. They had cheap imitations of numerous articles turned out at very small cost by the Chinese but, as so often happened, they overdid the business and soon withdrew.

By the 'forties, the house of Low began to assume leadership among the South Street importers of Chinese products. The elder Seth Low had moved his East Indian drug business from Salem to New York and in 1834 had been advertising a large assortment of such things as "Mocha gum arabic, Bombay arrowroot, musk in pods, asafœtida, gum benzoin" and the like. His son, Abiel A., a Russell partner at Canton for a while, went further. In co-operation with several brothers, he made the name of A. A. Low & Bros. foremost in the China trade. One brother resided for a while in Canton as a member of Russell & Co., who handled that end of the Low's business.

The new firm, together with the Howlands, were active in developing the China clippers for faster service on the run. The older ships had seldom made the trip from Canton to New York in less than a hundred days, even in the early months of the year when the winds were most favorable. They generally sailed from China in January and arrived pretty much in a group early in April. Out of season, the trip lasted much longer and there was one case of a ship which took 174 days, but she was headed for Philadelphia. The era of fast trips dated, perhaps, from the 91-day run of a discarded Liverpool packet, the *Silas Richards,* in 1837. "This is, we believe," wrote one New York newspaper, "one of the shortest voyages on record." Then, Howland &

Aspinwall's *Natchez,* a one-time New Orleans packet, began to lower that record under Captain Robert H. Waterman, one of the most celebrated or notorious "drivers" of the period, finally achieving a 78-day record in 1845.

In the meantime, some fast new ships were being built especially for the run. Back in 1843, William H. Low, the family's representative in Russell & Co., was returning from Canton in one of the Low ships under Captain Nathaniel B. Palmer, possibly New York's most outstanding mariner. In the course of the long trip, Palmer outlined to Low his ideas concerning designs for a really fast ship intended for the trade. In view of the high value of the cargo and the extra prices which early arrivals commanded, carrying space could be sacrificed to speed. The Lows ordered a ship on those lines to be built in one of the best East River yards, named her the *Houqua* after the highly esteemed old hong merchant, and gave her command to Palmer. At almost the same time, Howland & Aspinwall departed from their usual practice of using second-hand ships and ordered the *Rainbow* from another yard, which employed the services of New York's first noted specialist in ship designing. Then, as a reward for his fast work in the old *Natchez,* Howland & Aspinwall had the *Sea Witch* built for Waterman and under his vigorous command, she set up a remarkable record for speed. The Lows then built the *Samuel Russell* for Palmer and the era of the "China Clipper" was on, a prelude to the still more spectacular era of the California clipper.

Some of these China clippers of the 'forties, as a matter of fact, were in a position to increase their earnings radically by taking advantage of the gold rush to California before the later and greater ships designed especially for that run were launched. Until 1848, most of the ships had followed the initial track of the *Empress of China* by way of the Cape of Good Hope to Canton. The alternate route by way of Cape Horn had been used only occasionally and then only by the vessels which intended to pick up furs, sandalwood, or some other Pacific cargo on the way out. For the average China trader, the outward trip yielded little in the way of freight receipts. With the gold rush, there came an opportunity to make extra earnings by carrying provisions to San Francisco, where they could be sold for specie wherewith to purchase teas at Canton. From that time on, the voyages to Canton were generally made by way of Cape Horn and California, but the clippers still returned ordinarily by the old route around Africa.

The difference which this made to the owners is reflected in the earnings of the *Houqua,* revealed in the annual reports to the widow of William H. Low, a part owner, who had listened to Palmer's suggestions as to her design. The ship had originally cost some $45,000 in 1844 and had paid for herself even before the gold rush gave the opportunity for extra profit from the outward cargo. The reports also reveal that freight money was invested at Canton in tea, cassia, and firecrackers on the owners' account, so that they were able to make an additional profit on the difference in the cost of these at Canton and New York. She had come on the scene in time to reap the richest profits from both the China and California trade.

Another Low ship was the first to break into a new rich field, which appeared in the year of the gold rush. The repeal of the British Navigation Acts in 1849 opened to outsiders the carrying trade between China and London, formerly restricted to British vessels. The American clippers were so much faster than the British ships that, once those restrictions were removed, they were able to race to London in record time with the first teas of the new crop. The pioneer in this new activity was the Low clipper *Oriental* which in 1850 broke the record with a 97-day run from Hongkong to the Thames. The freight receipts for that single trip amounted to $48,000, more than two-thirds of her initial cost. Such news as that, however, was partly responsible for the overproduction of speedy clippers and, by the late 'fifties, scores of those splendid ships were prowling from port to port in the Far East, ready to carry coolies to California or Australia or take on any other sort of freight at sacrifice rates. The Lows were more fortunate than those ships for the firm lasted on long after the Civil War.

By the eve of the Civil War, New York had the China trade securely in its own hands. In the last five years of our period (1856-60), the annual arrivals from China averaged 50 vessels, totalling 48,500 tons, at New York; 33, of 23,400 tons, at San Francisco, many of which proceeded on to New York; and only four, of 3300 tons, at Boston, while the other American ports had virtually none.

Those figures, however, do not tell the whole story of the American trade in eastern waters at that time. If one adds to the arrivals from China those from British India, the Philippines, and the Dutch East Indies, Boston is virtually tied with New York. Boston averaged 108 ships a year against New York's 101, but the larger vessels at New York gave it the scant lead in tonnage of 92,800 to 89,000. The two ports ran neck and neck in the trade with the Dutch East Indies and the Philippines, but Boston still retained its old leadership in the trade with India, averaging yearly 81 ships of 67,400 tons against 31 ships of 26,200 tons for New York. The annual imports for the nation averaged $1,200,000 from the Dutch East Indies, $3,000,000 from the Philippines, while the total imports from newly opened Japan amounted to only $295 in 1859 and $55,000 in 1860. The average from India, however, was $9,800,000, which was almost equal to the China average of $10,600,000.

The opening of American trade with India had been almost simultaneous with the first trip to Canton. Just a month after the *Empress of China* had sailed from New York, the ship *United States* left Philadelphia. On Christmas Day of 1784, she showed the Stars and Stripes for the first time in India, off Madras, and proceeded to the near-by French port of Pondicherry for a cargo. Before long, the Americans were trading at the British ports of Madras and Calcutta as well—a privilege which the East India Company's monopoly denied to Englishmen outside the company. The trade, long overlooked, has recently received attention from several quarters. The British outsiders finally secured the repeal of the company's monopoly in all except the trade between India and Canton in 1813. New York, however, had taken little part in that early contact with India. Started by a Philadelphia ship, the trade was carried on principally by mariners from Boston and Salem.

As soon as peace came in 1815, however, a New York ship led the way in reopening the trade. The *Emily* arrived at the exposed roadstead of Madras on August 20, 1815, in 98 days from New York, "the first ship that took in a cargo since the peace in India." Among her passengers was Jacob Leroy of Leroy, Bayard & Co., the foremost New York house of the day and one that would be most active in the trade with India and the East Indies. After taking in part of her cargo at Madras, the *Emily* proceeded up the east coast to Sand Heads, where she picked up a pilot for the tortuous 130 miles up the river to Calcutta to load the remainder.

Calcutta offered commodities of a more variegated nature than the conventional tea, silks, chinaware, and cassia from Canton. One cargo which reached New York from there in 1818 consisted of sugar, alum, shellac, sago, twine, hides, indigo, cassia, turmeric, white cord, cotton, carpeting, straw matting, feather tippets and "merchandise."

That last expression covered the cheap cotton textiles which India offered in profusion before Lancashire began to force its own calicoes upon the Indians. The exotic names of those Calcutta cloths appeared frequently in the New York newspaper advertisements during those early years—"sooty romals, red gallas, beerboom gurrahs, frocketsay romals, gauzipore baftas" and so on; the dry-goods clerks simply called them "hum hums." Because of their cheapness, they were the first victims of the increasing protective tariffs and before long were imported only to be re-exported, with duties refunded, to Latin America. Saltpetre was also a frequent offering of Calcutta as were drugs of the type which the elder Low was selling in the 'thirties. In 1834, one ship tried to bring a menagerie from Calcutta to New York. The tiger, leopard, and rhinoceros arrived safely but the elephant "died off the Cape, 81 days out," and the "giraff" and "cameoleopard" died just before reaching Sandy Hook. Fifteen years before a ship from Bombay landed safely in the East River "an elegant Arabian horse, of best breed, reared at Bussorah under the eye of the East India Company's Resident."

But while New York was drawing ahead of Boston at Canton, the reverse process was taking place in the ports of India. Occasionally, a ship would sail from Boston and return to New York. An advertisement in 1830, for instance, read "For Calcutta direct. The fine A No. 1 coppered ship *Sapphire,* 400 tons burthen, Warren Gould master and joint supercargo with George S. Noble, will sail from Boston on or before the 15th October next, to return to New York." Such an arrangement was also common in the China trade, but more often the Boston ships returned from India to their home port, as the customs figures for the late 'fifties demonstrate. Boston had a unique offering for that market in the ingenious shipments of ice, originated by Frederick Tudor. There, as in the Baltic, Boston bested New York—one of the very few cases of sustained success by an outside port during the whole period. It was therefore appropriate that Boston, rather than New York, should have an "India Wharf."

The Dutch islands to the southeast of India have been termed the "Salem East Indies," from the amazing success of that little port in that distant trade. New York participated in it moderately from the outset and in the later days, after Salem dropped out of the picture, shared the business about equally with Boston. "Java" coffee, frequently grown in Sumatra, furnished numerous cargoes from Batavia, Sourabaya, or Samarang but it was only occasionally that pepper came direct to New York—that was Salem's specialty. There was danger in that trade, for in 1831, the ship *James Monroe* arrived at New York from the west coast of Sumatra with "5000 piculs of pepper" for the Howlands just a month after the U. S. S. *Potomac* had sailed from New York to avenge the massacre of a Salem crew on the Sumatra coast. Frequently a ship would load part of its cargo in the Dutch islands and then stop at India for the rest. C. C. Cambreleng, New York's perennial Congressman, for instance, advertised for sale in 1816 "an entire cargo, consisting of 330,000 lbs. Java coffee, 80,000 lbs. Calcutta sugar and 20,000 lbs. Bengal indigo." At times, ships from Canton would also stop at Batavia to complete their lading and they frequently chose the alternative of Manila, where sugar, hemp, and other commodities were to be had. It is significant that while several important New York houses became specialists in the China trade, the commerce with India and the islands was almost never more than a side line.

The quest for cargoes which might replace specie in the China trade led to some of the most exciting episodes in the history of the port. Except for the Astoria affair, New York had not participated as vigorously as Boston in seeking the skins of the sea otter on the Northwest coast but it partly made up for that by its adventures in the waters around Cape Horn. The chief actors in these adventures were the hardy mariners of Stonington, the little Connecticut port furthest away from New York; but their financial backing often came from New York. Some of their vessels were built there and they usually sailed to and from there on their distant wanderings.

One man stands out conspicuously as the promoter of this activity. He was Edmund Fanning, one of a large group of seagoing Stonington brothers. One of them early became a naval hero by claiming credit for dropping a grenade into the hold of the *Serapis* from the fighting top of the *Bonhomme Richard;* that seems to have unfitted him for useful work in later life. Edmund, however, did enough for several men. His whole career was influenced by an unusually successful voyage in 1797 when he was twenty-eight. In command of the 93-ton *Betsey* he sailed from New York with a few trinkets aboard as his only cargo. Rounding Cape Horn, his men slaughtered thousands of seals on the barren island of Juan Fernandez and then headed for Canton. Out in mid-Pacific, Fanning suddenly woke from a dream, rushed on deck, and saw breakers ahead, unnoticed by the lookout. That lucky awakening has left the name of Fanning Island as one of the dots on the map of the Pacific. During the next few days he also discovered Washington and Palmyra Islands, some two thousand miles due south of Hawaii. Proceeding to Canton, he exchanged his sealskins for a cargo which fetched $120,000 upon his return to New York, leaving a net profit of $53,000 for the voyage.

From that time on, for more than thirty years, Fanning devoted himself to propaganda in favor of developing such business, persuading New York merchants to put up capital, government officials to send exploring expeditions, and, easiest of all, Stonington seamen to carry on the actual work. In 1816, he himself sailed from New York in the *Volunteer* for seals in the South Pacific. He was seized and threatened by the Spanish officials in Chile. He claimed that his vigorous protests to Washington had much to do with the regular stationing of a naval vessel in those waters. Perhaps the most celebrated of the eighty expeditions which he boasts that he promoted was one in 1819 which left another Stonington-New York name on the map. Captain Pendleton sailed with several small vessels in company for the South Shetland Islands, just east of Cape Horn, the favorite sealing ground of the Stonington group. Distant ice was sighted to the southward and young Captain Nathaniel B. Palmer was sent down in the little sloop *Hero* to investigate. He found that it was apparently continuous ice and evidently a new Antarctic region. While he was there, he encountered a Russian exploring expedition whose commander suggested that the new discovery be named Palmer Land, and so it found its way onto the maps. Palmer's name crops up again and again in the history of the port—it was he, we recall, who suggested the *Houqua* as a fast China clipper and who commanded her and some of her Low successors in fast runs from Canton. He likewise served with distinction as a Liverpool packet captain and later acted in useful advisory capacities ashore.

Another of the Fanning-inspired voyages received wide publicity because of the adventures encountered. In 1829, Captain Benjamin Morrill of Stonington, accompanied by his young wife, set out for the South Seas in the schooner *Antarctic,* fresh from the East River yard of Bergh and Westervelt, whose names Morrill would later give to islands which he discovered. His first stop was at the Cape Verde Islands for salt wherewith to preserve the sealskins he hoped to obtain.

Then, rounding Good Hope, he set his course for New Zealand, hoping to find seals there but was disappointed. Next, he set sail for Manila, discovering en route the two groups of islands which he named for the builders of the schooner. At Manila, he decided to fit for a voyage to the Fiji Islands, despite the fact that the crew of a previous Fanning expedition had been eaten there nearly thirty years before. One day, "a little bird as black as ink" came on board the schooner and could not be induced to leave. Some of the superstitious sailors wanted to kill it as a bird of ill omen, but the captain saved its life. The next day an island was discovered and the bird flew to land. The superstitions were, for once, confirmed, and Morrill would have occasion to name it Massacre Island. It abounded in bêche-la-mer, sea slugs or "sea cucumbers," esteemed by the Chinese as food. Part of the crew were ashore gathering this commodity when a large force of natives fell upon them with murderous results. Unable either to rescue them or to continue work with his depleted forces, Morrill sailed back to Manila where he recruited more sailors.

With his crew thus reinforced, he returned at once to Massacre Island still hoping to gather some bêche-la-mer. Soon after he arrived, a small canoe put off from shore containing Leonard Shaw, one of the old crew, who had hidden in the woods and escaped the fatal attack. For fifteen days he had lain concealed, sustained only by four cocoanuts, and then was discovered by the natives who, after wounding him, put him to work making knives out of iron left by the landing party. He said that the skulls of the thirteen who had been slain and eaten were hanging at the chief's door and that there had been talk of treating Shaw the same way. That ceremony was postponed because of the absence of certain chiefs and the *Antarctic* appeared in time for the rescue. Nothing daunted, Captain Morrill had four brass swivel guns mounted in a treetop battery to protect the workers but the natives so persisted in the hostility that it was necessary to abandon the attempt. Two of the natives were brought back to New York and exhibited first in Tammany Hall and then at Peale's Museum, where for twenty-five cents one could not only see the "cannibal" headliner but also hear Shaw's account, along with other attractions. Both Morrill and his wife wrote accounts of the voyage and the captain himself later returned to the South Seas, where he was last heard from in the Marquesas.

American whalers were familiar visitors in those distant waters but only occasionally were they from New York. Nantucket and New Bedford, of course, were the great centers of whaling activity and a few other places in southern New England also shared in it. Many old New York packets and other merchantmen were sold as whalers, but most of them seldom ever visited the port again. A very few were owned and operated at New York itself, including the former Havre packet *Desdemona,* which was owned by two packet captains and a New York merchant who operated her. She later was sold to the whalers at New Bedford, where she remained active until almost the end of the century and even after that lasted on, tied up at a wharf as one of the picturesque bleached veterans of that exciting pursuit. Somewhat more numerous than the whalers owned at New York itself were those which used its harbor en route to or from their home ports at Newark or up the Hudson. The particular center of activity was the town of Hudson, composed of whaling families who had come there from Nantucket when the Revolution had interrupted their island business. During the late 'thirties whaling companies were chartered at Hudson, Newburgh, Poughkeepsie, and Newark. This was one of the few instances of corporate ownership of sailing vessels. Old packets, released from the stormy and circumscribed routine of service on the Atlantic shuttle, still sailed out through Sandy Hook, to return two or three years later from the Arctic or from the milder waters around Japan, Tahiti, or New Zealand loaded down with whale oil and yarns of high adventure.

The cod fishery, that other great Massachusetts specialty, was even more neglected than whaling at New York. A South Street firm sent a hurry call in 1823 to its New London correspondent, remarking that a certain captain was about to go on a fishing voyage and requesting information as to "what papers are granted to vessels bound on fishing voyages that proceed, with their fare, to Europe." "At our Custom House," they continued, "they are so little used to fishing voyages as to express entire ignorance of the course to be adopted." A quarter century later, in an article on New York shipping, a writer called attention to the meager total of 148 tons in the cod fishery, "which is, we believe, the extreme upper limit of New York enterprise in that direction." New York was willing to depend upon Marblehead or Gloucester for its salt cod; its own fishermen seldom ventured beyond the bass grounds off Sandy Hook.

Another objective of the distant wanderings of New York vessels was Africa, still pretty much the neglected and unknown "dark continent." In the first months of peace in 1815, Captain James Riley of the New York brig *Commerce* had an adventure with which he regaled the public in a book which went through two editions. His brig had been wrecked on the barren Atlantic coast of Morocco, where the Moors made technical slaves of himself and his crew. They were carried some distance into the interior, but it was actually more kidnapping for ransom than anything else. The captives were given a chance to communicate with the near-by port of Mogador, where the British consul and a merchant from New York, resident there, raised the sum necessary for their release. That was perhaps the last instance where the old Barbary custom affected mariners from New York.

Over on the east coast of Africa, an effort was made during the 'thirties to open commercial relations with the "Imam of Muscat," who controlled most of the region. In 1833, the Government sent Edmund Roberts in the U. S. S. *Peacock,* to negotiate commercial treaties with Muscat, Siam, and Japan. Roberts was successful in the first two instances and almost at once the young New York firm of Scoville & Britton sought to exploit the East African market. Valuable presents were sent to the Imam and members of the firm went out to handle the business at Muscat and Zanzibar. A series of misfortunes, however, brought the episode to a speedy termination, even before the Imam sent a ship of his own, the *Sultanee,* to New York in 1840 with presents of Arab horses for President Jackson and other gifts for the partners in Scoville & Britton, whose creditors seized them. The *Sultanee,* with her Arab crew, attracted much attention in the East River during her visit, but the matter had been long since forgotten a century later, when the Imam's descendant appeared at Washington to return the ceremonial visits of Roberts. The failure of Scoville & Britton proved fortunate for those who are interested in the history of the port, for the senior partner, driven to the use of his pen for support, became the chronicler of the old merchants.

Most of New York's African business was transacted not with Morocco or Zanzibar but with the familiar slaving regions of the Guinea Coast. In fact, the port of New York participated in the "birth of a nation" in 1820. On February 7th of that year, the ship *Elizabeth* sailed with the Negroes who were to establish Liberia. She managed to clear Sandy Hook, but contrary winds detained the U. S. S. *Cyane,* her escort. Months passed without word of the pioneers and there was fear that they might have been snapped up by a slaver. Reassurances finally came from her master, Captain William Sebor, who would later command London packets for many years. He had missed the *Cyane* and sailed alone for Sierra Leone where he arrived on March 9th. Ten days later, he reached the Sherbro River, the site of the settlement. When the passengers and supplies had finally laboriously been carried to the distant shore, he came back by way of Turks Island to pick up a cargo of salt. Most of the other sailings to Liberia were from Norfolk and two old coastal packets went onto that run after their line service was ended.

A few vessels, usually brigs, arrived at New York each year from the Guinea Coast, but only very occasionally were any of these from Liberia. Ivory was the most valuable commodity brought back legally from this region, with palm oil also frequently forming a part of the cargoes. The Guinea Coast, then, as later, was one of the most pestilential spots on earth and many a brig came back to report the death of captain, mate, or seamen from the terribly prevalent fever. This African trade was only a drop in the bucket, as far as New York's total commerce was concerned. Other American ports also sent their brigs thither and in 1860, ivory was one of the two commodities in which Salem still stood first in the nation's imports.

By no means all the vessels which sailed from America to the Guinea Coast went for honest business. The slave trade had been abolished by England in 1807 and by the United States a year later, while England had secured the grudging acquiescence of the other nations in this matter at Vienna in 1814. British and American naval vessels patrolled the fever-ridden coast and the *Cyane,* which had been supposed to escort the pioneers to Liberia, was kept on that station and soon sent back to New York for trial three captured slavers, one of which came from Baltimore. It is difficult to tell how far the New Yorkers were involved in this sorry business, but it seems certain that some of the fast products of the East River yards were sold in Cuba or Brazil for this purpose. The criminal dockets of the federal courts reveal numerous charges of "engaging in the slave trade" and "voluntarily serving on board of a slaver." On one occasion, the schooner *Falmouth* was stopped by the federal authorities as she was trying to leave New York; her officers and crew were conducted to prison by a guard of marines.

This New York participation in slaving lasted until the very end of our period. There was, for instance, among the New York vessels prowling in the by-ways of the seven seas, the swift yacht *Wanderer,* which had been built in the East River and at one time had flown the flag of the New York Yacht Club. She was still flying that flag in 1858 when she carried a cargo of slaves from the Guinea Coast to Georgia with the brother of Semmes of the Confederate raider *Alabama* as her sailing master. In the summer of 1860, the ship *Erie* sailed out past Sandy Hook bound for Havana and on to the Congo, where she loaded 800 slaves. Only fifty miles out, she was caught with that incriminating cargo by the U. S. S. *Mohican*. The slaves were released at Liberia, while the *Erie* was sent back to New York. Her captain, a native of Maine, was convicted in the federal court and hanged at New York. More reprehensible even than the schooners, built on the East River as opium runners for the China coast, these slave ships were unworthy successors to those stouter and slower craft which long before had plowed through distant seas to open the lucrative trade route to Canton.

CHAPTER XI

WATERFRONT AND OFFICIALDOM

NOWHERE outside the national capital are the agents and agencies of government as numerous and obvious as in a busy seaport. Except for the Secretary of the Interior, every Cabinet member of our period had supervision of at least one activity at the port of New York. The Governor of the State likewise had a long list of appointees carrying out various maritime functions, some of which would later be taken over by the Federal Government. The city, too, had officials of a type which would not be found in an inland town. Even if one excludes the artillerymen in the harbor defenses and the bluejackets and marines at the Navy Yard, there were hundreds of national, State, and municipal officials at the port, some of whom were so well rewarded in salaries and fees that their appointments were matters of acute political concern.

No story of the port would be complete without taking into account these various official activities, together with the numerous private occupations essential to maritime operations. Leaving the workings of the business district and the shipyards for later consideration, this chapter will be devoted to a brief summary of these manifold functions as they would be encountered by a vessel entering port. Such a treatment, which resembles a group of individual beads loosely strung together, involves a cruel amount of compression, for there is material enough at hand on this aspect alone to fill a volume of comfortable size.

The swift and seaworthy little revenue cutters might be called the advanced outposts of the port. Only occasionally did a vessel encounter them and then it generally meant trouble of one sort or another. Their name came from their British prototypes, designed for the suppression of smuggling. For that reason, they flew the Treasury flag with its special design; and for a while were under the immediate control of the collector of customs. On occasion, they were sent into the Sound to check the clandestine landing of broadcloth and at times they investigated strange vessels suspected of violating the neutrality laws. More than once, they put men aboard a ship to quell a mutiny or to take off mutineers in irons. Their principal business, however, was the relief of shipping in distress. When a vessel ran ashore in the sandy angle, a cutter was generally the first on the scene to offer assistance.

Their chief service came during the protracted winter gales when incoming vessels with their rigging cased in ice, their crews half-frozen, and their provisions running low, were liable to be driven ashore. In December, 1831, for example, a Treasury order read: "In the present inclement season, it is thought proper to combine with the ordinary duties of the cutters, that of assisting vessels found on the coast in distress and ministering to the wants of their crews." On the New York station, the *Rush* was to cruise between Sandy Hook and "Montaug," and the *Alert* between Sandy Hook and Cape May, "keeping as close to the mainland as may be consistent with the safety of each vessel." A month later, Lieutenant Oscar Bullus reported that the *Rush* was wrecked on Long Island, high and dry at low water and "bilged." Anchored in Huntington Bay, she had parted her chain in a "hurricane," dragged her hemp cable, and run ashore.

The early cutters were small craft for such strenuous work—the *Active,* long attached to the New York station, measured only 122 tons, being about 80 feet long and 20 feet in beam. By the mid-'forties, the New York merchants were urging steam cutters for the winter service and were finally gratified in that respect. When, in 1843, a separate revenue cutter bureau was established, its first head was a New York captain.

Two other squadrons of fast little schooners were more likely to encounter the incoming vessel before she reached Sandy Hook. The adventurous news boats, sent out by the New York editors to catch the latest word from abroad, are mentioned elsewhere. Until the late 'thirties, they usually reached the new arrivals ahead of the pilot boats, which, guarded by a State monopoly, were not inclined to operate too far from shore.

Most incoming craft of any size were virtually required to take a pilot, or at least to pay half the cost of pilotage if they chose to omit the service. From their base at Staten Island, the thirty or so licensed pilots operated in their small schooners of sixty to eighty tons. Each normally carried three or four pilots with a few apprentice boys and a cook. Every incoming vessel was fair game for the first to reach her, but the pilots scrambled for the larger ships since their compensation was based on the draft of water, an important consideration in crossing the bar. Vessels drawing 14 feet or less paid $1.50 a foot; if more than 18 feet, the rate was $2.25, so that a schooner might be only $10, while a packet might yield $40 or more. During the winter months, there was a further charge. Once aboard, the pilot took over the control and responsibility from the captain until the vessel had crossed the bar, traversed the harbor, and come safely to her wharf or mooring. It was an unwritten custom that the pilot who brought a vessel into port was entitled to take her out again, an easier job because it might be arranged in advance. On the outward job, however, the wind might be too strong for the pilot to be dropped into his little boat. On one occasion, a packet thus carried a pilot to England and back for a free trip in addition to the legal compensation of $3 a day.

Pilotage was a monopoly guarded by State law in the beginning of our period. The pilots themselves were appointed by the Governor, 28 and later 30 for Sandy Hook and a dozen or so for Hell Gate. Outside competition was barred, although the New York merchants were complaining of the monopoly as early as 1825. It was charged that the pilots were not sufficiently diligent during nasty winter weather in going out to meet ships.

Matters came to a head in the winter of 1836–37 with two terrific wrecks, blamed on pilot negligence. The *Bristol* arrived off Sandy Hook on a stormy Saturday night and sent up rockets for a pilot. None came and all next day, in a freezing gale the ship struggled to claw off a dangerous lee shore. Finally she piled up on the Long Island coast, with heavy loss of life. The outcry against the pilots swelled a few weeks later when the *Mexico* had an almost identical experience, with an even heavier casualty list among her immigrant passengers.

Widespread indignation against the monopoly led to Federal legislation which threw the business open to competition. New Jersey began to license pilots to compete with the New Yorkers and some of the packet operators and other big shipowners retained a group of their own pilots. The matter received wide publicity, particularly in the *Herald* from Bennett, who championed the old guard and published lists of the vessels grounded or wrecked in the hands of the Jersey or "merchant" pilots. The new competition, however, resulted in greatly improved service on the whole. Whereas, the old monopolists had formerly clung fairly close to Sandy Hook, the new scramble for work led them further and further afield. In 1843, for instance, an enterprising pilot boat secured the lucrative pilotage of the steamship *Great Western* by boarding her 180 miles southeast of Sandy Hook and the packets sometimes took on their pilots even further from port.

Up to 1837, the pilots had played so safe that scarcely a single accident was recorded; but the new extension of their cruising radius took its toll. During a gale in 1839, two pilot boats, the *Gratitude* and *John McKeon,* were lost with all hands; and in other cases the little schooners ran ashore or lost men overboard. It is said that fifteen pilot boats met with disaster between 1838 and 1860.

At times, because of their speed, pilot boats were chartered for distant service. One raced and beat a packet to England to head off an absconding bank clerk; and others went on mysterious missions at times when news of cotton or flour fluctuations was at a premium. It was a tribute to pilot skill that Capt. "Dick" Brown, a leader in the Sandy Hook group, was selected to sail the yacht *America* in the race where she won the celebrated cup in 1851.

The lighthouse service, another branch of Treasury jurisdiction, under the collector of the port, also greeted the incoming vessel before she reached the bar. Back in 1764, New York had erected Sandy Hook light on New Jersey territory, the fifth beacon to be established in the Colonies and the first south of New England. Its original masonry tower was the oldest to continue in service into the twentieth century. At first, it had been close to the tip of the spit; but the shifting of the sands gradually left it at some distance from the shore; and the New York shipping interests sought additional guidance in the dark. The answer was the "Floating Light," the first lightship, which was moored a few miles off Sandy Hook in 1823. Now and then it broke loose and drifted to sea, but was towed back. Its successor, built in 1837, was a vessel of 230 tons, 87 feet long with a 25-foot beam and carrying two lanterns hung between two pairs of masts, a 700-pound bell and a one-ton mushroom anchor with 90 fathoms of chain cable. Between the building of the first and second lightship, the approach to Sandy Hook was marked even more effectively by the erection of the twin Navesink lights on the Highlands above the Hook. The lights, some 250 feet above the water, were visible for 40 to 50 miles at sea in clear weather when they first went into operation in June, 1828. By that time, there was a lighthouse on Fire Island on the outer Long Island shore and at least a dozen along the Sound. Ten years later a lighthouse was built on Robbins Reef inside the harbor. By 1827, a lighthouse tender was in operation, the marine news noting the arrival of the "U. S. schr. *Hayti,* Humphries, from supplying the lighthouses with oil between Boston and this port, and bound to the southward for do."

Closely related to lighthouses were buoys marking the entrance to the port, chiefly spar buoys in red, white or black, though can buoys were appearing by the end of the period. In 1831, the collector of the port, who was charged with supervision, advertised for bids for the maintenance of these, adding that "none but pilots need apply."

By the time the incoming vessel had taken her pilot aboard and passed the lightship, her arrival had ordinarily been signalled to the city. Bad weather might detain a ship two or three days off Sandy Hook and it was useful to know that she was below. Back in the Dutch period, a flagstaff at the Narrows, visible from the Battery, had been used to announce arrivals and in 1815 several New York ship-owners had such "signal poles" there. In 1816, for instance, the marine news announced that "E. Morewood's private signal is flying at the Narrows—supposed for the ship *Elizabeth,* Borden, from Malaga and Gibraltar." In 1821 came the message "The lightning yesterday struck John Graham's pole and hurt it some. Palmer & Hamilton's is in ten thousand pieces; inform them of it."

That message came over the newly installed semaphore "telegraph" which had been erected by the Black Ball operators and other ship-owners. This semaphore on Staten Island with various movements of its arms could spell out whole messages visible to the watcher with his telescope at the Battery. It went into operation on June 23, 1821, with a series of messages which indicated the nature of its service. First came word that no vessels were sighted. Then came code letters for "light winds from the eastward" and "foggy at sea." By that time, a single schooner had come into view. The Vice-President's wife, with a group of friends, strolled past, and the message came "Lady Tomp-kins is here," and after that "We have done." By that semaphore or its rival established later, New York often had its first information of incoming packets and sometimes learned of such events as foreign wars and revolutions even before the news boats had time to reach the city.

As time went on, a semaphore was established at Navesink Highlands above Sandy Hook, whence messages were relayed to the city by way of the Narrows. By the mid-'forties, an electric telegraph line was run out to Coney Island, where it was possible to give quicker and more complete information.

The bottle-neck at the Narrows was a convenient place not only for pilots and signalmen but also for quarantine and preliminary customs inspection. A "boarding officer" from the Custom House was rowed out to inspect the vessel's papers while the health officer or a deputy from quarantine nearby examined the health of the ship. The latter was a State function at the time and the laws were very specific. Vessels arriving from Asia, Africa, the Mediterranean, the Caribbean, or from America south of Georgia; those from foreign ports with forty passengers or more aboard; and those on which any one had died on the homeward passage from a foreign port were under liability of detention at all times, while, during the pestilential summer months, those from the Carolinas and Georgia were added to the list of suspects. If the vessel arrived from a port where "yellow or other pestilential fever" was prevalent, she was to be detained at quarantine at least thirty days after arrival and twenty days after discharging her cargo, while her crew and passengers were detained for twenty days after her departure from the other port or after the last death on board. There were many further very specific regulations, with fines as penalties for violation.

In time of epidemics along the coast, real panic settled down upon the seaports, which became suspicious of every rival. New York had serious visitations of yellow fever in 1819 and 1822, with a terrible cholera epidemic in 1832. On one of those occasions, two officials boarding a vessel in a Mexican port leaped overboard in terror when they learned that she was from New York. Such quarantine inspection meant real danger for the officials. In September, 1819, while the first epidemic was in full swing and the New York merchants had moved their places of business to the remote quiet of Greenwich Village, the *Post* contained the following grim notice:

Died, this morning at the quarantine ground, in the 46th year of his age, Benjamin DeWitt M.D., health officer of his port, vice president of the College of Physicians and Surgeons of this city, and one of its professors. This makes the fifth health officer of this port who have [sic] fallen victim to the performance of their hazardous duties, viz. Drs. Treat,

Smith, Bailey, Ledyard, DeWitt, facts that speak with an emphasis irresistible.

The doctor designated as his successor declined the appointment.

Knowing what yellow fever or cholera could do to the city, the New Yorkers were furious at efforts to dodge the quarantine. In this respect, as in certain others, Perth Amboy on several occasions presented an opportunity for evasion. Passengers avoided quarantine by landing there and coming to town on the ferries. On one occasion the health officer posted notice of a $50 reward for the apprehension of such a man. The captain and mate of a Havana packet at another time were haled into court for falsifying the date of leaving that port, where yellow fever was raging, in order to cut short the time of detention at quarantine. When, in the 'fifties, the crowded immigrant ships began to arrive with victims of smallpox and other pestilence by the score, the Staten Islanders urged the removal of quarantine to Sandy Hook or some other less populated spot. To stress their point, they went so far as to burn the whole colony of quarantine buildings in 1859. For a while after that, an old coastal steamship was moored in the lower Bay for quarantine cases; then the establishment was shifted to two little artificial islands constructed below the Narrows.

Somewhat related to quarantine was another Staten Island institution known as the Sailors' Retreat or Marine Hospital, not to be confused with the heavily endowed Sailors' Snug Harbor, a home for aged seamen. For years, the authorities had been collecting a dollar from every sailor arriving from foreign ports for such a purpose, but only a limited range of extremely infectious diseases such as yellow fever, smallpox, or typhus would be admitted to the quarantine hospital and the other poor devils had to wander the streets of New York looking for assistance. Finally, a New York sea captain was elected to the State legislature for the express purpose of securing State backing for a hospital, to which the dollars collected from the seamen might be applied. The result was a four-storied stone building about a mile from the quarantine ground, with forty acres of land for vegetables and pasturage. It was opened in October, 1831. Six months later, more than 300 patients had been admitted, with an average of about 90 at a time. During that time there had been 12 deaths, "all hopeless," and among the diseases syphilis led with 62, followed by rheumatism at 29, intermittent fever at 27, and frostbite at 18.

Proceeding up the harbor from Staten Island toward the city, the arriving vessel came within the jurisdiction of a State official known as the harbor master, whose duty it was to maintain harbor regulations about mooring and the like, and to assign berths for docking. Fees from every vessel made this one of the most lucrative posts in the whole State patronage, the income being estimated, and presumably overestimated, at $20,000 in 1818. Many of the incumbents were simply deserving party henchmen whose main interest was in the fees, but one sea dog accomplished much during his incumbency around 1820. This was Captain Samuel C. Reid, whose exploits in the *General Armstrong* ranked high in the privateering annals of the War of 1812. He helped to improve the pilot regulations and did more than any one else to establish the semaphore service at the Narrows and the "Floating Light" off Sandy Hook.

Associated with the harbor master was a group of other State appointees known as the port wardens. Their chief function was to act as arbiters in case of damage sustained by a vessel or cargo and occasionally they authorized the sale of damaged goods at auction. The position was, on the whole, a sinecure worth securing for the occasional good fees.

The final destination of the incoming vessel was one of the numerous wharves along the New York waterfront. These presented a decidedly informal appearance to the Englishman accustomed to the great stone docks at London or Liverpool, where ships were floated in at high water and then, with the locks closed, were kept at that level even when the tide receded. With tides rising 20 feet, more or less, in the Thames and Mersey, such docks were necessary, but New York, where it rose only 4 or 5 feet, could get along with less expensive structures. Fenimore Cooper explained this contrast in a letter to a visiting foreigner in 1824:

The time has not yet come for the formation of massive permanent quays in the harbor of New York. Wood is still too cheap, and labor too dear, for so heavy an investment of capital. All the wharves of New York are of very simple construction—A frame-work of hewn logs is filled with loose stone, and covered with a surface of trodden earth. . . . The Americans . . . are daily constructing great ranges of these wooden piers, in order to meet the increasing demands of their trade, while the whole of the seven miles of water which fronts the city, is lined with similar constructions; if we except the public mall, called "the Battery," which is protected from the waves of the bay by a wall of stone.

The wharves of New York form a succession of little basins, which are sometimes large enough to admit thirty or forty sail, though often much smaller. These irregular docks have obtained the name of "slips."

Some of those older slips in the East River were the conventional waterfront landmarks, particularly Coenties Slip, Old Slip, Coffee House Slip, Fly Market Slip, Burling Slip, and Peck Slip. A Glasgow printer who visited the "overgrown sea-port village" of New York in 1823 left an unfavorable picture of them:

The slips run up a considerable way in the center of the buildings, as it were in the middle of streets; and being built or faced up with logs of trees cut to the requisite length, allow free ingress and egress to the water, and being completely out of the current of the stream or tide, are little else than stagnant receptacles of city filth; while the top of the wharves exhibits one continuous mass of clotted nuisance, composed of dust, tea, oil, molasses, &c., where revel countless swarms of offensive flies.

The slips were eventually filled in but for years travellers complained of having to pick their way among the boxes, barrels, and lumber which cluttered up wharves ankle-deep in mud in spring, dust in summer, and slush in winter.

Physically, the waterfront had undergone a marked change since colonial times, when the tide had lapped along shallow, sloping shores which were two or three blocks inland by the middle of our period. South Street and West Street, which skirted the wharves of East River and North River, respectively, were on "made land," far out beyond the low-water mark of earlier days. A survey in 1862, attempting to find from old maps and records where the original high- and low-water marks had been, estimated that since 1688 the average width of reclaimed land to the "bulkhead line" at the inner end of the wharves amounted to 626 feet. The Jersey side of the Hudson did not begin to figure as an important part of the port's waterfront until 1847, when Cunard built his wharves at Jersey City.

From the single East River wharf built by the Dutch around 1650, the waterfront had gradually expanded until by 1840, the East River had 60 wharves and the Hudson, 53. In 1815, the city fathers had voted that these be numbered, the separate series for each river starting with No. 1 at the Battery, the system still in force. Brooklyn, too, had a few wharves in addition to the partly enclosed Atlantic Dock and Erie Basin. The East River wharves were still more important than those of the North River. On a particular day in the spring of 1836, for example, a survey showed 921 vessels tied up along East River and only 320 in the Hudson. The latter total was made up chiefly of little schooners and sloops. Of the square-rigged ships and brigs, the aristocrats of the sea lanes, 305 were moored in East River and only 39 in North River.

As time went on, the average wharf underwent changes not only in size but also in structure. The old cribwork filled with stones was gradually replaced by open piling which allowed freer movement of the tidal currents. By the mid-'fifties, most of the docks ranged from 200 to 300 feet in length, while some were even longer. A thorough investigation of "harbor obstructions" in 1856 and 1857 brought out some interesting testimony on the details of wharf construction and economics. The pine planking with which they were covered had to be replaced every four or five years; the use of horses, travelling in a circle as they hoisted cargoes out of the holds, wore out the planking more rapidly than in the old days when all such work was done by hand. The wharfingers estimated that thirty years was the normal life of a pier; at the end of that time it had to undergo a thorough repair, with the adding of much new piling, at a cost of about $15,000, which represented about a third to a quarter of its original value.

Many of the wharves were built by the city and were leased to private individuals who operated them. Some remained fairly permanently in the use of a particular firm. Certain lines of packets kept the same wharves year after year throughout the period. Others, used for general purposes, were bid for at auction each year and the lessee collected his profits from the legal rate of charges, which were 75 cents a day for vessels of 100 tons and progressed upwards at the rate of a New York shilling (12½ cents) for every extra 50 tons, so that a 600-ton ship paid $2.00 a day. Vessels lying at the outer end of the wharves, which involved a longer hauling of freight and rendered them liable to be damaged by floating ice, paid half rate. Those low rates, while distasteful to some of the city's financial officials and private wharf owners, may be reckoned as one of the causes of New York's success in competition with its rival ports. The city controller declared in 1852 that "We have adhered to low rates of wharfage to keep up the name of the cheapest port on the continent." He cited the case of a New Orleans packet which discharged its whole cargo of 1700 bales of cotton at a North River pier in two and a half days. Her wharfage charge came to only $4.88, whereas, he claimed, the charge for similar accommodations at Baltimore would amount to about $50 and

fter a lithograph by G. Hayward   *From "Valentine's Manual," 1857*

PECK SLIP, NEW YORK, 1850

From "Valentine's Manual," 1860

MARKET SLIP FROM THE CORNER OF CHERRY STREET, 1859

These pictures represent two of the old slips after they had been filled in

at Boston, Charleston, Mobile, and New Orleans to about $68. The commissioners in 1856 demonstrated that the charges at New York were also much lower than at foreign ports and pointed out that New York's reasonable rates were often in themselves enough to determine shippers to use that port in preference to others where the costs were higher. The controller in 1852 reported that the total value of the city's piers, wharves, and bulkheads amounted to $3,250,000. The gross rentals came to some $127,000 and the repairs to about $37,000, leaving net receipts of about $90,000, equivalent to 3½ per cent upon the capital invested. Back in 1824, some of the Common Council had favored selling all the public wharves and slips, as "this species of property produced but a poor interest," but Mayor Philip Hone upheld municipal ownership, which still continues for a considerable part of the waterfront. When one considers the high charges imposed by private docking interests at other ports, the wisdom of the mayor's decision can be appreciated.

The wharves, naturally, involved their own set of officials. At first they were under the supervision of the Commissioner of Streets, while the Common Council had a standing committee on "wharves, piers, and slips." Each ward which faced on either river had a "dock-warden," with two for the busy first ward at the tip of the island. They exercised supervision of sorts and received fees. By 1843, the city had a municipal "superintendent of wharves" whose annual income was reckoned at $700. The lessees appointed a wharfinger, who was in immediate charge of the activities on his particular wharf.

The most numerous personnel associated with the wharves were the laborers who came to be known as longshoremen, the counterpart of the English dockers, who worked under the supervision of stevedores. Some firms had their own permanent personnel of stevedores and longshoremen—the house of Grinnell, Minturn & Co., for instance, had seventy at one time. For the stevedore himself, and for the first mate who was responsible for the stowing of cargo, the work required a considerable amount of skill. For the ordinary longshoremen, however, it was largely a matter of muscle, necessary for hoisting freight into or out of the hold. The longshoremen came to realize their strategic position, for they could delay a vessel's sailing if they refused to work. As early as 1825, they staged a strike:

Turn Out—Yesterday the wharves were thronged with crowds of labourers standing out for higher wages. Nearly all the ships in port were deserted by their men, to join in the general combination; several vessels nearly ready for sea are delayed for want of hands. Two very active and noisy individuals who employed themselves in going about and preventing those disposed to work from doing so, were taken up and committed to Bridewell.

The wharves also spawned another less active breed whose chief concern was to find a shady secluded spot on the lee side of a hogshead of rum, away from the eye of the wharfinger, insert a straw, and drink themselves into insensibility. One of the first appearances of the word "loafer" in print occurred in a *Journal of Commerce* editorial in 1837, describing the practices of this group. By night, a more sinister sort often prowled the wharves, carrying off valuable freight in small boats or looting the cabins of vessels. "Old Hays," the city's high constable, was the terror of this sort during much of our period and made many single-handed arrests. By the mid-'fifties, the city found it necessary, however, to establish a marine police to patrol the waterfront in boats, while private concerns were formed for "ship watching," providing watchmen for the purpose. The reminiscences of Jerry McAuley picture night life on the waterfront at the end of the period, although, like many other reformed rascals, he perhaps painted his early escapades in more lurid colors than they really deserved.

The sojourn of a ship in port was apt to cost several hundred dollars for all the various services from pilotage and towing to wharf rent, stevedoring, repairs, watering, and provisions. An account list of such costs for the China clipper *Houqua* appears in the appendix.

In the more sober realms of officialdom, there were ashore in New York several groups which overshadowed those outposts at Staten Island and off Sandy Hook. These included the courts with marine jurisdiction, the consuls, and, above all, the custom house.

The New York Custom House enjoyed a special significance. It was the principal source of revenue of the Federal Government. In fact, the duties collected there in 1828 were enough to pay the whole running expenses of the national Government, except the interest on the debt. The extensive personnel of the custom house was the largest group in New York port officialdom and the collectorship was regarded as the choicest of the local political positions.

While the collection of duties on incoming goods was the original purpose for establishing custom houses, many other functions fell upon its staff, who kept their fingers upon the pulse of the whole maritime activity of New York. For every voyage to foreign parts, and for many coastwise voyages as well, a vessel had to be formally entered and cleared. Every vessel which claimed New York as her hailing port had to be "documented" with a register for foreign trade, an enrolment for domestic trade, or, if less than twenty tons in size, with a license. Supervision extended over many other branches of marine activity, for new tasks were added from time to time in keeping track of crews, incoming passengers, and the like. The collector likewise had control of the local revenue cutter, lighthouse, and marine hospital services and was charged with enforcement of the neutrality laws. Even that list by no means exhausts the range of business handled by the custom house. The New York customs district, moreover, included not only the port proper but the whole Hudson River as far as Troy, the adjacent parts of New Jersey, and most of Long Island, except for the distant and inactive custom house at Sag Harbor.

In spite of its widespread duties, it was some time before the customs force secured adequate quarters. In 1799, the old "government house" on Bowling Green was taken over for the purpose, but when that was torn down in 1815, quarters were merely leased, occasioning complaints of "doing the immense business of the first port in the Union in a miserable stable." Eventually, in 1834, ground was broken for a fine new building of adequate size at Wall and Nassau Streets. This eventually became the Sub-Treasury, which still stands on that spot, with its massive pillars; while the custom house was shifted to the new Merchants Exchange diagonally across the street, now part of the National City Bank building.

The three principal officers at the Custom House were the collector, who was in general charge; the naval officer, who had had nothing whatsoever to do with the Navy since Colonial times when such an officer was appointed to check the collector's accounts; and the surveyor, who had general supervision of outdoor activities. The inrush of imported textiles after 1815 called attention to the need of expert opinion for the levying of ad valorem duties, so that two appraisers were added to the principal officers. Below them came scores and later hundreds of clerks, inspectors, weighers, gaugers, and other lesser officials. In 1827, the whole Custom-House staff numbered 164, with total salaries of $112,000; by 1843, the personnel had jumped to 503 and the payroll to $489,000.

Such patronage made the Custom House a particular object of political solicitude. In the earlier days, the staff had contained many veterans of the Revolution who managed to survive changes of administration with ranks relatively unbroken. The change became noticeable at the very time when we should most expect it—at the coming of Andrew Jackson into the presidency in 1829 and the application of the spoils system. The new regime was especially significant at New York because it ousted one of the best collectors the port ever had and brought in one of the worst. Jonathan Thompson, who had held the office since 1817, had administered the post with honesty and energy. Samuel Swartwout, Jackson's appointee, soon provided the Custom House with one of its most unsavory scandals. From that time, with only occasional exceptions, the collectorship was a plum of the first magnitude, rivalled only by the unprofitable appointment to the Court of St. James's. Not only did the combination of salary and fees yield a generous legitimate income, but the patronage involved in the ever-increasing staff was a matter of prime importance. For weeks after a national political overturn, the New York papers were filled with speculation about the new collector and as soon as he was appointed, he was almost hounded to death. In April, 1841, for example, when Harrison had just supplanted Van Buren as President, the *Herald* stated:

> There was a terrible rush at the Custom House yesterday. . . . The poor devils of locofocos behind their desks eyed the crowd of hungry loafers in front as mice might a cat about to devour them. The small apartment fenced off to protect the collector from the crowd was thronged by the boldest of the office seekers, and those who had not the impudence to obtrude themselves within the enclosure were gazing with envy upon the more daring, who were determined to have the collector's ear.

Six to seven thousand applied, the article continued, while only about two hundred changes were to be made in the five hundred positions. It would appear that a few of the staff were kept on to maintain the traditions and technique of the work, for an obituary notice appeared in 1842 of "Mr. Joseph Leonard, for the last 46 years a clerk in the Custom House." He was not apparently in charge of the registers of shipping, for in going through those old volumes, one may detect the presidential overturns by the change from neatness and accuracy to scrawls and corrections. Herman Melville, the author, served as an inspector for twenty years or so. The collector, in view of his political duties, became more and more of a figurehead—after a while all the fittings needed for his personal office were cigars and cuspidors.

It was almost inevitable, considering the millions involved in duties, that dishonesty crept in now and then. Not only were efforts made to defraud the customs, but time and again graft was exposed inside the service itself.

Only occasionally did the defrauding take the colorful form of nocturnal landing of precious wares in some remote cove. When the "Tariff of Abominations" increased the duties in 1828, two revenue cutters were told off to watch for such smuggling in the Sound, to be sure, and at another time the customs authorities ferreted out a valuable group of smuggled gems, which had been stolen from the Prince of Orange.

Defrauding ordinarily, however, took the more prosaic form of attempting to undervalue imported textiles. With duties ranging from 25 per cent to 50 per cent under different acts, it might mean a tremendous saving if woollens, for instance, could be brought in described as of cheaper quality than they were. One protectionist newspaper charged that the imports from England included a swarm of Yorkshiremen brought over for the purpose of false swearing of values.

More than one congressional document in those early days was devoted to the investigation of frauds at the New York Custom House, ranging from amazing expense accounts for stationery to irregularities in connection with the public warehouses. Jackson's collector, Samuel Swartwout, however, seems to have set the record for individual peccadilloes. "Old Hickory" had been impressed with Swartwout's fine sense of "honor" in duelling and similar frontier activities, but the millions passing through his hands were too much for the collector. Before he had been in office a year, he had diverted more than a million to some of his private ventures and he skipped to Europe when the storm began to break.

It would be unfair, however, to judge the customs officials by the conspicuous instances where a few of them slipped from honest performance of duty. More business was done at New York than at any other port and, on the whole, it was done conscientiously and well.

In one respect, at any rate, the political shifts from Democrats to Whigs and from Whigs to Democrats apparently failed to injure the service. Incoming foreign travellers at New York, as at other American ports, commented upon the invariable courtesy of the customs inspectors. According to Charles Dickens, upon his arrival at Boston, this stood in sharp contrast to the cringing servility of the continental officers and the churlish boorishness of the British.

The courts were another aspect of New York's maritime official business. Various tribunals were charged with the settling of maritime troubles, both civil and criminal. The most august of these were the federal courts, which had been granted admiralty jurisdiction under the Constitution. These included both the district court, with its resident federal judge, and the circuit court, over which in that day some member of the Supreme Court presided. The cases they tried, which one may exhume from their manuscript records or the printed federal reports, ranged from bottomry, a dull matter of marine mortgages, to barratry, the scuttling of a ship at sea. Some of New York's ablest lawyers were adepts at admiralty law. Their appearances were usually in connection with civil cases involving fat fees but these make less interesting reading than the occasions where pirates or slavers were sentenced to hang. The marshal, a sort of federal sheriff, was naturally concerned with much of this sort of business.

The dockets of admiralty cases in the district and circuit courts show that two types of cases predominated. One consisted of individual libels against a vessel, with "her tackle, apparel and furniture," to satisfy claims for wages or other debts. The other type consisted of customs cases, frequently expressed as "U. S. vs. 7 Bales of Woollens." The papers connected with such cases reveal a wealth of detail concerning business methods. Aaron Burr handled a large proportion of this sort of cases in his later days; at times he and his partner, Benedict, appeared as counsel in more than half of the cases on the docket. The criminal dockets of those federal courts suggest livelier subjects. Alleged shipboard offenses loomed largest. "Assault with a dangerous weapon" was the most common charge, followed by "endeavor to make a revolt." Out and out "revolt" or "revolt and mutiny" were less common, but "larceny on the high seas" was frequent and generally drew heavier sentences than physical violence. Captains or mates were the complainants in many of those cases, but they were usually defendants in the numerous charges of "cruel and unusual punishment," or the less frequent instances of "withholding sufficient food," or "abandoning a seaman in a foreign port." They were also occasionally defendants against charges of "excess of passengers" in violation of immigration laws, while the steamboat legislation brought in one defendant charged with fastening down a safety valve. Seven men were indicted for manslaughter in connection with the burning of the Hudson River steamer *Henry Clay*. There were occasional cases of prosecution for passing false invoices of imports at the Custom House or for obstructing customs officers in the performance of their duties. The chief interest, however, lay in the major charges for murder, piracy, and slaving. Considerable drama lies filed away in the records of such cases.

Far less majestic was the Marine Court, established by the State to give seamen a chance to obtain redress of grievances with jury trial. Its records contain scores of cases of captains and mates put on trial for alleged abuses of seamen. These were difficult matters to judge, since officers and foremast hands, both principals and witnesses, generally offered flatly contradictory testimony. A little group of shyster lawyers fattened on this business. Frequently, the warrant would not be served upon a captain until he was ready to sail, in the hope that the case might be settled quickly out of court. Since such marine disputes were apt to be too infrequent and irregular to provide a steady grist of business, the Marine Court was also given a "small claims" jurisdiction in cases involving less than $100 and at times such non-marine business occupied its full attention for weeks.

Those two courts received the bulk of the marine disputes, but other methods might be employed for solving certain types of cases. While a murder on the high seas would lead to the federal court, murder on a ship in port would come under the regular state criminal jurisdiction. Sailors' brawls ashore were generally handled by the municipal police courts.

In many instances, the merchants preferred to settle their disputes out of court. The legal routine was not only expensive but it was also slow. The merchants likewise felt that experts could settle technical disputes in a more intelligent manner than the average jury. Consequently, the Chamber of Commerce every month appointed a committee of arbitration, composed of some of the leading merchants, from whom a speedy decision might be secured for a five-dollar fee, provided that both parties agreed to abide by its decisions. The Chamber still possesses a little chest full of the committee cases, which fortunately survived the fire of 1835. Stripped of the pompous verbiage of the legal records, they set forth the essentials of the cases in a minimum of words. Disputes of all sorts were handled by this arbitration committee. On one occasion, in 1823, a cat figured in its deliberations:

We the subscribers wish the committee of arbitration of the Chamber of Commerce to adjust for us the following difficulty. John Griswold in behalf of the owners of the ship *Comet* claims from Mr. Jos. F. Carroll the payment of a bill or freight on goods by that vessel from London. Mr. Carroll claims that in consequence of mice having found their way into a case containing furs imbraced in said shipment, that he is intitled to indemnity from the owners of the ship for the damage done thereby. We wish the committee to state whether the freight is due without any allowance or not. It is not contended that any palpable neglect has been visible in any way as respects the case and attention appertaining to the ship. The captain states that while in London, a cat was kept on board the ship, but he did not think it necessary to continue her on the voyage.

At times, the merchants were willing to go still further in informal arbitration and place the disputed question in the hands of an individual whose judgment was respected. When Oliver H. Hicks died in 1832, his obituary remarked:

For several years past a large portion of his time had been occupied in adjusting marine losses and determining questions of mercantile difference, in which he acted by common consent as final arbiter. There is no other man among us whose loss in regard to such matters would be so severely felt. His decisions were equally satisfactory with those of the highest tribunal.

The foreign consuls formed a varied, colorful, and important group in the life of the port. Their functions were not uniform for all countries; but in general they consisted of keeping track of the ships of their flag and cargoes from their country, together with the relieving of distressed seamen and other countrymen. In 1836, when Germany and Italy still awaited unification, thirty different countries were represented at New York by consuls general, consuls, or vice-consuls: Austria, Baden, Bavaria, Belgium, Brazil, Bremen, Denmark, France, Frankfurt, Great Britain, Hamburg, Hanover, Hesse, Holland, Mexico, New Granada, Oldenburg, Portugal, Prussia, Rome, Russia, Sardinia, Saxe Weimar, Saxony, Sicily, Spain, Sweden (and Norway) Switzerland, and Venezuela. Six years later Chile, Greece, Hesse-Darmstadt, Lubec, Mecklenburg, Montevideo, Nassau, and Texas also had representatives. The British consulate and a few others had two officers of different rank, because of the large amount of "paper work" involved.

Most of these men were natives of the country which they represented, but sometimes a New York merchant assumed the function. William H. Aspinwall, of the firm of Howland & Aspinwall, for example, was vice-consul for Tuscany and Benjamin Aymar was vice-consul for Denmark. For some of the consuls, the position was a full-time job, particularly at the British consulate. Others conducted it in connection with their business. Henry Casimir DeRham, the Swiss consul, we recall, was head of the firm of DeRham, Iselin & Moore, who stood at the head of the importers from Havre. When young August Belmont arrived at New York with Rothschild backing to begin his brilliant financial career, he received the appointment as Austrian consul to strengthen his position.

Scoville tells of one Figaniere, a proud Portuguese who thus mixed official and commercial duties. In addition to being Portuguese consul, he was also bookkeeper for Low, Harriman & Co.:

When anyone called on business connected with the Portuguese consulate, (captains of vessels, or merchants with papers to be certified,) Mr. Figaniere would retire into his private office, where he kept his uniform, sword and cocked hat, and array himself in the paraphernalia of Portugal —then come out with all the dignity of a King's representative, sign the paper, administer the oath, attach the seal of Portugal, and take his fees. He would then undress and resume his old office coat, and return to private life as bookkeeper.

The British consulate naturally overshadowed the others because New York stood first among all the foreign ports which traded with England. In fact, the "Little Englanders," who regarded the colonies as costly burdens, pointed out that the nation carried on a heavier trade with New York, where the only cost was a few thousand pounds for consular expenses, than with Canada, Australia, New Zealand, and the other colonies of settlement which entailed a drain of millions for administration and defense.

During most of our period, this important post was held by two men, James Buchanan and Anthony Barclay. The latter's status was interesting because he was a native New Yorker but claimed to be a British subject as he had been born in the British consulate. His father, Thomas Barclay, son of a colonial rector of Trinity Church at New York, had served in the Loyalist forces during the Revolution and migrated to Nova Scotia where he rose high in the provincial government before returning to New York as consul general. The younger Barclay, who had married a wealthy widow in Georgia and whose appointment was opposed because his marriage had made him a slaveowner, was removed in 1856 for unneutral actions in recruiting for the Crimean War. The British consuls seem to have gone beyond the minimum requirements of their arduous task, for a newspaper notice in

1818 stated that "His Britannic Majesty's subjects, confined as debtors in the City Prison at New York, return their grateful acknowledgement to James Buchanan, Esq., H. M. Consul, for his very polite visit as well as for his liberal donation to enable them the better to commemorate the birthday of His Majesty."

The members of one family in a semiofficial capacity rendered a valuable service to mariners in general and made their name a byword among seagoing men. These were Edmund M. Blunt, who came down from Newburyport to New York about 1806; and his sons George W. and Edmund. Even before he left Newburyport, the elder Blunt had published the first edition of his celebrated *American Coast Pilot*. At New York, this went through edition after edition. By 1827, when it had reached the eleventh, the full title ran:

The American Coast Pilot, containing the Courses and Distances between the Principal Harbours, Capes and Headlands on the Coast of North and South America, with Directions for sailing into the same: Describing the Soundings, Bearings of the Light-Houses and Beacons from the Rocks, Shoals, Ledges, &c., with the prevailing Winds, Settings of the Currents &c. and the Latitude and Longtitude of the Principal Harbours and Capes, together with a Tide Table. By Edmund M. Blunt. Corrected and Improved by Information derived from Official Documents, Actual Observations, and the most experienced Pilots. New York: Published by Edmund and George W. Blunt, 154 Water Street, corner of Maiden Lane.

They also published a large series of charts, many of which were established after their own private surveys, including one of New York Harbor in 1816. On one occasion, they sent a chartered schooner to the eastward to investigate the report that Wood Island Light was not visible from the sea; and they cut short the route to Europe by determining that the Nantucket Shoals did not run out as far as previously supposed. George had an official capacity as first assistant of the U. S. Coast Survey, which began its own publications with plates purchased from the Blunts. The family rendered a service to mariners comparable to that of Lieut. Maury in his study of ocean currents and Nathaniel Bowditch with his *Practical Navigator,* which, incidentally, the Blunts published in several editions.

Associated in the same sort of work were numerous young naval officers, assigned to service with the Coast Survey. An excellent chart, published in 1845, bore the inscription,

Map of New York Bay and Harbor and the Environs. Founded upon a

Trigonometrical Survey under the direction of F. R. Hassler, superintendent of the Survey of the Coast of the United States. Triangulation by James Ferguson and Edmund Blunt Assistants. The Hydrography under the direction of Thomas R. Gedney, Lieutenant U. S. Navy.

Gedney won a lasting place in the port charts, for his discovery of the new "Gedney Channel" off Sandy Hook gave, as we recall, two extra feet of water in minimum depth and a much better line of approach than the old channel. The Army also played its part through the work of the engineers, who were entrusted with the deepening and maintenance of channels, but relatively little work of this sort was done before the Civil War.

One of the particularly lucrative political plums was that of Navy Agent. He handled the purchase of supplies for the Navy at the port, which was one of the chief centers of procurement. In 1841, an indignant ship chandler complained in print that the Navy Agent, a prominent Whig, had thrown his contracts at a rate 30 to 40 per cent higher than normal market rates, to a friend, Marshall O. Roberts, who will later be heard of as one of the prominent steamship operators. These naval contracts have sometimes been regarded as the first step in Roberts's rise to fortune.

Finally, there were the actual military and naval establishments. They were located at New York because it was a seaport, but since they were not a part of its essential port functions, they need not detain us long. The government purchased a site for the Navy Yard at Wallabout Creek in Brooklyn, just across the East River from the great Manhattan bulge at Corlear's Hook. A navy yard, of course, serves the dual function of a rendezvous for warships and a place for supply, repair, and construction. Some of the naval officers opposed New York as a rendezvous but at no other port might sailors be recruited as easily or were as many skilled shipwrights and marine engineers available. The annals of the yard became interesting at times, with an occasional duel among the hotheads who were doing their bit to create vacancies in an overcrowded service; with pompous captains going aboard ship for a court martial; or with expeditions sailing on important missions to distant parts, to punish Algerians or Malays, or to establish Liberia. Probably the dramatic high point at the Navy Yard during our period was the arrival of the U. S. brig *Somers* from a cruise with the astounding news that the midshipman son of a cabinet officer and others had been hanged from the yardarm for alleged mutiny. Her captain, a native New Yorker, stood his courtmartial aboard the *North Carolina* in port and, contrary to the general public indignation at his conduct, most of the eminent New York shipowners upheld his conduct as essential to discipline at sea.

The artillerymen at the harbor forts broke into print much less often, except when a soldier or two was drowned in the capsizing of a sailboat which he could not handle. General Scott and others, inspecting New York's defenses just after the War of 1812, felt that "Castle Clinton" at the Battery was not enough—by the time the enemy came within range of its guns, it would be too late to save the city. A fort was built on Governors Island, and Forts Tompkins and Hamilton were built to command the Narrows, supplemented by Fort Lafayette which rose out of the water at the Long Island end of the bar. Two other forts, Schuyler and Totten, covered the approach from the Sound into East River. Nothing much seems ever to have happened. Major Thomas J. Jackson found the life so boring after two years at Fort Hamilton that he threw up his commission in 1851 and taught school until the Civil War gave him a chance for excitement as "Stonewall." None of the guns of those New York defenses, fortunately, ever had to be fired in earnest; but their very presence was enough to give the port reasonable security in that day.

New York had still other officials and waterfront functionaries whom we have not mentioned, but the inspectors of flour and steamboats have been dealt with elsewhere; and there seems no need to discuss the sordid details of the crimps and harlots who handled the port sojourn of too many visiting seamen, despite the efforts of missions and "bethels." The survey has already gone far enough to indicate that it took more than merchants and mariners alone to operate a first-rate seaport.

CHAPTER XII

MERCHANT PRINCES

APPARENTLY there never has been a typical New Yorker. "On the island of Manhate, and in its environs, there may well be four or five hundred men of different sects and nations; the Director General told me that there were men of eighteen different languages." Thus was the infant Dutch colony described by a famous Jesuit missionary who visited it in 1643. A melting pot from the very outset, New York was still one two centuries later, in our period; and is still more of one today, at the close of its third century.

The merchants of Manhattan, in consequence, present more of a problem in description than do the more homogeneous group who made Boston a great port. The latter, almost to a man, came from families which had taken root in that immediate region some time before the Revolution. Boston had such an abundance of commercial talent that outsiders found little room for a foothold. With a common racial background, and brought up in the same distinctive New England traditions, the Boston merchant was a more definite type. In contrast with the New York situation, the men who developed the maritime business of New England came for the most part from families which had been settled in the region since the reign of George II, if not from that of Charles I. Among the great names of Salem, for example, the Peabody family had settled near by in 1635, the first Derby had come in 1671, and even the un-Puritan name of Crowninshield had been identified with Massachusetts since about 1688. Few of the important Boston merchants had come farther afield than Cape Cod. Far from having to import maritime talent, New England was able to export it in large quantities.

That was far from true of the New York merchants of our period. Such little homogeneity as the group gradually possessed was to be impressed upon it by the newcomers who gradually slipped over the border from New England.

Men of decidedly varied background dominated New York's commerce in 1815. The old Dutch stock was conspicuously absent; but many of them did not need to undergo the toil and worry of trade, for their ancestral acres were yielding ever-increasing rents as Manhattan rapidly grew in population. Some of the British, Huguenot, and other elements of the old Knickerbocker society, however, did their part. As for newcomers, John Jacob Astor was foremost among the merchant princes. He was already rich from his fur empire and his China trade; but many New Yorkers still remembered how he had peddled in the streets, an immigrant fresh from Waldorf in Germany. Archibald Gracie, another important merchant, was a Scot, born in Dumfries, and trained in Liverpool. He had migrated to Virginia and then moved north to take advantage of New York's superior opportunities. Another Scot was Robert Lenox, who had come to New York after a sojourn in New Jersey. The last great commercial house managed by the old New York aristocracy, if one excepts the near-greatness of the Barclays, was the firm of LeRoy, Bayard & McEvers (at times LeRoy, Bayard & Co.), whose Huguenot and Scottish forbears had long been prominent in the city. Its primacy ended with the death of the elder William Bayard in 1826.

The foreigners and the old Knickerbocker society shared the honors for the innovations which gave New York its lead over its rivals in the years immediately following 1815. Probably the man who did most of all was the Yorkshireman, Jeremiah Thompson, who was, we recall, credited with the original inspiration of the Black Ball packets and who also seems to deserve much credit for establishing the "cotton triangle." DeWitt Clinton, whose unflagging energy made the Erie Canal a reality, could trace his distinguished New York ancestry back to 1729. The idea of the *Clermont* came from Fulton, a Pennsylvanian of Irish descent; her engines were made in England by Boulton & Watt; her hull was built at New York by an Englishman; and the essential financial backing came from the deep Knickerbocker pocket of Chancellor Livingston.

Once that group had set New York upon the road to success, outsiders flocked in from every direction. Many came "on their own," but a considerable part of the migration resulted from the common practice, already noticed, of sending a partner, relative, or junior em-

JOHN JACOB ASTOR
1763–1848

WILLIAM BAYARD
1761–1826

DE WITT CLINTON
1769–1828

ROBERT LENOX
1759–1839

All four portraits by courtesy of the Chamber of Commerce of the State of New York

ployee of a firm to handle the business at another port and thus keep all
the profits and commissions under control. This practice was so prevalent that it must be taken into account in considerations of port rivalry
—outside of New England, few ports had their business concentrated
in the hands of native sons. On the whole, the more active the port,
the more such "commercial exiles" it sent out and the fewer it received in return. If Boston represented extreme self-sufficiency, the
newly developed ports of New Orleans and Mobile were just the reverse, receiving a host of outsiders and sending back relatively few in
return.

New York was in an intermediate position in this respect. It sent
men out to almost every port in the world with which it did business,
except to New England. At the same time, it received a considerable,
but probably smaller, number of outside representatives in return.

As far as Europe was concerned, New York seems to have exchanged business men on a fairly even basis. Many New Yorkers were
among the members of the American Chamber of Commerce at Liverpool with a fair number in the similar body at Havre. A few established themselves in other trading centers on the Continent. Their
numbers were offset by the many representatives of British and Continental firms who settled in New York. With the passive commercial
regions of the Caribbean and Latin America, as with the ports of the
southern states, New York's exports of commercial talent far exceeded
its imports, while no hong merchants came from Canton in exchange
for the young New Yorkers who settled there to do business.

While many of these men returned home after they had "made their
pile," it was a significant feature of this interchange of talent that a
large number became naturalized and settled down as permanent residents of their adopted country, eventually merging quite completely
into their new surroundings. New York experienced both sides of
this. A Captain Delano, for instance, who had come from New Bedford to New York, settled at Valparaiso, where a permanent branch of
that versatile family was established—the genealogy shows, in later
generations, a large number of Don Jaimes, Don Tomasos, if not Don
Juans, who had become good Chilians in spite of the good old Yankee
surname of Delano. On the other hand, such well-established families as the Belmonts and the DeRhams at New York today are descended from men who first came to the city as representatives of European business houses a century or so ago.

Before turning to the New Englanders, who were far and away the most numerous and successful of the invaders, we might note briefly some of those from other regions who were shrewd or lucky enough to rise to the status of "merchant prince." Considering the fact that according to the census of 1840, New York had 417 commercial houses engaged in foreign trade and 918 commission firms, it is obviously out of the question to do more than look at some of the more important merchants, examining whence they came and how high they rose; but to make no attempt to list them individually or even to estimate how many came from each region.

Because of the volume of trade with Liverpool, more business men came from England and Scotland than from any other foreign country. They swelled the membership of the societies of St. George and St. Andrew, while Wales, with its proximity to Liverpool, furnished members for the St. David's Society. These transplanted Britons had a journal of their own in the weekly *Albion;* and they used to take the ferry over to Hoboken to eat turtle in celebration of the King's or the Queen's birthday. Despite their numbers, not very many of them reached first rank in New York commercial circles. Many of them were manufacturers' agents, the "damned Yorkshiremen" of the protectionists, who transmitted the incoming Liverpool textiles to the auction rooms and lived in the numerous boarding houses which catered to British business. Most of them never appeared in print until, one day, the papers would announce the death of so-and-so, a native of Huddersfield or Bolton, "long a resident of this city."

None of the later comers from Great Britain approached the eminence of Jeremiah Thompson, who had come from Yorkshire before our period. His closest rivals for high honors would also be found among that little group of Black Ball pioneers. Benjamin Marshall eventually went upstate to supervise his cotton factories. Jeremiah's uncle Francis, besides helping to manage Black Ballers, was one of the first to raise the steerage trade to the level of big business. Samuel Thompson, another nephew of Francis, continued this in an even more extensive fashion and acquired ownership of several large immigrant "packets." James Boorman, who came from England, and his Scottish partner, John Johnston, headed a leading iron importing firm; Boorman also became first president of the Hudson River Railroad. The Irish members of the St. Patrick's Society could point with pride to John Flack, a prominent but not outstanding shipowner early in the period, and to Dominick Lynch, the debonair wine merchant. John Haggerty, whose auction business built up one of the largest fortunes early in the period, had a good Irish name but was not a first-generation newcomer. Most distinguished of those directly from Ireland was Alexander T. Stewart of Ulster, who amassed millions in the dry-goods business.

Several distinct waves of Frenchmen came to New York at various periods and some of them succeeded remarkably well. The Bayards, LeRoys, and Pintards were of French Huguenot stock which had been settled near New York for about a century by 1815, as was James P. Allaire, the foremost builder of marine engines. They, however, had become members of the old New York stock by the time our period opens. The Grinnells and the Delanos were also of Huguenot descent, but their long New Bedford background places them among the New Englanders. A wave of *émigrés* came direct from France when the French Revolution started to get rough and a few went into business; but most of them were returning to Havre or Bordeaux in the opening months of peace in 1815. More conspicuous in New York business circles were those other Frenchmen who fled at the same time from another terror—the Negro uprising in Santo Domingo. That wave, which gave Philadelphia its greatest merchant in Stephen Girard, enriched New York business with Francis Depau, son-in-law of Admiral DeGrasse and founder of the Havre packet service, as well as Stephen Jumel. The latter was the leading wine merchant in the early years of the century and his wife, an unscrupulous charmer from Rhode Island, tricked him out of his fortune and later married Aaron Burr. All three of those groups came to New York to escape persecution or death. The fourth group came more gradually and more voluntarily during our period, principally to participate in the western end of business on the New York-Havre shuttle. Conspicuous in this category were the eccentric Louis Salles, who made more than a million in the trade, and Charles Sagory, the New York representative of Lewis Rogers's vast tobacco business, involving Richmond, New Orleans, New York, Havre, and Paris.

A few highly successful merchants came from other parts of the Continent. Switzerland's most distinguished representative was Henry Casimir DeRham, already mentioned as consul, and so valuable a patron of the Havre packets that one was named for him. From Holland came Frederick Gebhard, and his sons-in-law, Frederick Schuchardt and Frederick Favre, who made a fortune in bringing gin from

Amsterdam in their fast regular traders. Though Sweden sent no merchant of importance, John Ericsson contributed to the port's development with his original work in marine engineering. The outstanding Spaniard was the somewhat mysterious millionaire, Peter Harmony, who owned many vessels and traded heavily with Spain and the Caribbean.

The Jews had not as yet made their remarkable inroads into New York business circles. Plenty of them, to be sure, were to be found on and around Chatham Street, but relatively few had risen to the wealth and importance which many enjoyed a century later. The most distinguished was the Rothschild representative, August Belmont, who married into the family of the Perry commodores, and built up a fortune in finance; but the Chamber of Commerce contained few Jews among its members.

Relatively few of the principal business men came from the states to the southward. Some of them were natives of Pennsylvania, Maryland, and Virginia, but almost none were from the far South. The best known of this group were James and Stewart Brown, who handled the New York end of the private commercial banking business, established by the Irish Alexander Brown at Baltimore.

Even near-by New Jersey contributed amazingly few, when one contrasts its influence with that of Connecticut which had slightly fewer people and was little farther from New York City. Save for the all-important Stevens family, whose spacious grounds in Hoboken bordered on the waters of the port itself, practically the only merchant of the front rank from New Jersey was John C. Green, born near Lawrenceville. Propinquity, then, was not everything.

Upstate New York, however, did a bit more than New Jersey, with Eli Hart, one of the foremost flour traders, and three men whose start to fortune was based on steamboats—Isaac Newton, who helped to develop the "floating palaces"; Daniel Drew, the sharp and sanctimonious operator; and George Law, son of a farmer who had migrated from the County Down in Ireland. Long Island was represented by three families of Quakers: Isaac Wright and his son, the Black Ball pioneers; Samuel Hicks and his sons, wealthy shipping magnates; and the Lawrences, noteworthy in several fields. New York's presiding genius in marine insurance, Walter R. Jones, also came from Long Island. Closer at hand, Staten Island produced the greatest transportation genius of them all in Cornelius Vanderbilt.

Though the old stock of New Yorkers were losing their control of trade in 1815, it was only to be expected that occasional native sons rose high from modest backgrounds. Particularly conspicuous were John and Philip Hone, of German and French descent, sons of a carpenter in modest circumstances. They established one of the two most successful auction houses, and amassed comfortable fortunes, though Philip later lost most of his. He had other claims to fame, however, especially as author of a valuable and oft-quoted diary. Another marked success was Moses Taylor, son of a confidential agent of Astor. After a good beginning in Cuban trade, we recall, he became head of the City Bank and eventually amassed several millions. There were others in various fields, such as Robert Kermit, a sea captain's son, who became an operator of Liverpool packets.

All of these, however, whether born in England, France, Holland, Long Island, or New York City itself, were swamped by the mighty invasion of business and maritime talent from New England in general and Connecticut in particular.

The tales of ships and skippers leave the impression that New England enjoyed a virtual monopoly of America's seagoing enterprise. The arid tables of imports and exports, however, show that the center of commercial activity lay not in New England but thirty miles beyond its frontiers in New York City. By the eve of the Civil War, the foreign commerce of New York was nearly six times that of all New England.

The answer to this apparent conflict between tradition and statistics is that the New Englanders captured New York port about 1820 and dominated its business until after the Civil War. Applying a little genealogy to the occupants of New York's countinghouses, shipyards, and quarterdecks, we find New Englanders in most of the important positions. They built and commanded most of the ships engaged in New York's ever-increasing commerce. They were, moreover, the leaders among the merchants and shipowners who set those ships in motion and made fortunes from their comings and goings.

There had been New England participation in New York commerce ever since Isaac Allerton, reputedly the wealthiest of the Pilgrim Fathers, became one of the leading traders of New Haven and New Amsterdam. Since that time, a gradual infiltration had been in progress from the eastward. The chief rush came around 1800 and twenty years later New England had the situation well in hand. The movement was part of the remarkable expansion of New England into many spheres of national activity beyond its own frontiers. The same motive which lured farmers from the barren, stony acres of western New England to the richer fields of the Middle West was attracting other New Englanders to the thriving seaport just beyond the Connecticut border.

Compared with the rather easy-going old Knickerbocker element, the newcomers from the eastward were "more conservative in character, more grave in temperament, and at the same time, more enterprising, and more insistent in action than the descendants of the Dutch and English settlers" of New York. Scoville, describing one of them, remarked that he "was the personification of a Yankee—if there is such a race—long legs, hatchet face, skin and bones, slight, pokey, and keen as a briar."

Most of them came from southern New England. Beyond Cape Cod, plenty of commercial and seagoing opportunities were to be found at Boston, Salem, Newburyport, Portsmouth, Portland, and other "down east" ports to absorb most of the commercial talent in that region; but an ever-increasing number of ships and mariners came from those more remote New England ports and compensated for the lack of recruits to the ranks of the merchant princes.

It was perhaps natural that Connecticut should be most heavily represented among the invaders from the eastward, since it was the nearest New England state to New York. Yet the even closer New Jersey had made no such contribution. Long Island cut off New Haven and the other western ports from direct contact with the open sea and, since the Connecticut Yankee was famous for his trading proclivities, it was not surprising that he took advantage of the excellent opportunity close at hand. Talent poured in from all parts of the State, Stonington being particularly prominent for its sea captains and Stamford for its shipbuilders, while potential merchant princes came from all over the State. Others came from Rhode Island and from southern Massachusetts, particularly from New Bedford, Nantucket, and the Cape.

The New England recruits for New York's commercial circles fell into four main groups. Some men who had already built up a moderately prosperous business in a New England port moved it to the wider sphere. Others came to handle the New York end of a business which remained in New England. A third lot were Yankee captains who came ashore to set up countinghouses at New York, and finally there were the self-made men who came to New York young and worked up from the bottom in the New York business district.

The constant commercial intercourse between New York and New England meant that good connections with one of the ports to the eastward gave a prospect of adequate commissions. Both ends of this business were usually retained in New England hands. If a Boston cargo of tea from Canton or a Salem shipment of pepper from Sumatra was to be sold at New York, the commissions were apt to go to a son of the owner, a friend of the family, or a junior employee who had moved to New York for the purpose. It was the same with shipments of domestic cotton goods from Lowell and Fall River, or shoes from Lynn and Haverhill, to say nothing of Maine lumber and New Bedford whale oil. Equally lucrative were the possibilities of the ship brokers, whose business it was to offer ships, brigs, and schooners from one's home port in New England for "sale, freight, or charter" and to find as constant employment for the vessels as possible, frequently acting as agent at a generous commission. Both the ready-made merchants from eastern ports and the young representatives of firms which remained there were very numerous among the South Street countinghouses.

The quarterdeck was not as common a preparation for the countinghouse at New York as it was to the eastward where a few years in command of a brig or ship had figured in the background of many of the leading merchants. The number of shipmasters who became merchant princes in New York was considerably less than of those whose whole education lay in the countinghouse; only a few of them even had experience as supercargoes, who, we recall, were a sort of business men afloat. Preserved Fish was a conspicuous graduate of the quarterdeck. Three others, Charles H. Marshall, Elisha E. Morgan, and Silas Holmes made fortunes in operating packets after previously commanding them. Several more utilized the contacts which they had developed either with passengers or with merchants during their frequent periods in port, to establish themselves as ship brokers, commission merchants, or ship chandlers, but only those four, all New Englanders, rose to the front rank during our period. Captain Rowland H. Macy, of a prominent old Nantucket whaling family, however, started a little store in 1858, which would one day grow to gigantic size. The resultant absence of ex-mariners made the New York commercial magnates a somewhat less colorful group than were the merchants of Boston, Salem, and Portland.

Finally, there were the poor boys, particularly from Connecticut, who made good. Old Scoville, who had been one of them himself, wrote several passages which remind one of Horatio Alger—and Scoville was apt to be more accurate in some of his generalizations than in his specific facts.

His winter schooling generally ends when the boy is fourteen years old. He can by that time (if he is smart) parse pretty well, and has reached the "double rule of three" in Daboll. He needs no more towards his future success than a trunk, "Sunday-go-to-meeting" clothes, and a Bible. This the family provide, and with a few dollars and a mother's prayer, the young hero goes forth to seek his fortune in the great mart of commerce.

He needs but a foothold. He asks no more, and he is as sure to keep it as that light will dispel darkness. He gets a place somewhere in a "store." It is all store to him. He hardly comprehends the difference between the business of the great South Street house, that sends ships over the world, and the Bowery dry goods shop with three or four spruce clerks. He rather thinks the Bowery or Canal Street store the biggest, as they make more show. But wherever this boy strikes, he fastens. He is honest, determined and intelligent. From the word "go" he begins to learn, to compare, and no matter what the commercial business he is engaged in, he will not rest until he knows all about it, its details—in fact, as much as the principals.

Another characteristic of the future merchant is this—no sooner has he got a foothold, than the New England boy begins to look for standing room for others. Perhaps he is the son of a small farmer who has several other children. The pioneer boy, if true blue, does not rest until one by one he has procured situations for all of his brothers. If he has none, he has friends in the village, and ere a year, Bill, Jo and Jim have been seduced off to New York.

Later, Scoville explains why these young New Englanders were more successful than the New York boys with their superior connections:

It is a singular fact that a foreign-born boy, or one from the New England states, will succeed in this city, and become a partner in our largest firms, much oftener than a born New York boy. The great secret of this success is the perfect willingness to be useful and to do what they are required to do, and cheerfully.

Take for instance such a firm as Grinnell, Minturn & Co. In their counting room, they have New York boys and New England boys. Moses H. Grinnell comes down in the morning and says to John, a New York boy— "Charley [sic], take my overcoat up to my house on Fifth Avenue." Mr. Charley takes the coat, mutters something about "I'm not an errand boy. I came here to learn business," and moves reluctantly. Mr. Grinnell sees it, and at the same time, one of his New England clerks says, "I'll take it up." "That is right. Do so," says Mr. G., and to himself he says, "that boy is smart, will work," and gives him plenty to do. He gets promoted—gets the confidence of the chief clerk and employers, and eventually gets into the firm as partner.

It's so all over the city. It is so in nearly every store, counting room or office. Outside boys get on faster than New York boys owing to two reasons. One is, they are not afraid to work, or to run of errands, or do cheerfully what they are told to do. A second reason, they do their work quickly. A New York boy has many acquaintances—a New England boy has none, and is not called upon to stop and talk, when sent out by the merchant.

Those old remarks, written during the Civil War, seem worth quoting *in extenso,* because they explain the beginnings of so many prominent New York mercantile careers. The story goes that a Scot, returning to Glasgow from a business trip to London, was asked how he liked the English. "I canna tell," was the alleged reply, "as I talked only with the heads of firms." A New Englander visiting New York during the second quarter of the last century might well have carried back a similar story.

Any list, however restricted, of the leading New York shipping houses between 1820 and 1860 would certainly include six New England firms, four of which were headed by sets of brothers. The Griswolds from Old Lyme and the Lows from Salem were in the China trade; the Howlands from Norwich in the Latin-American trade; and from New Bedford the Grinnells were among the greatest shipowners of the day. Ranking with them were the great commission house headed by Jonathan Goodhue from Salem and Pelatiah Perit from Norwich, together with the extensive metal importing and cotton exporting concern of Anson G. Phelps in successive partnerships with Elisha Peck and William E. Dodge, his son-in-law, all of whom came from Connecticut.

In 1794, the vanguard of that group appeared in New York. George Griswold at twenty-one grew restive at the limited opportunities of Old Lyme, where Griswolds had been settled for more than a century, furnishing Connecticut with more than one governor. George went to seek his fortune in New York, followed two years later by his brother Nathaniel. The brothers, "stout, fine looking young men, six feet high each, and well proportioned," in 1796 formed the firm of N. L. & G. Griswold. An early letter book, one of the few to survive a fire which later gutted their countinghouse, indicates that they started as brokers for the shipping from the lower Connecticut River and as flour exporters. Then they sent their flour to the West Indies, importing sugar and rum in return. From that, their activities stretched down the coast of South America and a considerable fleet of vessels flew their blue-and-white-checkered house flag. While continuing their general commerce, they became leaders in the Canton trade, we recall, with a succession of ships named *Panama*. Scoville was probably exaggerating when he wrote, "I do not suppose there is a country store however insignificant, in the whole United States, that has not seen a large or small package of tea marked 'Ship *Panama*' and 'N. L. & G. G.' upon it." At any rate, the Griswold business was so prosperous that the wits translated the initials "No Loss and Great Gain." "Old Nat," quiet and retiring, handled the shipping end of the business and made an added fortune in dredging on the side, while George did not limit his bold financial ability to the company's affairs but played a conspicuous role in the city's banking and real-estate development. Two cousins from Old Lyme, John and Charles C. Griswold, made a conspicuous success with the "Black X" packets to London, John serving for many years as operator while Charles lived for a while in Savannah, buying up cotton, before retiring to Connecticut, a part owner in most of the line's ships.

Joseph Howland, descended from John Howland of the *Mayflower*, was reasonably prosperous as a shipowner and merchant in Norwich, in 1800. Shortly afterwards, he moved his business and his family from Connecticut to New York. His own transplanted commercial activity attained no particular magnitude; our interest centers in his sons Gardiner Greene and Samuel Shaw Howland. Gardiner started his training with his father and with the Bayard firm, married an heiress, and in 1816, at twenty-nine, joined his brother in the firm of G. G. & S. Howland. We have already noticed their remarkable success in the Latin-American trade, conducted with their numerous second-hand ships, and we shall hear shortly of the "Greek frigate" scandal which left them richer in cash but poorer in reputation for business honesty. The brothers retired from active direction of the firm in 1834, retaining a special interest. Gardiner became one of the chief promoters of the Hudson River Railroad. His son, William E., and his nephew, William H. Aspinwall, whose mother was a Howland, continued the business as Howland & Aspinwall. The house gradually engaged in merchant banking and Aspinwall later will be seen in his important role in connection with the California trade, running the Pacific Mail steamships and developing the Isthmus of Panama.

Late in 1807, Jonathan Goodhue moved from Salem to New York with far better backing than the average New England invader. He had been trained in the Salem countinghouse of John Norris, who sent him as supercargo on two voyages to the East. Son of a United States senator, young Goodhue came well armed with letters of introduction to business and social circles and was aided besides by the patronage of John Norris, Joseph Peabody, and William Gray, who threw many good commissions his way. Constant trade interruptions, beginning with the Embargo, gave him a slow beginning, but gradually Goodhue & Co. became one of the outstanding commission houses of the city. His principal silent partner was Pelatiah Perit of Norwich. The influence of the house was increased by its close relations with the British banking house of Baring which loaned half the money for the Goodhue purchase of the Black Ball Line in 1834, in conjunction with two of the captains. Graduates of their countinghouse were established as correspondents of the firm in handling their imports and exports. Perit and another silent partner, Calvin Durand, also from Connecticut, carried on the business after Goodhue's death in 1848.

A fourth great house had its origins entirely in the New Bedford region. Preserved Fish, an eccentric whaling captain, decided that selling whale oil was more profitable than gathering it and moved to New York. In 1815, he formed a partnership with his cousin, Joseph Grinnell, also from New Bedford. Fish, contrary to a legend that he was picked up as a baby adrift at sea, came from Portsmouth, Rhode Island, where the family had settled in 1643, a year after the first Huguenot Grinnell (originally Grennelle) reached there. The firm of Fish & Grinnell (later Fish, Grinnell & Co., and finally Grinnell, Minturn & Co.) began as commission merchants for New Bedford whale oil, selling, according to Scoville, "two kinds of oil, good and bad." The success of the Black Ballers lured them into packet operation and by 1824 their Swallowtail liners were running both to Liverpool and to London. By 1829 both the original partners had retired, Joseph Grinnell returning to New Bedford, where he later became a Congressman, a railroad president, and the pioneer in that city's cotton industry, while Fish, after various ventures which ended in disagreements, settled down as a New York bank president.

Their places were taken by Joseph's younger brothers, Henry and Moses Hicks Grinnell, who had already come from New Bedford, and by Henry's brother-in-law, Robert Bowne Minturn, whose grandfather had moved a prosperous business from Newport to New York and whose father had headed the house of Minturn & Champlin until ruined by the War of 1812. Their swallowtail house flag eventually flew over more than fifty ships, and they seem to have been among the most extensive shipowners in America. Their fleet included not only the numerous packets of their two lines, but also general freighters and the most famous of the clippers, the *Flying Cloud*. Trading extensively with England, China, Cuba, and elsewhere, the firm was conservative in policy but, as Scoville remarked, "all is fish that gets into their nets." Celebrated for their unostentatious generosity and their public-spirited cooperation in local and national affairs, the three partners were among New England's finest contributions to New York port.

The Lows from Salem came on the scene somewhat later than the others. It was not until 1829 that the elder Seth Low, a native of Gloucester, moved his business in China and India drugs and other wares from Salem to New York, where he also served as agent for glass bottles manufactured in New England. He was soon followed thither by Abiel A., the eldest of his twelve children. Abiel went to Canton in 1833, and, like his brother later, became a partner in Russell & Co. In 1840, he returned to New York and went into the China trade on his own account. In 1845, he took his brother Josiah into partnership and later others of the family also became partners, but Abiel's leadership was reflected in the firm name of A. A. Low & Bros. Their *Houqua* and her successors, we know, were among the fastest of the early China clippers and one of her commanders was another brother, Captain Charles P. Low, who won a reputation as a "princely host" at Canton. The firm was still active in 1865 when it took into partnership Abiel's son Seth, who later became president of Columbia University and mayor of New York City.

More typical of the experience of poor Connecticut boys who "made good" was the career of Anson G. Phelps. Born in Simsbury, he was left an orphan while still young and learned saddlery under his older brother. He established his own business in saddlery at Hartford and began to sell his products in the South. In 1812, he moved to New York and joined in partnership with Elisha Peck from Hartford. Soon he was engaged in his great specialty, the importation of iron, copper, brass, and other metals, an activity in which he attained first place among American merchants. To pay for these abroad, he shipped cotton from New York and was one of the promoters of the pioneer

JONATHAN GOODHUE
1783–1848

*Courtesy of the New York Society Library and
Frick Art Reference Library*

ANSON G. PHELPS
1781–1853

JACOB BARKER
1779–1871

HENRY C. DE RHAM
1785–1873

Three of the above portraits by courtesy of the Chamber of Commerce

line of coastal packets to Charleston in 1822. Later, his partnership with Peck gave way to one with two of his sons-in-law as Phelps, Dodge & Co. The silent partner, David James from upstate New York, represented them in England. The other, William E. Dodge, a native of Connecticut, has left interesting memoirs of his start as a $3-a-week clerk in a New York dry-goods concern. Later, after running a country store back in Connecticut, Dodge became a dry-goods jobber before marrying one of Phelps's seven daughters and becoming a partner in the metal business. Eventually, Phelps, Dodge & Co. supplemented the importation of metals by developing the domestic supply of iron from western Pennsylvania and copper from Michigan and Arizona, as well as engaging in the manufacture of metal wares, particularly in the Connecticut town named Ansonia for Phelps. Both Phelps and Dodge amassed large fortunes and were very generous in their support of religious and philanthropic measures.

There were many other conspicuous New Englanders. Stephen Whitney from Connecticut, who became one of New York's first millionaires, is said to have laid the basis of his fortune by smuggling cotton out through Amelia Island during the War of 1812. The leading house of private bankers, Prime, Ward & King, were all New Englanders. Nathaniel Prime, according to Scoville, was a butler in a New England mansion before becoming a financial giant. The first of three generations of Samuel Wards came down from Rhode Island and the second was father of Julia Ward Howe. James Gore King was the son of the Maine-born Rufus, one of the first ministers to the Court of St. James's. Three different Morgans came from the eastward. Junius Spencer Morgan, born in western Massachusetts, came by way of Hartford to New York, where he spent two years in learning the banking business with which the name of his son, J. Pierpont, would be prominently associated in later days. Edwin D. Morgan likewise came from western Massachusetts by way of Hartford. He revealed his business genius in a clever deal while on a trip to New York, moved there about 1836, built up a large wholesale grocery business, and became one of the heaviest importers of sugar and coffee. He served as war governor of New York and later as senator. The third Morgan, Charles, a shrewd, quiet native of Killingsworth, Connecticut, came to New York as a boy and, starting as a grocery clerk, was soon a ship chandler and fruit importer. He soon was prominent in ship-owning, running one of the early lines of steamers to Charleston and then opening steam service in the western Gulf between New Orleans and Texas, where, operating from New York, he later became supreme. He also purchased one of the largest marine-engine works in New York and eventually went into railroads in the Gulf region. Edward K. Collins, the foremost individual operator of packets and steamships, was born at Truro, far out on Cape Cod, and joined his father at New York, specializing at first in the Mexican trade. In addition to the merchants proper, we shall see later that several of the chief shipbuilders likewise came from the eastward, as well as many others in important positions; but this brief account must not degenerate into too much of a catalogue.

Ample evidence shows that these New Englanders were leaders in New York commercial circles. The Chamber of Commerce of the State of New York, the mouthpiece of the merchants, had a New Englander as president for the entire thirty years from 1845 to 1875 save for one interlude of eight months. James G. King, Moses H. Grinnell, Pelatiah Perit, Abiel A. Low, and William E. Dodge all served in that position. Whenever the merchants assembled to protest against the tariff or to welcome an important guest, a Goodhue, a Griswold, a Grinnell, or a Howland usually presided at the ceremony. Most of these merchant princes were directors and many were presidents of banks and insurance companies. Their influence on New York business methods was so strong that it was remarked in 1845 that the city "borrows its institutions mainly from New England."

The Knickerbocker element resented the coming of the New Englanders fully as much, it is said, as a later New York resented the invasion of another acquisitive group. The New Englanders not only beat the old New Yorkers at the commercial game, but had the effrontery to boast about it. As early as 1805 they formed the New England Society in the City of New York "to commemorate the landing of the Pilgrim Fathers on Plymouth Rock and to promote friendship, charity, and mutual association, and to establish and maintain a library," with the membership open to "any person being of full age, being a native, or the son of a native, of any of the New England states, and of fair character." The carefully preserved accounts of their annual dinners reek with self-satisfaction. The toasts in 1831, for instance, included, "New England habits—industry, enterprise and shrewdness," "The rich and precious cargo of the *Mayflower*—Yankee capital—the real wealth of nations," and "The universal Yankee nation!

As universal, it would seem, as civil and religious liberty." In 1846, Brooklyn, the home of many "down east" shipmasters as well as merchants, established a New England Society of its own.

Washington Irving was particularly irritated at the invaders from the eastward and became prime mover in the organization of the St. Nicholas Society, of which he was the first secretary. Its start is recorded by Philip Hone, who apparently did not take it as seriously as Irving. In his diary for February 14, 1835, we find the following:

I attended this evening a meeting at Washington Hall of a number of New Yorkers, with a design to form a regular Knickerbocker society, as a sort of set off against St. Patrick's, St. George's and more particularly the New England. The meeting was large and exceedingly respectable . . . a goodly show of good fellows who will not disgrace their ancestors. . . . I suppose we shall have a few annual dinners which will be pretty much all that will grow out of it.

The annual dinners have continued for a century and with them the ceremony of turning the head of the society's gilded rooster to the eastward so that it might crow back at the Yankees.

Even a half century later, the irritation of the old New Yorkers had not completely died out. In 1883, the elder James W. Gerard delivered before the New York Historical Society a rambling paper entitled "The Impress of Nationalities upon New York." Remarking that there was no love lost in the old days, he continued:

There is good feeling and fellowship enough now, and a peaceable quiet invasion of New York in business and professional circles is continually in progress, without murmur. The laudation of New England and its sons, however, is rather too much dinned into our ears by those sons denizened here, and the changes are played on Plymouth Rock until we have become heartily tired of the continual *reveille*. With all due respect for New England, and admiration for its enterprising and cultured sons and daughters, the queer question arises continually in our minds, why, if it be such a delectable and superior place as is so abundantly lauded, should her sons and daughters desert it in such flocks and locate themselves in such an inferior place as New York.

However much pride New York might take in the swelling statistics of its commerce, it admitted the superiority of the Boston merchants in their cultural interests, at least in the early days before the New Englanders took over the port. The editor of the *Evening Post* wrote in 1823:

It is a truth, a humiliating truth to New York, that the character of the mercantile class of its citizens, generally speaking, is, in point of literature, politics and the fine arts, not upon a footing with that of the same class at Boston. This disparity, I have believed, is chiefly, if not altogether, owing to the great superiority of the public schools, English and Latin, in the latter place, and the far greater attention devoted to those institutions, by the public functionaries there, than here.

The occasion for those remarks was the establishing in 1820 of a Mercantile Library Association and an Association of Merchant Clerks under the auspices of the Chamber of Commerce. Like the similar organizations in other cities, these were designed to give ambitious young clerks an opportunity to improve their minds. At the time of organization, the preamble of the association called attention to the fact that

In a large and populous city, with excitements to pleasure surrounding them on every side, and hurried on by the warmth of early years, too many have become the votaries of vice and depravity; too many have sacrificed their health and their characters at the shrine of dissipation and run the giddy round of error before they have beheld the dawning of manhood. Our object is to oppose a barrier to the inroads of these moral foes, and to guard ourselves against their contaminating influence. The end we have in view is intellectual improvement.

The project received the blessing and support of many of the same merchants who were trying to provide better living conditions for the sailors in port. A reading room was opened, with a library which excluded "all works of an immoral or irreligious tendency," but at the end of three years it had only 200 members from the young clerks, whose total was estimated at 4000; and in 1827, a correspondent complained that the average clerk was "led to conclude that loquacity in a salesman, or a knowledge of Bennett's system in a bookkeeper, is the perfection of a mercantile character."

As late as 1840, the Mercantile Society announced a course of lectures by seven distinguished men, including "Mr. Longfellow, the poet," on Dante and Richter; Professor Torrey on "the Chemistry of Nature," Professor Silliman "on the curious subject of meteoric stars," Horace Mann on education, and "R. W. Emerson, an impressive speaker, possessing a peculiar style and mode of thinking," on the philosophy of history. This stern chase, to catch up with Boston in culture, however, seems to have been as fruitless as the efforts of Boston and the other ports to catch up with New York in commerce during those same years.

College graduates were rare among the New York merchant princes, but that would hold true for the business men of most other cities in that day. Jacob Le Roy had apparently been graduated from Princeton in 1783, the year before he formed his famous partnership with William Bayard. Pelatiah Perit of Goodhue & Co. was a Yale man, as was the elder John Austin Stevens, president of the Bank of Commerce, whose son of the same name, a sugar importer and author, attended Harvard. James G. King was also a Harvard graduate, while Charles King, a Gracie partner until the firm's failure and later president of Columbia, had attended Harrow with Byron and Peel and then the École Polytechnique. Mortimer Livingston, who operated Havre packets and steamships, was graduated from Columbia. A few other scattered examples might be found, but most of the merchant princes had not gone beyond the little red schoolhouse.

On that point, Scoville commented that "Old Archibald Gracie took ten times more pains with his clerks than is taken in Columbia College," and added

If I had a son, whom I wished to make a thoroughbred gentleman—a man of the world and a man of business, I would send him to college for three years, and then let him spend five more in the counting-house of a heavy merchant, where he should sweep out and end by being a thorough bookkeeper.

Aside from education and countinghouse training, there remained, of course, the two traditional aids to success: inheriting money and marrying it. A recent writer, in comparing Boston and New York in later days, attributes part of Boston's gradual loss of initiative to a practice which developed in its mercantile circles, sustained by a judicial decision around 1830. This was the so-called "spendthrift trust," whereby cautious merchant fathers tied up their sons' inheritances in trust funds which assured a comfortable income but prevented the use of the principal. This system, it was pointed out, produced a secure group of "four per cent coupon cutters" who had plenty of chance to develop the finer things of life, being deprived of the opportunity, if not the incentive, of risking their capital in new ventures. This Boston practice did not prevail at New York, where sons had more opportunity to risk their patrimony in new ventures, with the alternative prospects of increasing it or of losing everything. Consequently, New York offered many examples of sons working a comfortable inheritance into a substantial fortune while, conversely, there were more cases of "three generations from shirt sleeves to shirt sleeves" than among the sheltered sons of Boston.

Even for those who lacked the silver spoon at birth, marriage might often be a short cut to success. The self-made Connecticut Yankees showed uncanny luck in winning heiresses and in rising rapidly in the businesses established by their fathers-in-law. In many cases, it is difficult to tell whether the business or marriage ties were the first cause of success—sometimes sons-in-law were promoted to lieutenants and sometimes lieutenants were rewarded with a daughter's hand. Charles Morgan placed Connecticut sons-in-law in charge of different branches of his far-flung operations; William E. Dodge rose from comfortable profits in dry goods to a fortune in metals with his Phelps marriage; while the Howlands supplemented their modest patrimony with marriage into the circle of merchant princes. The Haggerty auction fortune established very comfortably three sons-in-law, including a son of DeWitt Clinton. The examples might be multiplied by the score.

As for the finished products of mercantile training, one wishes that space permitted a whole chapter on the mode of life and the attitudes of the New York merchant princes, for abundant material is at hand from many scattered sources. As it is, there is room to mention only very briefly a few of their outstanding characteristics.

In the opening years of our period, the elite of New York's social and business world—and the two were closely interlocked—might be found in comfortable residences in the aristocratic First Ward, close to the business district at the lower tip of the island, some of the finest houses being those which overlooked Bowling Green. Some of the early merchants actually lived over their places of business. Gradually the residential district moved uptown. Scoville's description of the experience of Daniel and Henry Parish, prominent merchants, was typical:

Daniel hired the house No. 12 Beekman street, and he lived there until 1831, when he and his brother Henry bought the lots Nos. 49 and 51 Barclay street, and put up two houses side by side, that were deemed in their day as palaces. . . . Our citizens would go out of their way, especially on Sundays, to look at them, then in a fashionable quarter of the town. The Parishes saw their happy days in those houses. They lived merry while they occupied them. When in after years, 1847, Henry moved up to a palace in Union square, corner of Seventeenth street, Daniel resided in his old house No. 51, years afterwards or until 1854, when he moved to Fifth Avenue and Sixteenth street. It is said that when Henry bade farewell to No. 49 Barclay, he visited every room, like a child, and the last words he said as he was

MOSES TAYLOR
1806–1882

JAMES BOORMAN
1783–1866

WALTER R. JONES
1793–1855

GEORGE W. BLUNT
1802–1878

All four portraits by courtesy of the Chamber of Commerce of the State of New York

leaving it, were: "Old house, good-by, I shall never know so much happiness anywhere else."

One of these old merchant homes, built in 1836, on Fourth Street, has been restored and opened by the Historical Landmarks Association.

More familiar to New Yorkers is the old Archibald Gracie mansion on the East River near Hell Gate, one of the more remote "country-seats" which many of the merchants maintained in addition to their town houses. An Englishman visiting New York in the spring of 1819 wrote:

All the road from the city, to the extremity of and beyond the isle, is adorned, on both sides, with the country-seats and pleasure grounds of rich citizens, who, like those of London, every morning and evening drive to and fro in great numbers. . . . The houses on the roads, thus leading thru the isle to the city, have each from five to ten acres of green pasture, park, or pleasure-garden.

Some of these country seats were as far distant as Throg's Neck and Flushing, where Gardiner G. Howland had a "noble farm," but many others were far down in what is now considered the heart of the city. Scoville wrote of Henry Coster, for example, that he "moved from No. 28 William to a new house in 85 Chambers street. He had a country seat in what is now First Avenue, between Thirtieth and Thirty-first streets. It was sold to Anson G. Phelps in 1835."

Whether at town house or country seat, a delightful social life existed among many of the merchant princes and their friends of the old New York society, whose real estate shielded them from the necessity for scrambling. One has only to open Philip Hone's diary to catch a glimpse of that existence, particularly of the constant succession of dinners where old wines of the best vintage were consumed in quantities which kept the Havre packets busy. Hone, a combination of the old New Yorker and self-made man, was in the inner circle of the day and missed nothing. The older edition of his diary includes many lists of the guests at these occasions—and two or three of the New England merchant princes were generally among the number. Hone, like some of his friends, winced at the ridicule which Dickens poured upon the generous hospitality accorded to him on his first visit to America in the 'forties.

In addition to the well-ordered good living among the great merchants, some among the commercial groups fell into the extreme categories of the "spartans" and the "sports." Scoville contrasted the career of two Pearl Street dry-goods merchants. John Robbins, who in 1846 was rated as worth $800,000, as much as Moses Taylor, Henry Grinnell, and Jonathan Goodhue combined, was put in the "spartan" category. Even at the age of eighty-two, during the Civil War, Robbins

goes regularly to market every morning; stopping first at the baker's for his loaf of bread for breakfast—and this, too, in all kinds of weather, in winter and summer. He never wore a pair of gloves in his life; but in very cold weather he wears his woollen mittens. Every morning, as early as the light, he is in his store. He opens it, sweeps it out, and makes the fire. . . . Mr. Robbins has never been a slave to luxuries, or felt their necessity. He never had a fire in his sleeping apartment, and he never had a wash-stand there. He did without Croton water for many years, and was content with the old-fashioned pump water. . . .

He was the very opposite of his old friend Henry Laverty. Laverty did love luxuries, from early strawberries and green peas to the finest woodcock and tenderest game. I remember him, an old man, long years ago, and yet with a remarkably keen eye for a young and pretty girl. His house in Broadway was once the seat of hospitality and festivity. I remember the son who accidentally killed Sykes, at Windust's saloon, near the old Park Theatre. . . . Henry Laverty was crippled in means for years. He was never out of trouble. He died poor, and left nothing, comparatively speaking.

Other examples of both sorts naturally were easy to find. "Old Salles," the millionaire French importer, was as famous for his slovenly appearance as for his enormous appetite. One formerly prosperous wholesale grocer and notorious "fast liver" wound up as a common sailor and ended his career by falling from a spanker boom.

In their social attitudes toward philanthropy and reform, the New York merchants covered a wide range. On one extreme were the elder Howlands, whose sharp practices in connection with the Greek frigates alienated many and who were conspicuously absent from many of the philanthropic movements of the day, although they made substantial bequests to charity in their wills. The opposite attitude was evident in another pair of New England brothers, Arthur and Lewis Tappan, natives of Northampton, Mass., and prosperous silk jobbers. They were reformers of the most aggressively meddlesome type—the *Herald* once referred to "Lewis, who keeps an office for looking after everybody's business but his own." Arthur started *The Journal of Commerce* in 1827, ostentatiously announcing that it would publish no theatre, liquor, nor lottery advertisements, nor would it gather news on the Sabbath. The brothers were identified with the Bible society, peace society, and mission boards. Arthur took a hand in the suppression of vice and was president of the Magdalen Society when it shocked New York with a report that there were 10,000 fallen women in the city. Their most conspicuous activity, however, was in connection with slavery. They became prominently identified with the cause of abolition and their houses were attacked by a mob in the Negro riots of 1834. The commandant of the Navy Yard sent marines to guard Arthur's home at a time when rumors told of a high reward, some said $100,000, offered in the South for his kidnapping, and of a mysterious pilot boat which had come to New York for the purpose.

The "cotton triangle" naturally led to close relationships between southern merchants and the Pearl Street jobbers. The southerners were in a dilemma because the Tappans frequently had the best bargains in silks. Threats were made from the southward of a boycott against any merchant who traded with the Tappans or certain other firms suspected of abolitionist tendencies; whereupon the firm of Bailey, Keeler & Remsen inserted a "card" in the newspapers in 1835:

Having learnt that some insinuations have been made (probably with the design to injure us) that our firm is in favor of the cause of Abolition, we hereby declare that such accusations are utterly false and unfounded; and we pledge ourselves that all the members of our house are opposed in principle to the views of the abolitionists, regarding the agitation of the slave question, and the interference with the rights of southern slave-holders as inexpedient, unjust, and pregnant with evils.

Sometimes the sale of property of southern debtors to satisfy accounts with New Yorkers temporarily involved the latter in slave-owning. Altogether, the close commercial ties with the South meant many embarrassments for New York merchants as friction developed between the sections and few were ready to follow the Tappans in their outspoken stand.

Midway between the Howlands and the Tappans with their extreme views stood a large number of merchants who were generous in their philanthropy and public spirit without attempting to force reforms on others. John Pintard was conspicuous in this respect in the earlier days. Robert B. Minturn, for example, like several other prominent merchants, gave of his time and energy as a commissioner of emigration, was instrumental in founding the Association for Improving the Condition of the Poor and St. Luke's Hospital, and supported his wife's agitation for the project to set aside Central Park. His partners, Henry and Moses H. Grinnell, were likewise decidedly generous and public-spirited; but they were by no means exceptional in this, for there were many others of that sort among the merchant princes. Captain Charles H. Marshall and other shipping men helped ameliorate the conditions for seamen in port. Anson G. Phelps is said to have given over half a million, chiefly for missionary and other religious purposes. In fact, his philanthropy was said to have saved his life; he had just left his desk to attend one of his many board meetings when his new warehouse collapsed, burying the head bookkeeper and several others in the ruins. The names of at least two New York merchants are borne by the colleges that they helped to establish; at Constantinople, that of Christopher Robert and in Indiana, that of John Purdue, a commission merchant who traded with the West. Drew Theological Seminary had its background in New York's steamboats, deriving its name and part of its support from Daniel Drew, who located it on the estate which was once owned by Thomas Gibbons. The list might be extended indefinitely.

As for their political views, Scoville, who had been private secretary to Calhoun, said "Very few merchants of the first class have been Democrats. The mass of large and little merchants have like a flock of sheep gathered in the Federal, Whig, Clay or Republican folds. The Democratic merchants could have easily been stowed in a large Eighth Avenue railroad car." That Democratic minority included Preserved Fish as well as Churchill C. Cambreleng, who sat in Congress for several sessions and was a right-hand man of Van Buren. A few merchants of the opposite faith also went to Congress, particularly James G. King and Moses H. Grinnell, together with Grinnell's brother Joseph, after his return to New Bedford. The Grinnell and Goodhue concerns threw their forces of clerks, longshoremen, and sailors into the riotous elections of 1834 and were accused of discharging Jackson men. Daniel Webster was a frequent visitor in New York merchant homes and married the daughter of one merchant, Herman Le Roy, as his second wife.

As for the wealth of these merchants, Carl Schurz, arriving at New York in 1852, was told that $150,000 was considered a fortune. Moses Y. Beach, editor of *The Sun,* set $100,000 as the lower limit of "wealth" in the, not too accurate, series of annual handbooks which he published between 1845 and 1855. The Europeans who sneer at the Americans as a race of money-worshippers could scarcely find better ammunition than this primitive "Who's Who." The sole prerequisite for inclusion in its columns was the estimated possession of at least $100,000. Official, social, or intellectual achievements were inadequate unless, in the opinion of the editor, one's fortune ran into six figures. Such a book would be out of the question today, except perhaps for the semisecret works of Dun and Bradstreet, for each individual would be torn between considerations of pride on the one hand and of the collector of internal revenue on the other. Mid-century New York, however, seems to have found it the most interesting and significant method of listing the relative importance of its citizens.

If we may credit Beach's estimates, which in many cases seem too low, New York had fourteen millionaires in 1846. Nineteen others had more than a half million, while a further 137 were rated at more than a quarter million. The book altogether contained about a thousand names. As New York City at the time had about a half million inhabitants, one individual in 500 was thus placed in the "wealthy" class. By 1855, the number of reputed millionaires had risen to twenty. From the remarks which accompany most of the estimates, not always complimentary in their nature, it is possible to gain a fair idea of the sources of this wealth. Finance and industry accounted for relatively few, while shipbuilding was conspicuously absent. Commerce and real estate bulked most prominently and in many cases the fortunes, as in the case of Astor, represented a combination of the two. Land values in Manhattan were rising with extraordinary rapidity and Scoville claimed that Pelatiah Perit made more money from the casual purchase of some uptown lots than he did from his long and strenuous service as a Goodhue partner. Those fortunes represented the fruits of New York's commercial success for the lucky minority and a heavy portion of them had been amassed by Connecticut shrewdness exploiting the opportunities of the rising port.

CHAPTER XIII

WITHIN THE COUNTINGHOUSE

LOADING tea at Canton, coffee at Rio, textiles at Liverpool, cotton at New Orleans, and other cargoes at scores of scattered seaports, New York vessels extended the city's commercial enterprise over most of the world. Their captains barked orders not only on the stormy North Atlantic but also off the Cape of Good Hope and Cape Horn and among the islands of southern seas. The packages of mechandise gathered at New York from the ends of the earth penetrated into little back-country stores all the way from Michigan down to Arkansas. Widespread as that activity was, the authority which decided upon those voyages, employed those captains, and called into being those vessels, was concentrated into a few blocks of brick countinghouses near the tip of Manhattan Island. In those surroundings, the merchant princes carried on the manifold aspects of their business.

Just as a common, seagoing hierarchy, ritual, and discipline were to be found aboard everything from China clippers to coastal colliers, so there were a fairly standardized personnel and routine in the countinghouses, whether of the South Street importers and shipping brokers, of the Pearl Street auctioneers and textile jobbers, or of the banking and marine insurance concerns of Wall Street. The business offices, moreover, had their uniform terminology just as did the ships. Sixty days' sight, *del credere,* and protests had all the significance, if not the color, of t'gallantsails, dog watches, and bilging. We might, therefore, look at the features which were common to the whole business community before turning to the more specialized functions of the different streets of the business district.

A building three to five stories high was the usual habitat of the business concern. Ordinarily, it was built of brick, though a few of the more pretentious were of granite from Quincy or the Maine coast.

Many such buildings were advertised back in the 'twenties as "fire-proof" until the terrific fire in the last weeks of 1835 disproved that hopeful claim by wiping out a large part of the district. Such a building at the outset cost about as much as a brig—as time went on, many cost as much as a full-rigged ship. Those who owned their counting-houses were generally better off than those who rented because New York real-estate values were mounting steadily during those years. The upper stories served as a warehouse for the storage of goods. The front part of the first floor was often used as a showroom where customers were received and goods or samples might be inspected. Further back on the ground floor was the real nerve center of the business, the counting room (or office, as it gradually began to be called).

Countinghouse practices, like shipboard routine, were based on British or other overseas models. Many of the older merchants had been trained in London, Liverpool, Glasgow, Amsterdam, or Hamburg houses; they transplanted to the streets of lower Manhattan the rigid discipline and meticulous practices of those older ports.

The most conspicuous difference in appearance between the old counting room and the modern office was the absence of women and of type-writers. The staff was entirely masculine; and instead of the clatter of machines there was simply the scratch of pens as the clerks on their high stools worked at manifests, bills of lading, accounts, and correspondence. This was slow work, for carbon paper still lay in the future and several copies had to be made out by hand.

At the bottom of the hierarchy were the boys, drudging from dawn to dark for a dollar or two a week; but, like the "r'yal boys" aboard ship and the apprentices in the shipyards, realizing that they were on the main road to advancement in their field. Above them were the ordinary copyists and above those the specialized clerks for outdoor work, custom-house work, translations, and the like. Then came the book-keeper and finally the confidential chief clerk. It was customary to work up through the ranks; Scoville wrote in the 'sixties:

In former years a clerk took his regular degrees. He was first set to delivering goods from the store—taking accounts of the marks and the number of the packages. He was also obliged to deliver goods and to keep correct accounts of such as he received in store or delivered to purchasers. Indoors he was obliged to copy letters; when the clerk could do that correctly and neatly without making an error or a blot, then he was promoted to making duplicates of letters to go by the packet ships. Then he was promoted to copying accounts. Next he was trusted with the responsible duty of making these accounts. All was a perfect system. One clerk instructed and one inspected the work of another. It was impossible to make mistakes. The bookkeeper too was an institution in the older times.

Gardiner G. Howland is said to have had absolute contempt for any businessman who had not gone, from the bottom up, through all these stages. Adequate rewards awaited those who made good. Aside from promotion in the countinghouse itself, constant outside possibilities were available. The Howlands set up many of their clerks as correspondents in foreign ports; so too did Goodhue and numerous others.

Many of the employers believed with Stephen Storm that "if you would have good clerks, you must keep them moving." If there were no customers, the clerks were kept moving goods from one part of the store to another, much as mates at sea tried to keep their whole watch busy. Few, probably, went to the extreme lengths of Arthur Tappan, however, who insisted that his clerks abstain from drink of every kind, from theatres, from late hours, and from houses of ill-fame ("Girls like silks, and Tappan kept a silk store"). He even required attendance at two prayer meetings a week, besides Sunday services—and then checked up on them to find out where they attended and the subject of the sermon. He also anticipated the time clock by making the clerks set down in a book the exact hour and minute of arrival.

The closest approach to the modern business school was the work of the writing masters, who advertised their success in teaching a "good hand" in a course of lessons "after candle light." The mass of surviving countinghouse manuscripts, in irreproachable copy-book writing, testify that they taught well. The heads of the firm, however, often lapsed from the fair hand of their apprentice days. Instead of dictating letters, they frequently scrawled out the original draft in the letter book. An old letter book of N. L. & G. Griswold contains letters drafted by both brothers; "Old Nat's" are fairly legible but it is almost impossible to read George's. In fact, the latter, according to a memorandum by his grandson, was often unable to read his own writing and retained one clerk for years as the only man able to decipher his scrawl.

Corresponding to a ship's quarterdeck, the heads of the firm generally supervised the operation of the countingroom from their desks in the rear—sometimes on a raised platform, sometimes in separate rooms. Frequently they had to sally forth to deal with the more important customers themselves. One merchant, "as a sort of incentive to pay the prices asked," kept a pipe of fine brandy on hand for the purpose. Arthur Tappan, according to his brother, was less hospitable. "It was his habit to have no spare chair to offer to callers," except for venerable persons, "if important." Otherwise he would "rise and receive him with much economy of speech, and as no seat was at hand, the person, whoever he was, soon took his departure from the taciturn and busy merchant."

Most of the New York concerns took the form of partnerships. Occasionally a man operated alone. John Jacob Astor was the outstanding example, although even he organized the American Fur Company for his most ambitious work. Others were William Whitlock (extensive shipowner, packet operator, and commission merchant who had been soured by an early partnership experience), Stephen Whitney, Silas Holmes, George Sutton, and Moses Taylor. Charters of incorporation were secured by banks, marine-insurance concerns, steamboat companies, and dry-dock companies, but were almost unknown for general commercial purposes. The usual thing was for two or three men to form a "copartnership." Ordinarily each partner contributed an equal amount of capital and shared equally in the profits and responsibilities. Each was entrusted with the "signature of the firm" and copies of the partners' signatures were sent to correspondents for identification. Anything signed by one partner for the firm was normally binding on the others. Generally the firm was designated by two names; silent partners were included in the expression "& Co." Thus the firm which began as Fish & Grinnell became Fish, Grinnell & Co., after the younger Grinnells and Minturn came in and the original partners retired. In 1833, the New York legislature passed an act requiring that a firm's designation contain only the names of those actively engaged; thereupon the firm, from which Fish had been absent for some time, became Grinnell, Minturn & Co. At the same time, H. & G. Barclay became Barclay & Livingston and S. Schermerhorn & Son, John S. Schermerhorn. At times, one partner managed to make both his partners silent, as in the case of Goodhue & Co., and A. A. Low & Bros. In 1832, the legislature authorized "limited partnerships" in which two general partners maintained the usual full responsibilities, whereas a third "special partner" was liable for only a limited amount. Thus James A. Coffin and Benjamin St. John became general partners in the firm of Coffin & St. John, "buying, selling and dealing in drugs, medicines and dyestuffs," while Benjamin Aymar, the Caribbean importer, became a special partner at $5000. The celebrated house of Howland later underwent such a change:

> W. H. Aspinwall had been brought up in the house of G. G. & S. Howland, his uncles. They gave him an interest in the business, and he signed the name of the firm as early as 1830 or 1831. He received twenty per cent of the commission account. He became an open partner, under the name of Howland & Aspinwall, about 1837. At that time, the two old Howlands went out, leaving about $150,000 each in cash as special partners. William Edgar Howland, a son of G. G., was one of the general partners, W. H. Aspinwall the other. William H. was the engineer of the house. When he went out of the house, his brother John Lloyd became a partner, with Mr. Comstock.

Often, each partner assumed special functions. Where a large concern included shipowning among its manifold lines, one partner was apt to serve as "outdoor" man and a sort of marine superintendent. Nathaniel Griswold, for example, handled that end of the firm's business while his brother George attended to the financial affairs.

Frequently, interlocking partnerships carried on business in each of two or more ports so that the same group of men might keep in their hands all the profits and commissions incident to the transactions. A slightly different name would be given to the firm stationed at each port, and at least one partner would be stationed there. Thus the partnership of Peter Crary, Jr., John S. Crary, and Benjamin F. Babcock assumed the name of Crarys & Babcock in New York and Crary, Babcock & Co. in Liverpool. Such relationships were particularly common in the commercial relationship between New York and the southern ports.

The merchant, like his clerks, usually followed a regular routine, albeit a much pleasanter one, if one may believe Scoville:

> To rise early in the morning, to get breakfast, to go down town to the counting house of the firm, to open and read letters—to go out and do some business, either at the Custom house, bank or elsewhere, until twelve, then to take a lunch and a glass of wine at Delmonico's; or a few raw oysters at Downing's; to sign checks and attend to the finances until half past one; to go on change; to return to the counting house, and remain until time to go to dinner, and in the old time, when such things as "packet nights" existed, to stay down town until ten or eleven at night, and then go home and go to bed.

To "go on change" was one of the important parts of the daily ritual for the merchants not only of New York but also of most of the other

Drawing by Alfred Hoffy; printed by J. T. Bowen

BURNING OF THE MERCHANTS' EXCHANGE, 1835

The first Merchants' Exchange, erected in 1827 on Wall Street just below William, was the most conspicuous victim of the great fire of December 16, 1835, which laid waste some 700 buildings in the business district. The Exchange also housed the Post Office and the Chamber of Commerce

larger seaports. In 1823, the prospectus of the new Merchant's Exchange declared:

In all commercial cities, such resorts are established; where at particular hours, merchants may be assured of finding each other; and, by having all brought together, may transact in a few minutes, the business, which, if each were to seek the other at his counting-house, would require as many hours to accomplish.

The practice was by no means a new one in New York at that date. As early as 1670, the governor had ruled that the merchants should gather every Friday. By 1753, regular quarters were established on Broad Street. In 1792, the Tontine Coffee House was built to afford more commodious quarters. The merchants met there daily until, by the early 'twenties, it was felt that still more adequate accommodations were necessary. Stephen Whitney and William B. Astor were promoters in selling a thousand shares at $100 each to erect the beautiful new exchange, completed in 1827. A few years after the fire of 1835 it was rebuilt on a more ambitious scale; and the merchants continued to gather there. This second Merchants' Exchange on Wall Street was later occupied by the Custom House and finally made over into the present quarters of the National City Bank. Throughout our period, therefore, either at the Tontine, the old Exchange, or its rebuilt successor, the leaders of the mercantile community might be found together for an hour or so every day. Letter bags for the various packets "up" for different ports hung in the hall, while office space in the building rented at a premium.

Another institution which involved the whole group of merchants, though at less frequent intervals, was the Chamber of Commerce of the State of New York, which dated back to 1768 and is still flourishing. It furnished, as we saw, a standing committee of arbitration for the settling of disputed questions out of court. Its chief function, however, seems to have been the facility which it gave for co-ordinated expression of the views of the merchants. It memorialized Congress time and again on many subjects; and it expressed the gratitude of the men of commerce to those who served them well. A review of its resolutions is a convenient way to learn what at least a considerable part of the merchants felt about various questions from time to time. A Chamber of Trade, composed chiefly of dry-goods dealers, came into being in the early 'thirties but did not enjoy the permanence or distinction of its venerable rival.

Although the countinghouses of the merchants were similar, many different sorts of business were carried on and each type of activity tended to concentrate along a particular street or streets. This was indicated in a survey of the downtown business district in 1852:

The principal business portion—that where the great commercial establishments are located—lies within the lines described by the lower end of Broadway, Fulton Street, and the East River. . . .

Wall Street is the focus of the great monetary operations, that are watched with great interest not only over the United States, but in Europe. Here are the great speculations in stocks, bonds, houses, lands, and other merchandises. It is occupied by the offices of brokers, banks, insurance companies &c, and contains also the Merchants' Exchange and the Custom House.

South Street is occupied by the principal shipping houses, and the offices of most of the foreign packet lines. The dry goods jobbing and importing business, formerly confined to Pearl Street, has extended to William, Broad, Pine, Cedar, Liberty &c. On Water and Front Streets, and the vicinity, are the wholesale grocers, commission merchants, and mechanics connected with the shipping business.

Broadway is not less an avenue of business than the promenade of beauty and fashion. It contains the chief bookstores, jewelry, upholstery, hat and cap, tailoring, millinery, retail dry goods, and other like establishments. The hardware trade is chiefly in Platt and Pearl Streets, and the leather dealers occupy Ferry and Jacob Streets.

All that lay below the City Hall, in what today is the extreme lower tip of the metropolis; but even that represented a wide dispersion when compared with the earlier days of the period when the three thoroughfares of South Street, Pearl Street, and Wall Street contained most of the concerns vitally connected with the workings of the port.

Of those three, South Street was most intimately connected with things maritime. It extended along the East River, on "made land," where the tide had ebbed and flowed until about 1800. Its countinghouses were on the north side of the street and opposite them were the East River piers, whence the bowsprits and jibbooms of the ships stretched well across the cobbled street. No South Street appears on the maps printed before 1800.

If South Street was the most maritime of the thoroughfares, so shipping was the most maritime of its varied functions. New York stood second only to London among all the seaports of the world in the tonnage of its shipping by the middle of the nineteenth century. Liverpool might still have a greater volume of incoming and outgoing commerce; but it fell behind New York in the vessels which claimed it as a hailing port. By 1850, the aggregate of vessels with "of New York" painted on their sterns exceeded the combined tonnage of Boston, Philadelphia, Baltimore, and New Orleans. This included both the shipping registered for foreign trade and the more numerous smaller craft, about equal in total tonnage, enrolled or licensed for domestic commerce. It did not necessarily mean that New Yorkers owned outright all that tremendous amount of shipping; but it implied that most of those vessels did their principal business at New York. Shipowners, ship brokers, and ship agents, consequently, loomed large among those who occupied the busy South Street countinghouses.

The majority of the vessels hailing from New York were not the products of the famous local East River yards, which were known far and wide for the excellence of their materials, workmanship, and design, as well as for their stiff prices. Only the port's best ships were ordinarily built locally; most of the rank and file came from New England. The New York merchant who wanted to buy or employ a new or second-hand ship or brig for ordinary trading purposes was apt to turn to Connecticut in the earlier and to Maine in the latter part of the period, because costs were less in eastern yards. The appendix tables will reveal the essence of the situation.[1] In 1860, for example, New York handled 52 per cent of the nation's combined imports and exports, had 33 per cent of the registered tonnage, but built only 5 per cent of the square-rigged vessels. Conversely, Maine, with less than 1 per cent of the national imports and exports, had 17 per cent of the registered tonnage, and built 43 per cent of the square-riggers, while New England as a whole built 77 per cent of them. This naturally implied a very close relationship between South Street and the craft from down east.

Except for steamers and whalers, vessels were almost never owned by chartered corporations. Each vessel, from an economic standpoint, was a sort of little corporation in itself with various owners holding a certain number of eighths, sixteenths, sixty-fourths, or whatever other fraction was convenient for dividing up the shares. The customs records of registry and enrollment always show the number of owners and usually their names; but only after 1847 did the New York certificates indicate the proportional shares held by each. Sometimes an individual owned one or more ships outright; frequently, especially in the earlier days of the regular traders, the partners in a commercial house joined in ownership. Still more common, as time went on, was

[1] See Appendix, i, ii, iii, xii, xiv,

the dispersing of ownership among a diversified group, often including the master and the builder, and frequently consisting of residents of other towns, besides New York. The normal interest in a vessel ranged somewhere between $1000 and $10,000. An extreme case of division of ownership was the 27-ton sloop *Emily*, whose enrollment certificate in 1838 stated that she was owned by Eliphalet Mowbray and 91 others—less than a third of a ton of shipping apiece! In contrast, an example of extremely concentrated ownership may be found in the case of Cornelius Vanderbilt, who by the late 'fifties was sole possessor of several large steamships and steamboats worth well over a million. In the course of his long career, Vanderbilt built some 34 steamboats and ferries in addition to half that number of ocean steamships, holding most, if not all, of the ownership in his own hands. He thus well merited his popular title of Commodore.

However many owners a vessel might have, one usually served as her managing agent or "ship's husband," as the phrase went. He attended to the active operation of the vessel, securing cargoes, selecting and instructing the captain, deciding upon repairs, and handling the entering and clearing at the custom house. Each year he would render an accounting to the other owners, after deducting a commission for his services. A vessel was generally registered in the port where the "ship's husband" resided. Numerous vessels built and partly owned at some little New England port would select some New York shipping merchant or ship broker who would be in a position to secure more business for the vessel than could be obtained on the Connecticut or Maine coasts. The Griswold manuscripts indicate that the South Street operator would sometimes advance part of the cost of construction. New York, consequently, did not own in full all that tonnage which bore its name on the stern.

In addition to such service as "ship's husbands," the South Street shipping men found business for vessels registered elsewhere, in whose ownership they had no part. Many New Englanders settled in New York primarily for the purpose of looking out for the shipping from their home towns. Their advertisements often were headed, "For Freight, Sale or Charter," and they received a commission for any one of the three. There was a lively market for second-hand vessels. Cautious buyers requested the "privilege of boring," to ascertain whether or not the timbers were still sound—the maritime equivalent of looking at a horse's teeth. Altogether, this sort of work was sometimes simply one branch of a great firm's activity, but more often it was carried on along with a more modest commission business. In addition, a few specialists known as ship brokers appeared on South Street. One old marine-insurance man defined a ship broker as one who acted for the shipowner and the merchant—and cheated them both. A longer and more respectable definition was given by a New York broker in his initial advertisement just a month after the peace news arrived in 1815:

> The owners of *ships* desire freights, and those who have *freights* search and advertise for ships; captains and mates want employment and ship owners often expend time and money searching for captains and mates; merchants with a view to sell their ships and shipping property are often driven to great labour and expense to procure the best purchasers; those who wish to make the best purchases are obliged to encounter the same disadvantageous circumstances; and almost every *trader* engaged in extensive business is frequently in need of a *commercial agent,* as every one concerned in *navigation* wants the services of a ship broker.

Several others blossomed forth in the new business within a year. The letters of Colonel Thomas W. Williams of New London show that when, on one occasion, he wanted to buy a second-hand ship for a whaler, he wrote to Henry Coit, a commission merchant who served as his New York correspondent. Coit replied that he had consulted Captain Thomas H. Merry, a ship broker who knew more about the business than any one else in the port, and described the relative merits of the available ships as the captain had analyzed them.

Characteristic of the "ship's husband" relationship was the record of John Howland during the first decade of our period. He was registered as part owner of eleven ships, four brigs, and a schooner, the other owners for the most part residing back in the New Bedford region; he was sole owner of only one ship and one little schooner. He was essentially a shipping specialist. Several other South Street houses had started in that way, but gradually they used the ships as auxiliaries to their general commercial activities. The largest number under a single house flag during that decade was that of the 34 vessels, totalling 9184 tons, of N. L. & G. Griswold. Of those, they owned 20 outright and were part owners of the rest. G. G. & S. Howland were registered as owners of 36 vessels, but many were brigs and schooners and their total tonnage was only 7431, divided about equally between sole and part ownership. Very few of those vessels were new and still fewer were built in New York; they averaged about five or six years old at the time of acquisition and were doubtless snapped up as good bargains in the "used ship" market. Some, particularly in the G. G. & S. Howland fleet, were quickly resold. The analysis of the customs registers, upon which those figures are based, reveals so many qualifying considerations of new or second-hand and sole or part-ownership that it seems risky to hail any one positively as the most extensive shipowner of the period.

Closely linked with the South Street shipping interests were the marine insurance companies of Wall Street. For centuries, the spreading out of marine risks had enabled the shipowner to minimize the financial loss involved in the perils of the sea and underwriting had become a well-established business. By the time our period opens, New York had several companies individually incorporated by the legislature, each with a capital of a quarter to a half million dollars. Throughout the period, there were generally about eight to a dozen companies at a time; as some failed, others rose to take their place. With the banks and the fire-insurance companies, they represented the largest concentration of capital at the time and their stocks were traded on Wall Street, with frequent fluctuations. The president and the directors were usually prominent shipping magnates; a secretary handled the routine work; while a retired captain served as inspector.

Three different things were normally insured—the ship itself, her prospective freight earnings, and her cargo. The ship was often insured by the year, at a rate somewhere in the neighborhood of 7 per cent as long as she was in first-rate condition. The more valuable the ship, the lower the rate; small or old craft were charged much more. In 1860, for instance, a ship worth $30,000 might be insured for $2100 a year, at 7 per cent, while a vessel worth $3000 might be charged $600 at 20 per cent.[1] For the freight earnings and the cargo, separate policies were usually taken out for the particular trip. A single company seldom took the whole risk. It was ordinarily spread out among two or three and, in the case of particularly valuable cargoes, companies at other ports might be called in to assume part of the insurance. When a Liverpool textile cargo or a shipload of tea from Canton was lost, one might often guess which companies had suffered from the way their shares were apt to fall off a few points.

Each port usually worked out a table of rates for the risks on vari-

[1] See Appendix, xix.

SECTION OF A MAP SHOWING NEW YORK'S BUSINESS DISTRICT IN 1856

South Street is shown skirting the East River waterfront; the parallel streets behind it were Front, Water, and Pearl Streets respectively. Wall Street is indicated by the ferry leading to it. The piers are shown with their official numbering; the shaded piers were owned by the city. The shipyards were in the vicinity of Corlear's Hook at the lower right

ous runs. A premium of 2 per cent did not mean that one vessel in fifty was expected to be wrecked. The companies left an ample margin of safety, as their dividend records demonstrate. At the same time, the fact that the directors included shipowners, who would have to pay the premiums, kept the rates from being excessive.

At first glance, the estimates of relative danger on the different routes present some astounding contrasts. Mileage was apparently the least important factor, but, as we recall, vessels out on the high seas were relatively safe and it was only when they approached the coast that danger increased. That, of course, accounts for the fact that in 1835 the trip from New York to most of the North Carolina ports, although only about 500 miles in length, commanded as high a premium (1¼ per cent to 1½ per cent) as the trip halfway around the world to China! The answer lay, as we know, in the fact that, except for Wilmington, the approach to all the North Carolina ports involved the crossing of Ocracoke Bar with its heavy seas and shifting channels. The Canton trip, moreover, was usually made by select ships with select masters, which was scarcely the case with the little coasting schooners. The rate from New York to New Orleans was at times considerably higher than from New Orleans to New York; the former entailed the threading of the Bahama Banks and Florida reefs, while the latter was a simple matter of following the Gulf Stream. The normal rates included permission to enter only one port; the extra risks in visiting others entailed an extra premium. The average rate to Europe and the Caribbean ranged from 1 to 1½ per cent (on the eve of the Revolution it had been about twice as much) and a moderate reduction was made if a policy was taken out for the round trip. The rates were higher at the beginning and end of our period than in the 'twenties and 'thirties.[1]

Those quotations for the routes were simply base figures; other considerations were also taken into account. The age and condition of the ship and the reputation of the master might affect the rate, if these did not entail rejection of the policy. The packets often proudly advertised that insurance could be effected at the lowest rates. During the hurricane season of late summer and early autumn, the Caribbean rates were, of course, often increased; while the menace of pirates, privateers, and revolutionary hostilities kept the Latin-American premiums at an abnormally high rate for several years. The na-

[1]See Appendix, xix.

ture of the cargo also made a difference. It was very rare for a ship to founder at sea; most of the damage came from running ashore, where there was a chance to save some of the cargo. Consequently specie commanded a very low rate, since it could normally be saved with little difficulty, whereas hardware, stowed in the lower hold, could not be salvaged as easily as the dry goods 'tween decks and was liable to be rusted if water entered the hull, and was accordingly charged four or five times as much as specie.

Marine insurance, like other forms of underwriting, presented a constant temptation for fraud. New York seems to have suffered relatively little from the practice which reached a shameful prevalence in the British timber ships of sending worn-out vessels well insured in the hope that they would founder. The most glaring case of fraud was perpetrated by a French resident in New York who chartered a Maine brig, put his own captain aboard, and sent her to Havre. A valuable lot of silks was purchased at Paris and received the necessary inspection marks from the customs authorities there, making further examination at Havre unnecessary. Before reaching that port, the silks were removed and rubbish substituted for them. Well out at sea, holes were bored in the hull, but a zealous mate, who was not in the conspiracy, plugged them up. More holes had to be bored when he was not on watch; the crew abandoned the sinking brig, but the expected insurance payments on the missing silks were not forthcoming. A French captain at New York, who had been cautiously approached about assuming command, had indignantly refused and communicated his suspicions to the president of one insurance company. The merchant was tried for fraud and the brig's captain was charged with the more serious crime of barratry for sinking his vessel.

Although each insurance company operated as a separate unit, the successful example of Lloyds suggested a certain amount of co-ordination. The various New York companies consequently organized the Board of Underwriters in 1820. Steps were taken to secure the freshest information possible, since that was highly essential to the business. Correspondents were appointed in most of the important ports of the world; and tough lighters were kept in readiness to hasten to any ship which might run aground in the sandy angle. The first consideration was the cargo stowed 'tween decks—generally worth more than the ship herself and very much easier to salvage. By 1858, the co-operation had gone still farther, for a group of the inspectors had organized an "American Lloyds" and begun to publish a register rating all American ships as well as some of the foreign ones which frequented the ports. Linked with this was the American Shipmasters' Association, formed just after our period closed, to set a stamp of approval upon captains who passed muster, and thus to help blacklist the less competent.

The name "Atlantic" indicated a sure primacy in New York underwriting circles during a considerable part of our period. The first Atlantic Insurance Co., organized in 1824, was short-lived; but a second company of the same name, established in 1829, soon achieved an easy leadership. In 1842, in accordance with the new vogue started by the Mutual Safety Insurance Co., three years before, it was transformed into the Atlantic Mutual Insurance Co., the name which it still bears. This meant that the insured, rather than the old stockholders, would share its profits and would elect trustees in place of the old directors to guide its policies. The Atlantic Mutual achieved a dividend record rivalling that of the old Dutch East India Co.; on three occasions before 1860, it reached 40 per cent, in addition to the 6 per cent interest on its scrip. In 1860, it handled half as much business as the other eleven companies combined. It still retains a proud position in the underwriting world, doing business at the same Wall Street corner where it has been located since 1851, the only survivor of the mutual companies of that day.

The company's success can be attributed in no small degree to the superlative genius of a Long Islander, Walter Restored Jones, who was easily the outstanding figure in New York marine insurance circles in his day. Vice-president of the old company and president of the Atlantic Mutual, he also served as secretary of the Board of Underwriters for many years and did much in that capacity to co-ordinate the port's activity in the field. He was also first president of the Life Saving Benevolent Association, formed in 1849 to establish stations with suitable apparatus along the Long Island coast; its directors were almost identical with the Atlantic Mutual's trustees. After his death in 1855, he was succeeded in the company's presidency by a relative, John Divine Jones, whose forty-year administration maintained the business at its high level.

The magnificent series of "disaster books," carefully preserved by the company, throw light upon some of the more spectacular aspects of marine insurance. The "black year" of 1854, for instance, established a high record for casualties, caused in part by a succession of smashing gales, forced even the Atlantic Mutual to pass a dividend for the only time in its long career. In addition to a large number of ordinary freighters wrecked or damaged, several crack members of New York's fleets of steamships, packets, and clippers were totally lost. In the most conspicuous disaster of all, the sinking of the Collins liner *Arctic,* the Atlantic Mutual was lucky, with only $20,000 on the hull and $739 on the valuable cargo. It was less fortunate when the *Franklin* of the Havre Line ran ashore on Long Island, having not only another $20,000 on the hull, but also $176,000 of the $472,000 insurance on her cargo, part of which was salvaged. Its risks on the cargoes of the two British steamships of the Inman Line lost that year totalled nearly $54,000. Three lost ocean sailing packets—the Red Star *Waterloo,* finally given up as missing; the London Swallowtail *Prince Albert,* abandoned at sea; and the Black Baller *Montezuma,* wrecked on Long Island—were insured by the company at $7000, $30,000, and $43,000, respectively. As for the clippers, the Atlantic Mutual had policies of $28,000 on the *Trade Wind,* sunk in collision at sea; $39,-000 on the celebrated *Oriental,* lost in Chinese waters; and, the heaviest single blow of the year, $254,000 on the *San Francisco,* wrecked at the entrance of the port for which she was named. Altogether, the company's losses for the year totalled some $4,500,000, exceeding the premiums by more than a quarter million. The strain of those terrible months probably hastened the end of Walter R. Jones, who died of apoplexy the following April.

The general business of the port, of course, involved many functions less distinctly maritime than shipping and underwriting. In addition to the great mercantile houses, whose functions included many different spheres, the principal categories were the importers, commission merchants or factors, the auctioneers, the jobbers or wholesalers, and the brokers.

The word merchant may be used, as it is generally used in this book, in the general sense of one prominently engaged in trade, whatever his particular special function might be. In the stricter and older sense, the merchant proper was one who bought and sold outright in foreign trade. Merchants of that type, frequently owning some shipping as well, were common up to the period when this study opens, but changes in method reduced their number radically. At the opposite extreme from that strict interpretation was the loose use of the word in some of the census reports. In 1860, for instance, New York State was credited with 21,677 "merchants"—all the little city retailers and country storekeepers must have been included to arrive at such a total.[1]

Midway between those two extremes was the classification adopted in Doggett's *New York Business Directory* in 1846.[2] Leaving the numerous "importers" in a separate category, it listed 31 "general merchants," 51 "importing and commission merchants," 138 "shipping and commission merchants" and 8 "shipping and importing merchants." Those South Street groups, particularly the "shipping and commission" lot, included most of the names which loomed largest in the New York mercantile world. The possession of crack ships, flying a distinctive house flag, gave lasting prominence to the Grinnells, Griswolds, Howlands, and Goodhue, though the tax lists and wealth estimates show that the fortunes which they accumulated were rivalled and sometimes exceeded by numerous importers and jobbers who conducted their more prosaic business on Pearl Street.

The commission merchants, who were to be found on South Street in large numbers, were commercial jacks-of-all-trade. In their relation to the goods passing through their hands, they occupied a position midway between the merchant proper, who actually acquired title to the wares which he bought and sold; and the broker, on the other hand, who simply brought buyer and seller together without handling the wares on his account. The principal function of the commission merchant was the selling of goods consigned to him by outsiders, but the table of commission rates reproduced in the appendix shows that there were many additional excuses for levying anywhere from $\frac{1}{2}$ to 5 per cent for services of various sorts.[3] The commission merchant, or factor, as he was sometimes called, was more apt to take any sort of business that came along, rather than to specialize in particular commodities. That 1846 business directory, for instance, showed that while there were 91 specializing in dry goods, 86 in flour and other produce, and 8 in domestic hardware, there were 317 "general" commission merchants. Some of the early advertisements, as the reproduction indicates, threw together in a single notice scattered commodities of every sort, brought from many parts of the world. The old collections of mercantile papers are full of announcements of new firms soliciting consignments far and wide, while the established houses occasionally sent a member abroad to drum up trade. Naturally, the commission

[1]See Appendix, xxx.   [2]See Appendix, xxxi.   [3]See Appendix, xx.

house which was able to make generous advance payments and to sell goods to the best advantage gradually acquired an increasing amount of business. Particularly well placed were those which had intimate connections with business houses in other ports, who would throw business their way. In reverse, no small part of New York's exports were sent on consignment to commission merchants in other ports.

Brokers of various sorts did not even handle the goods as did the commission merchants. Their function was merely to bring the interested parties together and they generally received a modest commission for so doing. Then there were also bankers and auctioneers, whose functions were obvious, in addition to agents of various sorts.[1]

Between the original foreign producer and the ultimate American consumer, goods normally passed through the hands of an exporter, an importer, a jobber or wholesaler, and a retailer. In the American export trade, the order naturally ran pretty much in reverse.

In 1815, the New York auction intruded prominently into the previous well-ordered system by which imports had reached the jobber and retailer. Formerly, the manufacturer had ordinarily sold his goods to a Liverpool exporter, who, in turn, sold them to a New York importer, each holding full title to the goods while they passed through his hands. With the coming of peace in 1815, both the exporting and importing merchants were pretty much sidetracked. The manufacturer began to retain the title to the goods until they reached the auctioneer, sending an agent to New York to handle them there and get them to the auction rooms.

The auction was not a novelty in New York or in many of the other American ports. It was found to be a quick way of disposing of goods, even though the prices obtained there might not be as much as an importing merchant or commission house might receive by waiting awhile. The system, however, had never reached the heights to which it was suddenly pushed with the first arrivals of foreign merchandise in the spring of 1815. The British manufacturers, we recall, had a huge surplus of products from the war years, when outside markets had been cut off, and were anxious to realize what they could upon them quickly. Merchants, having to order at prices determined months in advance, could not compete with the unpredictable fluctuations of the auction rooms; their countinghouses were deserted by the New York jobbers who, like many retailers from other parts of the coun-

[1]See Appendix, xxxi.

TOBACCO.

SEVENTEEN hhds. prime Richmond Tobacco, landing from schr. Logan, for sale by
D. BETHUNE & CO.
nov 24   92 Coffee House-slip.

BULLOCKS CHEESES.

THREE hundred and forty of the above, of excellent quality, an entire Dairy, just received and for sale by
JOHN BARTINE,
nov 24-1w*   183 Fulton street.

RHODE'S BLACK BOMBAZETTS.

A Few bales of Rhode's Black Bombazetts, just received per Magnet, for sale by
DAVID DUNHAM,
nov 24   144 Pearl-street.

RHODE'S BLACK BOMBAZETS.

A Few bales of Rhode's Bombazets, just received per Magnet, for sale by
D. DUNHAM,
{nov 25   144 Pearl-street.

DIVIE BETHUNE & CO. offer for sale, at 92 Coffee House-slip—
50 hhds. James' River Tobacco
170 do. prime Kentucky do
150 kegs Manufactured do
100 bbls. Georgetown Flour.
ALSO—
A large assortment of Cotton Bagging and Dundee Osnaburghs
10 bales Sheetings, 1 case Scotch Ginghams
4 cases Scotch Dry Goods assorted
Hemp and Tow Sacking, Sail Cloth
No. 1 to 7 English and Scotch Seine Twine, Sail and Herring Twine
1 bale fine Shoe Thread
L. P. Madeira Wine, of several approved brands, in pipes, qr. casks & hhds.
London Bottled Porter
18 pipes French Brandy
Wine & Porter Bottles
An invoice of well assorted Glassware
English Crown Window Glass, from 4 by 6
London refined Salt Petre   [to 10 by 14
Spirits of Salts, Duplex Aqua Fortis
White Lead in oil
Bristol Brown, French Ochre
Ivory Black, Venetian Red
18 casks Gun Flints
12 do Virginia Hoes
10 boxes roll Brimstone
West India Coffee.   nov 23

VIRGINIA WHEAT.

TWELVE hundred bushels, very superior quality, on board the schr. William, at Dover-street wharf, for sale by
BYRNES, TRIMBLE & CO.
nov 22   159 South-street.

LOST.

A Note drawn by Barker & Ferrier, in favor of J. W. Hunter & Co. and endorsed by them, dated Nov. 1, at 4½ months, for $314 92. The finder will be suitably rewarded by leaving

For freight from Alexandria, or the vicinity.

The schr. THETIS, W. Hedge, master, a substantial and well found vessel and good sailer; 4½ years old; burthen about 1000 barrels. It is expected she will be ready to receive a cargo by the 10th of Dec. The owner would wish a freight to Bermuda, or any permitted port in the West-Indies, or to any Southern port. Apply to
D. BETHUNE & CO.
nov 25-6t   92 Coffee-House-slip.

FOR LIVERPOOL,
(A regular trader,)

The fast sailing coppered ship MANHATTAN, David Tarr, Jun. master, wants from 100 to 150 bales of cotton, and will sail positively on Sunday, the 5th of next month, full or not full, weather permitting. For freight or passage, (having elegant accommodations furnished with beds and bedding,) apply to the captain on board, at pier No. 24, east side Peck-slip, or to   BYRNES, TRIMBLE & CO.
nov 24   159 South-street.

FOR FREDERICKSBURG,

The good schr. CONVOY, Capt. Gifford, lies at Dover-street wharf, and will sail on Sunday next. For freight or passage, apply to the captain on board, or to
BYRNES, TRIMBLE & CO.
nov 24   159 South-street.

FOR SALE,

At the Tontine Coffee House, on Wednesday, 1st December, at 1 o'clock, the ship RUFUS KING, burthen 513 tons, sound and in good order, British built, but sails with an American register, and stows a very large cargo; her sails, rigging, cables, &c. being in good order, with a full inventory, she can be sent to sea at a small expense; she was coppered to the bends in Amsterdam with heavy copper, where she underwent a thorough repair, having since made but a voyage to Batavia and back. The ship may be viewed at Edgar & Schermerhorn's long wharf, N. R. and her inventory examined at the office of
nov 23   LE ROY, BAYARD & CO.

FOR DARIEN,

The schr. ANN, Moderen, master, daily expected here, will be dispatched as soon as possible after her arrival. For freight or passage, apply to   JOHN DAY,
nov 22   3 Coenties-slip.

FOR SALE AT AUCTION,

By FRANKLIN & MINTURN, on Wednesday the 24th inst. at 1 o'clock at the Tontine Coffee House, (sale peremptory to close a concern,) as she lately arrived from London, the well known and very fast sailing coppered ship ELIZABETH, 305 53 95 tons. Stows 3300 bbls. was new coppered 18 months since; was built at New-Bedford, Mass. is now ballested, and could be sent to sea at little expence. Lies at pier 14, foot of Cedar-street, N. R. Inventory at auction room.   nov 22.

try, haunted the auction sales in search of bargains. Country newspapers advertised the stocks of local storekeepers, "recently purchased cheap at auction." Articles of every sort—houses, land, tea, crockery, hardware, and much else were put up for sale, but British textiles overshadowed all the rest at the Pearl Street "vendues."

By 1817, as we saw, it looked as though the New York market was pretty well glutted and the British seemed likely to divert their stream of manufactures to Boston, Philadelphia, or elsewhere. The New York auctioneers commissioned one of their number, Abraham Thompson, to propose to the governor a special form of legislation which would, as Thompson later boasted, "cause all the Atlantic cities to become tributary to New York." This bill became law on the same April day as the Erie Canal authorization. The scale of duties collected by the state was radically reduced from the previous 3 per cent level. Wines and spirits were to pay 2 per cent, "East India goods" 1 per cent, and all other imports, including the important item of textiles, 1½ per cent. Not only was that reduction a bid for retaining the business at New York, but the act contained another feature in which Thompson took particular pride. As he explained later in *Hunt's Merchant's Magazine:*

Every piece of goods offered at auction should positively be sold, and to encourage a sale, the duty should always be paid upon every article offered at auction. . . . The truth was, that both in Boston and Philadelphia, the free and absolute sale of goods by auction was not encouraged. (It did not appear to be understood.) In Philadelphia, goods were allowed to be offered, and withdrawn, free from state duty, and the purchaser went to the auction rooms of that city with no certainty of making his purchases. He was not certain that the goods would be sold to the highest bidder.

Whether or not one agrees with Thompson that the auction act deserved a pedestal alongside the starting of the Erie Canal and the announcement of the Black Ball packets in that *annus mirabilis* of New York port history, it is anyway certain that the British textiles kept pouring into New York and the buyers kept pouring in from the back country and from along the coast.

That combination helped to build up a few of the largest commercial fortunes achieved at New York during the first half of our period. For twenty years, the right to sell at auction, like the right to pilot ships, was a monopoly restricted to a small group named by the governor and the council of appointment. Many of the appointees, if one may judge by the published list of duties paid, failed to make much of the privilege; the lion's share of the business fell into the hands of two houses, one headed by John and Philip Hone and the other by John Haggerty and David Austin. Four others, at the four corners of Pearl and Pine Streets, also did a substantial business—Abraham Thompson & Co., Shotwell, Fox & Co., David Adee & Co., and Wolsey, Ward & Beach, though they seldom approached close to the Hone or Haggerty totals.

Those two houses annually paid duties between $30,000 and $50,-000, but their annual profits ran far beyond that. Not only did they receive a commission of 2½ per cent, but also an additional 2½ per cent for *del credere,* or guaranteeing of the payments by the purchaser. The profits, consequently, amounted to several times the sum of the duties paid. It is said that the Hones made a net annual profit of $159,000; at any rate, Philip was soon able to retire with a fortune.

The price fluctuations were sometimes violent, requiring constant vigilance and appealing to the gambling spirit. A writer in *Niles' Register* in 1828 declared:

I have known an article sold in the morning at 65 cents per yard, and the same article precisely, from the same package, sold in the afternoon of the same day, at 43 cents. I have known prints sell at 28 cents and go down to 21 cents in less than five minutes. I have known an article that was not very plenty advance in a few days from 35 to 65 cents, by the competition in the auction rooms.

All through the 'twenties there were strenuous attacks against the system. In 1821 and 1822, large numbers of New York dealers in various commodities, who wanted a more stable basis upon which to do business, signed pledges not to purchase at auction sales. Federal legislation, taxing or checking the system, was sought time and again, but nothing effective resulted. The sales reached their peak in 1827 and the following year saw a well-organized "anti-auction movement" which even put political candidates in the field. Thereafter, the sales failed to increase proportionately to the general rise in import figures; and one student of the subject picked 1830 as the date of the transition to more normal methods. During the decade 1821–30, the New York City auction sales of imported goods amounted to $160,000,000, or 44 per cent of the port's total imports. In fact, those few auction houses handled one-fifth of the whole nation's imports. The sales for the next decade, 1831–40, were almost identical, at $158,000,000, but were only 21 per cent of the New York imports, or one-eighth of the national total. State figures by commodities for the years 1818–41 show that European dry goods had a long lead over all else, amounting to almost half of the total sales.[1] In 1838, the appointment monopoly was ended and in 1846 the duties were cut exactly in half. Though their relative importance as a distributing agency steadily declined, the auctions in their heyday had played no small part in centering the nation's importing at New York.

As the auctions declined, the number of "importers" increased. In 1846, for instance, nearly sixty different fields of importation were listed, with more than a hundred importers of dry goods and allied commodities, 89 in wines and liquors, 86 in hardware and cutlery, 69 in coffee, and 53 in china, glass, and earthenware, to mention only the more numerous groups.[2]

The Pearl Street jobbers or wholesalers, who were the principal customers at the auction rooms, served the vital role of distributing the imported goods to the country storekeepers. They deserved the name of real merchants, for they actually bought the goods outright and sold them again. They were a very numerous group, but their names have not come down in tradition as have those of the South Street shipping and importing firms—partly perhaps because they did not own ships or trade with distant lands. Selling calico to Carolina or flannels to Ohio lacked glamor, but there was good money in it. The wholesalers of those days seldom considered it necessary to send out travelling salesmen among their customers, for, as we know, the storekeepers themselves swarmed to New York by packets from the South and by Hudson steamers from the West. Once there, they made a real visit of it, prowling from countinghouse to countinghouse of the jobbers to find the best bargains in what they wanted to fill their shelves for the coming year. Some of the jobbers instructed their clerks to move to the lodging houses where the visiting storekeepers stayed, in order to talk up the merits of their particular concern. The term "mercantile drummer" was used in the 'fifties for the aggressive runners who sought to lure the countrymen to their employers' jobbing houses. It is said that as late as 1860 there were only a thousand travelling commercial salesmen in the country.

At last, with their business done, the storekeepers left for home, their purchases often accompanying them in the same vessel. The

[1]See Appendix, xvii.   [2]See Appendix, xxxi.

PRICES CURRENT.

ARTICLES.	PER	PRICES.	DUTIES.	REM.	ARTICLES.	PER	PRICES.	DUTIES.	REM.
ASHES, pot -	ton	$ 280 285		scarce	Iron, Swedes, bar,	ton	$ 110	} 25 p. ct	
—— pearl -		255 260			—— Russia		112,50	} ad val.	
Allum,	cwt	6,50 7.00	free		—— Amer.can		110		
Almonds, soft shell	lb	c 25	4 cents		Logwood, Camp'y	ton	$ 60 65	} free	
Bark, Jesuit's -		75 a 100	3 p.c.ad		—— Bay		$ 55 60		
Beans, white -	7 bu.	$ 19 a 20			Lumber, Pipe staves	1200	$ 105 110		scarce.
Brandy, Fr. 4th pf.	gall	2,50 2.62	} 64 cts	scarce	—— hhd do WO		$ 70 75		
—— Spanish,4th		2.00 2.25			—— bbl do WO		$ 42,50 45		
—— Cider -		1.06 1,09			—— Red oak		$ 34		
Bread, pilot - -	bbl.	$ 7,50			—— Boards, O.	1000	20 21		
—— navy -		5 00			—— Scantling		$ 16 25		
—— middling		4 50			—— Shingles, p		$ 3 4		
Beef, Mess, new	bbl	16 18			—— Hoops -	1000	$ 30		
—— prime „		12 14	} dull		Lignumvitæ - -	ton	$ 45	free	scarce
—— Cargo „		10 12			Leather, soal	lb	,22 ,25	} 30 v.	
Bees Wax - -	lb	c 31 32			—— dressed, upper	side	$ 2.50 3.25		
Candles, mould -		22 26			Mahogany, St. Do.	su.ft.	,20		
—— dipped		20 21			—— Bay		,20		
—— sperm.		44 a 45			Molasses, West In.	gall	,87 93	} 10 cts	sales
Cheese, American		10 a 13			—— Havana	„	85 ,90		scarce
Cinnamon,			40 cts.	scarce	Naval Stores, Tar	bbl	4.00		
Cochineal,		6,50 7,00	free		—— Pitch		4,50 4,75		
Cocoa, Island -	cwt	$ 23 24	4 cts lb.		—— Turpentine		3,75 4,00		scarce
—— Carraccas			4	none	—— Rosin		3.50		
Coffee, green -	lb	c 25¼ a 27	10	scarce	Nicaragua Wood	ton	$ 135 145	free	scarce
—— common		24 25	10		Oil, sweet	doz.	9,00 9,50	30 p c. ad.	
Coal, Liverpool,	chal.	$ 22	4 cts pr lb		Pork, Mess - -	bbl	30 31		
Copper, pig	lb	c 17 18			—— Prime - -		24 25 50		
—— Sheathing		31 33			—— Cargo - -		20 22		
Copperas,	cwt	3,75 4,00			Pepper - -	lb	,31 ,32	12 cents	
Cordage, American		$ 10			Pimento - -		,43	3	
—— Russia		15 16 50	4 cts. lb.		Plaister Paris -	ton	10.50 11.00	free	plenty
Cotton, Sea-Island	lb	c 46 a 51		scarce	Quercitron		,65 ,80	30 ad v	dull
—— N. Orleans		33 35		brisk	Raisins, Smyrna	cask	,20·	3 cts. p.lb	
—— Geo. upl.		24 a 30		do	—— Muscatel	box	7.50 8.00	4	
Duck, Russia -	bolt.	$ 23 24	27 1-2p c		Rice, -	cwt	4.75 5.25		
—— Ravens		14,50	ad val.		Rum, Jam. 4th pf.	gall	1.87 1.90	64	} in dem
Flax-Seed, clean }	cask	11.50		} sales	—— St. Croix An.		1.56 1,63	50 & 56	
—— rough }	7 bu	11.50			—— Windward Is.		1.50 1,53	50 & 56	
Fish, Cod, dried	quin	4·50 4.75	100 cts.		—— of Molasses		1,15 1,18		
—— Herrings, N. R	bbl	5.00			Salt, Turk's Island	bush	,97 ,98		
—— salmon,		$ 22 a 24	200		—— St. Ubes		,90 ,92	} 20c per	
—— shad, Con.		18 20		scarce	—— Lisbon - -		,90	} 56 lb	
Flour, superfine		8.00 8,25		dull	—— Liverpool blo.		,80 ,85		
—— Philadelphia		9,00		do	Sugar, Muscovado	cwt	$ 19 22	5 cts. p lb.	} sales
—— Baltimore		8.50		do	—— Clayed bro.		23 24	6	
—— Richmond,		8.50 8,75			—— Hav. white		30 32	6	
—— middlings,fi.		6,25 6.75		do	—— do brown		23½ 24	5	
—— common		5,25 5,50		do	—— Loaf	lb	,44 ,45		
—— Rye - -		6,00		brisk	—— Lump		,42		
—— Corn meal		6.00		brisk	Teas, Imperial -		2,75 3,00	} 64 c.p.	} sales
—— Do	pun	$ 30			—— Hyson - -		2,12½ 2.25		
Fustic - - -	ton	35.00 40.00	free		—— Young Hyson		2,00 2,25	} 40	
Furs, Beaver ,north	lb.	4,00 4.50			—— Hyson Skin		1.60 1,70		
—— do south		2.00 2.50			—— Souchong		1,12 1,18	36	
—— Otter	skin	3.00 4.50			—— Rich'd best lf		,16 ,22		sales
—— Mink		36 40			—— do 2d qual.		,10 ,16		
—— Red Fox		1.00 1 25	} free		—— Peters'g best		,12 ,16		
—— Racoons W.		50 62½			—— do 2d		,8 ,10		
—— Muskrats		30 33			—— Kentuc'y best		,12 ,16		
Gin, Holland 1st pf.	gall	1.40 1,45	50 cents		—— Man'd Cavdh.		,25 ,35		
—— American -		1,03 1,06			—— Ladies' twist		,40	,	
Ginger, race -	cwt	1,00 1,12½	35 p c a.v	none	—— Sweet scent'd		,25 ,30		
Grain, Corn, white	bush	1,19 1.25			—— do 2d		,16 ,22		
—— do yellow		1.19 1.25			—— Common		,12 ,16		
—— Rye - -		1.10 1,12½			Verdigris		,52 ,54	free	
—— Wheat. sou.		1.56 1.62½			Whiskey, Rye,1st pf	gall	,98 1,00		
—— Do N. Riv.		1.56 1.62½			Wines, Madeira		3,25 5.00	100 c.p. g	
Hams, - - -	lb	,25		scarce	—— Sherry -		2,37½ 2.50	80	carce
Hemp, Russian -	ton	$250 2.75		sales	—— Port -		2,25 3,00	30	
—— Amer. -		$200 a 240	} free		—— Lisbon -		2,12½ 2,25	60	
Hides, dried -	lb	,16		scarce	—— Tenneriffe,		1.31 2.25	56	
—— salted -			} free		—— Claret,		$ 60 65	48	
Honey - -		,18 ,20	25 c ad v		—— Do	doz	7 10	70	
Hog's Lard - -		,25		scarce	Wool, Merino	lb	,70 1,2		dull
Indido, Flotant -		2.68 2.75			—— common,clean		,50 60		

PRICES CURRENT

From *Shipping and Commercial List*, October 3, 1815

goods, acquired along Pearl Street and vicinity, eventually found their way into the hands of the ultimate consumers, after paying toll to New York in ocean freight, auction commissions, jobbers' profits, and coastal or inland freight. As time went on, jobbing houses came into being at Cincinnati, Chicago, St. Louis, and other inland centers, serving in an intermediate distributing capacity between the New York importers or jobbers and the country retailers.

Some of the goods which went through the auction rooms remained in the city to be retailed in the shops on Broadway. The familiar name of Lord & Taylor dates back to 1824 and Captain R. H. Macy started his store in 1858, but for that day, all others were overshadowed by the ambitious and sumptuous establishment of A. T. Stewart, who had come from the north of Ireland with a well-selected stock of laces in the 'twenties and in 1848 built a retail "palace" on Broadway. One feature of those retail establishments disgusted the "he-men" from the back country. The clerks were men—dandified, smooth-tongued "ribbon clerks," who could murmur most delightfully to their feminine customers over the sheen of a bolt of silk or the exquisite weave of their muslin. Stewart did not rely on Pearl Street for his supplies; he imported direct from overseas; and eventually set up his own establishments on the other side.

The course of the flour barrel, the cotton bale, and other articles of export also went through well-developed channels from the interior through New York to Liverpool or some other foreign port. In the export trade the domestic commission merchant found his most fruitful business. The mechanics of the cotton trade have already been discussed. The flour trade, which we also recall, had its beginnings with the selling of the farmer's wheat to the country storekeeper, where it was credited to his account, or to some other gatherer of that commodity. Much of it, as time went on, found its way to the merchant millers, who ground it and then offered it as flour to the world of trade. Sometimes they dealt directly with the outside; sometimes through merchants at Albany, Rochester, Buffalo, Cincinnati, or some other inland point. Frequently the title to the flour barrel rested in the hands of that inland trader until it reached the other side, just as the title to the cotton bale remained in the hands of the planter or southern merchant. Many of the New York flour dealers were commission merchants, who simply took their percentage on the barrels passing through their hands without acquiring title to them.

By the late 'forties, the flour traders were beginning to gather daily to determine how the laws of supply and demand, influenced by reports, rumors, and "hunches," would affect the price of flour at the port. The Merchants' Exchange gradually became too crowded; the specialists began to gather by themselves. Out of informal beginnings came the Produce Exchange, which took fairly regular form by 1851. The flour dealers were the first to progress through the cycle which dealers in cotton, coffee, and other commodities would follow later——first gathering in the open air on a street corner; then acquiring an awning for shelter; then renting quarters and incorporating as an "exchange," and finally erecting a building. At the outset, articles of widely varied sorts were run through the general auction rooms but, as time went on, the auctioneers devoted more and more attention to textiles. The traders in tobacco, sugar, coffee, leather, cotton, and various other commodities were apt to gather in a particular locality where they could concentrate upon their specialized interest. The arrival of a tea cargo generally meant a special auction, with catalogues sent far and wide, so that distant buyers might send instructions to their New York correspondents.

Most of this extensive importing and exporting rested upon a credit basis. Cash was seldom paid, despite the efforts of certain merchants to handle their business in that way. Almost everything rested on deferred payments of thirty, sixty, or ninety days. The country storekeeper was seldom able to impose such fixed terms upon his customers—he "trusted" them until they should bring in enough wheat, butter, ashes, or other "cash crops" to balance his account. Because the storekeeper had to wait, the jobber likewise had to wait, and so, too, did the auctioneer or the foreign manufacturer or exporter. In the same way in the exporting game, it became necessary to advance money to the producer of cotton or flour often before his cotton was planted or his flour ground. The New York commission merchant or exporting merchant who advanced those funds had to wait not only to be repaid for those advances but also for payment by the overseas purchasers. Nearly every one, consequently, had to be granted credit for periods from one month to six months or more; sixty days being the most common term in the major dealings at New York and Liverpool.

If every one had to wait until the ultimate consumer finally paid off his creditor and he his creditors in turn, business would be seriously slowed down. That is where banking came in—the surplus capital concentrated in the hands of public or private bankers made it possible to keep things going, with capital available, during that period of lag in payments. Suppose, for instance, a Pearl Street jobber sold $1000 worth of goods to an Ohio storekeeper at ninety days. If he had ample resources, he could simply hold his draft for the three months and then receive his full $1000. If, however, he wanted to release his capital at once for other business, he might be able to discount the draft at once, either at the branch of the United States Bank, while it still existed; at one of the regular public banks, of which New York had a considerable number; or possibly at some private banking concern, the outstanding one of which was Prime, Ward & King. In the same way, the New Yorker selling cotton or flour to Liverpool could draw at sixty days' sight against the purchaser on the Mersey and likewise discount it, if all conditions were favorable. Naturally he did not receive the full amount; the interest, at the current discount rate, was deducted. That interest, of course, was part of the reward which the bankers obtained for their services; the remainder of the reward lay in their power to grant or withhold credit.

New York gradually became the money center of the United States, definitely outstripping Philadelphia after Jackson smashed the second United States Bank. It was consequently in a position to carry the southern planters and the western flour millers during the long months in which they enjoyed cash advances; because of that, they could direct that the cotton and flour would be shipped in a manner which would profit New York rather than some rival port.

There was, however, a greater financial center than New York and that was London. It had replaced Amsterdam as the world's money center; its commercial bankers could extend services to New York similar to those which New York extended to New Orleans or Cincinnati. Several great "American houses" of private mercantile bankers engaged actively in this business, permitting generous credits to American firms who would throw business their way. Conspicuous in this field was the house of Baring Bros. Co., one of whose partners was a native of Massachusetts; and W. & J. Brown (later Brown, Shipley & Co.), brothers of Stewart and James Brown, engaged in the same business on Wall Street. The Barings dealt through Goodhue & Co., for their more commercial transactions, and through Prime,

Ward & King in their financial dealings. Altogether a steady chain of credit extended from the London bankers, and behind them the Bank of England, down to the country storekeeper of the United States, who allowed his customer to build up a debit account.

In boom times, all went well; but the periodic panics and depressions tended to dry up the sources of credit and brought failures by the hundreds. Both sides of the Atlantic and all parts of the country were so closely interwoven in the meshes of credit that trouble was inclined to drag down widely scattered firms. The first serious depression of our period extended from 1819 to 1822. The Panic of 1837 ushered in a five-year slump, while as early as 1854, New York was feeling the effects of another decline which would culminate in the Panic of 1857. Between those depressions, boom periods came, particularly around 1825, 1836, and the late 'forties. Shipyards and their products afloat both reflected these fluctuations; so too did auction rooms, jobbing houses and banking concerns, as well as lesser businesses scattered on the fringes of the nation.

The Panic of 1837 concentrated attention upon the importance of determining the soundness of applicants for credit. The Barings had an American representative from Massachusetts with an uncanny sense of knowing the soundness of business men; nearly all of his first-rate list survived 1837 and its aftermath intact. He, however, dealt chiefly with merchant princes; the jobbers of Pearl Street wanted to know the stability of the country storekeepers from Georgia, Louisiana, Kentucky, and Indiana whom they were annually trusting with millions of dollars worth of goods. Shortly after the 1837 crash, Arthur Tappan offered them the services of his Mercantile Agency—the direct ancestor of Dun's—which secured confidential reports upon the merits of storekeepers, made by local representatives whose judgment could be trusted. Abraham Lincoln served in that capacity for a while out in Illinois. These reports were available to customers who inquired about individual applicants for credit. At first, detailed statements were submitted; eventually a list was published, which adopted the marine insurance ratings of "A1" and the like. Rival establishments sprang up; and doubtless did much to prevent the former losses from untrustworthy or irresponsible customers.

A friend once asked "Old Nat" Griswold, "How many merchants have succeeded among all those you have known for fifty years?" Griswold replied, "The average who have succeeded have been about seven in the hundred. All the rest, ninety-three in the hundred of untold thousands, have been bankrupts." South Street, Pearl Street, and Wall Street took their toll, but many, as we have seen, prospered well in those countinghouses. The business of the three streets was closely interlocked; the decisions of Wall Street, and the demands of Pearl Street often determined when ships could be called into being and what cargoes they could carry on their voyages.

CHAPTER XIV

THE EAST RIVER YARDS

I N THE transitional period when steam and iron were coming into use and the old wooden sailing vessels were being brought to their peak of perfection, many of the most significant developments occurred along the banks of two rivers—the Clyde near Glasgow and the East River at New York. The builders of Clydebank were working along the lines of future changes by taking the lead with iron hulls and screw propellers, but for the time being the East River won a commanding position with its stout packets, its swift pilot boats and clippers, and its very successful wooden sidewheel steamers.

These New York yards were noted for the quality of their ships. In design, materials, and workmanship, the products of the East River could scarcely be equalled in the world. Stiff prices were charged, but it gradually became known that these vessels were well worth their cost. Not only did the East River yards provide New York's best ships, but they received many outside orders, even from foreign nations. At the same time, the high prices caused New York to turn to New England for its ordinary run of shipping and these excellent local vessels, as we have seen, were but a fraction of New York's total tonnage. The East River represented the greatest concentration of shipbuilding activity in the country. Though some of the New England states produced more shipping as a whole, no other single customs district turned out as heavy an aggregate tonnage of new shipping during any year of our period covered by the records, except for Boston and Bath in 1856 and Boston again in 1859.[1]

A certain amount of genius was essential to keep in the van during this transitional period of shipbuilding. The "master carpenter," as the head of a shipyard was officially termed, had to combine many

[1]See Appendix, i, xiv, xv.

of the qualities of the artist, the engineer, and the man of business as well, if he were to succeed. The simple old "rule of thumb" methods might suffice for a while if one were simply turning out ordinary freighters in an outport; but the keen competition of the East River called for originality, efficiency, acumen, and a fair amount of luck. Space forbids mention of many of those who served in this role and only a few leaders, whose products won national and international reputation, will be noted in passing.

Shipbuilding at New York may date back to 1613, or 1614, when Block, the Dutch explorer, built the little "yacht" *Onrust* or *Restless* apparently on the shores of Manhattan to replace his burned vessel; although some claim that she was built up the Hudson. A moderate amount of shipbuilding was going on at New York during the Colonial period, but then the East River products were distinguished neither in quality nor in quantity. By the last years of the eighteenth century, two builders were winning moderate reputations. One was Forman Cheeseman, the son of another New York shipbuilder. He built the frigate *President,* a sister ship of the *Constitution* and often reckoned as an even faster, although less fortunate, craft than "Old Ironsides." The other was his sometime partner, Charles Browne, who came from England and built the hull of Fulton's *Clermont*. The names of Peck and Sheffield were also prominent on the East River during those early years.

By 1815, these men were overshadowed by a group, whose three yards or firms (for sometimes a builder might shift to another site on the river), under themselves or their successors, held a commanding position on the East River throughout most of our period. At the outset, the three yards were operated by Henry Eckford, Christian Bergh, and the brothers, Adam and Noah Brown. Their successors respectively were William H. Webb, Jacob A. Westervelt, and Brown & Bell.

The Eckford-Webb combination was probably the most distinguished of the three. Henry Eckford, born in Scotland in 1775, had migrated at sixteen to Quebec, where for five years he studied the principles of shipbuilding under his uncle. In 1796, he came to New York and soon established himself on the East River. His rigid training at Quebec soon bore fruit, and he began to incorporate original features into his ships, particularly the lightening of the heavy stern frame timbers. In 1805, he built the celebrated and long-lived *Beaver* for John Jacob Astor and fifteen years later he built the hull of the pioneer coastal steamship *Robert Fulton* for the New Orleans service. Warships, however, were his particular forte. During the War of 1812, when the British blockade meant a cessation of New York's normal shipbuilding, he was one of the group of shipbuilders, like Bergh and the Browns, who went to Lake Erie, Lake Ontario, or Lake Champlain with their shipwrights and helped to turn out at amazing speed some of the vessels which won control of those waters for the Americans. Returning to New York, he built a few merchantmen but in 1817 was placed in charge of government construction at the Brooklyn Navy Yard. During this appointment, he produced the ship-of-the-line, *Ohio,* one of the largest vessels built on the East River until many years later. Official friction terminated his position in three years, but by that time his reputation won for him fat contracts for several large warships for the Latin-American states as well as for one of the notorious "Greek frigates," of which more later. His last ship at New York was a Turkish corvette in which he sailed for Constantinople to become naval constructor for the Sultan. He died in 1832 while organizing a navy yard there and returned to New York preserved in a cask of wine.

His mantle fell upon a former assistant, Isaac Webb. Webb represented the beginning of the New England invasion of the East River yards, for, like two others of whom we shall hear shortly, he came to New York from Stamford, Connecticut. His own work, while sound, was not as brilliant as Eckford's, but he trained in his yard two men who were to be the leaders in the early 'fifties, the "golden age" of American shipbuilding. One was Donald McKay, the gifted Nova Scotian, who later produced masterpieces of clipper construction at East Boston. The other was Webb's own son, William Henry, who succeeded him by 1840 in charge of the yard. During the next twenty years, the younger Webb produced the greatest aggregate tonnage of any American shipbuilder up to that time. He showed remarkable versatility in the building of packets and steamships as well as of clippers, which came close to the exquisite perfection of those that gave McKay his superlative reputation. Short, curly-haired, and bullet-headed, William Webb was not impressive in appearance, but all the way from his first Black Ball packet to the ironclad warships which he built for European navies, his ships were as distinguished for their performance as for their numbers.

At almost the same time that Henry Eckford was coming down from Quebec, another young man, with the commanding height of six feet four, was also moving from British North America to try his fortune in the East River yards. For Christian Bergh, however, it was a return to familiar ground. He had been born near Rhinebeck, up the Hudson, descended from the first Christian Bergh, who had come over from Germany in the Palatine migration of 1710. During the Revolution, his father had been punished for his Loyalist stand by the confiscation of his lands. The family had taken refuge in Tory New York and in 1783, when Christian was twenty, had joined the Loyalist migration to Nova Scotia. There Christian had learned and begun to practice shipbuilding. Before long, he returned to New York and set up his yard on the East River. There seems to be no foundation for the oft-repeated story that he completed the *President,* started by Cheeseman. He turned out a number of sharp little schooners and brigs, some of which won distinction as privateers in the War of 1812. After an interlude of naval building on Lake Ontario, he returned with the Peace to the East River and devoted himself chiefly to the construction of merchantmen. The "close rudder" seems to have been one of his particular innovations. Packets for the new transatlantic lines were the most lucrative business for the New York yards for many years to come and of this Bergh received the lion's share, particularly for the Havre and London service.

The dividing line in the management of this yard between Bergh and Westervelt is less sharply defined than that between Eckford and Webb. Jacob Aaron Westervelt was born in Tenafly, New Jersey, where his ancestor from Holland had settled in the last years of the Dutch occupation. A brief experience at sea had early disillusioned him about the glamor of the sailor's life and in 1817, at seventeen, he and Robert Carnley were admitted to silent partnership in the firm of C. Bergh & Co. This lasted until Bergh's retirement around 1835, eight years before his death. Westervelt travelled with Carnley for a year in Europe, studying the most advanced principles of shipbuilding and then returned for a short-lived partnership with Nathan Roberts. In 1841, he entered upon a more durable partnership with William Mackey as the firm of Westervelt & Mackey, which lasted until the early 'fifties, when Westervelt took his two sons into the business. He did not finally retire until 1868, the year before Webb. Altogether, he is said to have participated in the construction of 247 vessels, with a tonnage second only to that of Webb. The Bergh-Westervelt yard stood first in the total number of packets built, but few of their individual ships won the high distinction of Webb's vessels.

The third of the "big three" yards was established around 1807 by two brothers, Adam and Noah Brown, who had been born out on the New York frontier, just before the Revolution. Early in 1780, according to Noah's autobiographical sketch, a group of Indians under Brant raided the settlement, carrying off the father, whom they soon murdered, and three brothers. At the close of the war, the mother returned with the remainder of the family to her old home at Stamford, where Noah learned the trade of a house carpenter. In 1792, he moved to New York and practiced the same craft there for twelve years. In 1804, Adam and Noah began their shipbuilding career with a lake schooner built on the Canadian side of the Niagara River. The following year, they constructed a whaler at Sag Harbor and then worked for a New York shipbuilder until about 1807, when they set up for themselves. They built several gunboats for the Navy and a number of fast privateers. Noah has left a graphic account of the brothers' work on part of Perry's fleet on Lake Erie and of McDonough's on Lake Champlain before they joined forces with Eckford in construction on Lake Ontario. Back in New York, they apparently built the hull of Fulton's pioneer steam warship. Then, like most of other New York builders, they turned to merchantmen. Their products were well represented among the pioneer packets. One of their first ships, back in 1807, was that substantially built regular trader and original Black Baller, the *Pacific,* which lasted as a whaler until she was seventy-five years old. Adam also built in 1817 another pioneer Black Baller, the *James Monroe,* while between 1819 and 1822, Noah constructed three of the original four ships of the Old Line to Havre. The fourth of these, also built in this yard, indicated the change in control, for the "master carpenters" of this *Henry* were "Brown & Bell," a name that would become increasingly prominent while Adam and Noah dropped out of the picture.

One of the new partners was David Brown, Noah's adopted son: the other was Jacob Bell, another of the New Englanders from Stamford. They had the cream of the packet construction for about twenty years, until finally overshadowed by Webb. Their packets were not as numerous as those of the Bergh-Westervelt yard, but they were larger and performed better. This yard had all the Black Ball orders for many

years, built Collins's new ships for the Dramatic Line, and also those
for the "New Line" to Liverpool. Nearly all of these were the largest
ships afloat at the time of their launchings and several were among the
fastest on the run. David Brown died in 1848 at Princeton, where a
college dormitory bears his name, and Bell carried on alone for the
remaining four years of his life. During that last period, he built several
successful clippers and two of the original great Collins steamships.

A fourth yard, which nearly approached those three in the quality
and quantity of its output, was that of Smith & Dimon, at times with
a third partner as Blossom, Smith & Dimon, and again as Smith,
Dimon & Comstock. Stephen Smith, still another of the Stamford
builders, was originally an apprentice under Eckford, while his partner,
John Dimon, attended to repairs. Taking over the old Eckford yard,
they turned out a respectable total of packets, steamers, and a few
clippers in addition to numerous ordinary merchantmen. Sidney Wright,
a nephew of the Black Ball operator and foreman for the Browns during
their work on the Lakes, had made a good start in his yard with Black
Ball orders at the time of his premature death in 1822. Various combi-
nations of the Fickett family led in the building of the early coastal
packets. Finally, conspicuous among the later builders were William
H. Brown (apparently no relation of the other Browns), who rose
from a modest beginning with canal boats to the construction of steamships and clippers; Roosevelt & Joyce, who took over the Brown & Bell
yard after Jacob's death; also the yards of John Englis, Lawrence &
Sneden, and Bishop & Simonson, which were devoted chiefly to hulls
for steamers; but a further catalogue of names would serve no purpose
at this point. This concentration into a very few hands was remarkable
considering the importance of the East River yards. For the capital
involved and the scope of the plants, the New York builders had few
rivals in the country.

Aside from the private yards, the Navy Yard at Brooklyn also
played its part in the East River construction. Various considerations,
political and otherwise, led to the spreading of building among the
various navy yards along the coast, but this yard at New York had a
definite advantage in its nearness to such a large supply of skilled shipyard labor along the East River, and, more particularly, to the virtual
New York monopoly of technicians qualified to make machinery for
the steam vessels.

Virtually all of the important New York shipyards were concen-

From a painting by Antonie Roux

BRIG *AMERICAN* OF NEW YORK, 1820

Vessels of this rig were earlier known as "snows" because of a small extra mast supporting the spanker

Courtesy of the Pennsylvania Museum of Art, Philadelphia—and the Estate of Laurence John Brengle

Drawn and lithographed by L. Brown, Jr. *Courtesy of Vernon Tate*

MEXICAN WAR VESSEL, *MARY C. ALLEN*, 1851

This speedy and slender vessel was described in Spanish on the New York lithograph, as a Mexican brig of war, built by W. H. Webb at New York. She does not appear under that name in the published list of Webb's vessels, but his *Malek Adhel* was a similar type

trated along a scant mile of this East River waterfront, stretching from about the present site of the Williamsburg Bridge, just below Corlear's Hook, where Manhattan bulges out into the river, up to about 13th Street. Except for the Navy Yard, in Brooklyn on Wallabout Creek, opposite Corlear's Hook, and for Jabez Williams's later yard at Williamsburg, most of the building was done on the New York side. The Bergh-Westervelt yard lay at the foot of Scammel Street, just below Corlear's Hook, Brown & Bell operated at the foot of Stanton Street, just above the Hook; while Webb's plant stretched from 5th to 7th Streets. Along all this section, there was still a natural sloping shore and boys went swimming at Corlear's Hook in summer. The upper portion was marshy land, partly cut off at high tide, before the waterfront was finally filled in. It was known as Manhattan Island in the days before that appellation was extended to the more important land behind it. Staten Island produced a considerable number of small craft and towards the end of the period a few larger vessels were built on the Jersey side of the Hudson. With those exceptions, New York's shipbuilding was restricted to that important mile of turbulent East River.

The various major processes involved in shipbuilding were fundamentally the same for most vessels, whether one were building a brig with a handful of men on some distant tidal river in Maine or fashioning a crack packet in an East River yard to compete for the blue ribbon of the Atlantic.

In either case, during the early years of the period, the master carpenter himself generally began the work by taking a block composed of strips of wood pinned together with dowels. From this he would cut a "lift" or "waterline" model to a predetermined scale representing half the hull from stem to sternpost and embodying the particular dimensions and lines of the vessel. Next this was sent to the "mould loft," where the lifts of the model were separated and the loftsmen would "lay down" the lines of the vessel to the full size of the actual vessel on the loft floor. Using this huge plan they made thin wooden "moulds" or patterns of each frame and timber which went into the hull. These were placed in the hands of the shipwrights who chose from their store of crooked and straight timbers a piece closest to the shape of the mould. Then with saw, axe, or adze they cut the log to the exact size and shape required.

Then on the "building ways," sloping down to the water's edge, actual construction would begin with the laying of the huge keel pieces. These might be called the backbone of the ship, while the rest of the skeleton consisted chiefly of the heavy stem and sternpost, together with numerous curved frames or ribs, each composed of several pieces, and large cross beams, supported by knees, to support the decks. Next came the planking or "skin" of the ship, fastened on with wooden treenails or "trunnels." Caulkers filled the seams with oakum to make the hull watertight while deck planks, which would be worn white with holystoning, were set in place, hatchways framed, and various odd jobs performed by the carpenters. There still remained the "stepping" of the big pine sticks for lower masts and the adjusting of the numerous lighter pieces for topmasts and yards, while the painters gave the hull its protective covering, gayer in color in the early days than after sombre black became prevalent. Riggers set in place the miles of rope for the stiff, tarred "standing rigging," which held the masts in place, and the more flexible "running rigging" with which the sails would be hoisted or shifted. The sailmaker would meanwhile be making the sheets, giving each sail its proper stiffness and "belly." Finally came the climax of the launching, which might occur either before or after masts and rigging were in place. The sheathing of the hull with copper had to wait until after the launching and might be deferred until the vessel reached England, where the process could be done more cheaply.

Towards the middle of the century the builders in the larger shipyards placed less dependence on the half model and more on plans drawn by professional ship draftsmen. As years passed these contained not only the lines of the hull, but also a complete delineation of the various members of the frame, the location of all hatches, deck beams, cabins with their various partitions, mast positions and the like. Instead of laying down the ship on the mould loft floor from the model, the full-sized drawings were made from data on the plans. Cutting half models was never entirely abandoned because many owners were not able to visualize what the projected vessel would be like from plans alone. However, they could run their hands over a model, squint along its side and bottom and see the finished product in their minds' eye.

All those stages were common to shipbuilding in general, so that there is no occasion to follow them in detail in the study of a particular port. In certain aspects, however, the East River yards presented special features, which contributed to the high quality of their products and resulted in certain extra efficiency, but at the same time tended to make the New York ships more expensive. Only a few outside yards at

Boston and elsewhere approached the East River establishments in their elaborate equipment, costly materials, and high labor costs.

Ship timber was one essential item in which New York's situation differed from that in many smaller ports "down east." One of the significant reasons for the success of American shipbuilding was the availability of an adequate supply of wood near enough the yards so that it could be brought to them at reasonable cost. This enabled the United States to turn out vessels at a much cheaper rate than the British yards, which had to look to the Baltic or America for much of their timber. New York, however, was not as favorably situated in this respect as most of the "down east" ports, where the builders, for a while, could secure all the oak and pine they needed close at hand. It took a hundred years, more or less, to grow an oak of adequate size for shipbuilding and the near-by regions were not producing new trees quickly enough to replace the steady drain of the East River construction. Even for white oak, the most popular and generally used of ship timbers, it was necessary even at the outset to send some distance up the Hudson or into New Jersey. Occasionally an advertisement in the New York newspapers would announce a supply of "pasture white oak" for sale. Such trees, growing in relative isolation and consequently subjected to the buffeting of the elements, were more apt to take on the strange shapes required for certain parts of a ship's frame than were the straighter trees which grew in sheltered forests. As the available oaks in the Hudson valley were gradually cut off, New York reached further inland to the regions tapped by the Erie and Champlain Canals. Probably even the white oak used in the New York yards had to travel an average of at least a hundred miles.

The East River builders, however, were more particular than the usual run of shipbuilders and white oak did not content them for their best products. Like the navy, they wanted live oak for those portions of the frame which would bear the greatest strain. This live oak, which produced the choicest of the American ship timbers, rivalled only by teak from India, grew in a long narrow strip along the southern coast, with the best trees in the swamps of Georgia and Florida. The short, crooked trees produced all the queer shapes which delighted a shipwright's eye, while the compact, fine-grained wood had a tensile strength and durability far beyond that of ordinary white oak. It was expensive, for the cutting was difficult and most of it had to be carried at least 800 miles. One versatile New York builder took his shipwrights to Florida, built a ship close at hand to the live-oak supplies, and sailed her home with the timbers for another ship in her hold. She was the *Citizen,* built by Charles Porter for the Canton trade. But she was an isolated case. For years, a steady procession of little schooners and brigs came northward past Hatteras, loaded with live oak for the Navy Yard, for particular builders, or for timber merchants. Henry Eckford had a small vessel of his own fairly constantly in the business. Enthusiasm for live oak was not universal, however; not only did it cost around $1.50 a cubic foot at a time when white oak cost around 65 cents, but it weighed around 80 pounds a cubic foot as compared with 50 pounds for white oak. This, it was felt by some, added too much weight to the ship. Finally, its tough texture made it much more difficult to work into shape with the adze; while spikes could not be used since it split so readily. The fact remains that most of the packets and Indiamen had this choice wood in their tough frames and this contributed to their lasting far beyond the normal span of twenty years.

Three other southern woods also found their way into the New York yards in large quantities. From Chesapeake Bay came light red cedar and tough locust. Both were less liable than white oak to be pulverized by dry rot and the cedar helped to offset the excessive weight of live oak. Both were used in the upper timbers and locust was also popular for treenails or "trunnels," those wooden pins which were used along with copper bolts to hold the hull together. Light pitch pine from the Carolinas or Georgia was often employed for part of the inner, upper, and deck planking, as well as for the beams which supported the decks and gave lateral strength. The particular uses of these various timbers, as indicated in the specifications for a warship built at New York, may be appreciated by those familiar with the technical names for the different parts of a ship's anatomy:

> The vessel is to be built of the best materials cut when the sap was down, her frame, bottom, planks, wales and thick stuff, the clamps, spirkettings and thick stuff of the deck of white oak, free from defects, except the apron, knight heads, hawse pieces and main transom which are to be of live oak, the ceiling, deck plank, beams, ledges, and plank of the topside of yellow pine, free from sap and all other defects, the top timbers on each side of the ports to be locust, as also the timber heads, all the other top timbers and half top timbers to be of red cedar.

The Black Baller *Columbus,* built in 1834, was described in *Lloyd's Register* as constructed of live oak, white oak, locust, cedar, and pitch pine. New York seldom resorted to hackmatack or larch, which was commonly employed "down east" for knees and other timbers.

While one procession of little coasters was bringing southern timber to the East River, another was coming down from Maine with "spars," a phrase which included masts and yards. The favorite wood for this purpose was white pine, which grew in great profusion in those eastern forests and furnished good straight sticks large enough for mainmasts of the most important ships. Four or five hundred miles was the normal trip for such cargoes from forest to the East River.

Proximity to the timber supply, therefore, did not explain the success of the yards at New York in the same way that it did in New England, where oak and pine grew close at hand. Rather, the increasing concentration of commerce at New York called for certain first-class ships and the owners were ready to pay the extra costs incidental to timber transportation in order to have their vessels constructed by skilled builders whom they knew personally and whose work might be easily inspected stage by stage.

In physical equipment, the East River yards generally had a larger number of specialized buildings and more mechanical labor-saving devices than the ordinary little New England yards. Most of the New York yards had several separate building ways in order that a number of vessels might be constructed at one time. Instead of having the frames and the workers exposed to the elements, they often had covered "ship sheds" over the ways. Noah Brown, for instance, had them even at the beginning of our period. One of the worst time-consuming tasks in the whole operation was the sawing of plank by hand, with one sawyer standing below in a pit while another, above, bent over the other end of the long two-handled saw. The New York yards before long substituted steam sawmills for this backbreaking work. They also provided machinery which quickly turned out "trunnels" of uniform size, instead of having them laboriously whittled down by hand. Steam derricks, too, lightened the work of raising the heavy frames into place, and steam pumps were used to fill the space between inner and outer planking with water to determine how tight the seams were. The New York yards, unlike those at Medford, Massachusetts, seldom called upon the local fire department for this service.

The smaller shipbuilders elsewhere generally limited their activity to the building of the hull itself. For the necessary finishing processes, such as mastmaking, rigging, sailmaking, and sometimes painting, they were inclined to rely upon independent firms, operating under special contract. The larger East River plants were more likely to retain such specialists as part of their permanent personnel. Only three of these stages were generally left to subcontractors at New York—sailmaking, boatbuilding, and the interior finishing of the cabins for the finer liners.

The sailmakers, who generally had their separate establishments, worked in sail lofts, which had to have a floor space large enough for spreading, cutting, fastening, and binding the huge sheets. It was a work of art to fashion sails which would have the proper amount of stiffness and of "belly." This became simpler when around the beginning of our period American cotton duck, manufactured at Baltimore, Paterson, or around Boston, began to replace the stiff, heavy canvas imported from England or Russia. Experiments in the Navy demonstrated the superior sailing qualities of the cotton-duck sails, which played their part in the excellent performance of the ships that used them. A vessel was normally provided at first with two or three complete "suits" of sails, sometimes with heavy ones for winter and lighter ones for summer. Many would carry as part of their personnel a sailmaker who could make new sheets as they were needed; other vessels continued to furnish business for the New York sailmakers long after their original job was finished.

The vessel's long boat and jolly boat were also apt to come from one of the numerous New York establishments, which specialized in that work. One enterprising boat builder inaugurated rowing races in the harbor to stimulate business and another, Joseph Francis, won lasting fame through the development of effective lifeboats. In regard to the interior finishing of vessels, ordinary carpenters were entrusted with most of this work. The packets, however, which were built to catch the best passenger trade, generally had their cabins finished by some outside shipjoiner. Birdseye maple and other woods, highly polished, were in favor for panelling during the early period, but white, finished with gold trimmings, gradually replaced that vogue. Skilled carvers fashioned the figurehead and other external ornaments.

The East River plants generally had their own blacksmith shops to make the many fastenings and fittings needed for hull, deck, and rigging, whereas the smaller yards ordinarily secured this material from outsiders. One extra item of expense in the better New York ships was the use of copper for fastenings, and copper, of course, cost much more than iron. Both iron and copper were generally imported during most of the period before the Civil War, particularly from England. A few American plants turned out domestic anchors, but they, like the chain cables, which gradually after 1815 replaced hempen anchor cables, were ordinarily brought from England. The question of duties on such materials was a matter of perennial dispute in tariff debates. One finds Daniel Webster, for instance, during his protectionist arguments in 1828, showing that the duties on iron, hemp, duck, and the like increased the cost of an ordinary 300-ton ship by $662, while if she were copper-fastened, the toll jumped to $1056.

The New York yards were in a position of unique advantage in the lucrative matter of repairs. Not only did their own creations have to come back again and again to replace cracked masts, wrenched timbers, and battered planking, but the constantly increasing volume of shipping at the port brought them a large amount of outside business. Repair work was often more profitable than original construction. The junior partner of Smith & Dimon was credited with the remark, "Smith builds the ships and I make the money." Some men, like the Poillon brothers, seem to have specialized in repair work exclusively, while Charles Porter, one of the most versatile and financially successful of the East River shipbuilders, had a very modest score in new ships, but did a flourishing business in salvage and repairs.

In one aspect of this repair work, New York had a decided advantage over the other ports. In the older days a vessel which needed repairs below the waterline had to be "careened" or tipped over in order that one side of the hull would lie exposed at low tide. In 1824, a group composed chiefly of New York shipbuilders and shipowners was incorporated as the New York Dry Dock Co., and three years later had equipment which enabled vessels to be drawn out of the water so that repairs might be made under more satisfactory conditions. The shipwrights engaged in repairs might use the dock upon payment to the company. This also made it possible to have ships copper-sheathed at New York without having to send them to England. Before long, a rival New York Screw Dock Co. was formed and by 1847, when the Cunarder *Britannia* was repaired, it was remarked that the port had eleven such establishments. Most of them seem to have been marine railways rather than dry docks proper. One of the latter, on a large scale, was finally constructed of masonry at the Brooklyn Navy Yard between 1841 and 1851 at a cost of more than $2,000,000, until then the bigger naval vessels had had to go to Boston to use the Navy Yard dock there.

The financial rewards from shipbuilding are somewhat elusive. Beach's figures for the estimated $100,000 fortunes in New York in 1846 do not include a single shipbuilder; yet a sailmaker, who was also later a mayor of the city, is on the list, indicating that there was money to be made in that line. By 1855, only the names of William H. Brown and Porter appear. There is, however, a certain amount of evidence to the contrary. Eckford made a considerable profit out of his fat contracts for foreign warships and was able to buy an estate which ranged from Sixth to Eighth Avenues between 21st and 24th Streets, but then he became involved in the failure of an insurance company which perhaps influenced his decision to go to Turkey. Christian Bergh left his son so comfortably fixed that he was free to devote his time to establishing the American branch of the Society for the Prevention of Cruelty to Animals. Part of the Brown & Bell profits went to build a dormitory at Princeton University and Webb was able to leave a very substantial sum to found and endow the Webb Institute of Naval Architecture.

Several shipbuilders played a prominent part in New York politics and Westervelt became mayor. They were in a decidedly advantageous position for such activity because they were among the largest employers of labor and in the days before the secret ballot it was not healthy to vote contrary to an employer's views.

The most detailed figures indicating the scope of the East River plants are to be found in the state census for 1855, when the building had reached and almost passed the peak. Including both New York and Kings Counties (Brooklyn, Williamsburg, etc.), the shipbuilding establishments proper numbered 31, employing 2313 hands and turning out finished products that year worth $3,538,000 from materials worth $1,501,000. Aside from the "iron works" which manufactured marine engines and boilers and have been mentioned elsewhere, the auxiliary plants—sailmaking, sparmaking, rigging, blockmaking, "ship smithing," boatbuilding, "steamboat finishing," and factories for treenails, blocks, capstans and windlasses—brought the total number of plants to 96. The work of these auxiliary plants seems to have nearly doubled the value of the hulls, for the grand total came to $6,263,000 in finished products from raw materials costing $3,185,000. The special plants, however, required only a fraction of the number of hands employed in the shipyards proper—470 as compared with 2313.

The labor relationship was a survival of the old craft system, with masters, journeymen, and apprentices. Nearly every one of the prominent East River builders worked up through those various stages. The would-be shipwright was normally apprenticed to a master-carpenter for a period of years, usually four at New York, to learn the "art, trade, and mystery of a ship-carpenter." That was the period for which John Englis, later an important builder of steamships, was bound to Stephen Smith in 1825. His indenture stipulated:

during all which time the said apprentice his master faithfully shall serve, his secrets keep, his lawful commands everywhere readily obey; he shall do no damage to his said master, nor shall see it done by others without telling or giving notice thereof to his said master: he shall not waste his said master's goods, nor lend them unlawfully to any; he shall not contract matrimony within the said term: at cards, dice or any unlawful game he shall not play, whereby his said master may have damage: with his own goods not the goods of others without license from his said master he shall neither buy nor sell: he shall not absent himself day nor night from his master's service without his leave; nor haunt ale-houses, taverns, dance-houses, or play-houses; but in all things behave himself as a faithful apprentice ought to do during the term. And the said master shall use the utmost of his endeavor to teach, or cause to be taught or instructed, the said apprentice in the trade or mystery of a ship carpenter, and the said master shall pay to the said apprentice the sum of two dollars and fifty cents weekly for each and every week he shall faithfully serve him during the said term. And also shall pay to him, the said apprentice, the sum of forty dollars per year, payable quarterly, for lieu of meat, drink, washing, lodging, clothing and all other necessaries.

When the great age of American shipbuilding came, scores of men, who had gone through such spartan discipline and instruction on the East River, were to play conspicuous roles both at New York and at many points to the eastward. Donald McKay himself, it will be recalled, received his instruction at the hands of the elder Webb and with others also there was a direct continuity from the old masters of 1815 to those who were turning out masterpieces in their turn in the 'fifties. It was the counterpart of the training of the boys who began their brilliant mercantile careers in the routine drudgery of the counting-houses of Leroy, Bayard & Co., or G. G. & S. Howland, or those outstanding shipmasters who in their boyhood had gone to sea with Captain Nathaniel B. Palmer and other autocrats of the quarterdeck.

With the apprenticeship completed, the young shipwright was graduated to the status of journeyman. As everybody knows, this word implied working by the day rather than "journeying," but the fact remained that, once relieved from the rather oppressive apprenticeship, these young men were inclined to shift around from yard to yard and even from port to port. In part this may have been simply for the sake of change, but also, for the more ambitious, it was probably with the purpose of learning the technique of various masters. In this way, developments in shipbuilding tended to spread throughout the port and along the coast. In the smaller yards, a journeyman might be expected to participate in all the various stages of building the hull, but the big yards gave an opportunity for specialization, with some men devoting themselves to sawing, others to carpentry, still others to caulking, and so on.

The working day was long at the outset, extending from "sunrise to sunset." In the summer, that meant from 4.30 in the morning to 7.30 at night, with an hour out for breakfast and two for dinner, together with a brief time off in mid-forenoon and afternoon for a three-cent glass of grog at a neighboring shop. For all that, the wages were only $1.25 a day. Gradually, however, the workers began to realize their strategic position and the difficulty the builders would face in obtaining skilled substitutes in a hurry. There was an organization, not exactly a labor union, called in 1817 "The Union Society of Shipwrights and Caulkers" and a quarter century later "The Journeymen Benevolent Society of Shipwrights and Caulkers." At any rate, some well-timed strikes finally won a ten-hour day in the East River yards; and the journeymen, to be sure that this was rigidly observed, raised money to buy a bell which was set up on a tower in the heart of the shipyard district and rung four times a day, at the beginning and at the end of work and at the dinner hour. They also gained an increase in wages: $1.50 and then $1.75 per day. By the time of the clipper boom, when skilled shipwrights were at a premium, wages sometimes ran as high as $2.50 a day, which was the main reason that the cost of construction was higher at New York.

As for the vessels turned out by these yards, a thorough search of the certificates of registry and enrollment at the New York Custom House has yielded a wealth of information, although often annoying gaps prevent a complete analysis. It will be well to notice some of the essential features and developments, taking up in turn, in increasing

order of size, the sloops, schooners, brigs, barks, ships, and war vessels. Steamboats and steamships are discussed elsewhere, for their machinery was a more unusual feature than the fashioning of their hulls,
which did not differ radically from the conventional shipbuilding
methods.

The New York customs district, we recall, included not only the

Sloop   Schooner   Brig   Ship

port proper, but at first the whole Hudson valley, western Long
Island, and part of New Jersey. The vessels registered for foreign
trade were chiefly the square-rigged brigs, barks, and ships. These were
a virtual monopoly of the East River plants and it was unusual when
a brig was built at Brookhaven on outer Long Island. The certificates
of enrollment for the domestic trade, on the other hand, reveal that
while the East River builders might turn out occasional square-rigged
vessels for the coastal trade and a number of smaller craft, most of the
sloops and schooners were built by small builders at scores of different
outside points in the district.[1]

In the early years of the period, even many of the little sloops and
schooners might be classed among the square-rigged craft, but as time
went on, the fore-and-aft rig became increasingly more popular. The
single big sail for each mast could be hoisted or lowered without the
necessity of going aloft; the vessel, therefore, could be operated by a

[1]See Appendix, vi, for number of each type employed between New York and various
foreign and coastal ports in 1835; xv for number of each type built each year in New
York, Maine, and Massachusetts; and xvi for dimensions of vessels of each type.

smaller crew. The fore-and-aft rig was also an advantage in working to windward or in clawing off a lee shore in a gale. The accompanying cuts show the sloop and schooner with the fore-and-aft, rather than the older "topsail" rig. The distinguishing feature between a sloop and schooner lay in the number of masts; the sloop had only one and the schooner generally had two; three-masted schooners were rare in that day.

The little sloops remained throughout our period the favorite method of conveying heavy freight on the Hudson, the Sound, and the Bay. Occasionally, they carried passengers as well, but that business was soon taken over by the steamboats which made their successful debut in those same waters. Sloops were also used in the earlier years for trips along the coast from New York as far as Boston or Chesapeake Bay, but most of that business soon went to the schooners. It was not that sloops were too small for deep-sea voyages. The little 84-ton *Enterprise* had made the second American China voyage, from New York to Canton and back, just after the Revolution. In 1817, Christian Bergh built the 111-ton sloop *Illinois* for the adventurous Stonington sealers. She was both the largest sloop built at New York in the period and one of the last registered for foreign voyages. Relatively few sloops were built by the crack yards. A few were turned out at Staten Island but the bulk of sloop construction in the New York district was carried on at some distance from the city and often under very informal conditions with a minimum of equipment. One or two men could build a sloop alone and frequently the "master carpenter" also appears as the skipper in the records. On the other hand, the writers of the day paid tribute to the skill of William Dickey and Caleb Welsie as New York specialists in sloop construction.

Midway between sloops and schooners proper came a type of little craft rather peculiar to New York. Known as the "periagua" or "pettiauger," it was technically a schooner because it had two masts. It was a sharp-ended craft with shallow draft, particularly useful for working its way up the little streams which tapped the rich region of eastern New Jersey. In 1824, which seems to have been the peak year for such craft, five of them, ranging from 22 to 60 tons, were built and enrolled at New York. The largest, from the Smith & Dimon yard, was 62 feet long, 23 feet wide, and, as its most distinctive feature, only 5 feet in depth of hold. Staten Island built and owned a number of these, some of which were enrolled in the name of its most illustrious son, Cornelius Vanderbilt, at the beginning of his career. Accounts of the actual details of pettiauger construction are conflicting and inadequate; the subject is one which deserves further investigation.

The schooner was by far the most common type in the American merchant marine. Of the total vessels built in the nation in 1815, 680 were schooners; 274, sloops; 224, brigs; and 136, ships. At the end of the period, they still held the lead. The total vessels constructed in 1860 consisted of 372 schooners, 289 sloops, canal boats, etc., 264 steam vessels, 141 ships, and only 36 brigs. In size, the schooners usually ranged from about 75 to 150 tons, though occasional exceptions went beyond those extremes. The schooners formed the rank and file on the "lesser" coastal runs from Maine to North Carolina and were also the usual type on the routes to the Caribbean and the Spanish Main.

From the standpoint of shipbuilding and naval architecture, the schooners fell into two groups. The ordinary coastal cargo carrier might be built by rule-of-thumb by amateur shipwrights who never bothered with lift models or the other niceties of the art. On the other hand, certain specialized types of schooners were among the fastest vessels afloat; and an able analyst of American ship design stresses the important early influence of the sharp Baltimore "clipper" schooners on the later developments which produced the clipper proper. Pilot boats offered the most common opportunity for artistry in this line, together with yachts, which began to appear gradually toward the end of the period.

The expensive East River plants were not normally called upon for ordinary freighters. As in the case of the sloops, these were apt to come from outlying parts of the district, particularly from Brookhaven and adjacent Long Island communities. At Staten Island, which may be considered a part of the port itself, Henry Rutan, Henry Seguine, and other builders concentrated upon schooners, both freighters and pilot boats. Upon one occasion, a group at Staten Island purchased a pilot boat from Baltimore and apparently proceeded to turn out others modelled upon her lines.

The big East River yards did not scorn orders for pilot boats, however. Webb, in his published collection of plans, included those of the pilot boat *John McKeon*, maintaining that she had fast lines and was a good sea boat. He did not add that she was lost with all hands in a bad storm. Closely related to the pilot boats were the swift schooners operated by the New York editors to gather news from incoming vessels.

The Journal of Commerce sent to Baltimore for the fast schooner which bore its name, but Webb and Allen in 1832 built the rival 100-ton *Courier & Enquirer*, 71 feet long, with a 21-foot beam and 7-foot depth of hold. The most celebrated of all the East River schooners was the yacht *America*, built by George Steers in the 'fifties; and her name lives on in the cup which she won. The most notorious was another yacht, the *Wanderer*, which, as we recall, ended as a slaver. Some of the other schooners from the East River utilized their speed for unworthy purposes, ranging from privateering and piracy in the Caribbean to opium running in Chinese waters or slaving on the Guinea coast.

The brigs, two-masted, occupied an intermediate position between the schooner and the ship and were gradually squeezed out between these two types. In tonnage, their normal range was from 150 to 250. The total number built, as we just saw, dropped from 224 to 36 between 1815 and 1860. New York produced only a very few each year; when New Yorkers wanted brigs, they usually sent to Maine, which built a large proportion of the national total. Brigs were used chiefly on the longer coastal runs and to the Caribbean and Latin America. They were more common than schooners on the routes to Brazil and Buenos Aires. Boston used relatively more brigs than did New York. They did not present such interesting developments in design as did either the schooners or the ships. Now and then, however, a brig of unusually sharp design was produced in the East River and generally aroused suspicion, as in the case of the *Malek Adhel*, built by Webb in 1840. It was learned that she was ordered by a merchant in the Gulf of California and the newspapers were certain that she was destined for no honest business. The regular brig was square-rigged on both masts and could be easily distinguished from a fore-and-aft schooner. The "topsail schooner," however, resembled the "half brig" (hermaphrodite or brigantine), square-rigged on the foremast only. Even the experts were sometimes confused; the inspector for the Atlantic Mutual Insurance Co., for instance, entered against the name of the Maine-built *J. L. Whipple* in the schooner volume, "I think this is a ½ brig but she is sometimes called a schooner. See Bg. Book."

The bark was a minor type, ordinarily included with the full-rigged ship in general categories. She had three masts but carried fore-and-aft rig on the mizzen. Generally, the barks overlapped in size the smaller ships and usually ranged from about 275 to 350 tons. Sidney

Wright produced the little 185-ton bark *Packet* in 1819 but scarcely another one was built at New York until the mid-'thirties, when they became more popular. Ships of the smaller class were occasionally re-rigged as barks, since they could then be handled aloft by fewer men. From the standpoint of shipbuilding, there was no essential difference.

The full-rigged ship, of course, was the capital ship of the merchant marine and the particular specialty of the East River yards. Whereas the other types changed relatively little during the period, there was a tremendous development both in the size and the design of ships.

In size, most of the ships built at New York in the first years after 1815 averaged somewhat under 400 tons. The smallest full-rigged ship built at the port during the period was the 176-ton *Sea Fox* turned out by Noah Brown in 1817. She was only slightly larger than the maximum schooner of that day and much smaller than many brigs. Possibly she was overrigged, for she capsized off the Delaware Capes. Some of the crew, trapped inside the hull, were rescued by chance, when the boat's crew from another ship, curiously rowing around the water-logged wreck, happened to hear tapping. Other ships ran to the opposite extreme in size. In fact, the first East River product regis-tered in 1815 was the 899-ton *General Brown,* built on speculation by Adam and Noah Brown. She was finally purchased as a regular trader to Cadiz but proved too large for the trade of the day. It was twenty years before the East River ships caught up with her in size; even the celebrated Dramatic packets, *Garrick, Sheridan,* and *Siddons,* built in 1836 and 1837, a hundred tons larger than any other packet of the time and surpassing most merchantmen, measured four tons less than that first ship of 1815. By the 'forties, ships of a thousand tons ceased to be novelties, and by the early 'fifties, clippers, packets, and freighters were approaching two thousand tons. Sometimes an occasional ship would even exceed that amount. Webb's 2145-ton *Ocean Monarch,* launched in 1856, was apparently the largest square-rigged merchant-man built on the river, though a few warships and steamships exceeded her in size.

Such tonnage increases, however, were far less significant and re-flected less honor upon the builders than the evolution in design dur-ing those same years. There is no room here to follow the intricate evolution of ship design; able analysis of that elusive subject is avail-able elsewhere. In general, it may be said that the trend was gradual, away from the bulky and "burthensome" ships of the early part of the period, toward the streamlining which found its extreme expression in the clippers. That process was the result of a long, steady evolution and cannot be pinned down to any particular year or man or locality, though the East River certainly played a very conspicuous part in the development. Designing was a tricky game, for the same yard sometimes turned out a slow ship immediately after a particularly fast one. In 1836, for instance, Webb produced his first Black Baller, the *Oxford*. She performed exceedingly well and the line ordered another from him, but the *Cambridge* averaged a whole week slower on the westbound crossing from Liverpool.

Speed had been at a premium during the War of 1812, when it was important to elude British frigates, if not to overhaul weaker British merchantmen, but with the return of peace, cargo capacity was deliberally sought even at the sacrifice of average speed. The tonnage laws had a pernicious effect, for the "old custom house measurement," used to estimate registry tonnage as a basis for port dues and the like, was determined by the too simple formula of subtracting ⅗ of the beam from the length, multiplying the difference by the beam, and that product by the depth of hold, which for a while was arbitrarily reckoned as half the beam. By dividing that result by 95, the supposed capacity of the hold was obtained in tons of 40 cubic feet each. The consequent effort to reduce running expenses by evading port duties led to the designing of abnormally deep vessels with a uniform beam for a considerable section of their length. The resultant bluff-bowed, square-sterned, "kettle-bottomed" tubs were able to carry cargoes far in excess of their registered tonnage, and their owners were ready to overlook slow passages in view of the reduction of tonnage duties.

The bars at the mouth of the Mississippi indirectly led to an important development around 1830 through the desire to combine large carrying capacity with moderate draft. As a compromise, five large New Orleans packets were built with "flat-floored" or U-shaped cross-sections instead of the previous V-shaped sections with their sharp "dead-rise," which increased the draft but was also supposed to increase speed. To the general surprise, these "flat-floored" packets made excellent time and consequently the principle won widespread adoption. Webb was a particular enthusiast upon the subject. With that change came a gradual tapering of the bows, which became less convex or "apple-cheeked," while the sterns were also rounded and the widest part of the ship was moved aft. These changes were soon incorpo-

THE CHINA CLIPPER *HOUQUA*

THE HAVRE PACKET *EMERALD*

Both ships were built by Brown & Bell on the East River, the sturdy 518-ton *Emerald* (later a Baltimore-Liverpool packet) in 1835, and the graceful 582-ton *Houqua* in 1844. Both had the same beam; the packet was deeper and the clipper longer

rated in the ocean packets, which were, of course, the most important products of the East River down to the mid-'forties. Their speed records, as analyzed in the author's separate study of the packets, showed an immediate gain.

Down to about the end of the 'thirties, Bergh, Webb, and the other "master carpenters" had done their own designing, whittling away at the lift models to express their own individual views of what made a good ship. Webb and some others continued this way, but in the 'forties appeared the naval architect, who specialized in designing ships for others to build. Outstanding in this field was John Willis Griffiths, son of a New York shipwright, who gave him a thorough, practical instruction in shipbuilding. The younger Griffiths served as a draftsman at the Norfolk Navy Yard and then entered the employ of Smith & Dimon, with whom he was to be most intimately associated.

The principles which he preached and embodied in his designs were an important factor in accelerating the developments of the clipper-ship era. The first tangible expression of his scientific approach to the subject was the *Rainbow,* built on his design by Smith & Dimon, as one of the first of the new China clippers at New York. In that trade, speed was the prime essential and cargo capacity might more profitably be sacrificed than in the ocean packets. Soon afterwards, for the same owner and the same driving captain, Griffiths and Smith & Dimon built the *Sea Witch,* which is said to have broken more speed records than any other American ship. Close upon that came the gold rush and the still larger California clippers, of which more later in their proper setting.

During the early 'fifties, the East River shipbuilders were at their zenith, sharing almost equal honors in clippers with McKay and the other builders at Boston. In addition, they were turning out packets and other merchantmen larger than ever before, besides finding time to produce most of the crack American steamships of the day. Griffiths wrote in 1851 that New York shipbuilding was "the standard for nearly all parts of the commercial world. I speak advisedly, having been called on from all parts of Europe for New York models, both in regard to the form of the hull and the manner of doing work."

Aside from building vessels for the merchant marine, the New York plants had a particularly lucrative and flattering specialty in the production of warships for various foreign nations, both in Latin America and in Europe. It was a high tribute to their position in the world of shipbuilding that they received, and continued to receive, such orders. Henry Eckford had begun this in a big way, with several frigates and other large vessels for five different Latin-American nations in addition to one for Turkey. Brown & Bell profited during the middle period from a number of warships for Spain, to be used around Cuba. The climax of this business came at the close of the period when Webb built the huge 4600-ton steam frigate, *General Admiral,* and a smaller screw warship, the *Japanese* for the Russian navy. During the Civil War, just after our period ends, he ventured into iron construction with two ironclads for the new Italian navy, the first such vessels to cross the Atlantic—only to be sunk by the Austrians. Next came an even larger ship from the Webb yard, the 5090-ton ironclad ram *Dunderberg,* destined for the Union navy but sold, after the peace, to the French.

One of the most unsavory scandals in the history of the port during this period arose from this foreign shipbuilding in the episode of the "Greek frigates" in 1825 and 1826. The Greeks, in their war for freedom from the Turks, sent agents to New York to negotiate for two frigates. The ensuing scandal involved not so much Eckford and Smith & Dimon, who did the actual building of the ships, as it did the commercial houses of G. G. & S. Howland and Leroy, Bayard & Co., who handled the financial end of the matter. These houses presented reasonable estimates of the probable cost of the frigates to the Greek agents, but when the time of reckoning came, the two houses had run up such a terrific charge for commissions, interest, and the like that the vessels were not handed over to the Greeks for their estimated price. A board of New York merchants arbitrated the matter and decided pretty much in the favor of the two houses. Consequently the Greeks, after paying more than the amount estimated for the two frigates, were given only one, the *Hope.* The other, the *Liberator,* which was withheld, was then sold to the United States Navy, where she served under the name of the *Hudson* for a short while, only to be soon affected with dry rot. This should not have appeared in her had she contained as much of the expensive live oak as had been stipulated in her original estimates. The ensuing scandal was especially embarrassing for old William Bayard, who had served as head of the committee to raise money in New York for the cause of Greek independence. He died before the close of 1826; the responsibility seems to have rested chiefly with his sons, who failed almost immediately afterwards. The hard-bitten and close-fisted Howland brothers, however, survived the affair intact except in their reputation for business ethics.

Finally, the Brooklyn Navy Yard did its share in contributing to the output of the East River. The *President* had been built before the navy yard was established, we recall. One of the yard's products, the ship-of-the-line *Ohio,* exceeded 2800 tons in size and was the largest vessel built at New York down to the 'fifties. In addition to warships, a number of staunch little revenue cutters were also built. On the whole, the New York output was about the same as that of the other navy yards. The government even distributed the construction of steam vessels with a fairly even hand, despite New York's leadership in marine-engine building. On one occasion, learning that a steam vessel was to be built at the easternmost navy yard, the *Herald* printed an indignant article entitled "Where is Kittery?"

If any single day were to be selected as the high-water mark of East River construction, it might well be January 21, 1851, when Webb launched in rapid succession three vessels, each of a different type. One was the 1072-ton Havre packet *Isaac Bell,* a good addition to his long total of successful sailing liners. The second was the 1244-ton clipper *Gazelle,* one of the group that was to give Webb a name second only, perhaps, to his one-time fellow apprentice McKay in that splendid but ephemeral phase of shipbuilding. The third, more prophetic of the future, despite her wooden hull and paddle wheels, was the 2067-ton steamship *Golden Gate* for the Pacific Mail. None of these was Webb's particular masterpiece in any of those three categories, but the thousands gathered at every vantage point on the East River cheered lustily at the threefold evidence of the great shipbuilder's versatile genius.

CHAPTER XV

LINERS AND SUBSIDIES

WHILE 1817 and the adjacent years were the most significant in the history of New York port, the activity of the middle period reached its glorious climax in the five years from 1848 to 1852. Crowded into that brief period were spectacular achievements in many spheres. New York kept its hold on the western trade by the completion of two railroads just ahead of its rivals' efforts to stretch rails across the Alleghenies. Dislodged by famine in Ireland and unrest in Central Europe, immigrants reached New York in unprecedented numbers; many remained in the metropolis to swell its population. The discovery of gold in California brought the clipper era to its height. Dozens of slender, fast, and beautiful vessels built in the East River, and dozens more owned on South Street, established lasting records for sailing-ship accomplishment in rounding the Horn to the Golden Gate. Fast side-wheelers, too, from the East River provided even faster service for passengers and gold to and from both the Atlantic and Pacific sides of the Isthmus of Panama. The sailing packets on the Atlantic shuttle reached new heights in speed and size but were outclassed by the Cunarders, which in their turn had to yield for a while in luxury and speed to New York's own splendid steamships of the Collins Line. Those new features will occupy the remaining portions of this study, beginning with the introduction of steam on the Atlantic shuttle.

The successive substitutes for sails required new additions to the vocabulary. The *Clermont* had been called a "steam boat" and that name, as one word, lasted on for her successors on the quiet waters of river, Sound, and Bay. It was not considered, however, a dignified enough title for the stouter craft which gradually ventured outside Sandy Hook on the high seas. In the initial stages of experimentation, the phrases "steam schooner," "steam brig," and "steam ship" denoted the particular rig of the seagoing craft; but the two former soon disappeared. So, too, did the functional designation of "steam packet" gradually fall into disuse, except in official titles of incorporation. For about a century, "steamboat" and "steamship" have been the usual appellations of the two major branches of steam navigation. The colloquial "steamer," which became common in the 'thirties, was applied to both the minor and the major groups. Our concern here will be with the "steam ships" which began to crowd the sailing packets on the Atlantic shuttle and the longer coastal runs.

"As to the project which was announced in the newspapers of making the voyage directly from New York to Liverpool by steam it was," he had no hesitation in saying, "perfectly chimerical and they might as well talk of making a voyage from New York to the moon." Such was the report of a lecture by Doctor Dionysius Lardner, a popular authority on science, before the Association for the Advancement of Science in 1835. He would probably have given anything not to have uttered that pompous pronouncement. Within three years came that red-letter day in the history of the port and of navigation in general when the *Sirius* and the *Great Western* arrived from across the Atlantic within a few hours of each other. Their achievement marked the beginning of permanent steam service on the Atlantic shuttle. Except for a few intervals, moreover, New York has ever since been the western terminus of the finest steamships afloat.

The *Sirius* and *Great Western,* of course, were no more the first steamships to cross the Atlantic than Fulton's *Clermont* had been the first vessel propelled by steam. In both cases, however, their maiden trips were more significant than those of their predecessors because they led to permanent successful service. Some of those earlier steamships deserve more of our attention than did the pre-Fulton steamboats because they involved New York more closely.

The story goes back twenty years before those simultaneous arrivals in 1838. The original initiative for attempting a transatlantic steam crossing may perhaps be credited to a New York mariner, Captain Moses Rogers, a native of New London. As master of John Stevens's *Phœnix* on her run from Sandy Hook down the exposed Jersey coast to the Delaware, he had taken the first steam vessel from sheltered waters into the open ocean. Eager to achieve a more ambitious "first time," Rogers tried without success to interest New York capital in financing a transatlantic steamship, but he had better luck in the little cotton port of Savannah. With this southern backing, the *Savannah,* a regular full-rigged ship with a 380-ton hull, was launched from the East River yard of Fickett & Crockett on August 22, 1818. Her boiler and engines were made across the bay in New Jersey as were her detachable iron paddle wheels, which could be, and too often were, folded up like a fan and taken inboard.

The *Savannah* left New York on March 28, 1819, and reached Savannah in eight days and fifteen hours, using her engine only forty-one and one half hours. President Monroe, who happened to be visiting Savannah, was taken for a ride down the river. The *Savannah* left the Georgia port on May 24, 1819, for her famous trip across the Atlantic and reached Liverpool on June 20, a passage of twenty-seven days. Her title to first honors for a transatlantic crossing, however, was obscured by the fact that she used steam for only eighty hours of the entire trip and on 18 different days. Her stack was belching smoke, however, as she approached the Irish coast, and a revenue cutter, whose commander thought that she was afire, rushed to her assistance. From Liverpool she proceeded to St. Petersburg, touching at several Baltic ports and using steam two hundred and thirty-nine hours in 33 days. She finally arrived back at Savannah late in November after a rough passage and was sent up to Washington on the strength of Monroe's suggestion that she might be purchased for the Navy. Failing in that hope, she proceeded to New York where, since there was no prospect of financial success, her engines were removed and she became an ordinary sailing ship. New York could claim her at the end, as at the beginning, for in 1822 she missed Sandy Hook during a storm and piled up, a total loss, on the near-by sands of Long Island.

New York, while building Rogers's ship, had refused him the financial backing he needed. The men of South Street and Wall Street apparently soon thought better of the matter. On April 7, 1819, two weeks after the *Savannah* left the East River, the New York legislature granted to ten New Yorkers a charter for the "Ocean Steam Ship Company." The preamble stated that the incorporators were "desirous of constructing and employing steam ships in navigating the ocean" and that they were confident "that vessels may be so constructed as to unite all the safety and other advantages of common ships, to the additional velocity to be gained by the application of steam." In view of the later competition between steamships and sailing packets on the Atlantic shuttle, it is interesting to note that Preserved Fish appeared among the ten incorporators. He was thus toying with the idea of ocean steamships three years before he started the Swallowtail line of Liverpool packets. No transatlantic service resulted from this project; for nearly twenty years New York's splendid "square-riggers on schedule" would have the cream of the business on the Atlantic shuttle pretty much to themselves.

On the longer coastal runs, however, New York made several experiments with "steam ships" during that interval. The first venture was undertaken in 1820 by David Dunham, an energetic New York auctioneer, another of the ten organizers of the abortive "Ocean" company the year before. His 702-ton paddle-wheeler *Robert Fulton* performed for several years with mechanical, if not financial, success on the stormy run down past Hatteras to New Orleans, touching at Charleston and Havana. She began that service a year before the first line of sailing packets to New Orleans was organized and two years before the first line to Charleston. Had Dunham placed three such steamships in service, the coastal packets might never have gotten a foothold in the rich trade between New York and the cotton ports. As it was, the "canvas-backs" made money where the *Robert Fulton* did not, partly because they carried more cargo and partly because shippers and passengers would not wait for her infrequent sailings. Dunham was drowned when the boom of a Hudson River sloop knocked him overboard in a squall; and the *Robert Fulton* passed from hand to hand. After unsuccessful attempts to sell her as a steam warship to the Greek and United States navies, her engines were removed, and she ended her days as a Brazilian warship under sail.

Except for the "steam brig" *New York* which went to and from Norfolk for a while in the 'twenties, New York's next major venture came in the 'thirties. Between 1834 and 1838, five "steam packets" were placed, two at a time, on the route to Charleston. Part of them were operated by James P. Allaire, the prominent builder of marine engines; the others by Charles Morgan, who would later make a fortune with steamers in the Gulf. These Charleston steamers gave frequent service, which the *Robert Fulton* had failed to do, but they lacked her sturdiness. Sailing every Saturday from each port, they matched the sailing packets in frequency of service and, when all went well, arrived in three days, which was just half the packet average and faster than the land mail route. They lured much of the passenger and some of the mail business between the two ports, although, like most of the early steamers, they did not carry much freight.

Passenger service, however, depends upon public confidence; and a series of accidents undermined that. The run past Hatteras called for tougher vessels than the New Yorkers were accustomed to build for the quieter waters of the Hudson and Sound. Time and again after wallowing in the waves which strained their hulls and machinery, the steamers had to put in for shelter at Norfolk or some port of refuge along the Carolina coast. The disastrous climax came in 1837 when Allaire's steamer *Home* broke down near Hatteras and went to pieces with the loss of nearly a hundred lives. Apparently her hull had not been braced strongly enough to support the weight of her engines in such rough waters, so that she had broken her back. Not long afterwards an even heavier loss of life followed a boiler explosion on the Baltimore-Savannah steamer *Pulaski* and most of the travelling public turned away from coastal steamships as too dangerous. Not until 1846 was service resumed on the New York-Charleston route by the very adequate steamship *Southerner,* but she was at that time overshadowed by the transatlantic steamships plying to and from New York.

By the mid-'thirties, New York, London, Bristol, and Liverpool were all entertaining projects of transatlantic steamship service. Two successors of the *Savannah* had demonstrated that it was possible. In 1830, the Dutch steamer *Curaçao* had crossed from Holland to the West Indian island for which she was named; and had continued in a satisfactory manner for three years until withdrawn for use as a warship. The first *Royal William,* after running for a while between Nova Scotia and Quebec, went from Pictou, N. S., to Liverpool in 1833. The fact remained, whatever the enthusiastic backers of each might say, that none of these had led to permanent service.

The times were ripe for such a venture. Cargoes and travel were reaching new heights in 1835 and went still higher in 1836. The New York sailing packets were flourishing. The ships had increased in size and Collins was ordering still larger ones for his new Dramatic Line. It was in this booming state of affairs that the steam projects made headway. Though the panic of 1837 destroyed much of that prosperity, it emphasized to business men on both sides of the Atlantic the need for speedier and more dependable transmission of commercial correspondence.

New York had its own plans for such service. The enterprising promoter was Captain Nathan Cobb, originally from Stonington, Connecticut, a veteran packet captain and part owner of the Black Ball Line after it had changed hands in 1834. During the next two years, he energetically sought financial support in New York and in Canada—packet captains naturally had excellent opportunities to make useful contacts during the long Atlantic crossings. In the autumn of 1835, it was announced that Cobb and his associates would petition the legislature to charter the Atlantic Steam Navigation Company, with a half million capital. The following summer it was reported that the "vessel that has been so much talked about is now rapidly building; her frame is up, and her machinery in progress." About 500 tons in size, with engines of 300 horsepower, this *Despatch* was to be commanded by Cobb himself, "to whose energy and perseverance will the publick be indebted for the first steamboat to run between this port and Europe." That dream, unfortunately, never came true. The *Despatch* seems to have become a victim of the Panic of 1837 and Cobb lost his chance for immortality.

The rival British projects, on the other hand, survived the financial crisis and went steadily ahead. The London one was the first to get under way. Junius Smith, its promoter, was a native of Connecticut, like Captain Rogers of the *Savannah* and Captain Cobb with his abortive venture. Smith had been graduated from Yale in 1802 with Pelatiah Perit, the New York merchant, and had studied law at Litchfield with John C. Calhoun. In 1805 he settled in England, where he was to live for nearly forty years. He traded with New York, where his nephew was his correspondent. It is said that a 54-day trip to New York in a British sailing vessel in 1832 convinced him of the need of a line of steamships and that from that time he devoted himself to creating public opinion and raising capital for such a project. Failing to receive support in New York, he returned to London, where he began to issue prospectuses wherein he preached of the possibilities of ocean steamships. For a while he encountered ridicule and rebuff, but in 1835, having secured a powerful ally in MacGregor Laird of the important Birkenhead shipbuilding family, Smith organized the "British & American Steam Navigation Company." At last, he began to get tangible results from his call for a capital of a million pounds.

By the summer of 1836, he had powerful competition. The directors of the Great Western Railway, which was being pushed through from

London to Bristol, were gradually brought around to the idea of extending their line across the Atlantic by means of steamships from that famous old west-coast port to New York. It is possible that the initiative came from their versatile and capable engineer, Isambard Kingdom Brunel. At any rate, Brunel was to be the prime mover in promoting and designing their ships for years to come. A third rival, the Transatlantic Steamship Company, was being projected at Liverpool.

A scramble followed to be the first to get a steamship ready for the ocean passage. The keel of the *Great Western* was laid at Bristol on July 28, 1836; she was launched the following July; and then taken around to the Thames to receive her engines at Blackwall. Measuring 1340 tons, she had a single funnel and also four schooner-rigged masts. She cost at least £50,000—one report said £63,000. Late in March, 1838, she made her first trial trip down the Thames. Meanwhile, Smith and Laird were having their difficulties. They had ordered a 1700-ton steamship in October, 1836, but the failure of one of the contractors left the *British Queen* (so named after Victoria came to the throne in 1837) hopelessly unfinished while the *Great Western* approached completion.

Despite that heartbreaking disappointment, Smith and his company were unwilling to accept defeat. To forestall the *Great Western,* they decided to charter a steamer and hurry her across to New York. The little *Sirius,* a London-Cork steam packet, was selected as the "pinch hitter" and suddenly given this opportunity for fame. Measuring some 700 tons, she was about the size of the larger New York sailing packets and little more than half the size of her rival. She left Cork on April 4, 1838, under the command of Lieutenant Richard Roberts of the Royal Navy. Four days later, under another naval lieutenant, James Hosken, the *Great Western* set out from Bristol.

The *Great Western,* though she followed a course which meant bucking the Gulf Stream almost the whole way, gradually gained on the little *Sirius.* Unlike the *Savannah,* each used steam the entire way and each burned about 450 tons of coal. The *Great Western* had an adequate reserve, but it is said that the *Sirius* had to burn some of her wooden fittings after the bunker supply approached exhaustion.

On the night of April 22, the *Sirius* arrived off Sandy Hook; but it was more than twelve hours before she reached the upper harbor. It is said that she had to have extra coal hurried down from the city to complete the trip; another account stated that she ran aground on

From a painting by Joseph Walker, 1838

N. Y. P. L.—*Eno Coll.*

ARRIVAL OF THE *GREAT WESTERN* IN NEW YORK HARBOR ON APRIL 23, 1838

The steamship from Bristol, arriving a few hours after the *Sirius*, is shown with the Long Island side of the Narrows in the background. In the left foreground is a typical pilot boat, and in the right foreground a Bay steamer

the bar and stuck there till the tide rose. At any rate, the New Yorkers were ready to give her a rousing reception when she finally came up the harbor the following forenoon. As one newspaper described it:

The news of the arrival of the *Sirius* spread like wild fire through the city, and the river became literally dotted over with boats conveying the curious to and from the stranger. There seemed to be an universal voice of congratulation, and every visage was illuminated with delight. . . .

Whilst all this was going on, suddenly there was seen over Governors Island, a dense black cloud of smoke, spreading itself upwards, and betokening another arrival. On it came with great rapidity, and about 3 o'clock its cause was made fully manifest to the multitudes. It was the steamship *Great Western*. . . . This immense moving mass was propelled at a rapid rate through the waters of the Bay; she passed swiftly and gracefully around the *Sirius*, exchanging salutes with her, and then proceeded to her destined anchorage in the East River. If the public mind was stimulated by the arrival of the *Sirius*, it became intoxicated with delight upon view of the superb *Great Western*.

After years of waiting for transatlantic steam service, New York received two steamships within four hours. Every one realized that he was watching history in the making; observations and prophecies of the most exuberant sort appeared in every newspaper and were voiced at the many festive occasions where the two commanders were feted.

The *Sirius* had crossed in 19 days at an average speed of 6.7 knots; the *Great Western* in 14½ days at 8.75 knots. By the beginning of the Civil War, the running time of the *Sirius* was to be cut almost exactly in half and her average speed, consequently, just doubled. Many different steamships, under several different flags, had, in the meantime, come to New York, for, from that famous April day in 1838, the Atlantic shuttle knew continual steam service. It will be unnecessary to follow those varied steamships beyond a few of the salient features most significant from the standpoint of the port, since, unlike the packets, they are not a virgin subject.

There was a rush of ocean steamships to New York during the remaining months of 1838. The Transatlantic Steamship Company at Liverpool sent the Dublin steam packet *Royal William* (not to be confused with the Canadian pioneer of 1833), in July and the *Liverpool* in November. Altogether, there were ten arrivals during the year, for the *Great Western* made five voyages, the *Sirius* and *Royal William* two each, and the *Liverpool* one. An eleventh sailing was made by a British steamer which had come by way of Jamaica.

By 1839, Smith's *British Queen* was at last ready for service; and first arrived at New York in July. Both the other companies continued in the business. By 1840, the Liverpool company had withdrawn its ships and the Bristol group continued to send the *Great Western* alone. Nothing as yet could really be called line service. A steamship could make six voyages a year, twice as many as a sailing packet. Two steamships, therefore, could provide the same monthly service as the conventional four-ship line of sailing packets. By the summer of 1840, Smith's company began to offer such service. The *British Queen* acquired a running mate in the *President*. Measuring about 2000 tons, she was the largest steamship afloat, while her elaborate appointments were the source of widespread admiration. Smith was at the peak of his career. Credited with the initiative which had produced this sudden steam shuttle, he received an LL.D. from Yale and there was talk of knighthood.

His success was short-lived, for the first major steam tragedy of the Atlantic carried off his masterpiece. The *President* sailed from New York on March 11, 1841, under the command of Lieutenant Roberts, who had brought over the *Sirius* on her first trip. The next day, a former Black Baller sighted the huge side-wheeler between Nantucket and the Banks—"rising on the top of a tremendous sea, she appeared to be pitching and laboring tremendously." That was the last that was ever seen of the *President*. A terrific gale swept the Atlantic for two days, but no one knows what happened in the last hours of Lieutenant Roberts and the 135 others aboard. Among them was the Irish actor, Tyrone Power, who had left a delightful account of his packet crossing eight years before. For a while, it was hoped that she might have been disabled and put into some remote port under sail. Rumors drifted in from mariners who had sighted floating derelicts. The British consul at New York summoned a court of inquiry; but after weeks of agonizing suspense it was finally realized that she had disappeared without a trace. New York was to have a repetition of that agony fifteen years later with one of its own great steamships. Smith's line did not long survive that crushing loss. He gave up his long London residence and moved to South Carolina. There he was making a successful experiment in tea raising until some ruffians, who opposed his antislavery views, gave him a cruel beating which led to his death, not long afterwards, in a New York hospital.

After the loss of the *President*, New York's steam service was reduced to "the good, old-fashioned steady going *Great Western,*" which performed regularly for eight years after her famous initial voyage. In 1845, she received a running-mate which embodied the two main features of future development. All of the earlier transatlantic steamships, and many which would follow in the next fifteen years, were wooden side-wheelers. Thanks to Brunel, the 3270-ton *Great Britain,* built at Bristol, was not only the first steamship to have an iron hull, but also the first with a screw propeller. She began her New York crossings in the summer of 1845; but a year later, in a heavy fog ran ashore on the Irish coast and lay there more than a year. Finally hauled off fairly intact, she demonstrated to the skeptical that iron hulls could stand more punishment than was generally supposed. The company, however, had abandoned the New York run shortly after the accident. In December, 1846, the *Great Western* was withdrawn and sold. During the eight years following her initial voyage, she alone, with her six trips a year, had given New York anything like regular, sustained service. She and the others on that route better deserved the name of regular traders than of liners.

Boston, during most of those years, had been enjoying a steam connection with Liverpool, superior in frequency, dependability, and safety, provided by the four-ship line of Samuel Cunard.

With the Cunarders, a new element had entered the steamship business. The New York sailing packets had prospered without a cent of government aid; but the Cunarders were the first to profit by heavy government subsidies. Steamships, of course, not only represented a much heavier initial expense but coal was a constant added cost in operation. By the fall of 1838, the success of the first steamships to New York led the British Government to advertise for bids for regular mail service to that port. Then and afterwards, two different branches of government activity were used as reasons, or excuses, for official financial aid to steamships. For a century or so the government had supported its packet brigs for the carriage of the mails. That made a precedent for postal subsidies. To finance the building of the new steamships, the navy also entered the field, upon the theory that the fast mail steamers could be used as cruisers in time of war. It was the Admiralty, therefore, rather than the Post Office, that advertised for the bids.

The Great Western group not only had valid claims of priority but also enjoyed powerful political backing. It looked as though they had the subsidy easily but they and the other original bidders were turned down in favor of a "dark horse." This was Samuel Cunard of Halifax, born there shortly after his Philadelphia Quaker father had moved to Nova Scotia at the close of the Revolution. He had been trained in a Boston countinghouse and had strong business connections there. For several years he had administered the distribution of mails from Halifax by sailing vessels with great regularity. Hearing of the subsidy project, he crossed to England in the fall of 1838. He lacked political influence at the capital but it is said that one of London's most charming hostesses made it possible for him to meet the men who counted most. Associated with a group of able Glasgow Scots, Cunard, in 1839, secured the coveted subsidy contract. In its final form, Cunard was to receive £60,000 a year for carrying the mails twice a month from Liverpool by way of Halifax to Boston. The Admiralty had originally designated New York, but Cunard's personal connections were with Boston; the business men of that port made urgent pleas and generous offers; and, too, Boston was closer to Halifax.

For this service, Cunard introduced another important feature. The various steamships serving New York, even those owned by the same company, lacked uniformity of any sort. Cunard ordered four almost identical ships, varying not more than a foot in any of their principal dimensions. Measuring only 1150 tons apiece, they were smaller than the *Great Western* and most of the other ships running to New York. They were, however, given tough hulls and good engines at Glasgow. The personnel was selected from the cream of the British merchant marine and subjected to a rigid discipline which has characterized the line ever since. The celebrated instructions to the captains stressed the fact that while speed was desirable, safety was the first essential—in fogs, storms, and ice fields, security was the prime consideration. Other lines might have bigger and more spectacular ships; those rivals might at times make much faster speed records; but no other line has matched the remarkable Cunard boast that for seventy-five years, until a German submarine sank the *Lusitania* in 1915, it had not lost a single passenger or piece of mail entrusted to it, while only two ships of its great fleet had been lost during all that time.

The *Britannia* left Liverpool for the first regular Cunard sailing on the Fourth of July in 1840. Boston gave her a tumultuous reception and with good cause. It had stolen a march on New York and for nearly eight years it would enjoy superior connection with England. Bennett and the other New York editors argued that commerce was so well established on the Sandy Hook route that Cunard had made a mistake and that the sooner he shifted to New York, the better it would be for him. For the time being, however, the subsidized Cunarders coming and going with clocklike regularity twice a month at Boston gave a service superior both to the sailing packets and the uncoordinated steamships at New York.

The Americans had long taken pride in the achievement of their sailing packets; even the British had admitted their superiority. With the coming of steam, initiative and honors passed to the British and that hurt. Quickly there was a demand that the United States Government do something to "drive the Cunarders off the sea." As early as February, 1841, in the dying days of the Van Buren administration, a lobby was at work under Collins, who argued for government aid to build mail steamers as potential cruisers. For a while it looked as though he might be successful, but Van Buren is said to have told him curtly that this country needed no navy at all, much less a steam navy. Four years later, however, in 1845, the combination of Cunard success and injured national pride influenced Congress to commit itself to a general policy of mail subsidies for steamships which could be used by the navy in time of war. It happened that New York during the next two years acquired practically all of these subsidy lines, both for transatlantic service and for the routes down the coast to Havana, New Orleans, and Panama.

New York's first transatlantic subsidy line was not a success. Instead of to Collins or some other recognized shipping operator, an annual grant of $200,000 was made to Edward Mills, virtually unknown in marine circles. His name commanded no confidence; the *Herald* expressed the fear that the new company would become a Wall Street plaything like the Harlem and Erie railroads. Nevertheless, the Ocean Steam Navigation Company was organized. The energy of the American consul at Bremen secured that port as the eastern terminus; at the time it was well ahead of its rival Hamburg in American trade. The ships were also to touch at Southampton or near-by Cowes, on the south coast of England; for years the New York-London sailing packets had been making similar calls at adjacent Portsmouth.

For this line, New York built its first ocean steamship, the 1700-ton *Washington*. Westervelt & Mackey, better known for the quantity than for the performance of their Havre packets, built the heavily timbered hull; the Novelty Works produced the boilers and engines. She left

New York on her maiden trip June 1, 1847; the Cunarder *Britannia* left Boston the same day and beat the *Washington* to England by two days. The British gave her a chilly reception. Southampton showed a dull apathy entirely different from the rousing welcome given to the British ships at New York and Boston. The local correspondent of the London *Times* reported that "in point of size she looked like an elongated three-decker, with only one streak around her; but about as ugly a specimen of steam-ship building as ever went through this anchorage." Bremen, which had contributed generously to the line's capital, received the *Washington* with real enthusiasm. Ten months later, she had a running-mate in the *Herrmann*. They did a fair business in "fine freight," particularly in Continental dry goods; on one trip the cargo amounted to some $750,000 in value. In sailing performance, however, they left much to be desired. Their machinery had to be altered several times. The original paddle-wheels were too large and the boilers too small. They continued on that route for ten years but their speed was slower than that of their rivals.

The withdrawal of the *Great Western* at the end of 1846 meant the last of the three original British lines to New York. By the following summer not only was the *Washington* on the Bremen run, but also, six weeks after her sailing, New York received the *Union,* the first arrival of a new line subsidized by the French Government, running first from Cherbourg and later from Havre. The line's performance was a comedy of errors. The first trip was almost the only one completed in a satisfactory manner. Ship after ship ran out of coal and had to finish the trip under sail, while the New York-Havre sailing packets sped past them. Some clumsy accidents occurred in New York harbor, where the helmsmen, not knowing English, did not understand the pilots' orders. French pride was hurt by the constant jokes on the subject; some eighty of New York's most prominent French residents held a meeting to inquire into the matter. The hearing revealed one shortcoming that was regarded as more unforgivable than running out of coal or bumping brigs. It was at least to be expected that Frenchmen could feed their passengers well, but that was apparently not the case. Lieutenant Maury told the tale of one of the French liners putting to sea without sugar; when it was discovered, the captain offered to put back to New York but, as Maury remarked, "it was too late. The passengers had already become *sour*. This sugar business broke up the line." At any rate, its service was short-lived.

In 1848, another American subsidy line began service to Havre with the New York-built *Franklin* first, and then the *Humboldt*. Operated by Mortimer Livingston and others experienced in the Havre packet service, it was an improvement upon both the Bremen line and the first French line, and continued on a profitable basis for some time; but it still lagged behind the Cunarders in importance.

More significant than any of those other attempts was Cunard's decision to extend his service to New York. For eight years, his ships had given Boston a transatlantic connection far superior to New York's spasmodic steamship service or the slow westbound runs of its sailing packets. It was too late, however, to divert the flow of transatlantic traffic away from Sandy Hook. The old sailing packets had done such a thorough job in directing business to New York that much of the trade clung to that old route in spite of its inferior facilities. Since Cunard could not lure the business to Boston, he decided to run ships to New York.

He made a new contract with the Admiralty whereby, for the increased subsidy of £145,000 a year, he would double his fleet from four to eight ships and provide weekly sailings—one week by the old Boston-Halifax-Liverpool route; the next week by direct runs between New York and Liverpool. Cunard's son, Edward, moved down to New York as agent; new piers were built across the Hudson at Jersey City; and sailing ships began to bring a supply of bunker coal from Liverpool. On December 29, 1847, the *Hibernia* arrived from Boston. On New Year's Day of 1848, she sailed on the first eastbound Cunard trip from New York, while the same day the *Cambria* left Liverpool for New York. For the first time in the ten years of ocean steam, New York at last had effective line service. As was to be expected, this New York route soon overshadowed the old one by Boston and Halifax. In 1848, the duties collected on Cunard cargoes at New York averaged $40,501; at Boston, only $29,508. In 1850, the score stood New York, $118,055; and Boston, $62,970.

By that latter date, the Cunarders were encountering some of the most spectacular competition in steamship history. After the first voyage of the *Washington* to Bremen in 1847, it became obvious that she was not the kind of ship that Congress had hoped for in granting subsidies to "drive the Cunarders off the ocean." At last Edward Knight Collins saw his opportunity and made the most of it. He was the outstanding figure in shipping circles. For twenty years he had operated sailing packets with pronounced success—first to Vera Cruz, then to New Orleans, and, for the past ten years, with his Dramatic Line to Liverpool. His picture shows a more suave and sophisticated face than most of his rivals in the packet game. Part of his packet success had come from his sumptuous dining and wining of passengers; doubtless that same practice helped him to win a subsidy contract from the Postmaster General on November 1, 1847. Collins promised the fastest steamships afloat and apparently it was mutually understood that expense did not matter. With the powerful financial backing of James and Stewart Brown, the New York branch of the international banking family, he organized five weeks later the United States Mail Steamship Company—known from the start as the "Collins Line."

The rise and fall of the Collins Line was almost simultaneous with the rise and fall of the clippers. They had much in common. Together, they represented the high-water mark of the old American merchant marine. Speed was the prevailing passion of the American public at the moment. Clippers like the *Flying Cloud* and Collins liners like the *Pacific* gratified that passion almost simultaneously with fast records which no British vessels could approach. The contemporary triumph of the New York yacht *America* rounded out the national gratification for speed. Their quick passages have lived on in legend and enriched our maritime tradition.

The fact remains that most of the clippers and all the Collins liners did not pay. That does not bother the modern reader who wants sea romance, which is not surprising—their trips make much livelier reading than the steady-going, money-making voyages of the packets and the Cunarders. The strange thing is that the hard-bitten, levelheaded businessmen of South Street do not seem to have been particularly concerned, either, that red ink would be used in large quantities in the ledger accounts of those gloriously fast craft. For a few years around 1850 they seem to have thrown to the winds the conservative prudence that had amassed the fortunes they were ready to spend for speed.

No pains were spared to give the Collins liners the best of hulls and engines. The hull contracts were divided between the yards of Brown & Bell and William H. Brown; the machinery between Allaire and the Novelty Works. George Steers helped to design the stout but graceful hulls; the chief engineer of the Navy resigned his post to take over the machinery plans. Commodore Matthew C. Perry, not yet gone to open up Japan, was detailed to observe and advise, for these ships were to be potential cruisers. In the lengthy congressional reports one may find the commodore's solemn opinion that paddle-wheels were and would remain preferable to screw propellers. In the expansive mood of all concerned, the size of the ships was fixed in the neighborhood of 2800 tons apiece, nearly a thousand tons larger than the latest new Cunarders. The first keels were being laid when the *Hibernia* opened the New York service; two years later, the ships were approaching completion. One feature of design, prophetic of the future, caught the eye in particular. Instead of the conventional slanting bow of the sailing vessel, copied in the earlier steamships, the Collins liners had the straight stems which later became almost universal.

Meanwhile Collins was looking over the merchant marine in general and the packet service in particular for men who could squeeze the utmost in speed out of their ships. Typical of the four commanders selected was Ezra Nye, a veteran of the Liverpool packet service, "with a propensity for carrying sail." Cunard's instructions to his captains emphasized speed with safety; Collins stressed the necessity to "beat the Cunarders."

On April 27, 1850, the *Atlantic* opened the service when she sailed from New York for Liverpool, followed in the course of the year by the *Pacific, Arctic,* and *Baltic*. The race was on, and the honors went to Collins. The New York newspapers joyfully published the times of each passage of the rival liners, drew up averages, and revelled in statistics to their hearts' content. No longer were runs simply recorded in days, which had been enough in the packet era—the new figures gave the precise number of hours and minutes. The old records toppled. The *Great Western* on her maiden trip had taken 14½ days on the westbound passage; in 1848, the Cunarder *Europa* reduced it to 11 days 3 hours; by 1851 the *Baltic* made the run in 9 days 18 hours, an average of 13 knots, which was equalled by the *Pacific*. The latter made a single day's run of 330 miles, which stood as the record until 1864. On the whole, the Collins ships averaged about a day faster than the Cunarders.

While enthusiasm over that speed performance was still high, Collins determined to take full advantage of it. In February, 1852, came his masterpiece in lobbying when he sent the *Baltic* around to the Potomac and gave one of the best parties which the capital could remember. A past master at dining and wining, Collins outdid himself in entertaining the President, the Cabinet, the senators, the congressmen, and others, to the total number of 2000, who were brought down to the great ship by steamer loads from Washington. The heavy liquor bill proved an excellent investment for Collins.

Congress was gratified, and that summer the line's subsidy was raised from $385,000 to $853,000 a year. As far as business went, the Cunarders carried more mail. In 1851, the total of letters carried was —Cunard, 2,613,000; Collins, 843,000; Bremen, 313,000; and Havre, 139,000. The passenger traffic, however, was attracted by the prestige, speed, comfort, and food of the Collins liners. (It was said that the Cunard table was not all that it might be.) In the first eleven months of 1852, the Collins liners carried 4306 passengers and the Cunarders, 2969. With all that, however, the Cunarders were making money and Collins was not. The extra speed not only meant heavy coal consumption, but strained the engines so that, according to rumor, hasty, secret, and extensive repairs had to be made by the Allaire or Novelty workmen after every voyage. The Cunard apologists claim that the British steamers were not racing, but that is hard to believe.

In any case, the Cunarders went on through ice and fog without mishap, while two tragic disasters cut the Collins fleet in half. On September 27, 1854, the *Arctic* was hurrying through a dense fog off Cape Race, bound for New York with a valuable cargo, 233 passengers, and a crew of 135. Suddenly there was a crash; she had collided with the little French steamer *Vesta*. The latter's forward bulkhead kept her afloat but it was soon found that the big Collins liner had sustained mortal injuries. Captain Luce headed her for Cape Race, but the water, rushing in through three holes, extinguished the fires and she soon began to founder. Widespread confusion ensued; the crew seem to have gotten out of hand; there was a rush for the boats and some were wrecked in launching. Two boats, with 35 of the crew and 14 passengers, reached Newfoundland; a solitary survivor was rescued from a raft from which 75 others had been washed overboard. Altogether, 318 perished in the disaster, including the wife, son, and daughter of Collins.

The line survived that first disaster. Orders were placed for a still larger ship, the *Adriatic;* in the meantime chartered vessels took the *Arctic's* place. Then, on January 23, 1856, the *Pacific* sailed from Liverpool; she had a crew of normal size, but because of the season there were fortunately only 45 passengers. Like the *President* fifteen years before, she "went missing"—not even a floating piece of wreck-

From C. B. Stuart's "Naval and Mail Steamers," 1853

COLLINS LINER *ARCTIC*

Engraving, based on a daguerreotype by Beckers & Piard; one of the few actual photographs of ships of that period. The liner is shown lying at the foot of Canal Street in New York, receiving coal from a schooner

From "Leslie's Weekly," January 5, 1856

THE DETENTION OF THE S.S. *NORTHERN LIGHT*

Suspecting that the Nicaragua Transit liner was carrying recruits to Walker, the filibuster, the federal authorities at New York had the revenue cutter towed down the bay by a steamer on December 24, 1855. The cutter is shown firing a shot across the liner's bow (see p. 371)

EVENING POST MARINE LIST

CLEARED

Brig Eleanor, Owen,	Matanzes
	Wm Ling
Hope, Backus,	Spain
	P. Harmony
Schr Five Sisters, Hallock,	Richmond
Schr Hiram, Pye,	Halifax
Caledonia, Kelly,	Yarmouth, N S
	Jno Hurry
Hiram Weeden,	Porto Rico
Sloop Susan, Tripp.	Westport
Sloop True American, Godfrey,	Taunton
Lark, Snow,	Boston
Herald, Smith,	Winton N. C.
Little Jim, Sheverick,	Lubeck
	J. Tremain.
Hetty & Sally, Long,	Indian River
Elizabeth, Hickman,	Do
Buck, Rhodes,	Newbern
Omega, Bunker,	Nantucket

ARRIVED SINCE OUR LAST.

Ship Margaret, Colfax, 10 days from Savannah with cotton to Hicks, Jenkins & Co. Thadeus Phelps, Pott & M'Kinne. A. K. Smedes, J. Adams, James M'Gee, and Charles W. Gordon, owner.

Brig Savannah Packet, Mott, 8 days from Savannah, with cotton, rice, steel, leather, vitriol, &c. to T. Whitmore. J. King, J. Harned, Lawrence & Remsen, Williams & Mott, G. Lee, W. Berry, R. L. Murray, J. Longworth, Pott & M'Kinne, Wells & Neptune, S. Whitney, A. Ogden & Co. and C. Bostwick. The Brig Sea Island, Jocelin, sailed the day before for New-York. Left brigs Tybee, Thompson ; Commerce, Capt. Bradley ; Eliza Lord, Capt. Wheeler, to sail next day, for N York ; the sloop Union, Ward, had just arrived from N York ; also, brig Superior, Champlin, ship Woodbine, Burnham, ship Triton, ——, brig ——, Barton, all from New-York, arrived on the 6th of May—The Savannah Packet has 8 passengers—Off Cape May spoke a schooner from Norfolk for New-York ; same time spoke a pilot boat, informed us that she boarded a brig from Liverpool for Philadelphia.

British brig Sarah, Brown, 44 days from Liverpool, with dry goods, crates, iron, and coals to Messrs. I. W. Schmidt & Co. G Goggill, Richards, Upson & Co. C. M'Evers, S. M. Brewer, and Major & Gillespie. May 10, lat. 38, long 69, spoke brig Trumbull, from New-Haven for Barbadoes. May 5th, lat 38, 30, long 65, 30, spoke a ship from New-York for Liverpool. April 28, lat 41, 30. long 56, spoke ship Percival, from Cork for Philadelphia.

Barque Gideon, Coffin, from Brunswick, in ballast.

Schr. Two Brothers, Ames, Plymouth. N. C. 6 days from the Bar, with naval stores to Tredwell & Thorne. The ship Aurora, Burrows, 7 days from Newport, had just arrived.

French schr. Jeune Baudoun, Alene, 30 days from Port Royal, (Martinique,) with 166 hhds. 18 tierces and 6 barrels of molasses to the captain—Left at St. Pierre, Martinique, the brig Mary,

New York *Evening Post*, May 16, 1815

MARITIME INTELLIGENCE.

Movements of Ocean Steamers.

Names.	Leaves.	Date.	For.
Great Britain	Liverpool	May 1	New York.
Atlantic	Liverpool	May 5	New York.
City of Manchester	Liverpool	May 5	Philadelphia.
Africa	Liverpool	May 8	New York.
Humboldt	Havre	May 9	New York.
Baltic	New York	May 15	Liverpool.
United States	New York	May 15	Aspinwall.
Europa	New York	May 19	Liverpool.
Prometheus	New York	May 20	San Juan.
Illinois	New York	May 20	Aspinwall.
Wm Penn	New York	May 22	New Orleans.
Washington	New York	May 22	Bremen.
Sierra Nevada	New York	May 24	Aspinwall.
Cherokee	New York	May 24	Havana, &c.
City of Pittsburg	N Y or Phila	June 1	S Francisco.

ALMANAC—MAY 15.

SUN RISES	4 45	MOON RISES	morn 3 23
SUN SETS	7 08	HIGH WATER	even 6 39

PORT OF NEW YORK, MAY 14, 1852.

Cleared.

Steamship Baltic, Comstock, Liverpool, E K Collins & Co.
Ship Flying Cloud, Cressy, San Francisco, Grinnell, Minturn & Co.
Ship Gazelle, Dollard, San Francisco, Taylor & Merrill.
Ship Gottenberg (Ham), Jorgensen, Hamburg, Schmidt & Balchen.
Ship Indiana, Bennett, New Orleans, Frost & Hicks.
Bark Rhein (Ham), Popp, Hamburg, E Beck & Kunhardt.
Bark Brunette, Preble, Lisbon, J W Elwell & Co.
Bark Telegraph, Crockett, Campeachy, Nesmith & Sons.
Bark Lolland (Nor), Nielson, Miramichi, E Beck & Kunhardt.
Bark Grampus, Dyer, Cardenas, Peck & Church.
Bark Ross (Br), Brown, St John, NB, H & F W Mager.
Bark Theo Korner (Brem), Schurenburg, Baltimore, Rodewald Brothers.
Brig Naritiska, Nelson, Ponce, PR, M M Freeman & Co.
Brig Times, Hinckley, Aguadilla, M M Freeman & Co.
Brig Atkinson (Br), Jackson, Quebec, Montgomery Brothers.
Schr Providence (Br), Mahon, Londonderry, J S Whitney & Co.
Schr Clinton, Rogers, Matagorda, N L McCready & Co.
Schr Gold Hunter, Brookett, Humacoa, L W & R Armstrong.
Schr Alethea, Rice, Harbor Island, C Akerly.
Schr J H Johnson/Johnson. Harbor Island, G J Whitlock.
Schr Richard Cobden (Br), Morrison, St John, NB, J S Dealey.
Schr Sybil (Br), Rodolf, St Johns, NF, Gillospie, Dean & Co.
Schr Iowa, Wheelwright, Philadelphia, master.
Schr Catharine, Collins, Philadelphia. J W McKee.
Schr Sacramento, Nickerson, Philadelphia, J W McKee.
Schr Thos H Thompson, Nickerson, Philadelphia, J Hand.
Schr Mary Clark, Allen, Newburyport.
Schr Hester, West, New Haven, Durham & Dimon.
Steamer Cayuga, Nelson, Philadelphia, J & N Briggs.
Steamer Oneida, O'Niel, Philadelphia, W H Thompson.

Arrived.

Steamship Great Britain (Br), Mathews, Liverpool, 13 days 5½ hours, with mdse and 160 passengers, to R Irvin & Co.
Ship Harpy (Danish), Backmann, Batavia, 105 days, with coffee, to Pavenstadt & Schumacher.
Bark Figaro (Brem), Beckmann, Bremen, 60 days, a ballast, with 94 passengers, to Pavenstadt and Schumacher. The F has experienced heavy weather on the passage.
Bark Pallas (Br), Young, Cork, 56 days, in ballast, with 143 passengers, to Grinnell, Minturn & Co.
Bark Brothers, Duran, Newry, 38 days, with iron and 196 passengers, to order.
Bark Rouble (of Boston), Chase, Pernambuco, April 4, with sugar, to W H Sale.
Bark Sir Fowell Buxton (Br), Woodcock, Sagua, April 25, with sugar, to M Taylor & Co, vessel to master. Has had a pilot on board four days.
Bark Guilford, Leslie, Savannah, 10 days, with cotton and rice, to J & R Osborn. Has experienced heavy weather, lost part of deck load, consisting of 12 bales of cotton.
Brig Rockcliff (Br), Forter, Newcastle, E, 57 days, with mdse, to Barclay & Livingston. May 6, lat 35, lon 69 30, spoke Br schr James Willetts, from West Indies for Yarmouth NS.
Brig Refuge (Br, of Sunderland), Pike, Bordeaux, 53 days, with brandies and wine, to D St Amant. Has had heavy weather; lost main yard, bulwarks, and received other damage.

New York *Herald*, May 14, 1852

MARITIME INTELLIGENCE

These are typical of the daily "marine news" at the beginning and end of the period. Note the changes in types of vessels.

age was found. The crack new Cunarder *Persia,* the first of the line's
iron ships, was crossing at the same time and reported sighting an iceberg. It is possible that Captain Asa Eldridge of the *Pacific,* a veteran
of packet and clipper service, was hurrying to beat the *Persia* and
crashed into ice.

That was the beginning of the end for the Collins Line. Congress
almost immediately reduced its subsidy to the original $385,000. Serv-
ice was maintained with chartered ships; in 1857, the *Adriatic,* which
had cost $1,200,000, went into service but made only a voyage or two
in the line, whose days were numbered. In 1858, the death-blow came
when Congress abandoned the policy of mail subsidies. Acrimonious
debates, in which Jefferson Davis and other southerners took the lead,
revealed bitter jealousy of New York, which had cornered most of the
subsidy lines. The *Baltic* made the final Collins sailing from Liverpool
on February 3, 1858. With that trip ended the spectacular attempt of
New York and the American merchant marine to challenge the Cunarders. The line had never paid a cent in dividends; but for several
years the American public had had keen pleasure in reading the speed
statistics.

The last years of our period witnessed many changes in the transatlantic steam service to New York. The only constant element was the
Cunard Line, which continued its uninterrupted service. The withdrawal of government aid ended not only the Collins venture but also
the mediocre subsidy line to Bremen. The better-managed subsidy line
to Havre managed to continue on its own. With the somewhat irregular sailings of Cornelius Vanderbilt's large, fast steamships to various European ports, it succeeded in keeping the American flag on the
shuttle for a while. The ocean steamship business, however, centered
more and more in foreign hands, where it was to remain. Two new
German lines began their distinguished careers of steam service to
New York. The Hamburg-American, which had been operating sailing packets to New York since the late 'forties, sent its first steamship,
the *Borussia,* thither in June, 1856. Just two years later came the first
Bremen from the port of that name, advance guard of the North German Lloyd.

The most substantial competition to the Cunard Line, however, was
to come from another British concern, the Inman Line, which extended its Liverpool service from Philadelphia to New York in 1857.
The line had begun in 1850, almost simultaneously with Collins. A

MARITIME HERALD.

The Latest Dates,

Anjier	Oct 2	Maracaibo	Oct 17
Africa	Nov 11	Mansanilla	Dec 6
Antigua	Dec 21	Matanzas	Dec 9
Aux Cayes	Dec 5	Mayaguez	Dec 29
Augustine Bay	Sep 14	Mazatlan	Sep 23
Batavia	Sep 28	Matamoras	Nov 24
Bay of Islands, NZ	July 14	Mexico (City)	Dec 14
Bermuda	Dec 21	Monterey, Cal	Sept 11
Buenos Ayres	Nov 4	Monterey, NM	Nov 16
Belize, Hon	Dec 1	Montevideo	Nov 3
Barbadoes	Dec 11	Merida, Yucatan	Oct 5
Bogota	Mar 10	Nassau, NP	Dec 22
Bonaire	Nov 6	Neuvitas	Dec 10
Bahia	Nov 12	Oahu, SI	Aug 1
Bombay	Nov 2	Oregon	Aug 1
Brazos Santiago	Dec 21	Para	Dec 6
Canton	Sept 21	Paris	Dec 16
Cape Town, CGH	Nov 5	Port au Prince	Dec 21
Calcutta	Oct 30	Porto Cabello	Dec 10
Cardenas	Dec 25	Point Petre, Guad	Dec 5
Chagres	Nov 29	Pernambuco	Dec 7
Cienfuegos	Dec 9	Panama	Mar 22
Cape Haytien	Nov 27	Payta	Oct 14
Curacoa	Dec 1	Puebla	Nov 15
Carthagena	Nov 28	Queretaro	Nov 23
Campeachy	Oct 21	Rio Janeiro	Nov 21
Coquimbo	Aug 29	Rio Grande, S A	Nov 2
Callao	Oct 11	San Juan de Nic'a	Nov 15
Demerara	Nov 23	San Diego	Dec 6
Fayal	Nov 23	San Francisco	Sep 18
Gibraltar	Dec 5	St Helena	Nov 29
Guayama, PR	Dec 20	St Thomas	Dec 10
Guatamala	Oct 29	St Jago de Cuba	Dec 9
Gonaives	Dec 11	St Johns, PR	Dec 22
Guayaquil	Sept 17	Segua la Grande	Dec 31
Gallipagos Islands	Sept 16	St Croix	Dec 3
Havre	Dec 15	St Domingo	Nov 14
Havana	Dec 23	St Ubes	Oct 22
Hobart Town, VDL	July 14	Surinam	Nov 19
Jeremie	Dec 2	Singapore	Sep 4
Jacmel	Dec 10	Santa Fe, NM	Nov 7
Kingston, Jam	Nov 29	Sydney, NSW	Aug 13
London	Dec 18	Trinidad de Cuba	Dec 9
Liverpool	Dec 18	Talcahuana	Sept 15
Laguayra	Dec 7	Tahiti	July 15
Laguna	Dec 4	Tampico	Dec 16
Manila	Sep 18	Tabasco	Sep 22
Madras	Sep 20	Turk's Island	Oct 26
Malaga	Dec 6	Valparaiso	Dec 24
Madeira	Dec 2	Vera Cruz	Dec 24
Mauritius	Sept 17	Zanzibar	July 23

Movements of the Ocean Steamships.

To arrive at New York.		To sail from New York.	
HAVRE.		**HAVRE.**	
Missouri, Morin,	Dec 23	Missouri, Morin,	Jan 23
Philadelphia, Besson,	Jan 22	Philadelphia, Besson,	Feb 21
New York, Ferraud,	Feb 21	New York, Ferraud,	Mar 31
LIVERPOOL.		**LIVERPOOL.**	
Cambria, Judkins,	Jan 1	Cambria, Judkins,	Jan 29
Sarah Sands, Thompson	Jan 22	Sarah Sands, Thompson	Feb 25
SOUTHAMPTON, &c.		**SOUTHAMPTON, &c.**	
Washington, Johnston,	Dec 18	Washington, Johnston,	Jan 20
Hermann, Crabtree,	Mar 18	Hermann, Crabtree,	Feb 20
To arrive at Boston.		**To sail from Boston.**	
LIVERPOOL.		**LIVERPOOL.**	
Britannia, Harrison,	Jan 15	Caledonia, Lott,	Jan 15
Caledonia, Lott,	Feb 12	Britannia, Harrison,	Feb 12

Movements of the Sailing Packets.

Ships to Arrive.		Ships to Sail.	
LIVERPOOL.		**LIVERPOOL.**	
Oxford, Goodmanson,	Nov 16	Waterloo, Allen,	Jan 11
Henry Clay, Nye,	Nov 21	New York,	Jan 16
Cambridge, Peabody,	Dec 1	Queen of the West,	Jan 21
Constitution, Britton,	Dec 6	Sheridan, Cornish,	Jan 25
Garrick Hunt,	Dec 11	Oxford, Goodmanson,	Feb 1
Montezuma, Louber,	Dec 16	Henry Clay, Nye,	Feb 6
PORTSMOUTH.		**PORTSMOUTH.**	
St James, Christianson,	Nov 8	Westminster, Hovey,	Jan 8
Switzerland, Fletcher, Nov 24		Northland, Griswold	Jan 21

New York Herald, January 11, 1848

THE LATEST ADVICES
RECEIVED AT THE
NEW YORK HERALD OFFICE,
APRIL 14, 1852.

Acapulco, Mexico	Mar. 11	Mayaguez, P. R	Mar. 19
Adelaide, S.Aust'lia.	Nov. 11	Mazatlan, Mexico	Mar. 6
Alexandria, Egypt	Mar. 7	Mexico (City)	Mar. 29
Angostura, Venes'la.	Feb. 20	Monrovia, Africa	Jan. 27
Antigua	Feb. 21	Montevideo, S. A.	Feb. 19
Antwerp, Belgium	Mar. 24	Nassau, N. P.	Mar. 25
Aguadilla, P. R.	Feb. 28	Neuvitas, Cuba	Mar. 24
Aux Cayes, Hayti	Mar. 15	Oregon	Mar. 11
Bahia, Brazil	Feb. 18	Panama, New Gra.	Apr. 1
Bankok, Siam,	Jan. 15	Para, Brasil	Mar. 6
Barbadoes	Mar. 11	Paris	Mar. 26
Batavia, Java	Jan. 20	Payta, Peru	Jan. 17
Belize, Hon.	Mar. 22	Pernambuco, Brazil.	Feb. 23
Bermuda	Mar. 16	Ponce, P. B.	Mar. 20
Bogota, New Gra.	Jan. 10	Port au Platt, St. D.	Mar. 7
Bolivia	Jan. 22	Port au Prince, Hayti	Mar. 21
Bombay, E. I.	Feb. 15	Port Spain, Trinidad.	Mar. 4
Bonaire	Jan. 15	Porto Praya, C. V.	Mar. 4
Buenos Ayres, S. A.	Feb. 16	Puerto Cabello, Ven.	Mar. 10
Calcutta	Feb. 8	Punta Arenas, C. R.	Mar. 5
Callao, Peru	Feb. 16	Raiatea, Soc'y Isl's.	Jan. 15
Campeachy, Mexico	Feb. 24	Rangoon, Birmah	Feb. 1
Cape Haytien, Hayti	Mar. 18	Rio Grande, Brasil	Feb. 5
Cape Town, C. G. H.	Feb. 4	Rio Janeiro, Brazil	Mar. 3
Cardenas, Cuba	Mar. 31	Sagua la Grande, Cu.	Mar. 26
Carthagena, N. G.	Feb. 29	Salt Lake City	Dec. 1
Cayenne, Fr. Guiana.	Feb. 28	San Antonio, Texas.	Dec. 26
Chagres, N. G.	Apr. 3	San Salvador, C. A.	Feb. 27
Cienfuegos, Cuba	Mar. 27	San Antonio, Texas.	Mar. 18
Constantinople, Tky.	Mar. 6	Santa Cruz, Teneriffe.	Jan. 14
Curacoa	Mar. 12	Santa Fe, N. M.	Feb. 28
Demerara, Br. Guiana	Mar. 12	Santa Martha, N. G.	Feb. 15
Dominica, W. I.	Feb. 18	San Diego, U. C.	Mar. 4
El Paso, N. M.	Feb. 11	San Francisco. U. C.	Mar. 17
Fayal, West. Is.	Jan. 27	San Jose, Costa Rica.	Mar. 13
Ft. Good Hope, M. R.	July 17	San Juan de Cuba.	Mar. 27
Fort Independence,	Jan. 28	San Juan, Nic'ua.	Apr. 4
Fort Kearny	Jan. 2	Shanghai	Jan. 23
Fort Laramie	Jan. 9	Sierra Leone, Africa.	Feb. 15
Fort Simpson, H.B.T.	Oct. 4	Singapore	Feb. 4
Gibraltar	Mar. 16	Sisal. Mexico	Mar. 5
Gonaives, Hayti	Mar. 20	Smyrna, Turkey	Mar. 8
Guadaloupe	Feb. 20	St. Paul, Minnesota.	Feb. 21
Guatemala	Mar. 5	St. Croix, Virgin Is.	Feb. 15
Guayama, P. R.	Mar. 25	St. Domingo City	Mar. 7
Guayaquil, Ecuador.	Mar. 14	St. Helena	Feb. 5
Havana, Cuba	Apr. 2	St. Jago de Cuba.	Mar. 21
Havre, France	Mar. 26	St. Johns, P. R.	Mar. 17
Hobart Town, V.D.L.	Nov. 15	St. Kitts	Feb. 21
Hong Kong	Jan. 30	St. Lucia	Feb. 20
Honolulu, S. I.	Feb. 26	St. Thomas	Mar. 20
Jacmel, Hayti	Mar. 14	St. Ubes. Portugal.	Dec. 20
Jeremie, Hayti	Feb. 24	St. Vincent, W. I.	Feb. 17
Kingston, Ja.	Mar. 24	Sumatra	Dec. 29
Laguayra. Venezuela.	Mar. 25	Surinam, Dutch Guin.	Mar. 2
Laguna, Mexico	Mar. 12	Sydney, N. S. W.	Dec. 15
Lahaina. S. I.	Feb. 1	Syria	Mar. 5
Liverpool	Mar. 27	Tahiti. Society Isl's.	Dec. 20
London	Mar. 27	Talcahuana, Chili	Jan. 28
Madeira	Mar. 7	Tampico, Mexico	Mar. 26
Malaga, Spain	Mar. 13	Tobago	Feb. 17
Malta	Mar. 9	Tabasco, Mexico	Mar. 5
Manilla. Philip. Isls.	Jan. 8	Trinidad de Cuba	Mar. 24
Manzanillo, Cuba	Mar. 17	Truxillo, Honduras.	Jan. 12
Maracaibo, Ven'a.	Mar. 13	Turks Island	Mar. 2
Martinique	Feb. 20	Valparaiso, Chili	Feb. 26
Maranham	Jan. 15	Vera Cruz, Mexico.	Mar. 17
Matanzas, Cuba	Mar. 30	Whampoa	Jan. 13
Mauritius, Ind.Ocean. Jan. 17		Zanzibar, Ind.Ocean. Dec. 26

New York Herald, April 14, 1852

RELATIVE SPEED OF NEWS TRANSMISSION

The 1848 list appeared while the first Cunarder to New York was on the high seas; by 1852 New York also had Collins service. In addition to the moderate speeding-up of European news, note the tremendous reduction in time from Chagres and San Francisco by means of mail steamers. The packet movements, long a regular feature, were dropped soon after 1848.

Clyde shipbuilder had constructed, as a venture, the 1600-ton *City of Glasgow*. Like the *Great Britain* five years before, she combined the two new features of iron hull and screw propeller. After a trip or two to New York in 1850, she was purchased by William Inman for regular service between Liverpool and Philadelphia. He added other "City" ships and soon developed an effective line. Not only was he playing the game of the future with iron and propellers, but he also went after the steerage trade. Cunard and Collins were leaving that to the sailing packets, but Inman provided relatively comfortable steerage quarters. The service proved attractive because steamships could reduce so radically the length of the trying passage. Just as Cunard had learned to add New York to Boston as a western terminus, Inman very soon found that the Sandy Hook business outstripped the old Philadelphia trade; by 1860 he was providing weekly service on the New York run.

There are two significant deductions from that Inman experience. In the first place it reflected upon the conservatism of the East River iron works. The Collins liners had been the fastest of their day, but a new day was already dawning. Before their keels had been laid down, the iron screw *Great Britain* had demonstrated her ability to cross the Atlantic, while the *City of Glasgow* was being built at the very same time. Until then the East River had held its own with the Clyde; from that time the shipbuilders of the Scottish river drew ahead steadily. In the building of iron hulls, to be sure, the British had a decided advantage, for the iron industry was still in its infancy in America. The East River builders, however, had less excuse for clinging to paddle-wheels and walking beam so tenaciously, for John Ericsson had been in their midst since 1839 preaching screw propellers. New York steamship construction was a case of arrested development which reached its limit in the Collins liners. When slowly, in later days, the United States made a tardy effort to catch up, the Delaware rather than the East River would be the scene of the new developments.

While the Inman experience reflected upon the engine builders, it bore witness to the potency of South Street and New York commerce in general. For eight years, Boston had had Cunard all to itself; for seven years, Philadelphia had enjoyed the advantage of Inman's excellent service. In each case, the British operators realized that they could not effectively divert transatlantic business from New York; and increased profits had followed their shifts to Sandy Hook. The same thing had happened at the other end of the shuttle. The pioneer *Great*

Western had been unable to divert much business from Liverpool to her ancient home port of Bristol; before long her eastern terminus had been shifted to the Mersey.

A final and rather freak climax to the steamship development of the period came with the arrival of the immense *Great Eastern* in 1860, already described in connection with the Sandy Hook bar. Originally designed to carry passengers and freight on the long run around Good Hope to Colombo, Ceylon, where smaller steamers would carry on the trip to India, China, and Australia, she might have been a success at that work. Her original owners were forced to sell her, partly because of extra costs arising from launching difficulties. The new owners placed her on the Atlantic shuttle, for which she was poorly adapted. She made several trips to New York during the next few years, but proved a costly "white elephant." Her only really useful service came in laying the second, and successful, Atlantic cable later in the 'sixties.

In the meantime, the old sailing packets, which had once monopolized the best business on the shuttle, had naturally felt the impact of steam competition. As we have already analyzed the effects of that competition in another volume, it is enough here to mention that the chief advantage steam had over sail lay in making the westbound crossings shorter and more regular. The eastward passages under sail were faster and more uniform; sometimes the packets even beat the steamships. During the first decade of steam, with the irregular service to New York, the packets held their own remarkably well, keeping a good part of the passenger and fine freight business. Some travellers preferred to make the westward run to Boston by Cunarder and the return trip by a more comfortable "canvas-back" from New York. This decade demonstrated that the difference between liner and regular trader was almost as important as the difference between steam and sail. When, however, New York acquired its own excellent steam line service with the coming of the Cunarders in 1848, the packets lost most of their former choicest business in cabin passengers and fine freight.

Strange as it may seem, the packet ships themselves reached their highest peak of perfection after the steamship competition began. The *Roscius,* the first to exceed 1000 tons, was not launched until several months after the first steamships came in 1838. A new spirit followed the long depression by 1843. The Black Baller *Yorkshire,* the fastest of all the regular packets, dated from that revival. The size and speed crept steadily upward; even the coming of the Cunarders did not check it. Though fine freight and cabin passengers might be lost, there was heavier business than ever with breadstuffs eastward and immigrants in return. The largest of the packets, the 1771-ton *Amazon,* was not built until 1854. The steerage quarters in the new Inman liners, however, presaged the loss of that valuable westbound source of income. Though the Black Ball rounded out a full sixty years and the London Swallowtail ran until 1881, the fine old ships were simply carriers of heavy freight in their later days.

From the very outset, the steamships had robbed the packets of much of their old importance as bearers of the latest news from Europe. Most of the foreign news came to Boston by Cunarders from 1840 to 1848. The New York newspaper editors, eager to retain their old function of purveying the latest news to the nation, went to extraordinary lengths to get it as soon as possible. Their little news boats still cruised off the Long Island shore not only to meet the New York steamships but also on the off chance that some packet might, as the *Yorkshire* occasionally did, bring in the latest word. Special "expresses" by rail and steamer were run from Boston, with compositors setting type as they travelled so that not a minute would be wasted in getting the news on the streets. Then the scene shifted to Halifax, the first port of call for the Cunarders. Fast steamers or pony expresses raced from there to Portland or Boston. For a while the ingenious and enterprising Daniel H. Craig beat all competitors by the use of carrier pigeons. The excitement was particularly tense in the mid-'forties when the Americans anxiously awaited England's action on the Oregon question and Corn Law repeal. Telegraph lines were stretched to Boston, then to Portland, and finally under water to Newfoundland, where sailboats waited off Cape Race for the liners to throw off floating containers with the latest news. It was a group of New Yorkers who sponsored the laying of the Atlantic Cable. It worked for a few weeks in 1858 and then went silent for eight years and America once more depended upon the liners and the auxiliary speed devices.

While the ocean steamships became an increasingly important element in New York's shipping, they seem to have done much less than their square-rigged packet predecessors to promote the port's remarkable expansion. The sailing packets had done much to draw foreign trade in New York's direction; two of the great British steamship lines had actually sought to divert trade from New York to rival ports, only to find that the packets had done too thorough a job in plowing a course toward Sandy Hook. New York's own steam liners enjoyed only a transient period of glory; but from the day Cunard moved down from Boston, the crack liners of the Atlantic have made New York their western port of call.

CHAPTER XVI

HUMAN FREIGHT

MISERY, disease, and shameless exploitation featured one major branch of the port's business during the years of this period. Along with the textiles and hardware brought westward across the stormy Atlantic came millions of Irish, German, English, and other European immigrants to seek their fortunes in the New World. Some close parallels may be drawn between the traffic in living and in inanimate freight. The same ports participated in each in about the same proportion. On the other side, Liverpool had a long lead, followed by Havre, London, Bremen, and Hamburg. On this side, New York received the same overwhelming share of immigrants as of manufactures. There was, however, one significant difference. Whereas New York became the nation's richest city by managing to disperse most of its commercial imports throughout the country, it increased its lead as the nation's biggest city by keeping a much larger share of its human imports within its own environs.

It was natural that New York received the heaviest impact of the incoming foreigners, for the immigrants simply followed the shipping routes already determined by the course of regular commerce.

From various causes, the city of New York is doomed to be the landing-place of a great portion of the European population, who are daily flocking to our country for a place of permanent abode. This city is the greatest importing capital of the United States, and a position from which a departure into the interior is generally considered the most easy and practicable. On being possessed of a more extensive and active trade than any other commercial emporium in the union it naturally occurs to the minds of emigrants that we possess more means of employment. Our situation is peculiarly healthy, and no local objection, either physical or moral, exists to arrest the approach of foreigners.

So the managers of the Society for the Prevention of Pauperism in the City of New York reported as early as 1819. During the remaining forty years of our period, the same conditions continued with increasing force. Of some 5,400,000 immigrants arriving in United States ports during that time, about 3,700,000, more than two-thirds, entered at New York. New Orleans was a poor second with about 550,000, followed by Boston with some 380,000, and Philadelphia and Baltimore, each with about 230,000. In 1854, the peak year of the movement, New York received 327,000 immigrants, almost three-quarters of the national total.[1]

The hundreds of books written on immigration have been primarily concerned with the forces which pried the Europeans loose from their old homes or with their assimilation into American life. Here brief attention will be given rather to the circumstances of the crossing itself and to the reception of the newcomers at New York.

In recent days, it has been customary to contrast the "new immigration" with the "old immigration." From the mid-'eighties, a marked change began to appear in the sources of supply. More and more, the new arrivals came predominantly from southern and eastern Europe. In our period, the "old immigration" from northwestern Europe practically monopolized the situation. The Irish and Germans loomed far above all the others, followed by the English and then the French. Switzerland and Scandinavia sent about equal but much smaller numbers. Holland and Belgium together furnished still fewer, yet even their modest figure exceeded the number from Spain, Italy, and the southeastern regions which would dominate the later immigration.

The flow of newcomers was not steady; a glance at the appendix tables will show that it fluctuated much more violently than did the importations of commodities from those same regions. Immigration was extremely sensitive to economic changes on either side of the Atlantic. Economic conditions in the United States affected its volume noticeably; both in boom periods, when the newcomers swarmed to this side, and in times of depression, when the arrivals fell off sharply and many, already here, actually returned home. On the other hand, there were constant complaints, particularly from New Yorkers, that Europe was using this country as a dumping ground for its paupers, criminals, and other undesirables, with many a prince, parish, or landlord paying the passage to be rid of the burden. Political considerations, too, in that period of revolutionary epidemics on the Continent,

[1]See Appendix, xxvii, with annual totals for major ports.

may have influenced a moderate number to make the momentous decision to try America, but the vast majority apparently came in the hope of escaping poverty and making their fortunes in what seemed to be a land of opportunity.

The early years of peace after 1815 gave New York and the other ports their first taste of wholesale immigration. For several years war had, of course, interfered with the traffic and now England, in particular, was caught with a severe unemployment crisis. England, we recall, was centering most of her dumping of textiles at New York at the time; and the immigrants followed the same route. The federal government did not begin to gather immigration statistics until 1819, but local figures indicate much business in those first years. In 1817, the arrivals totalled 7634: England, leading with 3131, followed by Ireland at 1703, and France at 674. The mayor of New York stated that from March 1, 1818, to November 1, 1819, 18,930 immigrants had reached the city and had reported at his office. In the three-year depression, which followed, the influx dropped off sharply. For the year ending September 30, 1820, only 3800 out of a national total of 10,300 came to New York. From that, the numbers crept up only very slowly until 1832, when an almost threefold jump over the preceding year brought the level to about 30,000. That figure had almost doubled again by 1836 and 1837. Then the panic of that year cut the total in half, after which a fairly rapid recovery followed in the early 'forties.

The chief boom occurred from 1847 to 1854. During the first part of that interval, most of the gain resulted from the potato famine which sent Irishmen overseas in tremendous numbers. This Irish influx attained its peak in 1851, when 163,000 reached New York. Meanwhile, economic discontent, coupled with the reaction to the 1848 revolutions, caused large numbers of Germans to migrate. In 1852, the German and Irish totals were almost identical at 118,000. The German migrations continued to rise, but the Irish grew less. The year 1854 witnessed the largest immigration total before the Civil War. The 327,000 immigrants arriving at New York in that year included nearly 177,000 Germans, 82,000 Irish, and 36,000 from England, Scotland, and Wales. By that time, New York was feeling the approach of a depression and by the next year, 1855, the total at New York fell to 136,000. The two years following the panic of 1857 saw the port's immigrant arrivals fall to 78,000 and 79,000.

In that first rush after 1815, the handling of the immigrants (the word emigrant was generally used then, even on this side of the water), was on pretty much of a catch-as-catch-can basis. They somehow managed to reach Liverpool, Havre, or the other ports of embarkation and there, collectively or individually, made their arrangements with the captains of vessels which happened to be sailing for America. Like the freight business in the pre-packet days, regularity and organization seemed to be completely lacking. The seaport journals carried advertisements of vessels which announced not only their readiness to convey merchandise but also human freight as well. In May, 1818, for instance, a notice in *The Liverpool Mercury* stated that the ship *Timoleon,* sailing for New Bedford,

is well calculated for steerage passengers, being lofty and capacious between decks; her cabin accomodations are likewise very good. Capt. Allen will arrange with any passengers going to New York, to forward them without delay from New Bedford, free of every charge.

The irregularity and uncertainty of the arrangements tended to work hardships upon the poor immigrants. Often they fell into the clutches of boarding-house keepers and had to spend most of their substance while waiting for a ship. Sometimes, after they had paid for their passages, dishonest agents absconded with the money, or sailings were indefinitely postponed, because the vessels were libelled for debt.

It did not take business men long to see the profits which might follow the systematic organization of this traffic. The business had, by the mid-'thirties, fallen into the hands of a small group of Englishmen, with closely related houses in Liverpool and New York. Outstanding among these pioneers was the Grimshaw-Thompson combination. A principal center of the business in Liverpool was the firm of "Caleb Grimshaw & Co., 12 Goree Plazas." That address had a sinister significance: before Liverpool had become the outlet for industrial Lancashire, it had specialized in the slave trade and Goree on the African coast had been one of its ports of call. Profits in the trade in "black ivory" required the compression of a maximum number of human beings into a minimum of space in a vessel's hold; and that art was to characterize Liverpool's flourishing new business in the shipping of white cargoes, although Grimshaw had a somewhat better name in that connection than did some of his rivals.

Linked to the Grimshaw concern both in business and in marriage was the "Old Established Emigrant Office" of the Thompsons in New York. It was founded about 1829 by Francis Thompson, one of the

Black Ball Line's owners. Packets did not seek immigrant business to any extent but, after Jeremiah Thompson's failure in 1828 forced Francis to sell out his share in the liners, the latter went into business with two other nephews. After he died of the cholera in 1832, the business was carried on by Samuel Thompson, one of those nephews, with two nephews of his own. They continued active through most of the remainder of the period. Next to them in prominence at New York came the firm of W. & J. T. Tapscott, while the houses of Douglas Robinson & Co., Rawson & McMurray, and Roche Bros. & Co. were also important in the immigration business. A conspicuous American was William F. Harnden, pioneer organizer of express service, who is said to have brought 100,000 immigrants to the country.

These houses would contract for the whole "'tween decks" space of a westbound vessel for a fixed rate and then proceed to fill it up with immigrants at somewhere from $15 to $25 a head, $20 being the average steerage fare for the period. Frequently they advertised "immigrant lines" from Liverpool to New York; these implied no permanent ownership and control as in the case of the regular packets; but were simply a series of transients, whose steerage space had been chartered, organized to sail in regular succession. As the regular packets gradually descended to the immigrant trade, these houses provided passengers for them. Eventually, the Thompsons and a few of the others built or purchased immigrant liners of their own and provided a service similar to that of the regular packet lines. Many of them also copied the service, which was inaugurated by Francis Thompson, enabling immigrants, settled in the United States, to transmit funds for the passages of relatives and friends who were to follow them from the old country.

One conspicuous additional function of these houses was the drumming up of business by agents, who penetrated every little community in Ireland and elsewhere to paint in glowing colors the fortunes that might be made easily and quickly in the United States. This propaganda was nothing new; William Penn had employed it long before to lure recruits for his colony. Undoubtedly the persuasive methods of these agents did much to increase the flow of immigration westward across the ocean.

A disgruntled Irishman, who said that he had given up a good job at home as a canal engineer, testified at New York in 1837 concerning these recruiting tactics:

And this deponent further says, that there were hand bills, placarded on every corner, tree, and pump and public place in the city of Dublin, and for forty or fifty miles in the surrounding country, stating, in substance, that the people were fools not to leave the country, where there was nothing but poverty staring them in the face. That laborers were so much wanted in America, that even women were employed to work at men's work—that work was plenty in America, and wages high, to wit, 9 or 10 shillings a day, British money, and his diet. And deponent further says that William Wiley of Dublin, the agent of Rawson and McMurray of New York, told this deponent that he, deponent, could get ten pounds British money per month, and his diet as wages; that every one was on a perfect equality in America. . . .

And this deponent further states, that there is one or more agent in every principal town in Ireland, who receives a commission for collecting and forwarding emigrants to Liverpool, where they take ship for America.

Dislodged from their old surroundings by such glowing promises, or shipped by the parish authorities, who wanted to be rid of pauper charges, the crowds of immigrants made their way to the ports. In the early days, New York received many shiploads from Londonderry, Belfast, Sligo, Cork, or Dublin direct, but gradually the agents began to send them instead by steamer over to Liverpool for embarkation for the United States. Meanwhile, the Germans, too, in pathetic caravans would be making their way overland to Havre. Accommodations would generally be arranged for them in boarding houses at the ports by the agents. Those establishments exerted every effort to extort extra profits and sold equipment and provisions at outrageous prices. Herman Melville, in his fairly autobiographical *Redburn,* described the sorry state of such Irish immigrants, waiting at Liverpool for their ship.

Then came the grimmest part of the whole arduous migration, the ocean crossing itself. The ordinary ship of the period had two decks; and the immigrants were normally carried in the " 'tween decks" between the upper and lower. The orlop, beneath the lower deck, was ordinarily used for heavy freight, but there were times when even its musty space was utilized for immigrants. Frequently there was less than six feet between decks, so that a tall man could not stand erect. Seldom were there any port holes: the only ventilation came through the hatchways, which were generally fastened down in bad weather. A few hanging lamps gave a fitful light in an atmosphere which grew every hour more foul. Eager to make the most of the space which they had chartered, the shippers erected tiers of wooden bunks so close together that there was barely room to pass between them and that scant space was inevitably cluttered with luggage. Naturally the number of immigrants who could be crowded into the bunks was not as great as the number of slaves, who, chained together and lying "spoon fashion," had been jammed into Liverpool vessels of similar size. Nevertheless, the steerage shippers got extremely effective results with their overcrowding at that.

The British and American governments, to be sure, passed a series of acts designed to eliminate the worst features of that and other attendant evils in immigrant ships. These varied from time to time in specific details and in the effectiveness of their enforcement. The United States act of 1819 apparently afforded better safeguards than the earlier British acts. Conditions seem to have been worse in the British ships bound for Canada than in those which had to meet the United States regulations at New York or elsewhere, while the ships flying the American flag seem, on the whole, to have had less evil conditions aboard than the British. Hamburg and Bremen, by stringent regulations and intelligent accommodations, set an excellent example. The New York Commissioners of Emigration in 1848 reported:

> The American packet ships, and the majority of transient vessels under the American flag, still maintain a superiority in their arrangements and management over the generality of British emigrant vessels; but there is a marked improvement in the latter. . . . The foreign vessels from ports in the north of Europe, more particularly those from Hamburg and Bremen, have landed their passengers generally in as good condition as the best of the American ships.

The three-decked packet *Queen of the West,* built at New York with an eye to the immigrant trade in 1843, was described at the time of her construction as having "perfect" steerage accommodations, "with a clear flush deck fore and aft, ventilated thoroughly from stem to stern, cool and pleasant in summer and warm and comfortable in winter." Such features became common in her numerous successors launched by the East River yards, but they were a far cry from the stuffy steerage quarters of the rank and file of the sailing vessels which brought most of the millions to America. The epidemics and disasters which attended the great rush of immigration in the late 'forties and early 'fifties finally led Parliament and Congress to draw up more comprehensive and stringent codes in 1854 and 1855, respectively, but they were too late to affect the boom period.

THE CROWDED FORECASTLE; LEAVING LIVERPOOL

Both from "Leslie's Weekly," January 12, 1856

THE "'TWEEN DECKS" STEERAGE

SCENES ON AN IMMIGRANT SHIP

Even the legal minimum of space was woefully low—generally the equivalent of two tons of cargo or eighty cubic feet. That meant that each adult would have a space some six feet high, two feet wide, and not quite seven feet long, most of that room being taken up by his rough pine bunk! The earlier steerage quarters made no allowance for privacy. Both sexes and all ages were jammed indiscriminately into the hold. Adequate toilet facilities were lacking and the stench became almost unbearable.

Food, too, was another source of difficulty. The packets carried their "farmyards" with a cow for milk and with sheep, pigs, and poultry; but those were for the cabin passengers, who were fed bountifully and served by obsequious Negro stewards. None of that was for the poor devils 'tween decks. Their passage money entitled them only to bread, salt meat, and a few other supplies. They not only had to bring most of their own food, but cook everything themselves. Grates were arranged on deck, but only a few might crowd around them at a time and the less aggressive might have to wait hours to get near a fire. In stormy weather, the grates were too exposed to be used at all and, as no fires were allowed below decks, it was a case of eating uncooked food or going hungry. When adverse winds stretched out the passage beyond the usual five or six weeks, the immigrant's private stock of food would sometimes become exhausted. The law required the ship to carry a minimum amount of provisions for each passenger, whether steerage or not, of bread, salt meat, and the like, adequate for a trip of ten weeks or so; but this was often evaded. At times vessels arrived at New York as did the *Henry Bliss* in December, 1843, fifty-six days from Liverpool, with "passengers in a state of starvation." Water, too, was a problem. Each adult was allowed only a gallon a day for drinking, washing, and all other purposes.

Conditions were not, of course, always bad. The journal of a skilled Englishman, who crossed in the steerage of a London packet in 1842, indicates that he had a fairly comfortable time of it; and his was undoubtedly not an isolated case.

The attitude of the ship's officers was at times an added source of unpleasantness in the steerage. They might be delightfully gracious to the cabin passengers, because the captain secured a generous share of their passage money and it paid to give the ship a popular reputation. The courtesy which went with a $140 fare, however, was not wasted on the $20. The income from the steerage all went to the own-

ers and the immigrants would probably not be travelling again anyway. The result was an attitude which descended from cold indiffer-
ence to rough brutality, depending upon the individuals. The mates
revelled in breaking up steerage fights, generally sailing in and knock-
ing down all in the vicinity without often trying to determine the
aggressor.

A letter exposing conditions on one of the better New York immigrant packets in 1850 found its way into a Parliamentary "blue book."
The writer, Mr. Vere Foster, was a philanthropic Englishman who is
said to have paid the fares of some 15,000 women to America as immigrants. To learn at first hand the conditions, he crossed incognito
in the steerage of the *Washington,* one of the immigrant liners of
Frost & Hicks, who also operated New Orleans packets. He wrote that,
on the first day out, the 900 steerage passengers were summoned on
deck for their daily supply of water; the mates cursed, abused, and
kicked them without provocation; and only 30 got their water. No
provisions were served for two days. When the starving passengers
drew up a letter of complaint to the captain, the bearer was knocked
down by the first mate. The next day, they at least drew half the stipulated supply of provisions. During the trip, several immigrants were
severely injured by the mates. Vere Foster was so indignant that he
sought legal action against the captain in New York, but stated that
he found it would be too slow and costly a process.

The ship's company apparently sometimes went still further. Early
in 1860, Congress passed an act "'for the better protection of female
passengers," which gives some weight to the observation that it had
been difficult for an unattended girl or woman to arrive safely at New
York. The act resulted from a petition signed by many residents of
New York and Brooklyn, including the mayors of those cities. It provided that if any officer or seaman of an American vessel seduced a
passenger "under promise of marriage, or by threats, or by the exer-
cise of his authority, or by solicitation, or the making of gifts or presents," he was liable, unless willing to marry the girl, of imprisonment
of not more than a year or a fine of not more than $1000. That sum
was to go toward the support of any offspring of the affair; the New
York authorities were tired of maintaining the large number of ille-
gitimate children.

All those foregoing hardships—overcrowding, failure of food and
water supply, and the rest—were apt to occur on any immigrant pas-

sage. In addition, three potential emergencies might result in whole-sale tragedy. Far more than in ordinary merchantmen, fire at sea, shipwreck, and contagious epidemics held grim possibilities when im-migrants were aboard. Marine insurance might cover the loss of an ordinary cargo, but human freight involved a moral responsibility which was an added reason for the unpopularity of immigrants with captains.

In the first place, a ship seldom carried more than four boats; often only two. In case of disaster, this gave little more than enough room for the crew and perhaps the cabin passengers. If the accident occurred far from shore or no rescuing vessel was close at hand, most of the immigrants were doomed.

New York was, on the whole, fortunate in the matter of fire at sea during our period. It was not until 1866 that the former Havre packet *William Nelson* caught fire in midocean when a hot iron was thrown into a pot of pitch, the usual method of fumigating the hold. The cap-tain with a few of the crew and passengers took to the boats; they were still in sight when the poop collapsed, and plunged some 400 immigrants into the blazing hull. The other comparable disaster oc-curred during the period, in 1849, but to a Boston rather than a New York ship. Enoch Train's fine new packet *Ocean Monarch* was only four hours out of Liverpool and still close to the coast when some im-migrant tried to light a fire in a ventilator. In almost an instant the great ship was ablaze; and more than 400 lives were lost. Though none of the New York ships encountered such disasters before 1860, a few burned with considerable loss of life. In 1849, Samuel Thomp-son's immigrant packet, the *Caleb Grimshaw,* caught fire in midocean. A Nova Scotia bark made a providential appearance in time to rescue 356 survivors but nearly a hundred were lost. Later, a German steam-ship bound to New York burned with heavy loss of life.

Many New York immigrant ships suffered shipwreck, some with appalling loss of life. None, however, could quite parallel the horror aroused by the loss of the *William Brown* in 1842. She was bound for Philadelphia rather than New York, but the story is an amazing illustration of the extremes to which the callousness of the officers might go—a story so striking that it was the basis of a motion picture, "Souls at Sea," nearly a century later. On an April night, five weeks out from Liverpool, the *William Brown* crashed into an iceberg and began to sink. Some 32 of the crew and passengers put off in a boat under the mate, Alexander W. Holmes. In his opinion, the boat could not properly carry that many; and he decided that some of the immigrants should be thrown overboard, just as freight might be jettisoned under similar circumstances. When he was tried for manslaughter in the Federal Court at Philadelphia, the testimony of one of the Irish witnesses included the following unbelievable episode:

The sailors came to Frank Carr. He said to them, "I'll not go out, you know I wrought well all the time; I'll work like a man till morning, and do what I can to keep the boat clear of water; I have five sovereigns, and I'll give it for my life till morning, and when morning comes, if God does not help us, we will cast lots, and I'd go out like a man if it is my turn," says he, "don't put me out till I get a speaking a few words to Mrs. Edgar." "Mrs. Edgar," says he, "can't you do nothing for me?" She made no answer that I could hear; then they put him out.

Mary, his youngest sister, was crying about him; "Oh," she says, "don't put out my brother—if you put him out, put me out too. I'm willing to die the death of my brother, but don't part me and my brother." Immediately they laid hold on her and threw her out after him. . . . When they put over Mary, Ellen, the other sister, was crying; they catched hold of Ellen and when they had her up, "Oh," says she, "don't put me over naked; all I request is to give me my mantle." Some of the sailors lifted up something and threw in after her, but it was not her mantle.

The boat was shortly afterwards rescued by a passing vessel. Holmes was convicted of manslaughter.

The two wrecks which ended the old pilot monopoly at New York in the winter of 1836–37 both involved a heavy loss of life among their immigrant passengers. The *Bristol* and the *Mexico,* unable to secure pilots at Sandy Hook, were driven ashore, a few weeks apart, on the Long Island coast near Hempstead. After the latter wreck, the frozen bodies of scores of immigrants were laid out in a morgue to be visited by frantic relatives and friends, who had vainly awaited the bark's arrival in East River.

The year 1854, when the immigrant business was at its peak, saw one of the worst epidemics of shipwrecks in the history of the port. The loss of the Collins liner *Arctic* overshadowed all the rest; but three other crack steamships were also wrecked. The *Franklin* of the Havre subsidy line and the Inman liner, *City of Philadelphia,* both ran ashore without loss of life; but the pioneer Inman ship, the *City of Glasgow,* sailed from Liverpool on March 1 with 460 souls aboard, chiefly immigrants, and was never heard from again. Two sailing vessels bound for New York, each with nearly 500 immigrants, foundered at sea in a fierce mid-April gale, but not until rescuing vessels had taken every one off safely.

That same gale, however, caused one of New York's worst immigrant wrecks. The *Powhatan,* a seventeen-year-old Baltimore ship of moderate size, was bound from Havre to New York with some 200 German immigrants. On a stormy Saturday night, the fierce northeaster drove her onto the Jersey coast just above the site of Atlantic City. The "wreckmaster" of that region discovered her Sunday morning, "thumping on the bar one hundred yards from the shore," her decks crowded with passengers. He sent helpers to get the government life-saving apparatus six miles away, but they did not arrive until next morning, when it was too late. All day Sunday, the ship lay there, close enough so that the captain, through his speaking trumpet, could bellow appeals for help across the "mountain-high" waves. Some of the passengers were washed overboard and their bodies drifted ashore. Finally, just at dusk, a tremendous wave struck the *Powhatan* "and in one moment the hull was scattered into fragments." The wreckmaster could hear shrieks but could do nothing; no one survived.

In contrast was the record of the regular New York packets. Just a month later the Black Baller, *Montezuma,* with some 500 immigrants from Liverpool, ran ashore under very similar circumstances at Jones Beach on Long Island. Her captain managed to get ashore to direct the rescue; tugs came out from New York, and saved the whole 500, who had thought that their end had come. Those New York sailing liners carried tens of thousands of immigrants in their later days; sometimes, as in this case, they were wrecked, but scarcely a score of immigrants in a score of years lost their lives. Perhaps it was luck; perhaps it was the unusually tough construction of their hulls; perhaps it was the discipline and keen presence of mind of their officers.

More common than fire or wreck was the danger of an epidemic which might sweep through the crowded, fetid steerage. Considering the fact that many came aboard weakened by hunger or disease, the wonder is not that there was frequent sickness on the immigrant ships, but that it was not universal. The most common cause of steerage sickness was "ship fever," which, like "jail fever," "camp fever," and "putrid fever," was another name for typhus. It was highly contagious and often fatal. The names of cholera and smallpox, being more familiar, spread more terror but probably carried off a smaller total of victims.

An Englishwoman, crossing on the packet *Hottinguer* in 1845, told of hearing a man, who emerged from the steerage, murmur to the captain: "I believe it is the *Small Pox!*" She then wrote, "The tempest had not shaken the firm nerves of the Captain, but he quailed at the hideous name of this scourge of God." It actually was smallpox and two children died of it; it was a wonder that it did not sweep through the whole five hundred.

During the last four months of 1853, 312 vessels arrived at New York with 96,000 passengers; 47 of the ships were visited by cholera, of which 1933 died at sea, while 457 more were sent to the marine hospital in New York. It was remarked that in a group of the largest ships, leaving Liverpool and arriving at New York within a month of each other, all in relatively quick passages, some escaped completely while others suffered heavily. The *Washington,* the same ship about which Mr. Vere Foster had complained three years before, lost 81 out of 952 passengers; and the Black Baller *Isaac Webb* lost 77 out of 773, while the *Montezuma* of the same line lost only 2 out of 404 and the *Great Western,* a third Black Baller, landed all her 832 passengers safely. Mrs. Maury, the Englishwoman who had remarked the smallpox scare on the *Hottinguer,* wrote that when she boarded the vessel, she had noticed a sign reading, "A Surgeon sails on this Ship," but there was no regular doctor in that capacity and it was only by luck that one was found in the steerage. She thereupon began energetic lobbying at Washington and London; no immediate legislation resulted, but she so aroused opinion that many of the ships began to carry doctors.

The last years of our period, we recall, saw steamships beginning to take over the steerage business from the sailing ships. The early steamships, like the early sailing packets, had concentrated upon cabin passengers and had not sought the immigrant trade. William Inman, however, provided ample steerage accommodations in the iron screw steamers which, as we know, he began running to Philadelphia in 1850, later extending his service to New York. He and his wife are said to have travelled back and forth studying the opportunities for improving the service. Among other reforms, the quarters for single men and women were placed at opposite ends of the ship, with the married couples in between.

The chief advantage of the steamships in the eyes of the immigrant, was the fairly sure prospect of a two weeks' crossing in place of the uncertain length of the sailing passages, which often stretched three or four times as long. Consequently, once begun, the shift to steam was rapid. In 1856, 136,000 immigrants arrived at New York in sailing vessels and only 5000 in steamships. Four years later, 74,000 came by sail and 34,000 by steam. By the end of the next decade, nearly all of them were travelling by the quicker and more dependable steamships.

As to the reception of the immigrants at New York, one might say that, whereas Liverpool's slogan was "Pack them in," New York's was "Keep them moving." The city regarded the influx of foreigners with mixed emotions. The merchants of South Street welcomed them as a lucrative source of employment for their shipping. The rest of New York resented them as a severe drain upon their relief funds. Many complained bitterly that overseas communities were shifting the burden of their paupers, imbeciles, and criminals to New York. Philip Hone was unfair to the industrious portion who made their way west immediately or quickly found useful employment, when he wrote in his diary of June 2, 1836:

All Europe is coming across the ocean; all that part at least who cannot make a living at home; and what shall we do with them? They increase our taxes, eat our bread, and encumber our streets, and not one in twenty is competent to keep himself.

There was also constant fear that the contagion from the fever-laden ships might spread throughout the city.

Those two fears of pauperism and epidemic lay behind the early municipal and State regulation of the traffic. The federal government did not assume control at the port until 1890.

The local health officer was in charge of the quarantine regulations, with power to detain "sickly" vessels and send contagious cases to the marine hospital at Staten Island. As in the case of sailors, a hospital tax was levied upon incoming passengers, entitling them to free service during their first year ashore.

In order to relieve the burden upon the almshouse, the State in 1824 required the master or agent of any vessel bringing immigrants to post a bond of $300 for each passenger that he or she would not become a burden upon the community.

The immigrant agents found means to avoid or lighten this potential expense. Once again, Perth Amboy appears as a back door for the evasion of New York's strict regulations. Thomas Smith had sent his tea ships there; vessels had found it an easy way to dodge quarantine;

and now, in view of New Jersey's more lenient law on the subject, it afforded a chance to dodge the bond. Many ships had landed there even before this law, in 1816; two years later, the revenue cutter seized a British schooner from St. John for illegally landing passengers at Sandy Hook and Perth Amboy without formal entry; and shiploads were deposited now and then during the ensuing years.

The great exploitation of Perth Amboy, however, came in 1837, when 5006 were landed there—more than the whole Boston or Philadelphia total that year. Widespread indignation followed the landing of some 320 immigrants from the ship *Phœbe,* consigned to Douglas Robinson & Co. There was sickness aboard; several had already died and scores were put ashore still sick. The little town had no marine hospital and the poor wretches had to lie outdoors in a grove during a rainstorm. The aroused residents of Perth Amboy did what they could in their homes, while New York refused to admit the illegal entrants to the Bay steamers. Eventually, the agents sent wagons to bring them to New York. The New York almshouse commissioners sued Douglas Robinson in the case of one Ann McGuire, who had been landed sick "and would probably have died but for the humane intervention of some kind ladies of Amboy." She had been taken to New York by wagon and immediately admitted to the almshouse hospital. The Marine Court jury gave a $50 verdict against Robinson—more than double the whole passage money from Liverpool.

That scotched the practice, for it showed that the bond-dodging did not pay. Thereupon, some of the agents established their own private hospitals and almshouses to care for ex-passengers, who would otherwise have become public charges. A later investigation of the Tapscott almshouse, however, revealed a diet of "blue mold" bread and rotten fish, as well as other shocking conditions.

Ordinarily, once quarantine was passed, the immigrants were landed at some New York pier. There they encountered still further trials. Fleeced in Liverpool or Havre, and bullied aboard ship, they now ran the danger of another thoroughgoing fleecing. Aggressive "runners" for immigrant boarding houses pounced upon them, sometimes carried off their luggage by sheer force, and by hook or crook lured them to their establishments. There they were charged outrageous prices which mounted so rapidly that their funds were often soon exhausted and their luggage seized for debt. The New Yorkers were careful to point out that this exploiting was not done by Americans, but by their own countrymen, who were able to lure them by speaking the same language and inspiring their confidence.

Others of their countrymen, however, did what they could to remedy the situation. Several philanthropic organizations—the German Society, the Irish Emigrant Association, the Hibernian Provident Society, the British Emigrant Society, and the Union Emigrant Society—all at one time or another sought to give assistance. Most of their help fitted in with the "Keep them moving" policy. They preached steadily against the folly of remaining in the city, while their employment agencies corresponded throughout the nation to find where labor was in demand. The British consul helped to send some of the newcomers through to Canada. Despite all this pressure, thousands remained in the city where they landed.

The sudden sharp increase of immigration in 1847, following the Irish famine, awoke the New Yorkers to the need of a more co-ordinated control of the situation at the port. In May of that year, the State legislature created the Commissioners of Emigration, with extensive authority. This body, serving without pay, carried on its valuable but arduous task until the federal authorities assumed control in 1890. The mayors of New York and Brooklyn and the presidents of the German Society and the Irish Emigrant Society were ex-officio members, together with six other appointees. Robert B. Minturn was one of the original commissioners and the packet operators were also represented later by Captain Charles H. Marshall. Gulian C. Verplanck served as president for many years.

The act which created the commissioners abolished the old $300 bond, which had been unsatisfactory to every one, and substituted for it a $1.50 tax on each passenger, in addition to the old hospital charge. With these funds, the commissioners assumed responsibility for both the poor relief and the hospitals. The marine hospital at Staten Island was reserved for contagious cases. For the non-contagious hospitalization and dispensary treatment, to which each immigrant was entitled for a year, as well as for a place of refuge for the infirm and indigent, a large establishment was set up on Ward's Island at Hell Gate. From 1847 to 1860, the commissioners spent more than five millions in caring for 893,000 immigrants, just a third of those who arrived at the port during those years.

In 1855, the commissioners added a third essential establishment, designed to eliminate the evils of the runners and their boarding houses. As long as the vessels arrived at separate piers, it was almost impossible to protect the immigrants from those harpies. The commissioners, therefore, acquired Castle Garden, the old circular stone building at the Battery, originally a fort, later an amusement hall, and at present the aquarium. It served its most distinctive function, however, as the reception hall for the bulk of the entering immigrants. Undisturbed by the rapacious runners, who at first had to be fought off by the police, the immigrant had a chance to make his transportation arrangements at normal rates and with honest advice, while his baggage was removed from the ship and checked through to his destination. This was one more "Keep them moving" device—the immigrant was in most cases gotten safely aboard the river steamer before the boarding houses had a chance at his money and his luggage. It is said that several hundred of the runners soon left for California. Castle Garden continued in that role until the end of the State regime in 1890; two years later the federal government transferred those functions to Ellis Island out in the harbor.

Despite the consistent efforts to keep the immigrants moving, a very large number remained in the city, accelerating its rapid rise in population. This was particularly true of the Irish; the Germans and English were more apt to go inland at once. The appendix contains an analysis of the nativity of the residents of the leading seaports in 1850. It is surprising to note that Philadelphia had more native Americans than did New York. The latter's foreign population gave it an easy lead as the metropolis of the nation. Were this a history of the city instead of the port, one might say much of the effects of the newcomers upon New York in politics, in business, in religion, and in much . else, but that is another story. The new additions to the melting pot added to its unique cosmopolitan quality, while many of the sons or grandsons of those who crossed in the " 'tween decks" of the square-riggers would later be found in the seats of the mighty.[1]

The pleasanter journeying of those who paid their thirty guineas and crossed first-class has been recounted in a separate study of the packets and will not detain us here. For twenty years, the New York packets carried the "best people" back and forth across the Atlantic. Lafayette and Longfellow both crossed in the Havre packet *Cadmus;* Morse had the inspiration for his telegraph returning from Havre in the *Sully;* Robert Owen came and went frequently by Black Ballers;

[1]See Appendix, xxviii.

Drawn by C. Burton

Engraved by Wm. D. Smith

NEW YORK HARBOR FROM THE BATTERY

Castle Garden was the circular building at the right

Audubon crossed a dozen times and was almost invariably seasick; Joseph Bonaparte took the whole cabin of Captain Morgan's "Black X" liner, whenever he travelled; but William Cobbett was "blackballed" when he sought passage on a Black Baller.

Even after steam came, the packets kept a fair share of the eastbound cabin trade for a while. James Gordon Bennett, to be sure, was in the *Sirius* on her return trip, but Dickens and Barnum compromised between Cunarders for the westbound trip and square-riggers eastward. After Cunard moved down to New York and Collins joined in fast rivalry, the beau monde deserted the old canvas-backs. Jenny Llind was given a tumultuous ovation when the Collins liner *Atlantic* brought her over for new triumphs; Kossuth received a similar welcome when he arrived in the *Humboldt* but slipped out quietly a few months later in Cunard's *Africa*. From the first Black Baller to the latest Cunarder, captains, cooks, and stewards sought to make the cabin passages as pleasant as possible, in surroundings which represented the last word in ship furnishing.

"All the world (our world) is going to Europe. The packet ship *Europe* sailed this morning for Liverpool with thirty-five passengers," wrote Philip Hone. His celebrated diary, however, bore witness more than once to that far more numerous, if less conspicuous, swarm of travellers, who kept coming from Europe under infinitely less comfortable circumstances and who were to leave an indelible impression upon New York and upon the nation.

CHAPTER XVII

CALIFORNIA BY CLIPPER AND ISTHMUS

NEW YORK, like the rest of the Atlantic coast, paid little attention to the first news that a gold nugget had been found in a California millrace on January 24, 1848. It took a while for the news to sink in; but when it did, the gold rush of "Forty-nine" gave New York the most exciting episode in its maritime history since the days of Captain Kidd.

A hundred thousand men, more or less, found their way to the west coast in that memorable year and many more followed in the next half decade. With the journeys of those who went overland by covered wagon, the port was not particularly concerned; but it played a noteworthy part in transporting the rest in sailing ships around Cape Horn or in wooden sidewheelers by way of Panama. After the goldseekers had arrived, there was for some time lively business for the ports in furnishing them with food and supplies at fabulous prices. Out of this situation came the swift and slender clippers, those masterpieces of shipbuilding art. Their races from Sandy Hook to the Golden Gate became, with the contemporary swift victories of New York's Collins liners over the Cunarders, the first national sporting events. New York built about half of the fastest clippers and owned about two-thirds of them, while an even greater proportion sailed from there for San Francisco. It had almost a monopoly of the steam routes via the Isthmus, which became anything but prosaic when rival New York shipowners hired armed filibusters to overthrow Central American governments in the interest of their particular liners.

Up to that time, the west coast trade had been of slight concern to any one except a few Boston merchants. A few vessels had sailed from New York with settlers and supplies around 1840 for disputed Oregon; but as for California, the reading public knew of it as a primitive backward region offering little but hides, from the experiences of a young Harvard student a dozen years before in the classic *Two Years before the Mast*. Mild excitement was stirred in 1846 when the marines hoisted the Stars and Stripes at Monterey, but that had been a distant episode of the Mexican War overshadowed by the operations of Zachary Taylor and Winfield Scott closer at hand. A few chartered transports had sailed from New York with troops to hold the new conquest.

A year later, the government had decided that it was advisable to develop regular communications with the newly acquired territory in California and Oregon. Groups of New York capitalists obtained generous subsidies to organize two steamship lines, one to run from New York to the Isthmus of Panama by way of New Orleans and the other to go from Panama up the Pacific coast. Those lines anticipated only moderate business from the undeveloped trade of the west coast when the gold rush brought them unexpected rewards. As their new steamers from the East River yards and iron works were nearly ready to go into operation, the news from California revealed their strategic advantage.

That was by no means the only stimulus to American shipping in those years. Two years earlier, the potato famine in Ireland had given our merchant marine new chances for profit in carrying flour and wheat to British ports and bringing Irishmen back. Now the route to California would offer advantages which even the Atlantic shuttle did not possess. Its 16,000 miles or so of sea lanes were barred to foreigners because the route was construed as coasting trade. The combined impetus of these two new opportunities was to bring American tonnage in the early 'fifties to a new high level and to produce ships which excelled all earlier ones.

The news of the gold discovery in January, 1848, had been kept quiet for a while by Sutter, on whose land the nugget was found. A young naval officer with despatches left California the first of August, sailed down the coast to Mazatlan, hurried overland via Mexico City and Vera Cruz, and thence by sail to Mobile and up the coast. On the 19th of September, a Washington newspaper contained the news, which was speedily copied in New York, of the rush to the gold fields, concluding with the remark, "The danger in California is from want of food for the residents, and still more for the stream of emigrants. Would not some of our merchants find it a profitable speculation to send cargoes of biscuit, flour, etc., round to the Pacific coast?" The public does not seem to have become excited even yet until after President Polk called attention to the situation in his annual message in December.

A few New York merchants, however, were quicker to grasp the unexpected situation and they profited greatly thereby. The tens of thousands pouring into California and rushing out to the gold fields were ready to pay high prices for food and supplies. Flour worth $5 or $6 a barrel in New York fetched ten times as much in San Francisco. The same was true of other supplies; even newspapers, costing a penny or so in New York, fetched fifty cents or a dollar, when four or five months old in California. According to Scoville, this group of enterprising merchants included George A. Ward, one of the worst snobs in the city. When the government chartered two Havre packets to carry additional troops to California, he sent $40,000 worth of goods in one of them and made a reputed net profit of $80,000.

This situation, combined with the determination of thousands to reach the gold fields, caused a feverish demand for anything that would float. For the time being, San Francisco caught the dregs of the merchant marine. Old ships by the score were sold at auction for a few thousand dollars to carry gold seekers and flour barrels around the Horn. Some of the former packets used for this purpose had long passed the twenty years which was the normal life of a ship. Some of the motley fleet put into Rio or Valparaiso in distress, leaving hundreds of passengers stranded; but somehow most of them, after five or six months, managed to reach the Golden Gate. Once arrived there, the crews joined the passengers in the scramble for the gold fields. The bay became a mournful graveyard of hundreds of deserted vessels, rotting at their moorings. One naval officer wrote of the danger in this fleet of old vessels, should a windward one catch fire. That did not happen, but many of the old craft found their final resting place in the mud of San Francisco Bay.

With the merchant marine thus purged of its least valuable vessels, San Francisco was about to become the terminus of the magnificent new clippers. From the first, New York was the leader in this new trade with the west coast. Of the 775 mongrel vessels which cleared from eastern ports for California in 1849, 214 were from New York and 151 from Boston, while no other port sent more than 42. That proportional distribution among the ports was maintained throughout

om a painting by Charles Robert Patterson   Courtesy of the Columbian Rope Company

"THE FORTY–NINERS"

Showing a ship in the Upper Bay at New York, departing for San Francisco

the clipper era; at the beginning and among the best ships, New York's ratio was even heavier.

No purpose would be served here to go into the details of the clipper era, for unlike other aspects of the port history, which are unexplored subjects, this has been the object of more minute and painstaking research than any other branch of the old merchant marine. Back in 1910, Captain Arthur H. Clark, himself a veteran of the service, wrote his classic, *The Clipper Ship Era;* since then, author after author has sent the *Flying Cloud* and her contemporaries around Cape Horn, for no other episode of American days of sail can compete with the clipper as far as romance and royalties are concerned. Of Clark's successors, Howe and Matthews, taking up clipper after clipper in alphabetical detail, and Cutler, with his glamorous chronological synthesis, are particular leaders. Among them scarcely a single trip, to say nothing of a single ship, has escaped statistical, if not narrative, attention. Inasmuch as New York played the foremost role in that thrilling era, however, a history of the port would be incomplete without some brief mention of the clipper exploits.

The authorities are not wholly agreed as to what, exactly, constituted a clipper. Cutler is the most catholic in his view of the subject, including in his analysis not only all the "sharp" and "medium" ships, but also the numerous barks which fell into that category. Clark is more exclusive and stresses only those ships which made the run to San Francisco in 110 days or less. The term clipper had begun to appear as early as 1815, principally in reference to the swift, slender schooners and larger craft in whose construction Baltimore was the first to play a leading role. The ship *Ann McKim,* built at Baltimore and soon owned at New York, has often been regarded as the prototype of the celebrated class. The clipper, on the whole, was more slender and "streamlined" than the ordinary solid, frigate-built, and "burthensome" cargo-carrier which reached its highest expression in the New York packets. The clipper, for one thing, had its "bows turned inside out," cutting through the waves, whereas the older bluff-bowed ships butted through them. It also had slenderer lines aft; and its point of maximum beam was farther from the bows than previously. The clippers, moreover, were, on the whole, more heavily sparred and carried more canvas; this is said to have reached a maximum in Webb's *Challenge,* the top of whose mainmast was a full 200 feet above the water. Altogether, these features enabled the clippers to travel faster than ordinary ships, but they could not carry as much cargo per registered ton. Only on long runs, where special conditions put a premium on speed, would clippers pay.

New York, fortunately, had several clippers on hand when news of the gold rush arrived. They were the China clippers, built in the middle and later 'forties. Griffiths, we recall, had embodied some of the new ideas in the *Sea Witch,* with which Howland & Aspinwall rewarded Captain "Bob" Waterman for his 78-day run in a second-hand packet; the new ship had established an all-time record of 74 days from Canton to New York in 1848-49. The Lows, profiting by the suggestions of that versatile "Stunington" sea dog, Captain N. B. Palmer, had the *Houqua* and *Samuel Russell* and were about to add the *Oriental,* all of which "Cap'n Nat" first commanded. By going to Canton by way of San Francisco instead of by Good Hope, these ships earned valuable extra freights for their owners. It was said that the *Samuel Russell* earned some $84,000 on her first trip around the Horn to 'Frisco, more than her original cost. The papers of the *Houqua* show that the Lows profited also by her change of course to the Orient.

New York, with its head start in the construction of China clippers, took the lead in building clippers for the Cape Horn route. It is small wonder that, with a chance of paying for them in a single four-months' trip to the west coast, the merchants of New York and the other eastern ports hastened to order such fast new clippers for this route to California. The first of the new 1850 crop to be launched in the East River was Webb's *Celestial.* Her name was characteristic of the poetic swing which would mark the names of the whole clipper fleet; very different from the packet lines, whose ship names had about as much homogeneity as the names of an ordinary collection of Pullman cars.

New York was to be concerned with the major proportion of the clippers. With Boston, it was to overshadow the other ports in the building and ownership (registry) of them. A tabulation of the collection of some 350 clippers described by Howe and Matthews demonstrates that New York built 53 and owned 116; Boston built 140 and owned 163; Maine built 54 and owned 7; whereas New England as a whole built 226 and owned 188. Of the 82 clippers which made the trip to San Francisco in 110 days or less, the New York proportion was much higher, since apparently it was able to afford the best ships. Of this 82, it built 25 and owned 39; Boston built 37 and owned 38; New

England as a whole built 55 and owned 41. Many of the ships owned in New England, however, sailed quite regularly from New York, which outranked all others as a hailing port for clippers. Of the 128 voyages made in 110 days or less, 94 started from New York, 33 from Boston, and one from Baltimore. In other words, in this select group of clippers, New York built 30 per cent to Boston's 45 per cent; owned 48 per cent to Boston's 46 per cent; but was the starting-point for 73 per cent, whereas only 26 per cent began their trips at Boston.

While the profits of the first clippers were impressive and induced the rapid building of more which paid for themselves quickly until the market was glutted, public attention centered upon speed records. Most of the clipper studies concentrate upon the number of days to San Francisco. The ordinary shipping which took the long route to California required somewhere between 150 and 200 days for the trip; one vessel took 240 days, a full eight months. The occasional appearance of arrivals in 100 days or less resulted partly from the new design of the ships, partly from the relentless driving by steel-nerved captains, partly from luck, and partly from the researches of Lieutenant Matthew F. Maury. The latter's patient, intelligent analysis of thousands of logs resulted in the publication of annual volumes of *Sailing Directions,* indicating the best way to take advantage of the prevailing winds and currents at various seasons along the major sea routes.

Since speed was the outstanding characteristic of the clippers, few other trips can compete in interest with the record-breaking maiden run of the *Flying Cloud* in the summer of 1851. Perhaps the most famous of all the clippers, the beautiful 1782-ton ship was built at East Boston by Donald McKay, the talented Nova Scotian who had learned part of his art on the East River and who, profiting by the initial experiments of Griffiths, Webb, and the other New Yorkers, became the outstanding builder of clippers. She had been built for his patron, Enoch Train, the Boston packet operator; but he, to his eternal regret, quickly sold her for $80,000 to Grinnell, Minturn & Company of New York. Josiah Perkins Cressy, a native of Marblehead, with experience in the China trade, was selected to command the *Flying Cloud* for her famous maiden voyage. The old log has come down to us; snatches of it are worth quoting. Between the lines, with their crisp brevity and informal punctuation, one may still catch the thrill of those days when her spindrift flew.

She left the foot of Maiden Lane in the East River at 2 P.M. on June 2, 1851; by seven that evening she dropped the pilot off Sandy Hook with "moderate breezes fine weather." Three days later, approaching Hatteras, with "good breezes," she "lost main & mizen topgallant mast and main sail yard." The clippers, of course, kept carrying full sail in winds which kept ordinary shipping under reefed topsails. On June 14, in mid-Atlantic in the latitude of Cuba, "discovered main mast badly sprung 4 feet below the hounds." By June 26, crossing the equator, she was rounding Cape St. Roque, tip of the great Brazilian bulge—"midnight tacked ship to clear Rocas Shoal at 2 A.M. Tacked south." July 10 found her off the Rio Plata, where fierce pamperos blew off the Argentine plains—"middle very heavy squalls with much & very severe thunder & lightning Double reefed the topsails; Latter part blowing hard gale—No observations." It *was* blowing when a clipper double-reefed the topsails. The next day was worse—"heavy gales, close reefed topsails split fore staysail & main topmost staysail at 1 P.M. Discovered main masthead sprung (same time brig in company to leeward lost fore and main topmast) sent down royal and topgallant yards & booms off lower & topsail yard to relieve the mast, very turbulent sea running Ship laboring hard & shipping large quantities of water over lee rail." The next day, two holes were found bored in the side by one of the crew—"put him in irons." Then, on July 23, fifty days out of New York, "Cape Horn N 5 miles at 8 A.M., the whole coast covered with snow—wild ducks numerous." It was winter, of course, down at "Cape Stiff" during the months of the northern summer. The last day of July, far off Valparaiso, "Latter part high sea running ship very wet, fore and aft. Distance run this day by observation 374 miles, an average of 15 7-12 knots per hour, during the squalls 18 knots of line was not sufficient to measure her rate of speed." That was the fastest day's run yet made by a ship—nearly forty miles better than any steamship travelled in a single day up to the Civil War. All through the month of August, the *Flying Cloud* sped northward with nothing eventful to mark her steady progress. Finally, on the last day of August, just a month after she rounded the Horn, "Light breezes and pleasant; middle strong & squally at 2 A.M. hove ship too for daylight at 6 A.M. made South Farallone NE 2 degrees E 6 miles, at 7 took a pilot, at 11 hour 30 mins came to anchor in five fathoms water off North Beach San Francisco Harbor." That record of 89 days and 21 hours stood until, three years later, the *Flying Cloud* herself bettered it by thirteen hours, a permanent record from "anchor to anchor."

Her first voyage was surrounded by a series of events which made the middle months of 1851 one of the most thrilling of periods for the New Yorkers, keyed up as were all Americans by the all-pervading lust for speed. Just two weeks before the *Flying Cloud* first sailed, the Collins liner *Pacific* arrived at Liverpool, the first vessel to reduce the Atlantic crossing below ten days. While the *Flying Cloud* was sweeping up the West Coast, the New York yacht *America* was winning her famous cup off the Isle of Wight at the expense of British yachtsmen. Three weeks before the clipper sailed, the first through train passed over the Erie Railroad to Lake Erie. On October 1, a month and a day after her arrival at San Francisco, the first train over the new Hudson River Railroad went from New York to Albany in five hours, more than two hours faster than any river steamboat had linked the two cities. New York thus had at last its double rail connection with the West. Probably at no similar period have New Yorkers enjoyed quite such a series of exciting achievements.

That same summer witnessed another clipper trip from New York which became famous, not for its speed but for other less pleasant attendant circumstances. The abnormally rapid expansion of the American merchant marine meant that there were not enough good seamen to go round. Clippers and packets alike too often had to sail with greenhorns or ruffians in the forecastle. Captains and "bucko mates" had to be ready in emergencies with pistol or belaying pin, while juries of landlubbers ashore were called upon time and again to determine whether mutiny or abuse of authority had occurred. On July 13, while the *Flying Cloud* was battling gales off the Argentine coast, the 2006-ton clipper *Challenge,* fresh from Webb's yard and flying the house flag of N. L. & G. Griswold, left the East River to try for a record. Her commander's reputation gave hope for that. He was none other than Robert H. Waterman, one-time Black Ball mate and master, who had later smashed all records on the Canton run in the *Natchez* and *Sea Witch.* He encountered nasty weather off Cape Horn; arrived at San Francisco in 109 days; and before he had been ashore long, a mob was howling for his life. Some of the crew, it seemed, had, in their cups, regaled saloon audiences with tales of brutal atrocities: men starved to death and shot from the yards off Cape Horn. It was true that Waterman had had a particularly rough and worthless crew; that

he had bashed in the skulls of two with a belaying pin to save the
mate's life; and that three men had fallen to their death from aloft off
the Horn. The passengers, however, denied that he had shown unnecessary cruelty while some of the crew expressed their willingness
to sail on to China under Waterman. The better San Francisco elements, with their vigilance committee, saved Waterman from the mob.
He left the sea after that trip, however, to live on in California, a respected citizen, for many years.

The success of the first clippers, and the high freight rates which
they commanded, led to a tremendous output of the slender craft in
1852 and 1853. Not only was there San Francisco to be supplied, but
the repeal of the British Navigation Acts in 1849 opened up new opportunities in carrying tea to London, while Australia's gold rush in
'51 meant a third important run where cargo space could be sacrificed
to speed. Maine joined Boston and New York as a leader in production, while many other places along the coast also turned out a fair
quota of clippers. According to one estimate, 270 full-rigged ships of
clipper model, in addition to many barks, had been built in the decade up to the beginning of 1854; 125, nearly half of them, had been
added in the single peak year of 1853.

By the end of 1853, a sad fact was beginning to become obvious:
there was not enough business for all the new clippers. By 1854, the
slump was underway; new and old clippers had to wait longer and
longer for cargoes and were glad to accept freight rates far lower
than the old $60 a ton. Even the Canton-London tea carrying and the
Australian gold rush of 1851, added to the California business and
even the occasional transatlantic runs to Liverpool, were not enough
to keep all the clippers busy.

Although the golden yield of the first years was over, the fetish for
speed continued on through the mid-'fifties. On the main racecourse
around the Horn to San Francisco, the four fastest trips by clippers
all started from New York, although only one of those was made by
an East River ship. That was Webb's *Swordfish*, which made the run
in 90 days 18 hours, which was not only slower than the two swift
trips of the Boston-built *Flying Cloud*, but was also exceeded by the
oft-argued run of the *Andrew Jackson*, built at Mystic, Connecticut.
The statisticians of the clipper era have fought back and forth over
the latter's claims to superlative speed, achieved in the last year of
our period. Leaving New York on Christmas Day in 1859, she arrived

off San Francisco on the evening of March 22 but could not secure a pilot until next morning. The consensus of opinion seems to be that while her "anchor-to-anchor" run of 90 days 12 hours leaves her well behind both trips of the *Flying Cloud,* her "pilot to pilot" passage was some four hours faster than the better run of McKay's great ship. When it comes to a matter of hours, however, two or three days of unavoidable baffling calms may have cheated equally good ships and captains of their chance.

Other routes, too, had their speed records. McKay's splendid *Sovereign of the Seas* on a trip from Honolulu to New York, with oil collected from the whalers, in 1853 not only established an 82-day record; but on a single day, March 18, logged some 421 nautical miles, which was faster than any steamship would do for years to come. The closest approach to that came a year later in the course of a record 13 day 1 hour crossing from New York to Liverpool in the Maine-built *Red Jacket* under Captain Asa Eldridge. On a single day, she logged 413 knots; and that was faster than her captain was to travel in the swift Collins liner *Pacific,* in which he soon afterwards "went missing." Meanwhile, the clipper record for size was attained by McKay's immense 4555-ton *Great Republic,* launched in October, 1853, at East Boston and carried around to New York. On the night after Christmas, unfortunately a waterfront blaze set her afire at her East River pier, where she was loading for her maiden voyage, and she burned nearly to the waterline.

Fascinating stories of heroism and hardship have come from many of the hundreds of clipper trips. As examples, there were the experiences of two ships which set out from New York for San Francisco early in 1856. Off Cape Horn, the weather was unusually stormy and every ship faced a grim battle. The *Rapid* had to give up after several weeks; of her crew of 24, ten were dead, ten were disabled, and the others could only put back to Rio. Meanwhile Captain Patten of the *Car of Neptune,* overcome by the strain and exposure, lay in his bunk stricken with brain fever and temporarily blind. He had already demoted the first mate for incompetence; no one else knew the mysteries of navigation except his young Maine wife. She assumed command, and, along with nursing her husband, carried the ship the rest of the way to San Francisco for a 145-day passage. The feminists pointed to her as proof that a woman could accomplish even that most masculine of duties.

By 1857, the clippers were deeply in the red financially. During that year of panic, 775 vessels were counted at one time in New York harbor, including many fine clippers. The *Flying Cloud* lay idle for two years; agents were glad to get cargoes at $10 a ton for San Francisco. Clippers descended to carrying lumber and flour, where their reduced cargo space was a handicap. They lay waiting at the guano chutes on the coast of Peru or brought coolies from China to California or Cuba. Many passed to foreign flags and others roamed eastern seas looking for cargoes or purchasers, with instructions to accept offers at a fraction of the cost.

Unlike the packets, which paid well for forty years, the clippers flourished scarcely more than half a decade. Yet, for the brief time that they lasted, they provided a glorious stock of romance for contemporaries and for later generations.

Meanwhile, the California trade was providing another whole decade of extremely profitable business for the New York side-wheel steamers, which were exploiting the shorter route by way of the Isthmus. The clippers, although they carried most of the freight for California, were too slow, for all their record three-month passages, to be the main line of communication between the east coast and the west. With steamships approaching Panama or Nicaragua on the Atlantic and the Pacific, New York and San Francisco could communicate with one another in a month, more or less—more in the beginning, less as time went on. Consequently, these steamships, exclusively a New York venture, carried most of the news, mails, express, and gold dust as well as a large part of the passengers who could afford their service.

Few corporations have had success thrust upon them so unexpectedly as the New York steamship lines on these Isthmus routes. Congress enacted a general policy of mail subsidies, we recall, in 1845; two years later, while the Mexican War was in progress, it became more specific. Oregon was the chief objective in the decision to subsidize, along with the Bremen line, steamship service from New York by way of Havana and New Orleans to Chagres on the Isthmus of Panama; and from Panama on the Pacific side up the coast to Astoria, Oregon. San Francisco, along with Acapulco, San Diego, and other west-coast ports, was mentioned as a way stop. The contracts were awarded to two men practically unknown in shipping circles—a Colonel Albert G. Sloo, of Cincinnati, got the Atlantic run and one Arnold Harris of Arkansas, the Pacific. By the end of 1847, those contracts had passed into the hands of wealthy New Yorkers who knew something about ships.

The chief figure in the United States Mail Steamship Company, which was to receive $290,000 a year for semi-monthly service to Chagres and way ports, was George Law, the burly, bewhiskered son of an Irish immigrant, but himself an ardent "Native American." "Live-Oak George" was a self-made man who had begun as a canal contractor and had graduated to river steamers. His *Oregon,* we recall, beat Vanderbilt's boat in that classic river race in 1847. For a while, the Atlantic service would be known as the "Law Line." His lieutenant and successor was. Marshall O. Roberts, the sharp son of a Welsh doctor. His active politics stood him in good stead in business; his fortune is said to have dated from some contracts, at prices higher than those of bidders of the wrong party, thrown his way by a friendly navy agent.

The Pacific Mail Steamship Company, with its $199,000 subsidy for monthly service from the far side of the Isthmus, was headed by a figure better known and longer prominently established in New York business circles. He was William H. Aspinwall, whose mother was sister of "G. G. & S." Howland. He and his cousin, William E. Howland, had taken over that great firm, with its commanding position in the Latin-American trade, a decade before. Aspinwall seems to have had his full share of the Howland shrewdness without those other qualities which had marred the reputation of his uncles.

It was easy to see that the Atlantic run would be good business. There was plenty of trade to be depended upon between New York, Havana, and New Orleans, even if the Chagres end of the route amounted to little. That was the reason for the service twice a month. Early in 1848, however, the Pacific part of the route looked decidedly like a gamble. With relatively few settlers as yet in Oregon or California, business, it seemed, would be slow to develop.

That was why Aspinwall's first steamship, the *California,* was being built by Webb with a tonnage of only 1050, while the *Ohio,* which Bishop & Simonson were building for Law, ran to 2397 tons. In comparison, the new subsidy liners to Bremen were just midway between the two; the first Havre liner was of identical size with the *Ohio;* and the new Cunarders built at just that time averaged around 1825 tons. The ships of the Law Line compared favorably in size and speed with all the ocean liners except those of Collins. Gradually, as business increased, the Pacific Mail's ships approached even those in size.

On Friday, October 6, 1848, the *California* left New York for the long run around South America to her distant post. Like the *Oregon,* the *Panama,* and other successors in the Pacific Mail, she might never pass Sandy Hook again. Nevertheless, they remained essentially New York ships; built there, owned there, and operated as integral parts of an important route which led to New York.

When the *California* left New York, the early news of the gold discovery, we recall, was causing only a slight ripple of interest. When she put in at Panama 106 days later, on January 20, 1849, her captain was amazed to find, instead of the anticipated modest handful of passengers, a swarm of eager gold-seekers anxious to get to California ahead of those struggling overland or coming by sail around the Horn. She proceeded on to San Francisco with far more than her normal capacity of passengers. The Pacific Mail had certainly "struck it rich," even if it did go into operation on a Friday.

After the first year or two, when a large number of passengers went out to the west coast in that mongrel fleet of sailing vessels, the steamships carried most of those who did not go overland. By steam, one was fairly sure of arriving in five weeks at the most, whereas ordinary square-riggers were apt to take five or more months and the clippers at their best took three months. A first-class passage by steam from New York to San Francisco on the subsidy lines cost $600, about four times the first-class fare to Europe. Steerage cost $300, about the same as the slower but more comfortable trip by clipper. It is small wonder that the steamship lines paid well, even though the Pacific Mail had to send most of its coal by sail around the Horn.

The increasing volume of business on the isthmian route soon led Law and Roberts to establish two separate routes, instead of combining all their ports of call into one as originally contemplated. One went from New York to New Orleans by way of Havana; the other direct from New York to the Isthmus. It was part of the agreement with the government that these mail steamers should be commanded by naval officers on leave. Two men who were to be conspicuous in the Civil War engaged in this service—David D. Porter, later an admiral, and Gustavus V. Fox, the highly efficient assistant secretary of the navy during that conflict.

Porter was in command of the *Crescent City* at the beginning of an episode which threatened international complications. The early 'fifties were a period of revolutions and filibustering in Cuba. In September, 1851, the captain general of Cuba forbade the *Crescent City* to land mails or passengers at Havana because her purser was accused of furnishing the press with "incendiary" articles about Cuba. Though urged by President Fillmore to go easily and penalized by the removal of the mails, Law sent the ship with that same purser aboard into Havana time and again. That audacity started a presidential boom for Law.

Disaster occasionally, but only occasionally, struck these routes. In 1851 the *Union,* belonging to an irregular rival line, was off Lower California, on her run from San Francisco to Panama. Her crew celebrated the Fourth of July until they were in a state of complete inebriation. A few hours after midnight, with no watch on deck and the helmsman too drunk to handle the wheel, she piled up on a reef. All were rescued but the ship was a total loss. One Pacific Mail liner never reached the Pacific. This was the *San Francisco,* fresh from Webb's yard, which sailed from New York late in 1853 with a regiment of regulars and numerous other passengers aboard. Barely sixty hours out, she encountered a heavy gale which washed nearly a hundred persons overboard and left the crippled sidewheeler wallowing helplessly in the trough of the heavy seas. Three sailing vessels finally rescued most of the rest, some of the troops being carried to England. One of New York's worst marine disasters in the whole period was the loss of the *Central America,* formerly the *George Law,* of the U. S. Mail Company's fleet. Bound from Havana to New York, she foundered at sea in a heavy gale on September 12, 1857. Blame was laid upon the engine room force, which had allowed the fires to go down so that she lost headway and was battered to pieces in the trough of the sea. Some 423 lives were lost, in addition to several millions in gold.

The most uncomfortable part of the short route was the crossing of the Isthmus from Chagres to Panama, a distance of nearly fifty miles. In the last days of 1846, the United States had made a treaty with New Granada (the later Colombia), securing a right of way and transit across the Isthmus by any existing means or any which might develop in the future. The existing means were woefully primitive. Between mules and open boats, it was apt to take from two to five days, with inadequate facilities for food and shelter, together with constant danger of catching the malarial "Panama fever." In the early days of the rush, when thousands were crossing, conditions were sometimes appalling. Aspinwall decided that a railroad was the immediate solution of the problem (a canal had been discussed since early Spanish days). In 1848, he and his associates secured a New York charter for the Panama Railroad and John L. Stephens, "the American traveler," who knew Central America well, was chosen president. A contract with New Granada secured exclusive rights and other privileges for 29 years in exchange for 3 per cent of all dividends. An island in Limon Bay, some ten miles east of Chagres, was made the Atlantic terminus and soon christened Aspinwall, later becoming Colon. Work was begun in the malarial swamps in 1850. Laborers were imported from many parts of the world but some soon died. Early in 1852, the eastern half of the road was open for business; by 1854,. it reached the summit at Culebra, leaving only eleven miles or so by muleback; and a rainy midnight in January, 1855, saw the last rail laid. Passengers would now go through in much less discomfort from the steamship arriving at one end to the second awaiting them at the other for the final stage of their trip. For more than a decade, the road paid regular 12 per cent dividends. This Panama Railroad, like the two subsidy steamship lines, was purely a New York affair.

Meanwhile, keen competition had developed to the northward; but it, too, came from New York, in the form of the redoubtable Cornelius Vanderbilt, whom we recall, more than thirty years before, helping Thomas Gibbons to buck the Livingston monopoly in the little steamer on New York Bay. In the meantime, his wits had been further sharpened and his wealth vastly increased by his steamboat exploits on the Hudson and the Sound. Even if Law had not beaten him in that Hudson steamboat race, Vanderbilt would probably not have long stayed out of the highly lucrative steam route to California.

Until the final decision for the Panama Canal a half century later, the Nicaragua route was a close rival to Panama. The Isthmus, to be sure, is about three times as wide in Nicaragua, but with Lake Nicaragua and the San Juan River, all except eleven miles on the Pacific side could be travelled by water. Seeing the Law-Aspinwall combination well entrenched at Panama, Vanderbilt negotiated with Nicaragua in 1849 for permission to dig a canal. That fell through, partly because of British intervention in the Clayton-Bulwer treaty in 1850. Vanderbilt, however, got from Nicaragua a charter for the Accessory Transit Company. He would carry passengers by steamship from New York to San Juan del Norte, or Greytown as it was called by the British. Then with small steamers, he would take them up the river and, in somewhat larger steamers, across the lake to Virgin Bay, whence it was only eleven miles to San Juan del Sul on the Pacific. For that final brief land travel, he would soon have a macadam road and big blue-and-white buses drawn by mules. His Pacific steamships would complete the route to San Francisco. On August 12, 1851, while the *Flying Cloud* was sweeping up the Pacific coast, Vanderbilt's *Prometheus* arrived at New York with the first passengers and gold from San Francisco by way of the Nicaragua Transit.

The new route was four to five hundred miles shorter than the Panama run and, once it was organized, could be accomplished in about two days' less time. Vanderbilt had no mail subsidy; but his Hudson River days had taught him about price wars. He cut the old rate a third, offering the through trip for $400; the Panama lines reluctantly had to follow suit.

The nature of the two services, once both were well under way, is indicated by rival passages, selected at random, both leaving San Francisco on the afternoon of December 31, 1853, in the last hours of the old year. Vanderbilt's *Brother Jonathan* arrived at San Juan del Sul on January 12 at night; the transit took 38 hours; his *Northern Light* left Greytown just before midnight on the 15th and arrived at New York at 9 A.M. on the 25th. Meanwhile, the Pacific Mail's *Oregon* reached Panama early on the 17th; there was an 18-mile mule ride and then the new railroad carried the passengers through to Aspinwall by that evening. Law's *Ohio* left Aspinwall on the 18th and arrived in New York on the 29th, four days behind the rival steamer. The *Ohio* brought the "regular mails"—that was what the government paid her for; but most of her west-coast news was stale. As for passengers and gold, they broke about even. The *Northern Light* brought 313 passengers and $850,000 in "'freight"; the *Ohio,* 300 passengers and $976,-000. Each brought packages by the Adams and Wells Fargo express services. During the summer season, passenger travel was generally heavier and nearly always more persons went out to San Francisco than came back.

Along with such prosaic details, the Nicaragua route provided some of the most bizarre episodes in the whole story of New York shipping. There was excitement from the very start, for the *Prometheus* was fired upon by a British warship as she left Greytown on her third trip to New York in October, 1851. Through a puppet "king of the Mos-quito Coast" the British exercised a protectorate over what was the only Atlantic entrance for the Nicaraguan route. As the *Prometheus,* with the last of her 500 passengers just arrived through the Transit, started to weigh anchor, a boatload of dusky Greytown officials rowed out to demand $123 in port dues. Captain Churchill denied their authority to collect this; refused to pay; and headed out for sea. Thereupon Her Majesty's brig *Express* sailed over and "fired a round shot over our forecastle, not clearing the deck house ten feet." Another shot passed over the stern. Captain Churchill sent a boat over; the British commander threatened to use grape and canister unless the steamship anchored. Churchill paid the sum under protest and was allowed to sail for New York. Within two months, the British Government disavowed the conduct of the naval commander, but the friction continued. In 1854, the U. S. S. *Cyane* bombarded Greytown while a smaller British warship stood by, too weak to do more than protest.

By that time, still stranger things were happening on the Transit. Vanderbilt was taking a vacation in Europe in his big steam yacht, leaving the management of the company in the hands of Charles Morgan, the Gulf steamboat operator, at New York, and William H. Garrison, another New Yorker, at San Francisco. They first began to manipulate the stock to their own benefit and Vanderbilt's detriment in New York.

Then they hit upon a more audacious scheme. Quite openly, both began to back William Walker, a filibuster from Tennessee, in his efforts to seize the government of Nicaragua. In return, they expected him to annul the Transit grant to Vanderbilt and issue it to them instead. Volunteers by the score rode south on Transit ships, passage free, to swell Walker's forces. In 1855 and 1856, the situation grew acute. In one of his operations, Walker used Transit lake steamers, filled with passengers; and some of them, including women and children, were killed. At New York, the federal district attorney, trying to uphold the neutrality laws, sought to check the flow of recruits which every Transit steamer was carrying southward, but the public was all for Walker. The authorities, moreover, found it hard to distinguish Walker recruits from ordinary passengers bound for California. On one occasion, the *Northern Light* sailed out of the harbor, carrying off a deputy marshal, who had been sent to serve a warrant on the captain in connection with this neutrality violation. The latter, who revelled in the name of Tinkelpaugh, was arrested on his return, tried, and acquitted. At another time, the same steamer was stopped by a revenue cutter in New York Harbor, but the suspected recruits could not be recognized. Eventually, Walker secured control in Nicaragua and was able to persuade its reluctant president, early in 1856, to shift the Transit award from Vanderbilt to Morgan and Garrison.

That roused Vanderbilt to action. Earlier, when he found what Morgan and Garrison had been doing in his absence, he is said to have shouted at them, "I won't sue you, for the law is too slow. I will ruin you." They managed to survive, but now Walker was to be ruined. Vanderbilt determined to close the Transit, which would cut off Walker's source of recruits and supplies and would make the shifted concession valueless to Morgan and Garrison. He sent one Spencer, a former engineer on a Transit river steamer, to co-operate with the Costa Ricans in shutting off the route. Spencer did the job thoroughly and Walker was through, for that particular episode.

Then, returning to more strictly maritime considerations, Vanderbilt resumed the familiar "blackmail" game, which he and Daniel Drew used to play on the Hudson and the Sound. He let the Pacific Mail and U. S. Mail know that he planned to shift his Atlantic and Pacific steamships to the Panama run, which naturally would have meant ruinous competition. To prevent this, they bought him off; and his price was stiff. Not only did they have to buy one of his ships, but they agreed to pay him $40,000 a month, the equivalent of their total government mail subsidies, for staying off the run and either using his ships in the transatlantic trade or letting them lie idle. Not only did they pay it, but before long, when Vanderbilt threatened to resume business, they raised the payment to $56,000 a month! Even at that, he finally returned to the Isthmian rivalry at the end of our period.

The cancellation of the federal mail subsidies in 1858 meant the end of the U. S. Mail. Law had withdrawn to go into New York street railways and Roberts played a sharp game. When the ships were sold at auction, he bought them for a song. It was a lucky investment, for, with his good political connections, he chartered them to the government at outrageous prices during the Civil War. The *Empire City,* which cost him $12,000 at auction, for instance, yielded $833,000 from the army, in addition to naval charters, but that is another story. In 1859, there was cutthroat rivalry of the most bitter type on both the Atlantic and Pacific runs. Vanderbilt, in company with Roberts and others, ran steamers on both routes, in competition with the Pacific Mail which for a while had three of the former Collins liners on the Atlantic side. Vanderbilt, seeking to purchase the Pacific Mail steamers and establish a monopoly, cut the first class fare from New York through to San Francisco to $100 and the steerage fare to $50, $25 of which went to the Panama Railroad. The Pacific Mail met this and lowered the steerage rate to $45; at one time, steerage passengers were carried all the way for $20, which meant actual loss in view of the heavy railroad fare. The rate war led to a lively boom in travel. Vanderbilt did not get the Pacific Mail, and soon withdrew. Frequent shifts of service followed on the Atlantic end of the run.

The sidewheelers of the Pacific Mail, however, maintained their steady course up and down the coast between Panama and San Francisco for years to come. The overland mail, the pony express, and the telegraph took over some of their functions; but they remained the most fashionable and desirable conveyances for passengers until the final spike was driven into the first transcontinental railroad in 1869. Since the late 'fifties, they had been one of the few seagoing branches of the American merchant marine to yield steady profits, for they had long outlasted, economically, the glorious clippers which had followed the more sporting route around the Horn to California. Both with sail and steam, New York had made the most of the opportunities suddenly offered by the gold rush.

CHAPTER XVIII

THE DISAPPOINTED RIVALS

ALL THE way from Canton to Chicago, New York encountered the stubborn opposition of rival ports as they sought to stem the increasing concentration of American commerce at Manhattan wharves. The other ports had missed their chance in 1815; late in 1823 the New England Society toasted "The City of New York—The emporium of America; commerce her glory, rivalship hopeless." Yet those rival ports hopefully struggled for a quarter century or so, if not to wrest the primacy from New York, at least to retain a fair share of the nation's commercial transactions. The rivalry spread out over the seas to many distant regions but its most conspicuous feature was the fight for the western front. Each port raced to spread rails beyond the mountains to draw the rich trade of the interior toward its own wharves.

It is not the purpose of this chapter to gloat over the customs figures, which show that those efforts failed to check the growth of New York's trade.[1] For some of the ports, the story of that rivalry is a proud and creditable one and their efforts bore fruit. New York's sum total of trade overshadowed the business of its rivals but many comfortable fortunes were built up at other points along the coast. The New York merchants did not necessarily become richer, man for man, than those in the rival ports—there were simply more men at New York who prospered in the process.

Various ports, up and down the coast, entered into the contest. New England had several small but very busy ports, notably Portland and Salem, whose enterprise brought substantial returns. Their role stood in sharp contrast to the cotton ports, which, despite their impressive export totals, were essentially passive and allowed themselves

[1]See Appendix, i, ii, iii.

to be exploited by outsiders. The three great ports which led in the attack on New York were Boston, Philadelphia, and Baltimore, and our story will naturally concentrate upon their efforts.

Both Boston and Baltimore came out of the contest with high honors, however far their customs totals might fall below those of New York. Laboring under definite geographical handicaps, they seemed to do about all that could be done, once they awakened to the situation, and more than once they gave New York cause for alarm. The role of the two ports was essentially different. Boston, remote from the rich hinterland beyond the mountains, looked primarily to the sea, where it frequently competed closely with New York in the quality, volume, and activity of its shipping. Baltimore, the upstart among the rivals, was handicapped by the long Eastern Shore barrier in the race for coastwise and transatlantic trade, and its particular preoccupation lay in exploiting successfully its proximity to the rich wheat fields of the interior.

Philadelphia was the hindmost of the "Big Four" in any distribution of honors in this competition. Looking backwards, it might find comfort in remembering the latter half of the eighteenth century, when it had for many years stood an easy first among the seaports of America, but in the current rivalry its role was only a defensive one. It bent its efforts toward trying to regain lost trade and to preserve as much of its remaining business as possible from the aggressiveness of New York and Baltimore. Conservative, if not actually "sleepy," Philadelphia fell behind relatively not so much from lack of effort, but because its effort was not well-timed. It had led the way in projects to reach the West, but they were premature and discouraging in their failure. Later it spent fully as much money and energy as the other rival ports in seeking western contacts, but missed a golden opportunity by selecting the wrong methods until too late. At sea, Philadelphia's enterprise, or lack of it, was completely outclassed by all three of the other major competitors.

The rivalry aroused, particularly during the second quarter of the century, an outpouring of pamphlets, newspaper and magazine articles, and oratory. The main theme of each promoter was the alarming threat that, unless his port supported his project, grass would soon be growing on the wharves and merchants would be making reservations at the poorhouse. The "decayed ports" of earlier times were paraded time and again to emphasize this point. While neither Boston, Baltimore, nor Philadelphia ever sank to such a state, there was a striking example of what might happen to a port which lacked initiative and foresight. Norfolk, close to the mouth of Chesapeake Bay, had been endowed by nature with advantages second only to those of New York. In the late colonial period, it had ranked, like Newport, among the leading ports of America, at a time when Baltimore did not even have a custom house. Then, like Newport, it fell behind to such a degree that its commerce and shipping in the nineteenth century were not only relatively but actually lower than they had been in colonial times. Such an example was enough to scare the merchants of other ports into buying stock in one canal or railroad after another.

In the seagoing aspects of the rivalry, Boston, of course, was the leader. In the volume of its shipbuilding and its registered shipping, it usually ranked second only to New York.[1] In 1856 and 1859 it actually went ahead in the total tonnage of new vessels constructed. In registered tonnage, its total averaged from a half to two-thirds of New York's impressive aggregate, while Bostonians held shares in many of the vessels which had "of New York" painted on their sterns. Boston also had a very generous share of the imports entered at New York, for, as we saw, Boston merchants would often send their cargoes from China and elsewhere to be sold at New York, but they derived a larger share of the profits than the customs figures indicate.

In several regions of foreign commercial activity, Boston retained its leadership until the end. At Canton, more vessels generally arrived from Boston than from New York, even though they generally headed for Sandy Hook on the return trip. India, as we have seen, was essentially a Boston sphere of influence, while in the Philippines and the Dutch East Indies, Boston divided the trade about equally with New York. As late as 1860, Boston stood first in the arrivals from the Baltic, from Turkey, and in the much larger volume of trade from British North America. Boston also cut heavily into New York's total in numerous other spheres of trade.[2]

Baltimore's overseas competition was most keenly felt in the trade with Brazil, which had, we recall, a predilection for Howard Street flour. As a result, the coffee cargoes, brought back in exchange, made Baltimore for many years an important center for that commodity. In the odoriferous guano trade from Chile, Baltimore also outranked New York for a while, because it lay closer to the agricultural regions which

[1]See Appendix, i, xii, xiv. [2]See Appendix, vi, viii.

needed such fertilizer. Baltimore's geographical position, of course, did not handicap the port as seriously in its trade with Latin America as with Europe. Baltimore also won seagoing distinction through the speed of the vessels which it built, although the volume of tonnage built or registered could never compare with New York's or Boston's.

Philadelphia, on the other hand, achieved little on any of the distant sea lanes. It ranked with, or ahead of, New York and Boston in the China trade at the very outset of our period, but after the failure of Thompson and the death of Girard, it dropped quite completely from that field. The Cope packets to Liverpool, started in 1821, maintained a quiet and respectable record throughout the period, but were overshadowed in quantity, if not in performance, by the New York sailing liners. Philadelphia had a moderate amount of business in various distant regions but practically everywhere it lagged behind the other rivals. Of all the thousand-odd different articles listed as imports in 1860, the only one in which Philadelphia led the country was German wine. In the coal trade, however, as we know, Philadelphia found one rather prosaic maritime field in which to be prominent. Its enrolled tonnage, often three times as large as the volume registered for foreign trade, included the large number of schooners which carried anthracite along the coast and gave the port its chief seagoing trade.

Turning to the more general and to the internal aspects of the rivalry, we might notice the various successive stages between 1815 and 1860. A search of the London archives revealed some interesting comments of the British consuls, stationed at the various Atlantic ports. They were naturally inclined to be more objective about the trade than were the local residents, and they show clearly that New York's rivals had been caught napping during that first decade after 1815. In 1822, the consul at New York reported "while the commerce of Boston, Philadelphia, Baltimore, and the other principal ports has fallen off, that of New York has increased." In 1819, the widespread slump was reflected by the Baltimore consul, who declared "the trade of this city was never more depressed, pecuniary embarrassment beyond anything ever before known, many failures, more expected, and no one knows who to trust." One year later, some signs of initiative at Charleston were summarized by the consul there as "these do not amount to much." The consul at Philadelphia remarked: "There is a spirit of enterprize in the State of New York for improvements which has not been followed up by its neighbors, . . . at the same time there is in Philadelphia a manifest superiority as regards manufactures." As late as 1824, this same consul declared that the commerce of Philadelphia was "on the decline in all its branches. . . . Commercial men here seem to have lost all their accustomed enterprise."

The completion of the Erie Canal aroused the rivals from their lethargy; and saw the beginning of that flood of propaganda which would continue for years. Not all were as generous in spirit as Hezekiah Niles of Baltimore, who wrote, "The New Yorkers *deserve* success for their enterprise. There is a good spirit among the citizens to advance the business of New York. Let it be imitated—not envied." Whether the motive was emulation, envy, or fear, there was widespread conviction that something must be done, and done quickly. Boston and Philadelphia had already started packet lines to Liverpool, but the opening of the Erie Canal centered attention on the western front. The rivalry of the seaports thus became a major factor in the development of the nation's transportation systems. Legislatures, cities, and individuals were ready to spend millions to divert the golden stream from New York and to engage in any means, fair or foul, to check the efforts of rival ports.

The situation was complicated by the fact that in September, 1825, just one month before the Erie Canal was finished, George Stephenson had run his pioneer locomotive over the Stockton & Darlington railway in England. As early as 1812, John Stevens of the Hoboken family had urged railroads as the proper method of communication with the West, but the canal idea seemed easier to grasp at the moment. Now, however, as one consul reported, the "rage for canals" had become mixed with the "Rail Road mania." New York, enthusiastic over the success of the Erie Canal, did no more than toy with the idea of railroads for many years to come. Boston, after drawing up a comprehensive and very intelligent analysis of the situation created by New York's initiative, wisely rejected any project for a canal to the West and bided its time for its successful railroad venture.

New York's pioneer work in the first decade of peace may be called the "first act" in the rivalry of the ports. What we might term the "second act" centered in the efforts of Philadelphia and Baltimore, during the next decade or so, to cross the Alleghenies to the Ohio.[1]

[1]See Appendix, xxvi, for details of rival routes.

Philadelphia was alarmed at the situation. Its prestige, if not its prosperity, seemed to be at stake. In volume of trade it had dropped in thirty years from first to fourth place. It had, moreover, given place to New York in population. Officially, fears were expressed that unless Pennsylvania "awakes to a true sense of her situation . . . she will be deprived of the sources of public prosperity . . . and instead of regaining the high commercial rank she once held, she will be driven even from her present station in the system of the Confederacy."

The State set to work to remedy the situation, by undertaking the task of connecting Philadelphia with Pittsburgh on the Ohio. Between 1827 and 1835, it spent some fourteen millions, double the cost of the Erie Canal, in building its 395-mile "Main Line" between those two cities. It bungled the affair badly, however, by failing to appreciate the relative merits of canal and railroad. A canal had well served the purposes of New York, as it had been able to take the Alleghenies in flank, but Philadelphia's route to Pittsburgh had to go over mountains at 2200 feet above sea level. Those fourteen million dollars might have been spent to excellent advantage on an all-rail route, which might have done wonders, in the formative years, in diverting the western trade from New York. Instead, the Main Line was a mongrel compromise between rail and canal. The first stage was a railroad from Philadelphia to Columbia on the Susquehanna. Then came a series of canals to the foot of the Alleghenies. The mountains were, of course, too steep for canals; too steep even, it was believed, for the crude locomotives of the day. The unusual solution for spanning the crest between Johnstown and Hollidaysburg was the 36-mile Allegheny Portage Railroad, in which stationary engines hoisted the cars up and lowered them down steep "inclined planes." The rest of the way to Pittsburgh was completed by canals through river valleys. The mixed system was both costly and slow and was never a particularly formidable rival of the Erie Canal.

Baltimore proved more successful during this "second act." While Philadelphia was declining in importance, Baltimore was definitely a port "on the make." Its growth, both in commerce and in population, was surprisingly rapid. Merely a hamlet in the colonial period, it had begun, after the Revolution, to concentrate the rich grain and tobacco trade of the upper Chesapeake region, until then widely scattered. By 1800, it ranked third among all the cities of the Union in population.

Its chief asset in this rivalry was the fact that it lay closer to the West than any of the other ports and that it had an excellent approach up the Potomac valley to Cumberland on the western border of Maryland. Beyond there, to be sure, were the Alleghenies to be crossed at a half-mile above sea level, which was even higher than on Pennsylvania's route. George Washington, in his keen interest to develop this "natural pathway to the West," had warned that, if New York or Philadelphia were to get into contact with the West first, Baltimore would face "the difficulty of diverting trade after connections are once formed." This route had been selected for the national project of the Cumberland Road, begun, we recall, in 1811, and which had for some time given Baltimore a considerable advantage over its rivals. Baltimore now met with energy and intelligence the threat of the Erie Canal, which, despite its greater mileage, was a cheaper and easier route to the West.

Instead of copying Philadelphia's muddled compromise between rail and canal, which was less satisfactory than either system alone, Baltimore was quick to grasp the possibilities of the railroad. Two of its prominent business men visited England in 1826 to examine what Stephenson was doing. On their return, they organized the Baltimore & Ohio Railroad. Unlike the Erie Canal and the Main Line, which were State undertakings, this was a private venture; but the city of Baltimore contributed generously to the stock. On July 4, 1828, Charles Carroll of Carrollton laid the "first stone" of the B. & O., remarking afterwards, "I consider this among the most important acts of my life, second only to my signing the Declaration of Independence, even if it be second to that." At almost the same hour that day, however, John Quincy Adams was officiating at the opening of the Chesapeake & Ohio Canal near Washington, and both were designed for that same route up the Potomac to Cumberland. From the outset the Baltimore & Ohio thus ran into the rivalry which was to hamper the whole course of its construction. Maryland supported both ventures, but Baltimore was more interested in its railroad. Many fights took place among lawyers and laborers before the Baltimore & Ohio received the right to parallel the canal route up the Potomac. By 1835, when the Main Line had been put through to Pittsburgh, the Baltimore & Ohio had progressed as far as Harpers Ferry and was tapping the rich wheat fields of the Shenandoah valley. But another seven years were to elapse before it reached Cumberland and beyond there lay the rough

Alleghenies and hostile, jealous states whose grudging permission was necessary before further extension was possible.

In addition to the rich but distant prize of western trade, the exploitation of the immediate hinterland was a source of port rivalry also. Baltimore, as well as Philadelphia, struggled for the prosperous business of the nearer Susquehanna valley. In this competition, the Chesapeake & Delaware Canal, built in 1829, was a score in Philadelphia's favor, for it gave access to Chesapeake Bay and the Susquehanna outlet. Baltimore, however, successfully countered by pushing a railroad to York, Pennsylvania, and thereby tapping one of the most flourishing agricultural regions in the country. New York likewise invaded Pennsylvania territory by building the Delaware & Hudson and other canals, as we have seen, to bring anthracite direct to New York without having recourse to the port of Philadelphia.

The Panic of 1837 might be taken as the end of the "second act," for it temporarily retarded further developments along the western routes. Neither Philadelphia nor Baltimore had succeeded in offering dangerous competition to the Erie Canal. Philadelphia had, to be sure, been connected with the Ohio River, but by means of a mongrel and inefficient system, whereas Baltimore's railroad had gone only halfway. Baltimore had caught up with Philadelphia in exports by 1832 and was to outdistance the latter port still further, but both, in spite of the millions they had sunk in communications, lagged far behind New York.

In the "third act," during the decade following 1837, New York's source of anxiety lay to the eastward. Seagoing Boston had quietly bided its time during the earlier stages of the competition. Now it suddenly blossomed forth as the first of the four rivals to enjoy through rail communications with the West; and at the very time that the Cunard liners were giving it the best connections with Europe. Boston, moreover, had weathered the Panic of 1837 better than the other three ports. The British consul there wrote in 1842 of "the superior situation in Boston in almost all matters of business, in comparison with New York, Philadelphia, and other rival cities which are suffering under great commercial depression." The real cause for this, he continued, lay in Boston's financial policy, "based on specie and steady principles of banking." As a result, Boston was in a position to drive energetically ahead in the railroad race.

Its immediate objective was Albany, which was not only the eastern terminus of the Erie Canal but also of a series of short railroads, running parallel to the canal. The first of these railroads, the Mohawk & Hudson, had been chartered in 1826, even before the Baltimore & Ohio. The initiative in the building of these parallel roads, which would one day be joined into the New York Central, came chiefly from upstate New York. The State, in granting the charters, made many stringent restrictions to prevent freight competition with the canal; for some time the roads were pretty much limited to passenger traffic. As yet, however, no railroad connected New York and Albany, which meant that during the winter when the Hudson was frozen, flour and other commodities accumulated at Albany with no outlet to the port.

The shrewd Bostonians wanted to tap this supply and realized that they would be able to do so, if they pushed rails across the Berkshires to Albany. They hoped to lure the Erie Canal traffic away from New York and anyway they could give Boston and its surrounding manufacturing region a cheaper supply of western products and an outlet for their own wares by such a rail link. They began with a railroad to Worcester and then extended it by the Western Railroad to the New York state line, where another short road connected it with Albany. As a result of this enterprise, Boston had by 1842 through rail service to Buffalo. Traffic on this future Boston & Albany road increased all through the 'forties and resulted in good dividends.

For almost the only time in the whole period of port rivalry, New York was definitely worried. Long overconfident in its canal, it had neglected railroads. The enterprise and initiative of its great decade seemed to have passed to its rivals. One particularly bad dream haunted New Yorkers during the mid-'forties. They knew that England was planning to repeal its Corn Laws, which would naturally mean a tremendous boom for American grain and flour in the opening of such a new market. They could also foresee that this news might reach America in December or January when the Hudson would be in all probability frozen; and that the Cunarders would undoubtedly be the bearers of the news. Boston would thus not only hear of it first, but might capture all the initial advantages of the boom by rushing through all available western grain by rail to its wharves at a time when 150 miles of river ice would leave New York hopelessly at one side.

The New York legislature, acting in the same spirit which most of the other State bodies showed throughout the rivalry, continued to hamper the rail route from Albany to Buffalo as much as possible by hostile legislation, while New York financiers refused to subscribe to the stock of the Western Railroad. Yet in constructive work, New York did little. The Erie Railroad, chartered in 1832, was even then described as a matter of "delays and disappointments"; and a million dollars invested in its original stages was wasted from a faulty system of building the railroad on wooden piles. The Hudson River Railroad, designed to link New York with Albany, existed only on paper in 1845. Freeman Hunt, editor of the *Merchants' Magazine,* sounded a warning to New York in that year:

The rapid increase of the city in population, wealth, trade and commerce during the last fifteen or twenty years is attributable, for the most part to the opening of the Erie Canal and other internal improvements. At the present moment, the tide of prosperity threatens to be checked by the superior enterprise of other cities on the seaboard, which are beginning to share in the advantages of those improvements, and thus to draw away much of the trade that flowed in this direction. Without great outlays of capital and enterprise, beyond what has already been made, New York must soon lose her proud pre-eminence among the cities of the Union, and add another example to the many the world has already seen, of the rapid decline of a commercial mart, by the operation of a decayed spirit of enterprise and successful competition in other places.

The Massachusetts menace lasted until about 1847, when New York, Philadelphia, and Baltimore all resumed the rivalry in the "fourth act." By 1852, the three cities had their own through rail communications with the West, four great systems all being completed within two years.

We left the Baltimore & Ohio stranded at Cumberland, at the head of the Potomac and on the western edge of Maryland, in the early 'forties. Financial stringency and the tough ridges of the Alleghenies were not its only sources of trouble. New York and Philadelphia were able to build their systems to the West entirely within the boundaries of their respective states. Cumberland, however, was the farthest point to which Maryland might extend support to the Baltimore & Ohio. To reach the Ohio River from there, it was essential to gain the permission of Pennsylvania to run the road up to Pittsburgh or of Virginia to push it through the Alleghenies to Wheeling. Both States were jealous and hostile. In the Virginia legislature Baltimore was referred to as a "foreign" port, while Philadelphia naturally fought such an attempt to divert Pittsburgh's business to Baltimore. Not until 1847 did Virginia finally give its consent; and the Baltimore & Ohio engineers began to wrestle with the problem of piercing the ridges with their irregular contours and 2600-foot maximum altitude.

Even when that obstacle was overcome, and the objective was being approached, Pennsylvania once more interfered in the interesting "Wheeling Bridge Case." Stanton, Lincoln's future Secretary of War, led the argument that the proposed railroad bridge over the Ohio, necessary in order to reach Wheeling on the far bank, would interfere with river navigation. To demonstrate the point, steamers with abnormally high stacks paraded the Ohio, but the Baltimore & Ohio finally won the case. The last rail was laid and the last spike driven in on Christmas Day, 1852, more than twenty-four years after Charles Carroll had laid the first stone. It had taken some twenty millions to build the 379-mile line. Wheeling in itself was not an important terminus, but the road, after emerging from the mountains, sent off a branch further south, which led to an excellent through route from Baltimore to Cincinnati and St. Louis. Baltimore ultimately gained a fair share of western trade, but just before that final spike was driven near Wheeling, Philadelphia had completed its through rail route to Pittsburgh, while New York had finished two rail lines to the West.

Indirectly, the approach of the Baltimore & Ohio through the mountains had hastened Philadelphia's move. The inhabitants of Pittsburgh were angry with the Pennsylvania legislature for denying them the opportunity to have something better than the Main Line for an outlet to the sea. They had no love for Philadelphia and, not being permitted to trade with Baltimore, even flirted with New York. Early in 1846, some of the Pittsburgh papers inserted the notice: "To New Yorkers—Some of our respectable merchants, who have formerly purchased almost wholly in Philadelphia, have requested us to suggest to the merchants of New York, that they will find it to their advantage to visit this city or send on agents to form business acquaintances," the merchants being "fully resolved to withdraw their business wholly from Philadelphia."

At any rate, shortly after this, the legislature incorporated the Pennsylvania Railroad, which began in 1847 to connect Philadelphia with the West by a real railroad over the route of the mongrel Main Line. The original railroad to Columbia was utilized; but along the previous canal routes rails were laid. This was completed, except for the mastering of the crest of the Alleghenies, during 1852. The Allegheny Portage was continued in use for six years more, but eventually the through regular rail connection was completed between Philadelphia and the Ohio River and beyond. In 1857, the old Main Line was put up at auction and the "Pennsy" purchased it at half its original cost. This new connection proved disappointing to Philadelphians, for they found that their port was not getting full advantage of it. Much freight from the West simply snubbed Philadelphia and continued by rail to New York, which thus acquired an extra western route in addition to two of its own.

Those two New York rail connections had put that port ahead in the western race the year before Baltimore and Philadelphia completed their long quest for rail connections across the mountains. President Fillmore had come North for the formal opening of the Erie Railroad on May 14, 1851, while the first train over the new Hudson River Railroad ran up to Albany on October 1 of that same year.

The Hudson River road followed the river up to Albany, where it connected with the series of roads running parallel to the Erie Canal westward to Buffalo. Such a road had been discussed for some time; but nothing definite happened until 1847, the same year which saw the start of the Pennsylvania and the renewed advance of the Baltimore & Ohio beyond Cumberland. The initiative came from Poughkeepsie, which, like the other river towns, felt keenly the lack of adequate communications during the winter months. The route ran along the river's east bank all the way, involving slow and costly work in cutting through the flinty rock of Anthony's Nose and Breakneck Hill, but resulting in a "water level route" almost without grades. The first train made the run in five hours, whereas the fastest of the steamboats required more than seven hours. Just after our period, in the 'sixties, Cornelius Vanderbilt would weld this new run with the old Albany-Buffalo roads into a single New York Central and Hudson River Railroad; but, in the meantime, New York enjoyed its new all-the-year connection with Lake Erie over the route by which the Erie Canal traffic had come for more than a quarter century.

The other New York venture, which reached completion a few months earlier, was the Erie Railroad. Instead of being a gradual assembling of little lines, it had been planned from the first as a single system. From the beginning, as we have noticed, it had encountered constant financial difficulties. Its route was shorter than the Hudson

River one, for it skirted the southwestern edge of the State. It had been promoted in deference to the inhabitants of Binghamton, Elmira, and other towns of the "southern tier," who were jealous of the benefits which Rochester, Syracuse, and the more northern communities had been gaining from the expenditures of State funds in the Erie Canal. Almost no other towns of any size lay along the whole 446 miles of the Erie's route. This meant that there would be little local freight for the road, which would consequently be chiefly dependent on through business. In order to avoid the jealous action of the legislatures of Pennsylvania and New Jersey, the Erie's original route lay entirely in New York, from Dunkirk out on Lake Erie in the northwest corner of the State, to Piermont, near Nyack-on-the-Hudson, about 25 miles above New York. At Piermont, a great stone pier ran out into the river so that the steamboats might pick up the passengers and freight for New York City. Later, the railroad secured a place on the New Jersey waterfront across the Hudson from New York City. It was also extended along the lake shore beyond Dunkirk to Erie, Pennsylvania. The road suffered from chronic financial troubles which made it a byword in railroad circles. Nevertheless, it gave New York port a good, direct freight route to the Great Lakes.

These various roads to the West did not stop at their original objectives. By 1852, when the four big lines were completed, connecting ones were being extended to Chicago and to other centers of importance.

Once more New York had triumphed. The Baltimore & Ohio and the Pennsylvania had not been completed in time to divert the long-established western connections with New York. The New York railroads simply took over gradually the traffic which had travelled the Erie Canal. The advertising columns of the Cincinnati newspapers, for instance, during the early 'fifties, contained more advertisements of New York commission merchants than of those from all the other ports combined. It was reported that in 1858 the Pennsylvania brought 141,000 tons of western freight to tidewater, exceeded in turn by the Baltimore & Ohio at 171,000, the Erie at 224,000, and the New York Central at 229,000, while the Erie Canal with its 1,273,000 tons still held first place with a heavier total than all four railroads combined.[1]

The West was not the only direction in which New York was sustaining its commanding position. As we have already seen, Boston and

[1] See Appendix, xviii.

Philadelphia found themselves sidetracked as the termini respectively of the Cunard and Inman steamship lines. In 1848, it was New York's good fortune that the Cunard Line was shifted from Boston to meet the coming competition of the Collins Line and that of other American steamships. This loss of the advantage it had enjoyed as the sole western terminus of the Cunarders put Boston behind in the port rivalry. Philadelphia, too, suffered when the British line of iron screw Inman steamships, which had been coming there for a while in the 'fifties, extended their western terminus to New York before that decade was over.

Thus, on the eve of the Civil War, New York's prosperity had reached a point which was certainly enough to incite the envy of its rivals. In spite of all that they had been able to accomplish, its lead had increased steadily. By 1860 New York was handling two-thirds of all the nation's imports and one-third of its exports. The combined imports of Boston, Philadelphia, and Baltimore were less than New York's imports of textiles alone. Those three rivals together exported less grain and meat products than did New York, whose hold on the West had not been seriously affected by the Baltimore & Ohio, the Boston & Albany, and the Pennsylvania roads, all of which had been begun with such high hopes. In fact, out of well over a thousand individual items distinguished in the customs reports, New York ranked first among the American seaports in all except seven articles of domestic export and twenty-four imported commodities. In the value of its imports and exports, as well as in the volume of shipping which entered and cleared, New York not only stood an easy first among American ports; but in all the world only London and Liverpool exceeded it. Although the decline of American shipping, already under way, would gravely affect the little ports down east after the Civil War, New York would still retain its commanding share of the nation's commerce, under whatever flag the cargoes might arrive or depart. World primacy still lay sixty-odd years in the future; but in the meantime New York waxed steadily greater in trade, wealth, and population, thanks to the well-timed enterprise of its citizens in the decade following 1815.

APPENDICES

BIBLIOGRAPHY

INDEX

I. RELATIVE MARITIME ACTIVITY OF PRINCIPAL PORTS, c. 1821–1860

Showing percentage of national total for the period; based principally upon annual tables in the following appendices.

	IMPORTS (STATE)	TOTAL EXPORTS (STATE)	DOMESTIC EXPORTS (STATE)	FOREIGN REEXPORTS (STATE)	TONNAGE ENTERED	TONNAGE CLEARED	REGISTERED TONNAGE	ENROLLED & LICENSED TONNAGE	TOTAL STEAM TONNAGE (1828–1860)	REGISTERED STEAM TONNAGE (1828–1860)	SHIPBUILDING TONNAGE (1833–1860)	IMMIGRATION
CHIEF GENERAL PORTS												
New York	60.3	32.9	29.5	58.6	26.0	21.2	26.8	21.0	21.0	75.9	15.4	68.6
Boston	15.7	8.4	6.6	21.9	10.0	9.1	16.9	3.7	.9	.7	9.4	7.1
Philadelphia	7.5	3.6	3.2	8.3	3.6	2.9	4.7	5.7	3.0	-	4.9	4.4
Baltimore	3.2	3.7	4.2	3.0	3.0	3.2	5.1	3.1	2.7	.1	4.0	4.2
COTTON PORTS												
New Orleans	6.6	24.5	26.9	7.3	9.0	10.8	4.3	5.2	20.4	8.6	-	10.2
Charleston	.9	6.7	7.9	-	2.3	3.3	1.3	1.1	1.3	1.6	-	.4
Savannah	.3	4.0	4.6	-	1.4	2.1	.8	.4	1.2	.4	-	-
Mobile	.3	6.3	7.6	-	1.8	2.7	.5	.9	2.7	-	-	-
OTHER PORTS												
Portland	(.3)	(.5)	(.5)	(.9)	1.2	1.7	3.8	1.3	-	-	3.7	.4
Bath	-	-	-	-	-	-	4.1	1.3	-	-	7.3	-
Salem	(.4)	(.4)	(.4)	(.4)	.7	.7	1.5	.7	-	-	-	-
Norfolk	-	(.1)	(.1)	-	.7	.7	.6	.8	-	-	-	.1

The imports and exports of the last four ports cannot be determined before 1856 because, unlike the other eight ports, they represented only a fraction of their respective state totals. The figures given in parentheses represent their share in 1860. The concentration of the national maritime activity at these few ports can be appreciated when it is realized that there were 92 separate customs districts, some of which included several ports, in 1821 and 79 in 1860. It will be noted that Boston ranked second in five of the above categories, New Orleans in six, and Philadelphia in one.

APPENDIX II

EXPORTS OF PRINCIPAL STATES

Compiled from annual *Reports on Commerce and Navigation*

(Millions of Dollars)

	TOTAL U.S.	CHIEF GENERAL PORTS				COTTON PORTS				OTHER STATES				
		NEW YORK (N.Y.City)	MASS. (Boston)	PA. (Philadelphia)	MD. (Baltimore)	LA. (New Orleans)	S.C. (Charleston)	GA. (Savannah)	ALA. (Mobile)	MAINE (Portland Quoddy)	VA. (Richmond, Norfolk)	FLA.	TEXAS	CALIF. (San Francisco)
1815	52	10	5	4	5	5	6	4			6			
1816	81	19	10	7	7	5	10	7			8			
1817	87	18	11	8	8	9	10	8			5			
1818	93	17	11	8	7	12	11	11	-		7			
1819	70	13	11	6	5	9	8	6	-		4			
1820	69	13	11	5	6	7	8	6	-	1	4			
1821	64	13	12	7	3	7	7	6	-	1	3			
1822	72	17	12	9	4	7	7	5	-	1	3	-		
1823	74	19	13	9	6	7	6	4	-	-	4	-		
1824	75	22	10	9	4	7	8	4	-	-	3	-		
1825	99	35	11	11	4	12	11	4	-	1	4	-		
1826	77	21	10	8	4	10	7	4	1	1	4	-		
1827	82	23	10	7	4	11	8	4	1	1	4	-		
1828	72	22	9	6	4	11	6	3	1	1	3	-		
1829	72	20	8	4	4	12	8	4	1	-	3	-		
1830	73	19	7	4	3	15	7	5	2	-	4	-		
1831	81	25	7	5	4	16	6	3	2	-	4	-		
1832	87	26	11	3	4	16	7	5	2	-	4	-		
1833	90	25	9	4	4	18	8	6	4	1	4	-		
1834	104	25	10	3	4	26	11	7	5	-	5	-		
1835	121	30	10	3	3	36	11	8	7	1	6	-		
1836	128	28	10	3	3	37	13	10	11	-	6	-		
1837	117	27	9	3	3	35	11	8	9	-	3	-		
1838	108	23	9	3	4	31	11	8	9	-	3	-		
1839	121	33	9	5	4	33	10	5	10	-	5	-		
1840	132	34	10	6	5	34	10	6	12	1	4	1		
1841	121	33	11	5	4	34	8	3	10	1	5	-		
1842	104	27	9	3	4	28	7	4	9	1	3	-		
1843 *	84	16	6	2	2	27	7	4	11	-	1	-		
1844	111	32	9	3	5	30	7	4	9	1	2	1		
1845	114	36	10	3	5	27	8	4	10	1	2	1		
1846	113	36	10	4	6	31	6	2	5	1	3	-		
1847	158	49	11	8	9	42	10	5	9	1	5	1		
1848	154	53	13	5	7	40	8	3	11	1	3	1	-	
1849	145	45	10	5	8	37	9	6	12	1	3	2	-	
1850	151	52	10	4	6	38	11	7	10	1	3	2	-	
1851	218	86	12	5	5	54	15	9	18	1	3	3	-	
1852	209	87	16	5	6	49	11	4	17	1	2	2	-	
1853	230	78	19	6	7	68	15	7	16	2	3	1	1	-
1854	275	122	21	10	11	60	11	4	13	2	4	3	1	3
1855	275	113	28	6	10	55	12	7	14	4	4	1	-	8
1856	326	119	29	7	11	80	17	8	23	2	5	1	1	10
1857	362	134	30	7	13	91	16	10	20	3	7	3	1	12
1858	324	108	22	6	10	88	16	9	21	2	7	1	2	15
1859	356	117	18	5	9	101	17	15	28	3	6	3	3	15
1860	400	145	17	5	9	107	21	18	38	3	5	1	6	10

* 9-month period; shift from Sept. 30 to June 30 as end of fiscal year. No satisfactory figures for individual ports exist before 1856; a few such lists which have been published contain obvious discrepancies. The figures for the first eight major states, except Massachusetts, are virtually those of their chief port. The Massachusetts figures include Maine to 1820, as well as Salem and other ports beside Boston, which had about 85% to 90% of the total. About 10% of the later New York figures represent the lake trade with Canada.

APPENDIX III

IMPORTS OF PRINCIPAL STATES

Compiled from annual *Reports on Commerce and Navigation*

(Millions of Dollars)

	TOTAL U.S.	CHIEF GENERAL PORTS				COTTON PORTS				OTHER STATES	
		NEW YORK (N.Y.City)	MASS. (Boston)	PA. (Philadelphia)	MD. (Baltimore)	LA. (New Orleans)	S.C. (Charleston)	GA. (Savannah)	ALA. (Mobile)	MAINE (Portland Quoddy)	CALIF. (San Francisco)
1815	113										
1816	147										
1817	99										
1818	121										
1819	87										
1820	74										
1821	62	23	14	8	4	3	3	1	-	-	
1822	83	35	18	11	4	3	2	-	-	-	
1823	77	29	17	13	4	4	2	-	-	-	
1824	80	36	15	11	4	4	2	-	-	-	
1825	96	49	15	15	4	4	1	-	-	1	
1826	84	38	17	13	4	4	1	-	-	1	
1827	79	38	13	11	4	4	1	-	-	1	
1828	88	41	15	12	5	6	1	-	-	1	
1829	74	34	12	10	4	6	1	-	-	-	
1830	70	35	10	8	4	7	1	-	-	-	
1831	103	57	14	12	4	9	1	-	-	-	
1832	101	53	18	10	4	8	1	-	-	1	
1833	108	55	19	10	5	9	1	-	-	1	
1834	126	73	17	10	4	13	1	-	-	1	
1835	149	88	19	12	5	17	1	-	-	-	
1836	189	118	25	15	7	15	2	-	-	-	
1837	140	79	19	11	7	14	2	-	-	-	
1838	113	68	13	9	5	9	2	-	-	-	
1839	162	99	19	15	6	12	3	-	-	-	
1840	107	60	16	8	4	10	2	-	-	-	
1841	127	75	20	10	6	10	1	-	-	-	
1842	100	57	17	7	4	8	1	-	-	-	
1843 *	64	31	16	2	2	8	1	-	-	-	
1844	108	65	20	7	3	7	1	-	-	-	
1845	117	70	22	8	3	7	1	-	-	-	
1846	121	74	24	7	4	7	-	-	-	-	
1847	146	84	34	9	4	9	1	-	-	-	
1848	154	94	28	12	5	9	1	-	-	-	
1849	147	92	24	10	4	10	1	-	-	-	
1850	178	111	30	12	6	10	1	-	-	-	-
1851	220	111	32	14	6	12	2	-	-	1	6
1852	212	132	33	14	6	12	2	-	-	1	-
1853	267	178	41	18	6	13	1	-	-	1	8
1854	304	195	48	21	6	14	1	-	-	2	5
1855	261	164	45	15	7	12	1	-	-	2	
1856	314	210	43	16	9	16	1	-	-	1	7
1857	360	236	47	17	10	24	2	-	-	2	9
1858	282	178	42	12	8	19	2	-	-	1	8
1859	338	229	43	14	9	18	1	-	-	2	11
1860	362	248	41	14	9	22	1	-	1	1	9

* 9-month period. In this, as in other tables, the figures have been reduced to millions or thousands by omitting the final digits rather than by giving the nearest million. Thus, 7,990,000 would appear as "7" rather than "8." A dash (—) indicates an amount less than a single unit of measurement. Import figures by states not available before 1821, but can be estimated approximately on basis of customs duties.

APPENDIX IV

TONNAGE ENTERED FROM FOREIGN COUNTRIES AT PRINCIPAL POI

Compiled from annual *Reports on Commerce and Navigation*

(Thousands of Tons)

		CHIEF GENERAL PORTS				COTTON PORTS				OTHER PORTS				
	TOTAL U.S.	NEW YORK	BOSTON	PHILADELPHIA	BALTIMORE	NEW ORLEANS	CHARLESTON	SAVANNAH	MOBILE	QUODDY	PORTLAND	SALEM	NORFOLK	
1821	846	(170)	(160)	(74)	(72)	(81)	(49)	(35)	-					
1822	888	(240)	(184)	(85)	(65)	(51)	(46)	(20)	(4)					
1823	894	(226)	(202)	(78)	(62)	(69)	(53)	(24)	(4)					
1824	952	(247)	(187)	(81)	(62)	(87)	(57)	(29)	(12)					
1825	973	(294)	(177)	(88)	(68)	(72)	(45)	(16)	(6)					
1826	1047	274	139	87	72	72	56	21	14					
1827	1055	287	123	78	59	97	64	29	17	12	40	17	18	
1828	1018	284	117	88	60	116	50	20	17	13	34	17	9	
1829	1003	270	122	73	58	100	51	20	17	14	30	18	11	
1830	1099	305	113	77	61	118	72	26	15	24	26	17	14	
1831	1204	333	126	80	65	131	53	28	21	53	33	13	17	
1832	1342	400	157	81	71	125	52	29	22	69	40	16	23	
1833	1608	420	178	92	82	133	49	31	21	101	37	16	21	
1834	1642	443	183	83	65	136	54	26	18	101	33	14	18	
1835	1993	465	194	78	63	156	53	35	30	65	30	10	19	
1836	1935	534	224	84	70	146	56	32	31	69	30	10	14	
1837	2065	579	242	91	96	136	58	32	27	75	25	14	14	
1838	1895	422	198	83	77	182	64	46	39	69	33	10	14	
1839	2116	563	230	111	78	183	54	29	39	67	30	15	14	
1840	2289	545	245	87	82	255	60	63	66	80	24	18	19	
1841	2368	547	291	99	89	264	54	46	60	58	27	14	21	
1842	2242	570	276	94	86	255	63	40	57	57	26	20	16	
1843*	1678	312	144	47	51	351	79	61	105	39	14	11	9	
1844	2894	576	288	89	82	310	74	46	80	58	29	18	13	
1845	2946	579	308	91	80	363	71	48	110	59	34	20	7	
1846	3110	655	318	88	89	315	56	57	77	72	37	23	9	
1847	3321	853	325	139	123	402	74	48	59	70	28	20	42	
1848	3798	932	432	119	102	366	61	37	61	59	35	26	13	
1849	4368	1117	451	142	110	425	98	64	87	74	41	33	9	
1850	4348	1145	478	132	99	349	96	57	96	58	64	36	20	13
1851	4993	1448	512	159	113	328	92	47	55	62	67	47	12	24
1852	5292	1699	518	178	128	423	101	49	87	77	57	40	20	23
1853	6281	1755	582	183	119	511	94	52	79	106	62	45	12	25
1854	5884	1840	653	191	156	492	89	53	86	115	43	39	57	20
1855	5945	1735	707	185	165	435	88	47	69	107	67	38	45	17
1856	6872	1681	682	173	153	663	121	70	169	128	53	43	32	16
1857	7186	2035	714	189	163	612	126	108	107	82	69	43	84	14
1858	6605	1694	665	156	156	583	126	66	115	74	74	36	73	14
1859	7806	1890	734	180	189	659	129	86	131	69	89	34	62	22
1860	8275	1973	718	185	186	632	126	92	160	73	115	31	67	23

* 9-month period; shift from Sept. 30 to June 30 as end of fiscal year. Figures in parentheses, 1821–25 state rather than port totals, but were almost the same.

392

TONNAGE CLEARED FOR FOREIGN COUNTRIES AT PRINCIPAL PORTS
Compiled from annual *Reports on Commerce and Navigation*

(Thousands of Tons)

	TOTAL U.S.	CHIEF GENERAL PORTS				COTTON PORTS				OTHER PORTS					
		NEW YORK	BOSTON	PHILADELPHIA	BALTIMORE	NEW ORLEANS	CHARLESTON	SAVANNAH	MOBILE	QUODDY	PORTLAND	SALEM	NORFOLK	RICHMOND	SAN FRANCISCO
1821	888	(168)	(130)	(73)	(66)	(74)	(64)	(56)							
1822	911	(203)	(141)	(76)	(68)	(58)	(63)	(43)	(2)						
1823	929	(216)	(143)	(80)	(70)	(84)	(78)	(47)	(2)						
1824	1021	(240)	(139)	(82)	(79)	(76)	(79)	(48)	(8)						
1825	1055	(275)	(150)	(84)	(70)	(77)	(74)	(28)	(10)						
1826	1052	227	94	73	64	91	82	44	17						
1827	1111	262	89	72	70	120	93	50	16	23	42	18	19		
1828	1048	242	92	67	64	124	73	31	20	21	47	15	17		
1829	1077	233	92	57	61	120	90	55	19	22	37	17	19		
1830	1105	243	93	67	58	142	72	58	26	33	38	19	15		
1831	1244	276	102	72	75	150	77	48	25	54	42	16	23		
1832	1362	309	148	60	64	147	89	63	31	67	43	20	30		
1833	1639	333	157	71	71	146	86	62	38	101	42	17	40		
1834	1711	329	156	62	58	183	100	60	39	101	41	15	30	24	
1835	2031	366	181	68	68	196	82	56	45	65	44	14	28	19	
1836	1990	401	204	64	57	195	96	66	52	67	53	15	27	24	
1837	2022	410	184	63	74	221	88	61	64	72	50	17	24	17	
1838	2012	346	163	62	66	259	106	80	82	63	46	13	24	17	
1839	2089	446	195	77	68	232	81	48	65	61	45	16	23	20	
1840	2353	408	181	83	93	350	105	86	118	79	38	16	20	24	
1841	2371	405	234	83	87	317	87	55	83	56	42	16	25	31	
1842	2276	451	225	78	82	317	95	61	89	57	41	18	22	25	
1843*	1792	285	140	47	56	373	112	84	135	39	28	14	19	14	
1844	2917	498	257	79	91	338	93	62	101	61	42	20	21	24	
1845	2984	483	266	76	92	373	117	75	142	70	40	19	20	18	
1846	3189	553	290	84	119	348	75	58	97	75	50	23	23	29	
1847	3378	758	281	143	169	440	91	55	66	75	44	23	53	24	
1848	3865	788	394	98	120	436	89	49	116	68	47	27	24	28	
1849	4429	931	414	120	149	487	143	84	148	79	60	34	24	27	
1850	4361	982	437	111	126	369	121	72	112	63	77	35	26	24	180
1851	5130	1230	494	140	105	421	138	69	121	66	77	45	26	24	422
1852	5278	1279	510	139	128	544	140	61	163	81	69	40	24	22	352
1853	6065	1384	590	151	143	630	131	81	143	108	77	45	23	27	442
1854	6019	1598	613	170	191	603	123	68	118	125	56	37	31	24	421
1855	6179	1445	687	142	158	604	140	93	145	123	103	40	33	28	322
1856	7000	1520	647	129	159	773	161	87	213	142	84	43	19	36	305
1857	7070	1756	666	141	188	728	143	120	156	97	104	38	22	47	262
1858	6802	1460	612	119	164	733	145	88	149	83	116	35	26	53	225
1859	7915	1476	642	125	171	808	161	138	206	81	130	30	25	53	354
1860	8789	1678	633	135	174	894	179	149	255	91	155	32	23	51	351

* See notes, opposite table.
  The effect of the cotton triangle is evident in comparing arrivals and clearances; at New York, the arrivals outnumbered the clearances; at the cotton ports the reverse was true. The same phenomenon shows in the New York-San Francisco-China-New York clipper runs, the "coastwise" clearances for California not showing in this list.

FOREIGN AND COASTWISE ARRIVALS AT NEW YORK, BOSTON, AND PHILADELPHIA, 1835

In the absence of ready-made figures for the period, based on the activity of particular ports especially in the coasting trade, this represents an attempt to indicate the relative volume. Absolute figures are out of the question in view of the available material.

The New York foreign arrivals, both in numbers and tonnage, are alone based on official figures, being compiled from the N. Y. customs MSS., Foreign Arrivals, vol. XXVIII; the customs Coastwise Arrivals are not complete enough to indicate more than the average size of the various types of vessels employed. The remaining figures are tabulated from individual arrivals listed in the *Shipping and Commercial List*, checked against marine news in local newspapers.

The tonnage estimates are calculated on the average size of each type of vessel used in particular fields of trade, as indicated in the customs records.

Local coastwise shipping arrivals were seldom reported fully in the marine news; in order to have a fair basis of comparison between the three major ports, the *arrivals from the same state and the two adjacent states are omitted.*

Tonnage figures represent *thousands of tons*, with one decimal. The figures cover the calendar year; whereas the official statistics are based on the fiscal year ending September 30.

FOREIGN	TONNAGE ESTIMATED			NEW YORK					BOSTON					PHILADELPHIA				
	N.Y.	Boston	Phila	Ships	Bks	Bgs	Sch	Sl	Ships	Bks	Bgs	Sch	Sl	Ships	Bks	Bgs	Sch	Sl
Liverpool	87.1	16.4	16.5	168	7	5	1		38	2				34	6	5		
London	23.4	3.2	.5	44	7	1			7		5			1		1		
Greenock	6.7			13	4	9												
Dundee	3.2			2	2	5												
Bristol	2.9	.6	.3	7	1	1				1	2					2		
Newport	1.6	.5	.5	1	3	2					3					3		
Newcastle	1.6	1.2	.1	1	2	4			1		5					1		
Gt.Brit.misc.	6.2	1.4		4	5	13	2		1	1	5							
Belfast	2.0			5		1												
Londonderry	.9		2.0	1	1	1	1							4	1	2		
Ireland,misc.	1.7				1	8												
Havre	34.2	.6		70		1			2									
Marseilles	9.0	1.2	1.2	8	3	25	1				7			2		3		
Bordeaux	3.6	.1	1.6	2	2	14					1				1	8		
Rochelle	3.2	.5	.1	1	1	16					3					1		
Cette	1.5			1		7												
Amsterdam	3.5	1.0	.6	3	1	10	1		1		4				2	1		
Rotterdam	3.4	1.0	.3	1	1	10					6			1				
Antwerp	2.6			4		6												
Flushing		.1									1							
Bremen	6.8			10	7	8	1											
Hamburg	4.9	.7	.2	7	2	7			2		1					1		1
Gothenburg	4.2	4.9		2	1	11	1		3	7	12							
Stockholm	3.3	1.2		5	1	8			2		3							
Gefle	2.3			3	3	3												
Cronstadt (St.P.)	3.9	6.5	.3	10	1	1			6	5	18			1				
Baltic,misc.	1.1	.6		1	1	2	1			1	2							
Archangel		.1									1							
Oporto	1.3		.3			6	2									2		
Lisbon	.9	.2	.3		1	4				1						2		
Setubal (St.Ubes)			1.9						3	2	2							
Malaga	6.7	3.5	1.5	2	1	32	3			2	17					9		
Cadiz	4.4	2.2	1.1	4	1	11	1		5		3			1	1	3		
Spain,misc.	.4	.7		1				1			4							
Gibraltar	1.6	.1	.1	1		6	1				1					1		
Palermo	3.4	4.6	.1	3	1	12			1	3	20					1		
Messina	2.8	2.4	.5	1	1	12			2		10					3		
Leghorn	2.5	1.7	.1	2		10			1		8					1		
Italy,misc.		.7							1		3							

FOREIGN,Ctd	TONNAGE			NEW YORK					BOSTON					PHILADELPHIA				
	N.Y.	Boston	Phila	Ships	Bks	Bgs	Sch	Sl	Ships	Bks	Bgs	Sch	Sl	Ships	Bks	Bgs	Sch	Sl
Trieste	3.9	.5	.1	4	1	11					3			1				
Malta		.1									1							
Syra		.1									1							
Smyrna	.5	1.8				3			1		9							
Madeira	1.8		.4	2	1	8									1	1		
Teneriffe	1.4	.8	.5	1		4	3		1		3			1	1			
Other Canaries	1.0	.1				5					1							
Azores	.6	1.0				2	2				6							
Cape Verdes	.1	.1				1					1							
Mogador	.5					4												
Africa, misc.	2.1	.7				10	4		1		2							
Canton	9.9	2.4	.4	24	2				7					1				
Calcutta	.3	3.3	1.6	1					8						4			
Manila	.8	1.9	.4	2		2			4	1					1			
Sumatra	1.4	.4		3		1			1									
Batavia	.3	.4	1.2	1					1					3	1			
Singapore		.4	.4						1					1				
Hawaii	.2	.2				1			1									
whaling	1.9	.4		5	1				2									
San Diego, Cal.		.6							2									
Mazatlan	1.0			1		2												
Guyaquil	.7			1		2												
Valparaiso	.9	.6		3		1			1	1								
'Iquique		.4							1		1							
Coquimbo		.3							1									
Buenos Aires	3.7	1.4	.2	3	2	10			1	1	5			1				
Montevideo	.5		.1			3								1				
Rio de Janeiro	7.1	1.8	3.2	14	3	8			2	1	5			5	1	7		
Rio Grande do Sul	2.2	2.2	.1			13				2	10					1		
Pernambuco	1.0	1.2	1.8			5					7					10	1	
Para	1.0					4	4											
Bahia	.6	.3			1	2					2							
Maranhao	.6					2	2											
Brazil, misc.	.6	.1		1		3					1							
Surinam(DutchGuiana)		5.5							1		30							
British Guiana	.9	.1				7					1							
Cartagena	1.8					11	3											
Maracaibo	1.3		.9			5	5									5	1	
LaCuaira	1.2	1.1	2.8			6	3				6	1				14	4	
Puerto Cabello	1.0	.8				6	3				3	3						
Angostura	.4					3												
Colombia-Venez.misc	1.0	.3	.2		1	4	1				2					1	1	
Honduras	2.7	.5			1	12	5		1	7	1							
Central Am., misc.	.6	.7				2	4				4							
Vera Cruz	5.9			6	8	7	2											
Sisal	3.6			2		12	12											
Tabasco	1.7					3	17											
Tampico	1.1	.1	.1			3	8				1						1	
Mazatlan(of.Pacific)																		
Mexico, misc.	3.5	.2	.1	1	2	11	7		1		1					1		
Havana	13.7	16.3	3.1	16	4	40	8		11	7	63	4		1	1	9	9	
Matanzas	10.6	9.9	2.1	2	2	49	6		3	6	42					9	5	
Trinidad de Cuba	5.0	6.4	5.9	2	1	21	6			4	29	3			5	24	4	
Manzanilla	2.2	3.3				9	4			2	15	2						
Neuvitas	2.1	.1		1		8	3				1							
Santiago de Cuba	.9	.4	1.2			4	3				2	1				7		
Cuba, misc.	1.6	.9	.4			6	7				3	4				3		

FOREIGN,Ctd	TONNAGE			NEW YORK					BOSTON					PHILADELPHIA				
	N.Y.	Boston	Phila	Ships	Bks	Bgs	Sch	Sl	Ships	Bks	Bgs	Sch	Sl	Ships	Bks	Bgs	Sch	Sl
Ponce,Puerto Rico	4.4	.3	1.5	2		18	7				2			1		6		
Guayama "	4.3	.3		4		18	5				2							
San Juan "	1.9	.5	1.4	1		3	10					5				7	2	
Mayaguez "	1.4	.9	2.5			6	5				4	2				11	6	
Puerto Rico,misc.	4.2	.5	.3	1		16	13				2	2				1	2	
Port au Prince	4.4	1.3	1.0			25	5		1		4	13				6		
Santo Domingo city	3.7	2.0				12	15				11	1						
Porto Plata	2.1					9	4											
Jacmel	1.9	2.2				6	10				2	10						
Gonaive	1.2	.6				2	10				2	3						
Aux Cayes	1.2	1.7				2	10				3	9						
Cap Haitien	.6	2.0	.1			3	3		2		13					1		
Haiti, misc.	.7	1.2	.3			1	5				4	5				2		
St.Croix	7.3	1.6	.5			35	14				5	7				3		
St.Thomas	3.0	.3	2.5	4	1	9	3				1	2				13	3	
Curacoa	2.8		.3			13	8				2					2		
Guadeloupe	1.5	.4	.3	5							1	3		1				
Martinique	1.1	.3		1		3	3				2							
West Indies,misc.	.6	.1					8					1						
Jamaica	8.1		.8	14		21	8									5		
British W.I.,misc.	1.8	.5	.3		1	8	2	1			1	4				2		
Turks Island	9.5	1.0	.5	6	3	31	7			2	2	2		1		1		
Bahamas	3.7	1.8	.9			11	16	2	1	1	3	7				2	5	1
Bermuda	1.7	.2				2	16				1	1						
St.Johns, Newf.	2.0	.8	.1			10	3				2	5					1	
King's Cove, Newf.	.1						1											
Labrador		.3										3						
Quebec	.1	.1					1					1						
Prince Edward Isl.		.2										2						
Halifax, N.S.	5.1	5.9	.8			24	9				20	23				3	3	
Windsor, "	3.3	5.1				10	15				10	32						
Sydney, " (C.B.)	1.6	4.9	.1			8	2		1	2	14	15				1		
Pictou, "	1.2	4.0	.1	1		4	2				7	27				1		
Yarmouth "	.9	2.2				1	7					21						
Digby "	.3	1.5				1	2					16						
Cumberland "	.4	1.5				1	3					15						
Annapolis "	.2	1.5					2					15						
Liverpool "	.1	1.5					1					15						
Bridgeport " (C.B.)		1.2									1	10						
Nova Scotia,misc.	2.1	2.2			1	2	15					21						
St.John, N.B.	6.0	6.4	2.4		1	13	20				5	53				3	18	
St.Andrews (Quoddy)		1.8	.4								1	16					4	
N.B. Misc.		.5	.3				5					3						
"LESSER COASTERS"																		
Eastport (Quoddy)	6.4	5.5	5.2			17	35				3	48				9	35	
Lubec "	9.4	1.9	3.8			27	45				1	13	6			9	12	
Calais "	3.8	3.7	1.4			5	28				7	24				4	7	
Machias	4.9	1.3	.3			2	43	1			1	11				1	2	
Bangor	2.5	8.8	1.7			7	13				22	48				4	10	
Camden	2.8	.2				1	24				1	1						
Thomaston	4.7	1.3				3	40				1	11						
Bath	3.2	6.6	.6			6	20	1	1		4	53					6	
Hallowell	1.4	4.9				2	10					47					5	
Portland	4.2	12.4	1.4			2	37	1		1	3	101				1	12	
Maine, misc.	4.3	27.0	1.2			4	33	3	1	1	19	217	3			1	10	
Portsmouth, N.H.	1.1		1.2				10	1									12	
Newburyport,Mass.	.6		3.9				6										38	
Salem	5.6		2.5				54										24	

	N.Y.	Boston	Phila	Ships	Bks	Bgs	Sch	Sl	Ships	Bks	Bgs	Sch	Sl	Ships	Bks	Bgs	Sch	Sl
Boston	52.7		35.0	2		16	469	7								119	135	1
New Bedford	1.7		4.4				6	23									41	2
Cape Cod	3.0		.1.0				27	5									10	
Nantucket	.7		1.3				4	7									12	1
Mass. misc.	3.9		1.9			3	37	4								2	15	1
Providence #	2.7		6.4	1		2	7	27								3	55	2
Rhode Island,misc.	1.0		.7	1			6	1								1	5	
Hartford		1.1	3.9									9	3				37	1
New Haven		.2	2.0									2				2	16	1
Connecticut,misc.		.2	2.4									2	1			1	21	1
New York City		70.3	39.0						6	2	35	600	24	5	1	25	372	116
Albany		13.8	2.8									128	9				27	
Kingston, N.Y.		4.5									6	33						
Hudson River,misc.		1.4	.3									14					3	
Long Island, misc.		.1										1						
New Jersey, misc.		.9										9						
Philadelphia	42.3	54.1		1	2	8	354	57		1	174	335	9					
Delaware,misc.	2.2	1.5					21					14	1					
Norfolk	10.2	4.3	3.5			5	89				10	26	1				32	3
Baltimore	14.8	22.8	3.8			31	141				110	34					24	26
Richmond	17.3	8.5	5.9	1		4	165				16	54	1			1	55	7
Petersburg	4.3	.6	.4				41					6					4	1
Alexandria	5.1	5.2	.5			2	45	1			21	15				1		7
Georgetown (D.C.)	2.9	.6	.1			3	23					6					1	1
Fredericksburg	.8	5.7					8				3	50						
York River	3.2	.2					30	1			1	1						
Snow Hill	3.1		.2				29	1									2	
Folly Landing	3.5		.1				34										1	
"Virginia"	10.7						104	4										
Chesapeake, misc.	6.2	2.0	1.1				60	1			2	16					9	4
Wilmington, N.C.	14.5	3.8	4.2			29	90				9	22				6	31	
Washington "	8.3	6.5	1.6			2	76				7	51				1	14	1
Newbern	11.3		.7			2	105										7	
Edenton	4.2					6	30											
Elizabeth City	2.3	.8					22	1				8						
Swansboro	2.6	.3	.6			1	24					3					6	
NorthCarolina,misc.	8.2	1.4	.5			3	76					14					5	
"MAJOR COASTERS"																		
Georgetown, S.C.	5.1						24	9										
Charleston, S.C. *	28.8	12.2	5.2	58		42	14	1	9	14	26	8	1			18	17	
Savannah, Ga.	26.8	4.1	5.1	44	6	45	20	3	3		13	8				25	7	
Darien, Ga.	4.3		.5			17	13									2	2	
St.Mary's,Ga.	.6	.1	.5				6				1					2	2	
St.Mark's,Fla.	5.9	.6				27	12				3	1						
Key West, Fla.	1.0		.1			5	2									1		
Appalachicola,Fla.	14.2	.3		15	1	36	11				2							
Florida, misc.	1.8	.3	.7			3	13				2	3				3	2	
Mobile,Ala.	23.1	9.3	4.0	42	6	21	10	1	12	8	10	2				14	3	
New Orleans,La.	59.4	25.2	16.5	92	9	90	12		31	16	38	8		22	7	25	5	
Louisiana,misc.	1.0		.4			3	5									1	3	

	N.Y.	BOSTON	PHILA	SHIPS	BARKS	BRIGS	SCHOONERS	SLOOPS
TOTAL LESSER COAST	302	285	151	19	8	837	5661	391
" MAJOR "	172	43	33	328	67	499	157	6
" COASTAL	474	328	184	347	75	1336	5818	397
" FOREIGN	460	194	75	705	189	1691	874	4
GRAND TOTAL	934	522	259	1052	264	3027	6692	401

* In addition to 39 steamer arrivals from Charleston and daily steamer arrivals from Providence.

NEW YORK DOMESTIC AND FOREIGN EXPORTS VESSELS AND CREWS ENTERED

Compiled from annual *Reports on Commerce and Navigation*

Export figures for New York State; others for port

	Exports (Million $)		Tonnage Entered (Thousands of Tons)		Vessels Entered (Number)	Crews Entered (Thousands)
	Domestic Exports	Foreign Reexports	American Vessels	Foreign Vessels		
1815	8	2				
1816	14	5				
1817	13	5				
1818	12	4				
1819	8	5				
1820	8	4				
1821	7	5				
1822	10	6				
1823	11	7				
1824	13	9				
1825	20	14				
1826	11	10				
1827	13	9	251	35		
1828	12	10	242	42		
1829	12	8	244	26		
1830	13	6	273	31		
1831	15	9	278	55		
1832	15	10	298	102		
1833	15	9	314	106		
1834	13	11	342	101	1950	
1835	20	8	374	91	2008	22
1836	18	9	396	137	2205	24
1837	13	9	391	187	2222	25
1838	15	6	342	79	1625	19
1839	24	11	427	135	2138	23
1840	19	10	417	128	1955	21
1841	22	7	423	124	2098	21
1842	17	5	419	150	1987	23
1843*	17	5	247	64	1151	13
1844	26	8	434	141	2123	24
1845	25	10	439	139	2008	39
1846	29	7	493	161	2132	26
1847	44	5	543	310	2238	33
1848	38	14	639	293	2870	36
1849	36	9	711	406	3218	43
1850	41	11	734	410	3163	44
1851	68	17	956	491	3647	52
1852	74	13	1221	477	3874	58
1853	66	12	1284	470	3927	59
1854	105	16	1377	462	4037	60
1855	96	17	1377	358	3773	55
1856	109	9	1381	299	3529	54
1857	119	15	1584	450	4068	67
1858	89	19	1273	420	3330	56
1859	104	12	1320	569	3902	63
1860	126	19	1356	617	3982	66

* 9-month period; shift from Sept. 30 to June 30 for end of fiscal year.

APPENDIX VIII

TONNAGE CLEARED AT PRINCIPAL PORTS FOR VARIOUS FOREIGN COUNTRIES—1860

Compiled from *Report on Commerce and Navigation, 1860*, pp. 526–7, 564–84

(Thousands of Tons)

	TOTAL U.S.	CHIEF GENERAL PORTS				COTTON PORTS				OTHER PORTS				
		NEW YORK	BOSTON	PHILADELPHIA	BALTIMORE	NEW ORLEANS	CHARLESTON	SAVANNAH	MOBILE	PORTLAND	SALEM	GALVESTON	SAN FRANCISCO	LAKE PORTS
Total	8789	1678	633	135	174	894	179	149	255	155	32	47	351	3522
United Kingdom	1557	493	73	27	12	485	81	111	164	31		31	1	1
Canada	3574	28	5	1	2			1	–					3520
Other Br.No.Am.	891	163	342	17	9	–		3		53	17		74	
France	360	128	2	–	8	124	21	6	53			1		
Germany	204	119		1	17	32	9	5	1			5		
Holland	57	20	3		21	4	3	–	–			1		
Belgium	38	25	–			9	–		–			1		
Scandinavia	13	–	–			5	4	–	1					
Russia	20	1	1			10	1	1	–				2	
Gibraltar & Malta	17	10	2	–	–	1	–	–	–					
Spain	79	11	1		1	31	17	4	11					
Portugal	7	6				1								
Madeira,Canaries&c	11	2	1	–	–	–				–		–		
Italy	48	6	1		–	30			–			–		
Austria	10	2	1	–		3			1					
Turkey	13	3	7						–					
Cuba	695	246	53	39	19	111	28	9	13	67		2		
Puerto Rico	43	23	2	1	7	–	–		–	–				
Haiti	41	17	17	3		1			–					
Santo Domingo	7	5	–						–					
British West Indies	149	66	6	10	22	1	1	1	–	–	–			
Dutch West Indies	6	4	–			–								
Other West Indies	44	19	4	4	–	–	–	–	–	–				
Mexico	82	13	–		1	26							3	33
Central Republic	4	1												1
New Granada(Col.)	205	110	1	1	6	1								74
Venezuela	12	6		5	–									
Brazil	92	19	4	9	21	4	–	–			1			
Uruguay	20	5	3	1	4		2	–			–			
Argentina	23	9	5	–	–	–	–		1	1				
Chile	38	9	5	1	4								16	
Peru	70	7	3	–									58	
Ecuador	1				–								–	
British Honduras	9	3				4								
British Guiana	18	8	1	–										
French Guiana	2											2		
British Africa	17	6	8	–	–							–		
Other Africa	34	10	4	2	2	–						9		
China	84	40	5	2	1								34	
Japan	1												1	
British East Indies	26	2	22										2	
Dutch East Indies	5	3	1										–	
Philippines	8		2										6	
Sandwich Isl(Hawaii)	16	–	3										12	
Australia	54	19	13		–								19	
Other Pacific	10												10	
TOTAL NO. OF VESSELS	23594	3402	3014	454	593	1293	391	276	343	671	265	100	514	6940

Note that if the lake ports are omitted, the proportion of New York and the other regular seaports is radically increased.

399

EXPORTS, 1860, BY PRINCIPAL COMMODITIES AND PORTS

Compiled from *Report on Commerce and Navigation, 1860*, pp. 310–402

Arranged in order of total value

(Millions of dollars)

	TOTAL U.S.	NEW YORK	BOSTON	PHILADELPHIA	BALTIMORE	NEW ORLEANS	CHARLESTON	SAVANNAH	MOBILE	PORTLAND	RICHMOND	SAN FRANCISCO	LAKE PORTS & CANADIAN BORDER
DOMESTIC EXPORTS Total	373.1	120.6	13.5	5.5	8.8	107.8	21.1	18.3	38.6	1.9	5.0	7.3	11.1
Cotton	191.8	12.4	.3			96.1	19.6	17.8	38.5				.1
Specie & bullion	56.9	50.3	2.3			.2						3.7	
Tobacco & mfrs. of	19.2	2.6	.6	.1	3.1	7.4					3.0		.8
Flour	15.4	6.6	1.0	1.0	2.1	.5					1.8	.3	1.2
Cotton goods	10.9	5.9	2.4		.5	.2						.3	.3
Iron & mfrs. of	5.7	3.2	.4	.6	.1							.2	.7
Lard	4.5	2.0	.1	.1	.3	1.2				.2			.1
Wheat	4.0	2.3		.1								.4	.9
Lumber, etc.	4.0	.8	.4			.3		.3		.2			
Naval stores	3.8	2.7	.1		.1		.2						
Pork	3.1	1.6	.3	.1	.2								.4
Wood, mfrs. of	2.7	.7	.5	.3	.1					.5			
Beef	2.6	1.8	.1	.2	.1								
Rice	2.5	1.0	.1		.1		.9	.1					
Indian corn	2.3	1.1	•	.2	.1	.1							.5
Staves & headings	2.3	1.3				.4					.1		
Whale oil	2.3	2.0	.1										.1
Hams & bacon	2.2	1.5								.2			
Live stock	1.8	.3											1.3
Copper, brass, etc.	1.6	1.4											
Oil cake	1.6	1.1	.1	.1									
Cheese	1.5	1.4											
Skins & furs	1.5	1.3											
Spirits, distilled	1.4	.5	.5										
Butter	1.1	.7											
Drugs & medicines	1.1	.8											
Household furniture	1.0	.5	.3										.1
Rye, oats, etc.	1.0	.4										.3	
Hides, raw	1.0	.2				.3							.3
FOREIGN REEXPORTS Total	26.9	17.5	1.6		.1	.6					.2	2.9	2.5
Coffee	2.2	1.9	.2										
Sugar	2.1	1.1	.1									.2	.5
Tea	1.9	.6	.2										.9
Hides & skins, raw	1.6	1.2											.2
Cotton goods	1.0	.1				.2							
TOTAL EXPORTS, DOMESTIC & FOREIGN	400.1	138.1	15.1	5.5	9.0	108.4	21.1	18.3	38.6	2.1	5.1	10.2	13.6

Note that the port totals, based on figures for the immediate customs district, are sometimes lower than the state totals as given in Appendix II.

APPENDIX X

IMPORTS, 1860, BY PRINCIPAL COMMODITIES AND PORTS

Compiled from *Report on Commerce and Navigation, 1860*, pp. 404–523

Arranged in order of total value

(Millions of dollars)

	TOTAL U.S.	NEW YORK	BOSTON	PHILADELPHIA	BALTIMORE	NEW ORLEANS	CHARLESTON	SAVANNAH	MOBILE	PORTLAND	SALEM	SAN FRANCISCO	LAKE PORTS & CANADIAN BORDER
Total	362.1	233.6	39.3	14.6	9.7	22.9	1.5	.7	1.0	1.2	1.3	9.5	18.8
Woollen goods	37.9	34.0	1.1	1.2	.2	.6	.1					.3	
Silk Goods	32.9	30.7	1.4	.1		.4							
Cotton goods	32.5	22.6	4.1	1.8	.3	2.9						.2	
Sugar	31.0	20.7	3.2	2.5	2.1	.6	.1					1.0	
Coffee	21.8	8.5	1.0	1.7	3.2	5.1		.1	.3			.1	.6
Iron, steel & mfrs. of	21.5	12.3	3.0	1.4	.5	1.7	.2	.2	.3			.1	.2
Linens & other flax mfrs	10.7	8.6	.7	.5		.5							
Hides & skins, raw	10.5	6.9	2.3	.4	.2						.3		
Tea	8.9	8.3	.2									.3	
Specie & bullion	8.5	2.3				2.2						2.2	
Tobacco & mfrs. of	6.0	3.3	.1	.1	.2	1.1	.1					.7	
Tin & mfrs. of	5.8	4.5	.5	.2		.4							
Molasses	5.2	1.6	.8	.5	.2	.2	.1	.1		.6			
Spirits, distilled	5.1	3.4	.4	.3		.5						.5	
Leather & mfrs. of	5.1	4.5	.2			.2							
Wool, raw	4.8	2.4	2.2										
Wines	4.7	2.9	.1			1.2						.3	
Chinaware, etc.	4.5	2.4	.5	.5		.6	.1						
Fruits, dried & green	4.2	2.4	.7	.1	.1	.4							
Laces	4.0	3.5	.3										
Clocks & watches	2.9	2.6	.2										
Linseed	2.7	.8	1.8										
Soda;(ash,sal & carb.)	2.5	1.3	.3	.6		.1							
Glass etc.	2.1	1.7	.2			.1							
Clothing,etc.,ready made	2.1	1.5	.1			.1						.1	
Gunny cloth & bags	2.0	.2	1.3			.2							
Lead & mfrs. of	1.8	1.6	.1										
Furs	1.8	1.7											
Jewelry,gems,etc.	1.7	1.5	.1										
Rubber & mfrs. of	1.6	1.3	.1										
Hats & bonnets	1.6	1.5											
Copper	1.6	.4	.4		.6								
Rags	1.5	1.0	.3										
Salt	1.4	.3	.1	.1		.3							
Indigo	1.4	.6	.7										
Silk, raw	1.3	1.3											
Spices	1.1	.6	.3										
Hemp & mfrs. of	1.1	.5	.5										
Saltpetre	1.1	.1	.8										
"Articles from British Provinces under the Reciprocity treaty"	20.4	.7	2.3	.1	.1						.2		16.1

In the original tables, some items such as tea and coffee appear in separate lists of free and dutiable articles. In several cases, such as cotton, woollen, and iron manufactures, the original lists are divided into numerous subheadings which have been consolidated.

APPENDIX XI

TOTAL TONNAGE (REGISTERED, ENROLLED AND LICENSED) BY CUSTOMS DISTRICTS

Compiled from annual *Reports on Commerce and Navigation*

(Thousands of Tons)

		CHIEF GENERAL PORTS				COTTON PORTS				OTHER PORTS AND DISTRICTS						
	TOTAL U.S.	NEW YORK	BOSTON	PHILADELPHIA	BALTIMORE	NEW ORLEANS	CHARLESTON	SAVANNAH	MOBILE	WALDOBORO	BATH	PORTLAND	SALEM	NEW BEDFORD	NORFOLK	SAN FRANCISCO
1815	1368	278	137	99	107	17	35	13	–	19	22	33	35	24	34	
1816	1372	299	143	101	101	13	36	12	–	19	20	30	34	22	31	
1817	1399	306	141	104	104	20	37	15	–	18	24	29	36	22	30	
1818	1225	238	125	82	67	35	27	11	3	18	21	29	33	25	30	
1819	1260	229	126	82	70	42	29	13	3	20	20	30	31	29	23	
1820	1280	231	126	83	68	38	28	10	6	21	21	33	33	32	23	
1821	1298	236	144	84	71	49	31	11	4	20	20	33	34	34	21	
1822	1324															
1823	1336															
1824	1389															
1825	1423	304	152	73	92	29	27	7	6	22	27	45	41	36	21	
1826	1534	316	171	73	96	39	28	8	8	24	30	48	43	39	22	
1827	1620	346	161	95	98	42	31	8	9	27	30	49	45	44	22	
1828	1741	339	176	104	106	51	32	10	10	32	36	56	48	50	24	
1829	1260	261	144	77	45	44	13	7	7	24	31	44	34	51	12	
1830	1191	256	135	71	35	45	13	6	5	21	26	42	28	55	10	
1831	1267	286	138	79	43	55	13	5	6	22	26	42	25	64	12	
1832	1439	298	171	77	47	61	13	6	7	24	33	47	30	70	15	
1833	1606	323	189	79	50	60	12	7	7	30	42	49	31	76	21	
1834	1758	359	212	83	59	74	13	11	11	35	47	57	35	74	18	
1835	1824	376	226	86	54	79	16	8	12	38	47	57	34	76	20	
1836	1882	404	226	91	62	81	14	8	6	38	42	57	33	81	16	
1837	1896	410	201	81	67	92	21	12	10	39	41	53	32	85	12	
1838	1995	400	207	87	60	104	24	16	16	46	45	53	34	85	16	
1839	2096	430	203	96	71	109	29	17	21	45	47	55	35	86	15	
1840	2180	414	220	103	76	126	29	17	17	52	64	56	37	89	19	
1841	2230	438	227	105	83	145	21	14	15	51	58	55	36	96	18	
1842	2092	459	193	100	75	143	21	13	12	56	48	54	34	98	17	
1843	2158	496	202	104	74	149	20	15	16	50	51	56	33	100	17	
1844	2280	525	210	114	76	161	19	14	15	57	57	57	34	104	18	
1845	2417	550	227	130	83	169	18	15	17	58	62	64	29	112	20	
1846	2562	572	240	127	92	180	18	16	22	60	64	66	28	117	21	
1847	2839	646	260	156	100	212	23	18	18	67	76	74	25	119	26	
1848	3154	733	285	175	122	225	24	18	22	85	83	82	26	123	24	
1849	3334	796	296	188	134	240	29	19	25	89	88	84	25	123	23	
1850	3535	835	320	206	149	248	33	19	24	96	103	86	28	127	24	17
1851	3772	931	342	222	160	251	31	22	27	103	103	97	30	131	23	58
1852	4138	1016	381	229	159	266	42	23	28	112	111	105	30	149	22	97
1853	4407	1149	450	252	158	153	42	20	28	113	129	104	30	155	27	97
1854	4802	1262	495	268	170	183	38	24	33	122	154	123	30	165	29	93
1855	5212	1288	546	294	183	200	56	27	36	148	175	137	30	169	35	87
1856	4871	1328	521	197	183	163	59	31	38	155	193	136	29	153	27	80
1857	4940	1377	447	211	191	173	56	33	46	153	182	145	28	152	23	84
1858	5049	1432	448	219	194	210	60	37	47	157	169	115	30	154	27	79
1859	5145	1444	455	220	195	215	61	37	52	151	167	115	29	153	25	78
1860	5353	1464	464	241	200	228	65	40	52	187	165	131	27	149	26	84

See Appendix XII for registered tonnage. The totals for enrolled and licensed tonnage can be obtained approximately by subtracting the registered totals from the above figures. Steam tonnage, included in the above, is also given separately in Appendix XIII.

TOTAL TONNAGE (REGISTERED, ENROLLED AND LICENSED) BY STATES
Ibid.

(Thousands of Tons)

	NEW YORK STATE	MAINE	NEW HAMPSHIRE	MASSACHUSETTS	RHODE ISLAND	CONNECTICUT	NEW JERSEY	DELAWARE	MARYLAND	VIRGINIA	NORTH CAROLINA	FLORIDA	TEXAS
1815	287	147	29	305	38	60	31	9	152	85	40		
1816	308	137	30	314	32	53	33	9	155	81	37		
1817	318	147	22	313	36	51	33	9	157	86	37		
1818	245	121	22	298	39	44	31	9	121	84	28		
1819	241	130	25	309	39	40	33	9	127	77	32		
1820	244	140	23	315	39	45	34	10	124	78	37		
1821	248	136	23	334	38	45	34	10	126	70	32		
1822													
1823													
1824													
1825	316	174	24	352	38	49	40	12	146	71	39		
1826	330	193	26	384	37	52	41	11	152	75	42	1	
1827	360	201	26	388	40	55	44	11	159	89	46		
1828	355	232	26	424	43	60	48	13	170	82	53		
1829	274	181	20	350	36	46	32	15	74	38	34	1	
1830	272	160	18	329	30	41	32	12	64	42	26	3	
1831	300	163	14	342	34	41	32	13	73	46	28	1	
1832	318	192	17	414	40	52	32	13	80	54	31	2	
1833	344	224	18	466	44	54	36	13	87	59	37	3	
1834	381	246	22	473	47	63	43	15	91	65	41	2	
1835	398	262	22	496	46	67	38	17	96	66	42	4	
1836	433	276	20	490	49	70	50	17	103	59	43	3	
1837	444	251	25	480	45	76	56	18	109	53	31	7	
1838	443	269	26	515	44	60	64	16	112	55	35	8	
1839	467	280	28	491	44	82	63	19	115	64	39	9	
1840	454	307	27	521	43	87	71	19	120	65	42	10	
1841	490	304	25	531	41	54	53	10	113	57	28	6	
1842	513	304	23	467	47	58	60	10	106	57	31	8	
1843	556	286	22	497	45	70	63	10	108	56	37	10	
1844	587	305	22	500	48	82	68	9	111	55	36	10	
1845	625	318	23	503	47	91	70	11	117	59	38	11	
1846	655	347	20	541	49	99	76	11	127	61	41	11	—
1847	746	384	20	568	47	102	83	14	139	68	37	10	2
1848	845	449	23	621	43	111	81	17	158	65	41	14	1
1849	911	465	25	636	43	113	82	15	172	70	44	14	2
1850	941	501	23	685	40	103	80	16	192	68	45	10	3
1851	1050	536	25	694	37	116	89	11	204	64	48	9	6
1852	1134	592	24	773	41	125	96	9	206	68	50	9	7
1853	1294	632	26	856	41	131	96	13	206	74	56	12	7
1854	1414	748	28	914	45	129	105	18	220	84	57	14	9
1855	1464	806	30	979	51	137	120	19	234	93	58	14	7
1856	1498	781	34	891	47	104	101	20	236	68	44	8	8
1857	1567	764	38	816	49	106	107	21	245	68	41	14	9
1858	1600	747	33	.794	48	104	114	22	249	68	43	20	11
1859	1627	738	34	836	40	115	119	22	250	71	42	20	12
1860	1661	784	32	835	41	111	104	23	254	76	47	28	12

In most of the other states, the total was virtually the same as for the principal port as given in the preceding appendix; the balance of the Pennsylvania total came from inland steamers enrolled at Presque Isle. The Virginia totals include Alexandria, which for a while was included in the District of Columbia, and exclude the river steamers of the Wheeling district.

APPENDIX XII

REGISTERED TONNAGE, BY CUSTOMS DISTRICTS
Compiled from annual *Reports on Commerce and Navigation*

(Thousands of Tons)

		CHIEF GENERAL PORTS				COTTON PORTS				OTHER PORTS						
	TOTAL U.S.	NEW YORK	BOSTON	PHILADELPHIA	BALTIMORE	NEW ORLEANS	CHARLESTON	SAVANNAH	MOBILE	WALDOBORO	BATH	PORTLAND	SALEM	NEW BEDFORD	NORFOLK	SAN FRANCISCO
1815	854	177	105	76	86	13	24	10	–	7	16	25	26	15	21	
1816	799	188	104	77	85	8	23	10	–	6	13	21	25	13	18	
1817	809	192	106	79	81	10	24	11	–	5	16	20	27	11	16	
1818	606	115	88	57	44	20	14	8	1	6	13	21	23	14	12	
1819	612	109	87	59	46	20	15	10	1	5	12	20	22	17	9	
1820	619	110	85	59	43	14	14	7	2	6	12	22	24	20	8	
1821	619	114	97	59	45	16	15	7	1	3	10	23	26	21	5	
1822	628															
1823	639															
1824	669															
1825	700	156	103	65	58	11	10	7	–	2	16	32	30	24	5	
1826	737	158	109	63	61	15	12	4	1	1	18	33	31	27	6	
1827	747	165	108	61	59	13	12	4	1	2	15	33	32	32	5	
1828	812	158	119	66	65	19	12	6	3	3	19	37	34	36	6	
1829	650	110	107	50	30	18	7	6	4	3	19	29	28	39	6	
1830	576	101	100	47	23	13	6	3	1	2	16	29	21	46	3	
1831	620	122	99	51	25	16	5	4	2	2	16	29	19	56	4	
1832	685	129	113	45	26	21	5	3	2	3	21	33	21	62	6	
1833	750	151	127	49	26	18	6	6	1	4	26	31	20	67	7	
1834	857	178	149	51	33	25	5	7	4	6	31	38	22	66	7	
1835	885	191	159	51	32	28	9	5	4	6	29	37	21	68	8	
1836	897	192	157	51	32	26	8	7	1	6	24	39	21	72	5	
1837	810	191	127	39	34	31	8	6	2	5	23	36	20	75	1	
1838	822	169	135	42	25	39	10	9	8	9	26	36	21	73	2	
1839	834	183	138	48	33	37	15	11	9	11	26	36	21	49	3	
1840	899	203	149	52	34	49	15	10	8	13	32	36	22	45	7	
1841	945	225	158	47	37	54	12	8	5	12	34	37	22	65	6	
1842	975	226	157	42	41	48	12	7	2	12	33	39	21	76	8	
1843	1009	237	165	39	41	49	10	2	6	15	36	40	22	83	10	
1844	1068	253	175	40	41	55	9	8	3	18	38	40	21	94	9	
1845	1095	248	187	39	44	58	8	8	5	20	41	44	18	103	10	
1846	1130	260	192	39	51	55	8	7	6	15	42	45	18	108	10	
1847	1241	297	210	43	56	80	11	9	4	21	47	51	16	111	14	
1848	1360	336	232	48	72	82	11	8	6	28	56	55	17	113	11	
1849	1438	378	247	53	79	81	14	9	7	31	61	57	16	115	9	
1850	1585	441	270	64	90	83	15	10	7	38'	76	60	20	115	9	15
1851	1726	504	296	69	95	81	15	11	8	46	78	69	21	122	9	38
1852	1899	571	326	67	95	81	22	13	7	46	84	77	20	139	7	55
1853	2103	667	396	72	92	84	21	12	8	47	101	75	20	146	9	55
1854	2333	754	437	74	102	103	13	15	11	53	124	90	20	156	13	46
1855	2535	737	482	77	110	114	32	17	12	77	147	102	19	157	17	57
1856	2491	765	472	58	110	99	36	21	14	85	162	109	19	144	14	53
1857	2463	802	401	59	112	113	33	21	19	84	155	100	18	145	10	46
1858	2499	840	399	59	114	130	36	25	20	86	141	96	20	146	12	45
1859	2507	844	404	57	115	128	36	25	22	76	143	93	20	145	10	44
1860	2546	838	411	67	114	132	38	27	22	79	138	108	18	141	10	47

APPENDIX XIII

STEAM TONNAGE

Compiled from annual *Reports on Commerce and Navigation*

(Thousands of Tons)

TOTAL TONNAGE (REGISTERED, ENROLLED & LICENSED)
REGISTERED (included in total)

	TOTAL TONNAGE												REGISTERED					
	TOTAL U.S.	NEW YORK	BOSTON	PHILADELPHIA	BALTIMORE	NEW ORLEANS	CHARLESTON	SAVANNAH	MOBILE	FALL RIVER	PERTH AMBOY	SAN FRANCISCO	TOTAL U.S.	NEW YORK	BOSTON	CHARLESTON	NEW ORLEANS	SAN FRANCISCO
1828	39	11	-	3	2	20	1	1	2	-	-							
1829	54	12	-	2	3	22	1	-	1	-	-							
1830	64	12	-	2	4	30	1	1	3	-	-		1					
1831	68	13	-	2	4	36	1	-	2	-	-		-					
1832	90	13	-	2	4	38	1	-	-	-	-	-	-					
1833	101	14	-	3	5	40	1	1	-	-	-		-					
1834	122	15	-	2	6	46	1	1	6	-	-		-					
1835																		
1836	145	19	-	4	6	50	3	2	5	-	-		-					
1837	154	24	-	4	6	54	4	5	6	-			1					
1838	193	25	-	5	9	57	5	6	6	1			2		-			
1839	195	30	-	4	7	63	4	6	3	2			5		-		2	
1840	202	34	1	2	8	55	5	6	3	2			4			1		
1841	175	31	1	5	10	27	3	3	6	-			-			-		
1842	229	35	1	4	7	85	3	4	6				4		-		4	
1843	236	35	2	5	7	85	3	4	5	2			5				-	4
1844	272	36	2	7	7	96	4	4	7	2			6		-		-	5
1845	325	42	3	9	8	102	3	5	9	3			6			-		5
1846	347	46	4	10	9	113	3	5	11		4		6	1	-			4
1847	404	52	5	11	9	120	4	5	10	1	4		5					5
1848	427	64	4	13	10	132	4	5	10	1	5		16	6	1			7
1849	462	71	3	13	11	146	5	6	13	1	4		20	10	1	1		8
1850	525	95	2	15	13	144	7	6	12	4	4	-	44	36		1		6
1851	583	121	2	19	14	149	6	8	13	4	5	4	62	52		1	6	1
1852	643	140	3	'24	12	170	9	8	16	4	4	4	79	63	-	2	7	4
1853	604	165	5	25	12	53	8	5	16	4	6	4	90	76	1	1	7	1
1854	676	184	4	25	14	64	9	6	18	5	1	3	95	82	1	1	7	11
1855	770	196	8	28	16	69	10	6	20	7	9	25	115	89	1	1	6	11
1856	673	176	7	19	15	55	8	5	18	7	8	28	89	68		1	3	14
1857	705	180	9	22	17	52	8	6	21	7	8	24	86	69	1	2	-	12
1858	729	184	11	22	18	70	8	7	21	6	8	20	78	65	1			9
1859	768	191	11	22	19	75	10	8	23	7	8	28	92	70	1	2		18
1860	867	205	13	25	21	84	11	8	24	7	9	29	97	72	1	2		18

Figures not included in reports before 1828. Steam tonnage included in general tonnage statistics. A considerable part of the steam tonnage at New Orleans and the other cotton ports consisted of inland river steamers. Inland totals in 1860 included St. Louis 58; Pittsburgh 45; Louisville 34; Cincinnati 33; Wheeling 17; and Nashville 4; lake totals, Buffalo 45; Detroit 31; Cuyahoga (Cleveland) 21; and Chicago 10. The registered tonnage figures show clearly New York's commanding position in oceangoing steamships after the start of the subsidy lines; the total figures show its long lead in tidewater steam navigation.

SHIPBUILDING, BY CUSTOMS DISTRICTS AND STATES

Compiled from annual *Reports on Commerce and Navigation*

(Thousands of Tons)

	TOTAL U.S.	CHIEF GENERAL PORTS					OTHER DISTRICTS					PRINCIPAL STATES									
		NEW YORK	BOSTON	PHILADELPHIA	BALTIMORE	COTTON PORTS S.C. to TEXAS (see below)	BELFAST, ME.	WALDOBORO, ME.	BATH, ME.	PORTLAND, ME.	NEWBURY-PORT, MASS.	MAINE	NEW HAMPSHIRE (Portsmouth)	MASSACHUSETTS	RHODE ISLAND	CONNECTICUT	NEW YORK	NEW JERSEY	MARYLAND	VIRGINIA	NORTH CAROLINA
1815	154																				
1816	131																				
1817	86																				
1818	82																				
1819	79																				
1820	47																				
1821	55																				
1822	75																				
1823	75																				
1824	90																				
1825	114																				
1826	126																				
1827	104																				
1828	98																				
1829	77																				
1830	58																				
1831	85																				
1832	144																				
1833	161	22	16	3	8	1	6	9	11	7	2	51	2	33	2	5	23	5	16	4	3
1834	118	17	10	2	5	3	3	5	7	4	3	28	2	24	1	3	18	5	10	3	1
1835*	46																				
1836	113	16	8	2	6	1	2	7	4	6	1	27	2	22	1	4	19	4	9	1	-
1837	122	20	6	3	5	3	3	4	5	4	2	23	1	20	1	4	14	7	10	-	1
1838	113	14	7	3	10	3	2	6	3	3	2	24	3	19	2	3	14	7	15	-	1
1839	120	16	11	5	9	2	2	5	6	6	3	27	2	24	1	2	17	6	13	-	1
1840	118	13	7	8	8	1	4	12	7	6	2	38	2	17	1	4	13	6	11	-	1
1841	118	16	15	5	7	1	3	7	4	4	3	26	3	28	1	3	17	3	10	-	1
1842	129	18	12	9	3	1	7	9	7	5	2	38	1	18	2	3	20	3	7	-	1
1843*	63	13	5	3	2	1	2	3	3	3	1	15	-	9	-	1	13	1	3	-	2
1844	103	18	5	6	4	1	1	6	3	3	-	20	-	9	2	2	21	1	5	-	-
1845	146	26	14	9		1	3	7	6	7	5	31	2	25	1	2	29	4	7	2	-
1846	188	29	12	8	10	2	7	7	9	9	1	49	2	24	2	3	33	5	13	3	1
1847	243	37	11	12	8	1	7	16	13	9	7	63	5	27	2	6	50	9	12	1	2
1848	318	57	17	19	11	3	6	21	19	14	8	89	5	39	4	7	68	8	17	2	2
1849	256	37	13	13	12	3	7	19	20	11	3	82	6	23	2	5	44	8	17	3	2
1850	272	55	23	18	11	2	6	23	22	11	4	91	6	35	3	4	58	6	15	3	2
1851	298	71	28	20	15	5	4	17	18	12	3	77	8	41	3	3	76	5	18	1	1
1852	351	69	24	16	15	3	5	27	24	16	6	110	9	48	3	9	72	3	18	3	2
1853	425	68	59	24	14	3	10	23	38	8	7	118	8	83	3	9	83	7	16	6	1
1854	535	93	69	24	16	4	12	31	58	16	8	168	8	92	5	10	117	8	20	3	2
1855	583	92	56	33	18	2	15	49	56	25	8	215	8	79	7	14	115	10	22	4	2
1856	469	49	62	19	15	6	11	30	50	21	7	149	10	80	4	7	76	9	19	3	2
1857	378	43	40	14	18	2	9	22	29	12	4	110	8	55	3	5	67	8	20	3	1
1858	242	25	21	10	4	3	3	11	14	7	4	55	5	32	3	7	37	6	6	2	1
1859	156	15	21	9	5	3	3	6	14	3	3	40	3	31	-	3	16	5	7	3	1
1860	212	23	21	11	6	3	6	10	16	5	4	57	3	33	1	7	31	4	7	4	-

* New York Port had the heaviest total of any single customs district every year of the period except 1856 (Boston, Bath) and 1859 (Boston). The figures show the almost complete absence of shipbuilding in the far south— the combined total of South Carolina, Georgia, Florida, Alabama, Mississippi, Louisiana and Texas was less than that of several single districts in Maine.

APPENDIX XV

SHIPBUILDING, BY NUMBER OF PRINCIPAL TYPES IN LEADING REGIONS
Compiled from annual *Reports on Commerce and Navigation*

	SHIPS & BARKS				BRIGS				SCHOONERS				STEAMERS					
	U.S.	NYC.	ME.	MASS.	U.S.	NYC.	ME.	MASS.	U.S.	NYC.	ME.	MASS.	U.S.	TOTAL TIDE-WATER	NYC.	ME.	MASS.	PITTS-BURGH
1815	136				224				680									
1816	76				122				781									
1817	34				86				559									
1818	53				85				428									
1819	53				82				473									
1820	21				60				301									
1821	43				89				248									
1822	64				131				260									
1823	55				127				260				15					
1824	56				156				377				26					
1825	56				197				538				35					
1826	71				187				482				45					
1827	58				133				464				38					
1828	73				108				474				33					
1829	44				68				485				43					
1830	25				56				403				37					
1831	72				95				416				34					
1832	132				143				568				100					
1833	144	26	37	54	169	7	99	30	625	36	167	99	65	14	5			24
1834	98	16	32	33	94	2	44	23	497	33	93	115	88	22	7			30
1835*	25				50				302				30					
1836	93	14	30	34	65	3	36	10	444	54	91	109	124	32	17			58
1837	67	10	18	27	72	5	45	8	507	25	82	121	135	43	16		1	46
1838	66	7	21	21	79	8	42	10	510	28	78	131	90	30	7	1	1	28
1839	83	10	26	31	89	7	48	14	439	17	68	100	125	51	16			7
1840	97	6	50	25	109	13	56	11	378	17	75	76	63	20	8			22
1841	114	13	35	50	101	5	47	17	311	8	48	43	78	13	5			12
1842	116	6	57	32	91	3	50	32	273	12	55	21	137	35	18	1	1	42
1843*	58	5	25	20	34	2	21	2	138	8	25	15	79	23	5			17
1844	73	11	27	18	47	6	15	5	204	16	52	19	163	30	14	2		34
1845	124	18	43	42	87	2	33	16	322	25	82	54	163	45	17	2	2	46
1846	100	11	47	26	164	3	97	26	576	37	140	108	225	62	23	3	4	49
1847	151	16	73	33	168	2	120	13	689	43	151	84	198	61	15	1	3	57
1848	254	26	130	53	174	3	118	17	701	59	114	107	175	39	19	1	2	42
1849	198	15	119	33	148	7	107	7	623	44	105	68	208	47	17	7	1	52
1850	247	26	127	51	117	2	75	19	547	42	115	46	159	76	28	6	2	14
1851	211	23	102	50	65	1	45	4	522	56	94	78	233	109	47	4		50
1852	255	24	138	51	79	2	63	6	584	46	148	97	259	100	43		4	55
1853	265	18	132	73	95	5	70	1	681	66	133	126	271	115	58	7	2	34
1854	334	40	156	82	112	7	78	4	661	63	99	87	281	109	49	3	3	61
1855	381	40	213	70	126	5	107	3	605	76	68	59	243	107	41	6	9	51
1856	306	24	155	84	103	7	70	10	594	35	83	35	221	60	17	4	4	55
1857	251	28	127	38	58	5	26	4	504	37	85	47	263	64	21	1	2	68
1858	122	7	56	33	46	2	28	3	431	21	77	70	226	78	26	4	3	37
1859	89	2	42	32	28		15	1	297	9	67	54	172	72	20	1	3	29
1860	110	4	43	30	36	2	20	2	372	15	95	91	264	99	28	2	7	53

* 9-month periods; shift of end of year of reckoning from Dec. 31 to Sept. 30 in 1835 and to June 30 in 1843
New York built very few brigs, which were almost a Maine monopoly. New York had a long lead over the other coastal ports in steamboat construction. Nearly all of the New York square-riggers and steamboats were built in East River but most of the schooners were produced elsewhere in the district.

407

APPENDIX XVI

DIMENSIONS OF PARTICULAR VESSELS OF VARIOUS CLASSES

These vessels, selected as illustrative of shipbuilding development, were all built at New York except three distinctive clippers, which were owned there. The figures are based upon the MS. Certificates of Registry and Enrolment at the New York Custom House, except for a few marked *, which, chiefly because of gaps in the official records, were derived from other sources which do not always agree in details. Tonnage figures are based on "Old Custom House Measurement," whereas some printed lists give inflated "Carpenter's Measurement." Few dimensions for the smaller sailing vessels are available in print.

	Year Built	Tonnage	Length Ft. In.	Beam	Depth of Hold	Remarks
SHIPS-GENERAL						
General Brown	1815	899	147	37	18-6	First ship reg. in 1815 (see text)
Sea Fox	1817	176	79	23-1	11-2	Smallest N.Y.-built ship (see text)
Roman	1825	492	118	30-6	15-3	China trade
Tallahassee	1828	489	128	29	14-6	Transient-cotton triangle,etc.
Helena	1841	597	134-6	31-4	20	China trade
Washington	1849	1650	205	41-9	28-10	Immigrant "packet," (see text)
Star of the West	1850	1122	170-6	38	22-2	" "
Ocean Monarch	1856	2145	240	46	30-3	Largest N.Y.square-rigged freighter
SHIPS-PACKETS						
Amity	1816	382	106-6	28-6	14-3	Pioneer Black Baller
Henry	1822	257	93-6	25	13-11	Smallest ocean packet (see text)
Saluda	1822	289	98-8	25-4	12-9	Typical Charleston packet
Charles Carroll	1828	411	121-2	27-4	13-8	Havre (see Frontispiece)
Natchez	1831	523	130-3	29-9	14-10	N.O.packet,later China (see text)
Roscius	1838	1030	167-6	36-4	21-7	Dramatic;first over 1000 tons
Yorkshire	1843	996	166-6	36-2	21	Black Ball, fastest packet (see text)
St.Louis	1850	938	161	35	21-2	N.O.,largest coastal packet
Amazon	1854	1771	216	42	27-5	Largest packet
SHIPS-CLIPPERS						
Houqua	1844	582	142-4	29-10	16-8	China (see text and picture)
Sea Witch	1846	907	170	33-11	19	" ,speed records (see text)
Celestial	1850	860	158	34	19	
Challenge	1851	2006	230-6	43-2	26	(see text)
Flying Cloud	1851	1782	229	40-8	21-6	McKay,E.Boston;speed record (see text)
Sword Fish	1851	1036	169-6	36-6	20	Fastest East River ship on S.F.run
Dreadnought	1852	1413	200	39	26-6	Newburyport;fast on Liverpool run
Great Republic	1853	4555	355	53	38	McKay,E.Boston;largest clipper; burned at N.Y;rebuilt,3356 tons.
BARKS						
Packet	1819	185	78-6	23-10	12-4	Caribbean trade
Navarino	1827	249	93-8	24-6	12-3	Havana packet
Mudara	1845	243	96	24-10	11-6	
BRIGS						
Janus	1816	293	91-6	26-6	13-11	Caribbean trade
Phebe Ann	1819	244	87	24-2	13-3	Pioneer New Orleans packet
America	1826	555	120	32-3	16-1	Largest N.Y.-built brig
Walkulla	1838	267	103-6	26-4	11	Coastal packet
Philura	1839	197	89-6	24-9	10-2	Rated as "brigantine"
Malek Adhel	1840	114	81-3	20-6	7-8	Fast (see text);later Mex.warship
SCHOONERS						
Hardware	1819	35	48-6	18-6	4-10	Note shallow depth
T.H.Smith	1820	63	60-6	17-10	6-10	Pilot boat
Croaker	1822	113	80	20-10	7-8	Caribbean trade
Antarctic	1828	172	87-9	23-2	9-2	South Seas (see text)
Swift	1828	324	111-6	24-6	13	Caribbean;one of largest schrs.
Courier & Enquirer	1832	100	71-1	21-7	7-7	News boat (see text)

	Year Built	Ton-nage	Length Ft. In.	Beam	Depth of Hold	Remarks
SCHOONERS,ctd.						
Aerial	1833	99	68-4	23-2	7-6	Typical dimensions for freight schrs.
Edward K.Collins	1844	75	65	19	8	Pilot Boat
America *	1851	170	87-6	22-6	9-3	Yacht; won "America's Cup."
SLOOPS						
Edmund	1815	94	66	22-6	7-7	By builder of Clermont's hull
Illinois	1817	111	59	23-2	8-4	Largest N.Y.sloop (see text)
Albany Packet	1820	99	64-6	24	7-10	Hudson River "packet"
Oyster Boy	1827	25	46	16-4	4	Built at Staten Island
MISCELLANEOUS						
Madison	1815	25	51-6	12-4	4-6	Pettiauger,"rebuilt from open boat"
Speedy	1819	32	51	17	4-6	" Staten Island
Cophorion	1835	64	75-3	18-4	5-2	"
Lady Clinton	1825	171	110-6	22-4	7-6	H.R."safety barge"(see text & picture)
Michigan	1825	86	75	19	6-10	" freight barge(called "towboat")
Hannibal	1827	93	79	22	6	" "scow"
Wave	1837	184	132	18-9	7-9	" freight barge
STEAMBOATS						
Clermont	1807	182	149	17-11	7	Dimensions after enlargement,1808
Fulton	1813	327	134	30-9	8-9	First Sound steamer (see text)
Olive Branch	1816	265	122	30	8-1	Bay,later H.R.(see text)
Stoudinger	1817	25	47-7	12-5	4-10	Bay,T.Gibbons,also called "Mouse"
Bellona	1818	142	102-6	20-10	7-6	Bay,in Gibbons vs.Ogden (see text)
James Kent	1823	346	135	31-6	9	H.R.
Linnaeus	1824	92	94	16	6-6	East River-Flushing
Rufus King	1828	131	102-6	19-8	7	One of the first regular towboats
Swallow *	1836	426	224	22	8-6	H.R.,wrecked (see text)
Isaac Newton *	1846	1332	338	40	10-8	" "floating palace" (see picture)
New World *	1848	1418	371	35	10-4	" longest N.Y.steamboat
" "	(1855)	1675	371	47	10-4	" rebuilt as night boat
Plymouth Rock *	1854	1742	330	40	12-8	Sound,largest N.Y.steamboat
STEAMSHIPS						
Savannah	1819	319	98-6	25-10	14-2	"First" ocean steamship (see text)
Robert Fulton	1819	702	159	33-9	14-3	On run to Havana & N.O. (see text)
Neptune *	1838	c 736	215	25	14	On Charleston run
Crescent City	1848	1290	233-7	33-11	22-8	On New Orleans run
Hermann	1848	1734	234-11	39-6	31	Bremen subsidy line (see text)
Ohio	1849	2397	248	45-6	24-6	U.S.Mail(Law)line to Chagres
Arctic	1849	2772	286	45-8	24	Collins Line (see text and picture)
Golden Gate	1851	2030	268-6	40	27	Pacific Mail
Adriatic *	1857	4114	351-8	48-8	33-2	Collins;largest N.Y.-built steamship
WARSHIPS						
Fulton the First *	1815	2475	156	56	20	First steam warship(see text&picture)
Regulus	1818	877	147	36-6	18-3	By Eckford,for Latin America
Ohio *	1820	2757	198	54-6	39-0	84 guns;largest N.Y.square-rigger
Liberator	1825	1765	183	46-6	23-3	"Greek frigate",U.S.S.Hudson (text)
Fulton II *	1837	1011	180	34-8	12-2	Steam "floating battery";rebuilt '51
Missouri	1839	1700	229	40		Steam frigate, side-wheel
Vixen *	1846	241	118	22-6	9-3	Steam;built for Mexico,used in U.S.N.
San Jacinto *	1850	1446	215-6	37-9	23-4	Steam screw;later in "Trent affair"
Niagara *	1856	c4580	328-10	55		Screw frigate; note relative size
General Admiral*	1858	c4600	302-10	55	34	" " Russia
REVENUE CUTTERS &c						
Morris *	1831	112	73-4	20-2	7-4	Rev.cutter,schr,model for class
Lightship(S.H.II) *	1837	230	87	25-6	12	Second Sandy Hook lightship(see text)
Legare *	1843	364	160	24	6	Steam revenue cutter;propeller
Harriet Lane *	1858	640	180	30	12-6	" " " ;later U.S.N.

NEW YORK CITY AUCTION SALES OF PRINCIPAL COMMODITIES

Adapted from N. Y. State, *Assembly Document*, 1843, no. 10, pp. 130–31; also in *New York Herald*, March 7, 1846; import figures from annual *Report on Commerce and Navigation*.

(Millions of Dollars)

	Total Auction Sales of Commodities	European Dry Goods	Domestic (American) Dry Goods	Teas, Silks, Chinaware, Caloutta Goods, etc.	Hardware, Groceries and Drugs	Wines & Liquors	Total New York Imports	Total U.S. Imports
1818	13.4	7.4	.8	2.3	2.3	.3		121.7
1819	11.1	5.8	1.1	1.8	1.8	.4		87.1
1820	10.4	6.3	.7	1.0	1.9	.4		74.4
1821	11.3	6.6	1.0	1.5	1.8	.2	23.6	62.5
1822	15.0	9.6	1.5	1.6	1.9	.2	35.4	83.2
1823	16.8	9.9	2.1	1.9	2.5	.3	29.4	77.5
1824	18.4	10.4	3.1	2.4	2.1	.3	36.1	80.5
1825	22.8	13.4	2.7	3.6	2.7	.2	49.6	96.3
1826	19.8	11.6	3.6	2.2	1.9	.4	38.1	84.9
1827	24.0	14.8	3.5	3.3	2.3	.1	38.7	79.4
1828	22.4	11.7	4.8	3.3	2.3	.1	41.9	88.5
1829	21.0	10.6	4.5	2.7	2.6	.4	34.7	74.4
1830	20.0	9.4	4.6	2.8	2.7	.3	35.6	70.8
1831	21.6	10.3	4.0	2.8	3.9	.3	57.0	103.1
1832	21.0	8.8	5.2	3.8	2.6	.5	53.2	101.0
1833	22.4	9.4	4.0	4.7	3.6	.5	55.9	108.1
1834	17.5	5.9	4.1	4.2	2.8	.4	73.1	126.5
1835	23.6	11.4	3.8	4.2	3.1	.9	88.1	149.8
1836	22.7	9.4	3.6	4.6	4.2	.7	118.2	189.9
1837	14.1	5.7	2.9	2.1	3.2	.1	79.3	140.9
1838	17.8	7.3	3.2	4.3	2.5	.3	68.4	113.7
1839	18.0	8.7	3.4	3.1	2.4	.2	99.8	162.0
1840	16.3	7.2	2.7	4.2	1.9	.1	60.4	107.1
1841	19.8	9.6	3.2	3.8	2.8	.2	75.7	127.9

The State auction figures cover the calendar year, while the federal import figures cover the fiscal year ending September 30. Obviously, in comparing the auction totals with the import totals, the domestic dry goods should be deducted (see text, pp. 279–80).

NEW YORK STATE CANAL TRAFFIC

From N. Y. State *Assembly Documents*, 1861, no. 5, p. 89; 1862, no. 112, pp. 26–37; 1882, no. 38, pp. 38–58; U. S. 32nd Congress, 1st Session, *Senate Document* 112, pp. 280–81.

Figures refer to both the Erie and Champlain Canals, including feeders, unless otherwise stated. "East" means eastbound traffic to tidewater; "West" means westbound traffic from tidewater.

Year	TOLLS (Thousand $)	TONNAGE (Thousand tons)						VALUE (Million $)				ERIE CANAL RATES (per ton) — FREIGHT including tolls		STATE TOLLS	
		Total Traffic, East & West, including local	East, arriving at tidewater	West, from tidewater	East, from States beyond New York	West, to States beyond New York	East; Flour & Wheat to tidewater	Total Traffic, East & West, including local	East, arriving at tidewater	East, Flour & Wheat to tidewater	West, to States beyond New York	West; Albany to Buffalo	East; Buffalo to Albany	West; Albany to Buffalo	East; Buffalo to Albany
1821	2														
1822	44														
1823	119														
1824	289		157	32											
1825	521		185	33											
1826	841		269	34											
1827	880														
1828	827			54											
1829	797			48											
1830	1017			66								20.00	9.07	10.22	5.11
1831	728			83								19.80	8.89	"	"
1832	1083											20.00	9.26	"	"
1833	1349			119								14.80	8.15	8.76	3.65
1834	1338		553	114						13		16.40	7.68	6.57	3.28
1835	1430		753	128		55				20		16.00	6.29	"	"
1836	1539	1310	696	133	104	61			26		9	21.00	7.13	"	"
1837	1273	1171	611	122	110	54	116	67	21	9	6	18.60	7.50	"	"
1838	1400	1333	640	142	125	77	133	55	23	9	8	17.80	6.76	"	"
1839	1576	1435	602	142	158	85	124	65	20	7	10	17.80	6.94	"	"
1840	1534	1417	669	129	214	63	244	73	23	10	7	16.60	7.50	"	"
1841	1892	1521	774	162	275	81	201	66	27	10	11	12.20	6.57	"	"
1842	1705	1236	666	122	272	54	198	92	22	9	7	13.20	6.02	"	"
1843	1863	1513	836	143	286	72	248	60	28	10	13	11.20	5.56	"	"
1844	2258	1816	1019	176	340	99	277	76	34	11	14	13.00	5.56	"	"
1845	2214	1977	1204	195	338	104	320	90	45	15	17	9.60	6.57	"	"
1846	2606	2268	1362	213	540	138	419	100	51	18	20	8.00	5.92	4.80	2.92
1847	3257	2869	1744	288	854	147	551	115	73	32	27	7.80	7.13	"	"
1848	2883	2796	1447	329	701	187	431	151	50	21	30	7.80	5.37	"	"
1849	3062	2894	1579	315	834	183	434	140	52	19	31	7.30	5.18	"	"
1850	3055	3076	2033	418	897	158	461	144	55	20	47	7.20	5.48	"	"
1851	3308	3582	1977	467	1047	246	457	156	53	16	62	6.20	4.71	4.40	2.19
1852	2915	3863	2234				576	159			22	5.20	4.90	2.92	"
1853	2928	4247	2505				618	196			30	5.60	5.18	"	"
1854	2754	4165	2223				240	207			18	5.00	4.81	"	"
1855	2436	4022	1890				301	210			23	5.00	4.81	"	"
1856	2498	4116	2123				474	204			29	5.40	5.56	"	"
1857	2310	3344	1617				263	218			14	4.80	4.26	"	"
1858	1882	3665	1985				454	136			19	2.80	3.14	1.46	1.46
1859	1652	3781	2121				250	138			9	2.40	2.87	.70	1.41
1860	2169	4650	2854				710	132			29	2.40	3.88	1.40	"

NEW YORK MARINE INSURANCE RATES, 1816–1860
Compiled from *Shipping and Commercial List*

The rates for the "round voyage" were generally less than double the one-way rate. Unless otherwise specified, these rates permitted a stop at only one port; there was an additional charge for extra ports. The figures below are one-way rates unless otherwise indicated.

It will be noticed that the rates were higher at the beginning and the end than during the twenties and thirties.

	1816	1825	1835	1845	1860
By the trip					
British Isles	2	1–1¼	1–1¼	1–1½	1–2¼
France	2–2¼	1–1¼	1–1¼	1–1½	1–1¾
North Sea	2⅛–2¼	1¼–1½	1–1¼		2–3
Lisbon or Cadiz	2½	1–1¼	1–1¼	1–1¼	1¼–2
Gibraltar or Malaga		1–1¼	1–1¼	1–1½	1½–2
Mediterranean		1¼–1½	1–1½	1–1½	2–2½
Madeira, Canaries, etc.		1–1½	1–1¼	1¼–1½	2–2½
Canton direct		1¾	1¼–1½	–1½	
" and return	8			–3	4–6
Batavia or Indian Ocean		1¾	1½		2–2½
Brazil		1¼–1½	1–	1–1¼	1½–1¾
Buenos Aires–Montevideo		1½–2	–1½	–2	–2
Valparaiso, West Coast		2–3		–1½	2–2½
"Spanish Maine"		1¼–2	1¼–1½	1¼–3	1½–3
Vera Cruz, Tampico			1¾–2	2–2½	2–3½
West Indies, general	2				
additional ports	¼	¼	¼–½	¼–½	
Windward Islands		1	1–1½	1¼–1½	1¼–2
Cuba		1¼–1½	1¼–1½	1½–2	1½–2¼
Santo Domingo		1¼–1½	1¼–1½	1½–2	2–2½
New Orleans, Mobile, to		1¼–1½	1½–2	1½–2	1½–2
" " from			1–1¼	1¼–1½	1¼–1¾
Charleston, Savannah		½	⅝–¾	⅝–1	¾–1
Wilmington, N. C.		¾–1	⅝–¾	⅝–1	1–1¼
N. C. "over Ocracoke Bar"		¾–1	1¼–1½	1–	1–1½
Chesapeake Bay, 1 port		½–¾	½–¾	½–1	½–¾
Delaware River, 1 port		½	½–	½–1	
"Southern Coasting"	1¼				
"Eastern Coasting"	1¼				
R. I.–Conn.		½	⅜	¼–½	¼–½
Mass.		½–¾	½	⅜–¾	½–¾
Maine–N. H.		¾–1	½	¾–1	½–1
Halifax		1¼	1¼–1½	–1	1–2
"By the Year" for vessels		5½–6	5–6½		
("By the Year," based on value of vessels)					
$30,000 and up				5–6	7–8
$20,000–$30,000				6–7	7–8
$10,000–$20,000				8–10	9–10
$5,000–$10,000				9–12	12–15
$3,000–$5,000				12–15	15–20
By specific cargoes					
Cotton, to Europe			¾–1	⅝–1	
Specie, to or from Europe			½	½	
Dry Goods from Great Britain			1¼	1¼–1½	2–2¼
Hardware from " "			1½–1¾	2–2½	2¼

APPENDIX XX

NEW YORK COMMISSION RATES, 1835

Quoted from *Shipping and Commercial List*, July 18, 1835

On Foreign Business	per cent
Sales of merchandise	5
Sale or purchase of stocks	1
Sale or purchase of specie	½
Purchase and shipment of merchandise with funds in hand; on the aggregate amount of costs and charges	2½
Drawing or endorsing bills in all cases	2½
Vessels, selling or purchasing	2½
Freight procuring	5
Collecting freight or general average	2½
Outfits or disbursements with funds in hand	2½
Effecting marine insurance in all cases, when the premium does not exceed 10 per cent —*on the amount insured*	½
Effecting marine insurance in all cases when the premium exceeds 10 per cent—*on the amount of premium*	5
Collecting dividends on stock	½
Collecting delayed or litigated accounts	5
Adjusting and collecting insurance losses	2½
Receiving or paying moneys, from which no other commission is derived	1
Remittances in bills, in all cases	½
Landing and re-shipping goods from vessels in distress, on the value	2½
Receiving and forwarding goods entered at the Custom House, on the value	1½
And on responsibilities incurred	2½

On Inland Business	
Sales of merchandise	2½
Purchase and shipment of merchandise, or accepting for purchase, without funds or property in hand	2
Sale or purchase of stocks	1
Sale or purchase of specie	½
Sale or purchase of bills of exchange, without endorsing	½
Sale or purchase of bank notes or drafts, not current	½
Selling or endorsing bills of exchange	2½
Vessels, selling or purchasing	2½
Chartering to proceed to other ports to load	2½
Procuring or collecting freight	2½
Collecting general average	2½
Effecting marine insurance (same as foreign)	
Adjusting and collecting insurance losses	2½
Collecting dividends on stocks	½
Collecting bills and paying over the amount, or receiving and paying moneys from which no other commission is derived	1
Receiving and forwarding goods, on the value	½
The same when entered for duty or debenture	1
Remittances in bills, in all cases	½

PORT EXPENSES OF CHINA CLIPPER HOUQUA, 1850

From MS. statement of A. A. Low & Bros., to owners of ship, for expenses incurred in port at New York between sixth and seventh annual voyages, from family papers of William Gilman Low, Esq., of Tuxedo Park, N. Y., grandnephew of Abiel A. Low. The items have been rearranged topically; the names in parentheses are those to whom the payments were made.

The Knox MSS. show that ordinary freighters spent only one-tenth as much on their more frequent visits to New York.

PORT SERVICES

Entry, telegraph, hospital money and Custom House	$74.90
Towing from sea	40.00
Pilotage from sea	54.00
Wharfage (Wm. Frost)	28.13
Dockage (Wm. Aymar & Co.)	46.88
" (W. C. Taylor)	21.50
Stevedore (N. G. Aymar)	110.45
" (Geo. Mills)	396.09
" (W. G. Hynard)	38.60
Running lines (C. Henry)	15.00
Shipkeeper (D. Miner)	48.00
Watchman (D. Miner)	45.00
Day watch	18.00
Day watchman & labour	32.62
Survey of hatches	4.00
Towing ship to Bell's yard &c.	24.00
Clearance of ship	6.70
Towing ship to sea (Str. *Ajax*)	50.00
Pilotage to sea	35.88

REPAIRS

Joiner (J. E. Jennings)	41.75
Punching copper (Tooker)	17.37
Weighing old copper	14.90
Painting ship (A. Hall)	148.00
Plank	.75
Jacob Bell's bill	874.20
Sails rep. &c. (Larkin & Snyder)	737.40
Nails (D. Cozer)	20.14
Screw Dock bill	197.88
Copper (Willetts & Co., cf. credit)	1603.80
Carpenter in full	11.25
Iron work (J. Barker)	8.41
Repairs (E. & G. W. Blunt)	1.00
Paints, oils &c. (Butler & Reynolds)	102.62
Superintending repairs, fitting for sea, 2 mos. (J. N. Low)	200.00

EQUIPMENT

Knives, Forks &c. (H. J. Cox)	20.50
Upholstery (H. A. Stevenson)	215.52
China ware (S. & E. Willetts)	2.00
Chairs	9.00
Cargo books	4.00
Carpets (Sloane)	18.13
Glass ware	14.44
Tin ware	59.52

STORES

Provisions (Cooper & Giraud)	$508.90
Wood (J. D. Brown)	114.56
Croton water	9.35
Ship chandlery	422.67
Stores (Russell & Copeland)	1266.17
Fresh provisions (Simonson)	38.30
Bread (Davidson & Young)	388.80
Tea (1 ch. Congo, ½ ch. oolong, 10 lbs. Hyson)	51.67
Coal (Worth & Co.)	5.75
Flour (Allen & Paxson)	98.11
Medicine (Thos. Ritter)	22.66
Live stock (D. Fowler)	182.60

CREW WAGES

Wages of crew & board of mate & steward (inward trip)	1607.09
Charles P. Low, master, wages at $100 per mo., Mar. 11 '49–Jan. 15 '50	1013.33
1st mate in full (J. C. Strong)	101.58
Shipping crew & advancing wages (Goin, Pool & Pentz)	487.50

MISCELLANEOUS

Insurance on ship, val. at $24,000, 6% policies	1414.75
Cooperage at ship (J. Coleman)	10.34
W. T. Chapman	65.75
Abm. Brower	21.37
Carboy vitriol thrown overboard	7.28
Cartages & washing	7.00
Labour (G. Potts, Francis)	36.65
Advertising ship in "leaded type" 3 papers	55.24
Commission at 2½% (A. A. Low & Bros., on all this business)	340.59

CREDIT

5475 lbs. old copper & 220 lbs. nails.	941.64

BALANCE

To Debit owners, 6th Voyage inward	3068.12
" " " 7th " outward	9955.14
	13023.26

(The corresponding debit amounted to $13,-920.94 in 1848 and $10,405.55 in 1849.)

SHIP STORES, 1825

From ledger of Dennis H. Doyle, New York ship grocer, in account with the first Sandy Hook Lightship, Capt. Barnard. (New York Public Library MSS.) The shillings in the incidental references are in New York currency, at 12½ cents.

1825

Jan. 3	½ gallon winter Lamp Oil	.37½
	2 Hogs, 271 lbs. Cartage 1s6	15.77
	10 lb. Butter	2.59
	21 do. Best Brown Sugar	2.62½
	6 do. Coffee	1.50
	2 do. Young Hyson Tea	2.37½
	6 Bottles Mustard	1.12½
	½ do. Pepper	.19
	8 Bushels Coarse Salt, cartage 2s	5.25
	23 gallons Rum	11.50
	2 do. Cognac Brandy	3.00
	2 do. Holland Gin	2.50
	2 Decanters	1.50
	1 quart Cherry Brandy	.37½
	1 do. Cognac do.	.37½
	1 do. Holland Gin	.31
	½ pound Salt petre	.19
Apr. 4	2 Barrels Navy Bread	6.78
	2 do. Mess Beef	6.00 (?)
	1 do. Prime Pork	11.00
	21 lbs. Sugar	2.62½
	2 lbs. Young Hyson Tea	2.37½
	4 lbs. Coffee	1.00
	½ Barrel Superfine Flour	3.50
	15 gallons New Rum	7.50
	2 Bushels Corn	1.25
	4 do. Salt	2.75
	10½ lb. Goshen Butter	2.62½
	1 gallon Holland Gin	1.25
	1 do. Cognac Brandy	1.50
	4 Bushels Kidney Potatoes	2.00
	1 Gallon Vinegar	.25
	1 Box Soap 20 lbs. Box 2s	2.02
	1 quart Brandy	.37½
	5 Gallons Molasses	2.19
	1 quart Rum	.31
	Bread and Butter	.50

Few of the regular merchantmen purchased quite that much liquor within a similar period; apparently it was the initial effort to overcome the tedium of lightship service. Presumably most of the lamp oil was furnished from other sources.

The Knox MSS. show that the stores and provisions consumed on the New York ship *Warsaw* on a six months voyage around the "cotton triangle" in 1840 amounted to 13 bbl. beef, 10 bbl. pork, 16 bbl. bread, 23 bbl. potatoes, 2 bbl. whiskey, 3 boxes soap, 1 firkin butter, 1 box herring, ½ bbl. beans, ½ tierce rice, ½ bbl. sugar, 2 bbl. molasses, 1 box tea and 1 box candles.

APPENDIX XXIII

TRANSIENT (TRAMP) VOYAGES

In contrast to the packets and regular traders, which ran regularly back and forth between two or more ports, the bulk of the merchant marine engaged in transient voyages, picking up cargoes wherever they could. An excellent example of the nature of this trade is found in the *Voyages* of Capt. George Coggeshall. This list is limited to those made during our period; he had made about an equal number prior to 1815.

1815–16 Ship *John Hamilton*—Baltimore, Savannah, Lisbon, St. Ubes (Setubal), New York.
1816–17 Schooner *Iris*—New York, Martinique, St. Eustatia, St. Thomas, Puerto Rico, Santa Cruz, St. Martins, St. Barts (St. Bartholomews), St. Martins, New York.
1818–19 Schooner *Iris*—New York, Teneriffe, St. Thomas, Havana, New York.
1819 (In U. S. Brig *Enterprise*—New York, Omoa (Central America); Schooner *Retrieve* —Omoa, Vera Cruz, New York.
1820–21 Sloop *Volusia*—New York, Santiago de Cuba, Omoa, New Orleans, Truxillo Bonaca, New York.
1821–22 Schooner *Sea Serpent*—New York, Lima (sold schooner); Brig *Dick*—Lima, Guayaquil (sold brig); returned as passenger by Panama, Chagres, Havana, Philadelphia, New York.
1823 Schooner *Swan*—New York, Havana, New York.
1823–24 Brig *Nymph*—New York, Cadiz, St. Thomas, Alvarado (sailed for Havana but put back leaky; brig condemned); returned as passenger by schooner, Alvarado, Philadelphia, New York.
1825–27 Ship *Governor Clinton* (as supercargo)—New York, Chile, Peru, Colombia (West Coast), Gibraltar, New York.
1830–31 Schooner *Julia and Laura*—as passenger New York, St. Barts; St. Thomas, Santa Cruz, Puerto Rico (various ports), St. Thomas; returned as passenger St. Thomas, New York.
1837–38 Brig *Brilliant*—New York, Isle of May (Cape Verdes), Rio de Janeiro, New Orleans, Boston; passenger to New York.
1838–39 Brig *Brilliant*—New York, Isle of May, Rio de Janeiro, New Orleans, Saybrook.
1839 Brig *Brilliant*—Saybrook, Sydney (Nova Scotia), Philadelphia.
1840–41 Brig *Brilliant*—New York, Rio de Janeiro, New Orleans (wrecked in river); returned as passenger by river steamer and overland to New York—last voyage.

APPENDIX XXIV

DISTANCES FROM PRINCIPAL AMERICAN SEAPORTS

In nautical miles, by shortest natural routes

Based on U. S. Hydrographic Office, *Table of Distances between Ports*, 1931

	Mont.	Port.	Bost.	N. Y.	Phil.	Balt.	Norf.	Char.	Sav.	N. O.	Liv.	Gib.	Hav.	Rio
Montreal	—	1205	1247	1459	1608	1768	1653	1939	2012	3049	2785	3188	2472	5356
Portland	1205	—	98	349	521	686	564	891	964	1986	2927	2999	1456	4772
Boston..........	1247	98	—	290	475	640	518	845	918	1940	2964	3036	1415	4741
New York......	1459	349	290	—	235	413	292	627	700	1711	3137	3209	1227	4770
Philadelphia	1608	521	475	235	—	381	260	597	670	1681	3280	3352	1156	4817
Baltimore.......	1768	686	640	413	381	—	172	548	621	1632	3418	3490	1107	4844
Norfolk.........	1653	564	518	292	260	172	—	426	499	1510	3367	3369	985	4723
Charleston......	1939	891	845	627	597	548	426	—	99	1171	3557	3619	646	4721
Savannah.......	2012	964	918	700	670	621	499	99	—	1133	3630	3689	606	4753
New Orleans....	3049	1986	1940	1711	1681	1632	1510	1171	1133	—	4614	4577	602	5186
Coast Av........	1771	818	774	675	714	762	655	794	846	1646				
" -Liv.-Hav.	7028	5201	5153	5039	5150	5287	5007	4997	5082	6862				

APPENDIX XXV

AMOUNT OF VARIOUS MATERIALS REQUIRED FOR COSTUME

Approximate yardage (1 yard wide) in the average costume of a well-to-do American woman and man, to illustrate the increasing demand for textiles in the mid-nineteenth century. Estimated for this study by Miss Lucy Barton, author of *Historic Costume for the Stage*.

WOMEN	1800	1855	1925
Underwear, cotton or linen.................	7½	63	3½ (silk)
" woollen......................	(4 oz.)	2½	
Dress, silk.............................	5	30	3 to 4
" woollen...........................	5	15	3 to 4
" cotton............................	5	30 to 40	3 to 4
Wrap, silk.............................	5	8	4
" woollen...........................	5	8	4
Stockings, cotton or lisle..................	(2 to 3 oz.)	(2 to 3 oz.)	(1 to 2 oz.)
Shoes, kid (yds.)........................	1½	1½ to 2	1½
Whalebone (yds.)........................	7 to 8	12 to 15	0

MEN			
Under linen & shirt......................	4 to 5	4 to 5	
Suit, woollen...........................	7½	8	
" silk or velvet......................	6½		
Stockings, silk or lisle....................	(2 to 3 oz.)	(1 oz.)	
" woollen.......................	(4 to 6 oz.)	(2 oz.)	
Shoes (boots), leather (yds.)...............	2 to 4	2	
Hat, Beaver or felt (yds.).................	1¼	1½	

APPENDIX XXVI

PRINCIPAL CANALS AND RAILROADS FROM MAJOR SEAPORTS TO THE WEST

Adapted principally from H. V. Poor, *History of the Railroads and Canals of the United States* (1860). The cost figures, which apply to the time of completion, vary somewhat in different sources.

	From	To	Length (Miles)	Begun (Year)	Finished (Year)	Cost (Millions)
Erie Canal	Albany	Buffalo	363	1817	1825	7
Pa. "Main Line" (canal and rail)	Philadelphia	Pittsburgh	395	1827	1835	14
Chesapeake & Ohio Canal	Georgetown	Cumberland	184	1828	1850	10
Baltimore & Ohio R.R.	Baltimore	Wheeling	379	1828	1852	20
7 roads (later New York Central)	Albany	Buffalo	298	1830	1842	6
Western, etc. (later Boston & Albany)	Boston	Albany	200	1832	1841	11
Erie R.R.	Piermont	Dunkirk	446	1836	1851	24
Hudson River R.R.	New York	Albany	144	1847	1851	10
Pennsylvania R.R.	Philadelphia	Pittsburgh	331	1847	1852	25

APPENDIX XXVII

IMMIGRATION

The port figures include foreign travelers as well as immigrants, since the two were not segregated in the annual federal reports until 1856. The statistics by ports are adapted from the Treasury Dept., Bureau of Statistics, *Tables showing Arrivals of Alien Passengers and Immigrants in the U. S. from 1820 to 1888* (1889), pp. 108–9. The figures by nationalities arriving at New York from 1847 to 1860, the boom years of the old immigration, include immigrants alone and are derived from the *Annual Reports of the Commissioners of Emigration of the State of New York from ... 1847 to 1860* (1861), pp. 288. The periods do not exactly coincide, as the latter are based on the calendar year throughout, whereas the federal figures were based on the year ending September 30 until 1851 and thereafter the calendar year.

(Thousands)

	ALIEN PASSENGERS ARRIVED AT LEADING PORTS										IMMIGRANTS LANDED AT NEW YORK							
	TOTAL U.S.	NEW YORK	BOSTON	PHILADELPHIA	BALTIMORE	NEW ORLEANS	CHARLESTON	PORTLAND	GALVESTON	SAN FRANCISCO	GERMANY	IRELAND	ENGLAND & WALES	SCOTLAND	SWITZERLAND	FRANCE	SCANDINAVIA	HOLLAND
1820	10	3	-	2	1	-	-	-										
1821	11	4	1	1	1	-	-	-										
1822	8	4	1	-	-	1	-	-										
1823	8	4	-	-	-	1	-	-										
1824	9	4	-	1	-	1	-	-										
1825	12	7	-	1	1	-	-	-										
1826	13	6	1	2	1	1	-	-										
1827	21	12	1	3	1	1	-	-										
1828	30	19	1	3	1	1	-	-										
1829	24	14	1	1	1	3	-	-										
1830	24	13	1	1	3	2	-	-										
1831	23	10	1	3	3	3	-	-										
1832*	61	35	3	4	9	4	-	-										
1833	59	39	3	4	4	4	-	-										
1834	67	46	2	4	6	4	-	-										
1835	48	32	3	1	3	3	-	-										
1836	80	58	3	2	6	4	-	2										
1837	84	51	3	4	6	8	-	-										
1838	45	24	2	2	5	7	-	-										
1839	74	47	3	3	6	10	-	-										
1840	92	60	5	4	7	11	-	-										
1841	87	55	8	3	4	10	-	-										
1842	110	74	8	3	5	12	-	-										
1843*	56	38	3	2	2	6	-	-										
1844	84	59	6	4	5	3	-	-										
1845	119	76	10	5	7	15	-	-										
1846	158	98	13	7	9	22	-	-	-									
1847	239	145	20	14	12	34	-	1	3		53	52	9	2	1	3	1	3
1848	229	160	22	9	7	19	-	2	1		51	91	24	6	1	2	1	1
1849	299	213	29	15	8	25	1	2	1		55	112	30	8	1	2	4	2
1850*	380	221	31	13	9	51	1	2	1	43	45	117	29	6	2	3	4	1
1851	408	294	25	18	8	52	1	2	1	?	69	163	30	7	4	5	3	1
1852	397	303	21	17	14	32	1	1	2	?	118	118	34	7	6	8	3	1
1853	400	294	25	19	11	43	1	-	2	?	119	113	28	6	4	7	2	1
1854	460	327	27	15	13	51	1	1	3	14	176	82	31	4	8	7	2	1
1855	230	161	17	7	6	20	-	-	2	4	52	43	24	4	3	4	-	-
1856	224	158	19	8	6	18	-	-	1	5	56	44	25	4	2	2	1	1
1857	271	204	17	5	9	21	-	2	-	6	80	57	29	5	2	3	1	1
1858	144	101	9	2	3	13	1	-	-	5	31	25	12	2	1	1	5	-
1859	155	113	12	3	3	11	1	-	-	4	28	32	10	2	-	1	?	-
1860	179	131	12	3	6	13	-	2	1	5	37	47	12	1	1	1	-	-

Total arrivals of alien passengers, 1820–1860, at leading ports

Total U. S. 5,457,914	San Francisco................. 91,029*	Key West...................... 4,487
New York.................3,742,532	Portland...................... 25,639	Mobile........................ 3,523
New Orleans............... 555,322	Galveston..................... 22,193	New Bedford................... 2,259
Boston.................... 388,195	Charleston.................... 22,163	Providence.................... 2,240
Philadelphia.............. 239,057	Norfolk....................... 5,664	Savannah...................... 2,013
Baltimore................. 231,314		

* 15-month period for 1832 and 1850; 9-month period for 1843. Year ending Sept. 30, 1820-32; Dec. 31, 1833-43; Sept. 30, 1844-50; Dec. 31, 1851 ff. San Francisco returns not available for 1851-53.

APPENDIX XXVIII

NATIVITY OF INHABITANTS OF LEADING SEAPORTS, 1850–1860

Adapted from J. D. B. DeBow, *Statistical View of the United States . . . being a Compendium the Seventh Census* (1854), p. 399, for 1850; and J. G. G. Kennedy, *Population of the United ates in 1860; Compiled from the Original Returns of the Eighth Census* (1864), pp. 608–615, 1860. Indicates effect of the active decade of immigration on the seaport population. Note at Philadelphia had more native Americans than New York in 1850 and nearly as many in 50. New York gained 152,000 native Americans and 148,000 foreign-born in the decade.

	Grand Total	Total Free Native	Same State	Total Foreign	Ire- land	Ger- many	Great Britain	France
(Thousands)								
50								
w York..........	515	277	234	235	133	55	31	4
iladelphia........	408*	286	242	121	72	22	20	1
ltimore..........	169	130	113	35	12	19	2	—
ston.............	136	88	68	46	35	1	4	—
w Orleans.......	116	50	34	48	20	11	3	7
arleston.........	42	17	16	4	2	1	—	—
vannah..........	15	6	4	2	1	—	—	—
ɔbile.............	20	9	5	4	2	—	—	—
rtland...........	20	17	15	3	2	—	—	—
5o								
w York.........	813	429	379	383	203	119	37	8
iladelphia........	565	396	348	169	95	43	23	2
ltimore..........	212	154	144	52	15	32	2	—
ston.............	177	114	86	63	45	3	5	—
w Orleans.......	168	94	72	64	24	19	3	10

The Philadelphia population for this table was based by DeBow on the enlarged area of 1854, when several ·ounding communities were included. The balance of the population in the southern ports consisted of slaves.

APPENDIX XXIX

GROWTH OF POPULATION OF THE LEADING SEAPORTS, 1790–1860

Adapted from DeBow, *op. cit.*, p. 192, and 1860 census

	1790	1800	1810	1820	1830	1840	1850	1860
(Thousands)								
w York...........	33	60	96	123	202	312	515	813
iladelphia..........	42	69	91	112	161	220	340	565
.timore............	13	26	35	62	80	102	169	212
ston..............	18	24	33	43	61	93	136	177
w Orleans.........	—	—	17	27	46	102	116	168
arleston...........	16	20	24	24	30	29	42	40
·annah............	—	5	5	7	7	7	15	22
bile..............	—	—	—	1	3	12	20	29
·tland.............	2	3	7	8	12	15	20	26

419

APPENDIX XXX

COMMERCIAL AND MARITIME OCCUPATIONS IN LEADING SEABOARD STATES, 1860

Compiled from J. G. G. Kennedy, *Population of the U. S. in 1860*

	N. Y.	Mass.	Pa.	Md.	La.	S. C.	Ga.	Ala.	M
Importers...........	474	19	49	5	6	—	4	—	
Commission Merchts.	921	209	176	114	307	42	225	131	
Brokers.............	1,817	503	520	94	405	51	90	43	
Auctioneers.........	257	124	160	28	54	5	18	19	
"Merchants"*.......	21,677	5,924	10,680	3,182	2,776	1,890	3,195	2,368	3,0
Bankers.............	660	52	148	37	23	8	23	18	
Speculators.........	665	31	72	77	47	8	34	52	
Ship-carpenters......	3,152	1,966	1,159	753	437	52	46	116	1,
Riggers.............	422	267	97	87	7	20	6	1	
Rope-makers........	579	474	289	73	32	—	3	19	
Sail-makers..........	685	471	239	177	55	8	9	14	2
Mast-makers........	102	80	55	8	4	—	—	—	
Block-makers........	189	76	36	39	2	—	—	—	
Boatbuilders........	704	210	758	99	6	12	2	13	
Shipmasters.........	459	1,143	133	82	25	15	8	12	
Sailing-masters......	400	26	74	10	3	—	—	2	
Steamboatmen	295	11	274	50	678	6	54	205	
Boatmen............	9,273	121	5,489	283	526	23	54	256	
Mariners...........	12,141	14,014	4,297	3,918	635	187	333	232	11,

* The term "merchant" was apparently used in the broadest sense, to include even country storekeepers. fact that these were official figures does not prevent one's questioning the validity of certain items, such as the number of "importers" and "sailing-masters" in Massachusetts. The bankers and "speculators" were about e in number at New York, which had the lion's share of each group.

APPENDIX XXXI

NEW YORK COMMERCIAL FUNCTIONS, 1846

piled from *Doggett's New York Business Directory for 1846 & 1847*, part II, "Classification of Professions
rade." The original list includes a very wide range of specialized functions, arranged in alphabetical or-
th the firms or individuals engaged in each. The groups are not mutually exclusive, for a general firm such
nnell, Minturn & Co., or Howland & Aspinwall might appear under several different headings. This list
the common functions not particularly distinctive of a seaport, such as retailers, lawyers, hotel keepers,
me of the more important functions have been rearranged in order for emphasis. For a discussion of the
al functions, see Chapter XIII. These lists indicate the wide range of commodities and the relative busi-
each.

ants

neral	31
nporting and Commission"	51
hipping and Commission"	138
hipping and Importing"	8

rters

ificial flowers	5
skets, willow	5
ting cloths	3
stles	9
nzes	2
rr blocks	2
ttons	6
ina, glass & earthenware	53
ths, cassimeres & vestings	36
fee	69
ugs	37
y Goods	89
ndee goods (burlaps, duck, etc.)	5
ential oils	4
icy goods	59
eneral"	17
it skins	4
ns & pistols	10
irdressers' articles	4
rdware & Cutlery	86
tters' trimmings	1
np	8
les	17
meopathic medicines	1
iery & gloves	16
igo	28
es & embroideries	24
en	2
king glass plates	6
rble	5
rocco	1
sical instruments	5
dles & fish hooks	6
paintings	1
e oil	9
umery	2
e glass	2
cious stones	3
e	30
sia goods	9

Importers, ctd.

Sail duck	4
"Segars"	44
Sewing silks	15
Silks & fancy dry goods	42
Slates	2
Stationery	4
Steel	1
Steel pens	1
Straw goods	8
Sugar	45
Suspenders	1
Tea	17
Toys	7
Twine	2
Watches	40
Watchmakers' tools	2
Wines & liquors	89
Woollens	6
Worsted goods	6

Commission Merchants

Dry goods	91
General	317
Hardware & cutlery, domestic	8
Produce (flour, etc.)	86

Auctioneers

Auctioneers	66

Jobbers

Boots & shoes	42
China, glass & earthenware	93
Clothiers	24
Cloths, cassimeres & vestings	14
Druggists	46
Dry goods	224
" " (also importers)	23
Fancy goods	30
Fruit, foreign	24
Grocers	221
Hardware & cutlery	35
Hats, caps & furs	42
Hosiery & gloves	8
Laces & embroideries	6
Ready made linen & stocks	3
Silks & fancy dry goods	40

Jobbers, ctd.

Tea.................................. 1
Wines & liquors.................... 22

"Merchants" or "Dealers"
(Not differentiated in respect to above
functions)
Carpet dealers...................... 33
Coal dealers........................ 95
Cotton merchants................... 3
Flaxseed dealer..................... 1
Flour dealers....................... 39
Fur dealers & furriers.............. 55
Grindstones & plaster.............. 55
Hide & leather dealers............. 33
   Leather only.................... 18
Iron merchants..................... 38
Lumber dealers..................... 60
Mahogany yards.................... 22
Military goods...................... 10
Molasses merchant.................. 1
Oil merchants...................... 42
Pot & pearl ash & saleratus dealers... 5
Produce dealers.................... 6
Rice dealer........................ 1
Salt dealers........................ 4
Stave yards........................ 4
Stone yards........................ 32

Brokers
Bill................................ 5
Bullion............................ 1
Commission........................ 5
Cotton............................. 13
Custom House...................... 9
Drug............................... 22
Dry goods.......................... 4
Dye woods.......................... 1
Exchange.......................... 114
General............................ 9
Hide & skin........................ 1
Insurance.......................... 4
Merchandise....................... 18
Metal.............................. 3
Money............................. 2
Note............................... 3
Oil................................ 2
Produce............................ 17
Rice............................... 2
Ship............................... 8
Tea................................ 3
Tobacco............................ 2
Wine............................... 4
Wood............................... 1
Wool............................... 3

Agents
Collecting......................... 3
General............................ 4

Agents, ctd.
Miscellaneous......................
Passenger..........................

Other Functions
Accountants........................
Bankers, private...................
Barometer & thermometer makers....
"Boarding houses—sailor"...........
Boat builders......................
Booksellers, foreign...............
Chain cables.......................
Chocolate & cocoa mfrs.............
Chronometer makers................
Coffee roasters....................
   "   "   & spice factors.......
Commercial agency.................
Consulates.........................
Cordage mfrs.......................
Cordage, rope & twine dealers.......
Cotton, damaged, dealers...........
   "   menders....................
   "   presses....................
Distillers..........................
Dock builders......................
Docks (dry, & marine railways)......
Expresses..........................
Forwarding & transportation merchts.
Gaugers............................
Harbor masters....................
Hide currier.......................
Inspectors (flour, tobacco, etc.) ......
Insurance companies, marine........
Leather dressers...................
Lighter offices....................
Map & chart publishers.............
Marine surveyor...................
Mathematical & nautical instrument
   makers.........................
Mercantile agencies................
Packet offices.....................
Passage offices....................
Port wardens......................
Rectifiers of spirits...............
"Refinishers, pressers & packers of dry
   goods".........................
Riggers & stevedores...............
Sailmakers.........................
Ship builders......................
Ship chandlers.....................
Ship joiners.......................
Ship smiths........................
Ship wrights.......................
Shipping offices...................
Spar makers.......................
Steam engine builders.............
Sugar refiners.....................
Weighers.........................

BIBLIOGRAPHY

This bibliography includes only those sources which have been particularly pertinent to this work; it is out of the question, in view of the many ramifications of the subject, to list all those which have been of incidental service.

For convenience, the bibliography has been divided into the following thirty sections:

1. Bibliographical Aids
2. Manuscripts
3. Newspapers
4. Periodicals
5. Government Documents
6. Annual Reports
7. Statistics
8. Manuals, Dictionaries, etc.
9. Memoirs and Diaries
10. Biography, collected
11. Biography, individual
12. Port of New York, History
13. New York City, General
14. New York City, Social
15. New York City, Description, etc.
16. Port Functions
17. Business Methods
18. Shipbuilding
19. Shipping, General, and Sea Routes
20. Shipping, Particular Groups
21. Steamboats and Steamships
22. General Commerce and Transatlantic Trade
23. Manufactures, Foreign and Domestic
24. The "Cotton Triangle" and Coasting Trade
25. Caribbean and Latin America
26. "Distant Seas"
27. Hinterland, Canals, and Railroads
28. Hudson River
29. Immigration and Passengers
30. Miscellaneous

Sources of particular pertinence or utility are marked with an asterisk (*).

I. BIBLIOGRAPHICAL AIDS

American Association of Port Authorities, *Bibliographic Notes on Ports and Harbors,* compiled by Perry Young (1926).
Most of the items deal with period later than this study.

E. B. Green and R. B. Morris, *A Guide to the Principal Sources for Early American History, 1600 to 1800, in the City of New York* (1929).
Designed for earlier period, but gives useful survey of collections.

Winifred Gregory, *American Newspapers, 1821–1936: A Union List of Files available in the United States and Canada* (1937).

G. G. Griffin, *Writings on American History* (annual since 1906).

*A. R. Hasse, *Index of Economic Material in the Documents of . . . New York, 1789–1904* (Carnegie Institute) (1907).
Invaluable guide to scattered references in annual state documents.

Library of Congress, Division of Bibliography, *Select Lists of References.*
An extensive and ever-increasing list of special bibliographies, some of which are mimeographed, including such as numbers 72, Harbors (1915); 452, Immigration (1920); and 1049, Early American Ships and Shipping (1928).

R. B. Morris, "The Federal Archives of New York City" in *American Historical Review,* XLII, pp. 256–72 (1937).

New York Public Library, *Bulletin.*
Includes numerous special bibliographies, such as "Financial and Commercial History, etc., of the City of New York" V, pp. 42–59 (1905), and "Waterfront of the City of New York, its Harbors, Docks, Ferries, etc.," *ibid.,* pp. 167–72.

*I. N. P. Stokes, *Iconography of Manhattan Island,* VI (1928); "Bibliography" by V. H. Paltsits.
The most comprehensive critical New York City bibliography of manuscript and published sources, compiled by the director of the Manuscripts Division in the New York Public Library. Supersedes earlier Osgood report on public archives.

II. MANUSCRIPTS

New York Custom House

These records have been the most serviceable of the unpublished records for this study. They contain a wealth of detail about the vessels, their movements, and their crews, but unfortunately reveal little about their cargoes, since manifests are preserved for only ten years.

*Certificates of Registry.

*Certificates of Enrolment.
Two separate series, for vessels in foreign and domestic trade respectively; about 500 certificates in each series each year until around 1850, when number increased. Steam vessels are segregated for most of the period. A new certificate was issued for every shift in ownership or structural change. Each certificate indicates tonnage, dimensions, place of building, master, and owners; the builder's name is generally given only for new vessels and proportional shares of ownership only from 1848 onwards. The records have been rebound in canvas and stored in steel cases, under immediate supervision of the Marine Division. Unfortunately there are serious gaps in each series.

*Foreign Arrivals.

*Foreign Clearances.
These indicate every movement in foreign trade, giving name of vessel, master, tonnage and, in early years, general nature of cargo.

Coastwise Arrivals.

Coastwise Clearances.
Only a minor portion of the vessels engaged in coastwise trade were

required to enter or clear at the custom house; consequently these do not present a complete picture, as do the foreign arrivals and clearances. Both of these series are also Marine Division records.

*Crew Lists.

Cover all voyages in foreign, but not in coasting, trade. Each list gives master's name, together with details of nativity, residence, age, height, complexion, etc., of the mates and other crew, with notes on desertion and the like. The personal details were often entered in too perfunctory a manner to be reliable. These papers, directly under the Records Division, are stored in the sub-cellar, in bundles with end boards; they are arranged in order of arrival by years in two series—"T. P." (this port) for vessels of New York registry, and "O. P." (other ports) for the rest.

Miscellaneous.

Various other customs collections were of occasional service. The passenger lists are not open to general inspection, but information concerning particular vessels, from 1819 onwards, may be had upon request to the Records Division. The state records of immigration have been destroyed by fire. The records of the custom houses at Perth Amboy and other nearby places are also preserved at New York.

UNITED STATES COURT, SOUTHERN DISTRICT OF NEW YORK

Extensive collection of records of the federal courts, both district and circuit, are preserved in the new Federal Court Building under the supervision of the clerk of courts. The papers have recently been cleaned, sorted and stored in steel cases by the Historical Records Survey.

*Dockets.

Admiralty and Criminal Dockets were of particular value, giving brief summaries of each case; do not start until latter part of period. Separate criminal dockets for District and Circuit Courts.

*Papers.

A very wide variety of material in connection with admiralty, criminal, customs and other types of cases, including many business documents of a sort difficult to find elsewhere. Some of the papers filed under heading "Embargo" contain material on slaving and customs violations. There are also papers dealing with "deceased seamen."

SURROGATE COURT, NEW YORK COUNTY (Hall of Records)

Wills.

Copies of all wills probated in Manhattan (the old New York City) from the mid-seventeenth century; indicate nature of estates and bequests. Excellent cumulative index series facilitates identifying approximate date of death. The similar records for Kings County (Brooklyn) are useful for many shipmasters. The Connecticut probate records help to identify numerous New York mariners and merchants, but search is difficult since they are preserved in separate towns rather than at the county seats.

National Archives (Washington, D. C.)

*Consular Despatches.

Recently removed from State Dept.; bound in volumes by ports. The despatches themselves contain only incidental material of value; but after the early 'thirties, each consul was expected to report semi-annually the movements of all vessels of American registry at his port. These indicated the master, tonnage, number of crew, the ports from which they arrived and for which they cleared, and, in the more complete records (Havre was better than Liverpool in this respect), the nature of the inward and outward cargoes, and, at some ports, the value of those cargoes. The despatches themselves, from 1856 onwards, were published in *Commercial Relations,* but the semi-annual reports were only summarized.

Public Record Office (London)

The despatches of the British consuls stationed at the principal American ports contain occasional interesting, objective comments upon the rivalry of the ports.

Free Public Library of Liverpool

American Chamber of Commerce Minutes.

Four volumes contain the minutes of the American Chamber at Liverpool, throwing considerable light on New York's vital relations with that port; numerous former New Yorkers were among the members of the chamber.

Chamber of Commerce of the State of New York

Minutes.

Four volumes contain the manuscript minutes of the Chamber down to 1858 when the printed reports began. The minutes contain part, but not all, of the Chamber's memorials, petitions and committee reports. Photostatic copies of these originals are in the Manuscript Division of the New York Public Library. The early portion of these minutes, 1768–1784, were published as "Colonial Records" in 1867.

*Arbitration Records.

A little old chest contains many of the papers of the Chamber's arbitration committees, particularly for the period of this study (see text). The earlier committee minutes, for 1779–1792, have been published.

New York Public Library

Bayard Papers.

Scattered correspondence of William Bayard and his great firm of Leroy, Bayard & McEvers during the years 1786–1826.

*Allan Melville Papers.

Business papers of the father of Herman Melville; 9 boxes and 2 volumes, especially useful for Havre trade. Include letter book of French business, 1818–25; accounts of importations and sales of goods, 1821–32; and bills of lading, 1803–26.

*Thomas W. Williams Papers.

Twenty-two boxes of "in letters" of New London merchant, in constant correspondence with New York about disposing of West Indian cargoes, purchase of ships for whalers, etc.

Cyrus Williams Papers.

Ledger, 1818–61, of merchant and cotton manufacturer of North Stonington and New Haven; useful details of country merchant's barter trade. Letters, two boxes, have scant New York connection.

*Dennis L. Doyle Account Book.

"Ship Book" containing ledger accounts of New York ship chandler, 1823–29; indicate nature of ship stores and amounts purchased for particular voyages.

*Levi Coit Letter Books.

Two volumes (1796–1804, 1808–1816) of New York commission merchant; particularly useful for operations in cotton.

Brown Bros. & Co. Business Records.

Of the 176 volumes of accounts of the great private bankers, the only particularly pertinent one is vol. 31, "Custom House Entries, 1827–33" with details of linen and tea cargoes.

Dodge Papers.

Personal and mercantile account books of William E. Dodge, 1830–70, 46 vols., and miscellaneous papers of Phelps, Dodge & Co., 1832–59; latter contain interesting statements of metal sales by consignees at cotton ports.

Thomas K. Jones & Co. Papers.

"In letters" of Boston auctioneers and commission merchants, 1808–32; particularly good for letters from Jeremiah and Francis Thompson concerning textile consignments, 1818–19.

*Frederick S. Wolcott Diary.

Two volumes, 1849–54, by New York dry goods jobber and agent for New England textiles; occasional details of that trade, in addition to brother's China trade, and social notes about Howlands.

Jonathan Bulkley Diary.

Photostat of first of three volumes in Pequot Library at Southport, Conn.; covers 1802–26; kept at Mill River, near Fairfield, Conn. Details of Sound sloop movements.

Hunt, Merriam & Co., Order Book.

Record of a few jobbers' sales of thread; together with informal pencilled notes of credit standing of various customers, 1851.

Customs Papers.
> Miscellaneous documents, 1792–1865, including interesting batch of applications and testimonials for customs berths in 1852 and business details of building of new custom house.

(Moses Taylor Papers.)
> This immense collection, filling some fifty large wooden packing cases, contains more than a thousand account books and much correspondence concerning the Cuban trade, New York banking, etc., but will not be available to scholars until sorted and arranged, a matter of several years of work.

The Manuscript Division also has a large amount of material for the period 1783–1815, including the letter books of Stephen Jumel.

NEW YORK HISTORICAL SOCIETY

While rich in material for that same 1783–1815 period, particularly with the letter books of P. P. & R. C. Livingston and the account books of Howland & Grinnell, the Society has little for the period of this study except for the 28 quarto volumes of the Philip Hone diary, thoroughly exploited and edited by Tuckerman and later by Nevins (see Memoirs and Diaries).

BAKER LIBRARY, HARVARD GRADUATE SCHOOL OF BUSINESS ADMINISTRATION

(Including the manuscripts of the Business Historical Society)

John Jacob Astor Papers.
> Collection of 22 volumes and 15 boxes, including material of New York China trade; thoroughly utilized by Porter (see Biography).

Pierson Receipt Book.
> Indicates diversified trade of Isaac G. Pierson & Bros., New York commission merchants, importing iron and dealing in many domestic products, 1827–33.

A. P. Gibson & Co., Letter Book.
> Covers wide range of New York business operations, 1816–18; including specimens of instructions to captains.

*W. W. Gordon & Co., Papers.
> More than 500 volumes of Savannah firm of cotton dealers (Reed & Tison at start), 1856–1916, including letter books, journals, ledgers, etc., but most of the material too late for this period. Useful in conjunction with Bostwick papers at Yale.

Perkins Papers.
> Ledgers and day books, 18 vols., of Andrew & Joseph Perkins, merchants of Norwich, Conn., similar in value to Cyrus Williams ledger above, in showing dealings of country merchant, with occasional West Indian dealings. Cover period 1783–1825.

*Mercantile Marine Insurance Co., Risk Book.
   Contains list of individual risks taken by this Boston company, 1830–73, including numerous trips from New York. Useful for indicating fluctuations in rates; supplements American Mutual papers, below.
Log Books.
   Logs of several vessels on voyages from New York during the period.

YALE UNIVERSITY LIBRARY (New Haven, Conn.)

*Bostwick Papers.
   Extensive collection of letter books, ledgers, journals, cash books, sales books, bill of lading books, and memorandum books of William Bostwick (including firms of E. Campfield & Co., Burton & Bostwick and Bostwick & Baird), commission merchant and cotton factor at Augusta, Ga., covering years 1826–45 (see text).

RUTGERS UNIVERSITY LIBRARY (New Brunswick, N. J.)

Neilson Papers.
   Large collection of manuscript material from the Neilson family of New Brunswick, N. J., covering a considerable part of eighteenth and nineteenth centuries, including material illustrative of trade in flour, etc., between New Brunswick and New York, with movements of the family's sloops.
Eveleth & Wood Papers.
   Letter books of Boston commission merchants in leather, boots and shoes around 1840 (see text).

STEVENS INSTITUTE OF TECHNOLOGY LIBRARY (Hoboken, N. J.)

John Stevens Papers.
   Extensive correspondence, accounts and memoranda on his pioneer experiments in steamboating, chiefly for years 1807–16; material well utilized by Turnbull.

ATLANTIC MUTUAL INSURANCE CO. (49 Wall St., N. Y. C.)

*"Vessel Disasters."
   Continuous series of more than 320 quarto volumes from 1852 to present (25 volumes to 1861). Designed to keep office posted on latest information concerning all accidents to American vessels and some foreign vessels frequenting New York. Usual entry in old books consisted of clipping from newspaper marine news, together with notations on company's insurance involved, if any, indicating amounts insured on vessel, freight, and cargo and, occasionally, amounts insured by other companies.
*Inspectors' Reports.
   Seven quarto volumes of confidential reports of the company's inspectors, 1847–52, upon various classes from sloops up to ships, in-

cluding many hailing from other ports. In addition to conventional data on ownership, dimensions, materials and rating as given in later printed reports, contain interesting informal observations of a sort not easily obtainable elsewhere, especially for smaller craft.

Financial Statements.

One volume of printed annual statements, accompanied by specimens of annual dividend certificates or "scrip."

Company Biography.

Entries for every officer and employe of the company from the beginning, indicating length of service and other data.

Essex Institute (Salem, Mass.)

Large collection of early log books, some of which give details of transient voyages touching at New York.

Private Papers

*Low Manuscripts.

Detailed annual reports of A. A. Low & Bros. to part owners of *Houqua* and other Low ships, giving a wealth of detail upon the economic side of shipowning, port expenses, etc., in possession of William G. Low, Esq., of Tuxedo Park, N. Y., grand nephew of A. A. Low.

*Knox Manuscripts.

Papers of Alexander Knox, Jr., New York merchant-shipowner; including "receipt book," 1838–42, indicating port expenses, etc.; passage book, 1831–35, with individual steerage and cabin accounts, indicating sureties, for immigrants, of ship *Camillus* on New York-Greenock run; log of ship *Warsaw*, 1840, on "cotton triangle" voyage; diary 1836–38, including account of a Black Ball passage; and two letters, 1842, with details of shipowning, etc. In possession of his great-grandson, Alexander O. Vietor, Esq., of New York City.

Griswold Manuscripts.

Early letter book of N. L. & G. Griswold around 1800, one of the few records escaping the fire which later destroyed their countinghouse; also memoranda and recollections by the late Frank G. Griswold, in the possession of George Griswold, Esq., of Greenwich, Conn.

III. NEWSPAPERS

The day-by-day search of the New York newspaper files for the almost half-century of this period has constituted the backbone of the research for this volume. The files of at least one New York daily, and generally more than one, together with the complete files of the semi-weekly *Shipping List* yielded an immense amount of information not to be secured elsewhere. The three chief items of value in the daily papers were (a) "marine intelligence," listing all arrivals and clearances, frequently with incidental remarks on the trips; (b) general marine news; and (c) advertisements, which revealed much of incidental value. The same newspaper was seldom best for all three, so that it was desirable to consult several. Most of them were used in the research room of the Newspaper Division at New York Public Library. For location of particular files, consult the Gregory *Union List,* mentioned under Bibliographical Aids. The dates given below indicate the whole period of the paper's existence, even though much of it falls outside the period of this study.

NEW YORK NEWSPAPERS

Commercial Advertiser (1797–1904).

Daily Advertiser (1817–1836).

*Evening Post (1801 to present).

Mercantile Advertiser (1792–1838).
> These four are all useful to 1827, after which others below are better. The *Post* was most useful for general news and editorials, but weak in advertising; the *Daily Advertiser* had much statistical material but was inferior in general news. The *Mercantile Advertiser* was consulted at the Library of Congress.

*Journal of Commerce (1827 to present).
> Best for 1827–35 and useful after that for detailed statistics, analyses, and advertising.

*Herald (1835–1924).
> Most useful general newspaper from 1835 onwards. Bennett's news schooners generally gathered the fullest and freshest marine news; his special correspondents sent intelligent reports from other cities; and his lively interest in things maritime led to frequent valuable special articles. As in some of the other papers, useful annual summaries of commerce, shipbuilding, etc., appeared around the end of each year. Advertising, however, was not as full as in some of the "Wall Street Press."

Times (1851 to present).
> Only New York daily file available at Princeton before 1861, so consulted frequently for details, but treatment of marine news not as full or lively as in *Herald.*

*Shipping and Commercial List and New York Price Current (1815–1926).
> Invaluable for statistics and factual details, though containing few general articles. Listed arrivals and clearances at all principal American seaports, with analyses of cargoes arriving at New York. For most of period contained monthly statistics of exports of chief commodities, and frequent statements of rates of freight, insurance, commissions, pilotage, etc., in addition to "price current" of commodities each issue. Later volumes well indexed for the year. Semi-weekly; title varies.

OTHER CITIES

Baltimore Price Current and Weekly Journal of Commerce (1850–1908).

Boston Commercial Gazette (1795–1840), merged in *Boston Semi-Weekly Advertiser* to 1876.

(Boston) *Columbian Centinel* (1784–1840).

Charleston Mercury (1822–1868).

Liverpool Mercury (1811–1904).

(London) *Times* (1785 to present), with useful separate index.

New Orleans Price Current (1822–1884, title varies).

(Philadelphia) *Grotjan's Philadelphia Public Sale Report* (1812–1827).

Philadelphia Price Current (1827–1931, title varies).

(Portland) *Eastern Argus* (1803–1921).

IV. PERIODICALS

Albion, a Journal of News, Politics and Literature (1822–1875).
A British weekly published at New York.

*DeBow's Review (1846–1862, title varies).
Edited by J. D. B. DeBow at New Orleans; devoted chiefly to economic matters, principally southern.

Harper's Weekly (1857–1916).

*Hunt's Merchant's Magazine and Commercial Review (1840–1869).
One of the most valuable single sources for this study. Edited by Freeman Hunt at New York; two volumes each year. A mine of pertinent material, both in general articles on commercial and maritime subjects, and in special items, together with much statistical matter, both current and in tables for periods of years. Contains studies of most of the first- and second-rate seaports of the world. Each volume well indexed.

Illustrated London News (1842 to present).

Leslie's Illustrated Weekly Magazine (1855–1922).
These two, with *Harper's* above, contain many woodcuts of varying merit, illustrating the shipping and port scenes. Several cuts from *Leslie's* are reproduced in this book.

Nautical Gazette (1871 to present).

Niles' Weekly Register (1811–1849).
Edited by Hezekiah Niles at Baltimore. Not as strictly commercial as Hunt, but useful for early years of period.

Sailor's Magazine and Naval Journal (1828 to present, title varies).
Issued by the American Seamen's Friend Society at New York; contains much about seamen's welfare and shipwrecks. Complete files in libraries of Society and Chamber of Commerce.

United States Commercial and Statistical Register (1839–1842).
Edited by Samuel Hazard of Philadelphia; some New York information is also contained in his *Register of Pennsylvania* (1828–1835).

V. GOVERNMENT PUBLICATIONS

(See also Annual Reports)

GREAT BRITAIN

Parliament, *Sessional Papers* ("Blue Books").
Occasional special papers, such as general inquiries on commerce, shipping, and emigration, were of service. Good cumulative indices available. See lists of pertinent papers in bibliographies of N. S. Buck, *Anglo-American Trade* and S. C. Johnson, *Emigration from the United Kingdom.*

NEW YORK CITY

Manual of the Common Council (see Annual Reports).

NEW YORK STATE

Legislative Documents (Senate Documents, House Documents, Reports, etc.). Thoroughly analyzed in Hasse.

Law Reports.
Various series for state courts, in addition to federal courts indicated below. Many of the pertinent commercial cases, as summarized in *Hunt's Merchant's Magazine,* are conveniently listed in W. F. Poole, *Index to Periodical Literature,* I, pp. 821–23; also consult various digests under appropriate topics.

Statutes.
Published annually; include many regulations concerning port, and, in earlier years, incorporation of insurance and steamboat companies. Titles of all acts affecting New York City, together with text of laws current in 1855, are given in H. E. Davies, *The Laws of the State of New York, relating particularly to the City of New York* (1855).

UNITED STATES

American State Papers.
Collection of early official documents in several series. The *Commerce and Navigation* series includes the annual reports on that subject to 1821, with other incidental material; the *Finance, Military Affairs* and *Naval Affairs* contain only occasional pertinent matter.

Congressional Documents.
This tremendous collection, arranged under *Senate Documents, Senate Reports, House (Executive) Documents, House Reports,* etc., for each session of Congress, includes most of the material published under government auspices during our period. In addition to the annual re-

ports (*q.v.*) on various subjects, they contain special papers indicated separately. Convenient cumulative indices are available.

Congressional Record (and other collections of debates).
Occasional material, concerning steamship subsidies, etc.

Law Reports.
Series of important cases in Supreme Court and lower federal courts. See remarks under state law reports.

Statutes at Large.

VI. ANNUAL REPORTS, OFFICIAL AND UNOFFICIAL

Boston Board of Trade, *Annual Reports* (since 1854–55).

*Chamber of Commerce of the State of New York, *Annual Reports* (since 1858–59).
Unfortunately, this invaluable series did not start until the very end of our period. Each issue, in addition to recording the business of the Chamber in continuation of the old manuscript records, contains detailed analyses of the trade in various commodities—dry goods, sugar, coffee, etc., with abundant statistics and accounts of the state of the market for the year; together with sections on marine insurance, lists of marine losses, etc. Each volume is well indexed; and a cumulative index, both for the early manuscript minutes and later printed reports, is being prepared by Miss L. Elsa Loeber, librarian of the Chamber.

New York City

Manual of the Corporation of the City of New York, 28 vols. (1848–1871).
Popularly known as "Valentine's Manual," having been edited until 1866 by D. T. Valentine. In addition to full lists of city officials and municipal activities, Valentine included much early historical material and reproduced many maps and pictures. The "new series" edited by H. C. Brown had no official status.

New York State

*Annual reports of Canal Commissioners, Canal Fund, Auditor of Canal Fund, Comptroller, inspectors of flour, etc., in Senate or Assembly Documents or Reports. For exact references, see Hasse.

United States

(The following reports are sometimes found separately bound; but they are also included in the regular series of Congressional Documents).

Commercial Relations of the United States with Foreign Countries.
Report by Secretary of State, starting with year 1855–56; summary of consular despatches from various foreign ports.

Commerce and Navigation.
Report by Secretary of the Treasury, starting in 1821; information for

earlier years in *American State Papers, Commerce and Navigation.* The original source for most of the statistics for the nation's foreign commerce. Includes exports, imports, tonnage entered and cleared, tonnage registered, enrolled and licensed, and shipbuilding. Imports and exports analyzed by ports or customs districts only from 1856 onwards. Much of the pertinent information in this series illustrating relative activity of various states or ports is summarized in appendix.

State of the Finances.
Another report by Secretary of the Treasury, since 1821. Duplicates some of commercial statistics; also gives per capita consumption of commodities, and reports on customs service, marine hospitals, light-house service, steamboat inspection, specie movement, etc.

Passengers Arrived from Foreign Countries.
Report by Secretary of State, starting in 1820. Shows, for each port for each quarter year, the countries of origin, occupations, sex, etc. For tabulations, see Immigration.

Coast and Geodetic Survey.
Reports new surveys and also includes new charts.

Census (decennial).
In addition to population, indicates occupational statistics for the various states or ports. Valuable special studies in some of the later reports (see Shipbuilding). One of the most useful single volumes is (J. D. B. DeBow) *Compendium of the Seventh Census* (1854).

Statistical Yearbook.
Compiled by Bureau of Foreign and Domestic Commerce since 1879. Wealth of statistics on many different subjects, including commerce and shipbuilding. For the period before 1860, however, most of the figures are simply decennial averages.

VII. STATISTICS

(In addition to above Annual Reports)

*J. S. Homans, *An Historical and Statistical Account of the Foreign Commerce of the United States* (1857).
A very concise and convenient arrangement of the Commerce and Navigation data on exports, imports, and tonnage, arranged by states and foreign countries for the period 1821–56, with useful brief notes on American and foreign seaports.

William Page, *Commerce and Industry, 1815–1914,* 2 vols. (1919).
The second volume consists of a compilation of commercial and other economic statistics from the British parliamentary papers.

Timothy Pitkin, *A Statistical View of the Commerce of the United States* (1835).

Adam Seybert, *Statistical Annals* (1818).

VIII. MANUALS AND DICTIONARIES

*Joseph Blunt, *The Merchant's and Shipmaster's Assistant* (1832).

*———*The Shipmaster's Assistant and Commercial Digest* (1837, etc.).
Separate editions of a highly useful manual by a New York lawyer. Sums up concisely the essential points on a large number of different subjects. The scope of the work is indicated by the chapter headings in the 1837 edition: "Ships, Navigation Acts, Custom House Laws, Fisheries, Revenue Cutters, Shipowners, Shipmasters, Seamen, Consuls, Freight, General Average, Salvage, Bottomry and Respondentia, Marine Insurance, Factors and Agents, The Navy, Pensions, Crimes, Slaves, Wrecks, Quarantine, Passengers, Pilots, Bills of Exchange, Exchange, Weights and Measures, Harbor Regulations, Commercial Regulations."

F. G. Clarke, *The American Ship-Master's Guide and Commercial Assistant* (1838).
A similar work, published in Boston.

*R. H. Dana, *The Seaman's Friend: Containing a Treatise on Practical Seamanship . . . a Dictionary of Sea Terms; Customs and Usages of the Merchant Service; Laws relating to the Practical Duties of Master and Mariners* (9th ed. 1857).
Invaluable reference work for practically everything concerning shipboard nomenclature and routine, by the author of *Two Years Before the Mast*.

B. F. Foster, *The Merchant's Manual* (1838).

*J. R. McCulloch, *A Dictionary of Commerce and Commercial Navigation* 2 vols. (1851), and numerous other editions, British and American.
Comprehensive and useful compilation of a wide range of material on various ports, commodities, business practices, etc., with a large quantity of statistics usually based upon the years immediately preceding the edition. Information about a particular country is apt to be found under the heading of its leading port.

J. Montefiore, *A Commercial Dictionary* (1804).

IX. MEMOIRS AND DIARIES

(Jacob Barker), *Incidents in the Life of Jacob Barker of New Orleans,* etc. (1855).
"Largely autobiographical, but ostensibly written by a friend." Barker was a prominent New York shipowner until banking troubles led him South.

R. J. Cleveland, *Narrative of Voyages and Commerical Enterprises,* 2 vols. (1842).
Includes a voyage from New York to the West Coast around 1818; an

abridged version was edited by his son, H. W. S. Cleveland, as *Voyages of a Merchant Navigator.*

Henry Clews, *Fifty Years in Wall Street* (1908).

*George Coggeshall, *Voyages to Various Parts of the World, made between the Years 1800 and 1831* (2nd ed. 1853).

*——*Second Series of Voyages . . . between 1802 and 1841* (1852).

*——*Thirty-six Voyages . . . made between the Years 1799 and 1841 . . . (Selected from his Manuscript Journal of Eighty Voyages)* (3rd ed. 1858).
The last volume is a combination and slight expansion of the first two series. This is perhaps the most valuable single narrative source illustrating the seagoing end of New York's commerce. (See text and appendix.)

Edmund Fanning, *Voyages round the World: with selected Sketches of Voyages to the South Seas, North and South Pacific Oceans, China, etc.* (1833).

——*Voyages and Discoveries in the South Seas* (1924).
The latter is an abridged edition, published by the Marine Research Society. (See text.)

R. B. Forbes, *Personal Reminiscences* (1878).
He was a versatile Boston mariner-merchant, who not only served as head of Russell & Co., in Canton, but also dabbled in early steam navigation and agitated for safety at sea.

*W. E. Dodge, "Reminiscences of a New York Merchant" in H. C. Brown, *Valentine's Manual,* new series.
Interesting and valuable account of the early experiences of a future merchant prince as a boy in a New York jobbing house and later as a young partner in a dry goods jobbing concern. Gives a description of methods not to be found elsewhere.

*Philip Hone, *Diary, 1828–1851,* ed. Allan Nevins, 2 vols. (1927).
One of the most celebrated and useful primary sources for New York in this period, by the wealthy and fashionable ex-auctioneer and mayor; concise comments on many of the events affecting the port. Selected from the 28 MS. quartos in the New York Historical Society. The Nevins edition is more useful than the earlier one by Bayard Tuckerman.

N. T. Hubbard, *Autobiography . . . with Personal Reminiscences of New York City from 1798 to 1875* (1875).
Hubbard was a prominent produce merchant.

*C. H. Haswell, *Reminiscences of an Octogenarian of the City of New York (1816 to 1860)* (1896).
Interesting year-by-year comments on New York events, by a one-time chief engineer of the U. S. Navy.

*(C. P. Low) *Some Recollections of Captain Charles P. Low, commanding the clipper Ships "Houqua," "Jacob Bell," "Samuel Russell" and "N. B. Palmer" in the China Trade, 1847–1873* (1905).
> Brother of A. A. Low; also gives early experience as boy in dry goods jobbing house and father's store, and cabin boy on London packet.

Vincent O. Nolte, *Fifty Years in Both Hemispheres* (tr. 1854).
> International financial adventurer; occasional visitor at New York; good account of situation at New Orleans during 1825 cotton boom.

*Samuel Samuels, *From the Forecastle to the Cabin* (new ed., with foreword, 1924).
> The tallest collection of yarns by any New York sea captain; wide range of experiences from serving as boy on a Philadelphia collier to command of the New York-Liverpool clipper "packet" *Dreadnaught,* including some lively mutiny accounts.

X. BIOGRAPHY, COLLECTED

*(William Armstrong) *The Aristocracy of New York: Who they Are, and What they Were; being a Social and Business History of the City for many Years* (1848).

*M. Y. Beach, *Wealth and Wealthy Citizens of New York City* (title varies slightly in the 13 editions) (1842–55).
> Compiled by the editor of the *Sun;* basis for inclusion was an estimated fortune of at least $100,000. Many of the entries accompanied by remarks, not always complimentary, upon how the fortune was made. Editions increased in size from 8 to 80 pages. Sixth edition (1845) reproduced complete in H. W. Lanier, *A Century of Banking in New York.*

W. H. Boyd, *New York City Tax Book, being a List of Persons, Corporations and Co-Partnerships, Resident and Non-Resident, who were Taxed, according to the Assessors' Books, 1856 & 1857* (1857).
> Similar compilation for 1850 by W. A. Darling.

*Chamber of Commerce of the State of New York—*Portrait Gallery of the Chamber—Catalogue and Biographical Sketches,* compiled by George Wilson (1890).

——*Catalogue of Portraits in the Chamber* (1924).
> The earlier work contains useful biographical sketches of a large number of merchants; the latter reproduces the portraits, with much briefer sketches.

Mrs. C. F. Diehm, *Merchants of our Second Century* (1889).

F. G. Griswold, *House Flags of the Merchants of New York* (1926).
> Reproduces many of the old house flags, with brief notes on the leading firms. Also included in his *Clipper Ships and Yachts* (1927).

Dictionary of American Biography ed. Allen Johnson and Dumas Malone, 20 vols. and index, 1928–36.

The most satisfactory up-to-date source for the numerous individuals included: brief bibliographical data with each sketch. The author of this work contributed more than fifty articles on men associated with New York Port.

Freeman Hunt, *Lives of the American Merchants,* 2 vols. (1858).
Most of the biographies appeared first in his *Merchant's Magazine;* devotes most of the space to making plaster saints of his subjects; disappointingly little on their business careers.

Income Record (The); a List giving the Taxable Income for the Year 1863 of the Residents of New York (1865).

*H. C. Kittredge, *Shipmasters of Cape Cod—a Chronicle of the Great Days of Sail* (1935).
A delightful and authoritative study, including several mariners prominent at New York; based in part on local private records.

H. W. Lanier, *A Century of Banking in New York, 1822–1922* (see Business Methods).
Chap. V. gives lists of wealthy New Yorkers at various periods.

*W. M. McBean, *Biographical Register of the St. Andrews Society of New York,* 2 vols. (1922–25).
Includes prominent Scots in New York business circles; same author also wrote a history of the Society.

Gustavus Myers, *History of the Great American Fortunes,* 3 vols. (1910).

New England Society of the City of New York, *Annual Celebrations* (1861, etc.).
Lists of members identify origin of many prominent merchants.

James Parton, *Sketches of Men of Progress* (1870).

*J. A. Scoville, *The Old Merchants of New York* (see Port of New York).

*G. W. Sheldon, "The Old Shipping Merchants of New York" in *Harper's Magazine* LXXXIV, pp. 457–71 (1892).
Well illustrated; one of his three valuable contributions to port history.

XI. BIOGRAPHY, INDIVIDUAL

C. S. Alden, *Lawrence Kearney, Sailor Diplomat* (1936).

E. M. Barrows, *The Great Commodore; The Exploits of Matthew Calbraith Perry* (1936).
The opener of Japan was closely associated with New York; and supervised for the navy the construction of the Collins liners.

D. B. Bobbé, *DeWitt Clinton* (1933).

C. W. Bowen, *Lewis and Arthur Tappan* (1883).

W. A. Butler, *A Memorial of Charles H. Marshall* (1867).
Includes autobiographical sketch of his early life.

E. J. DeForest, *John Johnston of New York, Merchant* (1909).
Scottish merchant, of Boorman & Johnston, leading iron importers.

——*A Walloon Family in America; Lockwood DeForest and his Forbears, 1500–1848,* 2 vols. (1914).
The DeForests were active in the South American trade.

——*John Taylor, a Scottish merchant of Glasgow and New York, 1752– 1833* (1917).

H. W. Dickinson, *Robert Fulton, Engineer and Artist* (1913).

D. S. Dodge, *Memorials of William E. Dodge* (1887).

W. M. Emery, *The Howland Heirs* (1919).

W. H. Hallock, *Life of Gerard Hallock* (1869).
Editor of the *Journal of Commerce.*

W. E. Harding, *W. E. Morrissey, His Life, Battles and Wrangles* (1881).
Deckhand on Hudson River steamers and runner for immigrant boarding house.

G. F. Heydt, *Charles L. Tiffany and the House of Tiffany & Company* (1893).

*W. H. Hillyer, *James Talcott, Merchant, and his Times* (1937).
Dry goods "factor"; good description of the trade.

David Hosack, *Memoir of DeWitt Clinton* (1829).
Useful material in extensive appendix.

P. M. Irving, *Life and Letters of Washington Irving,* 4 vols. (1862–64).
The writer's brothers were merchants in New York and, briefly, in Liverpool.

I. F. Judson, *Cyrus W. Field, His Life and Work* (1896).
The promoter of the Atlantic Cable started as a boy with A. T. Stewart and was later a paper merchant at New York.

*W. J. Lane (Life of Cornelius Vanderbilt, in preparation).
This promises to be the first adequate, scholarly biography of the Commodore; the author generously assisted in the preparation of this study.

Lewis Mumford, *Herman Melville* (1929).
Another dozen or so studies of Melville, whose father was a New York importer, and who served for twenty years as a customs inspector, are now in preparation.

(Oelrichs & Co.), *Caspar Meier and his Successors: C. & H. H. Meier, Caspar Meier & Co., L. N. von Post & Oelrichs, Oelrichs & Krüger, Oelrichs & Co., Oct. 12, 1798–Oct. 12, 1898* (1898).

E. L. Pond, *Junius Smith: a Biography of the Father of the Atlantic Liner* (1927).

*K. W. Porter, *John Jacob Astor, Business Man* (see Business Methods).

G. L. Prentiss, *A Sermon Preached at the Death of Anson G. Phelps* (1854).

James Renwick, *Life of DeWitt Clinton* (1840).

Benjamin Rodman, *Memoir of Joseph Grinnell* (1863).

L. H. Rogers, *A Sketch of the Life and Times of Eli Hart* (1931).

Sketch of Events in the Life of George Law, Published in Advance of his Autobiography (1855).
A campaign biography; the autobiography never appeared.

J. R. Spears, *Captain Nathaniel Brown Palmer, an Old-Time Sailor of the Sea* (1922).

*Lewis Tappan, *Life of Arthur Tappan* (1870).

Thatcher Thayer, *A Sketch of the Life of D. W. C. Olyphant* (1852).

R. H. Thurston, *Robert Fulton* (1891).

M. W. Tileston, *Thomas Tileston, 1793–1864* (1925).

J. W. Wayland, *The Pathfinder of the Seas: the Life of Matthew Fontaine Maury* (1930).

R. M. Weaver, *Herman Melville, Mariner and Mystic* (1921).

Bouck White, *The Book of Daniel Drew* (1910).
An "incisive, semi-fictional study."

S. T. Williams, *The Life of Washington Irving*, 2 vols. (1935).

XII. THE PORT OF NEW YORK—HISTORY

R. G. Albion, "New York Port and its Disappointed Rivals, 1815–1860" in *Journal of Business and Economic History*, III, pp. 602–29 (1931).

——"Yankee Domination of New York Port, 1820–1865" in *New England Quarterly*, V, pp. 665–98 (1932).

——"Commercial Fortunes in New York around 1850" in *New York History*, XVI, pp. 156–68 (1935).

——"The Primacy of the Port of New York" in A. C. Flick, ed., *History of the State of New York*, VIII (Chap. V), pp. 159–97 (1937).

——*Square-Riggers on Schedule* (1938) (see Shipping).

*(G. W. Baker) *Review of the Relative Commercial Progress of the Cities of New York and Philadelphia, tracing the Decline of the Latter to State Developments, and showing the Necessity of Trans-Atlantic Steamship Communication to Reestablish Foreign Trade* (1859).
A Philadelphia propaganda pamphlet of 72 pages, analyzing many aspects of the activity of the two ports, with ample statistics.

Bank of the Manhattan Company, *Ships and Shipping of Old New York* (1915).
Brief, readable, well-illustrated account of period to 1860.

C. C. Cutler, "Introduction" in *Descriptive Catalogue of the Marine Collection at India House* (1935).

F. V. Emerson, *A Geographical Interpretation of New York City* (1909).

Evening Post, Greater Port of New York Supplement (June 20, 1917).

G. Eyskens, *Le Port de New York dans son Rôle Economique* (1929).
An economic study from the University of Louvain, analyzing the modern period, with only a brief historical background.

E. M. Grace, Jr., *The Blockade of the Port of New York during the War of 1812* (MS. 1937).
An unpublished Princeton senior thesis, analyzing the effect of the British blockade upon shipping movements and prices.

E. H. Hall, "The New York Commercial Tercentenary, 1614–1914," appendix to New York State, New York Commercial Tercentenary Commission, *First Annual Report* (1914); also in American Scenic and Historic Preservation Society, *Annual Report, 1914*, pp. 441–500.

*V. D. Harrington, *The New York Merchant on the Eve of the Revolution* (1935).
The only thorough, scholarly monography devoted to the port's early activity. Though it analyses the period prior to 1815, it is decidedly useful as background.

*(John McCready) *A Review of the Trade and Commerce of New York from 1815 to the Present Time, by an Observer* (1820).

R. C. McKay, *South Street, a Maritime History of New York* (1935).
Interesting material for period 1783–1860 and well illustrated; but unco-ordinated, uncritical, repetitious, and often contradictory and inaccurate. Book withdrawn by publisher after attention was called to wholesale plagiarism, without acknowledgement or quotation marks, from numerous other works, including some of this author's articles.

R. P. Morgan, *The Decline of the Commerce of the Port of New York* (1901).
A midwest doctorial dissertation based on the wishful premise that New Orleans, Montreal and other ports would cut down New York's lead; deals principally with later period. The port, of course, did not bear out the author's thesis.

T. E. Rush, *The Port of New York* (1920).
Disjointed study, dealing chiefly with modern port problems of varying importance, by a former surveyor of the port; sketchy historical background based on secondary works.

*J. A. Scoville (Walter Barrett, *pseud.*), *The Old Merchants of New York*, 5 vols. in 3 (1863–66 and later editions).
The principal source of information and misinformation about the port's activity up to the Civil War, written by a "broken merchant," who later served as Calhoun's private secretary and wrote novels. Rambles along without any co-ordination or logical arrangement; mainly a series of biographical notes with occasional generalizations on methods, etc. A quotation prefaced by, "as Scoville says," indicates that this author does not underwrite its accuracy.

*G. W. Sheldon, "The Old Shipbuilders of New York" in *Harpers Magazine*, LXV, pp. 223–41 (1882).

*——"The Old Packet and Clipper Service," *ibid.*, LXVIII, pp. 213–37 (1884).

*——"The Old Shipping Merchants of New York," *ibid.*, LXXXIV, pp. 457–71 (1892).
These three interesting and admirably illustrated articles, written by a prominent New York art critic, represent the principal co-ordinated study of the old port activity, as contrasted with Scoville's ramblings. They have been incorporated, at times almost verbatim, errors and all, into numerous later works.

J. E. Wharton, *The Commercial Position of New York and a Way to Improve It* (1860).
Propaganda for a new railroad to the West.

XIII. NEW YORK CITY, GENERAL

R. M. Bayles, *History of Staten Island from its Discovery* (1887).

W. T. Bonner, *New York, the World Metropolis, 1623/4–1923/4,* 2 vols. (1925).
Commemorative edition of the city directory; useful, comprehensive compilation, reproducing many well-selected old pictures. Particularly useful for co-ordinating the history of particular branches of port and business activity.

H. C. Brown, *Valentine's Manual, New Series,* 12 vols. (1916–28).
Derives its name from the old Corporation manual (*q.v.*) but lacks its official status. Assembles a hodge-hodge of antiquarian material of strangely varying value; little pertinent to this study except Dodge recollections. Reproduces many old pictures.

*A. C. Flick, ed., *History of the State of New York,* 9 vols. (1933–37).
A co-operative work of varying but generally high merit; includes several chapters dealing with the city and its trade; each chapter has a useful bibliography.

Rodman Gilder, *The Battery* (1936).
Interesting, well-illustrated popular study.

R. S. Guernsey, *New York City and Vicinity during the War of 1812–15,* 2 vols. (1889–95).

H. R. Stiles, *A History of the City of Brooklyn,* 3 vols. (1867–70).
Useful sections on "Ferries," "Docks and Commerce" and "Navy Yard" in vol. III.

*I. N. P. Stokes, *The Iconography of Manhattan Island, 1498–1909,* 6 vols. (1915–28).
This monumental work, the product of years of intelligent diligence, has been called the most comprehensive history of a city ever written. Includes not only a general running account (vols. I and III), and analyses of various maps and records of buildings (vol. II), but also a highly useful chronological day-by-day collection of pertinent passages

quoted from newspapers, official records, travellers' accounts, etc. (vols. IV–V), and the excellent bibliography by Paltsits already cited (vol. VI). It is exhaustive on the antiquities of New York itself, but has less to say of the port's activities beyond Sandy Hook.

Spencer Trask, *Bowling Green* (1898).

J. G. Wilson, ed., *Memorial History of the City of New York,* 4 vols. (1893).
The most serviceable of the general histories, superseding the earlier works by M. L. Booth (1866) and M. J. Lamb (1877).

XIV. NEW YORK CITY, SOCIAL
(See also Memoirs)

Herbert Asbury, *The Gangs of New York* (1928).
Chap. III, "Sin along the Waterfront"; Chap. IV, "River Pirates."

A. C. Dayton, *The Last Days of Knickerbocker Life in New York* (1882).
Describes New York society in the thirties.

D. R. Fox, *The Decline of Aristocracy in the Politics of New York* (1919).

J. W. Gerard, Jr., *The Impress of Nationalities upon the City of New York* (1883).
Discusses New Englanders in addition to foreign groups.

T. B. Gunn, *The Physiology of New York Boarding Houses* (1857).

J. R. G. Hassard, "The New York Mercantile Library" in *Scribner's Monthly,* I, pp. 353–67 (1871).

H. W. Lanier, *A Century of Banking in New York, 1822–1922* (see Business Methods).

J. D. McCabe, *Secrets of the Great City* (1868).
Includes descriptions of sailors' boarding houses, etc.

M. H. Smith (Burleigh, *pseud.*), *Sunshine and Shadow in New York* (1870).

XV. NEW YORK CITY, DESCRIPTION, GUIDE BOOKS, ETC.

Blunt's Stranger's Guide to the City of New York (1817).
The earliest, for our period, of a large series of guide books, useful because they furnish many details about the waterfront, public functionaries, packets, steamboat lines, etc.

John Disturnell, *New York as it Is* (1833, etc.).
D. was a prolific compiler of guide books, travel guides, etc., for many years.

(John A. Dix), *Sketch of the Resources of the City of New York* (1827).

Doggett's New York Business Directory (1841–46).
The first part lists business men and firms alphabetically; the second part is arranged by functions, with the names of those engaged in each. Succeeded by Wilson's and later by Trow's.

Doggett's New York City Directory (1842–54).
The conventional city directory, succeeding Longworth's and succeeded in turn by Wilson's and Trow's. Useful for identification of individuals.

Doggett's New York City Street Directory (1851).
Useful for identifying merchants located on a particular street.

C. D. Francis & Co., *New Guide to the Cities of New York and Brooklyn and Vicinity* (1853).

J. G. Gobright, *The Union Sketch Book* (1860).

A. T. Goodrich, *The Picture of New York, and Stranger's Guide through the Commercial Emporium of the United States* (1818).

James Hardie, *The Description of the City of New York* (1827).

*T. Longworth, *Longworth's American Almanac, New York Register and City Directory* (1798–1841). Succeeded by Doggett's.

J. V. Loomis & Co., *United States Statistical Directory; or Merchant's and Traveller's Guide, with a Wholesale Business Directory of New York* (1847).

H. Phelps, *Stranger's and Citizen's Guide to New York City, 1857–58* (1857).

James Whitney, *The New York Shippers' and Consignees' Guide, designed to Facilitate the Commercial, Mercantile and Shipping Interests of New York* (1861).

*E. Williams, *New York Annual Register* (1830 and later editions).

(For descriptions by foreign travellers, see the chronological section in Stokes' *Iconography;* a few are quoted in Allan Nevins, *American Social History, as Recorded by British Travellers* (1923).

XVI. "WATERFRONT AND OFFICIALDOM"
(See also Business Methods)

W. H. D. Adams, *Lighthouses and Lightships; a Descriptive and Historical Account of their Mode of Construction and Organization* (1870).

*R. S. S. Andros, *The United States Custom House Guide* (1859).
Full details concerning all branches of customs routine.

Herbert Asbury, *Gangs of New York* (see New York, Social).

Atlantic Dock Co., *Prospectus* (1840).

J. G. Barnard, *The Dangers and Defenses of New York* (1859).

J. B. Bishop, *A Chronicle of 150 Years: The Chamber of Commerce of the State of New York, 1768–1918* (1918).

W. N. Black, *Storage and Transportation in the Port of New York; an Investigation into Methods of handling Merchandise*, etc. (1884).
Deals chiefly with later period.

G. W. Blunt, *Pilot Laws, Harbor and Quarantine Regulations of New York* (1869).

Hamilton Bruce, *The Warehouse Manual and General Custom House Guide* (1862).

Chamber of Commerce of the State of New York, *Annual Reports (q.v.).* Also see collection of memorials and petitions, in pamphlet form, on various aspects of port activity, for period prior to first published reports.

F. A. Collins, *Our Harbors and Inland Waterways* (1924).

Custom House Guide, 7 vols. in 1 (1932). "Port Section" describes different ports and lists principal customs officers at New York and elsewhere from the beginning.

C. P. Daly, *Historical Sketch of the Judicial Tribunals of New York from 1623 to 1846* (1855).

C. H. Farnham, "A Day on the Docks," in *Scribner's Monthly,* XVIII, pp. 32–47 (1879). Like the other magazine articles listed below, is well illustrated.

J. D. Goss, *Tariff Administration in the United States from Colonial Times to the McKinley Administration* (1891). Includes account of New York customs service.

Carleton Green, *Wharves and Piers, their Design, Construction and Equipment* (1917).

C. H. Haswell, *Report of the Result of Observations upon the Deposit of Silt in the Harbor of New York* (1857); also in *Journal of the Franklin Institute,* LXV (3rd series XXXV), pp. 161–68 (1858).

C. M. Hough, *Reports of Cases in the Vice-Admiralty of the Province of New York, and in the Court of Admiralty of the State of New York, 1715–1788* (1925). Edited by a federal judge; deals with earlier period but indicates nature of business of federal courts in admiralty jurisdiction.

Theodore Hunter, *Port Charges and Requirements on Vessels in the Various Ports of the World* (1878 and later editions).

R. S. MacElwee, *Port and Terminal Facilities* (1918).

——Port Development (1925).

——*Wharf Management, Stevedoring and Storage* (1921).

*Henry Mitchell, "Circulation of the Sea through New York Harbor" in *Science,* XIX, pp. 204–05 (1887). Brief, clear explanation of importance of East River current in keeping main channel clear of sand and ice.

New Jersey, Legislature, *Report of the Joint Committee . . . on the Encroachments upon the Bay and Harbor of New York* (1855).

*New York City, City Surveyor, *Maps of the Wharves and Piers from the*

Battery to 61st Street in the Hudson River and from the Battery to 41st Street on the East River, New York (1860).
This set of 23 maps is available at New York Public Library; for titles of earlier maps, from 1849 onwards, at the Dept. of Docks, see Stokes, *Iconography*, bibliography.

——Commissioners of Sinking Fund, *The Wharves, Piers and Slips belonging to the Corporation of the City of New York, 1868* (1868).

——Dept. of Docks, *Annual Reports* (from 1870).
The separate Dept. of Docks was not established until 1870; until then, the wharves were under the Comptroller's supervision.

*——Finance Dept., "Communication from the Comptroller, relative to leasing the Docks and Slips belonging to the City" in Board of Councilmen, *Documents, 1855*, No. 26.

*New York State, Commissioners of the Land Office, *Report . . . relative to New York Harbor Encroachments* (1862).
Contains an excellent large-scale map of the waterfront, indicating the original shore line of 1686 and the "made land."

——Committee on Commerce and Navigation, *Report . . . in relation to the Official Conduct of the Harbor Masters of the City of New York* (1857).

——Report of the Select Committee . . . to examine into the Affairs, and investigate the Charges of Malfeasance in Office of the Harbor Masters of New York (1862).

——Reports of the New York Harbor Commission of 1856 and 1857 (1864).
Published as a single volume by the Chamber of Commerce. Contain a wealth of detail about harbor currents, channel depths, etc., with official reports and testimony; also the best available account of the construction, leasing, operation and income of New York wharves, with testimony by several wharfingers; together with two excellent large-scale maps of the harbor and a list of maps and charts consulted.

J. S. Newberry, *The Geological History of New York Island and Harbor* (1878).

G. R. Putnam, *Lighthouses and Lightships of the United States* (new ed. 1933).

T. A. Richards, "New York Circumnavigated," in *Harper's Magazine*, XXIII, pp. 165–83 (1861).

W. H. Rideing, "The Harbor and Commerce of New York," in *Appleton's Journal*, XVII (n.s. II), pp. 481–90; XVIII (n.s. III), pp. 97–108 (1877).

*C. E. Russell, *From Sandy Hook to 62°, being some Account of the Adventures, Exploits and Services of the Old New York Pilot Boat* (1929).
Based partly on records of pilot association, partly on legend.

L. F. Schmeckebier, *The Customs Service, its History, Activities and Organization* (1924).

——*The Public Health Service* (1923).

D. H. Smith and F. W. Powell, *The Coast Guard, its History, Activities and Organization* (1929).
The above three are Service Monographs of the Institute for Government Research. A history of the revenue marine service is being prepared by Stephen Decatur.

E. B. Smith, *Governor's Island: its Military History under Three Flags, 1637–1913* (1913).

*W. O. Stoddard, "New York Harbor Police," in *Harper's Magazine*, XLV, pp. 672–83 (1872).

C. B. Stuart, *Naval Dry Docks of the United States* (1852).
Includes an account of the great dock at Brooklyn Navy Yard and the sectional dock built at New York for the Pacific coast.

*T. B. Thorpe, "New York Custom House," in *Harper's Magazine*, XLIII, pp. 11–26 (1871).

(United New York and New Jersey Sandy Hook Pilots Benevolent Associations) *Pilot Lore; from Sail to Steam, and Historical Sketches of the Various Interests identified with the Development of the World's Greatest Port* (1922).

United States, *American State Papers.*
Information concerning New York defenses, etc., summarized in *Military Affairs,* III, pp. 248–56, VI, pp. 400–03; *Naval Affairs,* IV, pp. 953–56.

——Army, Corps of Engineers, and U. S. Shipping Board, Bureau of Operations, *The Port of New York,* Port Series, No. 20 (rev. ed., 1932).
Useful data on physical aspects of port, preliminary to lengthy analysis of modern problems. Series includes similar studies of many other ports.

*——Coast & Geodetic Survey, *Annual Reports.*
Include charts of New York. Particularly useful are Chart No. 120 of New York Harbor and Environs in six parts (1844) and No. 143, a single sheet chart of the whole (1845). Excellent electroplate copies of these original charts are obtainable at reasonable rates.

*——*Tides and Currents in New York Harbor* (1933).

——*Congressional Documents.*
In addition to the various annual reports (*q.v.*), see for defenses 26th Congress, 1st Sess., *Senate Doc.* 451 and 27th Congress, 2nd Sess., *Senate Doc.* 2; for investigations of custom house frauds, including much incidental information about customs details, 37th Cong. 3rd Sess., *Senate Doc.* 44; 42nd Congress, 2nd Sess., *Senate Report* 227.

*——Lighthouse Bureau, *Fog Tables* (1929).
Mimeographed tables showing average hours of fog per year at all lighthouses and lightships.

L. F. Vernon-Harcourt, *Harbours and Docks; their Physical Features, History, Construction, Equipment and Maintenance,* 2 vols. (1885).
Good brief summary of New York problems, I, pp. 426–28, 622–27.

J. W. Watson, "The Wharves of New York," in *Harper's Magazine,* XXV, pp. 307–25 (1862).

D. W. Wheeler, *New York Harbor, and the Improvements necessary for the Accommodation of its Commerce, and the Removal of the Dangers at Hell Gate* (1856).
Paper read before the American Geographical and Statistical Society.

H. Worden, *Round Manhattan's Rim* (1934).
Modern rambles around the whole waterfront, with an account of the traditions.

XVII. BUSINESS METHODS

Joseph Blunt, *Shipmaster's Assistant and Commercial Digest* (see Manuals).

W. T. Bonner, *New York, the World Metropolis* (see New York, General).
Brief sections dealing with the various exchanges and with many special branches of business.

J. C. Brown, *A Hundred Years of Merchant Banking, a History of Brown Bros. & Co.,* etc. (1909).
Written by one of the second generation of the banking family; reproduces considerable original correspondence; more useful than the *Experiences of a Century, 1818–1918* (1919), also dealing with the same subject; see also Kent below.

*N. S. Buck, *The Development of the Organisation of Anglo-American Trade, 1800–1850* (1925).
The most generally useful study for this field; based in part upon British parliamentary papers. Scope indicated by chapters: "The Agencies of Trade," "The British Cotton Market," "The Organisation of the American Cotton Trade," "The Trade in British Manufactures, 1800–1815" and the same for 1815–1830 and 1830–1850.

Chamber of Commerce of the State of New York, *Earliest Arbitration Records of the Chamber. . . . Committee Minutes, 1779–1792* (1913).
Though dealing with the period before 1815, give an indication of the valuable amount of the illustrative material to be found in the manuscript records of the arbitration committee for the later period.

R. M. Devens (F. Kirkland, *pseud.*), *Cyclopædia of Commercial and Business Anecdotes,* 2 vols. (1865).

F. B. Dixon, *Hand-Book of Marine Insurance and Average* (2nd ed. 1866).

*John Duer, *The Law and Practice of Marine Insurance,* 2 vols. (1845–46).
A New York work, analyzing particular cases adjudged at the port.

J. V. Eaton, "An Old Street of New York," in *American History Magazine*, II, pp. 546–7 (1906).
A history of Pearl Street.

D. M. Evans, *History of the Commercial Crisis of 1857–58 and of the Stock Exchange Panic of 1859* (1859).

*W. Frothingham, "Stewart, and the Dry Goods Trade of New York," in *Continental Monthly*, II, pp. 528–34 (1862).

*R. W. Hidy, *The House of Baring and American Trade, 1830–42* (MS. 1935).
Unpublished Harvard dissertation, based primarily upon voluminous Baring MSS. Gives for the first time an adequate description and analysis of the workings of the British commercial credit system in connection with American commerce.

W. H. Hillyer, *James Talcott, Merchant, and his Times* (see Biography).

*F. M. Jones, *Middlemen in the Domestic Trade of the United States, 1800–1860* (1937).
Valuable study of distribution methods with particular attention to New York.

F. R. Kent, *The Story of Alexander Brown & Sons* (1925).

H. W. Lanier, *A Century of Banking in New York, 1822–1922* (1922).
More of a descriptive picture of Wall Street and the business district than an analysis like Myers; reproduces many interesting old pictures.

M. G. Myers, *The New York Money Market, Origins and Development* (1931).
The first volume of a comprehensive study of the money market.

Allan Nevins, *History of the Bank of New York and Trust Co.* (1934).

*K. W. Porter, *The Jacksons and the Lees*, 2 vols. (1937).

——*John Jacob Astor, Business Man* (see Biography).
Two valuable contributions to business history, analyzing early business methods and reproducing a large amount of early commercial correspondence illustrative of various aspects. The Jacksons and the Lees were Boston merchants, but the study contains much that is pertinent to New York.

Horace Secrist, "The Anti-Auction Movement of 1828," in *Annals of the Wisconsin Academy*, XVII, No. 2.

(W. H. Schieffelin & Co.) *One Hundred Years of Business Life, 1794–1894* (1894).
The account of a prominent New York house of drug importers.

*W. B. Smith and A. H. Cole, *Fluctuations in American Business, 1790–1860* (1935).
Significant statistical analysis, based in part on New York commercial and financial records for the period.

W. L. Thorp, *Business Annals* (1926).

J. Vaucher, *A Guide to Marine Insurances; containing the Policies of the Principal Commercial Towns in the World* (1834).

*E. N. Vose, *Seventy-five Years of the Mercantile Agency, R. G. Dun & Co., 1841–1916* (1916).

R. B. Westerfield, "Early History of American Auctions," in *Transactions of the Connecticut Academy of Arts and Sciences*, XXIII, pp. 159–210 (1920).

W. D. Winter, *A Short Sketch of the History and Principles of Marine Insurance* (1925).

XVIII. SHIPBUILDING

(See also Steamboats and Steamships)

R. G. Albion, *Forests and Sea Power* (1926).
A detailed study of ship timber.

(William Annesley) *Description of William Annesley's New System of Naval Architecture* (1818).

(Noah Brown) "The Remarkable Statement of Noah Brown," in *Journal of American History*, VIII, pp. 103–8 (1914).
Autobiographical data included in long affidavit.

*"The Building of the Ship," in *Harper's Magazine*, XXIV, pp. 608–20 (1862).
For the layman, this is one of the best available concise accounts of the various processes involved, well illustrated by diagrams and pictures.

*H. I. Chapelle, *History of American Sailing Ships* (1935).
Written by a naval architect, this is an able study of ship design; tends to concentrate upon a few types, to the exclusion of others. His studies of the Baltimore Clipper and American boats are also useful and suggestive.

Joseph Francis, *History of Life-Saving Appliances* (1885).
This New Yorker was an outstanding pioneer in the construction of lifeboats and in promoting lifesaving.

J. W. Griffiths, *A Treatise on Marine and Naval Architecture* (1850).
——*The Shipbuilder's Manual and Nautical Referee*, 2 vols. (1855).
See text for Griffiths' importance in American shipbuilding.

Henry Hall, "Report on the Shipbuilding Industry of the United States," in *Report of the Tenth Census*, VIII (1884).
Historical sketch, with discussion of various types, ship timber, etc.; special section on New York, pp. 115–21, including list of vessels built by Webb.

*J. G. B. Hutchins, *The Rise and Fall of the Building of Wooden Ships in America, 1607–1914*, 2 vols. (MS. 1936).

Able and thorough Harvard doctoral dissertation, now being prepared for publication. The first volume covers the period to 1860. Special attention devoted to reasons for building at particular localities, with considerations of comparative costs.

*Lauchlan McKay, *The Practical Ship-Builder* (1839).
Written by a brother of the celebrated Donald; designed as guide for builders in smaller ports and consequently gives one of the best descriptions available of the various stages, step by step. Only four copies are said to have been located at present.

R. C. McKay, *Some Famous Sailing Ships and their Builder, Donald McKay* (1928).

E. I. P. Morris, *The Fore-and-Aft Rig in America, a Sketch* (1927).

*J. E. Morrison, *History of the New York Shipyards* (1908).
Uncritical but very useful.

*G. W. Sheldon, "The Old Shipbuilders of New York," in *Harper's Magazine* (see Port of New York).
Fewer minute details than Morrison, above, but much better accounts of the principal builders, with portraits, etc.

*(W. H. Webb) *Plans of Wooden Vessels, selected as Types from One Hundred and Fifty of various Kinds and Descriptions, from a Fishing Smack to the largest Clipper Ships and Vessels of War, both Sail and Steam, built by William H. Webb in the City of New York from the Year 1840 to the Year 1869*, 2 vols. (1895).
Some of the dimensions do not tally with the customs registers, and it has been suggested that some of the plans are not thoroughly accurate.

(This list does not include studies of shipbuilding at various New England ports and elsewhere, even though some of those vessels were used at New York).

XIX. SHIPPING, GENERAL, AND SEA ROUTES

*E. M. Blunt, *The American Coast Pilot* (many editions).
(See text).

F. C. Bowen, *The Golden Age of Sail: Indiamen, Packets, and Clipper Ships* (1925).
Like several of his other works, useful particularly for the excellent collection of pictures from the Macpherson Collection.

E. K. Chatterton, *Sailing Ships, the Story of their Development* (1909).

C. G. Davis, *The Ways of the Sea* (1930).

R. A. Fletcher, *In the Days of Tall Ships* (1928).

The above four works are popular presentations but contain considerable useful information and compose a pleasant introduction to the subject.

*(India House, Inc., New York) *Descriptive Catalogue of the Marine Collection at India House* (1935).
Valuable notes on many individual vessels of New York, with reproductions of many of the valuable collection of ship pictures. Excellent introduction, on the port's history, by C. C. Cutler.

E. R. Johnson, G. G. Huebner and A. K. Henry, *Transportation by Water* (1935).

A. W. Kirkaldy, *British Shipping: Its History, Organisation and Importance* (1919).

*W. S. Lindsay, *History of Merchant Shipping and Ancient Commerce,* 4 vols. (1874–76).
Written by a prominent British shipowner. American sailing ships are discussed at length in vol. III and transatlantic steam development in vol. IV.

W. L. Marvin, *The American Merchant Marine . . . 1602–1902* (1902).
More useful than the similar works by Abbott, Bates and Spears.

*M. F. Maury, *Explanations and Sailing Directions to accompany the Wind and Current Charts,* 8th ed., 2 vols. (1858 and other editions).
Valuable not only for their immediate purpose of analyzing the winds and currents on the main sea routes, particularly from New York to Liverpool, New Orleans and San Francisco, but also for incidental information about New York shipping. The 8th edition reproduces photographically a New York-Liverpool packet log, one of the thousands of logs analyzed in Maury's researches and still preserved at Washington. Published by U. S. Naval Hydrographic Office.

——*Physical Geography of the Sea* (1858).

United States, Naval Hydrographic Office (see Maury, *Explanations,* above).

*——*Table of Distances between the Principal Seaports of the World* (1931 and other editions).
Similar tables also prepared by British Admiralty; some of New York distances tabulated in appendix of this work.

XX.   SHIPPING, PARTICULAR GROUPS
(PACKETS, CLIPPERS, ETC.)

*R. G. Albion, *Square-Riggers on Schedule: The New York Sailing Packets to England, France, and the Cotton Ports* (1938).
Systematic account of the major lines, 1818–1858, with a more cursory survey of the later years. Designed as complementary to this study, with details concerning captains and crews, packet passengers, sailing conditions, speed performance, etc.

F. B. C. Bradlee, *The Dreadnought of Newburyport, Mass., and some Account of the old Transatlantic Packet Ships* (1927).

*A. H. Clark, *The Clipper Ship Era* (1910).
The first of the sound clipper studies, by a one-time clipper captain.

*C. C. Cutler, *Greyhounds of the Sea, the Story of the American Clipper Ship* (1930).
A readable and exhaustive account, with detailed statistical information concerning dimensions and performance.

*O. T. Howe and F. C. Matthews, *American Clipper Ships, 1833–1858*, 2 vols. (1926–27).
Whereas Clark's treatment is topical and Cutler's chronological, this is a study of individual ships, arranged alphabetically.

W. G. Low, *Something about A. A. Low and Brothers' Fleet of Clipper Ships* (1919).

A. Basil Lubbock, *The Western Ocean Packets* (1925).
A collection of separate articles, not up to some of his other interesting works in quality and accuracy.

John Robinson and G. F. Dow, *Sailing Ships of New England*, 3 vols. (1922–28).
Excellent collection of pictures, with brief accounts; the third "series" edited by Dow alone; published by Marine Research Society.

*G. W. Sheldon, "The Old Packet and Clipper Service," in *Harper's Magazine* (see Port of New York).
The principal source for the packets until recently; utilized by other writers for many years; responsible for erroneous date of 1816 as start of packet service.

*C. P. Wright, *The Origins and Early Years of the Transatlantic Packet Ships of New York, 1817–1835* (MS. 1932).
Unpublished Harvard dissertation; able and valuable "biography of ships and men," analyzing minutely the manner in which the early lines were formed.

XXI. STEAMBOATS AND STEAMSHIPS

Account of the Delamater-Ericsson Celebration in New York City (1920).

F. M. Bennett, *The Steam Navy of the United States* (1896).

V. M. Berthold, *The Pioneer Steamer California, 1848–49* (1932).

F. C. Bowen, *A Century of Atlantic Travel, 1830–1930* (1930).
Interesting comprehensive survey, but often inaccurate in early period.

*D. L. Buckman, *Old Steamboat Days on the Hudson River* (1907).

J. O. Choules, *The Cruise of the Steam Yacht North Star, a Narrative of the Excursion of Mr. Vanderbilt's Party to England, Russia, etc.* (1854).

W. C. Church, *Life of John Ericsson*, 2 vols. (1890).

W. H. Cooper, *Incidents of Shipwrecks; or the Loss of the "San Francisco"* (1855).

W. K. Covell, "Steamboats on Narragansett Bay," in Newport Historical Society, *Bulletin,* No. 90, pp. 2–57 (1934).

*F. E. Dayton, *Steamboat Days* (1925).
Readable general survey, well illustrated; less detailed than Morrison.

C. H. Dow, *History of Steam Navigation between New York and Providence* (1877).

Henry Fry, *History of North Atlantic Steam Navigation* (1896).

C. H. Haswell, "Reminiscences of Early Marine Steam Engine Construction and Steam Navigation in the U. S. A. from 1807 to 1850," in *Transactions of the Institute of Naval Architects* (1898–99).

Historical Sketch of the Fulton Ferry and its Associated Ferries, by a. Director (1879).

*S. A. Howland, *Steamboat Disasters and Railroad Wrecks in the United States* (2nd ed., 1840).
Full accounts of several New York disasters, including the *Home* and *Lexington,* in addition to several wrecks of New York sailing vessels.

G. C. Jackson, *The Ship under Steam* (1928).

*J. H. Kemble, "The Genesis of the Pacific Mail Steamship Company," in *California Historical Society Quarterly,* XIII (1934).

——"The Panama Route to the Pacific Coast, 1848–1869," in *Pacific Historical Review* (1938).

——"Coal from the Northwest Coast, 1848–1850," in *British Columbia Historical Quarterly,* II, pp. 123–30 (1938).
Studies preparatory to a general history of the Pacific Mail. The author generously assisted in the preparation of this study.

*W. J. Lane, *History of Transportation in New Jersey to 1860* (in press).
Good details of steamboats on Raritan route; Gibbons vs. Ogden, etc. His study of Cornelius Vanderbilt, in preparation, also contains much on steamboats and steamships.

W. S. Lindsay, *History of Merchant Shipping* (see Shipping, General).

R. W. McAdam, *The Old Fall River Line* (1937).

*A. J. Maginnis, *The Atlantic Ferry, its Ships, Men and Workings* (1892).
One of the soundest studies on the subject; good tables.

*J. H. Morrison, *History of American Steam Navigation* (1903).
Comprehensive and extremely detailed.

New York State, Superior Court, *William Heilman vs. Marshall O. Roberts* (1861).
Valuable details of the cost of operating the U. S. Mail steamships.

H. Parker and F. C. Bowen, *Mail and Passenger Steamships of the Nineteenth Century* (1928).
Good pictures from the Macpherson Collection.

H. F. J. Porter, "The Delamater Iron Works, the Cradle of the Modern Navy," in *Transactions of the Society of Naval Architects and Marine Engineers,* XXVI (1919).

G. H. Preble, *A Chronological History of the Origin and Development of Steam Navigation* (1883).

Thomas Ranney, *Ocean Steam Navigation and the Ocean Post* (1858).
Discussion of situation created by cancellation of federal mail subsidies.

W. D. Renninger, *Government Policy in Aid of American Shipbuilding* (1911).

Richard Sennett and H. J. Oram, *The Marine Steam Engine* (6th ed., 1902).

H. J. Smith, *The Romance of the Hoboken Ferry* (1931).

Steam Fleet of Liverpool (The), (1865).
Detailed survey, by lines.

C. B. Stuart, *Naval and Mail Steamers* (1853).
Diagrams, pictures, statistics, and rhetoric concerning subsidy liners and warships, by chief engineer of the Navy.

*J. E. Tuel, *The Steam Marine of the Port of New York, examined in its Connection with the Southern Ports of the United States and the West Indies, and in Connection with the Atlantic and Pacific Oceans* (1853).
Published originally in the *Journal of Commerce.*

U. S. *Congressional Documents:* 29th Cong., 1st Sess., *Senate Doc.* 237; 34th Cong., 3rd Sess., *Senate Report* 440; 35th Cong., 1st Sess., *Senate Report* 326; 36th Cong., 1st Sess., *House Report* 648; 36th Cong., 2nd Sess., *Senate Report* 292; 37th Cong., 3rd Sess., *House Report* 49.
Contain much information concerning Collins Line, Pacific Mail, U. S. Mail and other subsidy lines.

A. J. Wall, "The Sylvan Steamboats on the East River, New York to Harlem," in N. Y. Historical Society, *Quarterly Bulletin,* VIII, pp. 59–72 (1924).

XXII. GENERAL COMMERCE AND TRANSATLANTIC TRADE, ETC.

(See also Manufactures)

*I. D. Andrews, *Report . . . on the Trade and Commerce of the British American Colonies and upon the Trade of the Great Lakes and Rivers, etc.* (U. S. 32nd Cong., 1st Sess., *Senate Exec. Doc.* 112) (1853).
Commonly known as the "Andrews Report"; more comprehensive than the title indicates; surveys many aspects of the nation's commercial activity, with detailed statistics on many subjects, and studies of the individual seaports.

E. Baasch, *Beiträge zur Geschichte der Handelsbeziehungen zwischen Hamburg und Amerika* (1892).

S. J. Chapman, *The History of Trade between the United Kingdom and the United States, with Special Reference to the Effect of Tariffs* (1899).

*C. M. Depew, ed., *One Hundred Years of American Commerce* (*1795–1895*) 2 vols. (1895).
Useful co-operative work, with individual studies of many branches of commerce and industry.

*R. W. Hidy, *The House of Baring and American Trade* (see Business Methods).

B. H. Holland, *The Fall of Protection, 1840–1850* (1913).
A study of the transitional period in British commercial policy.

E. R. Johnson, et als., *History of the Domestic and Foreign Commerce of the United States* (Carnegie Institute) 2 vols. (1915).

T. P. Martin, "Cotton and Wheat in Anglo-American Trade and Politics, 1846–1852," in *Journal of Southern History* (1935).

W. P. Sterns, "Foreign Trade of the United States, 1820–1840," in *Journal of Political Economy,* VIII, pp. 34–57, 452–90.

Herman Wätjen, *Aus der Frühzeit des Nordatlantikverkehrs: Studien zur Geschichte der deutschen Schiffart und deutschen Auswanderung nach den Vereinigten Staaten bis zum Ende des amerikanischen Bürgerkriegs* (1932).

XXIII. MANUFACTURES, FOREIGN AND DOMESTIC

(See also Commerce, "Cotton Triangle")

W. R. Bagnall, *The Textile Industries of the United States* (1893).

*Lucy Barton, *Historic Costume for the Stage* (1935).
The best account of just what sorts of materials were worn at different periods, and how much of them; the author also made special estimates for this study.

*V. S. Clark, *History of Manufactures in the United States* (Carnegie Institute), new ed. 3 vols. (1929).

A. H. Cole, *The American Wool Manufacture,* 2 vols. (1926).

*Thomas Ellison, *The Cotton Trade of Great Britain* (1858).

M. B. Hammond, *The Cotton Industry: an Essay in American Economic History* (1897).

Herbert Heaton, *The Yorkshire Woollen and Worsted Industries* (1920).

Arthur Redford, *Manchester Merchants and Foreign Trade, 1794–1858* (1934).

F. W. Taussig, *The Tariff History of the United States,* new ed. (1923).

U. S., Bureau of Statistics, *Exports of Manufactures from the United States and their Distribution, by Articles and Countries; also, Impor-*

tation of Manufacturers' Materials and Finished Manufactures, 1790–1902 (1902).

Andrew Ure, *Cotton Manufacture of Great Britain* (1861).

Perry Walton, *The Story of Textiles* (1912).

XXIV. THE "COTTON TRIANGLE" AND COASTAL TRADE
(See also Manufactures)

*R. G. Albion, *Square-Riggers on Schedule* (see Port of New York).
Chap. III, "Enslaving the Cotton Ports," analyzes major coastal packets and nature of cargoes; specimen cargoes from cotton ports to New York in 1835, together with freight rates, are analyzed in appendix.

J. S. Bassett, *The Southern Plantation Overseer* (1925).

J. E. Boyle, *Cotton and the New Orleans Cotton Exchange: a Century of Commercial Evolution* (1934).

*N. S. Buck, *The Organisation and Development of Anglo-American Trade, 1800–1850* (see Business Methods).

J. D. B. DeBow, *Industrial Resources, Statistics, etc., of the United States, and Particularly of the Southern and Western States,* 3 vols. in 1 (1854).
Includes full accounts of the later southern commercial conventions and their propaganda; later article by Maury on "Direct Trade" at beginning of vol. III.

W. E. Dodd, *The Cotton Kingdom* (1921).

G. S. Graham, "The Gypsum Trade of the Maritime Province," in *Agricultural History,* XII, pp. 209–23 (1938).

Meyer Jacobstein, *The Tobacco Industry in the United States* (1907).

(Daniel Lord), *The Effect of Secession upon the Commercial Relations between the North and South, and upon each Section* (1861).
Originally appeared in *New York Times.*

*(M. F. Maury) "Direct Trade with the South," in *Southern Literary Magazine,* V, pp. 2–12 (1839).
Analyzes "cotton triangle"; stresses importance of New York packets; and urges similar service from southern ports. A later amplification of same article appeared in DeBow above.

F. L. Olmstead, *Journeys and Explorations in the Cotton Kingdom,* 2 vols. (1861).
Abridges previous separate studies on Seaboard Slave States, etc.

U. B. Phillips, *A History of Transportation in the Eastern Cotton Belt to 1860* (1908).

——*Life and Labor in the Old South* (1929).

*R. R. Russell, *Economic Aspects of Southern Sectionalism, 1840–1860* (1924).

*The *"Southern Trade." An Epitome of Commerce North and South, movements of Exports, etc., with a Directory of New York Houses interested in Southern Trade* (2nd ed. 1860).
Consists of an article, "The Strength of the Union" by T. P. Kettell, with advertisements of New York "southern houses" on alternate pages.

*A. H. Stone, "The Cotton Factorage System of the United States," in *American Historical Review*, XX, pp. 557–65 (1915).

J. G. Van Deusen, *Economic Bases of Disunion in South Carolina* (1928).

G. S. Wasson, "The Old Rockland, Maine, Lime Trade," in *Old-Time New England*, XXI, 156–67 (1931).
Includes excellent photographs of coasting schooners.

——and Lincoln Colcord, *Sailing Days on the Penobscot* (1932).

J. L. Watkins, *King Cotton: an Historical and Statistical Review, 1790 to 1908* (1908).
Amplification of his Bulletin for the Statistical Division of the Dept. of Agriculture in 1895; it has been remarked that his figures are "wrong in themselves and have been a cause of error to others."

William Way, *History of the New England Society of Charleston, 1819–1919* (1920).

T. J. Wertenbaker, *Norfolk, Historic Southern Port* (1931).
A history and apology, written under contract with the Norfolk city government.

*H. Winder, *Southern Commercial Conventions, 1837–1859* (1930).

R. G. Wood, *A History of Lumbering in Maine, 1820–1861* (1935).
Includes an account of the lumber coasters.

XXV. CARIBBEAN AND LATIN AMERICA

G. W. Allen, *Our Navy and the West Indian Pirates* (1929).

J. M. Baker, *A view of the Commerce between the United States and Rio de Janeiro* (1838).
Detailed statistics, by former consul there.

H. C. Bell, *Studies in the Trade Relations of the British West Indies and North America, 1763–73; 1783–93* (1917).

F. L. Benns, *The American Struggle for the British West India Carrying Trade, 1815–1830* (1923).

H. M. Brackenridge, *Voyage to Buenos Ayres . . . 1817 & 1818*, 2 vols. (1819).
B. was secretary of the American mission which visited Latin America to investigate trade possibilities, etc. Accounts by Joel Poinsett and William Baldwin also describe same mission, giving a picture of the

region. A large number of other contemporary accounts by travellers or residents were consulted for descriptions and incidental remarks on trade; but few were of sufficient value to warrant inclusion here.

F. B. C. Bradlee, *Piracy in the West Indies and its Suppression* (1923).

C. L. Chandler, *Inter-American Acquaintances* (1917).

R. J. Cleveland, *Voyages* (see Memoirs).
Detailed account of a lengthy and adventurous voyage from New York to the West Coast.

*George Coggeshall, *Voyages* (see Memoirs).
The most valuable single account of New York trade with the West Indies and Latin America (see text).

W. E. Curtis, *Trade and Transportation between the United States and Spanish America* (1889).
A government survey, dealing principally with conditions after 1860.

R. H. Dana, *To Cuba and Back* (1859).

Edmund Fanning, *Voyages* (see Memoirs).
Account of a voyage from New York to the West Coast, with experiences similar to Cleveland's.

H. E. Jacob, *Coffee: The Epic of a Commodity* tr. Eden and Cedar Paul (1935).

A. K. Manchester, *British Preëminence in Brazil, its Rise and Decline: a Study in European Expansion* (1933).

*W. R. Manning, ed., *Diplomatic Correspondence of the United States: Inter-American Affairs* (Carnegie Endowment for International Peace), 8 vols. (1925–34).
Reproduces many documents which throw light on trade conditions, though much of the detailed statistical analysis in the consular despatches is excluded.

E. T. Parks, *Colombia and the United States, 1765–1934* (1935).

L. J. Ragatz, *The Decline of the Planter Class in the British Caribbean, 1763–1833* (1928).

——*A Guide for the Study of British Caribbean History, 1763–1834* (American Historical Association, *Annual Report*) (1937).

J. F. Rippy, *Rivalry of the United States and Great Britain in Latin America, 1808–1830* (1929).
Emphasis diplomatic rather than commercial; several of the other works of this authority on Inter-American affairs also have a bearing on the subject.

W. S. Robertson, *Hispanic-American Relations with the United States* (Carnegie Endowment for International Peace) (1923).
Chap. VI is one of the most useful summaries of the trade with South America.

W. O. Scroggs, *Filibusters and Financiers* (1916).
Able analysis of the relation of Vanderbilt and the other New York

steamship operators to the activities of William Walker in Nicaragua. Later popular study, *The Filibuster* by Laurence Greene (1937), adds little to the story.

Anthony Trollope, *The West Indies and the Spanish Main* (1860).
Good description of the various regions at the close of our period.

P. L. Vogt, *The Sugar Refining Industry in the United States; Its Development and Present Condition* (1908).

A. C. Wilgus, "Spanish American Patriot Activity along the Atlantic Seaboard," in *North Carolina Historical Review,* IV, pp. 174–75.

——"Spanish American Patriot Activity on the Gulf Coast, 1811–1822," in *Louisiana Historical Quarterly,* VIII, pp. 212–13.

XXVI. "DISTANT SEAS"

E. J. G. Bridgman, *Life and Labors of Elijah Coleman Bridgeman* (1864).
Missionary in China; briefly a New York merchant; supported by D. W. C. Olyphant at Canton.

M. E. Cosenza, ed., *Complete Journal of Townshend Harris* (1930).
New York chinaware importer, who played very prominent rôle in early American contact with Japan.

Tyler Dennett, *Americans in Eastern Asia* (1922).

F. R. Dulles, *America in the Pacific, a Century of Expansion* (1932).

*——*The Old China Trade* (1930).
An interesting, valuable and comprehensive account.

*(W. C. Hunter), *The "Fan Kwae" at Canton before Treaty Days, 1825–1844, by an old Resident* (1882).
Concise, clear and interesting account of the business methods, etc., of the "foreign devils" and their relationship to the Hong merchants; written by one of the New Yorkers who made a fortune as a partner in Russell & Co.

*Edmund Fanning, *Voyages* (see Memoirs).
Full account of the Stonington-New York sealing and exploring activities in the South Atlantic and Pacific, promoted by Fanning.

R. B. Forbes, *Reminiscences* (see Memoirs).
Excellent account of Canton around 1840 by a Russell partner.

Sidney & Marjorie Greenbie, *Gold of Ophir* (1925).
Account of the old China trade, written in a more verbose and flowery manner than Dulles.

T. J. Jacobs, *Scenes, Incidents and Adventures in the Pacific Ocean . . . under Capt. Benjamin Morrell* (1844).
See works by Morrell and his wife below.

*S. E. Morison, *Maritime History of Massachusetts, 1783–1860* (1921).
Delightful and valuable chapters on the China and East India trade,

with good bibliography. This classic of American maritime history is also useful for other aspects of the period.

Abby Jane Morrell, *Narrative of a Voyage to the Ethiopic and South Atlantic Ocean, Indian Ocean, etc., 1829–31* (1833).

Benjamin Morrell, *Narratives of Four Voyages* (1832).
Stonington-New York adventures in the South Seas; one of the liveliest single episodes in this period of the port's history (see text).

H. B. Morse, *The Chronicles of the East India Company trading to China, 1635–1834,* 5 vols. (1926–29).

——*The Gilds of China, with an Account of the Gild Merchant or Cohong of Canton* (1909).

James Riley, *An Authentic Narrative of the Loss of the American Brig "Commerce" wrecked on the Western Coast of Africa in 1815* (1817).
A New York captain temporarily enslaved by the Moors.

K. W. Porter, *The Jacksons and the Lees* (see Business Methods).

——*John Jacob Astor, Business Man* (see Biography).
Analysis of methods, illustrated by original documents, in trade with India and China.

Edmund Roberts, *Embassy to the Eastern Courts of Cochin-China, Siam and Muscat, in the U. S. Sloop of War "Peacock"* (1837).

W. S. W. Ruschenberger, *A Voyage around the World: Including an Embassy to Muscat and Siam* (1838).
The latter was an officer on the *Peacock;* the Roberts mission led to temporary trade between New York and Muscat.

(Samuel Shaw), *Journals of Major Samuel Shaw, with life of author by Josiah Quincy* (1847).
Shaw was supercargo of the *Empress of China* on the first trip to Canton from New York in 1784 and the first U. S. consul at Canton.

T. Thayer, *Life of D. W. C. Olyphant* (see Biography).
One of the leading New York China merchants.

XXVII. HINTERLAND, CANALS, AND RAILROADS

C. H. Ambler, *A History of Transportation in the Ohio Valley* (1932).

I. D. Andrews, *"Andrews Report"* (see Commerce).

George Armroyd, *A Connected View of the Whole Internal Navigation of the United States* (1826).

*P. W. Bidwell and J. I. Falconer, *History of Agriculture in the Northern United States, 1620–1860* (Carnegie Institute) (1925).
A great deal of valuable description and analysis not only for agriculture proper but also for the details of hinterland economic connections with the coast.

E. S. Clowes, *Shipways to the Sea: Our Inland and Coastal Waterways* (1929).

D. G. Creighton, *The Commercial Empire of the St. Lawrence, 1760–1850* (1937).

(Delaware & Hudson) *A Century of Progress: History of the Delaware & Hudson Co.* (1925).

John Disturnell, *The Western Traveller; Embracing the Canal and Railroad Routes from Albany,* etc. (1844).
Also numerous other railroad and travel guides by same compiler.

Seymour Dunbar, *A History of Travel in America,* 4 vols. (1915).
Reproduces many interesting old prints, timetables, etc.

A. T. Hadley, *Railroad Transportation; Its History and Its Laws* (1885).

James Hall, *The West; its Commerce and Navigation* (1848).

A. F. Harlow, *Old Towpaths, the Story of the American Canal Era* (1926).

H. W. Hill, *An Historical Review of Waterways and Canal Construction in New York State* (1908).
In publications of Buffalo Historical Society.

A. B. Hurlburt, *The Great American Canals,* 2 vols. (1904).

Edward Hungerford, *Men and Iron: A History of the New York Central* (1938).

——*Pathway of Empire* (1935).

——*The Story of the Baltimore & Ohio Railroad, 1827–1927* (1928).

C. L. Jones, *Economic History of the Anthracite-Tidewater Canals* (1908).

*C. B. Kuhlmann, *The Development of the Flour-Milling Industry in the United States* (1929).
Very useful for flour trade in general.

W. J. Lane, *History of Transportation in New Jersey to 1860* (see Steamboats).

A. C. Laut, *The Romance of the Rails,* 2 vols. (1929).
Includes a chapter on New York's delay in railroad construction.

J. W. Livingood, *The Rivalry of Philadelphia and Baltimore for the Trade of the Susquehanna Region* (MS. 1936).
Unpublished Princeton doctoral dissertation; able analysis of rivalry with canals and railroads.

*B. H. Meyer and C. E. MacGill, *History of Transportation in the United States before 1860* (Carnegie Institute) (1917).

E. H. Mott, *Between the Ocean and the Lakes; The Story of Erie* (1899).

New York State, Canal Commissioners, etc. (see Annual Reports).

H. V. Poor, *History of the Railroads and Canals of the United States* (1860).
Detailed account of cost and progress for each road and canal; continued by annual *Poor's Manual.*

J. L. Ringwalt, *Development of Transportation Systems in the United States* (1888).

Topical arrangement, with chapters on rolling stock, rails, etc., interesting topographical profiles of main routes to west, opp. p. 72.

H. W. Schotter, *The Growth and Development of the Pennsylvania Railroad Co.* (1927).

J. W. Starr, *One Hundred Years of American Railroading* (1928).

F. W. Stevens, *Beginnings of the New York Central Railroad* (1926).

G. N. Tucker, *The Canadian Commercial Revolution, 1845–1851* (1936).

R. J. Vandewater, *The Tourist, or Pocket Manual for Travellers* (1839).
Similar to Disturnell; gives useful details on Hudson steamer lines, canal travel, railroads, etc.

*N. E. Whitford, *History of the Canal System of the State of New York, together with Brief Histories of the Canals of the United States and Canada,* 2 vols. (1906).
Published as supplement to the Annual Report of the State Engineer and Surveyor of the State of New York for the fiscal year ending Sept. 30, 1905. The most exhaustive study of the Erie Canal, etc. Contains an extensive bibliography, II (continuous paging), pp. 1173–1366.

C. R. Woodward, *The Development of Agriculture in New Jersey, 1640–1880* (1927).

(No attempt has been made here to list the very numerous works dealing with the economic history of particular inland cities and regions.)

XXVIII. HUDSON RIVER

H. C. Brown, *The Lordly Hudson* (1937).
Elaborate reproductions of many old pictures.

*D. L. Buckman, *Old Steamboat Days on the Hudson River* (see Steamboats).

*J. S. Curtiss, "The Sloops of the Hudson, 1800–1850," in *New York History,* XIV, pp. 61–73 (1933).

Joel Munsell, *Annals of Albany,* 10 vols. (1850–59).

*W. E. Verplanck and M. W. Collyer, *The Sloops of the Hudson. An Historical Sketch of the Packet and Market Sloops of the Last Century,* etc. (1908).

William Wade, *Panorama of the Hudson River from New York to Albany* (1845).
Panorama view and descriptive text.

Paul Wilstach, *Hudson River Landings* (1933).

XXIX. IMMIGRATION AND PASSENGERS

*Edith Abbott, *Historical Aspects of the Immigration Problem: Select Documents* (1926).
One of the most valuable works on immigration; reproduces a large

amount of contemporary source material on reasons for migrating, adjustments in America, reaction of "native" Americans, etc.

W. F. Adams, *Ireland and Irish Immigration to the New World from 1815 to the Famine* (1932).
Like Hansen and Johnson below, covers one of the three main sources of New York's immigrants in a thorough, scholarly manner.

R. G. Albion, *Square Riggers on Schedule* (see Shipping).
Chap. IX, "Thirty Guineas, Wines Included," analyzes the cabin passage during the period in detail and includes a first-hand account of two immigrant passages; the bibliography lists many of the best travel accounts by cabin passengers, so that those are not duplicated here.

R. B. Anderson, *The First Chapter of Norwegian Immigration, 1821–1840* (1896).

T. C. Blegen, *Norwegian Migration to America, 1825–1860* (1931).
The first group arrived at New York in 1825.

F. C. Bowen, *A Century of Atlantic Travel* (see Steamboats and Steamships).

W. J. Bromwell, *History of Immigration into the United States*, etc. (1856).
Statistical tables of port totals, occupation totals and national origins totals, 1820–55, based on annual official reports; not as useful as the Treasury Dept. table, below (compiled chiefly by Bromwell), since it does not distinguish aliens from total passengers, including Americans.

Calvin Colton, *Manual for Emigrants to America* (1832).
Like Knight below, typical of the British volumes of advice to those contemplating emigration.

"Departure of Emigrant Vessels," in *Littell's Living Age*, XXVI, pp. 492–97 (1854).
Describes conditions on New York packets leaving Liverpool.

J. Duval, *Histoire de l'Emigration au XIXᵉ Siècle* (1862).

*"Emigrant Ship *Washington*," in *Chambers' Edinburgh Journal*, XVI, pp. 27–30 (1852).
Reproduces from parliamentary papers full text of Vere Foster's description of trip in New York ship (see text).

H. P. Fairchild, *Immigration* (1913).

A. B. Faust, *The German Element in the United States*, 2 vols. (1909; new ed. 2 vols. in 1, 1927).

A. C. Flick, ed., *History of the State of New York*, VII (1936).
Chapter on New York immigration.

R. L. Garis, *Immigration Restriction, a Study of the Opposition to and Regulation of Immigration in the United States* (1927).

J. W. Girard, Jr., *The Impress of Nationalities upon the City of New York* (see New York, Social).

*M. L. Hansen, *Emigration from Continental Europe, 1815–1860, with Special Reference to the United States* (MS. 1932).
Unpublished Harvard dissertation; able analysis of causes and methods. Good bibliography.

W. E. Harding, *John Morrissey, His Life, Battles, and Wrangles* (see Biography).

Harry Jerome, *Migration and Business Cycles* (1926).

*S. C. Johnson, *A History of Emigration from the United Kingdom to North America, 1763–1912* (1913).
Includes good bibliography of official British sources.

*Theodore Kapp, *Immigration and the Commissioners of Emigration of the State of New York* (1864).
Written by one of the commissioners, this is perhaps the most useful single source on New York immigration; detailed description of the various phases and problems affecting the port, including passage conditions, reception of immigrants, etc.

Charles Knight & Co., *The British Mechanic's and Labourer's Hand Book and True Guide to the United States* (1840).
Like Colton, a good example of the British emigrant manual.

T. F. Meehan, "New York's first Irish Emigrant Society," in *U. S. Catholic Hist. Record,* VI, pt. 2, pp. 202–11 (1913).

S. F. B. Morse, *Imminent Dangers to the Free Institutions of the United States through Foreign Immigration* (1835).
A strong and oft-quoted statement of the "nativist" opposition to immigration, by the inventor of the telegraph.

*New York State, *Annual Reports of the Commissioners of Emigration of the State of New York, 1847–1860* (1861).
A collection of the annual reports into a single volume, with useful statistics for the period; concentrates in particular upon the work of the commissioners at the Quarantine, the Ward's Island refuge, and Castle Garden. The bulk of the material is well utilized in Kapp's study.

*——*Report of the Select Committee Appointed by the Legislature of New York to Examine into Frauds upon Emigrants* (1847).
The investigation which led to the creation of the commissioners of emigration; findings also analyzed in Kapp.

T. W. Page, "The Distribution of Immigrants in the United States before 1870," in *Journal of Political Economy,* XX, pp. 676–94 (1912).

L. D. Scisco, *Political Nativism in New York State* (1901).

*U. S. Treasury Dept., Bureau of Statistics, *Tables showing Arrivals of Alien Passengers and Immigrants in the United States from 1820 to 1888* (1889).
The most compact tabulation of immigration statistics for the earlier period; arrivals by ports (pp. 108–9) reproduced in appendix in simplified form.

*U. S. Secretary of State, *Annual Reports of Passengers arriving from Foreign Countries* in Congressional Documents, 1820 ff.
The basis for the statistics in the above *Tables* and in Bromwell; indicates the number of each nationality and each occupation arriving at each port for each quarter-year.

*U. S. Congressional Documents "Report of the Select Committee . . . on the Sickness and Mortality on board Emigrant Ships," 33rd Congress, 1st Session, *Senate Doc.* 386 (1854).
Other pertinent government documents listed in Library of Congress bibliography on Immigration.

"Voyage in an Emigrant Ship," in *Chambers' Edinburgh Journal,* I, pp. 228–32 (1844).
The same immigrant's experiences ashore, from New York to Buffalo, are continued, *ibid.,* pp. 262–65, .302–04.

Herman Wätjen, *Aus der Frühzeit,* etc. (see Commerce).

XXX. MISCELLANEOUS

(Sarah Allen) *A Narrative of the Shipwreck and Unparalleled Sufferings of Mrs. Sarah Allen (late of Boston) on her Passage in May last from New York to New Orleans* (1816).

E. S. Bolton, *Clement Topliff and his Descendants in Boston* (1906).
Pioneer gatherer of marine news.

Confession of Charles Gibbs, a Native of Rhode Island, who, with T. J. Wansley, was doomed to be Hung in New York . . . for the Murder of the Captain and Mate of the Brig "Vineyard" (1831).
Notorious West Indian pirate (see text), culminating career with murder of officers of brig from New Orleans to New York and burying stolen specie in sand near Coney Island.

W. D. Edmonds, *Erie Water* (1933).
——*Rome Haul* (1929).
Sound and very interesting historical novels portraying the Erie Canal under construction and in operation; the author has recently written several good stories on New York Port episodes.

John Foster, *Account of the Conflagration of the Principal Portion of the 1st Ward of the City of New York . . . the 16th of December, 1835* (1836).

R. H. Gabriel, *The Evolution of Long Island, a Story of Land and Sea* (1921).

A. F. Harlow, *Old Waybills: The Romance of the Express Companies* (1934).

"The Great Fire of 1835" in New York Historical Society, *Quarterly Bulletin,* XX, 1 (1936).

Excellent pictures of the fire which wiped out a considerable portion of the business district. List of sufferers given in Foster above.

A. K. Laing, *The Sea Witch* (1933).
Lively historical novel based on the famous clipper and Captain R. H. Waterman; good "atmosphere," but takes a few liberties with history.

T. Lord, *A Concise Account of a Voyage made . . . in the Ship "Minerva" in the Winter of 1818* (1871).
Wreck of a New York-Liverpool regular trader.

Herman Melville, *Redburn* (various editions).
Novel, presumably partly autobiographical, describing voyage from New York to Liverpool and back in a regular trader around 1837.

Victor Rosewater, *History of Cooperative Newsgathering in the United States* (1930).
Good account of Sandy Hook newsboats, etc.

(*The Sun*, N. Y.) *Full Particulars of the Two Late Awful Shipwrecks near Sandy Hook. Narrative of the Wrecks of the Barque "Mexico" and of the Ship "Bristol"* (1837).
These wrecks, occasioned partly by pilot neglect, resulted in heavy loss of life and led to an overhauling of the pilot service (see text).

W. A. Weaver, *Lithographs of N. Currier and Currier & Ives* (1925).
Pictures of business district, waterfront, ships, wrecks, etc.

INDEX